WOMEN IN GAMING
100 PROFESSIONALS OF PLAY
PLAYER 1

TABLE OF CONTENTS

PROFILES

▶ A DAY IN THE LIFE OF

▶ ESSAYS

▶ IN THEIR OWN WORDS

A NOTE FROM THE AUTHOR

Hello!

Firstly, I want to thank you, deeply, for supporting *Women in Gaming: 100 Professionals of Play.*

Secondly, before you dive into reading, I want to make one point abundantly clear:

This book is not a complete history of the contributions and achievements of women in the video game industry.

In my opinion, that's a good thing. If we could fit the cumulative accomplishments of every professional woman associated with the video game industry within a 350-page book, we'd have a significantly longer journey ahead of us on the road to true representation and parity. There is certainly more work to be done, and this book aims to aid the cause. Every year more women around the world lend their voices—amplified by industry allies—and make the passage that much less turbulent for aspiring video game professionals.

With that in mind, filling a list limited to *only* 100 influential women was an incredibly daunting task. Accepting that I couldn't include every woman who made a mark on gaming, I instead carefully curated contributors to represent a diverse array of life experiences, skills, and opinions. I networked with organizations from around the world to help surface women making change everywhere; from established markets, to emerging ones in the Middle East, Sub-Saharan Africa, the Caribbean, Southeast Asia, and more. I sought out accomplished women from varying ethnic, religious, and sexual identities. I interviewed women with backgrounds in AAA titles, indie games, games-for-change, and beyond. The diverse tapestry of stories collected in this book illustrates the immense potential video games have as a medium—limited only by the most valuable resource within it—the people.

With that caveat out of the way, let's talk about *what this book is*:

- **It illustrates that women have always played a major role in the video game industry, despite widely-accepted beliefs that it originated as and continues to be the domain of men.**
- **It represents a diverse array of women's voices, including women of color, LGBTQ+ women, women from developing markets, and other often marginalized groups.**
- **It is a celebration of achievements, not a chronicling of challenges. Although we do touch on gender issues from both a personal and systemic standpoint, we don't want them to overshadow success stories.**
- **It highlights both industry icons and unsung heroes; those whose careers span decades, and those whose careers have just begun.**
- **It counters the exclusionary opinion that only core development roles are key contributors to success by highlighting women in user research, quality assurance, systems administration, marketing, public relations, community management, journalism, retail, esports, and more.**
- **It highlights women from varied facets of the industry; AAA, indie, mobile, casual, educational, experimental, and everything in-between.**
- **It works to dispel the notion that one woman must speak for all women by including direct quotes from diverse individuals. Opinions of contributors have not been edited or editorialized; they belong to each individual, as they should.**
- **It embraces making mistakes and offers candid reflections from industry veterans and newcomers alike, addressing how missteps resulted in valuable learning opportunities.**
- **It provides insight into specific industry disciplines through "Day in the Life of" features and a "Strategy Guide" of career resources, which is of value to all genders.**
- **It is accessible to those unfamiliar with the industry through a "tutorial" that defines common terms and colloquialisms, as well as high-level industry overviews to provide context to contributor profiles.**

My biggest hope for this book is that these collected stories will inspire young women to join our ranks as the next generation of video game talent. I want them to aspire to be woman #101.

On a personal note, writing this book has been both empowering and incredibly humbling. Interacting with over one hundred women of such caliber and character has been an unprecedented experience in my life.

The responsibility of writing this book is not lost on me. Over the last year I've had my fair share of sleepless nights working to ensure each profile got the time and attention it deserved, inspired to do right by both the participants and readers.

To all of our contributors: Thank you for trusting me to tell your story, for dedicating your time, and for challenging me with your feedback along the way. The book is better for it and so am I.

Enjoy,
Meagan Marie

FOREWORD

I fell in love with video games at the age of seven, when my family set up an Atari 2600 and I was transported to new adventures I'd never dreamed of. Whether I was commanding a tank, outshooting my fellow outlaws, racing in the dead of night, exploring jungles and nimbly jumping on crocodile heads, or rescuing E.T. after he fell into a pit for the thousandth time, video games made an indelible impression upon me at a very early age.

As I grew up and discovered new gaming platforms and worlds to explore, game developers were akin to rock stars in my mind. Mere mortals did not make video games! My imagination—so eager to take me to 1930s Los Angeles, the Zinderneuf blimp, or the kingdom of Hyrule—couldn't conceive of one day becoming a game developer.

But thanks to a quirk of fate and the Johns Hopkins University fencing team, I joined a company called Microprose in 1992 as a playtester. I was the only woman in the department at the time, starting both my career and my search for a sisterhood of other women who were as passionate about games and game development as I was.

Over the course of more than 26 years in game development, I've met amazing people of all genders. But I don't think I ever fully recognized the importance of highlighting women as gamers and game developers until I had two daughters of my own. Without fail, if they can choose a female character, they do so. They want to see themselves as the heroines of the story. They want to see girls and women saving the world. They want to see girls and women making the worlds they love.

When we see women as game players, game characters, and game developers, we see possibility and opportunity for everyone. We see that we don't need to conform to perceptions of who a gamer is, or what a game developer should look like, or sound like. Like those early game experiences I had so many years ago, we see new worlds and new experiences, new challenges and new opportunities, hope and love and wonder.

We see a community that recognizes that everyone has a place in the game.

Jen MacLean
IGDA Executive Director

Participants from the IGDA Foundation's Women in Games Ambassadors program at GDC 2017.

TUTORIAL

If you're not overly familiar with the video game industry, don't worry! We wanted *Women in Gaming: 100 Professionals of Play* to be accessible to as many people as possible, whether you're a longtime fan of video games or just learning about them through this book.

This tutorial is a basic primer on the structure of the game industry, it explains some commonly-used terms, and spells out popular acronyms. Keep in mind that the game industry is always innovating, and the language used evolves along with it. This is a solid snapshot of the video game industry in 2018.

GAME JOBS

Jobs in the game industry don't often have a unified description. A producer at one studio may have different responsibilities than a producer at another studio. Oftentimes, game development requires wearing multiple hats, so to speak. You can read more about key positions in the Day in the Life of entries in this book.

INDUSTRY OVERVIEW

DEVELOPER

A game developer is a company or entity that creates video games. Games can be developed by a single person (*Undertale*), by hundreds of people spread across several international studios (*Assassin's Creed*), and by teams of every size between.

PUBLISHER

A game publisher is a company that publishes games, which may include providing various services such as funding, marketing, distribution, public relations, etc. Publishers have long been a requirement for getting games onto most platforms, but digital distribution and new ways of financing independent titles (such as crowdfunding via Kickstarter and IndieGogo) have shaken up the status quo.

DISTRIBUTOR

A game may have a distributor in addition to a developer and publisher that helps manage relations with local retailers. This usually involves physical products, as digital distribution services such as Steam, GOG, and the iTunes App Store do not involve brick-and-mortar shops. Distribution deals may involve agreements with competing companies that have a better foothold in certain regions.

FIRST-PARTY

A first-party publisher refers to companies that make game platforms, such as Microsoft and the Xbox. First-party developers are internal studios or have been acquired by said companies and develop exclusively for those platforms (Microsoft Game Studios / 343 Industries / Rare Ltd., etc.). Aside from Microsoft, Sony (PlayStation) and Nintendo (Switch) are the two other major first-party companies in the current console generation.

SECOND-PARTY

Second-party is an unofficial term associated with third-party developers who act like first-party developers by taking platform-exclusive contracts.

THIRD-PARTY

Third-party companies may develop and/or publish games without being tied to any single platform. Activision Blizzard, Electronic Arts, Square Enix, Capcom, and Ubisoft are five of the most prolific third-party companies.

AAA

Triple-A or "AAA" refers to high-profile games by major publishers, generally with massive budgets and marketing efforts. The film industry equivalent to AAA is "blockbuster."

INDIE

Independent (indie) typically refers to self-funded game developers with much smaller resources and team sizes than AAA games. However, in the past decade indie games have surged in popularity and success, blurring the lines between AAA and indie in some cases. For instance, *The Witcher III* (developed and published by CD PROJEKT RED) easily rivals the biggest AAA productions, while ultra low-budget games created by solo developers (*Undertale*, *Stardew Valley*) have outsold many mid-tier and AAA titles.

HARDWARE

Hardware may refer to video game consoles, personal computers, and handheld devices, as well as physical accessories for those devices (mouse and keyboard, controllers, VR headsets, etc.).

SOFTWARE

In the video game industry, software most commonly refers to the actual video games themselves, regardless of platform and distribution method (physical/digital).

CURRENT GEN

"Current Gen" refers to the current generation of gaming hardware and the games available for them. The eighth (and current) generation of video game consoles was initiated in 2012 with the release of the Nintendo Wii U, followed by the PlayStation 4 and Xbox One in 2013, and the Nintendo Switch in 2017. Related terms include "Last Gen" and "Next Gen."

MULTIPLATFORM

A multiplatform game release is one made available on various platforms. This typically refers to third-party titles, but may apply to some first-party titles, such as those from Microsoft which can often be played on both Xbox and Windows 10, technically making them multiplatform.

CROSS-PLATFORM

Cross-platform gaming is a fairly rare practice that allows players to interact in the same game with players on a different platform. *Fortnite*, for example, allows cross-platform matchmaking across PC, Mac, Xbox, Switch, and mobile.

EXCLUSIVE

Exclusivity is a concept popularized during the console wars between Nintendo and Sega wherein a game (or specific features of a multiplatform game) is available exclusively on one platform. While first-party titles are exclusive by default, the practice extends to third-party games, such as Naughty Dog's *Crash Bandicoot* series, which was published exclusively on the Sony PlayStation before the studio was acquired by Sony in 2001. A related term, "Timed Exclusive," means a title's exclusivity has an expiration date, and it can be published to other platforms after that period of time, oftentimes one year.

REMASTER

A remastered game has had certain components, most commonly audio and visuals, upgraded to be closer in line with modern standards compared to when the game was originally released.

REMAKE

A remake is when a developer completely rebuilds an existing game—usually one released in a previous hardware generation—from the ground up. Aside from the audio/visuals, other core aspects such as narrative and gameplay are updated to make the game more appealing to a contemporary audience, while still retaining the same structure as the original title.

REBOOT

A reboot is similar to a remake in that it is an existing property rebuilt for a modern market, with the distinction that reboots will often see a "reimagining" of key characters, plot points, and themes.

ESPORTS

Esports (electronic sports) is synonymous with pro gaming—most commonly referring to organized video game competitions with some aspect of spectatorship (such as in an arena and/or being broadcast live online). Esports have surged in popularity thanks to titles like *Counter-Strike*, *Halo*, *Tekken*, *League of Legends*, *Hearthstone*, and *StarCraft*. Esports have become a massive financial opportunity for both competitive players and the organizations behind them, while also boosting the sales of popular esports titles.

VR

Virtual reality (VR) uses sensory feedback, often through the use of a VR headset, to create an immersive interactive experience.

AR

Augmented reality (AR) places computer-generated data in the user's real-world environment. *Pokémon Go* is one such example, wherein a computer-generated Pikachu may appear in the user's living room, backyard, or as they walk down the street.

MONETIZATION

DLC

Downloadable content (DLC) is digital content for games made available either for free or at an additional price. It can be released at the same time as the game, after it, or sometimes even before. Many developers utilize DLC as a way to generate additional revenue. DLC began in the form of "expansion packs" for PC titles (sizable expansions adding new missions and/or levels to the core game) but nowadays can range from a single weapon or outfit to season passes and soundtracks.

F2P

Free-to-play (F2P) is a business model where a game is available to download and play with no upfront cost to the player. F2P games typically monetize via microtransactions and/or—as is extremely common on mobile platforms—ads.

MICROTRANSACTIONS

A business model enabling the purchase of virtual goods with real money or hard/soft currency. Microtransactions (occasionally abbreviated as MTX) were popularized by F2P games such as MMOs and mobile games, but have since become common among full-priced releases. Microtransactions differentiate themselves from DLC by usually being smaller in scope and price, but this is not always true.

Cosmetic items (such as emotes, outfits, and characters that do not affect gameplay) are one of the more popular virtual goods, while weapons or items that give paying players an advantage can be highly controversial and are often to referred to as "pay-to-win."

F2P games featuring microtransactions, especially those that bar or heavily hinder progress unless purchases are made, are often referred to as "freemium" (a combination of "free" and "premium").

HARD CURRENCY

In-game currency (gold, platinum, stars, etc.) purchased with real-world money used to facilitate microtransactions.

SOFT CURRENCY

In-game currency obtainable without paying real-world money, such as completing missions or as a daily log-in reward. Soft currency typically does not allow players to buy the same (and generally more powerful) content as hard currency.

ENGINES

A game "engine" is a collection of software tools used to create the different aspects of the game, such as the visuals, gameplay, and audio. Some companies opt to develop proprietary engines, such as EA DICE's Frostbite engine (*Battlefield* series, *Mass Effect: Andromeda*), id Software's id Tech (*Doom, Rage*), and CryTek's CryEngine (*Crysis, Far Cry*). However, due to the rising costs of development, many studios license ready-made, third-party game engines with the two most popular being Unreal Engine and Unity.

UNREAL ENGINE

The Unreal Engine is the longest running and most popular AAA game engine in the industry, having been used in over 400 commercial releases across dozens of platforms. Developed by Epic Games, the Unreal Engine was initially used to create Epic's flagship first-person shooter *Unreal* (1998). The Unreal Engine is currently on version 4, and is available to anyone for free with a royalty agreement requiring 5% of revenue from products that earn more than $3,000 per quarter.

Notable games/franchises using the Unreal Engine include: *Unreal Tournament, Gears of War, BioShock, Lineage II, Tom Clancy's Ghost Recon/Rainbow Six/ Splinter Cell, Batman Arkham* series, *Infinity Blade, Borderlands, Life is Strange, Mass Effect, Mortal Kombat, SMITE, XCOM, Resident Evil*, and *Fortnite.*

UNITY

Launched in 2005 exclusively for Apple's OS X operating system, Unity (formerly Unity 3D) has since become the world's most-used cross-platform game engine, catering largely to indie developers. Designed by Unity Technologies with accessibility and ease of use regardless of intended platform, Unity greatly lowered the barrier of entry for game developers of any skill level. After Unity 5 launched in 2015, Unity moved to an annual naming scheme, starting with Unity 2018. Unity has changed its licensing model multiple times, currently has four levels (Personal, Plus, Pro, Enterprise), and a robust asset marketplace.

Notable games/franchises using Unity include: *Cuphead, Thomas Was Alone, Temple Run, BroForce, Cities: Skylines, Angry Birds 2, Her Story, Hearthstone, Monument Valley 1/2, Subnautica, Animal Crossing: Pocket Camp, Life is Strange: Before the Storm, Pokémon Go, Firewatch, Inside, Dreamfall Chapters: The Longest Journey*, and *Never Alone.*

ASSET FLIPPING

The term "asset-flipping" refers to software that is mostly or entirely comprised of assets purchased or downloaded for free from asset marketplaces for engines such as Unity and Unreal, rather than creating bespoke assets for a specific project.

SELECT GENRES

Adventure: *Myst*
Action/Adventure: *The Legend of Zelda*
Battle Royale: *Fortnite: Battle Royale*
Fighting: *Street Fighter*
Open-World: *Grand Theft Auto*
Platformer: *Super Mario Bros.*
Puzzle: *Tetris*
Racing: *Need For Speed*
Roguelike: *Spelunky*
Simulation: *The Sims*
Sports: *NBA Jam*
Survival Horror: *Resident Evil*

GENRE ACRONYMS

MMO/MMOG: Massively Multiplayer Online Game; *Planetside 2*
MMORPG: Massively Multiplayer Online Role-Playing Game; *World of Warcraft*
MOBA: Multiplayer Online Battle Arena; *League of Legends*
FPS: First-Person Shooter; *Call of Duty*
RPG: Role-Playing Game; *Elder Scrolls*
JRPG: Japanese Role-Playing Game; *Final Fantasy*
TRPG: Tactical Role-Playing Game; *Disgaea*
RTS: Real-Time Strategy; *StarCraft*

TERMINOLOGY & JARGON

AOE

AOE stands for area of effect, meaning the area that will be affected by an attack, ability, or spell. Similar terms include damage over time (DOT), wherein an effect has a prolonged damage-dealing attribute.

BUFF

Buffs are an increase to a character's prowess. For instance, casting a spell called Attack Up in an RPG would buff a character's attack.

HP

HP most often refers to "hit points" or "health points" and represents a character's total health. In most games, taking damage will deplete HP, and when HP reaches 0, the character will die or be knocked out. HP can usually be recovered using healing items, spells, or resting. Related terms include MP (Magic Points), SP (Skill Points), and AP (Action Points).

HUD

A heads-up display (HUD), sometimes known as a "status bar," is part of a game's user interface (UI) that most commonly displays key information for the player. In a racing game, this may include current lap, position, and a mini-map, while in an FPS it typically includes health and ammo.

LUDONARRATIVE DISSONANCE

Ludonarrative dissonance describes the conflict between a game's narrative and gameplay. A commonly quoted example is when likeable, relatable heroes are put into narrative frameworks where they have to kill a large number of enemy NPCs—usually in self-defense—yet the action has little or no influence on their emotional state or character arc.

NERF

Unlike buff, nerf is reserved for changes made to a game at a design level. For example, if a character or weapon is found to be OP (overpowered), the developer may reduce its stats or functionality to better balance the game.

NPC

Non-playable or non-player characters (NPC) are characters controlled by the game's artificial intelligence (AI). Many games, especially open-world titles and RPGs, are filled with increasingly lifelike NPCs to simulate a living, breathing society. In the original *Super Mario Bros.*, all characters except Mario (or Luigi in co-op) are considered NPCs. Conversely, the player or playable character (PC) refers to characters that can be controlled by the player. In *Super Mario Bros.*, the PC is Mario or Luigi.

PROCEDURAL GENERATION

Procedural generation, or random generation, is when a game uses an algorithm to create data, such as the layout of the game world. Although certainly not the first titles to use procedural generation, games like *Diablo*, *Spelunky*, and *Minecraft* popularized the concept.

RNG

RNG is an acronym for Random Number Generator, a programming technique used to randomize in-game events. Modern roguelike games rely heavily on RNG to create unique, unpredictable experiences. Loot boxes use RNG to determine the items players will obtain. RNG has evolved to be synonymous with "chance."

SALTY

Slang for saying someone is angry or upset. The term rose to prominence in reference to players who lost matches in competitive games.

HARASSMENT

GRIEFING

Griefing is the intentional harassment and annoyance of other players in a multiplayer game. Common forms of griefing include blocking doorways and teamkilling (using friendly fire to kill your own teammates and allies).

STREAM SNIPING

Stream sniping is the practice of using a livestreamer's active broadcast to locate and harass them in-game. By watching the stream, it provides viewers an advantage by knowing details such as the streamer's location, current equipment, and so on. Both Twitch and certain games such as *Fortnite* have provided tools to prevent stream sniping.

DOXING/DOXXING

Doxxing (derived from dox, an abbreviation of "documents") is the release of private information about an individual or organization online with the intention to shame, harass, or harm them. Doxxing can include home addresses, phone numbers, photos, financial information, and more.

SWATTING

Swatting, named after SWAT (Special Weapons and Tactics, a specialized law enforcement unit), occurs when a false report—such as a hostage situation—is made to emergency services with the intention of sending SWAT teams or other police units to the home of the swatter's target. Swatting is most commonly done to livestreamers (where the swatter can witness the results of their actions in real-time), and have resulted in accidental shootings and death. Swatting is a serious criminal offense, punishable by fines and imprisonment.

LAYING THE FOUNDATION

DECADE OVERVIEWS WRITTEN BY SEBASTIAN HALEY & MEAGAN MARIE

Play is inherent to who we are as humans. Through play we have entertained, expressed, taught, socialized, and competed since before recorded history. As such, an attempt to summarize the history of video games—a modern, wildly successful medium of play—would be impossible within the confines of this book.

That being said, we have provided a high-level overview of the technology that led to the creation of video games, and of each decade since as a means of contextualizing the achievements of contributors. These decade overviews merely form a basic skeleton of crucial events throughout the formative half-century leading to the present-day game industry. They focus primarily on key players such as Atari, Nintendo, Sega, Sony, and Microsoft. Some of it was good, some of it bad, but all of it was impactful in its own way.

For a compelling and expertly written account of the full history of video games, we suggest reading Tristan Donovan's *Replay: The History of Video Games*, among others.

TABLETOP GAMES & COMPUTERS

Modern day play has formalized through many mediums, including the proliferation of tabletop games. Women have made noteworthy contributions to the tabletop genre; *The Landlord's Game*, better known today as *Monopoly*, was patented by Elizabeth Magie (1904); Eleanor Abbott created *Candyland* (1948); Jennell Jaquays was the second person ever to publish a self-contained RPG adventure for *Dungeons & Dragons* (1976); Ora Coster co-created *Guess Who?* (1979); Leslie Scott invented *Jenga* (1983); and Laura Robinson co-created *Balderdash* (1984), to name a few.

Specific to the inception of electronic games, women played a key role in the evolution of computer programming, which would eventually collide with non-digital games, war, film, and real-life sports to create the industry as we know it. Ada Lovelace is considered the first computer programmer on record. In 1843 she created software in the form of punch cards (the world's first binary machine code) for Charles Babbage's theoretical "thinking machine," also known as the Analytical Engine. In 1980, the United States Department of Defense contracted a high-level, international computer programming language, named Ada, which continues to be used to this day.

Hedy Lamarr, best known as a celebrated Hollywood actress in the 1930s-1950s, was also an accomplished inventor. Among other things, Lamarr co-created a radio guidance system that would allow Allied torpedoes to circumvent radar jamming during World War II. Her work was used as the foundation for Bluetooth and Wi-Fi technology, which now powers much more than just video games.

Computer programming did not belong solely to nobility, Hollywood, or otherwise. The first "computers" were humans who carried out calculations and computations. In the mid-1940s, a handful of women became the first modern programmers, using the Electronic Numeric Integrator and Computer (ENIAC) to achieve the work previously done by hand by 80 female mathematicians. Rear Admiral Grace Hopper is considered foundational to the computer industry, having helped create the first computer compiler and for coining the term "debugging"; Kathleen Booth is on record as having written the first assembly language; Adele Goldberg collaborated in developing programming language Smalltalk-80, a precursor to modern graphical user interfaces.

According to Timeline[1], a news site dedicated to surfacing lost stories throughout modern history, between 30 and 50% of programmers in the 1950s were women. A 1967 article in *Cosmopolitan*, "Computer Girls[2]," detailed why the work was a natural fit for women. Sadly, programming shifted from being considered clerical work to associated with stereotypical male activities such as chess and mathematics. As women were socialized out of the profession, the pay and prestige for programming increased. This was all occurring during the 1970s, the fledgling years of the video game, when computers and software were expanding beyond their academic roots. Women were being expelled from an industry about to explode in popularity and cultural relevance, and the repercussions would echo strongly into the modern era.

Many of these stories are only starting to surface. The ENIAC women's contributions were not recognized for nearly five decades. Similarly, the achievements of NASA's African-American women computers weren't popularized until the 2016 book and film *Hidden Figures*. Initiatives such as The Computer History Museum's exhibit *Thinking Big: Ada, Countess of Lovelace* and The Center for Computing History's exhibit *Computing History: Her Story*, are helping to change the face of computing to more accurately reflect its true history.

THE 1970s: ESTABLISHING AN INDUSTRY

1972: MAGNAVOX ODYSSEY: THE FIRST HOME CONSOLE

Developed primarily by engineer Ralph Baer and hardware technician Bill Harrison, the Magnavox Odyssey was the first home console. It allowed three "dots" and a line controlled by players to be displayed on a connected television set via the game *Table Tennis*. The system included a dozen pre-installed games, with another 10 others sold separately. Due to the limited graphics, most games used plastic overlays attached directly to the television set or other gimmicky accessories.

The Odyssey wasn't particularly successful, but its influence was far-reaching. A company named Nintendo secured the rights to release the Odyssey in Japan, giving the future giant its first taste of the home console market.

1972-1973: PONG IS RELEASED

Founded by Nolan Bushnell and Ted Dabney in 1972, Atari entered the video game arena. Inspired by the Magnavox Odyssey's table tennis game, Atari's *Pong* was released and became an international phenomenon. It started a "craze" for ball-and-paddle video games in the arcade scene, laying the foundation for the coin-operated video game industry.

1970 1971 1972 1973 1974

1974: THE FIRST CRASH

With a relentless wave of *Pong* variants flooding the coin-op industry within a year, the market collapsed, leading companies like Atari and Midway to branch out into new genres such as shooters and racing games. At home, ball-and-paddle games were more successful, with a variety of Magnavox consoles (Odyssey 100 and 200, etc.) and Atari's Home *Pong* system being released in the mid-to-late seventies, yet they too faced their own crash in 1978.

1977: ATARI 2600 IS RELEASED

Known as the Atari Video Computer System (VCS) until 1982, the Atari 2600 was a moderately successful home console credited with popularizing hardware using games contained on separate ROM cartridges, whereas most game consoles up to that point were restricted to the games built into the system (including Nintendo's Color-TV Game series, released the same year in Japan). In the early 1980s, the Atari 2600 exploded in popularity thanks to titles such as *Space Invaders* and select third-party releases. Approximately 30 million units[3] were sold, with production for the Atari 2600 ending in 1992.

1977: BREAKOUT IS RELEASED

Video games and dedicated arcades had become well-established in the coin-operated amusement industry by the late 1970s, but still had not surpassed mainstays such as pinball. In 1977, Atari's *Breakout* was released. Developed by Atari co-founder Nolan Bushnell, Steve Bristow, Steve Wozniak, and Steve Jobs, *Breakout*'s influence extended beyond the game industry. Wozniak's technical accomplishments served as a reference point for the Apple II personal computer, also released in 1977[4].

1979: ACTIVISION IS FOUNDED

Four programmers at Atari—David Crane, Larry Kaplan, Alan Miller, and Bob Whitehead—became frustrated with the discrepancy between Atari's earnings and their salary, as well as a lack of recognition for their work (video game credits had not yet been standardized). The group estimated it had helped Atari earn $100M in revenue the previous year alone, yet they were being paid $30K each. They left and formed Activision Publishing (a portmanteau of "active television"), spawning one of the game industry's modern titans.

1978 & 1979: SPACE INVADERS & ASTEROIDS

Like *Pong*, *Breakout*'s success equated to countless imitators. Japanese developer Taito replaced *Breakout*'s bricks with aliens and released *Space Invaders* the following year. Alongside Atari's *Asteroids* (1979) and the increased popularity of coin-op games in public places such as bars and teahouses, these titles helped establish what would come to be known as the Golden Age of Arcade Video Games.

1975

1976

1977

1978

1979

1979: SIERRA ON-LINE IS FOUNDED

Founded by Ken and Roberta Williams, Sierra On-Line helped revolutionize the adventure genre by popularizing graphic-driven games such as those from the *King's Quest* and *Gabriel Knight* series. By the mid-1980s Sierra was an international contender, becoming the twelfth-largest microcomputer-software company in the world, according to *InfoWorld*[5]. Roberta Williams is considered one of the most influential women in video game history for her work as a writer and designer on *Mystery House*, the *King's Quest* series, *Phantasmagoria*, and over 20 additional games. She and Ken have remained out of the public eye enjoying retirement since 1999, aside from an appearance to receive the first-ever Industry Icon Award at The Game Awards in 2014.

1. Transnoodle. "Women Pioneered Computer Programming. Then Men Took Their Industry Over." Timeline. May 16, 2017.
2. Mandel, Lois. "The Computer Girls." *Cosmopolitan*, 1967, 52-53.
3. "Atari VCS (Atari 2600)." A Brief History of Game Console Warfare. *BusinessWeek*.
4. Connick, Jack. "...And Then There Was Apple." Call-A.P.P.L.E. Oct 1986: 24.
5. Caruso, Denise. "Software Gambles: Company Strategies Boomerang." Infoworld, April 2, 1984.

CAROL KANTOR

INTRODUCED USER RESEARCH IN THE VIDEO GAME INDUSTRY

 Business Builders  businessbuilders.com

EXPERIENCE

FIRST & FAVORITE INDUSTRY PROJECT: PLAYER RESEARCH ON PINBALL & COIN-OP VIDEO GAMES IN DEVELOPMENT AT ATARI

ACHIEVEMENTS UNLOCKED:

> FIRST GAMES USER RESEARCHER IN INDUSTRY HISTORY (1973)

> GAMES USER RESEARCH ASSOCIATION RECOGNITION FOR INDUSTRY CONTRIBUTIONS (2014)

STATS

INDUSTRY LEVEL: 12

CURRENT CLASS: FOUNDER

CURRENT GUILD: BUSINESS BUILDERS—CUPERTINO, USA

SPECIAL SKILLS: MARKETING, PROMOTION, SOCIAL MEDIA, GRAPHIC DESIGN, FUNDRAISING, USER RESEARCH

STANDARD EQUIPMENT

MUST-HAVE GAME: BREAKOUT

BIO

Carol Kantor got her foot in the door at Atari on a bet. "I met Gene Lipkin, the VP of Atari," she began. "I asked him how he could tell if a game was good or not. I bet him that in six months, I could tell him which Atari game would do better than the others using market research. If I could, then he would have to hire me full-time. I did, and then he did."

In her mid-20s, Kantor was already experienced in market research, having previously worked for the consumer products divisions of Fairchild and The Clorox Company. She had landed at Clorox after earning a degree in business statistics and a minor in computer science from the University of Texas, as well as a master's in management science and marketing from the University of Colorado.

Kantor played a few arcade games here and there, but was generally unfamiliar with the industry before she made up her mind to join it. She knew enough to see an opportunity for her skills to be put to good use, and took the time to study up. "I learned how the industry worked from the beginning," she said. "The flow and success from product development to distribution and to operation in the field."

Easter Egg

Has won over 193 logo design contests on a popular crowdsourcing website.

COIN-OP OBSERVATIONS

In 1973, Kantor was hired by Atari and became the first user researcher in video game history. "Atari was a young company and was not quite sure what they needed at the time," explained Kantor. "I challenged them to let me try to forecast game success. I took the techniques learned and applied them to game-player research. It worked and the program began and expanded from there."

As manager of the new market-research department of Atari's coin-op division, she was tasked with pre-market testing and evaluation, product analysis, forecasting, and planning. "I developed the entire research program, analyzed results, and worked with the design engineers and marketing group to improve the products," said Kantor.

Prior to her intervention, Atari used coin-collection data as their primary form of analysis. It boiled down to, "the more money, the better the game." Kantor's formal research program kicked off in 1973. A series of defined methods would help to tell if a game was going to be a success.

Field Observations: A prototype arcade game would be placed in a bar or arcade, and researchers would watch patrons play and take notes. They would look for behavioral reactions, try to evaluate their entertainment level, and carefully observe variations between different games.

Focus Groups: Kantor would also bring groups of individuals to Atari's office at different phases of development to solicit feedback.

Surveys: Formulating specific questionnaires, Kantor and her team would intercept people playing Atari games in the arcades and other locations and, over time, developed a comparative database of answers that all games could be measured against.

"My favorite times were when the game-development engineers came to observe players in the field and actually saw the results of observations."

The data provided actionable insights for Atari. It would indicate where a player would lose interest in a game and drop off, allowing programmers to implement a fix to keep them hooked. "My favorite times were when the game-development engineers came to observe players in the field and actually saw the results of observations," she recalled. "They would ask questions and listen to the players. It was rewarding to have them implement improvements based on the findings of my research."

THE ATARI FAMILY

While research was Kantor's main priority, Atari was quickly growing, which required multidisciplinary efforts from all employees. "I also took the responsibility of coordinating all trade shows, events, and materials for the marketing department," she said. "I especially enjoyed writing and editing the *Coin Connection* newsletter. I had to gather information from many sources and combine them into a publication that would be of value to the readers. I learned so much about writing, designing, and publishing from that one part of the job."

In 1977, Kantor began to grow her team to keep up with Atari's booming business. She hired Colette Weil, Mary Fujihara, and Linda Adam. Together, the four became the first industry user-research group. "Women at Atari were part of the family in all departments," said Kantor. "We were fortunate to work on a team that valued what we knew and what we could accomplish. In marketing there were other amazing women I worked with: Lenore Sayers Funes, Suzanne Elliott, Mireille Chevalier, Ruth Evans, Mariann Layne, and Evelyn Seto, just to name a few. We recently had a reunion and learned how these women continued their careers and successes. This makes me proud to be their friend and to have worked with them."

Women of Atari reunion in 2018.

"The early years at Atari were exciting and fulfilling because we felt like we were all working together to build an industry, provide 'fun' for the players, and profits for the operators," Kantor continued. "We worked hard and played hard together. Atari in the early days was like family. And it is terrific that we are still friends."

A LASTING LEGACY

Kantor left Atari in 1979 and founded her own company, Business Builders. "I started Business Builders to provide promotional services to the game industry and all kinds of other businesses," she explained. I have won several promotional industry awards for programs we developed over the years." Not long after founding Business Builders, Kantor put her industry research and marketing skills to good use, writing *Promoting Your Game Center*, a book to help arcade operators attract new players and build loyalty.

Kantor's work helped establish the foundation that modern day video games are built upon. "I am proud that I initiated the concept of doing player research in the video game industry, and having the findings used as part of the modern game-development process," she said. "At the time I didn't know that I was starting something that would evolve into the 'video game user research' industry—but it is fun to know that it is a thriving discipline today and still growing and discovering new ways to use player research as feedback for product development." In 2014, the original Atari game-research team—Kantor, Weil, Fujihara, and Adam—was recognized by the Games User Research Association for their contributions.

"I didn't know that I was starting something that would evolve into the 'video game user research' industry."

"The industry grew up over the past 45+ years," reflected Kantor. "It plays by the same basic rules that make games good—the 'easy to learn and hard to master' philosophy still applies. It is different because technology has opened many more opportunities for growth, expansion, and change. My career has moved from the game industry to the promotion industry, and also in youth-development class, teaching values to young students. I hope that I have a lasting impact to help others move forward."

EVELYN SETO

COLLABORATED ON EARLY ATARI GRAPHIC IDENTITY

 ejseto.com

EXPERIENCE

FIRST INDUSTRY PROJECT: MECHANICAL ART FOR ATARI LOGO (1976)

FAVORITE INDUSTRY PROJECT: REBRANDING ATARI PACKAGING (1978)

ACHIEVEMENTS UNLOCKED:

> MECHANICAL ART FOR ATARI LOGO (1972)

> SUPERVISED MAJOR ATARI CONSUMER GAMES REBRANDING (1978)

> CONSULTANT FOR "THE ART OF ATARI," AUTHORED BY TIM LAPETINO, MUSEUM OF VIDEO GAME ART (MOVA), (2016)

STATS

INDUSTRY LEVEL: 8

CURRENT CLASS: ARTIST & DESIGNER

CURRENT GUILD: EVELYN SETO ART AND DESIGN—SAN JOSE, USA

SPECIAL SKILLS: GRAPHIC DESIGN, PACKAGE DESIGN, BRAND IDENTITY, LOGO DEVELOPMENT, TYPOGRAPHY, PAINTING

STANDARD EQUIPMENT

MUST-HAVE GAME: BREAKOUT

BIO

Armed with degrees in commercial art and graphic design, Evelyn Seto's first job out of college was a production artist position at a small Palo Alto-based ad agency in Silicon Valley. The year was 1972, and the agency was Opperman-Harrington (O-H). "In those days, aerospace (Lockheed, NASA), scientific instrumentation (Hewlett-Packard, Perkin-Elmer), semi-conductors (Fairchild, AMD, Intel), computer technology (IBM, Xerox PARC), and their support industries were the main employers," shared Evelyn.

"O-H developed business-to-business and retail advertising, PR, and promotions for a variety of clients like Coates & Welter, Coherent Radiation, GRT Music, Cuvaison Winery, and Bullocks department store," she continued. "This start-up coin-op game company, Atari, was just one of their clients. So you could say I fell into the industry by association."

"George Opperman designed the now iconic Atari company logo," recalled Evelyn. "I was the production artist who inked the final camera-ready art. We didn't have desktop computers or publishing software. Everything was done by hand with Rapidograph pens, French curves, and various templates. Typesetting was probably the only automated technology available at the time."

Easter Egg

Worked on graphic concepts for a Wonder Woman pinball game at Atari, which was never put into production.

ARCADE ARTISTRY

In 1976, Evelyn was working as a graphic designer at a business unit of Hewlett-Packard when she got a call from Opperman. "He told me he was starting an in-house art department at Atari and wanted me to join as his assistant," she said. "George was a talented, one-man show. He was a designer, illustrator, and writer. He was the guy who started putting big, bold color graphics on the side panels of the arcade games. His art would convey excitement to the distributors and arcade owners so they could picture quarters dropped into the coin box by arcade gamers."

Excited for the opportunity, Evelyn joined Atari as a graphic designer. "As his number two at the time, I worked on the production art for printing the marketing materials," she explained. "The company was starting to grow fast as more game titles were waiting in the wings. We needed more designers and artists. I put out the word and pre-screened the illustrators and designers for George to interview. We grew to be about eight in the first years. I was the only woman on the team."

"Back in those days, on-screen images were simple pixel blips created by programmers, not the elaborate graphics you see today," Evelyn continued. "Once the backstory for the gameplay was revealed by the game programmers, the designers and illustrators had to create the visual excitement for the front display and side panel graphics. The graphics for the panels were designed with hard edges to be silkscreened in as many as 12 colors (a hand-cut stencil was created for each color). It was a registration challenge. At that size, we didn't have the technology to use process color for softer photographic images." Evelyn designed cabinet graphics for games such as *Super Bug*, *Mini-Golf*, *Fire Truck*, and *Soccer*, as well as providing production art for corresponding marketing materials.

Inspired by Disney, in 1977 Atari founder Nolan Bushnell set out to create a family-friendly game experience outside the typical game arcades. "Gaming in the early days was associated with gambling and pinball parlors. Game themes were targeted to boys and men," Evelyn said. "Enter Chuck E. Cheese Pizza Time Theater, the first family restaurant to integrate food, animated entertainment, and an indoor arcade."

Opperman and art director Robert Flemante created the look and feel for all the Pizza Time characters as part of the coin-operated division. Evelyn provided production support on marketing materials for the launch, including designing the metal token used to play arcade games instead of quarters.

ATARI CONSUMER PRODUCTS

In 1978, Evelyn transferred from the Coin-Op Division to the Atari Consumer Division design group under the leadership of director John Hayashi. "This is where I found my niche in packaging design and brand identity. The department grew from about 10 to over 50, the largest in-house art department in the valley. Eventually I became a design supervisor and managed three staff designers and a cadre of external suppliers for pre-press and print for the hardware and software packaging."

Evelyn took the lead on a major rebranding for Atari consumer games in 1978. This was both her favorite and most challenging project. "When I joined the Consumer Division, they had just launched the Video Computer System (VCS) console. The software game packages were in bright rainbow colors,"she explained. "Two new game consoles were in development, providing different features and price options to the consumer. The branding challenge was to create a graphic solution to differentiate between systems and to pump up the Atari name."

The game consoles were to be numbered: 2600, 5200, and 3600, the latter a working name for the Atari 7800. "We came up with a bright color system—a nod to the color system consumers were familiar with from the game cartridges: red for the 2600, blue for the 5200, and purple for the 3600. We also created a second, more modern concept with silver as the overall look, using color Atari logotype to differentiate the systems," said Evelyn. "Mock-up packages in both concepts were made and taken to a retailer to compare the shelf appeal with our competitor's packaging. Our new streamlined design removed the visual clutter that made our brand stand out on the shelf."

"Once we decided on the silver concept, we went through various treatments of the game cartridge packaging, exploring the compatibility of an original Atari game title next to a licensed arcade game title's graphics, such as *Kangeroo* or *Raiders*," she continued. "We also had to look at how to tie-in the children's licensed games with *Peanuts*, Disney, or the Children's Television Network to the silver packaging, or whether they needed their own look." The project was extensive—mock-ups were developed for studies, including packages of all shapes and sizes for product extensions and gaming accessories such as controllers. "There were a lot of considerations and people to please. It was a team effort, lots of work but lots of fun and in the end, a great cohesive look."

Unpublished box explorations for licensed games.

On a more personal level, Evelyn loved working with typography. "I loved lettering, combing through type books for the character styles to create new letterforms for a game or product logotype," she said.

> "This [at the Atari Consumer Division] is where I found my niche in packaging design and brand identity."

STAYING IN SILICON VALLEY

In 1983, Evelyn left Atari for a start-up opportunity as art director at Catalyst Technology. "Nolan Bushnell seeded money for a think tank, funding several pet projects that included Axlon (electronic toys and games), Etak (an early driving navigation mapping system), and I'ro, a computer color analyzer for the fashion industry," she explained. "I designed packaging graphics and marketing materials for Axlon's toys and games, and conceptual imagery and branding for I'ro."

Catalyst was Evelyn's last touchpoint with the game industry, although she worked in toys at the Tonka-Kenner-Parker Corporation in Minnesota for a few years before returning to Hewlett Packard in 1989. HP would remain her home for the next 15 years. She spent the first half as corporate communications art director, consulting with HP's numerous business units as they transitioned through the company's first major rebranding in 50 years. The second half of her tenure, Evelyn was the worldwide packaging manager for the home computer division. Evelyn moved to Apple in 2005, project managing software package printing. Witness to the launch of iPod extensions and the first iPhone, she recalls it as an exciting period of time at Apple. From packaging hardware and software, Evelyn rounded out her career by "packaging" a city with Team San Jose. Her job was to promote tourism by bringing conventions and visitors to San Jose and the surrounding area.

Looking back on her career, Evelyn feels it was an honor to witness—and contribute to—the landscape of technology that became Silicon Valley. "I got to see a lot, from HP's pocket-sized, programmable scientific and business calculators replacing the slide rule and adding machine, to watching the introduction of the Apple iPhone," she said. "In between were the Atari days. At its peak, Atari accounted for one-third of Warner Communications' annual income and was the fastest growing company in US history, making Silicon Valley a household name. It was exciting to be part of the Atari Consumer Games rebrand."

At the time, I thought video games were a fad. Boy was I ever wrong," reflected Evelyn. "I'm astounded. Who knew it would become a legit career path."

BRENDA LAUREL

EXPERT IN HUMAN-CENTERED DESIGN

 Blaurel

 Brenda Laurel

 Brenda Laurel

 neogaian.org

EXPERIENCE

FIRST INDUSTRY PROJECT: RUMPLESTILTSKINS (1977)

FAVORITE INDUSTRY PROJECT: DREAMWORK WITH HOWARD RHEINGOLD (UNRELEASED)

PROJECTS SHIPPED: 25 GAMES

ACHIEVEMENTS UNLOCKED

> INDIECADE "TRAILBLAZER" AWARD (2016)

> VIRTUAL WORLD SOCIETY "NEXTANT PRIZE" (2017)

> HIGHER EDUCATION VIDEO GAME ALLIANCE FELLOW (2018)

STATS

INDUSTRY LEVEL: 30

CURRENT CLASS: PRINCIPAL

CURRENT GUILD: NEOGAIAN INTERACTIVE—SANTA CRUZ, USA

SPECIAL SKILLS: PERFORMANCE STORYTELLING, WRITING, POETRY, PHOTOGRAPHY, TAI CH'I

STANDARD EQUIPMENT

FAVORITE PLATFORM: APPLE COMPUTER

GO-TO GENRE: ADVENTURE

MUST-HAVE GAME: STAR RAIDERS

BIO

A storyteller from the start of her career, Brenda Laurel's Master of Fine Arts in acting and directing would lead her to telling tales of an interactive nature. Laurel first fell in love with computers at the lab of a friend, Joe Miller. In 1976, Miller and his colleague, John Powers, formed their own company called CyberVision. Recognizing Laurel's talent, they brought her on board. "They wanted to do a fairy-tale series and asked me if I'd like to join as a designer," she said. "I never looked back."

Laurel worked as a designer, programmer, and eventually manager for educational product design at CyberVision until its closure in 1979. Looking for a new gig, she moved from Ohio to California, accepting a position with gaming giant Atari as a software specialist and was rapidly promoted to manager of the Home Computer Division for Software Strategy and Marketing. Laurel recalled how as the only woman on her floor, the women's restroom was being used as a smoking lounge when she first started.

ASKING THE BIG QUESTIONS

When Laurel felt she wasn't reaching her full potential in her current postion, she secured a new job across the street at the Atari Systems Research Laboratory, requesting a job studying interactivity and immersive media. Alan Kay, who had been hired to start the lab, welcomed Laurel and in doing so altered the course of her career. Motivated by technology and the sociology behind games, Laurel sought academic answers for fundamental questions. What are games? What is interactivity? How can we make games more intelligent? It was here she began a theory of first-person experiences in interactive environments and worked to improve the quality of interactivity in games.

In 1985, Laurel paused her career to write her dissertation and have her first baby, then joined Activision as Director of Product Development for Learning and Creativity. Inspired by her previous work in research, Laurel completed her PhD at The Ohio State University in the Department of Theater, Theory, and Criticism in 1986. Her dissertation—"Toward the Design of a Computer-Based Interactive Fantasy System—provided the foundation of her 1991 book, *Computers as Theater.*

ART & VIRTUAL REALITY

For the next seven years, Laurel would focus her work on research and consulting for major companies such as LucasArts Entertainment and Sony Pictures, as well as the development of virtual environments and remote presence systems for Telepresence Research, Inc., of which she was co-founder and president. In 1992, she became a member of the Interval Research Corporation's research staff, founded by Microsoft co-founder Paul Allen and CEO David Liddle. Here she collaborated on a cutting-edge project highlighting the artistic opportunities of virtual reality. The project was extremely well-funded by Interval, with the goal of showcasing that VR could be used for more than just training exercises.

Easter Egg

Is an experienced abalone diver.

> "I wanted to design games that met girls where they were and we finally succeeded in that at Purple Moon."

The 1993 project, installed in the Banff Center for the Arts, explored VR as not only a visual experience, but a multisensory one, focusing on visual, audio, and motion in her designs. "*Placeholder* was the first VR project to decouple gaze from direction of movement, provide two hands to participants, support two participants at once, represent multiple traversable locations, and capture imagery from the natural landscape. We meant to make a design statement about the value of the medium in the realms of art and fantasy," said Laurel.

"The world allowed interactors to take on the bodies of animals along with their particular sensory-motor characteristics," she explained. "One of the animals was a crow who could fly by flapping its wings. Interactors entered animal bodies by sticking their heads into petroglyphic avatars." Laurel witnessed surprising behavior with players when they would trade bodies to experience the unique aspects of each animal. "This was truly emergent behavior. We had no idea that body-swapping was one of the affordances of the piece!"

While at Interval, Laurel also led a four-year R&D effort to understand the relationship between gender and technology among children and teens, specifically tweenaged girls. They looked at play as a concept and researched social structures between young girls. Over one thousand girls were interviewed in eight cities. From this research, Laurel came to the conclusion that girls were interested in games, which was contrary to the commonly held belief at the time, but wanted a different kind of gaming experience than what was being offered on the market. She also resolved that intervention was needed at a young age to prevent girls from losing interest in STEM fields due to existing social constructs.

PURPLE MOON

In 1996, Laurel used her research into gender and technology as the underpinning of a new studio and co-founded transmedia company Purple Moon.

"It was not until I co-founded Purple Moon that I was in a workspace relatively free of sexist overtones, although the separatist feminists who dominated my first development team were just as toxic as many male managers had been," recalled Laurel, speaking to conflicting thoughts on how to design games for girls.

Should they cater to idealized notions of gender from the consumer world, or the equally idealized notion of gender from feminist ideology?, asked Laurel. "I had done extensive research on tween girls before starting the company, but some of the women in the first development team I hired did not respect that research. They, like most others, wanted to design games where characters were what they thought they should be as opposed to how girls really are. They wanted, like the men who dominated the industry, to present a notion of the feminine that was consonant with their ideology. I wanted to design games that met girls where they were and we finally succeeded in that at Purple Moon." The majority of Purple Moon's games starred a young girl named Rockett and focused on storytelling, exploration, and relatable scenarios in the life of many young women.

In 1999, Laurel's investors suddenly shifted their focus from video games to the new frontier of web content and pulled investment from Purple Moon. With 60 employees working on their eighth title, she had little choice but to let the company go. Mattel bought and closed the studio, as Laurel puts it, "to avoid competition for the Barbie franchise."

> "I like to think that I, among many others, contributed an ethical consciousness to video games."

After Purple Moon closed, Laurel shifted her focus fully to academia and research. She worked as a chair and professor at the Art Center College of Design, tasked with creating a fresh curriculum for the Graduate Media Design Program. Laurel also was a chair and professor for the Graduate Program in Design at the California College of the Arts and, subsequently, an Adjunct Professor in the game design program at the University of California Santa Cruz. She has also focused on her own research, consulting, and speaking gigs for academic and professional audiences. Laurel released her third book, *Utopian Entrepreneur*, in 2001 and *Design Research: Methods and Perspectives* in 2004. An updated edition of *Computers as Theatre* was released in 2013.

"I like to think that I, among many others, contributed an ethical consciousness to videogames. I think that my relentless insistence on authorship as time-displaced collaboration with a player has helped people to understand authoring in interactive media," said Laurel. "I'm proud of producing generations of students who understand and utilize the powers of human-centered design research. I am proudest of my work to bring games to girls with Purple Moon in the late 1990s." To this day, Laurel still receives at least one letter each week from the young women who played Purple Moon games, detailing how games changed their lives for the better.

A DAY IN THE LIFE OF...

A PRODUCER

Producers ensure that your favorite games make it to market by taking a project from concept to completion. A liaison between the devs on the floor and studio or publisher executives, they track against content milestones, budgets, and quality. Strong communication and critical thinking are imperative to the success in this role, as producers must balance small daily tasks such as taking meeting notes with more complex responsibilities like identifying and mitigating key project risks. Sarah Hebbler, Executive Producer at Psyonix, lives this lifestyle day in and day out, and used her skillset to help the indie hit *Rocket League* make a major splash in the market.

SARAH HEBBLER

 RocketLeague  Rocket League  Psyonix  rocketleague.com

PROFESSION: EXECUTIVE PRODUCER AT PSYONIX—SAN DIEGO, USA

YEARS IN PROFESSION: 8

ASSOCIATED WITH: ROCKET LEAGUE, NOSGOTH

▶ EDUCATION

"I have a degree in International Business, which doesn't directly apply to what I'm doing, but it does have some value since I've had classes in management, marketing, and working with organizations worldwide. In terms of production, I'm primarily self-taught through books and experience."

▶ BREAKING IN

"It was difficult to break into the industry and find organizations willing to take on a person with little to no experience, but I had a passion for games and was determined to find a way in. I took whatever opportunities possible to work on games. I worked as a designer with a group of friends for my first project. For a few years after that, I took on various contract design jobs for very small projects.

"I had been a project manager outside of games and believed that production would be an ideal fit, so I started seeking jobs in that field. I used my free time to learn about game production and I was fortunate to find an organization that took a chance on me joining their production team."

▶ KEY QUALITIES

"Communication skills are critical. Producers are working with the leadership, developers and publishing groups, so good written and verbal communication is crucial in order to be effective. Being a forward thinker is key, too. Producers need to always be looking ahead to set goals; identify opportunities and issues that may impact the projects. They must also have excellent interpersonal skills and be good at building and maintaining relationships. Producers are the oil that helps the development machine work and holds the team together, so strong relationships and trust help with those efforts. Also, a strong sense of ownership and a good attitude. Good producers have a strong sense of ownership with the outcome of projects and will be reliable with their responsibilities. There are also times when the work can get tough, so a positive attitude from the producer can go a long way with how the team is approaching the challenges."

▶ TOOLS OF THE TRADE

"My job's focus is on communication and working with the team, so I'm always on email and Slack. I'm also in Microsoft Office and Google Documents for risk reporting, budget tracking, process documentation, design reviews and other projects. I also monitor project progress through Microsoft Project management software, Axosoft task and bug database, and Mindjet Mind Manager where we track our short-term goals."

▶ AN AVERAGE DAY

"I typically start the day before the larger team gets in so I can go through my email, schedule, and to-do list without distractions. A typical day for me is full of interruptions, so this is my time to focus and organize myself. If new, high-priority work has come up, I go through my to-do list and reprioritize to ensure I'm tackling the most important tasks for the day.

"I then have a standup meeting with the production team to talk through what our personal and project focuses will be for the day and discuss any obstacles that need to be addressed.

"Following that, most of my day is focused on communication. I'm often in meetings with leadership and developers discussing project and studio updates and ways that production can support their efforts. I will dedicate some of my day working through issues that we are encountering.

"With the remainder of my time, I'll usually spend it looking ahead and backwards planning our next steps based on our long-term goals. I'm also looking for ways to improve our efficiency and methodologies at the studio."

▶ PROMOTIONAL PATH

"Assistant Producers are typically brand new to production, so we start them with basic project management responsibilities like taking meeting notes and following up on action items. Associate Producers' main focus is the day-to-day needs, like task management, creating schedules, and coordinating efforts with the various teams. Producers facilitate communication, build schedules and ensure milestones are hit, create resource plans, track budgets, identify and mitigate risks, and assist with other aspects of development. Senior Producers have a broader management and input into the project direction. Executive Producers communicate progress, project goals, and studio goals to stakeholders and the broader team. They help create processes and structure to promote efficiency and high-quality work."

▶ PROFESSIONAL PERKS

"I love working in game production. I get to work with every discipline in game development, so I experience a very comprehensive view of the game coming together and enjoy the personal relationships with the different disciplines as we work together. At Psyonix, we have so many fantastic perks. The snack closet alone keeps me happy, but we have monthly events, trips, and lots of really fun, team-building activities."

▶ CAREER CHALLENGES

"There are many challenges within production and I'm always encountering new and unique ones with every project. The following are challenges we typically encounter in production:

"Managing all the details and day-to-day of development, while looking ahead for what's coming next.

"Creating a schedule that takes into account possible risks, variance within reported estimates, and the inevitable unknowns that occur in a project.

"Limitations on resources and time and making the most effective and efficient use of what you have.

"Building effective and transparent communication. Producers need to take into account that people like communicating through different methods (emails, meetings, etc.) and they may need to adjust and duplicate communication in order for it to be properly understood. Information also needs to be to the point, but include details for those who need it, which can be tough to balance.

"Building consensus within a team with very different opinions. If a team believes in and agrees with the decisions being made, they will take accountability and be more motivated with the work.

"Keeping up the momentum and motivation on a project can also be difficult when the team has been working on the same thing for a long time, or are encountering a lot of obstacles.

"Managing expanding teams and products where you need to help facilitate integration, pipelines, and quality, all while new team members are being hired in the middle of the project can make communication more complicated."

"Get involved with games in any way you can and jump on opportunities. You never know what could end up being a doorway to a great job in the industry."

JENNELL JAQUAYS

MASTER OF GAMES ACROSS MEDIUMS

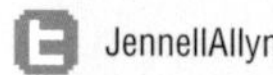 JennellAllyn

EXPERIENCE

FIRST INDUSTRY PROJECT: PAC-MAN TABLETOP ARCADE (1981)

FAVORITE INDUSTRY PROJECT: AGE OF EMPIRES III: THE WARCHIEFS EXPANSION (2006)

PROJECTS SHIPPED: 154 GAMES

ACHIEVEMENTS UNLOCKED:

> NOMINATED FOR THREE H.G. WELLS AWARDS FOR HER ROLE-PLAYING ADVENTURES

> SUMMER CES "ORIGINAL SOFTWARE AWARD"—WARGAMES (1984)

> MEMBER OF THE ACADEMY OF ADVENTURE GAMING ARTS & DESIGN HALL OF FAME (2017)

> LGBTQ NATION "TOP 50 SUCCESSFUL TRANSGENDER AMERICANS" (2017)

STATS

INDUSTRY LEVEL: 42

CURRENT CLASS: CONTENT DESIGNER & ARTIST

CURRENT GUILD: DRAGONGIRL STUDIOS—SEATTLE, USA

SPECIAL SKILLS: LEVEL DESIGN, CHARACTER CONCEPT ART, SCI-FI AND FANTASY ILLUSTRATION, CARTOONING, GAME ADVENTURE DESIGN

STANDARD EQUIPMENT

FAVORITE PLATFORM: XBOX 360

GO-TO GENRE: ACTION ROLE-PLAYING GAMES

MUST-HAVE GAME: SID MEIER'S PIRATES! (ORIGINAL VERSION)

BIO

Games of any form have been a passion for Jennell Jaquays all her life. Propelled by a relentless professional drive, her storied career includes work on games across mediums and genres—tabletop RPGs, board games, miniature games, arcade games, and home video games.

"I have a bachelor's degree in art, mostly focused on traditional media studio art," began Jaquays. "I took a lot of art classes, enough to have a major and a minor in art, if such a thing was possible. I also took fiction-writing classes, but abandoned thoughts of an English minor because that path entirely focused on being a teacher. I was aiming, hopefully, for a career as an illustrator."

Easter Egg

Is the second person ever to publish a stand-alone, self-contained role-play game adventure. In June of 1976, she published *F'Chelrak's Tomb* for *Dungeons & Dragons* in her fanzine, *The Dungeoneer*, missing first place by two weeks. Her first commercial *D&D* adventures are still in print 40 years after their initial publishing.

DUNGEONS & DRAGONS

Jaquays' career path began to gain focus with the 1974 release of a seminal fantasy tabletop RPG. "There was a moment in college when this new game called *Dungeons & Dragons (D&D)* entered my life," she recalled. "I didn't realize it at the time, but my college hobby of playing *Dungeons & Dragons* and then self-publishing adventures for the game established me as one of the pioneers in the tabletop role-play game industry, and then networking connections put me in a place where I almost stumbled into being a pioneer in video games a few years later."

In 1975, she began her career working as an illustrator for small role-playing game publishers. The illustrations for *Chitin I: The Harvest Wars* were her first ever professional game project. Jacquays also created content for *D&D* publisher TSR's *Dragon* magazine. "While I started creating art and writing adventures, it wasn't until I was 21 and just out of college, trying to find steady work as an artist, that the opportunity to work full-time in games occurred."

Steady work came when she joined game publisher Judges Guild in 1978, designing and illustrating adventures for RPGs like *D&D* and *RuneQuest*. "My *Dungeons & Dragons* game adventures *Dark Tower*, *Caverns of Thracia*, and *Book of Treasure Maps* are considered collectible classics of the genre," said Jaquays. After leaving Judges Guild, she returned to freelancing. A chance encounter led to a short contract position with Coleco, known best at the time for pools, big wheel tricycles, and hand-held electronic games.

COLECO

With an impressive array of tabletop RPG games already under her belt, Jaquays started full-time at Coleco as a game designer in 1981, tasked with creating new electronic game concepts and product prototypes. "When Coleco decided to enter the video game market, I was the only game designer still on staff and the only artist in Advanced Research & Development," explained Jaquays. "Coleco had the license for *Donkey Kong* and *Smurfs*, and with Toy Fair rapidly approaching, they needed to show what these characters and their environments would look like on our game screen. With markers and graph paper in hand, I blocked out our first look at what a ColecoVision Mario would look like."

Over the next five years, Jaquays built the foundation of Coleco's video game department. "I assembled, trained, and supervised both the game design and video game art departments during a time when there were no such things as video game designers or artists," she said. "My design team was responsible for the design end of the production of Coleco's non-educational video and computer games."

The 1981 *Pac-Man* tabletop arcade was Jaquays' first electronic game product, followed closely by the release of *Donkey Kong* for the ColecoVision in 1982. She also co-designed the 1984 title *WarGames* (based on the motion picture), which won the Summer CES Original Software Award in 1984.

> "With markers and graph paper in hand, I blocked out our first look at what a ColecoVision Mario would look like."

Jaquays and the few developers left on her team were laid off in June of 1985 as the collapse of the video game industry finally caught up to Coleco. Eventually, she began freelancing as an artist, writer, book editor, and computer game designer under her own studio name. "My clients were primarily fantasy role-playing game publishers like TSR, West End Games, and FASA, but I also worked for such diverse clients as Electronic Arts, Epyx, Interplay, Crossover Technologies, and *Guideposts* magazine," she revealed.

Jaquays' most notable projects at the time included design work on the first volume of Interplay's *Lord of the Rings*, the *Central Casting* character-generator series for Task Force Games, and the cover for TSR's *Dragon Mountain D&D* deluxe boxed adventure set. That painting and several others led her to working with them on staff from 1993 to 1997.

RETURNING TO THE ARENA

After a short hiatus from electronic entertainment, Jaquays joined id Software in 1997, where she would stay for five years. In that time, she constructed play areas for *Quake II*, *Quake III Arena*, and *Quake III: Team Arena*.

"*Quake II* represented my return to working on video games," she said. "I understood the concepts of designing complex play areas in 3D space needed to make tabletop game dungeon adventures, but extrapolating that to computer 3D space—with 1997's technical limitations on complexity—was a learning curve for me."

Jaquays adapted to the new medium of design and became a multidiscipline contributor on *Quake III*. "I designed, built, and decorated game levels for *Quake III*; wrote, outsourced, and edited bot chat copy; and even wrote the instruction book for how to use the level-creation tools," she said. "*Quake III Arena* took a risk by requiring a graphics-accelerator card to be played. It was a bold move. But the game established itself as possibly the best fast-action, first-person shooter—maybe even best shooter ever."

GUILDMASTER

In 2002, Jaquays left id to join Microsoft's Ensemble Studios. While developing games full time at the studio, she also worked with faculty and staff of Southern Methodist University (SMU) in the evenings to co-found SMU Guildhall, a graduate-level school focused on game design and development. As a "guildmaster," she collaborated on the school's art curriculum, and reviewed intake portfolios for the program. Valve's Gabe Newell was SMU's second commencement speaker—a graduate class that included Jaquays' son.

At Ensemble Studios, Jaquays worked as an artist, focusing on 3D world development. She created content for both the single and multiplayer campaigns of *Age of Empires III*. "My favorite project is still *The WarChiefs* expansion for *Age of Empires III*," said Jaquays. "Once *Age of Empires III* shipped, I joined a team tasked to create the first expansion for it. We decided to go with Native American cultures with a product that leveled the playing field for the Native Americans in a game about colonial expansionism. Our small team—a third the size of the original—spec'd out what we could do in less than a year, delivered on that, and then through our love for the project and were able to get more content in than originally planned. To top it all off, my son was one of the other artists on the project."

> "To top it all off, my son was one of the other artists on [*Age of Empires III* expansion]."

OLDE SKÜÜL

In 2009 Jaquays moved to CCP's North American office for three years, designing and developing the game world for the *World of Darkness* MMO. She is now a co-founder of Olde Sküül along with three other women game-industry veterans: Susan Manley, Maurine Starkey, and her wife, Rebecca Heineman. Jaquays directs the creative content for all company product and promotional material, including day-to-day management of outside creative resources. She also returned to freelancing under her brand Dragongirl Studios. Recent projects include concept art for licensed game miniatures based on her *Dark Tower D&D* adventure and a pair of RPG titles published under her Fifth Wall brand, *Quack Keep* and *The Dragon's Secret* (her first RPG adventures in nearly 30 years).

While Jaquays' four-decade career has innumerable points of pride, she feels her work at the SMU Guildhall—rated the top grad school for game design in the world by the Princeton Review—has made the biggest industry impact. "It has been producing top-tier game developers for the last 15 years, including people who go on to be leaders in the industry," she closed. Being a mother to one of those alumni undoubtedly makes the achievement that much more meaningful.

CAROL SHAW

RENOWNED ATARI AND ACTIVISION DESIGNER

EXPERIENCE

FIRST INDUSTRY PROJECT: POLO (1978)
FAVORITE INDUSTRY PROJECT: RIVER RAID (1983)
PROJECTS SHIPPED: 7 GAMES
ACHIEVEMENTS UNLOCKED:

> VIDEO GAME UPDATE "GAME OF THE YEAR"—RIVER RAID (1983)
> ARKIE AWARDS "BEST ACTION VIDEO GAME"—RIVER RAID (1984)
> NEXT GENERATION "TOP 100 GAMES OF ALL TIME"—RIVER RAID (1996)
> GAME AWARDS "INDUSTRY ICON AWARD" (2017)

STATS

INDUSTRY LEVEL: 6
CURRENT CLASS: RETIRED
CURRENT GUILD: HOME—CALIFORNIA, USA
SPECIAL SKILLS: COMPUTER SCIENCE, ELECTRICAL ENGINEERING

STANDARD EQUIPMENT

FAVORITE PLATFORM: ATARI 2600
GO-TO GENRE: RETRO
MUST-HAVE GAME: SIMCITY (1989)

BIO

Growing up in what would become Silicon Valley, Carol Shaw had the unique opportunity of being on the front lines of an emerging industry in her formative years. She had a high skill level in math from an early age; winning awards in math contests throughout junior high and high school. By the time Shaw left for college, she could already program in BASIC. Shaw attended the University of California at Berkeley and earned a bachelor's degree in electrical engineering and computer science. While finishing her master's, she began to interview for jobs and had several offers extended, including a position at Atari. Shaw had played early arcade games such as *Computer Space* and *Space Wars* and felt the job at Atari would be the most creative and fun out of the lot.

Easter Egg
Is signed up to be cryopreserved by the Alcor Life Extension Foundation at the time of her legal death so she can see the future.

"When I was a young girl, video games and personal computers didn't exist. My family played a lot of board games, including *Monopoly*, *Clue*, and *Careers*," explained Shaw. "In college, I had a Radio Shack video game that hooked up to my black-and-white TV set and played a game similar to *Pong*. Playing and programming video games for a living sounded like fun, and I had the assembly language experience that Atari needed."

ONE-WOMAN SHOW

Shaw started at Atari as a microprocessor software engineer in 1978, focused on programming games for the Atari VCS—later renamed the Atari 2600. As the only woman on her team, she remembers her gender not being relevant to her job or to her co-workers, with whom she shared a high level of respect.

Since these were the early days of gaming, developers rarely wore one hat. Shaw would not only design and program her games, but also create the graphics and sound. It was a one-woman show, aside from testing and feedback from peers.

Her first project at Atari was a *Polo* game in partnership with Ralph Lauren. Although the game was finished, the deal fell through and it was never published. Years later Shaw got permission from Atari to release the binary as part of a Starpath Supercharger game collection, *Stella Gets a New Brain.*

Over the next year, Shaw would design and program *Video Checkers*, *3D Tic-Tac-Toe,* and a port of *Super Breakout*—the latter a collaboration with fellow Atari employee Nick Turner. She and Ed Logg also teamed up on a version of *Othello.*

"At Atari, we typed the source code into a computer to be assembled by a cross-assembler. We didn't have any sort of paint or draw program to help us with the graphics. We would draw the images on graph paper, hand convert to hex ASCII, and then type the hex into our source code file. Designing the 'kernel,' the part of the software that generated the display on the TV for the Atari 2600, was also an interesting challenge. I also enjoyed programming the computer opponent in games such as *Video Checkers* and *3D Tic-Tac-Toe*."

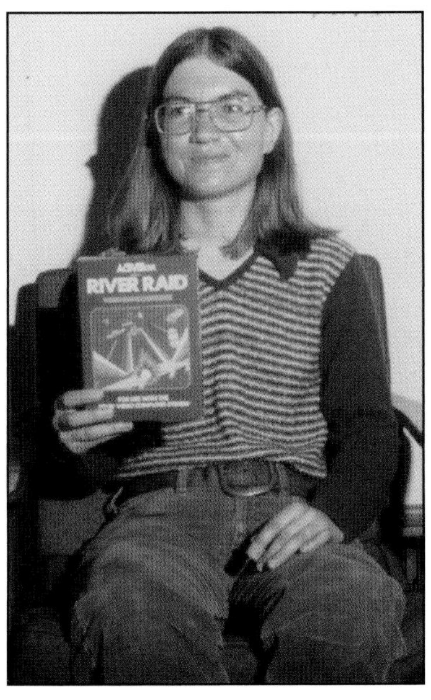

Outside of gaming, Shaw programmed a calculator to run on the Atari 800 computer. All of these releases were accomplished within the short window of time she was at Atari. Shaw left in 1980 just as the industry was starting a downturn; the stress of a lack of job security had deflated the fun of working there.

ACTIVISION

After a year-and-a-half stop at Tandem Computers working as an assembly language programmer, Shaw got an offer to join Activision in 1982, recruited by her ex-Atari co-workers. Her very first game at the company would become the most successful of her career—*River Raid*.

As it turns out, *River Raid* was nearly an interspace adventure. "I told Al Miller I was thinking of doing a space game, but he said there were too many space games, so he suggested that I come up with a different idea," said Shaw.

In *River Raid*, the player took control of a jet in enemy territory, flying above the "River of No Return" while keeping an eye out for hostile vehicles and fuel depots. Shaw's use of a vertical scrolling screen was an innovation at the time. "I wanted to do a scrolling shooter, and I was doodling on graph paper seeing what I could do with the playfield graphics," she explained. "I realized that if I scrolled horizontally, the graphics would jump four pixels at a time, whereas if I scrolled vertically, I could scroll smoothly, one television line at a time. The right and left halves of the screen could be identical, or they could be mirror images of each other. I realized that by using the mirror image mode, I could have a river with islands in the middle of it. I used a pseudo-random number generator with a fixed seed to generate a variety of landscape with a very small amount of memory."

Shaw became synonymous with the game due to Activision's practice of putting designer names on box art in a movie-poster presentation: "Carol Shaw's *River Raid.*" The game was a mega-hit for Activision—selling over a million copies. *River Raid* took home several end-of-year awards in 1984, and was noted as one of *Next Generation*'s "Top 100 Video Games of all Time" in 1996.

River Raid's success continued through ports to different consoles. Shaw was directly involved in the Atari 5200 home console and the Atari 800 computer versions. She also designed and programmed 1983's *Happy Trails* while at Activision, and began working on an unnamed graphic adventure before voluntarily returning to Tandem Computers, where she worked until 1990. Shaw took early retirement that year, thanks to *River Raid*'s success, smart investing, and having a working spouse. She would return to tech from time to time for volunteer work, including a part-time position as CIO at the Foresight Institute.

PRESERVING THE PAST

In 2017, Shaw donated her gaming memorabilia to the Strong National Museum of Play for their 2018 Women in Games Exhibit. Donations included video game cartridges, boxes, source code, design documents, sketches, promotional materials, and other assorted items from her time at Atari and Activision.

"We have the good fortune to be the home for several boxes of source code and design documents, and her attention to detail is staggering," said Women in Games Exhibit curator Shannon Symonds. "For her very first, unreleased game, *Polo*, she has printouts of encyclopedias discussing in-depth how the game is traditionally played. For her work on a calculator program, she has manuals and design specs for other calculators of the time. Her design documents show her incredible intelligence when it comes to math and coding."

"I am constantly amazed at her humble nature," continued Symonds. "She's been quite clear that she didn't think she was doing anything special or pioneering. She simply had a love of math and programming and put it to good use. I find her story incredibly inspirational, and whether or not she realized it at the time, she set herself up to be a wonderful role model for similarly minded young girls."

Shaw now lives the retired life with her husband Ralph Merkle. In 2017 she made a rare public appearance to accept the Industry Icon Award at the Game Awards, a recognition many video game veterans agree is well deserved.

A DAY IN THE LIFE OF...

A GAME DESIGNER

Game design is a coveted profession within development, but the specifics of the job are often nebulous to those who aspire to work in the industry. While it is true that creativity is needed in abundance to be a successful game designer, it must be tempered with an ability to identify and work within production and technology constraints, a deep understanding of the target audience, and honed communication skills. A critical eye is also imperative. Game designers don't just know if a game is bad, they can dissect exactly why. Is the core gameplay loop unfulfilling? Is the in-game economy unbalanced?

Principal Game Designer Katherine James knows her stuff, with seven years of experience leading her to head up one of Zynga's most successful brands. Specializing in the design of systems, economy, features, and content, James has her finger on the pulse of games in the social and mobile space.

KATHERINE JAMES

PROFESSION: PRINCIPAL GAME DESIGNER AT ZYNGA—SAN FRANCISCO, USA

YEARS IN PROFESSION: 7

ASSOCIATED WITH: WORDS WITH FRIENDS 2, GIFS AGAINST FRIENDS, DREAM CITY: METROPOLIS, BINGO!, FULL BLOOM, DISNEY ANIMAL KINGDOM EXPLORERS

▶ EDUCATION

"I have a Master of Entertainment and Technology degree from Carnegie Mellon University, where I focused on game design."

▶ BREAKING IN

"Unlike many of my colleagues in game design, breaking in was really easy for me but for a few specific reasons:

"1. I was applying for entry-level positions as a graduate student from a great university just as higher education was really starting to catch on to the games industry as a viable career space. I've seen a lot of student résumés over the past few years and my grad school's practice of critiquing résumés and cover letters definitely gave me an advantage over other applicants with similar qualifications.

"2. Unlike many of my male classmates considering the same opportunities, I had absolutely no qualms about working on Facebook games catering to a primarily older female demographic, so I had very little competition.

"3. I can be surprisingly sociable and outgoing when I want to be and I really turned it up at conventions when I was first job-hunting. I landed my first job by networking at a smaller industry convention in Austin in 2011 when I was still a grad student. I don't know if I would have been able to find a job so quickly had I gone through online channels alone."

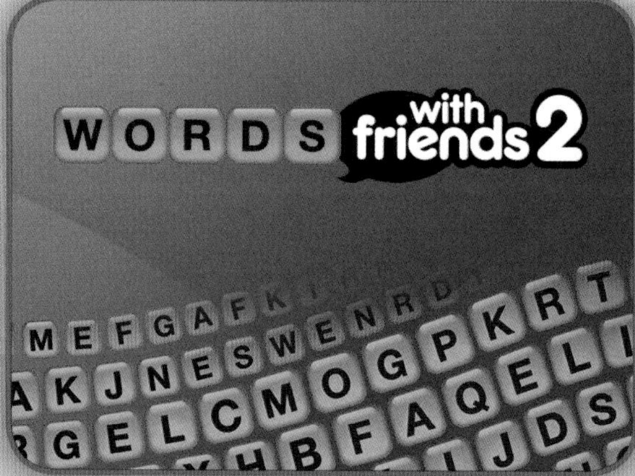

▶ KEY QUALITIES

"One of the biggest challenges I grapple with as a game design lead is balancing creative flexibility with my responsibility to preserve the game's identity and serve player needs. In the games industry, you never know when circumstances will change, necessitating reprioritization or modification of design decisions you thought were put to bed. In my role, it's important to understand how systems changes will impact the core player experience. Clearly articulating how potential design changes connect with the core loop and do—or do not—align with the game's pillars is crucial to finding solutions that meet leadership's goals while preserving overall game health.

"Being responsible for overseeing design decisions across multiple features and teams on the Words With Friends franchise, means I have to context shift on a regular basis.

"Regardless of what level you're at or your specialization, succeeding as a game designer requires excellent attention to detail. My teammates rely on me to produce design documents, economy spreadsheets, and presentations that are clear and accurate."

▶ TOOLS OF THE TRADE

"I use all things Google Drive: Docs, Sheets, and Slides. They are absolutely the best for collaborative work. I use Sheets for all of my economy work and to organize content. My team goes back and forth between using Slides and Docs for design documentation. We use Hipchat and Slack for online communication across the team."

▶ HOURS & ENVIRONMENT

"I usually work from around 9:30 am to 6 or 7 pm in an office with an open floor plan. Zynga has one of the most 'Silicon Valley' headquarters in the industry with our own culinary team that caters breakfast, lunch, and happy hours, a resident brewmaster, a gym complete with basketball court in the basement, and the building is dog-friendly! This is super important for me, because my four-year-old corgi has come to work with me every day since she was a puppy. Being surrounded by well-socialized dogs is really the best part of my work environment. There are also employee resource organizations supporting women and special interest groups."

▶ PROMOTIONAL PATH

"Most companies have a single career track that starts at Associate Game Designer and ends in Creative Director or some similar title, incorporating management at the Lead Game Designer level. Zynga makes room for game designers who are not interested in personnel management (like myself) by forking the career path after Senior.

"So the most common hierarchy is: Associate Game Designer > Game Designer > Senior Game Designer > Lead Game Designer > Director of Game Design > Creative Director.

"The individual contributor path at Zynga is: Associate Game Designer > Game Designer > Senior Game Designer > Principal Game Designer > Distinguished Game Designer > Game Design Fellow.

"Unlike the management track, ascending the individual track requires the designer to become a subject matter expert in one or more fields, mentorship in their areas of strength, and eventually impacting the discipline at a company-wide level."

▶ CAREER CHALLENGES

"I have always found that the greatest challenge in being a professional game designer in the social/mobile side of the industry is working with teammates who do not understand game design as a legitimate discipline with an actual skill set. Teaching someone the difference between having an opinion and having an expert opinion can be a real challenge in an industry where everyone is so passionate about what they are making.

"When teammates mistake passion for experience, problems arise. Unlike engineering, game design is largely a soft skill set; if your skills are lacking, the proof may not be immediately obvious. As a result, it can be extremely challenging for a non-game designer to identify quality game design candidates, or for a game designer with a solid skill set but underdeveloped communication skills to convince stakeholders that their decisions are sound.

James's corgi, Rini, accompanies her mom to work at Zynga each day.

"As a result, there are a lot of game designers in the industry who are either underleveled or overleveled, which exacerbates the general confusion around the value that a good game designer brings to a team. No matter which company or team I work on, no matter what my title, this has always been a struggle and I expect it always will be."

▶ FAVORITE PROJECT

"When I was working on Disney Animal Kingdom Explorers for Facebook, I got to take two business trips to Walt Disney World to meet with Animal Kingdom zoologists and conduct photo shoots of the park for content. We stayed at the Animal Kingdom Lodge hotel, had a private safari ride, and got to explore some of the parks before they opened to guests! We then had the afternoons free to visit all the parks, and entered for free with our employee badges and got amazing discounts. It doesn't get much cooler than that!"

PRO TIP!

"Learn some basic game design principals—core loops, economy inflows and outflows, primary aspiration—and be able to intelligently discuss popular games using that vocabulary. Anyone with access to the internet can tell you which games are and are not successful; a game designer's job is to know why. Endeavor to understand why a game works—or doesn't work—and you'll be well on your way to becoming a real game designer!"

THE 1980s: RISING FROM THE ASHES

1980: INTELLIVISION IS RELEASED

Touting the console's superior visuals in an aggressive marketing campaign against the Atari 2600, the Intellivision (a portmanteau of "intelligent television") was estimated to hold 20% of the home console market before the industry crashed in 1983[1]. Developers for the Intellivision included Activision, as well as Coleco, who manufactured the rival console, Colecovision.

1980: NINTENDO LAUNCHES GAME & WATCH HANDHELD LINE

In 1979, Nintendo designer Gunpei Yokoi observed a businessman killing time on an LCD calculator while using public transportation. This inspired Yokoi to develop the Game & Watch line of handheld gaming devices. Each release featured a single simplistic game, including *Ball, Helmet, Lion, Parachute, Octopus*, etc. Sixty Game & Watch titles were released between 1980 and 1991, popularizing the handheld gaming device market, and inspiring Nintendo's own Game Boy as well as rival efforts with the most notable coming from Tiger Electronics.

1980: PAC-MAN BECOMES VIDEO GAMING'S FIRST MASCOT

Developed by Namco and licensed for distribution in the US by Midway Games, *Pac-Man* was a pop culture phenomenon, generating over $1B in quarters in its first year, eclipsing the then-highest grossing film of all-time (*Star Wars*). Largely regarded as the first instance of a video game mascot, *Pac-Man* became a game industry icon with merchandising bringing in another $1B in revenue. The game was designed to appeal to a broader audience, and as a result, estimates suggest women comprised more than 50% of *Pac-Man*'s audience[2]. Adjusted for inflation, *Pac-Man*'s estimated total gross revenue is placed at around $7.5B based on the combined sales of unauthorized *Pac-Man* clones almost matching the number of units sold by the original[3].

1980 1981 1982 1983 1984

1980: VIDEO GAME CHAMPIONS

Rebecca Heineman became the first-ever person to win a national video game contest when she took the top spot in the *Space Invader*'s Championship, hosted in New York City. In 1984, then 58-year-old Doris Self scored an incredible 1,112,300 points in *Q*bert* at Twin Galaxies' Video Game Masters Tournament, becoming the highest scorer and the "world's oldest video game champion[4]."

1982: ACTIVISION VS. ATARI

After leaving Atari, the founders of Activision were part of a lawsuit claiming copyright and patent infringement. A court ruling solidified Activision's right to exist, changing the established business model of the industry. Whereas games had previously been released exclusively by the console makers, Activision and the court system had irreversibly established the third-party software market. Early Activision successes included *Chopper Command*, *River Raid*, and *Pitfall!*, the latter of which largely established the side-scrolling platform genre and was the best-selling home video game of 1982[6].

1981: DONKEY KONG HITS ARCADES

Supervised by Gunpei Yokoi, a young Nintendo designer named Shigeru Miyamoto created an arcade game titled *Donkey Kong*. After Nintendo failed to license *Popeye*, the game's characters were changed from Bluto, Olive Oyl, and Popeye, to Donkey Kong, Pauline, and Mario (originally Mr. Video/Jumpman), respectively. *Donkey Kong* was an industry-shattering success, earning Nintendo hundreds of millions of dollars in arcade unit sales and merchandising[5].

1981: WIZARDY ESTABLISHES CRPGS

Sir-Tech's 1981 *Wizardry: Proving Grounds of the Mad Overlord* for the Apple II served as the foundation for modern computer role-playing games. It inspired Origin Systems' *Ultima III: Exodus* (1983), which together popularized RPG mechanics such as turn-based battles and party-based systems and largely influenced other popular titles like *Final Fantasy* and *Dragon Quest*.

1982: DISNEY RELEASES TRON

Walt Disney Productions' 1982 film *Tron* focuses on a software engineer who is downloaded into a virtual world. The filmmakers, who were directly inspired by *Pong* and the growing possibilities of technology, featured groundbreaking visual effects for the time. While *Tron* was a moderately successful film on its own, it had a far-reaching cultural impact, such as influencing future Pixar Animation Studios head John Lasseter who would later go on record to say that "Without *Tron*, there would be no *Toy Story*."[7]

1983: M.U.L.E. MAKES AN IMPACT

Inspired by *Monopoly* and lead designer Danielle Bunten Berry's own real-time auction game, *Wheelers Dealers*, *M.U.L.E.* was one of the first notable implementations of a multiplayer video game, allowing up to four players to compete on a single console. While *M.U.L.E.* was not particularly successful at the time, it gained a cult following that included *Donkey Kong* creator Shigeru Miyamoto and future *SimCity* developer Will Wright. *M.U.L.E.*—and its creator—are remembered as revolutionary for the time.

1983: THE VIDEO GAME CRASH

As happened in the late 1970s with coin-op ball-and-paddle games, the North American home console market became oversaturated in the early 1980s, leading to a cataclysmic market crash. The legalized third-party software market and lack of platform-control measures on the Atari 2600 opened the floodgates to an abundance of low-quality games, with the most infamous being Atari's *E.T. The Extra-Terrestrial*. The personal computer market, led by the Apple II and Commodore 64, simultaneously applied pressure on home consoles, as it provided a better investment for fiscally-aware families. Many companies and products were dealt critical blows, or were outright eradicated, due to the video game crash.

1983-87: NINTENDO LAUNCHES THE FAMICOM/NES

Nintendo released the Family Computer (Famicom) in Japan in 1983, then later as the Nintendo Entertainment System (NES) in the West in late 1985. The platform was largely immune to the earlier video game crash and went on to sell (globally) over 60M lifetime units[8]. Flagship Nintendo titles such as *Super Mario Bros.*, *Metroid*, and *The Legend of Zelda* pushed the NES to the forefront of the market where it remained for the entirety of the third generation of home consoles. The NES was so successful that Nintendo had little reason to invest in a 16-bit console, despite competition from multiple SEGA consoles and NEC Home Electronics' TurboGrafx-16, the latter of which kicked off the fourth generation of consoles in 1987.

During this time, Nintendo established the now-standard industry practice of licensing the rights to release third-party titles on its hardware, which helped prevent the same quality control issues that caused Atari to lose its grasp on the market.

1985 1986 1987 1988 1989

1989: SIMCITY IS RELEASED

Designed by Will Wright and published by Maxis, *SimCity* was a financial and critical success, popularizing simulation games and spawning dozens of "Sim" spin-offs and imitators, the most notable being Maxis' own *The Sims* in 2000.

1989: NINTENDO RELEASES THE GAME BOY

Developed by Gunpei Yokoi and the Nintendo Research and Development 1 team, the Nintendo Game Boy was the first immensely successful handheld game console, combining elements of the NES and Game & Watch devices. Although it was technically inferior to rival devices such as the Atari Lynx and Sega Game Gear, the Game Boy succeeded in part thanks to Nintendo's strong branding and the breakout success of *Tetris*, which came bundled with the Game Boy.

(NO) WOMEN IN GAMING

By the time games became an entertainment staple, they were considered toys, and toys were sold in gendered sections of stores. Marketers had limited budgets and needed to focus on key demographics [9].The numbers showed video gamers were mostly male, and the marketing followed suit accordingly. While Atari ads in the early 1980s had pictured young girls and their mothers, advertisements industry-wide transitioned to appeal to boys and men, including the overt use of hyper-sexualized women as marketing tools. This practice only intensified as games became more successful and violent in nature, continuing well into the modern age.

Narratives followed suit, with some of gaming's biggest franchises reducing its female characters to damsels in distress needing constant rescue from the protagonist. Even anthropomorphic mascots were given sexualized trophies for love interests.

1. Sklarewitz, Norman. "Computerized Games Hit Profits Jackpot for Mattel Company." The Christian Science Monitor. May 24, 1982.
2. *How to Win Video Games*. Pocket Books. 1982. pp. 86–87.
3. "Top 10 Highest-Grossing Arcade Games of All Time". USgamer. January 1, 2016
4. Buck, Stephanie. "This Granny Gamer Set World Records against Players Half Her Age." Timeline. March 26, 2017.
5. Jörg Ziesak (2009), "Wii Innovate—How Nintendo Created a New Market Through Strategic Innovation," GRIN Verlag, p. 2029
6. "The Players Guide to Fantasy Games." Electronic Games. June 1983. p. 47
7. "In Tron We Trust | Disney Insider." Oh My Disney. July 08, 2016.
8. "Consolidated Sales Transition by Region" (PDF). First Console by Nintendo. January 27, 2010.
9. Lien, Tracey. "No Girls Allowed." Polygon. December 02, 2013.

REBECCA ANN HEINEMAN

PROLIFIC VIDEO GAME PROGRAMMER AND ENTREPRENEUR

 burgerbecky  burgerbecky.com

EXPERIENCE

FIRST INDUSTRY PROJECT: LONDON BLITZ (1982)

FAVORITE INDUSTRY PROJECT: DRAGON WARS (1989)

PROJECTS SHIPPED: 250+ GAMES

ACHIEVEMENTS UNLOCKED:

> ATARI "NATIONAL SPACE INVADERS CHAMPIONSHIP WINNER" (1980)

> SMITHSONIAN "ART OF VIDEO GAMES" SHOWCASE—BARD'S TALE III: THIEF OF FATE (2012)

> INTERNATIONAL VIDEO GAME HALL OF FAME & MUSEUM INDUCTEE (2017)

> HAS WON MULTIPLE AWARDS FOR "SAILOR RANKO," HER SAILOR MOON FANFICTION

STATS

INDUSTRY LEVEL: 40

CURRENT CLASS: CEO/CTO

CURRENT GUILD: OLDE SKÜÜL, INC.—EL CERRITO, USA

SPECIAL SKILLS: PROGRAMMING, GAME DESIGN, TECHNICAL DESIGN, WRITING, REVERSE-ENGINEERING, CODE OPTIMIZATION, SYSTEM ARCHITECTURE DESIGN, SHARPSHOOTING, BAKING

STANDARD EQUIPMENT

FAVORITE PLATFORM: APPLE II

GO-TO GENRE: COMPUTER ROLE-PLAYING GAMES

MUST-HAVE GAME: BARD'S TALE III: THIEF OF FATE

BIO

Rebecca Heineman has one of the most prolific careers in the history of video games, with four decades of programming, designing, and entrepreneurial endeavors on her résumé. It all started with some well-intentioned piracy.

"I was so poor when I was young, I couldn't afford to buy Atari 2600 cartridges," began Heineman. "I was able to teach myself how to copy cartridges and amassed a huge video game collection. Not satisfied with copying, I reverse-engineered how the games worked."

One of the games Heineman copied was *Space Invaders*, and at 14, her top scores were pretty impressive. "In 1980, a friend took me to Los Angeles to compete in the Atari 2600 National *Space Invaders* regional, which I had no hope of even making the top 100," she recalled. "I was shocked that I won, and even more shocked that I won the championships in New York a few months later."

As the first national video game tournament champion on record, the newfound visibility resulted in offers to write about video games for *Electronic Games Magazine*, as well as consulting for a book called *How to Master the Video Games*. "When I mentioned to a magazine publisher that I reverse-engineered the Atari 2600, he arranged for me to meet the owners of Avalon Hill and I was hired as a game programmer on the spot." Heineman, 16 at the time, moved cross-country, forgoing her high school diploma, and has been making games ever since.

Avalon Hill was primarily known for board games at the time, but was looking to enter the video gaming market. Heineman's initial responsibility was training their staff to program Atari 2600 games. "I wrote the entire manual for the programming team at Avalon Hill," she said. "I also wrote the main game engine, and another programmer did the game logic." Heineman worked on the foundational code for a few pieces of software—including *London Blitz*—which shipped after she departed Avalon.

"When I mentioned to a magazine publisher that I reverse-engineered the Atari 2600, he arranged for me to meet the owners of Avalon Hill and I was hired as a game programmer on the spot."

INTERPLAY

After a short while at Avalon, Heineman returned to California and briefly worked at a small developer called Boone Corporation, where she programmed *Chuck Norris Superkicks* and *Robin Hood*.

"I learned how to program the C64, Apple II, VIC-20, IBM PC, and other assembly languages in short order," she continued. "I learned so much about game hardware and game design while I was creating games."

In 1983 when Boone shut down, she founded Interplay Productions along with colleagues Jay Patel, Troy Worrell, and Brian Fargo. As lead programmer, her early Interplay work included *Wasteland*, *Bard's Tale*, *Out of This World*, and *Wolfenstein 3D* for Mac and 3DO.

Programming *Out of This World* is particularly memorable for Heineman. "When I was creating *Out of This World* for the Super Nintendo, I was told over and over that the game couldn't be done. I proved it could be done and made Interplay a lot of money," she said. "Being able to do the impossible is what makes me hover over my keyboard day in and day out."

Heineman earned more creative control over games with time, and was responsible for design work on *The Bard's Tale III: Thief of Fate*, *Dragon Wars*, *Tass Times in Tonetown*, *Borrowed Time*, *Mindshadow*, and *The Tracer Sanction*, among others.

Easter Egg

Earned the nickname "Burger" because she would purchase a bag full of 29-cent hamburgers from a nearby hamburger stand and bring them back to Interplay to eat throughout the day. She would sneak burgers into games as Easter eggs as a result.

Bard's Tale III stands out as one of her defining moments at Interplay and of her entire career. "Being able to head the project and be the decision maker was what started me on the path to being a studio head," she explained. *Bard's Tale III* would go on to be featured as part of the Smithsonian's "Art of Video Games" exhibit.

Heineman stayed at Interplay until 1995, watching it grow to upwards of 500 employees. She departed for a new entrepreneurial adventure, desiring a return to small but passionate teams.

A LOGICAL MOVE

In 1995 Heineman co-founded Logicware, primarily as a publisher of Macintosh titles, but eventually expanded to take on work for 3DO, Id, Activision, MGM Interactive, and both Avalon Hill and Interplay. Since she acted as both chief technical officer and lead programmer, core technologies fell under her remit. She additionally oversaw a handful of original titles for Windows 32, Mac, and Dreamcast, and led programming efforts on ports of *Out of This World*, *Shattered Steel*, *Jazz Jackrabbit II*, and *Half-Life* (Mac), which was finished but never released.

Heineman notes that the most difficult project of her career took place at Logicware. "*DOOM* for 3DO was literally the project from hell," she said. "Long story short, I had to port *DOOM* for the Atari Jaguar to the 3DO in 10 weeks while at the same time dealing with a client who had set expectations beyond the stratosphere." Despite the intense time constraint, she managed to do it within the allotted time.

CONTRABAND ENTERTAINMENT

Heineman founded Contraband Entertainment in 1999, and would run it for nearly 15 years as CEO, working on both original games and platform ports with a staff of 25 people under her wing. She personally took the lead on projects such as *Myth III: The Wolf Age*, the *Activision Anthology*, *Aliens vs. Predator* (Mac), *Baldur's Gate II* (Mac), and *Heroes of Might and Magic IV* (Mac).

While running Contraband, Heineman kept busy with consulting work. For three years she was a Senior Engineer III at Electronic Arts—self-described as a "troubleshooter and bug hunter"—and contributed to *Medal of Honor: Rising Sun*, *GoldenEye: Rogue Agent*, *Medal of Honor: Pacific Assault*, *Medal of Honor: European Assault*, *Battle for Middle-Earth II* (Xbox 360), and *Command & Conquer III* (Xbox 360).

Shorter contracts saw her helping companies improve their core technology, such as developing Wii, Xbox 360, PlayStation 3, and Nintendo DS engines for Barking Lizards Technologies. She went to work optimizing code for Sensory Sweep, as well as getting desired feature sets into their games.

At Ubisoft, Heineman maintained and upgraded their proprietary engines across various platforms. She spent a short period of time at Bloomberg and Amazon as a senior software architect, and tackled projects at Microsoft and Sony. She traveled to development studios around the world and provided training on how to make products perform their best on the latest Xbox 360 technology for Microsoft. At Sony, she primarily focused on kernel programming—the code at the core of a computer's operating system—for the PSP and PlayStation 4.

GOING OLD-SCHOOL

After the closure of Contraband in 2013, Heineman teamed up with three other industry veterans—Jennell Jaquays, Maurine Starkey, and Susan Manley—to form Olde Sküül, where she currently works as CEO. The company aims to create retro games with modern sensibilities.

Additionally, Heineman has been a member of the Video Game History Museum advisory board since 2011. She consults on the historical significance of artifacts, assists in fundraising efforts, and verifies the accuracy of content related to the history of video games.

FEELING GLAAD

Since Heineman came out as transgender in the early 2000s, she's made a point to celebrate diversity and make safe spaces for other LGBTQ+ community members within video games. While at Amazon, she was the Transgender Chair of Glamazon, the LGBTQ+ group within the company designed to encourage and support member growth. She also currently sits on the Board of Directors for GLAAD, advising on issues that affect the community as it relates to the tech and video game industries.

"I was at PAX Prime when I met a fan who told me that my work inspired her to overcome her fear of being LGBT, to teach herself programming, and create her own career in the video game industry," recalled Heineman. "Being told I'm a role model was a turning point in how I approach the gaming world."

BRENDA ROMERO

ILLUSTRATING THAT THE MECHANIC IS THE MESSAGE

 BR  blromero.com

EXPERIENCE

FIRST INDUSTRY PROJECT: WIZARDRY: PROVING GROUNDS OF THE MAD OVERLORD (1981)

FAVORITE INDUSTRY PROJECT: GUNMAN TACO TRUCK (2017)

PROJECTS SHIPPED: 40+ GAMES, 3 BOOKS

ACHIEVEMENTS UNLOCKED:

> WOMEN IN GAMING "LIFETIME ACHIEVEMENT AWARD" (2013)

> GAME DEVELOPER'S CHOICE "AMBASSADOR AWARD" (2015)

> BAFTA SPECIAL AWARD (2017)

> DEVELOP: BRIGHTON "DEVELOPMENT LEGEND AWARD" (2017)

 STATS

INDUSTRY LEVEL: 37

CURRENT CLASS: GAME DESIGNER & CEO

CURRENT GUILD: ROMERO GAMES—GALWAY, IRELAND

SPECIAL SKILLS: GAME DESIGN, LEVEL DESIGN, SYSTEMS DESIGN, GAME WRITING, SCRIPTING

STANDARD EQUIPMENT

FAVORITE PLATFORM: THE WORLD

GO-TO GENRE: NARRATIVE EXPLORATION

MUST-HAVE GAME: CIVILIZATION REVOLUTION

BIO

Brenda Romero's favorite gaming platform is the world. "There are no limits. I make my games in PC, console, mobile, and tabletop," began Romero. "Some of my games don't fit conveniently on a tabletop, though, and some simply wouldn't work when digitized. Limiting myself to a single platform limits my ability to express an idea. My game *One Falls for Each of Us* has 50,000 pieces. There's no other way to release that game."

As one of the most veteran and influential figures in gaming, Romero has been making games since the furthest reaches of her memory. As a child she would scavenge garage sales and salvage board games. "I would use pieces from board games and make my own," reflected Romero. "I built entire worlds—or so I thought—out of toys."

Easter Egg

Intentionally seeks out and sleeps overnight at haunted castles in Ireland, including Leap Castle, allegedly the most haunted in Europe. Has yet to see a ghost.

DUNGEONS, DRAGONS, AND WIZARDS

Drawing from her already long history of game design—and an informal education via the first edition of *Dungeons & Dragons*—Romero got her start in the industry at 15. "I was fortunate that a game company, Sir-Tech Software, started in my hometown thanks to Robert Woodhead and his programming genius," explained Romero. "He and his co-designer Andrew Greenberg created the *Wizardry* series."

"Limiting myself to a single platform limits my ability to express an idea."

Romero's primary responsibility was to know these games inside and out, starting with *Wizardry: Proving Grounds of the Mad Overlord*. In the days before the Internet, if people were stuck in a game they had to call for help and it was Romero they reached.

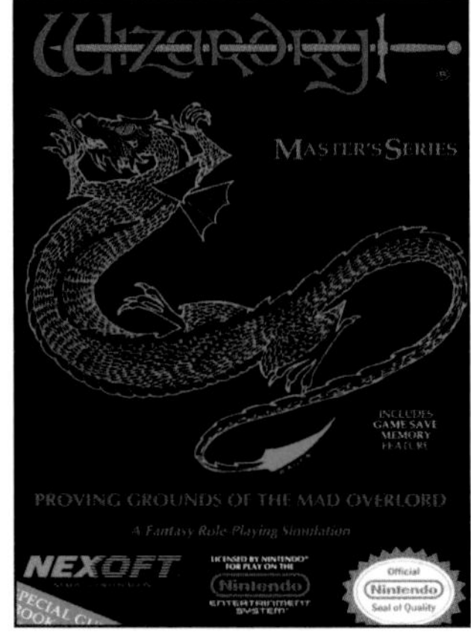

Sir-Tech would be her home for nearly two decades, until going defunct in 2003. While at Sir-Tech, she studied technical communications at Clarkson University.

"The curriculum was part programming and part writing—perfect for a game designer," said Romero. Over time, her role evolved from writing game manuals to writing entire games, and from testing games to designing them. Romero most heavily contributed to the ongoing *Wizardry* series, as well as the *Jagged Alliance* games. Her work as game designer and writer on the eighth installment of *Wizardry* earned five RPG of the Year awards and a variety of Editor's Choice honors.

STUDYING SEX IN GAMES

After a long time at a single studio, Romero designed for an array of publishers over the next several years. Two years were dedicated to designing *Dungeons & Dragons: Heroes* while at Atari, another two as lead designer on *Playboy: The Mansion* for Cyberlore Studios. She also spent a period of time at Electronic Arts working on *Def Jam: Icon*.

Designing a *Playboy* game sparked a new interest in Romero. She founded the IDGA Sex Special Interest Group—now called the Romance and Sexuality Group—in 2005, as a means of addressing the unique circumstances of developing and marketing adult-oriented games. In 2006, Romero formalized her research in a book, aptly called *Sex in Video Games*. The book examined the history of sexual content in games, while also exploring ethical concerns and the responsibility that parents and retailers play in keeping adult games away from minors. That same year Romero wrote *Challenges for Game Designers*, a collection of non-digital exercises to sharpen game design skills.

THE MECHANIC IS THE MESSAGE

In the mid-2000s Romero detoxed from the digital world and returned to her roots with analog games. She developed a series of six games under the umbrella of *The Mechanic is the Message*. "These games are part of a series of documentary games I made about profoundly difficult moments in human history," explained Romero. Over four years, she would explore the slave trade in *The New World*, the holocaust in *Train*, and the Trail of Tears in *One Falls for Each of Us*, the latter taking six years to complete. Each game was a one-of-a-kind installation, showcased at conferences, galleries, and museums. The most recent piece was released in 2009. *Train* won the Vanguard Award at IndieCade in 2009 and was covered in the *Wall Street Journal*. Romero discussed the series in a 2011 TEDxPhoenix Talk, *Games for Understanding*.

It isn't a surprise that these were—and continue to be—the most challenging projects of her career. "The subject matter was incredibly painful, and it was necessary to feel that pain to make it come through in the game," she explained. "When I made my documentary games, the notion that games had to be fun was strong, almost impervious. To make games about difficult subject matter was unheard of. However, books, photographs, paintings, movies, and music did. Games were stuck in a box of our own construction. So, in that sense, these games were transformational and certainly transformational for me."

SOCIAL GAMES & SCHOLARLY PURSUITS

Returning from her digital hiatus in 2009, Romero worked as creative director and designer on a variety of casual and social games. A result of her collaboration with fellow industry veteran and future husband John Romero, LOLapps' hit *Ravenwood Fair* was nominated for several large industry awards. The success inspired the pair to found Loot Drop in 2010, developing games for Rock You, Electronic Arts, Ubisoft, and Zynga before closing in 2015.

Romero's achievements were also recognized in academic circles. She served as chair of the Savannah College of Art and Design's Interactive Design and Game Development Department from 2008 to 2009. In 2012 Romero became the first game designer in residence at the Games and Playable Media Program of the University of California, Santa Cruz, also serving as director. In 2014 she was the recipient of a Fulbright award, allowing her to study the games industry, academic, and government policy in Ireland. Still residing in Ireland, Romero is the program director of Game Design and Development at the University of Limerick.

ROMERO GAMES

Settling down in Galway, Brenda and John co-founded Romero Games in 2015. "I really love where I am at now, genuinely. I work with such a great group of people," she said. "As each group has built out—programming, art, design—we have really taken care as a team to gate-keep and to make sure that those joining the team are great fits, not just technically, but personally. Building a game, building a company, and building a community are all intensely rewarding experiences." The studio has two games in production currently.

The work is rewarding on a more personal level, too. Romero Games' 2017 release *Gunman Taco Truck* was made in collaboration with her son. "It was amazing to take a kid's idea for a game—my then-nine-year-old son Donovan—and turn it into a game with my family," said Romero. "The joy on my son's face when I told him that *Gunman Taco Truck* had made its first $10,000 is one of my favorite memories. By game standards, that's not a lot of money. For a 12-year-old kid, though? That's all the money in the world." She's now working on a game with her daughter. "It's true that I've won awards and had some accolades that have surprised me, but you can't beat seeing your own kids happy," said Romero.

ASSOCIATIONS & ACCOLADES

Reflecting on Romero's career, it is clear those accolades are well-deserved. The recognitions Romero has earned include top rankings in "most influential" lists by *Forbes*, *Next Generation*, *Gamasutra*, and *Develop*. She has been recognized with various lifetime-achievement awards, women-in-games awards, ambassador awards, and a Women of the Year award. Her work has been celebrated by industry press, industry peers, and entities entirely outside of gaming.

With 37 years of experience behind her, Romero has evolved alongside the industry. "What hasn't changed since 1981? Surprisingly, there is at least one thing that hasn't—curiosity is still the greatest asset that I have," Romero concluded. "I research subjects exhaustively for as long as I remain interested. Who knows if they'll come out in a game? The game I'm making now has been an interest of mine since I was at least 17. I remember being fascinated by it when I was growing up. Here I am 30 years later, making a game about it."

"What hasn't changed since 1981? Curiosity is still the greatest asset I have."

A DAY IN THE LIFE OF...

A LEVEL DESIGNER

Level designers are architects of virtual worlds, establishing gameplay scenarios and constructing the environments in which they unfold. While goals vary by genre, successfully designed levels facilitate mission flow through scripted events, include visual landmarks to guide players to their objectives, and fit the overall aesthetic of the game.

Level Design is an iterative process, requiring regular user tests and fine tuning until the content meets the team's established goals for vision and quality. As a Level Designer, Dontnod Entertainment's Sophie Bécam closely collaborates with engineers who build and customize tools, artists who turn simple blockmesh into stunning worlds, and fellow level and narrative designers to ensure the game as a whole feels cohesive. Her work on *Life is Strange*'s Arcadia Bay helped provide the foundation for the mundane-turned-mystical adventure of Max Caulfield and childhood friend Chloe Price.

SOPHIE BECAM

 Sophie Becam

PROFESSION: GAME & LEVEL DESIGNER AT DONTNOD ENTERTAINMENT—PARIS, FRANCE

YEARS IN PROFESSION: 4

ASSOCIATED WITH: MONOPOLY, FRAGMENTS, LIFE IS STRANGE, CAPTAIN SPIRIT, LIFE IS STRANGE 2

▶ EDUCATION

"I have a Masters degree in Management, Game, and Level design. I studied at Supinfogame in France. At this school, I mostly studied video game history, analysis, management techniques, and game and level design. We used to do 'intensive weeks' where, in a small group, we would create a game. At the end of the week, we would submit it to the teachers and clients. The process helped us to understand the priorities of how to make a game.

"Besides that, I'm self-taught on most of the editors I use—Unity and Unreal 3, but mostly Unreal 4. I like to participate in game jams because I can set a goal and create a game on my own. That way I always learn new things in art, game design, or scripting. And, if the game isn't fun, I tell myself 'I made this in two days... it's not great, but at least I've learned something. I had fun making it!'"

▶ BREAKING IN

"The first step I faced was my own fears. I discovered that there were video game schools and wondered if working on a video game was a real job. Keep in mind that at that time I wanted to study Biology and had already found a university. I had to choose between a safe choice and an unknown path. I told myself that, if I ever fail at video games, it would be easier to come back to Biology rather than the other way around. Video games would also combine a lot of things I like: creativity, technicity, and technology. Then I had to convince my parents.

"During school, I discovered that I didn't have such a great understanding of video game culture, so I forced myself—and still do—to play and analyze a lot of different video game genres. Even if I don't really like the game, I try to pinpoint the good, bad, and what could be improved on the game's mechanics. Now that I am working, it's relatively easy for me. I know where I want to go and the things I like and don't like to work on."

▶ EARLY INDUSTRY IMPRESSIONS

"I was surprised by the diversity of jobs needed in the production of a video game. I often thought that a video game was about the gameplay, the environment and level design, the art, the sound, and the narration. But there are so many more jobs than that! There is also lighting, visual FX, testers, production, community management, the engine developers, the gameplay developers, and so on. Moreover, a lot of my coworkers come from other forms of media. Some worked on films, web design, or software. It's not necessary to study video games to make your way in the video game industry.

"What disappointed me a bit at first is that when you found a woman at a video game company, they were mostly in the administrative jobs, art, or production. There weren't many in the technical fields like programming or design. It's slowly changing and it's really something women should not be afraid of!"

▶ KEY QUALITIES

"If you want to work on a video game, you have to be curious! Never stop learning new things and never tell yourself that you know everything. Being able to work in groups is also important."

▶ TOOLS OF THE TRADE

"I mostly use video game editors—Unreal 3, Unreal 4, Unity—and Microsoft Word for documentation."

▶ HOURS & ENVIRONMENT

"I work about 37 hours a week, 10:00 am to 7:00 pm, in an open floorplan."

▶ AN AVERAGE DAY

"I'm a level designer on a new *Life is Strange*, but also an episode manager, so I need to check the episode consistency between all the level designers' work, and check with the producers to ensure the planning is correct. Generally, I have meetings to discuss features with the programmers. I also design and script levels in the editor and then review the level with the design and narrative team. I also talk with other project members to ease the production of assets."

PRO TIP!

"In level design, knowing how to guide a player's navigation in the environment is the key to a good map. You can study urban design to understand how architects deal with pedestrian paths, and you can study light and image composition to create an appealing and understandable environment. Get some notions in psychology to understand the frustration and reward balance!"

▶ PROMOTIONAL PATH

"The traditional promotional path begins with Level Designer, then Leads, Producers, and the Game Director overseeing the whole project."

▶ PROFESSIONAL PERKS

"As a level designer in a medium-sized company, I work closely with the narrative designers and game directors. I can easily discuss any concepts with them. Since they trust us, they usually don't force an idea, but rely on us to be creative and to present some gameplay."

▶ CAREER CHALLENGES

"Having to restrain yourself when designing something. Since we don't have an unlimited budget, even the best idea can be pushed aside because of the cost to produce it."

▶ FAVORITE PROJECT

"On the game *Fragments,* I was able to use the HoloLens from Microsoft. It was really awesome to see all the possibilities of these goggles. There is voice recognition, hand gesture recognition, and recognition of your surroundings. In *Fragments*, we could differentiate the player's couch from the table and use that to display different objects and gameplay. And as the video game industry is mostly about 'new technologies,' we often have the opportunity to try it early. For example, I've been able to prototype some personal games on the HTC Vive because the company had one."

▶ LIFE HACKS

"Know what your limits are and when to ask for help. Set achievable goals. If you want to fulfill difficult tasks, don't do it to be respected as a woman, do it for your own pride as an individual. Also, set some goals that are fun to accomplish!"

DONA BAILEY

GAVE CENTIPEDE ITS LEGS

 dona_c_bailey

EXPERIENCE

FIRST INDUSTRY PROJECT: CENTIPEDE (1981)
FAVORITE INDUSTRY PROJECT: CENTIPEDE (1981)
ACHIEVEMENTS UNLOCKED:
> ARKIE AWARDS "BEST COMPUTER ACTION GAME"—CENTIPEDE (1984)
> NEXT GENERATION "TOP 100 GAMES OF ALL TIME"—CENTIPEDE (1996)
> PHI KAPPA PHI (SINCE 2004)
> WOMEN IN GAMES INTERNATIONAL KEYNOTE SPEAKER (2007)

STATS

INDUSTRY LEVEL: 4
CURRENT CLASS: PROFESSOR OF RHETORIC AND WRITING
CURRENT GUILD: UNIVERSITY OF ARKANSAS AT LITTLE ROCK, USA
SPECIAL SKILLS: SOFTWARE DEVELOPMENT, RESEARCH, TEACHING, WRITING

STANDARD EQUIPMENT

FAVORITE PLATFORM: UNIX
GO-TO GENRE: NONFICTION
MUST-HAVE GAME: ROBOTRON: 2084

Easter Egg

Almost finished writing a script about working at Atari from 1980 to 1982 as programmer on *Centipede*.

BIO

Although programmer Dona Bailey pursued other professional goals after working in video games for a brief time, she left a mark on the world of coin-op arcades in the early 1980s. Intending to study literature and history, she arrived at college and found those fields overflowing with like-minded students. Bailey wanted to take a less-travled path, and decided to explore other areas of interest—psychology and biology. Along the way, Bailey unexpectedly discovered a love of programming, despite disliking math. She approached programming from a language standpoint, the syntax and structure of coding appealing to her greatly.

After college graduation, Bailey moved to California and found a job at General Motors, working as an assembly-language programmer using microprocessors in Cadillac engines. While working at GM, she overheard "Space Invader" by the Pretenders, and asked a friend about the song's title. Bailey was excitedly escorted to a nearby bar during lunch, where she was shown the arcade cabinet that inspired the song. Having never played a video game before, Bailey's first quarter did not last long. An interest was sparked within her, however. The display reminded her of the ones she programmed at GM, and so Bailey began investigating the video game industry. Eventually, she worked her way to Atari's coin-op division, after discovering Atari used the same 6502 microprocessors in their games that she programmed at GM.

Bailey remembers the culture of Atari being younger and rowdier than that of GM. "At Atari, we fit into age categories pretty well in my time in the early 1980s," she explained. "Programmers and hardware engineers who did not have other responsibilities were mostly in their 20s, supervisors and management people were primarily in their early 30s, and I think people who were higher up in the administrative hierarchy were in their late 30s to 40s. I spent most of my time at Atari with other people—guys—who were in their 20s, just as I was. It's funny, but I had always been the youngest person at any previous workplace. At Atari, where I was 24 to 26, I was not 'old,' but I was two or three years older than a lot of people. Overall, we were young and frequently immature, but doing our best." She remembers being the only woman in a 30-person department when she started. After a period of rapid growth, the team size jumped to over 100 when she left two years later.

At that time, Bailey and her colleagues knew they were on the front line of technology, and she acknowledges it was a once-in-a-lifetime experience. "It takes hard work and a lot of concentration and focus to embark on and then complete any creative project," Bailey shared. "But the one thing that was most different at Atari in those days, that I've never encountered anywhere else in my work, was the feeling of being on a frontier where there is no road map to look to as an example."

In an emerging industry, Atari rarely had the luxury of reflecting on past successes. Every day, every game, was something new. "That sense of moving forward without reflecting on the past can be unnerving and led to feeling lost sometimes, but it is also exciting and innervating at the same time," she continued. "I remember wanting to have time and energy to dream bigger. I wanted to find new ways to use games to make people happy and to teach them useful ideas and concepts at the same time. I think I've continued through the years to want to use digital tools in those same ways."

"I remember wanting to have time and energy to dream bigger."

BAILEY'S BUG

Atari kept a notebook in the coin-op department, filled with game ideas from employee brainstorming sessions. Most of them focused on sports or war, which didn't interest Bailey. She was assigned to create a game from concept to completion, and was hopeful she could find something inspiring. An idea with a one-sentence description captured her attention. In the notebook, Bailey read, "A multi-segmented insect crawls onto the screen and is shot by the player."

Part of a four-person team, Bailey learned the steps of programming a video game and collaborated on *Centipede*'s design with project leader Ed Logg. The first step in creating her new game was drawing the "motion objects," later referred to as sprites. At the time, motion objects were created by the programmer, using one square on paper to represent one pixel on a screen. Bailey first drew the player, followed by the shot, and the centipede's body segments. Motion objects for the Centipede board were 16 pixels by 8 pixels in size. Bailey patiently drew boxes on graph paper, then flipped the paper on its side, and coded each row—8 bits—of each box into one hexadecimal byte of information, resulting in a list of 16 bytes of hex representing each motion object. This list of hex values was then typed by hand into a PROM (a programmable ROM chip) graphics chip and inserted on the game board for testing and for play in the game.

From a visual standpoint, Bailey was inspired by a hot arcade title at the time—*Galaga*. "I found *Galaga* visually delightful at the time," she continued. "Any *Centipede* inspirations that seem to be derived from *Galaga* are tributes to my love of *Galaga* back then." Bailey wanted her game to stand out in a similar visual way. "My primary goal was to make a game that would be visually appealing to me. I wanted to make a game that was beautiful."

Bailey feels that part of *Centipede*'s beauty came from what she refers to as a "happy accident." "I noticed *Centipede*'s different color palette as I watched the screen while our technician was making adjustments to the prototype game," recalled Bailey. "I think our technician was maybe setting a potentiometer for the monitor, and whatever he was doing caused the color palette to change from primary colors to hot pastel colors. As I watched, I made a little yip of approval for our technician to keep those colors. It ended up that I could use the regular primary colors plus the hot pastel colors, and I loved having both to use."

Centipede came out in arcades in 1981, controlled by a trackball due to Bailey's preference for its ease of use over buttons as controllers. "I couldn't use buttons to play," Bailey laughs. "Using buttons was like a typing test for me—no fun at all." *Centipede* proved to be one of the first arcade games to garner a large player base of women, which Bailey feels is due in part to the game's visual appeal plus its ease of play. The success of the game spawned a number of *Centipede* clones from other developers eager to cash in on the craze.

A LASTING LEGACY

Centipede has stayed with Bailey for years, in part, literally. "At that time at Atari, the tradition in coin-op was to give the prototype game to the programmer on the game team after a game had been released and was completely wrapped up," she explains. "I kept my prototype *Centipede* in my home for about three years. In those days, an arcade game was really heavy, and most of the weight was up high in the cabinet due to the monitor, making a game especially hard to lift and to move. First I had my prototype *Centipede* in the kitchen of a house I lived in, then it was in the den of my next house, then in the kitchen of my small Palo Alto apartment, and finally, in the kitchen of a house in Portola Valley where I lived. I was exhausted from moving it around! When I moved from Portola Valley to Menlo Park, I donated my *Centipede* to the VA hospital where the author Ken Kesey worked when he was a student in the writing workshop at Stanford."

Centipede would be ported to a string of Atari home consoles as well as personal computers over the next several years, and released over a dozen times since as a part of various collections and greatest hits programs. Years later, Bailey laughs at the idea that if created today, *Centipede* would likely be considered a casual game. Bailey still samples these new styles of the retro classic, though. In 2012, she helped Atari promote the app *Centipede: Origins*.

Bailey started a second game at Atari, but soon used all the microprocessor's cycle time on animation and visual effects, leaving no processor time for gameplay. She left Atari shortly after learning to divide processor time between gameplay and visual effects. For a time she programmed arcade games at Videa, a company comprised of ex-Atari employees, that was purchased by Nolan Bushnell and renamed Sente. Later she took PC contract roles for Activision, working on a two-person team with Paul Allen Newell. In 1985, Bailey left gaming, working as a programmer in other industries.

After 25 years of programming and systems analysis, Bailey decided to take her career in a different direction. "I earned two master's degrees beginning when I was 48, and I worked hard to earn a position as a faculty member at a university. It's hard to take up a new profession later in life, and I'm proud of that work." Her first master's degree is in education, in instructional design, and the second is in professional and technical writing. She is retired from a faculty position at the University of Arkansas at Little Rock, where she taught in the department of Rhetoric and Writing.

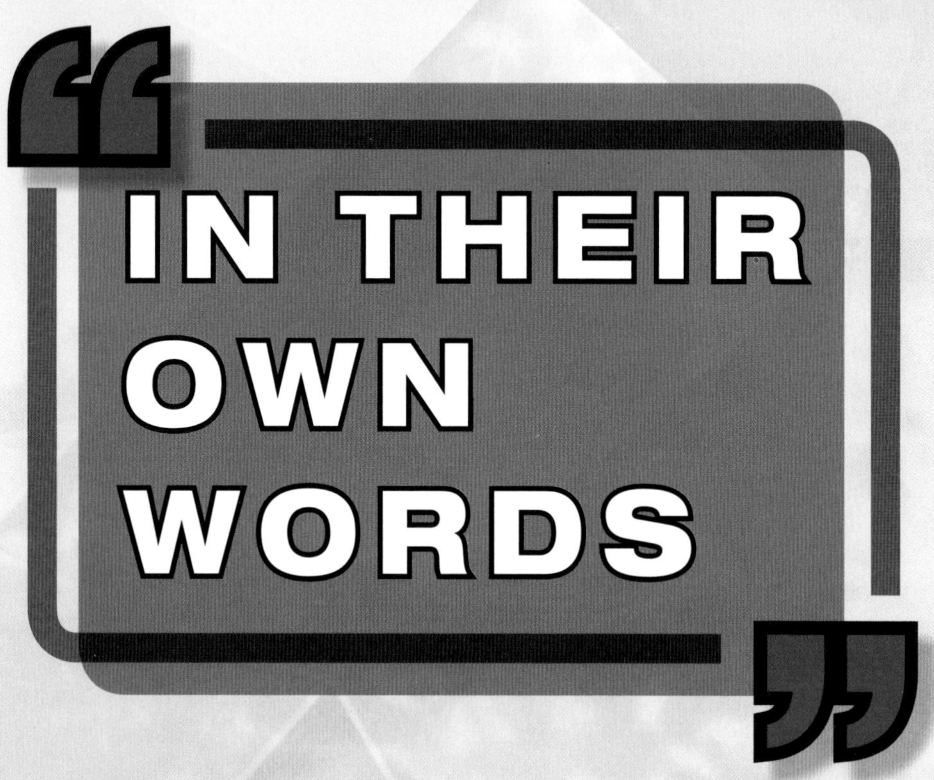

THE INFLUENCE OF GENDER

Do you feel that your gender influences your work?

"Who I am influences my work. Gender (both biological and societal) is one piece of that larger whole. I'm either embracing or rejecting a stereotype with every game I produce, but as a working professional, I have to be able to design for audiences that are not me. So influences? Yes, of course. Controls? No, not really."

Kimberly Unger | Mobile/VR Producer | Playchemy | Burlingame, USA

"I don't really feel like my gender influences my work, or the products I personally produce. I'm sure my gender influences the reception to that work in some cases, but on almost every article I write—including ones that have my byline—commenters will usually refer to me as 'he' by default, until someone corrects them."

Alanah Pearce | Writer/Producer | Rooster Teeth | Los Angeles, USA

"Sometimes yes, but that is changing rapidly. Being in the Middle East and a woman, it works in my favor most of the time, as it generates a lot of respect from the media and partners. However, the Middle East still being a little shy toward the female gender can pose hesitations from certain territories that are much more conservative. Having said that, I personally have never faced any problems or been shown disrespect. The industry is very close-knit, and everyone just wants to ensure that it progresses."

Divya Sharma | Marketing Manager | Shooting Stars | Dubai, UAE

"My gender is only a fraction of a thousand pieces of my own person. It may unconsciously influence my work, but I believe that what reflects it are my memories, my ideas, my experiences, and personality. I'm a one-and-a-half-meter-tall girl with very small hands and a passion for every kind of art. Drawing, creating music, sewing handmade notebooks, and creating games are some of them. In fact, *Tin-Heart*, the first game I've ever developed, has some of those experiences and influences."

Inês Borges | UI Designer & Game Artist | Elifoot 18 & GameNest | Lisbon, Portugal

---

"I've spent over a decade in the game industry, and although I am in a leadership position, I still struggle with being a woman and minority in our industry. I'm often ignored in business meetings if my male colleagues are present. Developers have told me that they can't add a female character to their game because it would be too difficult. All that said, I have taken my experiences and used them as a catalyst for change. My gender influences my work daily, and while sometimes that can be utterly exhausting, it has also been rewarding. Game development is very important to me, and I want it to be a place where women and marginalized groups are welcome and celebrated."

Kari Toyama | Senior Producer | Private Division, Take-Two Interactive Software, Inc. | Seattle, USA

"I feel gender plays a lot that's unsaid or written when it comes to culture. When working in a Japanese culture but being American, I feel I have a lot of gray areas that I maneuver between to take advantage of the two cultures. I can be direct yet not threatening, I can approach difficult subjects with delicacy, I can assure someone but with understanding of urgency. These do depend on someone's ability to communicate, but I am certain my gender plays a role in the recipient's impression."

Lola Shiraishi | Producer | SEGA of America | Los Angeles, USA

"One of the mistakes that I made when I started my profession was that I used to believe gender affects my job more than it really does, despite the fact that I'm living in a country with strong thoughts about gender differences. As I moved forward in my career, I found out that it really depends on how professional your colleagues are, and the more professional they get, the less important gender differences are to them. Then, the only thing that matters is my work capabilities.

Shohre Esmaili | Lead Game Designer | Karizma Game Studio | Tehran, Iran

---

"Absolutely. While I suspect we all like to think it doesn't, the way others treat you because of your gender influences the way you react to something. We all bring the sum of our experiences into our work. Do I think it makes me better or worse at my job because of my gender, however? The answer is no."

Pippa Tshabalala | Video Game Reviewer/Presenter | Glitched | Johannesburg, South Africa

---

"Growing up, it never occurred to me that my gender could in any way limit what I'd be permitted to do or what I could do. I've always operated under the principal of, 'I want to make games, so I will.' It would be naive to think that my gender has never influenced my work in the eyes of others, but I am one of those fortunate women who has never been made to feel like a 'woman in games.' I'm a game developer and I happen to be a woman, but I feel that my gender has no bearing on what I want to do in life or how I do it."

Robyn Tong Gray | Co-Founder & Chief Creative Officer | Otherworld Interactive | Los Angeles, USA

"It can't not do so! Because 'who we are' influences 'what we make.' As Creators and Makers. As Black or White. Male or Female. Gay or Bi. Cis or Trans. Neurotypical or Neurodivergent. And any other number of not-actually-binary choices in how we define ourselves (or how society defines us).

"So insomuch as 'gender' is a part of identity, gender influences everyone's work. But I'm not trying to be clever here. I, specifically, speak openly about my identity as a black woman in both a country and an industry where I'm a constituted minority. I'm explicit about how my identity—gender being a part of that—influences my consumption and creation of games, movies, music, literature, basically any and all media that's not nailed down. And I do this not because it's comfortable, but because it's uncomfortable to do so. We all need to learn how to become more comfortable with the discomfort of identity and how it shapes our world in strange and beautiful ways."

Shana T. Bryant | Senior Producer | Private Division, Take-Two Interactive Software, Inc. | Seattle, USA

"Absolutely it does. [The influence of gender] changes how I interact with people and the perspective I bring to the table. It does not, however, affect the quality of my work. That comes from years of experience and hard work."

Rachel Day | Senior VFX Artist | Blizzard Entertainment | Irvine, USA

"My experience does and a good part of that experience has been impacted by being a woman. So, yes, it does."

Catherine Vandier | Marketing & Communications Manager | Electronic Arts | Guildford, UK

"It would be impossible to not have my gender influence my work. From the moment I entered games media, my gender provided a reason to question my legitimacy. That's why every day, with the work that I do, I promote the voices of women currently working in games to hopefully encourage and inspire even more. I have a platform, so I see using it to spread the word of individuals and programs addressing the huge gender disparity in the games industry as an important responsibility. Wherever possible, I'll interview the women working on development teams. I'll speak to women running mentorship or training programs aimed at women. I'll get the word out there that even though this industry is overwhelmingly male, if you're not, you won't be completely alone. And with our collective strength, we can make a real and significant change."

Rae Johnston | Editor, TV & Radio Presenter | Junkee | Sydney, Australia

---

"At Blizzard, I don't feel any differences in interactions or responses to my work because I'm a female. In fact, our team is almost 50/50 women to men, which is pretty unusual in the industry."

Monika Lee | Associate e-Commerce Merchandiser for Consumer Products | Blizzard Entertainment | Irvine, USA

"I think my personality and strengths influence my work, some of which could be a result of my gender. It's hard to answer that question without generalizing, I think."

Kayse Sondreal-Nene | Senior Merchant, Video Games | Best Buy Co., Inc. | Minneapolis, USA

"That's a loaded question. I think I'm intuitive. Is that because I'm a woman, or is it because that's just who I am? I also have an easy time talking to people and have been told that I put people at ease. Is that because I'm a woman? Hard to say, because I don't have anything to compare it to."

Katie Nelson | Senior Recruiter | Inspired Hires | San Francisco, USA

"I do, in the sense that women are more empathetic and have more emotional intelligence. Both of these traits are needed to be successful in customer support, more so in gaming because the users have a high level of emotional investment in the game and their characters than most other companies. Being able to relate to the customer while solving their problem goes a long way to establishing trust between the brand and its customers."

Debbi Colgin | Director of Support | Hustle | San Francisco, USA

"I do not think my gender really affects or limits my profession in any way. Although most of industry professionals in Korea are males, especially in the concept art field, I never doubt that my work is any less comparable to them. Also, a lot of people judge me as a guy, and they get quite surprised when they see me in person at conventions or meetups and say they would never expect me to draw something like my artwork. I think it is a great misconception that people expect female artists will always draw something cute, and I want to break that misconception."

Yujin Jung (Sangrde) | Concept Artist/Chief Illustrator | SpeedPro Imaging | Global

---

"I think it does, and it probably has to do with the time at which I first started my career. Since I didn't see a lot of women working at the studios I started in, I felt that I needed to prove myself and put in my dues. This pressure might've been my own doing, but it got me to where I am today. I've grown into a senior professional who can manage teams of other artists as well as art levels of my own. I'm independently driven, and I hope that I inspire some of that in others too."

Daryl Hanna Tancinco | Senior Artist | Infinity Ward | Woodland Hills, USA

"I think it affects me in how people perceive me and my work. That affects how I have navigated working with people. It's made me think about how I need to work around these issues differently."

Jennie Nguyen | Systems Administrator | Crystal Dynamics | Redwood City, USA

"It makes me work a lot harder. I'm very aware of the disadvantages that women have in this industry. It's depressing, but I love what I do and I can't imagine being happy doing something else."

Sarah McNeal | Character Artist | Sledgehammer Games | Foster City, USA

"I think being brought up as a girl has trained me to consider what people mean instead of what they are literally saying. It has also trained me to try to anticipate other people's needs. These traits help me immensely as an effective lead artist whose job is to implement the art director's vision."

Jane Ng | Artist | Valve | San Francisco, USA

"I am both very masculine and very feminine. After I ran into one too many glass walls in my career due to being a woman, I felt a strong sense of responsibility to make the industry different for younger women and other underrepresented people coming up. I put my own career advancement on pause to pursue this goal. I left my job and started traveling and speaking and writing. However, by doing that, I removed myself from some pretty restrictive and oppressive environments and surrounded myself with a wider range of people, including many more feminine people. And this led to a number of realizations about game design and a number of prototypes, and those ended up leading to significant career advancement for me. If the industry was less sexist, I would have developed my talents earlier. But it is sexist. I'm happy that working to fix that also finally unlocked a path forward for me that uses my talents and hopefully will also create some space for people like me to develop their talents."

Brie Code | CEO/Creative Director | TRU LUV | Montréal, Canada

---

"Yes. There is a different expectation of a woman in front of a camera than a man because it is being viewed through the male lens. Like it or not, my male colleagues are judged first on the merit of their words, not on the cut of their shirt. Some people will never accept a female voice in a sportscasting arena—I'll forever be 'the nag' they didn't want to bring to the game. I'm 'condescending' and 'arrogant' instead of 'frank' and 'confident.'"

Indiana "Froskurinn" Black | *League of Legends* Shoutcaster | Riot Games | Shanghai, China

---

"Generally no, but that's only because I feel like I'm shaped by a lot of things—one of them is my gender. I identify as a woman, but I'm also Filipino-American, and I'm a child of immigrant parents with migrant farmworker backgrounds. The list goes on, but I think all of these distinctions inform my decisions, how I work, and how I see the world. I believe that being a woman plays a huge part in how I approach my work, but it's in a way that I'm not sure I can separate from all those other pieces that make me who I am. If anything, I think my being a woman more influences how others see me, rather than how I see myself."

Francesca Reyes | User Research Manager | 2K | San Francisco, USA

"Yes. I think my experience, knowledge, and skills are so intertwined with who I am that it's impossible to ignore my gender completely. My gender has shaped who I am and who I am shapes my work; you just can't have one without the other. While gender isn't directly related to my work in accessibility, I've been immensely inspired by others working for inclusion of all kinds, and my ability to empathize with other women and non-binary people in gaming got me to where I am today. I think my gender also made me tougher and more determined than I would have been otherwise. Before I started working in this capacity, I had been been facing adversity in games; it even went all the way back to my first experience gaming online in the 90s with *Command & Conquer*. I quickly learned that my gender would get me in trouble and I needed to be both tough, and probably hide who I am to some degree. In the end, the pushback I get for my gender in every aspect of games—including streaming—just makes me work that much harder. I also won't easily take 'no' for an answer, which really helps when it comes to accessibility."

Cherry Thompson | Game Accessibility Consultant | Freelance | Vancouver, Canada

---

NETWORKING 101:

By Sheri Graner Ray | *Senior Designer at Electronic Arts*

If you ask anyone the best way to get a game industry job, they will tell you to network. This industry is completely about "who you know."

While everyone will tell you how important networking is, rarely does anyone tell you exactly how to network. At best, they will tell you to "go to events and talk to people." While that is good advice, it's neither very helpful nor specific.

I have a secret. I do not like parties. The few times I tried "going to an event and talking to people," I wound up standing alone in a corner with a watered-down drink wondering what to do next.

It didn't take long for me to figure out this wasn't networking, so I decided to figure out exactly how to network. I started to watch people who were successful at networking. I wanted to figure out how they made "go to events and talk to people" work for them. Now I want to share with you what I learned.

There are three parts to successful networking. They are:

- **SOCIAL MEDIA**
- **CONTACTS AND CONFERENCES**
- **VOLUNTEERING**

Social media is your online presence. Contacts and conferences are the root system that grows your network, while volunteering is how you put a face to a name—yours and someone else's. By using all three elements in a systematic manner, you can build a very robust network that will be a huge asset for you as you grow your career.

SOCIAL MEDIA

The game industry is a bit different from other tech industries in that we tend to use social media as much as we use professional sites like LinkedIn. By using social media, you have an opportunity to make social connections with people who are important to your career. Conversely, people will be trying to make connections with you. That means one very important thing:

Clean up your profile.

Make sure the image you are presenting is mature and professional. This doesn't mean you can't post pictures of your pets or family, but please remove those embarrassing pictures of you at your BFF's bachelorette party!

Not only you should be careful what you post, but you will also need to monitor what your friends post about you. Be on the lookout and, if unflattering pictures show up, unlink or untag your name from them.

The same rule goes for Twitter. What you post is seen by many more people than just the ones to whom you are responding. In fact, Twitter is a great snapshot into a person's character. Anything that implies bigotry, hate speech, or just unprofessional behavior gets noticed for sure.

Even Reddit is not immune to this type of searching. The opinions you post publicly can—and will—determine how the hiring manager views you. Make sure what you post is something that conveys the image you want everyone to see.

There are other uses for social media beyond just putting a public face on you. These platforms are also great tools for making connections.

Social media is like the breakroom of the game industry. It's where people in the industry meet to chat about the things they would usually talk about around the coffee maker. Nothing of much substance is normally talked about in the office breakroom; it usually revolves around what was on TV the night before, a great restaurant someone found, or something similar. As trivial as these sound, they are the things we form social bonds over. If all the people important to your career were gathered in the breakroom, it would be awfully silly not to take advantage of this and at least say "good morning" to them and engage them in some social chat.

The difference is the "breakroom" in social media circles can be populated by the people who can influence your career.

Start by making a list of the people who are important to your career. They could be people you've seen speak, people who work at places where you would like to work, people you admire in the industry, and so on. Who would you like to grab a coffee with? Who would you like to talk about games with? Add them to your list.

Once you have a list, find those people on social media. Follow them. Friend them. Watch what they say and what they post. Then, when there is a subject you feel comfortable commenting on, do so. Keep your comments short, polite, and on subject. Tag their name, if you can. People can't help but look when they receive notice that their name has been mentioned.

It is very likely that person will see it. If you do this a couple of times (not all in one day) and you have smart, thought-provoking, polite things to say, then the person may reply to you. If you're very lucky, they may even follow you! Now suddenly you are having a conversation with someone who is very important to your career!

Just because you make a connection doesn't immediately make that person your new BFF. It is now up to you to farm that contact. By careful tending and maintenance, you can grow it into something very valuable.

CONTACTS AND CONFERENCES

You have probably heard a hundred times how important it is to attend conferences. This is true. It is where you are exposed to interesting opinions from different viewpoints. More importantly, it is where you will meet people who are important to your career. The question is, how do you make this happen and what do you do after meeting them?

First, make plans to see speakers who are interesting and important to you. Focus on people who work, or have worked, for companies you want to work for. Look for talks on subjects that are pertinent to what you are doing or want to do. After the talk, approach the speaker and ask for a business card. Most everyone who speaks takes a stack of business cards with them. They expect to hand out cards afterwards.

Those business cards are a golden ticket to the world of game development. When you get a card from someone you feel is important to your career, immediately turn it over and jot down a note about where you met them, what they were speaking about, and any other information that will remind you of this moment.

After the conference, sort through all your business cards. Pull out the cards from people you think can help you in your career, and then write those people an email.

Re-introduce yourself. Thank them for taking the time to talk to you. Mention something they said that impressed you, then sign off. Keep it to one short paragraph; no more than just a couple sentences. Now, here's the important part:

DO NOT EXPECT A RESPONSE.

Frankly, think of this as a thank-you note for a gift. The gift they gave you was their time. You don't expect a response to a thank-you note, so you shouldn't expect a response in this case either.

Your networking does not end there. Four weeks after sending that first email to those people, send them another email.

Do not make this a fan letter. Instead, mention how something they said or did influenced something you thought or did. Thank them again for their time and sign off. Keep it short. Keep it polite. Keep it professional.

Again, do not expect a response.

Now here's the trick and, frankly, where most people fail. In another four to eight weeks after that second email, you should write them again. Remind them who you are, and then ask them something they can answer in one sentence or less. For example, ask if they will be at PAX South, whether they recommend GDC or DICE, what books they recommend. This will make it easy for them to respond.

Whether they respond or not, continue that path. Every other month or so, drop them another email. Do *not* regale them with tales of your latest great game idea and, by all means, *do not ask them for a job*!

Networking is not about that important person hiring you. Networking is about keeping your name front and center so that when someone mentions a job opening, that important person says, "Hey, there's this interesting person I met at GDC last year. Let me forward their info to you." That is how networking works.

VOLUNTEERING

Volunteering is a fantastic way to meet influential people and move your career forward. There are a thousand ways to get active in the game community and one of the largest and most diverse is the IGDA. It has hundreds of local chapters all over the world.

Join your local chapter and then get active—and not just in the fun stuff. Help clean up after a meeting. Help haul off trash. Help with registration for the mixer. Why? First, because you will be present. Second, you will become known as someone who is dependable and gets things done. That is a desirable trait for an employee.

One of the very best jobs you can volunteer for is handing out name tags at a mixer. It is the best way to put names and faces together and see "who is who" within your local community.

What if you live in an area where there is no local IGDA chapter? First, make sure there isn't another organization like it. Is there a computer gaming group at the local college? Is there a casual games group? Maybe a social games group? If you live in a place that is devoid of game industry, then you must get active on a national level.

The IGDA has SIGs (Special Interest Groups) that cater to nearly every discipline and group there is in the industry. Find the SIG that best fits what you want to do and where you want to go in the industry. These groups can become some of the best networking tools out there. However, you won't get anything useful from the experience if you don't get active. Think of it as an investment in the future. You're trading time right now for connections that will help you get ahead in the future.

Now that you are putting the aforementioned suggestions to good use, there is one more thing you must do.

Make games!

It doesn't matter if you are an artist, designer, programmer, or marketing person. The way to make games for a living is to start making games today! There are enough free, sophisticated tools available for anyone to make a very passable game.

If you can't get your head around the tools, then make a board game or a card game. Make a game and have your friends try it out, get their feedback and try again. This provides invaluable experience and gives you something to show during your next interview.

Networking is not about asking people for jobs. Networking is not about being the life of the party, or a great conversationalist. Networking is about farming. It is about planting seeds of connection, tending those seeds as they start to grow, and then maintaining them as they form the foundation you need to support your career in games. You can do it. It just takes a lot of desire and self-discipline to keep at it.

Good luck and, the next time you get a business card from me, I expect to receive an email from you!

RIEKO KODAMA

ROLE-PLAYING GAME VISIONARY

 phoenix_rie  archives.sega.jp/segaages

EXPERIENCE

FIRST INDUSTRY PROJECT: CHAMPION BOXING (1984)

FAVORITE INDUSTRY PROJECT: PHANTASY STAR SERIES (1987–1993)

PROJECTS SHIPPED: 30 GAMES

ACHIEVEMENTS UNLOCKED:

> DUBBED "THE FIRST LADY OF RPGS" BY NINTENDO POWER

> EGM "TOP 100 GAMES OF ALL TIME" #80—SKIES OF ARCADIA (2001)

> EGM "THE GREATEST 200 VIDEO GAMES OF THEIR TIME" #26—PHANTASY STAR (2006)

> IGN "ALL-TIME BEST GAMES EVER MADE" #61—PHANTASY STAR IV (2007)

STATS

INDUSTRY LEVEL: 34

CURRENT CLASS: PRODUCER & DIRECTOR

CURRENT GUILD: SEGA—TOKYO, JAPAN

SPECIAL SKILLS: GRAPHIC DESIGN, PRODUCTION

STANDARD EQUIPMENT

FAVORITE PLATFORM: DREAMCAST

GO-TO GENRE: RPG

MUST-HAVE GAME: FINAL FANTASY III, FINAL FANTASY V

BIO

Over 30 years after she started her career at SEGA Japan, artist, producer, and current director of the SEGA AGES series Rieko Kodama has come full circle in her landmark work.

Kodama attended a trade school for graphic design in the early 1980s. She intended to pursue advertising before the still-young video game industry caught her eye. "I didn't really want to do advertisement-type work and wanted to create things instead. Game development was still a very new type of career at that time," Kodama explained.

Easter Egg

Was at one point considering archaeology as a career instead of art and, as such, enjoyed exploring ancient cultures in games she worked on, such as *Phantasy Star* and *Skies of Arcadia.*

PHOENIX RIE

Although interested in the potential of the medium, Kodama didn't know much about video games at the time. The Nintendo Famicom and SEGA's SG-1000 had only just hit the market. The Japanese video game industry was still arcade-heavy—and arcades weren't places she frequented. Video games were an entirely new world to explore.

When Kodama began to proactively look for a job in video games, she found a listing for an opening at SEGA at her school. The interview went well and Kodama officially started as a SEGA artist in 1984. Initially, she thought she'd be working on box art and marketing materials, but as she began to settle in, Kodama was drawn to developing the games themselves.

Kodama began learning the basics of making sprite art and put them to use creating the characters for the 1984 arcade title *Champion Boxing*. "I was taught about graphic design at school, but I didn't learn anything about computers," she said. As a student, Kodama wasn't fond of physics and mathematics and, as such, was relieved she'd never need to use functions and probability as an artist. "It was very surprising that I wasn't just drawing, but had to think in hexadecimal and quantifying colors!" she laughed.

In short succession, Kodama would provide graphics for *Ninja Princess* (called *SEGA Ninja* in the West), *Alex Kidd in Miracle World*, and an assortment of other titles. "When we worked on an 8-bit game, a team consisted of one or two programmers, a designer, one or two artists, and one who did sound," she recalled. "Teams were commonly composed of five members at the time." Not only were teams smaller, development time was shorter. She often worked on five or six games a year.

"[*Magic Knight Rayearth*] was my first experience creating a kawaii (cute) themed game that was appealing to female players."

During this period, Kodama was credited as Phoenix Rie in her published works. A common practice in the industry at the time, developers were asked to use pseudonyms to avoid the risk of them being lured away by another company in this competitive market.

A STAR IS BORN

In the mid-80s, role-playing games were starting to rise in popularity—such as Enix's 1986 release *Dragon Quest*. SEGA was eager to develop their own contender to showcase the power of the SEGA Master System. The fruit of their work released in 1988, called *Phantasy Star*. Kodama—a veteran artist by this time—helped establish the overall visual direction, in addition to creating in-game characters, 2D backgrounds, battle screens, and additional assets as needed.

Early on Kodama was inspired by Western sci-fi successes such as *Star Wars*, but wanted to add a unique flavor to the world. She decided to blend medieval aesthetics and sci-fi technology. To differentiate the game from what was already on the market, the development team challenged themselves to implement new features, including 3D dungeons, animated monsters, and a bold choice—a woman as the main protagonist.

The main character, Alis, as well as party member Lutz, were designed by Kodama. Alis was on a quest to avenge the death of her brother, and was conceptualized to blend femininity with her strength and forward-thinking nature. Lutz was intended as a strong, silent, and handsome type. While Alis went through nearly 10 iterations before Kodama was happy with her, Lutz remained the same from the first sketch she created.

Phantasy Star was a mega success and raised the bar for RPGs industry-wide. It birthed a series that continues to this day, encompassing sequels, spin-offs, online titles, and manga adaptations. Kodama worked on the series sequel in 1989, then took the helm as game director for the 1993 release *Phantasy Star IV: The End of the Millennium*. She has also guided remakes and compilations over the years, ensuring they met the mark set by the original development team.

BEYOND THE PHANTASY

Kodama continued to be a prolific creator outside of the *Phantasy Star* series, contributing art for SEGA Genesis titles *Altered Beast*, *Alex Kidd in the Enchanted Castle*, and in 1991, *Sonic the Hedgehog*. Sonic would become the most recognizable character and successful series in SEGA history.

Having shown her skills as a lead designer, Kodama stepped up as director on *Magic Knight Rayearth* for the SEGA Saturn in 1995. "Directing *Magic Knight Rayearth* was challenging," she recalled. "It was my first experience creating a kawaii (cute) themed game that was appealing to female players. The original story was based on the manga from famous manga artists CLAMP, so I had to keep in mind video game enthusiasts, but also the female fans of the original manga series when I made directions for this game. The target consumer was so different to the past titles I worked on, so I had lots of thoughts and worries early in the development."

In the 2000s, Kodama led production on *Skies of Arcadia* as part of SEGA's Overworks division, which released to critical acclaim on their new Dreamcast console. Alongside *Phantasy Star*, she marks the *Arcadia* series as a favorite, due in part to the improved hardware. "There were many things the hardware handled, like graphics processing," Kodama explained. "The hardware cared about the developer, and it was developer-friendly hardware."

As producer, she also worked on *Project Altered Beast*, *Mind Quiz*, and four entries in the *7th Dragon* series—another personal favorite.

SEGA AGES

Now, a 30-year veteran at SEGA, Kodama is the lead producer of SEGA AGES, a run of re-releases of classic SEGA titles. The series will launch on the Nintendo Switch in 2018 and includes 15 games, such as *Alex Kidd in Miracle World*, *Phantasy Star*, *Sonic the Hedgehog*, *Sonic the Hedgehog 2*, *Out Run*, and *Thunder Force AC*.

Working on the series is a trip down memory lane, and at times, Kodama has needed to draw from her memory to fill in developmental gaps. "If I could tell my past self I would be working on a project called SEGA AGES, which is a reproduction of the past games I've worked on, and games of the hardware of which I would work on, I would tell myself to properly manage the archives of these projects," she laughed. "Things like source codes, design assets, concept documentations. It's rarer to find these all intact, so I would tell myself to keep a firm check and make sure you properly archive it!"

Kodama is glad to see continued interest in past SEGA games, and the success of retro-inspired titles today. "The pixel art I was creating when I first started was already treated like an ancient lost skill by the time games transitioned to polygons everywhere," she explained. "But I am happy to hear that there is a resurgence of pixel art lately, and that it has become one of the art styles young people like or even prefer!"

MURIEL TRAMIS

LEGION OF HONOUR RECIPIENT FOR EXPLORING CULTURE AND EDUCATION IN GAMES

Muriel Tramis

 MisizMurielT

 Muriel Tramis

 mewilo30th.com

EXPERIENCE

FIRST INDUSTRY PROJECT: MEWILO (1987)
FAVORITE INDUSTRY PROJECT: MEWILO (1987)
PROJECTS SHIPPED: 22 GAMES
ACHIEVEMENTS UNLOCKED:

> CITY OF PARIS "SILVER MEDAL FOR HISTORICAL AND CULTURAL SIGNIFICANCE"—MEWILO (1987)

> EUROPEAN FEDERATION OF BLACK WOMEN BUSINESS OWNERS' CORPORATE AWARD (1997)

> FRENCH "LEGION OF HONOUR" AWARD (2018)

STATS

INDUSTRY LEVEL: 16
CURRENT CLASS: CEO
CURRENT GUILD: SENSASTIC PROD—FORT-DE-FRANCE, MARTINIQUE
SPECIAL SKILLS: PROJECT MANAGEMENT, SYSTEM ENGINEERING, GAME DESIGN, GAME WRITING, PROGRAMMING, INTERACTIVE PEDAGOGY

STANDARD EQUIPMENT

FAVORITE PLATFORM: PC
GO-TO GENRE: POINT-AND-CLICK ADVENTURE
MUST-HAVE GAME: LEMMINGS

BIO

The first sign that Muriel Tramis was destined to be a designer came at a young age. "I played board games, but I was more attracted to the design of the games than the games themselves," she began. "For example, I would rather build crossword puzzles and invent definitions than fill them out."

Despite an early affinity for creating play, as an adult Tramis ended up in a completely unexpected field. After finishing her engineering degree in high school, her first job was programming drones for the French army. "The field was extremely formative on my career from a technical point of view, but five years around weapons resulted in a crisis of conscience," Tramis explained. "I felt great creativity in me and knew that I could only exercise it in a more peaceful field. I quit and decided to start a second professional life."

Easter Egg

Has published two French books—one an autofiction novel taking place in Martinique in the 1970s, the second a collection of Creole and Cruel tales. A third is in the works, focusing on the historical and cultural origins of Caribbean expressions and proverbs.

CHANGING COURSE

At the age of 28, Tramis' combination of computer skills and innate taste for designing games led her to French video game developer Coktel Vision. The CEO—Roland Oskian—was eager to hire someone with both engineering and artistic abilities, and brought her on board.

"It was a period of extreme innovation," said Tramis. "Everything had to be discovered, like a first parachute jump—perilous but exciting. All of us in the studio were aware that we were having an extraordinary experience. We had only one instruction, to let our imagination run, but in the rigor of processes and methods."

EXPLORING CREOLE CULTURE IN VIDEO GAMES

Tramis had freedom from the start of her time at Coktel, and decided to investigate her French-Caribbean heritage with her first project—1987's point-and-click adventure *Mewilo*. "This allowed me to talk about my culture, still very little-known in a historical context, therefore realistic despite the fiction," Tramis explained. "Far from my native island, it was a way of going back to my roots."

"I asked my friend Patrick Chamoiseau, who was starting a career as a Creolist novelist, to write the dialogue," she continued. "I did all the programming. I spent long hours in the attic of Coktel Vision, where I slept episodically between two compilations of my computer."

The title was recognized in a major way. *Mewilo* became one of the first games ever to attract attention from outside of the video game industry. Tramis was awarded the Silver Medal of Paris because of the unique exploration of French-Caribbean themes.

Tramis continued to tackle complex and historical themes with her next release, 1988's *Freedom: Rebels in the Darkness*. The game featured a black slave on a sugar plantation. The player's goal was to incite a revolt within the slave population and gain their freedom. In this stealth-strategy game, four playable characters could be chosen at the start—two women and two men, each with his or her own stats in categories such as constitution and dexterity.

EXPLORING THE EROTIC

Tramis also found herself questioning the role of women in games. This exploration led her to the creation of a trio of erotic titles. A separate brand—Tomahawk—was created to publish them under. "At the time in Europe, the movie *Emmanuelle* was the symbol of the liberated woman who exposes her desires and claims her right to pleasure," Tramis explained. She convinced her boss to buy the licensing rights, and created a story set in Brazil. *Emmanuelle: A Game of Eroticism* released in 1989.

In 1990 she released *Geisha*. "I am quite proud to have invented the first virtual-sex system, via a hologram," said Tramis. "The game focused on caressing a female hologram to the point of ecstasy. It was also a technological advancement for the studio, because for the first time, real images were used within an illustrated setting."

Fascination released in 1991 and starred a female lead, Doralice Prunelier, at the center of a murder mystery. She could only solve her way out of it with logic and intuition, a mandate from Tramis due to her past career in armament.

BIZARRE ADVENTURES

In addition to exploring personal projects, Tramis collaborated with others. 1991's *Gobliiins* was developed with artistic director Pierre Gilhodes, and they would work together on two sequels. In 1995 they teamed up again on *The Bizarre Adventures of Woodruff and the Schnibble*, with Tramis as project lead and writer. "The game was a completely delirious universe, comparable to that of Monty Python, and because of that I had the most fun," said Tramis. "It was a very different world from mine, but I plunged into it with delight. Writing the dialogue was a very pleasant style exercise because all the situations were full of derision for it was the defects of our present world pushed to the absurd."

More adventures came, including *Lost in Time*, starring another female protagonist, who was accidently sent back to the 1840s.

EDUTAINMENT

Simultaneous to her work in adventure games, Tramis began to develop a range of ludic software, *La Bosse des Maths*, to better broach a subject many girls were scared away at high school levels.

From this series of games, it was decided that the public needed revamped educational curriculums to make schools more effective. "We sat around a table with teachers and ergonomists and we built a complete range from school to college: *ADI (Accompagnement Didacticiel Intelligent)* was an international success." The series was published in Spain, Russia, Italy, Canada, the United States, and other countries around the globe. It also branched into comic books and a television series.

BACK TO THE START

Tramis stayed at Coktel through 2003, weathering their purchase by Sierra On-Line in the mid-'90s, and their subsequent fusion leading to the gigantic multinational corporation Vivendi Universal Games. Since then, she's moved to the Caribbean island of Martinique and has worked as CEO of Avantilles, focusing on applications of virtual reality for urbanism and architecture. She is now working to on a remake of *Mewilo* for its 30th anniversary in her recently established studio Sensastic Prod.

LEGION OF HONOUR

Looking back on her career, Tramis' work is hard to define with such varied subjects and intended audiences. It's clear she pushed cultural, educational, and technological boundaries through her work, however.

In 2018, Tramis was recognized for her contributions to the medium when appointed to the rank of Chevalier of the Legion of Honour. The award requires a minimum of 20 years' civil service in France, and is the highest available in both military and civil service. Quantic Dream's David Cage is the only other game designer to have been awarded it.

"I have learned that no technology can transmit knowledge as effectively as a game," Tramis concluded. "The game is the best learning tool we have. I also learned that the best production is not done in pain but in happiness. If we want to be productive, we must first love what we do. If you are not happy in your job, you must first look for what makes you happy. It's not financial enrichment that has guided my steps so far, which makes me very poor today, but I'm satisfied with what I'm doing. And then I learned that anything is possible—just imagine it."

"I have learned that no technology can transmit knowledge as effectively as a game."

A DAY IN THE LIFE OF...

A GAME WRITER

There is a misconception that game writers work in a bubble, sitting at their desk, furiously typing and singularly focused on delivering a polished script to project leads. Far from the truth, game writing is an extraordinarily collaborative endeavor and one which requires constant testing, iterating, and when required, starting over entirely. ArenaNet's Samantha Wallschlaeger knows this firsthand from her contributions to AAA games such as *Mass Effect: Andromeda*. Her experience illustrates that game writing is much more than actually writing—it is working with an enormous creative team on a project that is greater than the sum of its parts.

SAMANTHA WALLSCHLAEGER

StillNotSam

PROFESSION: WRITER & NARRATIVE DESIGNER AT ARENANET—SEATTLE, USA

YEARS IN PROFESSION: 3

WORKED ON: STAR WARS: THE OLD REPUBLIC, MASS EFFECT ANDROMEDA, GUILD WARS 2

▶ EDUCATION

"I was a film and TV major in college, specializing in screenwriting. It taught me how to write dialogue-driven narrative, and how to think visually. I think this gave me the kickstart I needed to write for any visual medium. As for game development, I taught myself the only way I knew how: by playing everything, from massive AAA titles to bite-sized indie games made by a single person. I analyzed each game to determine what about the narrative was successful, and what fell flat. I also read dozens of books about game design and production, so that I could learn what my team members need from me. If you understand disciplines outside your own, you can make decisions that benefit everyone, which ultimately make for a better game."

▶ BREAKING INTO THE INDUSTRY

"It was extremely difficult breaking in! Writing takes years to master, and is incredibly subjective. And when you add that onto an already fiercely competitive industry, it's no wonder very few game writers are able to land that coveted job. When I applied for the assistant writer position at BioWare, they were giving preference to locals first. With that kind of disadvantage, I had to make my application so solid they couldn't possibly overlook it. I even sent two Twine writing samples instead of the one they required. And it worked! But it was a result of over two years of applying to multiple studios."

▶ TRAINING OPPORTUNITIES

"The GDC vault has a ton of extremely valuable talks by some of the most brilliant minds in the industry. Watching those videos is like absorbing an entire formal education in itself!"

▶ TOOLS OF THE TRADE

"In both the studios I've worked at, Final Draft is the main tool used for writing first drafts. After we get a few rounds of feedback from the narrative team, we put our scripts into the game's engine, which has a special tool for dialogue. From there, all edits to the dialogue happen inside the game itself."

▶ HOURS & ENVIRONMENT

"I currently work at ArenaNet, and I'm very lucky in that my studio promotes a healthy work-life balance. We work typical 40-hour weeks—sometimes a few more hours if we're really close to a deadline. I also work in a highly collaborative environment, so we have an open floor plan divided into large wings for each development team. I'm seated next to the rest of the writing team, but also near the designers I work with, and just down the hall from the cinematics and art teams. It makes communication and collaboration much easier when I can just pop down the hall for a conversation or sit down at a designer's desk to play through a level."

▶ KEY QUALITIES

"You have to be a good collaborator! Game writing is a completely different process than sitting alone writing a novel or screenplay. You have to understand others' point of view and be able to communicate effectively and with compassion. Humility is also essential if you want to be successful as a game writer. Your work is going to be reviewed by everyone—from the lead writer to the level designer to the game director—and every single person is going to ask for changes or point out inconsistencies and flaws. And it still may need to go through changes in order to fit the gameplay or art direction. You have to be able to roll with the punches and not get too precious about your own work."

▶ AN AVERAGE DAY

"A typical day for me often has very little 'writing' in the way you might imagine. One episode of content takes months to create, and it involves hours of story outlining by the entire team, followed by a detailed walkthrough of the gameplay design. Then I'll spend around two weeks writing the first draft of the episode. From there, the script will go through several months of rewrites to fit story needs, design needs, director feedback, and playtesting feedback. Meanwhile, I read and play my fellow writers' work and give them feedback, and also playtest my own content and give feedback on the level design, right up until the content launches."

▶ ADVANCEMENT OPPORTUNITIES

"Game writing typically follows a pretty normal hierarchy. Junior writers will handle side quests, combat barks, on-screen text and sometimes main story content. The main story, or "golden path," is normally done by the senior writers, as well as the character stories in bigger games. The lead writer does some writing—more, if it's a small team—but usually oversees the other writers' work and provides feedback and occasional rewrites. And some studios and projects have a narrative director who acts as an advocate for the writing team and makes sure the story of the game is strong and cohesive."

▶ CAREER CHALLENGES

"There's the problem, at some studios, of other disciplines not recognizing the narrative team as an 'important' part of the development process. Writing is sometimes treated as a pretty decoration to slap on top of existing design, rather than a vital component of the game. Because of that, it's often a struggle to tell a compelling story inside a strict set of rules laid down by the rest of the development team. You really need to have a strong sense of negotiation, and stand up for what you believe will serve the story in the best way."

▶ EXCITING ADVANCEMENTS

"I think game narrative is shifting to become less strictly linear. I think we're going to see a more modular system of storytelling, with vignettes or micro-stories that players can experience in any order, all culminating into a single narrative experience, almost like a cartoon series. It can be tough as writers for us to wrap our heads around this system of storytelling. We're used to stories having a strict beginning, middle, and end, but I'm excited to evolve the way I think about narrative."

PRO TIP!

"Teach yourself to write interactively! Game writing is so different from writing for any other medium, because players have control over how they experience the story. It takes practice to be able to account for player choice when writing a story. Download Twine and make a few text-based games to practice branching choices. Join a mod team for your favorite game and help them write a few quests. Play games and write down every time you go left when the game tells you to go right and observe what differences in story you see as a result. And don't give up! It's an incredibly hard profession to break into, but with enough hard work, you'll get there."

MANAMI MATSUMAE

MEGA MAN MELODY MAKER

 Chanchacolin

 Manaminsky

 Manami Matsumae

bravewave.net

STATS

INDUSTRY LEVEL: 31

CURRENT CLASS: COMPOSER & ARRANGER

CURRENT GUILD: FREELANCE—KYOTO, JAPAN

SPECIAL SKILLS: PIANO, COMPOSITION, ARRANGEMENT, SOUND PROGRAMMING

EXPERIENCE

FIRST INDUSTRY PROJECT: MEGA MAN (1987)

FAVORITE INDUSTRY PROJECT: MIGHTY NO. 9 (2016)

PROJECTS SHIPPED: 60 GAMES, 1 SOLO ALBUM

ACHIEVEMENTS UNLOCKED:

> ANNUAL GAME MUSIC AWARDS "OUTSTANDING CONTRIBUTION—INDEPENDENT COMPOSER" (2014)

> RELEASED SOLO ALBUM—THREE MOVEMENTS (2017)

> ANNUAL GAME MUSIC AWARDS "ALBUMS OF THE YEAR—ORIGINAL ALBUM" —THREE MOVEMENTS (2017)

STANDARD EQUIPMENT

FAVORITE PLATFORM: ANYTHING WITH CD-QUALITY AUDIO AND NO DATA STORAGE LIMITATIONS

GO-TO GENRE: SIMULATION

MUST-HAVE GAME: THE FIRE EMBLEM SERIES

BIO

In 1987—during her final year at university—Manami Matsumae spotted a notice from Capcom on the campus recruitment board, advertising music-production openings. "I played *Super Mario Bros.* and *Dragon Quest* when I was a student, so I liked games and ended up applying casually," she shared. "I majored in piano at university. It's the only instrument I played, while composing itself was something I only dabbled in during one of my composition theory classes. Despite all that, I was hired by Capcom."

Without formal composition or game-development experience, Matsumae recalls her first year in the industry as particularly tough. The first hurdle was learning how to use a computer. "My predecessors and mentors at Capcom taught me all the skills I have," she said. "However, because I liked games, the difficulties quickly went away. I steadily got used to the job."

Perhaps surprisingly for the time, many of those mentors were women. "When I joined my team at Capcom, it was actually comprised mostly of women. There was only one male, the section leader. Therefore, I was actually able to do my job with some freedom," she said, explaining how the recently passed Equal Employment Act had shaken up business in Japan. "When I left Capcom, I was the second-most-senior member of my team next to the section leader, despite there being other men around."

Capcom's success kept Matsumae busy. "When one project ended, a new one came at the same time, which would soon be joined by the next one," she said. "I was involved in composing for more and more games. I was very surprised at how my predecessors and mentors all found this to be typical. Actually, I thought I'd be able to take a holiday after finishing one project, but I was pretty naive," she explained with a laugh.

MEGA MAN

Listening to Matsumae's now-iconic early work, fans wouldn't notice the learning curve and ambitious production timelines that she was constantly up against. As an in-house composer for Capcom, Matsumae wrote music for games such as *Dynasty Wars*, *Mercs*, *F-1 Dream*, *Final Fight*, and most notably, *Mega Man*. Responsible for both music and audio, Matsumae also created and implemented all sound effects. The 1987 title was only her second project at Capcom, and it remains a defining part of her career.

Easter Egg

Grew up in the Kyoto countryside and intends to retire to a life of self-sufficiency through farming, following in her parents' footsteps.

Matsumae jokingly lists her favorite gaming platform as brand-agnostic, but rather anything that features CD-quality audio and no storage data limitations—for good reason. "I joined the industry during the NES era, so we had to compose with only three sound channels plus noise, and the sounds had to be converted into numbers and then implemented into the game using a custom programming application," she explained. These restrictions may have played a positive role in her melody-heavy compositions, however. The space limitations caused her to use repetitive drum and bass sounds, saving the data space for melody. Her melodies got more time and attention during development and, as with *Mega Man*, often are the most memorable pieces in her portfolio.

GOING FREELANCE

In 1991 Matsumae went freelance and remains so today. The freedom to work with more than one publisher opened doors for her, as well as granting an escape from obscurity. "When I was at Capcom, the industry was still young. There were relatively few people involved in development, so to avoid getting headhunted by other companies, we weren't allowed to include our real names or talk to creators from other companies," said Matsumae, explaining a common industry practice at the time. "After becoming a freelancer, I was finally allowed to use my real name." Prior to then, her work was credited under a variety of pseudonyms, including Chanchacorin, Chan Chakorin, and Chanchacorin Manami.

Throughout her freelance career, Matsumae has worked on nearly 50 games—including a large number for Japanese developer SunSoft. Titles ranged from licensed games such as *Looney Tunes* or *Batman: Return of the Joker*, to the long-running *Derby Stallion* series, and more recently *Dragon Quest Swords*, *LovePlus*, and a return to her roots with *Mega Man 10*.

Matsumae recalls composing for 2016's *Mighty No.9*—a collaborative reunion with *Mega Man* producer Keiji Inafune—as both the most challenging and rewarding project in her freelance career. "I was the main composer of the game, and worked with two others on the music," she began. "The sounds that the two other composers used to compose were completely different from mine, so if one listened to the soundtrack in its entirety, it might sound like it lacked cohesion. Therefore, I would take their MIDI data, listen to sample MP3 sounds, and then swap in the sounds I always use in order for that cohesion to be achieved. It was a tough job." The payoff for her hard work was big. "I was able to perform music from *Mighty No. 9* in front of a live audience of 4000 people at MAGFest. This is one of my cherished memories."

The industry has evolved greatly over the course of Matsumae's career, but she still composes much the same today as she did at Capcom. "I've been in my own studio composing by myself this whole time, so for me the changes have been more muted," she said. "I look at the game screens, game world, character movements, etc., and decide what kind of music would go well with them. I think about how players of my games look when they enjoy my music and try to make something that will fulfill them with a sense of satisfaction. That sends my motivation upward."

"I was able to perform music from *Mighty No. 9* in front of a live audience of 4000 people at MAGFest. This is one of my cherished memories."

THREE MOVEMENTS

To celebrate her 30-year milestone in gaming, Matsumae collaborated with Brave Wave Productions to release her very first solo album in 2017. The award-winning *Three Movements* features entirely original music, but offers fans a window into her growth as an artist. The first movement pays tribute to her early 8-bit compositions, and as the album progresses the music transitions to grander, more complex arrangements. *Three Movements* is reflective of the breadth of her portfolio and personal interests, drawing from a variety of genres.

It is impossible to overstate the influence of the original *Mega Man* on Matsumae's career. "This game is popular not only in Japan, but all around the world, too," she said. "This is how my name has become known worldwide and why I am given work offers. If I didn't work on *Mega Man*, I don't think I could have continued working as a game composer for 30 years. That's how important the game is to me."

Fans have just as strong a connection to the franchise as Matsumae does. "I've met people who played *Mega Man* as kids and then grew up, started their own indie studios, and have given me job offers," she shared. "These people hail from Taiwan, Indonesia, Mexico, the United States, etc. They say to me, 'Hey, I played your games as a kid, and having you compose for me is a dream come true.' And I say to them, 'Thank you!' It's an amazing feeling."

CHRISTY MARX

PROLIFIC POP-CULTURE WRITER, NARRATIVE DESIGNER, AND INDUSTRY ADVOCATE

 christymarx
 christy.marx
Christy Marx
christymarx.com

EXPERIENCE

FIRST INDUSTRY PROJECT: CONQUESTS OF CAMELOT: THE SEARCH FOR THE GRAIL (1989)

FAVORITE INDUSTRY PROJECT: CONQUESTS OF THE LONGBOW: THE LEGEND OF ROBIN HOOD (1991)

PROJECTS SHIPPED: 20 GAMES

ACHIEVEMENTS UNLOCKED:

> VIDEOGAMES & COMPUTER ENTERTAINMENT MAGAZINE "BEST COMPUTER ADVENTURE GAME"—CONQUESTS OF CAMELOT: THE SEARCH FOR THE GRAIL (1990)

> COMPUTER GAME REVIEW AND ENCHANTED REALMS "BEST ADVENTURE GAME"—CONQUESTS OF THE LONGBOW: THE LEGEND OF ROBIN HOOD (1991)

> WRITERS GUILD OF AMERICA "ANIMATION WRITERS CAUCUS LIFETIME ACHIEVEMENT AWARD" (2000)

> ASSOCIATION OF EDUCATIONAL PUBLISHERS "DISTINGUISHED ACHIEVEMENT AWARD"—HARCOURT ACHIEVE (2006)

STATS

INDUSTRY LEVEL: 30

CURRENT CLASS: WRITER & NARRATIVE DESIGNER

CURRENT GUILD: INDEPENDENT CONTRACTOR—NORTHERN CALIFORNIA, USA

SPECIAL SKILLS: WRITING, IP DEVELOPMENT, SERIES CREATION, STORY EDITING, SHOWRUNNING, GAME DESIGN, GAME WRITING, NARRATIVE DESIGN, STORY DESIGN, TRANSMEDIA IP ADAPTATION

STANDARD EQUIPMENT

FAVORITE PLATFORM: PC

GO-TO GENRE: MMOG

MUST-HAVE GAME: "DIFFERENT GAMES FOR DIFFERENT REASONS"

BIO

"Throughout my career, I've followed Marx's Three Maxims: 1) You never know unless you try; 2) The worst they can do is say no; and 3) Life is too short to work with assholes." Guided by this advice, multidisciplinary writer Christy Marx has led a career with an imprint on nearly every medium of entertainment—be it creating and writing the animated series *Jem and the Holograms*, penning comic scripts for *Red Sonja*, or leading game design for the *Conquests* series.

"I grew up before video games—or computers, for that matter—existed," began Marx. "I began writing animation scripts on computers early in my career, which gave me the edge of being computer literate when the opportunity came along. That opportunity was sheer luck—in 1988 Sierra On-Line was looking for artists willing to move to Oakhurst, CA to work for them. At the time, I was married to Australian artist Peter Ledger. When Sierra's headhunter called to see whether Peter would be interested, I asked, 'Are they looking for writers?' This was so early in the birth of games that they were willing to hire pretty much anyone to design a game. "There was no training, no established role, and no special requirements. If Ken and Roberta (Sierra founders) thought you could do the job, they hired you."

Easter Egg

Has collected comic books for over 50 years. She was particularly obsessed with comics as a kid and bought *X-Men* #1 off a spinner rack.

DIVING OFF THE DEEP END

Marx dove headfirst into her work at Sierra On-Line. "I'm a strong believer in having many different writing skills, so I jumped at the chance to learn how to write and design a game," she recalled. "I was experienced at visual, linear storytelling, but I had to teach myself from scratch how to be a game designer." Marx approached her improvised education in a systematic way. First, she played every Sierra game published to get a feel for what was fun, what wasn't fun, and to put herself in the player's mindset.

"Next, I sat down with the programmers and asked them to tell me what the technical limitations were; what I could or couldn't do," Marx continued. "They had their own game engine, but my first game was a parser-based DOS game. Even using a mouse wasn't yet a thing." The art department was the third stop on her studio tour. "I had them show me their tools, and explain what we could and couldn't do with our limited tech. My first game had only 16 colors," said Marx.

Lastly, she asked Sierra's veteran designers to share their documentation. She remembers there being outlines with varying degrees of detail, no consistency, and no established protocol. "Once I had the detailed story and design worked out, I created the first real design document at Sierra," recalled Marx. It was a hefty three-ring binder with every single detail of the design completely spelled out, down to the maps, the list of animations, the list of screen illustrations, and so on. They'd never seen anything this organized or detailed before."

THE HOLY GRAIL

That binder housed the soul of *Conquests of Camelot: The Search for the Grail.* As designer, Marx had her hand in nearly every aspect of development. "Back then it meant I created the entire design, wrote every word (including the hint book), plus I ran the game team, with help on scheduling and budget from a producer," she explained. "I made every creative decision from beginning to end. I sat and tested the game with the QA team, sometimes doing twenty-hour stretches, because I had to sign off on shipping it and I wanted it to be right."

The biggest hurdle Marx had to overcome was adapting to non-linear storytelling. Experienced designers at Sierra offered her advice, although it took a field trip to observe players directly for the new way of thinking to truly resonate. "I was astonished by the completely random way players would navigate the game or try to solve a puzzle. I realized that players were the agents of chaos, and that was what I needed to understand in order to write in a non-linear way. I learned more in those couple of hours than I had in the preceding six months. I finally *got it.*"

Released in 1989, *The Search for the Grail* was awarded "Best Computer Adventure Game of 1990" by *VideoGames & Computer Entertainment* magazine, and took home an Excellence Award from *Game Players* magazine.

"My second game, *Conquests of the Longbow: The Legend of Robin Hood*, was my favorite," she said. "*Longbow* was a point-and-click game, and the engine was modified to use a mouse rather than being parser-based. It provided me with new challenges, but overall I felt I had a better grasp on designing a game and I was happy with how it turned out. I developed fundamentals of narrative design that remain valid today."

An example of this foundational work was the inclusion of multiple interaction options for each NPC. "One was the best way, while other ways ranged from poor to bad," Marx continued. "This was not the same as branching dialog, but similar in principal. There were also moral choices to be made. That was something I introduced in the *Camelot* game and I was surprised by the enthusiastic response to that element. As a writer, I couldn't see creating a storyline that didn't have moral choices, but apparently that was a new thing for games." Which ending the player saw depended on the moral choices they made and how they interacted with NPCs. Those moral choices had a major impact on how the game played out, via varying story threads. All the unique decisions resulted in one of multiple endings. *Conquests of the Longbow* was awarded Best Adventure Game in 1992 by both *Computer Game Review* and *Enchanted Realms*.

"Nothing has been more fulfilling than being the sole designer, writer, and team leader of my first two adventure games," said Marx. "I was able to completely mesh storytelling with gameplay without having to sacrifice one for the other."

A UNIVERSE IN DISARRAY

When Marx wasn't afforded that level of ownership, she learned that projects were significantly more challenging. "*The Legend of Alon D'ar* was a 2001 console fantasy RPG that was well along in development when I was brought on board to create and write the story," she recalled. "They had already designed a world and its zones, created races and characters, and were well along on the overall design of the game when someone realized they had no story." Marx was tasked with taking existing assets and eclectic lore, and finding a way to cohesively weave them together. The project was challenging on many levels but, as with all opportunities, provided lessons for future projects.

Over the next several years, she created game bibles, metastories, quests, and characters for a run of MMOs, including *Earth & Beyond* and an unreleased game for Slipgate Ironworks. Shortly after, she provided story editing, dialogue, and cutscene writing for *The Lord of the Rings: War in the North.*

Just as Marx was on the cutting edge of MMOs in the early 2000s, in 2010 Marx joined casual-game giant Zynga as a narrative and principal game designer, lending her talents to the emerging Facebook and mobile games market. She wrote and implemented story, characters, and quests across well-known casual titles such as *Mafia Wars 2*, *Hidden Chronicles*, *CastleVille Legends*, and *FarmVille: Tropic Escape.* All the while, her career in animation, television, and comic book writing continued to flourish.

PASSION PROJECTS

Along with her fiction work across multiple media, Marx released nearly nine non-fiction educational books, including a series of biographies on subjects such as Jet Li, Admiral Grace Hopper, and The Wachowskis. She also authored *Writing for Animation, Comics and Games*, which she's currently updating for a second-edition release. With such prolific contributions to entertainment on her résumé, Marx is in a position to be selective with her time and attention. "I'm at the stage in my career where I want to work on my own personal passion projects," she concluded.

Although her focus has shifted, Marx leaves a legacy as an advocate for professional writing in games that lasts to this day. "You don't ask an artist to create game budgets, or a programmer to create art, or a composer to design a game engine. So why would you ask a programmer or producer or whoever happens to be standing around to write the story?" It seems an obvious question to ask, but one that required leaders like Marx to stand up and make the industry take note.

Original photo ©Osamu Nakamura

YOKO SHIMOMURA

CELEBRATED COMPOSER OF LANDMARK VIDEO GAMES

 midiplex

 midiplex.com
blog.livedoor.jp/midiplex

EXPERIENCE

FIRST INDUSTRY PROJECT: SAMURAI SWORD (1988)
FAVORITE INDUSTRY PROJECT: TOO HARD TO PICK!
PROJECTS SHIPPED: 80+ GAMES
ACHIEVEMENTS UNLOCKED:

> ORIGINAL ALBUM RELEASE—MURMUR (2007)
> NAVGTR "ORIGINAL MUSICAL SCORE OF THE DECADE"—KINGDOM HEARTS (2011)
> FORBES "THE TOP 12 VIDEO GAME SOUNDTRACKS OF ALL TIME"—KINGDOM HEARTS (2012)
> CLASSICFM.COM "HALL OF FAME" #30—KINGDOM HEARTS (2015)

STATS

INDUSTRY LEVEL: 30
CURRENT CLASS: COMPOSER
CURRENT GUILD: FREELANCE—TOKYO, JAPAN
SPECIAL SKILLS: PIANO, COMPOSITION, ARRANGEMENT

STANDARD EQUIPMENT

FAVORITE PLATFORM: GAME BOY ADVANCE SP
GO-TO GENRE: RPG
MUST-HAVE GAME: DRAGON QUEST

"All the women in [Capcom] were so talented, and I was surprised that a lineup of women could become the forefront of their industry."

BIO

Yoko Shimomura started studying piano at the age of five, and recalls creating her own compositions from a young age. At first her works started as an unstructured collection of notes, but soon evolved into distinct compositions she still remembers how to play.

"I was 20 years old and had majored in piano at Osaka College of Music," said Shimomura. "I wanted to get a job that involved music." Her original goal was to become a full-time piano teacher—a well-respected and stable career. "I just so happened to stumble across a job listing from a game company for new graduates, and I liked games, so I thought it would be interesting. I applied for the job."

Easter Egg
Collects LEGOS and Nanoblocks. Whenever in a creative rut while making music, she builds something to get through it.

CAPCOM

The company was Capcom, and the year was 1988. She was hired, much to the concern of her family and music instructors. Since the job was a non-traditional application of her skills in an emerging industry, they worried that her years of training would go to waste. Rather, Shimomura's three-decade career would help elevate the quality of video game music worldwide.

"I didn't have any formal training in game development," she explained. "It was my first time composing after I entered the industry, and I was severely lacking in a lot of skills. It was a continuously tough time." Her education was achieved through collaboration until she solidified her skills and found her musical voice within the technological constraints of the time.

Part of her on-the-job training was mentorship, and Shimomura remembers being surprised by the team makeup when she started. "When I was at Capcom, there were many female composers there already," she recalled. "It was quite unexpected because classic and pop composers are often men. All the women in the company were so talented, and I was surprised that a lineup of women could become the forefront of their industry." She appreciated that talent—not gender—was most valued at Capcom.

Shimomura stayed at Capcom from the time she graduated in 1988 until 1993. "My first console game release would be *Samurai Sword* for the Famicom Disk System," she said. "I handled music and sound effects." She then collaborated on the soundtrack for *Final Fight*, and composed *Street Fighter II: The World Warrior*, the latter marking the first soundtrack exclusively of her work. On the side, she occasionally played Capcom music at live events—including her own compositions—as part of the in-house band Alph Lyla.

SQUARE CO.

From 1993 until 2002, Shimomura resided as an in-house composer for Square Co., which merged with the Enix Corporation in 2003 to become Square Enix. It was during her tenancy at Square that she would create some of the most memorable work of her career, as well as landmark releases within the industry as a whole.

Shimomura desired to branch out into RPGs, which she felt would allow her to compose classically inspired soundtracks, as was the case with renowned *Final Fantasy* composer Nobuo Uematsu. Her first project at Square was composing for the genre-bending RPG *Live A Live*, which unfolded in settings ranging from the American Old West to a distant future featuring interstellar travel. The original soundtrack was released in 1994, and three of the tracks became part of her future "best hits" collection. During this time she also worked on *Super Mario RPG*, and was offered a collaboration on the 1995 title *Front Mission*.

The 1998 soundtrack to *Parasite Eve* marked a first for Shimomura's career with the inclusion of vocals, made possible by the technological advancements of the PlayStation. The music was celebrated for the unique blending of musical genres, ranging from classical piano, to electronica, to opera, and would release as a two-disc album later that year. *Parasite Eve* is often cited as the soundtrack that put Shimomura's work on the international map. This success story was followed by another as she composed, arranged, and produced the music for 1999's *Legend of Mana*.

CAPTURING HEARTS

While her popularity had grown immensely at Square, the 2002 release of *Kingdom Hearts* resulted in success that transcended the video game industry. Shimomura was given the difficult task of blending an established Disney soundscape and popular *Final Fantasy* themes, while creating an original voice for the music in the process.

Game reviews worldwide celebrated the soundtrack, noting the emotion and joy Shimomura was able to elicit through her work. After composing for the first *Kingdom Hearts*, Shimomura left Square on maternity leave, and went freelance from that point forward. She would continue to work closely with Square for years to come, remaining the composer for over 10 *Kingdom Hearts* releases—including a variety of spin-off titles—and is the composer of the highly anticipated 2019 release *Kingdom Hearts III*. Her work on the franchise would receive a variety of stand-alone album releases, in addition to piano treatments, remixes, and "best of" compilations. In 2007 IGN named *Kingdom Hearts II's* "Dearly Beloved" as one of the top five RPG title tracks of all time. It's also one of her favorite tracks ever composed.

MIDIPLEX

Going freelance allowed Shimomura to work on a variety of new projects. Under the umbrella of her new company, Midiplex, she composed soundtracks for over two dozen games, including *Mario & Luigi: Superstar Saga*, *Xenoblade Chronicles*, *The 3rd Birthday*, and more recently, *Final Fantasy XV*.

With an array of work to her name, Shimomura released a compilation album in 2008 titled *Drammatica: The Very Best of Yoko Shimomura*, which she curated with fan-favorite songs that had yet to be performed by an orchestra. The album was played live at Stockholm Concert Hall in 2008 as part of the Symphonic Shades event.

Shimomura's work has become a staple of video game concerts around the world, having been performed as part of Symphonic Fantasies and a Night in Fantasia. Her music is also regularly featured during the internationally-celebrated concert series Video Games Live.

In 2014 she performed in a 25th-anniversary retrospective of her work at the Tokyo FM Concert Hall, which included arrangements from *Kingdom Hearts*, *Street Fighter II*, and other highlights from her career. The solo concert was performed outside of Japan for the first time in 2015, first in Paris, followed by Mexico City. Shimomura also played a *Final Fantasy XV* concert live at Abby Road Studios in 2016, performed by the distinguished London Philharmonic Orchestra.

Recently, she's taken *Kingdom Hearts* on the road. "I've had the chance to visit multiple countries for the *Kingdom Hearts* Orchestra World Tour," she said. "I love orchestras as well as visiting different countries, so it's my dream job!"

A LASTING LEGACY

Over the years, Shimomura's fans have expressed their love for her work in a multitude of ways. "I love meeting fans after concerts, and hearing comments like 'I listened to your music, and the sadness saved me,' or 'I listened to your music and aspired to become a composer,' and 'I've listened to and studied your music for a year, which helped me get accepted into my desired university,'" she shared. "Hearing such comments makes me happy. I think each conversation like this is important."

Shimomura's legacy extends far beyond the fans, though. Her work has been ranked in the ClassicFM.com Hall of Fame the past four years, peaking at #30 in 2015. "To be in the same ranking as Tchaikovsky and Beethoven is amazing," she said. "It was a huge honor."

A DAY IN THE LIFE OF...

A PROGRAMMER

Programmers can be called by many names—software engineers, coders, computer scientists, and more. The unifying factor is that they all develop the base code that software, development tools, and entire game engines run on.

On smaller teams, programmers often work as generalists. On a large production, they are more likely to fall within a variety of disciplines, such as programming artificial intelligence, gameplay mechanics, sound, user interface, physics, or graphics tech. There are also network programmers who ensure online play runs smoothly, whether on a two-player cooperative title, or a 100-player competitive game.

Massive Entertainment's Simona Tassinari focuses primarily on Ubisoft's proprietary game engine—Snowdrop—that games such as *Tom Clancy's: The Division, Mario + Rabbids Kingdom Battle, South Park: The Fractured but Whole, Starlink: Battle for Atlas, Tom Clancy's: The Division 2*, and *The Settlers* are built upon. Her job is to coordinate development on Snowdrop across multiple teams, ensuring they collaborate efficiently. She also works on ensuring that Snowdrop stays on the bleeding edge of technology, doing R&D to continuously improve the engine.

SIMONA TASSINARI

PROFESSION: LEAD PROGRAMMER—SNOWDROP TEAM AT MASSIVE ENTERTAINMENT (UBISOFT)—MALMÖ, SWEDEN

YEARS IN PROFESSION: 14

WORKED ON: KINECT SPORTS, KINECT SPORTS: SEASON 2, KINECT SPORTS RIVALS, TOM CLANCY'S: THE DIVISION, SOUTH PARK: THE FRACTURED BUT WHOLE, MARIO + RABBIDS KINGDOM BATTLE, THE SNOWDROP ENGINE

▶ EDUCATION

"I earned a four-year computer science degree in Italy; my degree is roughly equivalent to a master's degree. I chose a number of classes in my degree that were very apt for computer games development. I took classes on animation, advanced math, physics, etc. I picked those classes because I found them interesting; I didn't plan to work in games."

▶ BREAKING IN

"Entering the industry was pretty much luck for me. I prepared my thesis in the US, aiming to find job opportunities abroad. But my first job was in my hometown in Italy, at a start-up developing web services. I then moved on to the Netherlands to work on what was, in hindsight, an extremely complex 'serious game' project. After about one more year of struggling to learn Dutch, I interviewed at Rare in the UK and was hired. I don't really feel I faced any specific obstacles to enter in the industry. I was full of enthusiasm at the time, and I took new experiences as they came without overly thinking about it."

▶ EARLY INDUSTRY IMPRESSIONS

"I remember my first couple of years in the industry as exciting and challenging, but in hindsight I didn't really understand the dynamics of the workplace or the development process for a long time. I was very enthusiastic and eager to learn, so that carried me through! I learned all I could and I was pretty ambitious, although I didn't really have any specific goals. I just tend to have a lot of ideas, and I try to connect different disciplines and be open-minded. My colleagues lived and breathed video games, while I had a more practical and technical approach that was complementary to their skills. I didn't really know what to expect."

▶ KEY QUALITIES

"Lots of different people can have a successful career working in video games. There are many different roles requiring different skill sets and attitudes. Personally I really enjoy working with people who are smart, curious, and humble. This normally correlates with continuous learning and improvement and good working relationships."

▶ TOOLS OF THE TRADE

"If I'm programming, I use Visual Studio, C++, and C#, but that's quite rare nowadays. I have a lot of expertise in Perforce (a source-control tool very common in the industry), and I normally spend some time working with Perforce, advising developers doing integrations or trying to understand the history of some code and data. If I'm coding, I will also spend some time in the Snowdrop editor to test and validate things."

▶ HOURS & ENVIRONMENT

"For most of my career, I've worked normal office hours (9-6) but since I have a son now, my husband and I work reduced hours to be able to do school pickups. I've worked hard in the past, but I feel that work-life balance is paramount, and I try to avoid overtime as much as possible for me and my team."

▶ PROMOTIONAL PATH

"The video game industry is very varied in how hierarchies are structured. Typically there will be multiple programmers being managed by a lead programmer; multiple leads will be managed by a producer or product manager.

"In general, programmers can develop their career in a couple of ways: they can specialize as technical experts and architects, sometimes called a 'technical track,' or they can decide to become managers and run teams."

▶ PROFESSIONAL PERKS

"For me, the major perk is the co-workers. My colleagues are all exceptional, creative, and inspiring in so many ways. From a technical point of view, I love the fact that we have to be cutting-edge; so much of the work we do is R&D, and it's never boring."

▶ CAREER CHALLENGES

"Because everything is R&D, it's very hard to plan work efficiently, and sometimes it's frustrating to have to stop feature development due to time constraints, or even failure. It can get very hectic, and working on AAA projects involves so many people that effective communication can be very challenging. To make things more complicated, I work on engine development, where the engine is used by multiple AAA projects in several time zones, so communication is a big part of my daily work."

▶ FAVORITE PROJECT

"From a technical standpoint, I had the opportunity to design and implement the localization pipeline in the Snowdrop engine. It's rare to be able to write something completely new in this industry, and I am glad I joined the company at the right time! From an infrastructure and project-management point of view, working on Snowdrop and on the engine-sharing design is definitely the most complex and exciting project I've participated in.

"There is so much to think about and so many challenges. But this is also the widest-reaching project I've ever been in, and the impact can be phenomenal."

▶ LIFE HACKS

"I always try to do too much, and then I'm disappointed when I can't achieve the ridiculous workload I've set for myself. For me to be able to recognize this, I focus on prioritization of areas and tasks and learning to say no sometimes is a continuous process."

▶ BIGGEST MISTAKE

"When I first became a team lead, I prioritized goals and achievements too much, and I sometimes lost track of my own beliefs and values along the way. I was unhappy, and my team also suffered. I moved away from management for many years after this, in favor of more technical roles, and I've only recently moved back into management. I think I learned a lot about how much I value integrity in myself and in my team, and how important it is to stay true to yourself, especially under pressure. I have learned to be extremely transparent and to not only discuss decisions, but also explain the whole reasoning around them, document it when possible, and store it for later review. I also focus much more on the wellbeing of the team in general."

▶ EXCITING ADVANCEMENTS

"This is probably really exciting only for me, but I'm very happy to see a paradigm shift in the industry on reusing technology and sharing tech more efficiently. It's a lot easier to write non-reusable tech from scratch, but it can be so much more efficient if things can be shared, improved, and built upon."

PRO TIP!

"Study computer science and become a good programmer. A good programmer can become a great video game programmer, but without a strong technical background, you are unlikely to be able to break into the industry and excel in it. There are many 'video game development' university courses (not all) that teach a lot about the development process and various specialties, but they give a very wide education that is not deep enough to have a solid background in programming. Having an understanding and interest in other disciplines is very important; we collaborate very tightly with lots of profiles, but it's fundamental to start with a good base."

AMY HENNIG

FORERUNNER OF CINEMATIC STORYTELLING IN GAMES

 Amy_Hennig

EXPERIENCE

FIRST INDUSTRY PROJECT: ELECTROCOP (1990, UNRELEASED)

FAVORITE INDUSTRY PROJECT: LEGACY OF KAIN: SOUL REAVER (1999)

PROJECTS SHIPPED: 14 GAMES

ACHIEVEMENTS UNLOCKED:

> WRITERS GUILD OF AMERICA "BEST VIDEOGAME WRITING" AWARD—UNCHARTED 2 (2009)

> BAFTA VIDEO GAME AWARDS "BEST STORY"—UNCHARTED 2 (2010)

> WRITERS GUILD OF AMERICA "BEST VIDEOGAME WRITING" AWARD—UNCHARTED 3 (2012)

> BAFTA "SPECIAL AWARD"—AMY HENNIG (2016)

> GAMELAB 2018 "HONOR AWARD"

STATS

INDUSTRY LEVEL: 29

CURRENT CLASS: SR. CREATIVE DIRECTOR & WRITER

GUILD: INDEPENDENT—SAN CARLOS, USA

SPECIAL SKILLS: WRITING, GAME DESIGN, PERFORMANCE CAPTURE, ANIMATION

STANDARD EQUIPMENT

FAVORITE PLATFORM: PLAYSTATION

GO-TO GENRE: ACTION/ADVENTURE

MUST-HAVE GAME: LEGEND OF ZELDA: A LINK TO THE PAST

BIO

For Amy Hennig, 1977 was a seminal year. "I had always been a gamer. I used to spend my allowance at the arcade every weekend—and this was back in the '70s when there wasn't much to play besides *Pong*, *Night Driver* and *Sea Wolf*," described Hennig. "I was obsessed with the Atari 2600—especially *Adventure*. I had just turned 13 when it came out and it blew my mind." Combined with the release of *Star Wars* and her discovery of *Dungeons & Dragons*, '77 set her imagination on fire.

"Even so, I never considered a career as a game developer; it wasn't even on my radar," Hennig said. "I studied English Lit and thought I might want to be a writer, and then pursued Film Theory & Production and thought I wanted to be a filmmaker." While in film school, Hennig was accepted into a pilot program for 3D modeling and animation using Wavefront on a Silicon Graphics workstation.

Hennig was taking odd jobs to pay her way through film school, including a contract position as an artist, animator, and designer on a side-scrolling game for the Atari 7800 called *Electrocop*. Having never made a game before, Hennig studied the state-of-the-art NES games for inspiration, poring over screenshots in *Nintendo Power* magazine. "We didn't have any tools to speak of, so we had to be creative," said Hennig.

"I used Graphist Paint—a precursor to Photoshop—and MacroMind Director to do all the art and animation on a Macintosh II, and transferred it over to the Atari ST. I designed all the levels on paper and then entered the layouts in hexadecimal, tile by tile, and column by column."

A NEW FRONTIER

Even though *Electrocop* was never released, working on the game was a lightbulb moment for Hennig. "I realized that games were a new frontier, a pioneer medium that had yet to be defined," she said. Hungry for more, she dropped out of film school in early '91 and applied for a junior artist/animator job at Electronic Arts.

Easter Egg

Collects vintage sci-fi toys from the 1930s including ray guns, rocket ships and books—mostly Buck Rogers. Her secret dream is to one day make a game in the style.

At Electronic Arts, Hennig first worked as an artist on *Bard's Tale IV* and *Desert Strike: Return to the Gulf.* "After a year or two I shifted into game design, which I ultimately found more fulfilling," she explained. "After studying and deconstructing a lot of games, I was more fascinated by—and opinionated about—mechanics and layout and what made a game 'fun' than I was by the aesthetic and technical aspects." Hennig took the role of Lead Designer on *Michael Jordan: Chaos in the Windy City.* The game reviewed well and, better yet, Jordan's kids loved it. He signed a basketball for her saying "To Amy, Great Game."

DESIGNING A LEGACY

In 1995, Hennig departed EA for nearby studio Crystal Dynamics, accepting a design manager position for the gothic action/adventure title *Blood Omen: Legacy of Kain.* She took the reins as director for the sequel—*Legacy of Kain: Soul Reaver*—and assumed the lead writer role as well. She remained writer and director for the two following titles—*Soul Reaver 2* and *Legacy of Kain: Defiance.*

"Every project has its high points and low points," said Hennig. "I'd probably say *Soul Reaver* was my favorite, though, because it felt the purest in terms of game design—the mechanics were born out of the story and vice versa. It was also the most ambitious game I'd done at that point, with a lot of 'firsts.' The first PlayStation game I'd worked on, the first time we'd used 3D graphics, the first game I wrote for, and my first experience working with actors. And even though it was our first game, we really pushed the limits of the hardware, using data streaming for a seamlessly loading open world, and geometry morphing when Raziel, our main character, shifted between the material world and the spirit plane. It was a really inspiring project to work on."

In 2003, Hennig moved on to Naughty Dog, the studio best known for *Crash Bandicoot* and the *Jak and Daxter* series at the time. After shipping *Jak 3* for the PlayStation 2, she took on the responsibility of writing and directing an entirely new IP—an action/adventure title starring a wise-cracking treasure hunter named Nathan Drake.

UNCHARTED WATERS

"Whether creatively, schedule-wise, or in terms of technical hurdles, it's never a breeze. Every project is challenging in its own way," said Hennig, speaking to developing the first *Uncharted* title. "We had to weather a hardware transition, rewrite our engine from scratch, and establish a whole new franchise. It was a tough transition for the studio in general to go from a stylized series like *Jak and Daxter* to something more realistic, and it took a long time to get our tools and engine up and running."

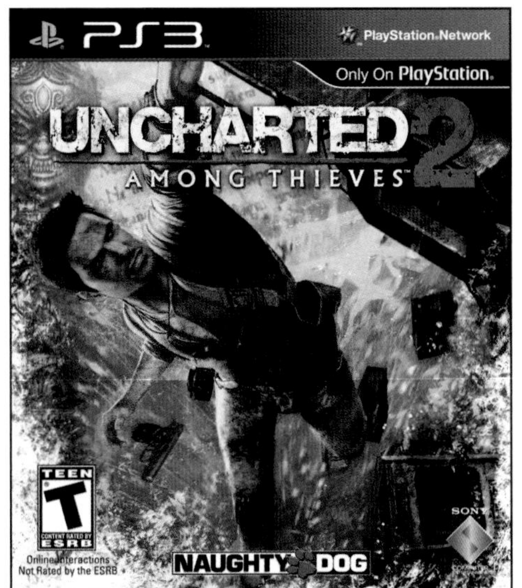

Uncharted was a massive success so anticipation was high for the sequel. Hennig would remain at the helm as Creative Director and Writer on *Uncharted 2* and *3*, and then worked for over two years on *Uncharted 4* before departing Naughty Dog in 2014. "The *Uncharted* series is one of the highest-rated and most-awarded franchises in the industry, particularly *Uncharted 2: Among Thieves*, which received over 20 Game of the Year awards and 10 Academy of Interactive Arts & Sciences awards," said Hennig. "The series as a whole has sold over 40 million units worldwide."

Celebrated for advancing games as a narrative medium with the *Uncharted* franchise, Hennig also introduced the seamless, cinematic story experiences that are common today. "With *Uncharted*, we pushed the state-of-the-art using performance capture in games, shooting more like you would for film or TV and working with actors as a collaborative ensemble. I love shaping story and drafting dialogue, watching the actors bring the characters to life, and seeing the scenes elevated by their talent."

Hennig measures success by more than just critical and commercial acclaim, though. "I've had letters from women in their fifties telling me how much they enjoyed *Uncharted*," she said. "Parents who bonded with their children while playing the game together. Grown children who played *Uncharted* with a terminally ill parent, saying how much the game brightened their final days. I'm profoundly grateful to have been in a position to reach so many people with our games."

"Whenever a young woman... tells me that my work influenced her to join the industry, that's the best."

Upon leaving Naughty Dog, Hennig returned to her roots at Electronic Arts as Sr. Creative Director and Writer on Visceral Games' unnamed *Star Wars* title. After the closure of Visceral in late 2017, she moved on to a new and unannounced endeavor. "I hope to keep pushing the boundaries of interactive narrative," said Hennig. "Whether in traditional games, VR, or some other platform."

"Whenever a young woman comes up to me at an event and tells me that my work influenced her to join the industry, that's the best," said Hennig, reflecting on her career so far. "As women in the industry, we're often so busy and focused on the task at hand, it's great to be reminded how much our voices matter, and how important it is for us to be visible role models for young women and girls who may aspire to a career in game development."

SHERI GRANER RAY

DUNGEON MASTER TURNED GAME DESIGNER

Sheri Graner Ray

EXPERIENCE

FIRST INDUSTRY PROJECT: ULTIMA VII—THE BLACK GATE (1992)

MOST RECENT INDUSTRY PROJECT: UNRELEASED SONY ONLINE ENTERTAINMENT MMO

PROJECTS SHIPPED: 25+ GAMES

ACHIEVEMENTS UNLOCKED:

> HOLLYWOOD REPORTER "20 MOST INFLUENTIAL WOMEN IN GAMES"—GAME (2004)
> GAME DEVELOPER'S CHOICE AWARD (2005)
> NEXTGEN "TOP 100 WOMEN IN GAMES" (2006)
> PCGEN "TOP 10 MOST INFLUENTIAL WOMEN IN GAMES" (2017)

STATS

INDUSTRY LEVEL: 29

CURRENT CLASS: SR. DESIGNER

CURRENT GUILD: ELECTRONIC ARTS—AUSTIN, USA

SPECIAL SKILLS: GAME DESIGN AND DEVELOPMENT, WRITING, TEAM DEVELOPMENT AND MENTORSHIP, GENDER AND TECHNOLOGY STUDIES

STANDARD EQUIPMENT

FAVORITE PLATFORM: PC

GO-TO GENRE: MMO

MUST-HAVE GAME: CITY OF HEROES

BIO

At the age of 29, Sheri Graner Ray worked at the American Diabetes Association as the communications manager and editor of a quarterly magazine. Fortunately for future fans of her games, the office was scheduled to close and she was looking for a new gig.

Ray ran a weekly *Dungeons & Dragons* group in her free time and it became the surprising catalyst for an entirely new career. "In this group, I wrote most of my own adventures and had my own set of 'house rules,'" she said. "We took in a new member who happened to be working at a company called Origin Systems, though none of us really knew who they were or what they did. After about three months of playing in my group, he said that because I had been writing my own stuff, that I would be a good match for an opening they had for a 'writer' at their company."

ORIGIN SYSTEMS

A week later, after passing along her résumé and writing samples, Ray landed an interview with Ultima Producer, Warren Specter. She got the job as a writer for the series. "I believe running table top games since I was in my teens is probably the best education I could have for making computer RPG games."

Easter Egg

While in middle school, Ray won a talent contest as a ventriloquist. She wrote her own material and created a puppet out of paper bags. She went on to win the local and district competitions.

The first task assigned to her on *Ultima VII* was a very specific.
"My job was to check all the dialogue and ensure we had used 'thee' and 'thou' properly," explained Ray. "We didn't have Google back then, of course, so I spent a lot of time at the St. Edwards University library, looking for books on the subject! Then I had to go through lines and lines of code to find the dialogue and check the grammar. The funniest part was, once I got it corrected, they changed a lot of it back because Richard Garriott liked the way the original sounded better!"

Ray worked at Origin Systems for five years, writing for the *Ultima* series—including the short-lived *Worlds of Ultima*—for the duration of her stay. She eventually departed for an offer from American Laser Games to work in their new division—Her Interactive. Her Interactive was the first company in the US dedicated exclusively to developing and promoting games for girls. Ray was brought onboard to get a product out the door in time for the holiday season, a game that was supposedly nearly finished.

> "The most meaningful contribution I've made is reflected in the women who have walked up to me or written an email to tell me that I had changed their life for the better."

"I showed up for my first day of work on the first of May. They handed me a box of shot movie film and a shooting script then said, 'There you go. Now make the game.'" recalled Ray, speaking to the uphill battle to get their first title—*McKenzie & Co.*—to market. Ray pushed through the hurdles, formed a team, and got it out the door on time. "I was and still am inordinately proud of that team and that product. We were the first girls' game to be made and released in the US."

With this success behind her, Ray was promoted from Associate Producer to Director of Product Development. She solidified the company vision, served as a spokesperson for the studio, managed a department of 65 people, and served as creative director on all Her Interactive products. She lent her design skills to the licensed game *Vampire Diaries* and the first title in the company's Nancy Drew Series, *Secrets Can Kill*. *McKenzie & Co.* was successful enough that when American Laser games went through bankruptcy, Her Interactive split off and remained in business.

GENDER INCLUSIVE DESIGN

While at Her Interactive, Ray began to develop concepts and theories on female entertainment criteria and its application to computers. This work, which included research, focus groups, surveys and studies, was formalized in her first book. *Gender Inclusive Game Design—Expanding the Market* was nominated for Game Developer's Book of the Year in 1996.

Ray didn't stop at the issue of diversifying games for consumers; she intended to help diversify the industry as a whole. The very first Women in Games conference, organized by Ray in conjunction with the 2004 Austin Game Conference, unfolded through presentations, group discussions, and brainstorming sessions. Notes were taken, consolidated, and transformed into white papers that detailed solutions for hurdles faced by women in the games industry. Ray expected 50 participants but to her amazement 168 attendees showed up that day, a memory that still puts a smile on her face.

In 1998, Ray put her research and conference learnings to further use by founding the Women in Game Development Special Interest Group, serving as its leader for a decade.

The organization's focus was achieving gender balance in the workplace and marketplace. Organizing and amplifying the voices of women in the industry continued to be a passion for Ray, as she also founded Women in Games International in 2005 and served as its Executive Director for 10 years.

Ray's design career wasn't slowed down by her advocacy; she worked at a variety of high-profile companies in the 2000s including the Cartoon Network, Big Noise Games, Schell Games, and Sony Online Entertainment. In addition, she founded two studios of her own. At SEO, she served as the content lead over a team of seven designers for *Star Wars Galaxies* and served as the lead designer on an original IP MMORPG, which was never released. Ray's game created as contract work for a defense industry company *GeoCommander* received the Best Serious Game, Government Edition award at the 2008 Serious Games Showcase and Challenge. After founding Zombie Cat Studios in 2014, Ray was wooed away to a Sr. Designer position at Electronic Arts, where she currently works.

A BRIGHTER FUTURE

Now considered the computer game industry's leading expert on the subject of gender and computer games, Ray notes that progress has been made but there is still work to be done. "When I started nearly 30 years ago, we were dealing with the institutional belief that women/girls simply did not—and would not—play games," said Ray. "We had to fight just to get the industry to acknowledge we even existed. Today we know that 48% of the market is female, so no one would even think to say that the women's market does not exist." She also notes a jump of women working in the industry from 3% to 22%, as the industry begins to have conversations about the importance of finding and retaining diversity.

"The most meaningful contribution I've made is reflected in the women who have walked up to me or written an email to tell me that I had changed their life for the better; that I had given them the courage to follow their dream," reflected Ray. "There is nothing more humbling or more amazing than knowing something you did helped someone else reach their life's goals."

THE 1990s: PIXELS TO POLYGONS

1991: STREET FIGHTER II: THE WORLD WARRIOR IS RELEASED

Capcom's *Street Fighter II* is unequivocally regarded not only as the most influential fighting game ever made, but also one of the most influential releases in video game history. Responsible for a renaissance in the coin-op gaming scene, *Street Fighter II* was also immensely successful on home consoles, with console sales exceeding $1.5B by 1993[1]. The vibrant visuals, unique characters, and revolutionary gameplay set the standard still used by modern fighting games and inspired many other franchises.

1991: THE CONSOLE WARS: NINTENDO VS. SEGA

A second generation of console wars erupted in the 1990s with the release of *Sonic the Hedgehog* (1991) for the Sega Genesis. Although the Genesis had been available since 1988, it had done little to challenge Nintendo's stranglehold on the market. However, *Sonic the Hedgehog*, combined with bare-knuckled, grassroots marketing efforts from Sega of America, allowed the company to overtake Nintendo as the leader of the home console market, a throne Nintendo had sat comfortably upon since 1985. Sega peaked with 65% of the 16-bit market in 1992[2]. Eventually, Sega's missteps enabled the Super NES to reassert its dominance with the introduction of technologically groundbreaking games such as *Star Fox* (1993) and *Donkey Kong Country* (1994).

1990

1991

1992: DUNE II ESTABLISHES THE REAL-TIME STRATEGY (RTS)

Inspired by 1990s *Herzog Zwei* for the Sega Genesis, Westwood Studios' *Dune II: The Building of a Dynasty* laid the foundation for the RTS genre as it's known today. The game was a spiritual predecessor to Westwood's own *Command & Conquer*, as well as Blizzard Entertainment's *Warcraft* (1994) and *StarCraft* (1998).

1993: ESRB IS ESTABLISHED

Due to growing concerns around increasingly violent video games (particularly *Mortal Kombat* and the FMV title *Night Trap*), two U.S. senators threatened the games industry with government regulation. Over the course of a senate committee hearing during which representatives from Nintendo and Sega appeared, the industry was given three months to develop its own appropriate answer to prevent the sale of hyper-violent and sexual games to minors. From this, the Electronic Software Ratings Board (ESRB) was created in early 1994, along with a ratings system that is still used today for modern game releases in the US. Other territories would eventually follow suit, such as the self-imposed PEGI ratings system used in over 40 European countries.

1993: DOOM POPULARIZES THE FIRST-PERSON SHOOTER (FPS)

Id Software's *Doom* is responsible for shaping not just a genre, but the entire video game landscape. Initially distributed as shareware, *Doom* was played by an estimated 15 million people within two years of release[3]. The game featured a single-player campaign and multiplayer mode, which *Doom* programmer John Romero noted was inspired by the competitive multiplayer featured in *Street Fighter II*[4], the latter of which gave rise to the competitive deathmatch subculture that would eventually shape the foundation of esports and some of the most successful video games in the following decades.

"*Doom* clones" came to be synonymous with 90s PC gaming, yet a few distinguished titles stood above the rest: *Quake* (1996), id Software's fully-3D follow-up to *Doom*; *Half-Life* (1998), Valve Software's award-winning, narrative-driven take on the genre; *Counter-Strike* (1999), a mod for *Half-Life* that would become one of the longest-running competitive FPS titles in gaming, among many others.

1993: ATARI JAGUAR AND THE END OF ATARI CORP.

With the console market at an all-time high, Atari re-entered the console race with the Atari Jaguar. Marketed as the first true 64-bit console, the Jaguar struggled to perform against Nintendo, Sega, and new comer Sony the following year. The Jaguar would be the swan song for Atari as a hardware manufacturer, as Atari Corp. merged with budget hard drive manufacturer JT Storage in 1996. Atari's intellectual property was sold to Hasbro Interactive in 1998, shortly before JT Storage filed for bankruptcy[5].

Hasbro's ownership in Atari would later be sold off to French publisher Infogrames in 2001, which would rename itself Atari Interactive and its US subsidiary Atari, Inc. in 2003. In 2004, the first in a line of Atari Flashback consoles was released, which featured an assortment of classic Atari 2600 and 7800 titles. In 2013, both Atari Interactive and Atari, Inc. filed for chapter 11 bankruptcy protection[6]. A third company, Atari Casino, was formed with a focus on *Asteroids* and *Centipede*-branded social casino games, and in 2014, the head of all three companies stated that Atari as a whole employed 10 people collectively[7].

In 2018, Atari raised $3M in crowdfunding for a modern Atari VCS, which is planned to release in mid-2019. A modern Intellivision console was also announced the same year, reigniting a 40-year-old rivalry.

1994: SONY PLAYSTATION AND SEGA SATURN ARE RELEASED

The third iteration of the console wars truly kicked off between two 32-bit, CD-based consoles: the Sony PlayStation and the Sega Saturn. The PlayStation was the wild card, as Sony had previously maintained working relationships with Nintendo and Sega. The PlayStation was originally conceived as a CD add-on for the Super Nintendo. However, prior to Nintendo's CES press conference in 1991, the company announced a partnership with Sony's rival, Philips, who eventually released the doomed CD-i Interactive home console. Sony's executives were not keen to enter the console market, but Nintendo's unexpected partnership with Philips was interpreted as an interntional act of disrespect, and was a large factor in the company's decision to move ahead with its own version of the PlayStation[8].

The PlayStation and its cutting-edge technology attracted a large number of developers and publishers, many of whom had grown weary of Nintendo's cartridge-licensing practices and Sega's waning brand power. With appealing franchises (*Tony Hawk*, *Resident Evil*, and *Tomb Raider* among others), along with a famously competitive price point $100 below the Saturn, this newcomer become a mainstay. The PlayStation would go on to sell 102 million lifetime units; 10 times that of the Sega Saturn[9].

Sega released most of the noteworthy Saturn titles, including *Panzer Dragoon*, *Virtua Fighter*, and others, but the lack of mainstream, system-selling games and a proper *Sonic the Hedgehog* game, as well as confusing and poorly marketed peripheral hardware, led to the system severely underperforming.

1995: NINTENDO VIRTUAL BOY LAUNCHES

In a partnership with Reflection Technology, Inc., Nintendo developed the 32-bit Virtual Boy console with Gunpei Yokoi leading the charge. Marketed as a form of virtual reality, the Virtual Boy was a critical and commercial failure. The Virtual Boy was discontinued half a year after release and stands as Nintendo's lowest-selling platform in the US at 770K units sold[11].

1995 & 1996: THE FIRST E3 AND TGS SHOWS ARE HELD

Up until the mid-90s, game companies generally utilized the Winter and Summer Consumer Electronics Show (CES) to announce and exhibit upcoming hardware and software. In 1995, the first annual Electronic Entertainment Expo (E3) was held in Los Angeles, CA, while the bi-annual Tokyo Game Show (TGS) started the following year. Both events were designed as a dedicated forum for the video game industry and became central to the announcement of key new products.

1995

1996

1997

1996: NINTENDO 64 LAUNCHES

Due to continually strong sales of the Super NES and the graphical achievements of the Super FX chip, Nintendo was the last to enter the 32-bit console wars. However, it skipped 32-bit entirely (Virtual Boy notwithstanding) and released the Nintendo 64 to compete with the Sony PlayStation and Sega Saturn.

Utilizing a much-touted chipset from supercomputer manufacturer Silicon Graphics, Inc., the Nintendo 64 was capable of advanced 3D graphics, which it showcased with its critically acclaimed launch title, *Super Mario 64*, which still stands as one of the most impactful 3D games of all-time.

Detracting from the Nintendo 64's initial success were an awkwardly-designed controller and a variety of limitations caused by Nintendo's insistence on using cartridges, which were more expensive and less capable than CD-ROMs.

1. Steven J. Kirsh (2006). *Children, Adolescents, and Media Violence: A Critical Look at the Research.* SAGE Publications. p. 228
2. "This Month in Gaming History." *Game Informer.* Vol. 12 no. 105. GameStop. January 2002. p. 117.
3. Armitage, Grenville; Claypool, Mark; Branch, Philip (2006). *Networking and Online Games: Understanding and Engineering Multiplayer Internet Games.* Chichester, England: John Wiley & Sons. p. 14
4. Consalvo, Mia. "Atari to Zelda: Japan's Videogames in Global Contexts." MIT Press, 2016.
5. Atari Corp Annual Report (Regulation S-K, Item 405) (10-K405) Item 7. "Management's Discussion and Analysis of Financial Condition and Results of Operations."
6. Current, Michael. "A History of HIAC XI / Atari Interactive." Atari History Timelines by Michael Current.
7. "Atari Files for Chapter 11 to Separate From French Parent." Prnewswire.com. 21 January 2013.
8. Takahashi, Dean. "Atari and FlowPlay team up to offer social casino games." VentureBeat. 26 March 2014.
9. Fahey, Rob. "Farewell, Father." Eurogamer.net. April 27, 2007.

1997: FINAL FANTASY VII IS RELEASED

Square and Nintendo were thought to be an inseparable power couple, with the former releasing a multitude of highly successful RPGs on the latter's hardware. Due to technical limitations of the Nintendo 64 and the ever-increasing cost of cartridges, Square opted to partner with Sony and release its next game, *Final Fantasy VII*, on the PlayStation. This alliance was notable for a couple of reasons. Firstly, *Final Fantasy VII* was a watershed moment in gaming history with its 3D graphics, CGI cutscenes, memorable characters, and more. Secondly, the game (and its handful of sequels and spin-offs) became system sellers for Sony, attracting entirely new audiences as well as players once loyal to Sega and Nintendo.

BOOTH BABES

The term "booth babe" was coined in the mid-1980s to describe the attractive, young, female promotional models employed by exhibitors at CES. Originally called "CES guides," the models' purpose was to attract attendees to their booth and hand out promotional materials such as pamphlets, answer questions, or take an attendee's contact information for follow-ups from sales representatives.

With the male-centric marketing focus in technology and gaming, both CES and trade shows such as E3 and TGS fully embraced booth babes. Although controversy surrounded booth babes as early as the 1990s, they would continue to be used by exhibitors for decades. In 2006, E3 began enforcing rules against "nudity, partial nudity, and bathing-suit bottoms that were once seen as almost standard booth-babe attire.[17]" The practice often resulted in female industry professionals being referred to as booth babes, done both unintentionally and intentionally, to demean their relevance at events and contributions to the larger industry. It also contributed to the feeling of "otherness" that many women felt at the time; that they were not welcome at such events, and games were not made for them.

Eventually, in the mid-2010s, as part of a larger discussion around sexism in entertainment, several conventions began strictly regulating exhibitor attire, or outright banning booth babes of any kind.

1998

1999

1999: EVERQUEST IS RELEASED

Following the groundwork provided by *Neverwinter Nights* (1991), the first online RPG to display graphics rather than text, and *Ultimate Online* (1997), which further established an open-ended fantasy world where thousands of players could compete with or against each other, Sony Online Entertainment's *EverQuest* was the first fully-3D, massively multiplayer online role-playing game (MMORPG) to achieve commercial success. While many MMOs have long shut down, with most failing to reach EverQuest's level of popularity (which peaked at 450K subscriptions in 2003[14]), the game and its 2004 sequel are still receiving updates and expansion to this day.

1999: THE SEGA DREAMCAST IS RELEASED

Sega released its final home console, the Sega Dreamcast on September 9th, 1999. The first sixth generation game console, the Dreamcast followed in its predecessors' footsteps with limited support and disappointing sales. While a commercial failure, the Dreamcast—like the Saturn—is often cited as featuring some of the more innovative games of the period, including *Jet Set Radio*, *Rez*, *Space Channel 5*, and *Seaman* (a voice-activated AI precursor to Siri and Alexa). Third-party titles such as Capcom's *Resident Evil: Code Veronica* and Namco's *Soulcaliber* also received high marks from critics, as did the console's built-in modem, a first for home consoles.

The Sega Dreamcast sold 9.13 million units worldwide[15] (just under the Sega Saturn's 9.26M[16]) and was eventually discontinued in 2001, leading Sega to shutter its console efforts and back out of the hardware race it once brazenly bullied its way into. However, Sega would go on to become a fairly successful third-party developer for Sony, Nintendo, and Microsoft's platforms.

10. "PlayStation Cumulative Production Shipments of Hardware." Sony Computer Entertainment.
11. "Consolidated Sales Transition by Region" (PDF). Nintendo. January 27, 2010.
12. Snow, Blake. "The 10 Worst-Selling Consoles of All Time." *Gamepro*. May 04 2007.
13. Sheff, David. *Game Over: How Nintendo Zapped an American Industry, Captured Your Dollars, and Enslaved Your Children*. Random House, Inc. 1993.
14. Woodcock, Bruce. "MMOG Active Subscriptions 21.0." mmogchart.com.
15. Zackariasson, Peter; Wilson, Timothy L.; Ernkvist, Mirko (2012). "Console Hardware: The Development of Nintendo Wii." The Video Game Industry: Formation, Present State, and Future. Routledge. p. 158
16. Snow, Blake. "The 10 Worst-Selling Consoles of All Time." *Gamepro*. May 04 2007.
17. Glaister, Dan. "Decline of the Booth Babe." *The Guardian*. May 16, 2006.

TRACY FULLERTON

PROFESSOR OF INTERACTIVE MEDIA AND GAMES

 tracyfullerton.com

EXPERIENCE

FIRST INDUSTRY PROJECT: RIDE FOR YOUR LIFE (1995)
FAVORITE INDUSTRY PROJECT: NETWITS (1996)
PROJECTS SHIPPED: 30 GAMES
ACHIEVEMENTS UNLOCKED:
> THE HOLLYWOOD REPORTER "WOMEN IN ENTERTAINMENT POWER 100" (2001)
> FORTUNE "10 MOST INFLUENTIAL WOMEN IN VIDEO GAMES" (2014)
> GAME DEVELOPERS CHOICE "AMBASSADOR AWARD" (2016)
> LOS ANGELES MAGAZINE "WOMAN OF THE YEAR" (2016)

STATS

INDUSTRY LEVEL: 26
CURRENT CLASS: DIRECTOR & PROFESSOR
CURRENT GUILD: USC GAME INNOVATION LAB—LOS ANGELES, USA
SPECIAL SKILLS: PRODUCTION, GAME DESIGN, CREATIVE DIRECTION, MENTORSHIP, SAILING

STANDARD EQUIPMENT

FAVORITE PLATFORM: IMAGINATION
GO-TO GENRE: SOCIAL STRATEGY GAMES
MUST-HAVE GAME: BASEBALL

BIO

Tracy Fullerton's forward-thinking contributions to the industry have long challenged the traditional boundaries of how we define games. In doing so, she has both helped establish and bring visibility to independent game design through her work, students, and advocacy.

"Very early on, my parents bought us a Commodore Vic-20, and then a Commodore 64, and I used them to program my own little games," said Fullerton. "I always knew I would do something creative, but I didn't know what form it would take until after grad school." Fullerton studied theater and literature as an undergraduate, followed by film production as a graduate student. Although she briefly worked in film, it didn't take her long to find a home in interactive entertainment.

CD BOOM

Fullerton's start came during a period of rapid change for video games, and as such, her film degree offered an advantage. "There was a huge boom in the media aspects of the game industry—right around the time that CD-ROMs were being introduced—and so there was a lot of opportunity for someone who understood both the creative aspects of storytelling and had a knack for the technical aspects of digital media."

Her very first design job—a 1995 experimental, interactive experience made in partnership with Sony—set the foundation for her future body of work. Produced by Interfilm, *Ride for Your Life* was released in 47 theaters nationwide and starred Adam West, Betty Buckley, and Matthew Lillard. The game required the audience to make collective choices with a three-button controller on the arm of their theater seat. "It was a massive undertaking for a small team, and we all took on many different roles to make sure it came together in the end," said Fullerton.

Easter Egg
Owned a 30-foot sailboat and regularly sailed it to Catalina Island.

Not long after, Fullerton became a founding member of the New York design firm R/GA Interactive. As a producer and creative director, she blended her experience in film and games for clients such as Sony, Intel, Microsoft, AdAge, Ticketmaster, Compaq, and Warner Bros. Notable projects included MSN's *NetWits*, and Sony's multiplayer *Jeopardy!*.

NETWITS

Two decades later, *NetWits* (1996)—a casual multiplayer game distributed through the Microsoft Network—remains a highlight in Fullerton's career. Every night fans would compete against each other through a series of social games. "It was so early on in online gaming that we had to build our own massively multiplayer server system," she explained. "Also, this was before web tools like Flash were available, so we had to build our own lightweight animation tool for the project." Everything was created from scratch by a passionate team connecting people through play. *NetWits* was named "Best of the Web" by *Time Magazine* in 1996.

Fullerton founded Spiderdance, Inc. in 1998, focusing their work on impressive proprietary technology—a massively multiplayer server system that could sync games to broadcast shows. Spiderdance regularly collaborated with media giants, developing NBC's *Weakest Link*, MTV's *webRIOT*, the WB's *No Boundaries*, and the History Channel's *History IQ*. Fullerton recalls her time at Spiderdance as the most challenging of her career, which is quite understandable. She was the president, the designer of the underlying technology, and a designer on the product level.

webRIOT—released in 1999—was noteworthy for allowing fans at home to compete with players on "Live on MTV." The first 25,000 users online had a chance to win a prize, or even be selected for a spot on the show. The *webRIOT* app also included live chat, which connected over one million participants during the product's lifespan.

GAME INNOVATION LAB

Spiderdance shut its doors in 2002 and two years later Fullerton took on her longest-running position to date. As the director of the University of Southern California's Game Innovation Lab, she and her students focus on experimental game design and research with the goal of challenging the path of the mainstream industry. "The students who have come through my classes have done just that, and I hope will continue to do so. Designers like Jenova Chen, Kellee Santiago, Ian Dallas, Asher Vollmer, Erin Reynolds, and more all exemplify the best of what we do at USC, and there are so many more like them."

In addition to her guidance as a professor, Fullerton recognized that more work could be done through building a like-minded community. Taking steps toward this goal, she served as an active advisor to the creation of festivals for students and indie designers to show off their hard work, including IndieCade and Games for Change. "These are all part of an ecosystem that allows independent work to be made, to be shown, and hopefully, to be played by the public, and to influence the path that the medium of games will take overall."

"We train students who can do more than just work in the game industry; our goal is to train them to innovate in ways that expand the industry, as independents, as entrepreneurs, as artists, and as visionaries."

WALDEN

Between teaching tasks, Fullerton moves along her own passion projects. Her most recent game has already received great acclaim. *Walden, a game* was funded by the National Endowment for Humanities as well as the National Endowment for the Arts and aims to attract gamers and non-gamers alike.

Fullerton first came up with the idea in 2002, when standing in Henry David Thoreau's footsteps at the site of his cabin near Concord, Massachusetts. Spiderdance had just shut its doors, and she wondered where the future would lead.

Walden invites the player to live in an abbreviated version of Thoreau's introspective period at Walden Pond. Players manage the essentials of survival, balanced with finding inspiration in nature. If the player works too much, they are leached of inspiration, and the world goes gray. A small core team of staff and students from the USC Game Innovation Lab helped bring the vision to life over the past decade.

Paradoxically, the game can be seen as a way to detox and detach from computer and mobile devices. Fullerton believes that because we're on these screens—for better or worse—they need to be used consciously and deliberately.

While *Walden* has won a fair number of awards that Fullerton can take pride in, including Game of the Year from Games for Change in 2017, the reward of developing it has been illustrated on a much deeper level, too.

"I got a letter from a *Walden, a game* player who suffered from post-traumatic stress," she said. "They wrote me that, coming home after work, when they were filled with anxiety, playing the game gave them the sense of peace that they really needed. That made me extremely happy, to think that my game had helped someone get through the day."

A DAY IN THE LIFE OF...

A CONCEPT ARTIST

Concept artists have the vital responsibility of establishing a game's aesthetic direction long before assets are rendered into a 3D world. The work is inherently exploratory; pieces that the end user never sees are just as important as the polished ones released publicly. Experimentation and elimination through feedback allow artists to home in on a game's visual expression.

Diverse by nature, concept art can include anything from expansive environment scenes to character and prop design. The range of deliverables is vast: loose thumbnail sketches, sequential storyboards, character sheets, technical orthographic illustrations, and more. Toward the end of the development cycle, concept artists may also be asked to assist with key marketing assets by creating polished works for magazine covers, billboards, and other public forums.

Yujin Jung—better known by Sangrde—began her career as a concept artist while still in Korea. Fast-forward seven years and she's graduated with a bachelor's degree in fine art and is working full-time in the United States as an illustrator. Jung has lent her unique style to everything from character designs for horror-Gothic indie games, to secret pieces for mega-publisher Nexon Japan. Now employed full-time, Jung is the lead artist on a sci-fi visual novel called *IGIST*, which hit beta in May of 2018.

YUJIN "SANGRDE" JUNG

 Sangrde  Sangrde  Sangrde artstation.com/sangrde sangrde.deviantart.com

PROFESSION: CONCEPT ARTIST & ILLUSTRATOR—GLOBAL

YEARS IN PROFESSION: 7

ASSOCIATED WITH: SPEEDPRO IMAGING, KIRARITO, NEXON JAPAN, GREY FOX GAMES, REDROOART, GIKUTAS JAPAN

▶ EDUCATION

"I originally majored in accountancy in college. I was already working and illustrating for companies overseas, so I decided to change my career path to arts, which I think was the best decision I made in my life. My school did not have a digital art major, so I decided to do fine art instead. This helped me with the basics of art since I did not have knowledge or education in art before. I believe the foundation in traditional art made a strong base in my digital art. YouTube and online tutorials were my teachers for digital art. There are many helpful resources online, but the difficult part was that I did not have someone to provide feedback. That is the most difficult part when you're self-taught. You have to believe in yourself that you are going on the right path."

▶ BREAKING IN

"I started working for companies as an independent artist and got commissions at an early age. But I had to do a lot of work promoting myself and get myself out there so I would be recognized, rather than waiting for someone to give me work. I regularly used social media and posted my works in many different places. I also studied the trends of the market.

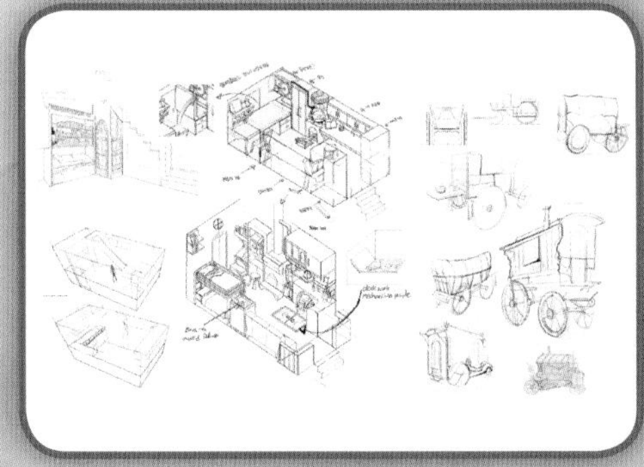

"After graduation, finding a company to hire me full-time was a whole different story. In a competitive market, I needed to stand out so I had to be extraordinary compared to other artists.

"I also realized that my art style and subject are quite different from US audience tastes after a lot of researching. I thought I had some industry experiences since I have been freelancing for many years, but most of it was from overseas clients who were looking for stylized illustrations for mobile games, while US companies were looking for a realistic style, focused on concept art. Then I realized I had been refusing to get out of my safe zone. So I started reworking and improving my portfolio. And I got a lot of interest from companies to hire me."

▶ EARLY INDUSTRY IMPRESSIONS

"I realized I would have to deal with a lot of stress sometimes, when clients ask me to make tons of changes. I don't get to draw what I want to draw; instead I am doing what clients tell me to do. It is the dilemma you always have to deal with being a commercial artist. Sometimes the clients will give me full freedom to design, which allows me to have more creativity. I am happy that I found a place that respects and values my creativity."

▶ KEY QUALITIES

"Being patient and consistent is absolutely crucial. I basically draw all day, every day. It is very tiring to do the same thing all the time. Being a professional, I have the responsibility to deliver the quality product that my clients expect from me every time. So I always try to be consistently good and make the best result I can. If I am not satisfied with the result, I will work extra hours if needed."

▶ TRAINING OPPORTUNITIES

"For aspiring illustrators, I recommend going to a convention and selling your artwork; it will help you promote yourself and also make money from your passion. I started going to Artist Alley four years ago, and I learned a lot from the experience, such as what people want to see from me, what the popular trends are, etc.

"There's a convention called CTN Animation Expo, an annual three-day convention that focuses on putting the talent center stage. They offer a lot of good opportunities for young artists, such as mentoring, Artist Alley, recruiting, and portfolio-review opportunities. I made connections and received helpful feedback on my portfolio there."

▶ TOOLS OF THE TRADE

"I mostly work with Wacom Intuos Pro as my main tool. I sometimes work with an iPad Pro to sketch ideas quickly. For software, I use many different ones, including Photoshop, ZBrush, Maya, Clip Studio Paint, SketchUp, Paint Tool SAI, etc. I enjoy learning and working on 3D programs. It helps me work faster with matte painting and thinking of 2D canvas as a 3D perspective."

▶ HOURS & ENVIRONMENT

"I work eight hours a day except weekends. Luckily, I work from home and don't have to go to work and drive two hours a day. It is a very comforting environment with my three cats and bed 24/7. But I always keep pushing myself to focus on work when I get distracted easily. I constantly update my progress and communicate with my coworkers and boss on Slack."

▶ PROFESSIONAL PERKS

"Being an artist is amazing! I can do what I enjoy all day and make a living from my hobby. How amazing it is! Also, the concept artist guides the direction of the game visuals, such as color scheme, design direction, etc.

"Being an illustrator, I carry the responsibility of entertaining the viewers' eyes. Art is one of the first things people judge before playing a game. When you go to a bakery, you would likely pick the most beautiful cake before tasting it. It is no wonder that artists get a lot of attention and love from people. Interacting with fans who supports me motivates me to create more, too."

▶ CAREER CHALLENGES

"While getting a lot of attention from people is very enjoyable, sometimes dealing with too much attention is very stressful. You have to have the mindset ready to take the critiques regularly."

▶ BIGGEST MISTAKE

"As I get commissioned from many different companies, I always try to keep up with the latest trends, such as what art style companies are looking for. There were times that I kept changing my art style depending on what clients wanted from me. I do appreciate all art styles and working on new ones, but it felt like copying the style of someone else and generating artwork like a factory. Changing constantly affected my art style and quality. I learned that I do not have to force myself to fit into the clients' requirements. I decided to push my own art style and improve it instead of copying the trend. I kept doing it and I got a lot of contacts from companies so I can be picky with what I want to work on."

PRO TIP!

"It may seem impossible to turn your hobby into a career. But enjoy what you are doing, like something you can do 24/7 such as playing a video game or eating fries. The time and effort you spend never betray you and eventually will pay off."

ALYSSA FINLEY

EXECUTIVE PRODUCER, EX-PROGRAMMER, PROFESSIONAL CAT HERDER

 Alyssa Finley

EXPERIENCE

FIRST INDUSTRY PROJECT: REBEL SPACE (1992)

FAVORITE INDUSTRY PROJECT: MINECRAFT STORY MODE (2015)

PROJECTS SHIPPED: 20 GAMES

ACHIEVEMENTS UNLOCKED:

> BAFTA "BEST GAME" AWARD—BIOSHOCK (2007)
> GAME INFORMER "GAME OF THE YEAR" AWARD—BIOSHOCK (2007)
> VARIETY "WOMEN'S IMPACT REPORT" (2008)
> "WOMEN IN GAMES: THE GAMASUTRA 20" (2008)

STATS

INDUSTRY LEVEL: 26

CURRENT CLASS: EXECUTIVE PRODUCER/DIRECTOR OF PRODUCTION

MOST RECENT GUILD: TELLTALE GAMES—SAN RAFAEL, USA

SPECIAL SKILLS: PRODUCTION, SCHEDULING, STORYTELLING, GAME DESIGN, EDITING, MENTORING

STANDARD EQUIPMENT

FAVORITE PLATFORM: NINTENDO SWITCH

GO-TO GENRE: ADVENTURE

MUST-HAVE GAME: ZORK

BIO

With 26 years of industry experience under her belt, Alyssa Finley has a deep understanding of what it takes to make great games. Her lengthy career includes roles as a customer-service representative, programmer, community manager, technical director, producer, project manager, studio head, and more.

In 1992—with graduation looming—Finley wasn't overly impressed by the aid provided from her university career center. They pointed her toward a vacant position at a local government facility, which may have been a fit for her computer science degree, but didn't appeal to her passion for collaboration and gaming. "Thankfully, a friend from California stepped in and suggested I come out over spring break and look for jobs," Finley recalled. "Within a week, I was able to land an entry-level position at a tiny video game company in San Rafael."

That company was Beyond Software, later known as Stormfront Studios. She was hired to work on *Rebel Space*—a play-by-email game hosted on Prodigy's online service. "I had spent much of high school playing an earlier email game—*Trade Wars*—on a local bulletin board system," explained Finley. "That, plus the fresh computer science degree, was enough to get me a chance at the company. Don Daglow, Stormfront's founder and the person who hired me for my first job, believed in team diversity and had incredibly strong values that he passed on to and enforced in his teams."

Finley didn't flex her programming muscles when she first started, however. She was hired as a customer-service representative. "My job was to run the daily 'turns,' which would process people's input, and generate emails to them with the current state of the game," said Finley. "I also dealt with anything that went wrong in the process, such as missed turns and bugs."

Over time, responsibilities naturally evolved to draw on her formal education, and Finley found herself programming upgrades to *Rebel Space*, assisting with the Mac port of *Eagle Eye Mysteries*, and eventually growing into a lead programmer position. Her technical trajectory continued at new studios, where she worked as a lead programmer at Psygnosis in 1997, and technical director at both Zowie Entertainment and LEGO leading into the 2000s. Finley was responsible for leading engineering teams, developing prototypes, researching and writing technical design documents, and evaluating new technologies.

"Programming wasn't my best strength, though," explained Finley. "What I realized over time is that coordination, planning, and process was much more my strong point, and my programming background served me better in giving me context and credibility in those interactions than as my passion."

Easter Egg

Skipped her college graduation to get started at Stormfront Studios. They mailed her the diploma later.

With this revelation, Finley's career took an entirely new direction. Returning to Stormfront Studios as a project manager in 2001, she was brought on as a "firefighter" to help get troubled projects to retail. Eventually, she was promoted to a production role, shipping projects such as *Lord of the Rings: The Two Towers* and *Forgotten Realms: Demon Stone.*

As a producer, Finley would have the opportunity to work on one of the seminal games of the new century. In 2005 she moved to Massachusetts to work at Irrational Games, leading production, planning, and execution for the dystopian title *BioShock.* The game was a critical and commercial success, taking home numerous accolades, including many Game of the Year awards. The emotional impact of the game ran deep. "I've worked with people who have gotten the wrist tattoo from *BioShock*," she said. "It's incredibly humbling to have worked on a game that people felt that strong a connection to."

With proven leadership skills, Finley was given the opportunity to bring a new branch of parent company 2K to life. In 2007 she moved cross-country once more to act as executive producer and studio head of 2K Marin. "Starting the 2K Marin studio from scratch and handpicking and hiring a team to make a game was an incredible experience," said Finley. "We grew from a core team of seven to over 100 people working on *BioShock 2*, and I believe we made something really special together."

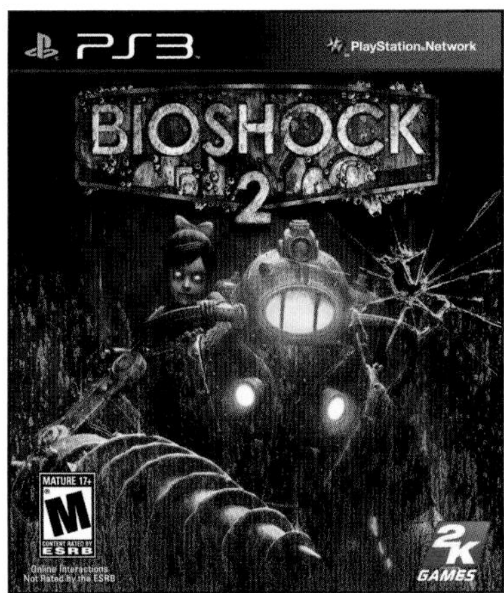

Running a studio meant managing the staffing plan, budget, and hiring and review processes across 2K Marin, as well as a 50-person sister studio in Australia. The studio shipped *BioShock 2* in 2009, and then transitioned to start working on both original IP and an FPS set in the XCOM universe that had been long incubated within the Australian team.

The challenges of developing a two-studio project proved to be considerable, particularly sharing a vision from a small, remote leadership team in Australia to the larger studio in the US. It was a hard lesson in the importance of creating and nurturing culture and ultimately the original IP was shelved in favor of consolidating XCOM development into the Marin studio, and splitting up the two locations to focus on different projects. This change shifted Finley's responsibilities to VP of Product Development, where she was hands-on in managing the production of 2K Marin's final game, *The Bureau: XCom Declassified.*

Unfortunately, in 2013 the Marin team faced the devastating news of studio-wide layoffs. "Shutting down the 2K Marin studio after our third release was incredibly painful, but we tried to treat people as well as we could, given the circumstances," said Finley. Although distressing, the studio shutdown presented important lessons to Finley that she has carried forward in her career. "The lesson: Decisiveness matters," she said. "If you try to make too many people happy, you'll end up only disappointing everyone—and it's better to give people a clear 'no' that they may not like short-term, than a murky 'maybe' that they then have to keep thinking about without clear resolution."

Finley found a home at Telltale Games, shipping the *Game of Thrones Series* as executive producer before accepting the role of director of production in 2014. The episodic nature of Telltale's development process provided the kind of challenges that Finley thrives upon. "Production is a storytelling discipline, where our job is to use collaboration, planning, and data to help shine a light in the darkness and explain exactly how we can assemble a coherent whole from a starting point of smart people, creative ideas, and good intentions.

Telltale also allowed Finley the chance to branch out of production and into a creative director role on *The Walking Dead: A New Frontier.* That role allowed Finley to apply her collaborative skills to the creative discipline. "A creative director needs to set vision to the point that the team understands the goals and boundaries, allowing that team to focus their best efforts within those constraints. Then she also needs to be both editor and evangelist for the vision and the team."

Telltale provided Finley not just with her own growth, but the inspiration for the next generation game developer. "My daughter was playing a lot of *Minecraft* and participated in an early playtest Story Mode before I was involved. She was incredibly enthusiastic about the game," recalled Finley. "It really cast a light on the fact that for most of my career, other than a brief stint at Zowie/LEGO Lab, I'd been primarily working on M-rated games that I couldn't really share with her. *Minecraft Story Mode* changed all that and acted as a gateway for her to play almost everything else in the Telltale catalog, leading to lively discussions about the art of narrative design and her heartfelt desire to be a developer when she grows up. I was so glad to be able to be a part of making that game, and then watch her play it, and talk to her about it."

With her extensive industry experience, Finley hopes her work in production has empowered others in the field. "I hope I've influenced some producers in the methods of their work and the values they espouse in a way that's made their future projects a little more successful or their future teams a little happier," she concluded. "I hope to keep working with creative teams, keep solving tricky problems, and keep finding better ways to work. I hope to continue teaching people things and to always keep learning."

JEN MACLEAN

GLOBAL GAME DEVELOPER ADVOCATE

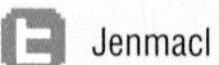 Jenmacl

Jen MacLean

EXPERIENCE

FIRST INDUSTRY PROJECT: DARKLANDS (1992)

FAVORITE INDUSTRY PROJECT: CIVILIZATION II (1996)

PROJECTS SHIPPED: 30+ GAMES

ACHIEVEMENTS UNLOCKED:

> NEXTGEN "TOP 100 WOMEN IN GAMES" (2006)

> GAMASUTRA "TOP 20 WOMEN IN GAMES" (2008)

> LAUNCHED IGDA FOUNDATION "NEXT GEN LEADERS" PROGRAM (2017)

STATS

INDUSTRY LEVEL: 26

CURRENT CLASS: EXECUTIVE DIRECTOR

CURRENT GUILD: INTERNATIONAL GAME DEVELOPERS ASSOCIATION (IGDA)—BOSTON, USA

SPECIAL SKILLS: STRATEGY, BUSINESS DEVELOPMENT, INTERNATIONAL RELATIONS, ADVOCACY

STANDARD EQUIPMENT

FAVORITE PLATFORM: MOBILE

GO-TO GENRE: RPG/STRATEGY

MUST-HAVE GAME: DRAGON AGE: INQUISITION

Easter Egg

Was the captain of her college fencing team, which indirectly led to her first job working in video games.

BIO

Growing up, IGDA Executive Director Jen MacLean thought game developers made magic in a nearly literal sense of the word. "I immersed myself in video games, but when I would read the little biographies of game developers included in the Infocom packages, they were as accessible and approachable as rock stars to me," she recalled. "Game development wasn't a career option; it was a mystical profession undertaken by wizards and geniuses." Once working in the industry—currently as an advocate for game developers worldwide—the illusion was dispelled, but that doesn't make video games any less magical in MacLean's eyes.

MacLean got her "in" with the industry in an unusual manner—fencing. "My friend and fencing coach began working at MicroProse Software as a playtester, and recommended me for a part-time position," she explained. "I was hooked. I love games. They're my favorite hobby, my way to relax and recharge and explore and achieve. Being able to make games, and support people who make games, is a dream come true."

> "Game development wasn't a career option; it was a mystical profession undertaken by wizards and geniuses."

PLAYTESTING

MacLean began her playtesting position in 1992. Her first official project was putting the isometric RPG *Darklands* through its paces. "I loved that game—even though it shipped with a 300-page bug list—and happily volunteered to continue to test it through the patches and updates," said MacLean, admitting she may have later regretted her initial enthusiasm when she was still testing the game eight months later. MacLean would test well over a dozen games for MicroProse, moving her way up the ranks to lead tester.

"My first game as lead tester was *Civilization II*, and that game will always have a special place in my heart," she recalled. "From the perspective of craft, it was fascinating to see how the sequel addressed some fundamental design flaws in the first game. The project was also led by Brian Reynolds, who believed in early prototyping and iteration long before it became a trendy design approach, so I was able to play the game, literally, for years. I don't know if anything will match the experience of working on *Civ II*."

Those first years were formative for MacLean, in more ways than one. "It wasn't an easy path," she shared. "As playtesters, we were considered the least-valuable members of the team by many developers; one engineer said we should be fired and 'replaced by trained monkeys' after a few too many drinks at a company party. I was also, for a significant period of time, the only woman in playtest and sometimes the only woman in all of development. I've faced frequent sexism, microaggressions, and sometimes blatant harassment throughout my career."

Other employees were allies to her, actively supporting MacLean at the start of her career. "They recognized that playtesters were generally more familiar with the current market than anyone else in the company," she explained. "I'll never forget the privilege of working with Sid Meier and Brian Reynolds on *Colonization* and *Civilization II*. They made me feel like a valued member of the team, and their kindness and graciousness to, and respect for, a young playtester taught me an invaluable lesson about recognizing the importance and contribution of everyone on your team, regardless of title or seniority."

BIG BUSINESS

In 1996 MacLean accepted the role of project manager for Games Channel at American Online, and would work her way up to programming director in the six years she spent there. Her director-level duties had her develop and implement an overall content strategy for the company's game branch. Additionally, she collaborated on the development of over 60 games at AOL and with partners at companies including EA, Mythic, Slingo, and Kesmai.

In 2002 MacLean moved to another big name in business—Comcast. As the senior director for sports, games, and entertainment for Comcast's broadband service, she was responsible for development across all three categories, often in partnership with leading media companies including Fox Sports, Major League Baseball, Disney and Electronic Arts. She was promoted to vice president and general manager for games at Comcast Interactive Media in 2006, and oversaw the launch of Comcast's casual PlayGames platform and their cross-platform editorial offering, GameInvasion.net.

After leaving Comcast, MacLean took up post as vice president of business development—and eventually CEO—at 38 Studios, working on *Kingdoms of Amalur: Reckoning* with NYT bestseller R.A. Salvatore and renowned artist Todd McFarlane. After the unfortunate closure of 38 Studios in 2012, MacLean took a brief hiatus from games to work at health IT company Ovuline, and tuition-assistance program EdAssist. She returned to interactive entertainment as president of StoryArc Media in 2015, tasked with reorganizing the company structure, adopting a new tech stack, and reinvigorating its product slate.

THE IGDA

MacLean first became involved with the International Game Developers Association (IGDA) as a volunteer and contributor to the first Casual Games Whitepaper in 2005 and was elected in 2007 as a member of the board of directors. The IGDA is the world's largest association for game developers and has a lofty purpose: "To make game development as a profession more diverse, more fulfilling, and more valued."

After departing StoryArc Media, MacLean took over as managing director for the IGDA, the IGDA's public charity and advocacy organization for diversity and inclusivity in game development. Now also the executive director of the IGDA, MacLean works as a full-time advocate for game developers on a global scale. "As the executive director of the IGDA and IGDA Foundation, my role is to support game developers around the world in creating sustainable and fulfilling careers, and in building a more diverse and inclusive game-development community," she explained.

"There's nothing else like it, for the opportunity to make a difference to tens of thousands of game developers and millions of game players." When required, as the IGDA head, MacLean represents video games in public forums, including national television programming appearances.

MacLean has several passion projects at the IGDA and IGDA Foundation, and the Next Gen Leaders program is clearly at the top of the list. "Recently, I launched a new program, Next Gen Leaders, designed to improve retention of underrepresented minorities in game development," she began. "The first year of the IGDA Foundation's Next Gen Leaders program was especially meaningful to me." The yearlong program kicks off at GDC. "They receive two days of personal and professional development workshops—as well as a travel stipend and conference pass. They then receive a year of mentorship and are brought back to GDC the following year for two additional days of personal and professional development, and opportunities to mentor aspiring game developers themselves."

When the first group of leaders met and mingled at GDC 2017, it was a moment MacLean will not forget. "The way they clicked with each other, and almost immediately found a support system and network, it was an incredibly powerful experience," she continued. "One of the best possible rewards is seeing how people you've mentored grow and excel in their own careers. Helping people succeed is the best possible outcome, and the very best motivator."

"Every year, literally thousands of people around the world participate in an IGDA Chapter, Special Interest Group, or event; travel to a conference and expand their horizons as part of an IGDA Foundation program; or give their time and energy to support the game-development community through the IGDA and IGDA Foundation," MacLean said in closing. "Enabling, empowering, and supporting this group of people is a gift; by giving people the tools, information, and support they need to help themselves and their communities, I'm able to, slowly but surely, make a lasting difference to the game-development community."

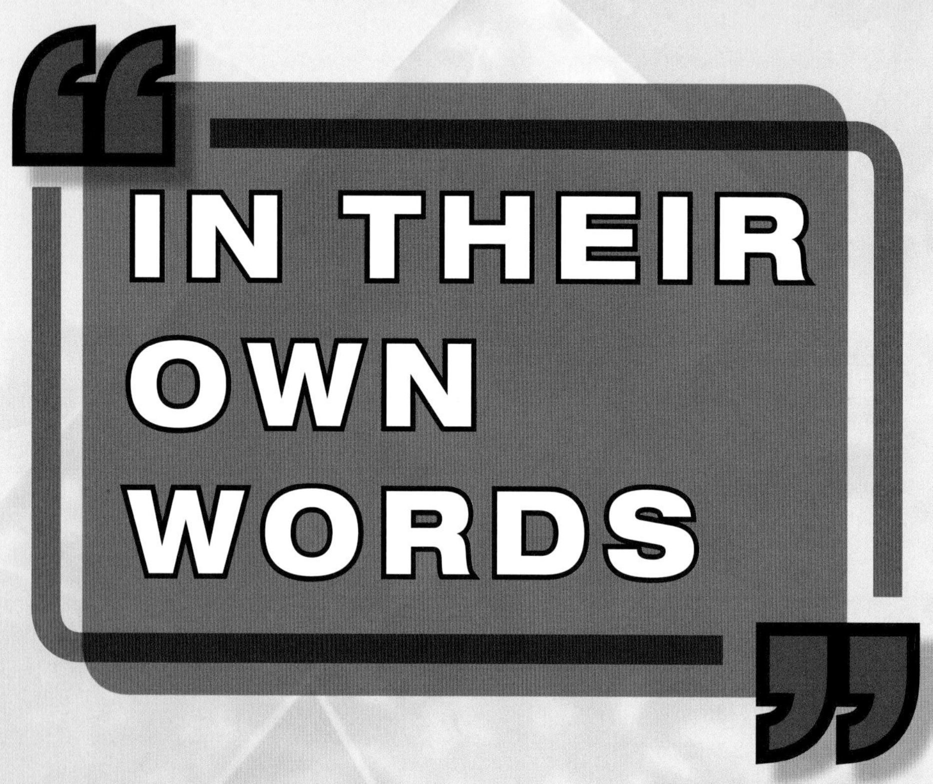

THE BENEFITS OF DIVERSITY

In your opinion, what are the benefits to having teams in the industry with diverse gender representation?

"The diversity of genders on a team generates more varied opinions on how to make a game, and that can greatly enrich the experience. For example, it helps to take into account the inclusion of different gender representations in the characters and the themes. I have worked on video game projects whose target players were women but which were developed by a majority of men. There you see the amount of prejudices that a male team can have on how to represent a woman in a video game and what a woman supposedly wants as a player. Games made in this way become transmitters and repeaters of prejudice. Women also have ours. In reality, it is not so much a question of diversity of genders on a team but of diversity of ways of thinking, but of course it helps to have mixed teams."

Alejandra Bruno | Narrative & Game Designer | QB9 | Buenos Aires, Argentina

---

"There are so many benefits to having a diverse team working on a game. People with different life experiences, perspectives, and skills bring more to the table than having a team with a similar viewpoint. Gamers as a whole are a diverse consumer group—they live all around the world; they're male, female, young, old. By having a more diverse representation in the development of games, the industry can continue to create better and better games that gamers will want to experience."

Amanda Erickson | Social Media Manager | Rooster Teeth | Austin, USA

"[Diverse teams bring] invaluable, different perspectives to the table. Video games can be extremely personal experiences, and broadening that spectrum for more people to benefit from them is just magical. It also deepens the social side of it all by allowing more people to have their voices heard, be able to share different life stories and experiences, and ultimately elevate us all as human beings."

Geneviève St-Onge | Co-Founder | PopAgenda | San Francisco, USA

"We as an industry tend to iterate and retread the same features, mechanics, and genres, which is a consequence of groupthink. Having diversity on your game development team invites new perspectives and increases the chances of there being unique ideas that have not been tried previously, which puts you at a competitive advantage. There is also the possibility that the resulting game will appeal to a broader audience, which would mean more sales for your game and a bigger community of gamers exposed to your work."

Anna Kipnis | Senior Gameplay Programmer | Double Fine Productions | San Francisco, USA

"We're all shaped by our experiences and lives we've lived, so we'll never all see 100% of the picture, no matter how much we may think we're able to see others' perspectives. We will all—always—have some blind spots. Having a diverse team makes sure we see things from different angles. It gives us the opportunity to understand how those experiences shaped us, and the people around us, and gives more depth to what you're creating so you don't tell just one point of view. The people who pave the way are inspiration for newer generations that want to work in games as well."

Cat Karskens | Senior Community Manager | Square Enix Europe | London, UK

"No matter your gender, your color of skin, or your nationality, each person is their own individual—with their own ideas, culture influences, and experiences—who brings a myriad of concepts that will help to develop and strengthen the project. What matters most is that each of those individuals shows interest and passion to learn more with others and help each other out. That they want to work on the project and be proactive about it."

Inês Borges | UI Designer & Game Artist | Elifoot 18 and GameNest | Lisbon, Portugal

---

"A diverse team can create products that appeal to a much wider audience. There's no better way to expand out of the male 18-35 group than to add more voices to your development team. I saw a presentation by Jen MacLean once, and she said something like, 'Hiring a diverse team is difficult at first, but then it becomes delightful.' I love that. It's been a joy to work with diverse people and to hear their feedback, ideas, and to watch how it has shaped the games we work on."

Kari Toyama | Senior Producer | Private Division, Take-Two Interactive Software, Inc. | Seattle, USA

"This answer feels obvious but I know it isn't—yet. I was explaining this to my own daughter and son the other day. They felt that the job should go to the 'best candidate.' I explained that, if candidates are close to equal on experience and knowledge, the job should go to someone who brings a new viewpoint to the team. Not just diverse gender, but any diverse demographic will add a broader worldview to the team and should be sought after for this reason. If you're not hiring, make your free beta testers diverse. If you're unable to use outside testers, seek out a diverse and culturally rich community of players. Whatever way you make your team or audience diverse, you make your game richer and more widely accepted for it."

Katherine Postma | Community Manager | Stoic | London, Canada

---

"I always think the more perspectives that you can get on a topic only make the work better. We all come to the table with our own unique experiences and look at each subject from a different angle. I think that a very homogenous group of people have been making games for some time now, and we're getting to a point where that stifles some amount of creativity. We can't keep telling the same stories and watching similar characters take the lead. For the games industry to continue to grow, we need to have more viewpoints represented and those diverse voices to drive game development and writing."

Kimberley Wallace | Features Editor | *Game Informer* | Minneapolis, USA

"Diversity saves lives. Having a diverse team in the medical field can be the difference between life and death. Media and entertainment nurture our daily life, and shape the way we see the world. If we keep on telling stories from a narrow segment of people, there's a lot we're missing, and there are so many people who we won't be able to reach."

Laia Bee | Co-Founder | Pincer Games | Punta del Este, Uruguay

---

"Studies in multiple areas show that diversity has a positive impact on the performance of teams, and game development is not an exception. I believe diversity is particularly relevant for teams working on creative tasks, as innovative ideas emerge from the convergence of diverse perspectives. In this sense, while working on game development, it's extremely valuable that each team member feels free to bring forward their own background and experience, because this way something unique might emerge."

Maureen Berho | CEO & Producer | Niebla Games | Valparaíso, Chile

---

"What aren't the benefits, is my question? Diversity in any way—be it race, gender, religion—helps provide a broader and more nuanced perspective to any industry. In an industry where character interaction and narrative are key, the better and more diverse the team, the better your finished product should be as a result."

Pippa Tshabalala | Video Game Reviewer/Presenter | Glitched | Johannesburg, South Africa

---

"Having a diverse team creates diverse feedback, both on the design of a project and the experience of playing it. For example, women are more prone to motion sickness than men. Having women widely test and create VR hardware and software is necessary to create more universally comfortable VR experiences that, in turn, encourage a broader consumer base. Diverse teams also create diverse content. To encourage more and different players to play games, we need to continue expanding on what games can be and what subjects they can be about."

Robyn Tong Gray | Co-Founder & Chief Creative Officer | Otherworld Interactive | Los Angeles, USA

"Diverse. Teams. Make. Better. Things. It doesn't matter whether those things are rocket ships or ad campaigns, taco trucks, T-shirts, or video games. A team with a wide variety of approaches, references, and experiences is a team with friction, and friction—when properly corralled and disciplined—can lead to some mind-blowingly creative results. But here's where I remind everyone that it isn't just the capital-D Diversity; it's also the capital-I Inclusion. Diversity and inclusion are necessary to build those types of high-functioning teams that appropriately challenge and adequately support. Diverse and inclusive teams have the potential for not just friction, but that good friction that leads to creative outcomes and sought-after solutions. Now for some myth-busting: "diverse" doesn't mean development is easy. On the contrary, building diverse and inclusive teams is very, very hard. It doesn't happen on accident or overnight. But speaking as someone who's both been on and built some highly functional, highly creative diverse teams in my time, there's no greater pleasure than to be a part of one."

Shana T. Bryant | Senior Producer | Private Division, Take-Two Interactive Software, Inc. | Seattle, USA

"It is easy to create a game about what resonates for yourself, your gender, and your own culture. But then you end up in an echo chamber, where storytelling only goes one way. A video game is pretty much like a prism; it is not a vertical story that you are telling to yourself. Each interaction with every gamer will reflect differently, based on their own life and experience. Every art in every culture in every civilization has started as an alternative movement. You can never really know what is going to take. All you can do, as an artist, is create something that means something."

Catherine Vandier | Marketing & Communications Manager | Electronic Arts | Guildford, UK

"Diverse gender representation, and diverse representation overall, leads to more creative solutions and a stronger end product. Everyone has a unique background and viewpoint to share, and when they're pooled together, the results can be incredible and unexpected."

Katie Swindlehurst | Associate Brand Manager | Crystal Dynamics | Redwood City, USA

"Well, studies show that you make more money. You also hold everyone on the team accountable to listening to a wide variety of perspectives, which is critical when it comes to playtesting, and identifying your audience. A team with a monoculture will have a lot of blind spots when it comes to making choices that make a better game for a wide audience that a diverse team does not."

Kellee Santiago | Partnerships Development Lead | Google Entertainment | San Francisco, USA

"It's not an opinion. It's fact. According to *Forbes* magazine, in a survey of Fortune 500 companies, it was shown that diverse teams have better ROI, make better business decisions, and show greater creativity and innovation. That last part is the key. Our industry lives or dies on creativity and innovation. That means diversity isn't an option; it's a mandate."

Sheri Graner Ray | Senior Designer | Electronic Arts | Austin, USA

"The audience of people who play games is very diverse, and like any product or industry, it benefits us to have diversity on the creator side. Diversity of perspective on a team means you have people with different ideas and opinions that, I think, make the team think about the creative choices in the experience differently. Ideally a diverse team means we really think about our customers differently, so that we continue to push ourselves to make new experiences that resonate, delight, challenge, surprise, make people think, and enable fun that attracts a larger audience.

Bonnie Ross | Corporate Vice President, Head of 343 Industries | Microsoft Studios | Seattle, USA

DIFFICULT WOMEN:

The Importance of Female Characters Who Go Beyond Being Strong

By Ally McLean | *Director of The Working Lunch*

In the debate that swirls around representation of gender in video games, we often fail by over-simplifying and underestimating the complexity and the range of roles that women and girls play in our lives. Expanding representation of women in games is about more than rejecting damsels and celebrating so-called "strong female characters." It's about creating room in this powerful, innovative, storytelling medium for women of all walks of life to see themselves represented and to take part in revolutionising what is possible for women in the playing and creating of video games.

I have long been drawn to what I would characterise broadly as "difficult women." These are characters who break tropes, defy our expectations, and demand to be more than the history of this medium would have them be. There are a handful of these women and girls peppered throughout my library of favourite games—games that inspired and challenged me, and games that ultimately made me the developer I am today. There are a select few, though, that lodged themselves in my heart and mind and undoubtedly changed me. I can quite easily map my career and the peaks and valleys of my life through the difficult women who pushed me forward. Here lies the power of complex, nuanced representation. These characters and their stories and the experiences around them are powerful things that through their defiance can change the way we view ourselves and what is possible.

As a younger sister to two older brothers, princesses—of the Peach and Zelda variety—were my bread and butter growing up. While I loved the social experience of playing games, I was never particularly impacted by a video game narrative until much later in life. Freshly moved out of home, I camped out on the floor of my shoebox bedroom in a leaky, roach-infested terrace house. Cradling an ancient laptop that would frequently overheat and burn grid marks onto my legs, I entered the floating city of Columbia for the first time.

Bioshock Infinite's world felt tailored to me as a young girl. Its bloomed-out sunshine, flowery monuments, and gleaming pastel architecture was far from the grimdark, grimy game worlds I'd become accustomed to emotionally detaching myself from. Columbia was a world within which I could identify connections to my own life, from the sunshine and barbershop quartets to the horrors that lurked behind closed doors.

Elizabeth at first presents as somewhat of a princess: locked away in a tower, protected or imprisoned by an otherworldly creature, aesthetically reminiscent of Belle in *Beauty and the Beast*, pining Ariel-style for a world beyond the confines of her home.

Referred to as "the Lamb," Elizabeth occupies a space in the collective consciousness of Columbia's occupants as a precious, mysterious, and delicate object. When we first meet her, we observe her through a one-way mirror fussing over her hair, pouting over a paper cut. Playing as Booker, we're no doubt anticipating a frustrating escort mission that games have trained us to expect from traditionally feminine, disempowered women. But Elizabeth has other plans. Mere moments later, she literally tears a hole in space-time and assaults Booker with a tome on quantum mechanics. "What makes the girl different?" muses Rosalind Lutece. "I suspect it has less to do with what she is, and rather more what she is not."

Elizabeth contains multitudes and that fact is plainly evident in the story of her creation. I spoke to Ken Levine about bringing Elizabeth to life with actor Courtnee Draper. "It's impossible to separate the actress from the character for me," he told me. "But in real life, Courtnee's also a prosecutor for Los Angeles County. She's nothing like Elizabeth and everything like her at the same time."

In this sentiment, Levine summarises the power of nuanced representation. Elizabeth is the damseled princess, but she is also the unfathomably powerful cosmic being. She is a tormented woman, a hero, a sidekick, and a villain. As a 19-year-old girl with laptop burns on my legs, this was a powerful revelation. If I could be Elizabeth—and Elizabeth could be anyone—my own potential was limitless.

Several years later, after I had begun my own pursuit of a career in games, I met Yennefer of Vengerberg. Few female characters of recent years have invited such uproar and debate among players, which no doubt adds to the appeal of Yennefer as an entity beyond her appearance in *The Witcher 3: Wild Hunt*. Ultimately, this game would take me around the world and kick-start my professional journey into game development.

Yennefer benefits from the rich lore of the *Witcher* novel series that informs her role in *Wild Hunt*. Polish novelist and *Witcher* creator Andrzej Sapkowski says of Yennefer, "When I created Yennefer's character, I wanted Geralt to fully grow, but then I decided to make things complicated. I created a female character who refuses to be a fantasy stereotype."

True to that sentiment, and far beyond her purpose as a love interest, Yennefer is a survivor of childhood abuse, an infertile woman who craves motherhood, a hunchback made conventionally beautiful by magic and somehow—most impressively of all—Yennefer isn't preoccupied with being liked.

Knowing this, and having fallen in love with her already, when Marcin Momot (the community manager at CD Projekt Red) proposed I create her costume and cosplay as her for promotion at events around the game for the years leading up to release, I was stunned.

I spoke to Marcin Blacha, story director of *The Witcher 3*, about how Yennefer's unique blend of cold indifference and deep compassion was translated into the game and received by players. "Presenting Yennefer in the game was a topic of long debates. From the start, we knew that we wanted to showcase her independence… She's the driving force of the search [for Ciri] and Geralt has a choice to either help her, by offering her his skill repertoire, or not."

Yennefer is presented as a self-sufficient entity, her story progresses and she continues to pursue her own agenda regardless of the male protagonist's actions. In this way, she stands above the leagues of women and girls summoned into male narratives to fulfill their needs and quietly move on when they are no longer required. In fact, it's difficult to imagine Yennefer quietly doing anything.

It's fitting then that Yennefer's portrayal compared to the softer, more genial women in the story has been a topic of heated debate. Blacha recalls, "Not long after the release of the game, groups of Team Triss and Team Yennefer were diving deep into conversations on the personalities of both characters." Working for CD Projekt Red in many ways marked the beginning of my career and becoming a public advocate for Yen and her eccentricities introduced me to the full spectrum of gamers' reactions to the epitome of a difficult woman in a franchise that had catered heavily to the male gaze.

The heartening experiences that shone through the muck, however, were the stories from women who saw themselves reflected in Yen's nature. One in particular from Amanda Erickson, social media manager for Rooster Teeth, comes to mind. "After doing a Myers-Briggs test, I got INTJ, which had Yennefer listed as a similar personality. It's pretty rare for women to have this personality type and it's often characterized with evil, scheming characters in fiction. I felt like it put a spotlight on the worst parts of my personality," Erickson said.

"But as I played *The Witcher 3* and read the books, I saw more and more the good parts of Yennefer and started to appreciate those aspects in my personality. Learning more about Yennefer and the different areas of her personality and drive helped me learn more about my own personality and how my brain works."

Yennefer embodies the revolutionary act for a woman to be difficult and still worthwhile, to be unlikeable but of value, to be inconvenient and still be loved.

With these formative experiences of trope-demolishing women in my back pocket, when it came time to step up and direct the creation of my own characters in a narrative game, my first thought was how exciting and terrifying it would be to try to shape my own difficult woman. When talking to someone who knows this process very well, writer Rhianna Pratchett said "There's a general lack of female antagonists and anti-heroes in entertainment in general, but particularly in games. From a writerly perspective, it was so much fun crafting the mistress characters in the *Overlord* games, or twisted women like Whiplash in *Heavenly Sword*. It's narratively juicy to play with expectations and explore the paths less travelled."

Embarking on the journey of being the Gamerunner on *RUMU* (the first feature-length game for which I would lead development), I knew that Sabrina—our house AI and grief stricken maternal villain—would present the biggest opportunity to explore the path less travelled.

Daniel McMahon, lead writer on *RUMU*, feels that Sabrina's character lives and dies by her maternal characteristics. "What I think is interesting is that from the earliest concept, even her name was never anything other than female. It's dumb and offensive to suggest that *RUMU* only works as a boy because curiosity, adventure, and mischief are exclusively male qualities. But I don't think it's offensive to suggest that Sabrina only works—or works much better—as a mother figure. The trauma she goes through, the way she reacts, the burden she carries, all feel truer to a woman, at least in the current climate. Bring on the day when a male AI could talk to us the way Sabrina does and we would believe it."

If *RUMU* presents the player with a more conventional, innocent and often naive definition of what it means to love, then Sabrina barks back with the darker, controlling, fractured and insecure love that comes with loss and betrayal. Sabrina embodies the suffocation of women assigned to be nurturing, to keep domestic order, and to serve the needs of others before themselves. Her surface is calm and in control, while chaos, deception and earth-shattering grief bubbles below. Sabrina's experiences—and her ultimate unravelling—stand in contrast to the countless depictions of women as service robots, holograms, and other helpful AI that live and die to progress male stories.

From overheating a laptop while opening portals in Columbia, to travelling the world as an unlikeable sorceress, to taking part in birthing my own fractured and insecure AI, these unexpected and defiant women have shaped not only my career, but how I see my role and the roles of women and girls in games as a whole. We have a ways to go in this young industry, and surely the greatest works of video game storytelling are yet to be made. It's my aim to continue to celebrate and create difficult women. Long may they reign, whether you like them or not.

PERRIN KAPLAN

PUTTING CONSUMERS FIRST BY SELLING JOY

perrinkaplan  perrinkaplan

 Perrin Kaplan  zebrapartners.net

EXPERIENCE

FIRST INDUSTRY PROJECT: ONGOING SNES PROMOTION

FAVORITE INDUSTRY PROJECT: LAUNCH OF WII AND POKÉMON

PROJECTS SHIPPED: 650 GAMES, 12 PIECES OF HARDWARE

ACHIEVEMENTS UNLOCKED:

> AD AGE "MARKETER OF THE YEAR"—NINTENDO (2007)

> BRANDWEEK "TEAM OF THE YEAR" (2007)

> ADVERTISING WEEK "TEAM OF THE YEAR" (2007)

> ALONG WITH A TEAM OF VOLUNTEERS HAS RESCUED AND PLACED MORE THAN 8000 DOGS ON DEATH ROW INTO HOMES SINCE 2007, THROUGH HER NON-PROFIT SAVING GREAT ANIMALS

STATS

INDUSTRY LEVEL: 25

CURRENT CLASS: CO-FOUNDER, PRINCIPAL

CURRENT GUILD: ZEBRA PARTNERS—SEATTLE, USA

SPECIAL SKILLS: CORPORATE COMMUNICATIONS, PUBLIC RELATIONS, MARKETING, CONTENT STRATEGY, BRAND DEVELOPMENT, PUBLIC SPEAKING

STANDARD EQUIPMENT

FAVORITE PLATFORM: MOBILE

GO-TO GENRE: PUZZLE

MUST-HAVE GAME: YOSHI'S COOKIE

BIO

When Nintendo of America (NOA) set out to recruit a corporate communications manager in 1992, they were hunting for someone who knew nothing about gaming to offer a fresh perspective. "That was definitely me," laughed Perrin Kaplan, former Vice President of Marketing and Corporate Affairs. "I didn't even know Mario was a character versus a real person! True story. I was hired in the 16-bit era by Senior Vice President Howard Lincoln and Nintendo of America founder Minoru Arakawa, and to this day am so grateful for the complete redirect of my career. It's been an amazing journey so far!"

From youth, Kaplan was taught to aim high across all of her pursuits. "My mother was so active when I was growing up," continued Kaplan. "She started Seattle's first ever shelter for battered women. She was a painter and writer. She worked with Gloria Steinem and wrote several books about the history of women and the force of power that we all are. She always told me to shoot for the stars. She was and still is my hero."

> "I didn't even know Mario was a character versus a real person! True story."

Kaplan graduated with a bachelor's degree in communications and political science from the University of Washington, but believes an innate ability is needed to truly succeed as a professional. "The field of marketing and communications and even business development comes from a sixth sense," she said. "You either have it, and this is your field of dreams, or you don't and should switch to something else. Marketing and PR and video games are not for the faint of heart."

Before joining Nintendo, Kaplan worked as a news editor and reporter, followed by years in politics at the Washington State Senate, working on presidential campaigns, and a position as Vice President of PR firm, The Rockey Company.

A BRAVE NEW WORLD

In the early 90s Kaplan found herself unexpectedly interviewing for a position in the foreign world of video games. "It was all brand new to me," she said. "At first, I really didn't get it. But then I began to understand. It has been a pleasure to work in this fantasy world of creative minds, intention for joy and play, and cutting-edge technology."

Kaplan's first official Nintendo project was the continued promotion of the Nintendo's recently-launched SNES console. "I was in the midst of developing an entire division from the ground up. At that time it was just me, myself and I," she said.

During her 16 years at Nintendo, she would help bring some of the most successful products in Nintendo and gaming history to market, from launching *Pokémon Red* and *Blue* in the US, to debuting the Game Boy Color, Nintendo DS, and the Nintendo Wii.

Easter Egg

Taught late Nintendo CEO and president Satoru Iwata a new English slang word or phrase each time he visited the US office. His favorite was trail-mix shorthand "gorp."

TOPEKACHU

Introducing *Pokémon* to the United States in 1998 is one of Kaplan's favorite memories. "When we were launching *Pokémon*, it was coming from Asia and we all just sat there and said, 'What are we going to do with this thing? What are these creatures?' We had a lot of meetings. We came up with the idea of launching it in Topeka, Kansas, and the city name was changed to Topekachu for the day."

Kaplan's team started brainstorming ways to get the word out, expecting it to be a small media-driven event. "We had planned the media tour with these Volkswagen Beetles," described Kaplan. "We had 10 of them done up as Pikachu with the eyelashes in front, the stripes, and the zig-zag tail—the works. Even the horn said, 'Pika, pika, pika,' and the game system was in the back. They were beautiful, shiny, and yellow, all lined up in this middle of this corn field ready to simultaneously drive off to multiple markets across the U.S. for consumers and media to see."

Media began to show up the day of the event, followed by an unanticipated number of fans. "Hordes of humans show up," she recalled. "All these kids, so excited! They flew in from everywhere. Some of them came internationally. It was unbelievable. They came to be the first to get their hands on *Pokémon*." That's when Kaplan and her team knew they had something huge.

"We were really the first to ever do something like that," she said. "We were creative. We came up with ideas that have been duplicated a million times over by many companies."

The innovative campaign ideas continued. "When we launched the Game Boy Color we had to figure out how to differentiate it from the highly popular Game Boy, which was already in millions of homes," said Kaplan. "We launched the Game Boy Color using a huge billboard, where people—including some of the team's family members—were hanging with splashes of colorful paint across their bodies and the canvas. It was a showstopper, for sure, as the first living billboard in the US."

CODENAME: REVOLUTION

Over the years Nintendo has been noted for their fan-first approach to creating and marketing products, and that is something NOA and Kaplan helped establish. "When we launched the Wii, we wanted to launch to consumers first, and media second. Nintendo was still super profitable, but not perceived as being in first place," she explained. "So we were very careful how we introduced something as dramatic as the Wii. The great trust Mr. Iwata and Mr. Miyamoto had in all of us was amazing. We had proposed very bold and different ideas and approaches and thank goodness they said yes to them!"

Kaplan and her team stressed the importance of grassroots brand ambassadors years before it was adopted in the wider industry mainstream. "We were literally the first to have these mom and family ambassadors. The first to do these Wii parties, Wii Generation bowling, and to go into senior citizen centers. It launched the whole 'ambassador movement,'" she continued. "We told media they could see and play the Wii, but that they should talk to an ambassador who tried it. I really didn't want us all telling everybody how great it was. I wanted the people who had tried it to say what they thought. And obviously, they loved it."

"Working at Nintendo was some of the best family feeling ever to be found in a company," she continued. "We all realize that it was an amazing and extremely special time in our careers and frankly, our lives."

NEW STRIPES

In 2008, Kaplan departed Nintendo for a new venture, founding strategic communications firm Zebra Partners with her Nintendo colleagues Beth Llewelyn, and Kelli Horner. "I had wonderful offers to transfer to other corporations. But at that time it seemed that the immense learning and skill we earned from Nintendo could benefit other companies. We wanted to help really large companies get back in touch with their consumers, and small to mid-sized ones be heard."

Over the past decade at Zebra, Kaplan has worked with many global brands including Nintendo, Microsoft, Facebook/Oculus, Qualcomm, Intel, Sony, and dozens of other companies. "And, I have such dear friends still at Nintendo who are super supportive," she said. "Several people from Nintendo have come to work with us. Our team is close to 30 now."

Kaplan has helped launch around 650 software titles and 12 hardware systems in her career so far, and isn't slowing down. "I hope to inspire others to keep pursuing their dreams in this industry. The glory of our industry is that you have so many different ways to enter it," she said. "While I learn from others every single day, I hope that by being a confident, seasoned, powerful female and leader in my field, I have inspired people to know that they can do whatever it is in their careers that they set out to do."

Kaplan is excited by the future of video games. "The changing face of business on a near daily basis inspires me," she said. "The gaming industry is the absolute cutting edge of how to do marketing, PR, content, distribution and so much more. We are a shining example for other industries to look to. I always remember that what I do for a living is sell joy. We are not curing cancer but joy and entertainment do have a very key role in all of our lives."

A DAY IN THE LIFE OF...

A 3D ENVIRONMENT ARTIST

Environment artists furnish game worlds by creating everything from coffee cups to cars. In doing so, they transform the basic block mesh handed off by level designers into captivating, virtual playgrounds. The work blends technical skills such as modeling, texturing, and art asset optimization with knowledge of art principles, including composition, color, and lighting. During development, environment artists often produce a catalog of assets and libraries of textures, which can be reused not only for cohesion in the world, but smartly repurposed to save on time and resources.

All this must be done in a way that feels organic to the world in question—whether stylized or photorealistic—and in a manner that doesn't confuse the player or hinder gameplay. Daryl Hanna Tancinco has a decade of experience in environment art, working for big hitters such as Infinity Ward, Sony Santa Monica, and Electronic Arts. Her work has expressed everything from the gritty realities of modern war to the excess and opulence of Ancient Greece.

DARYL HANNA TANCINCO

Daryl Hanna Tancinco

dhtancinco.com

PROFESSION: SENIOR ARTIST AT INFINITY WARD—WOODLAND HILLS, USA

YEARS IN PROFESSION: 10

ASSOCIATED WITH: CALL OF DUTY: INFINITE WARFARE, CALL OF DUTY: GHOSTS, GOD OF WAR: ASCENSION, BULLETSTORM, MEDAL OF HONOR, GOD OF WAR III, TRANSFORMERS: REVENGE OF THE FALLEN

▶ EDUCATION

"I was lucky enough to have a few schools in the Los Angeles area that offered a bachelor's degree in game art. In the end I enrolled into the Game Art & Design program at the Art Institute of Los Angeles. There I learned the bulk of my education and training. The rest came from fiddling around with new software tools and 3D packages to stay with the constant change in workflows and technology."

▶ BREAKING IN

"In my experience, it wasn't too hard to initially get your foot in the door. The hard part was staying there. I started my career with a string of contract positions, which is basically temporary employment for six months to a little over a year until they evaluate and determine whether or not you stay. I was told it was never a matter of 'are you good enough to be converted to full-time'; it was always the lack of headcount they could keep. School never mentioned it would be so tough to land a stable gig, but what it did do was prepare me to be part of a team, find my strengths, and identify what skills I needed to hone to get to where I wanted."

▶ KEY QUALITIES

"An average day in the industry involves a lot of collaboration. On a daily basis you're working with multiple departments to make an experience in the game. There's environment art, of course, but to get to the final product you see when you play at home, there's FX, designers, code, tech art, animation, weapons, vehicles, producers, and overall art direction. It's important to be open-minded with your work and never be 'married' to what you make. Sometimes direction changes and you have to start all over."

▶ TOOLS OF THE TRADE

"Basic tools of the trade for me in creating environment art, whether it be assets or textures, are software suites like Autodesk Maya, ZBrush, Marmoset, xNormal, Substance Designer, Substance Painter, some use of Marvelous Designer for fabrics, and Adobe Photoshop CC. Of course, you will also use whatever engine or editor is used in-house. Every studio has their own workflow, so in some places I might do all world building, where others I might do more asset creation. I use some of the above-mentioned tools versus all of them depending on the task I am responsible for.

"At my current position at Infinity Ward, we use our own editor where I do a lot of world building. World building is creating the environment over what a designer initially gives you. They do a block out to establish how big a level is and determine the gameplay experience that happens in that space. My job then is to art it and make it look like a real functional place. This takes a lot of collaboration with the designer to make sure the final product is both fun to play and visually impactful."

▶ HOURS & ENVIRONMENT

"Hours are the standard 40-hour workweek, but depending on how close we are to our game's release, hours tend to increase and can even go well over double that. Overtime—some studios call it crunch or hardcore—is a norm in the industry. They try to avoid it with planning milestones, but it's an inevitable thing, especially with the quality bar of AAA games constantly changing. It's both exciting and exhausting personally, but when you work with passionate people and people who have the same vision, time flies so fast."

▶ PROFESSIONAL PERKS

"I have a couple of games in the military genre under my belt now, and that comes with opportunities to better understand the world you're creating. To do that, there are times where we get to have hands-on experience with some of the weapons and gear that they use. We get opportunities to pick the brains of military operatives and, with their guidance, try out some of the tech they use, like night vision and laser sights."

▶ CAREER CHALLENGES

"The key challenges of my profession are the constant growth of technology and the demand for more. Making video games is very technology-based. We're limited by what the latest and greatest gaming console is capable of and the tech of the game engines we develop on. You are constantly learning and growing, and with every new game that you make, better techniques and software are made to create better results. Games have come a long way since the 8-bit days. It's never a dull moment, and it keeps things exciting."

▶ BIGGEST MISTAKE

"When I first started working in the industry, I was very quiet. I was a hardworking worker bee that kept to myself. Now that I'm much more confident in my work and myself, I realize what a mistake that was. I missed out on opportunities to really get to know my heroes and to learn from them. It's so important to communicate with your team. It makes work a much more enjoyable experience, and often it helps you to step out of your comfort zone. There are always opportunities for growth."

▶ EXCITING ADVANCEMENTS

"The biggest advancement in the video game industry is coming from scan data. Consoles nowadays are so powerful and can handle so much more data. Photo-based rendering was big, and games like *The Order* showed us how powerful that can be. The next step toward lifelike graphics is scan data. That is essentially hundreds of ultra-HD photos of real-life objects, like a military crate or a pile of rubble, for example. These photos are then processed and stitched together in a program to create the most realistic 3D model. *Battlefront* did an amazing job with this tech, and so many other studios are putting that into their workflows. I wouldn't be surprised if it became an industry standard alongside more traditional techniques."

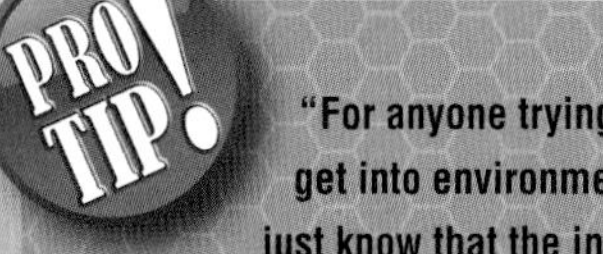

"For anyone trying to get into environment art, just know that the industry is full of already talented and driven artists. You will need to work hard. Find out what the trends are, and work toward them. Find what you're passionate about—an art style, weapons, creating materials—and excel at it. You don't need to know everything right away, but it's important that you at least know what the type of studio you're looking to get into is looking for. Hone your portfolio to that and never stop learning."

KIRSTEN DUVALL

SPORTS BROADCASTER TURNED BUSINESS EXECUTIVE

 BitterDiva  Kirsten Duvall

EXPERIENCE

FIRST INDUSTRY PROJECT: EA CLASSICS (LATE 1990s)
MOST RECENT INDUSTRY PROJECT: MIXCAST (2017)
PROJECTS SHIPPED: 97 GAMES ACROSS BUSINESS MANAGEMENT, BUSINESS DEVELOPMENT, SALES, MARKETING, BRAND MANAGEMENT, PRODUCT MANAGEMENT, AND PRODUCTION
ACHIEVEMENTS UNLOCKED:
> FORTUNE'S "10 POWERFUL WOMEN IN VIDEO GAMES" (2014)

 STATS

INDUSTRY LEVEL: 25
CURRENT CLASS: VP OF BUSINESS STRATEGY
CURRENT GUILD: BLUEPRINT REALITY INC.—SAN FRANCISCO, USA
SPECIAL SKILLS: BUSINESS DEVELOPMENT, PARTNER RELATIONS, SALES & MARKETING WITH A VR & MOBILE FOCUS, MARATHON RUNNING

 STANDARD EQUIPMENT

FAVORITE PLATFORM: ROOM-SCALE VR PLATFORMS
GO-TO GENRE: RACING GAMES
MUST-HAVE GAME: CENTIPEDE

BIO

Kirsten Duvall, a 25-year veteran in the business of games, got her start in sports. Switching industries after discovering the potential in video games, she quickly moved her way up to senior staff positions in marketing and found a way to keep sports as part of her daily routine in the process.

That career shift occurred through happenstance, when Duvall took a tech job in Silicon Valley at a video card company. "I didn't really care too much about video cards at the time, and the company itself had a very toxic culture," explained Duvall, "but during my short time working there, they started a multimedia game division. I decided, 'That's what I want to do!' although I didn't know exactly what role I wanted to play." Driven to gain access to the industry, she secured an entry-level position on the sales team at Spectrum HoloByte, a simulation specialty company and the first developer to publish *Tetris* outside the Soviet Union, and has remained in gaming ever since.

Duvall wasn't sure if the career path was sustainable at first. "I thought it would only last a few years and at some point I'd have to get a more serious job. But the game industry became big business, and although tumultuous sometimes, it's an industry that's here to stay, is constantly evolving, and offers a lot of opportunities."

EA CLASSICS

After a year and a half, Duvall moved on from Spectrum HoloByte, accepting a position at Electronic Arts. There, she worked in various roles for eight years, kicking off with the EA Classics line of games. "The EA Classics line consisted of older PC games that were updated to run on Windows 95. I received a producer credit on the Classics games. I coordinated everything from the development schedule to new documentation, new package designs, and sales and marketing materials." Following that, as a retail marketing manager, she managed the planning, creative, and execution of all retail-marketing activities, including developing national promotions for game launches, and partnering with online retailers to raise awareness of EA games.

In 1999, Duvall was promoted to EA SPORTS Marketing Manager and moved to EA Vancouver in Canada, where she developed and executed complete franchise marketing plans for the EA SPORTS baseball and hockey franchises. She also helped define product positioning, feature sets, and licensing applications across multiple territories. A plus for a big sports fan, she was additionally tasked with managing relationships with key sports licensors, athletes, and agents from the MLB and NHL. "The *Triple Play Baseball* franchise was my favorite," recalled Duvall. "I loved working on those games because I'm a big baseball fan, and I had the opportunity to attend many marquee baseball events and meet some baseball legends!"

Easter Egg
Duvall's first job after college was in sports broadcasting. She typed players' stats into the Chyron machine for live broadcasts of the San Francisco Giants and 49ers games.

"I'd like to do more to ensure a pipeline of women coming into the industry."

Duvall had a degree in Audio/Video Production, which was useful in her sports-broadcasting work, but wasn't getting much use in sales and marketing. She saw the potential for further education. "While I was at Electronic Arts, I went back to school at night to get my MBA. The MBA has been beneficial as I've gotten further along in my career and held more senior positions. And it's definitely helpful when getting a new venture up and running."

In 2004 Duvall took up post at Activision. Her role expanded to Global Brand Manager, with more diverse work than ever. Duvall drove the development and execution of worldwide product-marketing plans, including positioning, advertising creative strategy, media planning, PR and trade-marketing strategy, and promotions development.

MOVING TO MICROSOFT

Duvall moved to Microsoft shortly after, brought on as a product planner for Xbox Sports. She was quickly promoted to Senior Business Manager, responsible for business development and developer relations for Microsoft Game Studios developers, including Bungie, Lionhead Studios, and Big Huge Games. This provided her the opportunity to work on flagship titles such as *Halo 3*, and *Fable 2*. "One of my favorite memories is from the *Halo 3* launch day in New York, when some of the team members—including Master Chief—rang the Closing Bell on NASDAQ," she recalled.

In 2013, Duvall pursued a new opportunity with a mobile gaming start-up based in Finland that was looking to open an office in San Francisco. As the Sr. Director of Developer Relations, she helped establish Applifier's North American presence, managed partner relationships, and worked directly with developers to help grow the Everyplay mobile game recording and sharing service from three games to 1000+ games. Duvall also contributed to building Applifier's mobile advertising network, which became known as Unity Ads after they acquired the company in 2014. The ad network has continued to grow within Unity thanks to its strong foundation.

Having worked in gaming for 25 years, Duvall has a unique, long-term perspective on gender in the industry. "I think women were treated more equally when I first started working in the industry," she said, speaking from her personal experiences. "Back then, when video games were cartridge-based, they were considered 'toys' and were mostly sold by toy stores. In the toy business, there were a lot of women in senior roles. So there seemed to be a different attitude toward women and women holding senior roles, in the '90s."

Addressing the challenges women have faced in the industry as it evolved, Duvall hopes to help make positive change. "I'd like to do more to ensure a pipeline of women coming into the industry," she continued. "Create more awareness among girls and young women of what kinds of roles and opportunities are available in the game industry and help them acquire the skills they'll need to be successful."

A NEW REALITY

After working at some of the largest gaming entities in the world, Duvall has now found the sweet spot in a start-up. As the VP of Business Strategy at Blueprint Reality, she works closely with a development team that creates VR content and tools that make VR experiences more social. So far, the company has published *Awaken*, an immersive physics puzzle game, and *MixCast*, a tool that makes it easy for anyone to create professional-quality, mixed-reality videos and livestreams of VR experiences. "The position I have now is the most fulfilling," said Duvall. "Being able to work with a start-up from the beginning, developing strategy, setting direction, and coming up with sales and marketing ideas for a relatively new platform is really exciting. Seeing the impact I make on a daily basis is extremely motivating."

PATRICIA E. VANCE

INDUSTRY REGULATOR AND GLOBAL AGE RATINGS INNOVATOR

 PatriciaEVance  Patricia Vance

 esrb.org, globalratings.com

EXPERIENCE

FIRST INDUSTRY PROJECT: ABC'S MONDAY NIGHT FOOTBALL (1996)

FAVORITE INDUSTRY PROJECT: FOUNDING AND CHAIRING THE INTERNATIONAL AGE RATING COALITION (IARC)

PROJECTS SHIPPED: OVER 7.5 MILLION RATINGS ASSIGNED SINCE 2002 (INCLUDES MOBILE)

ACHIEVEMENTS UNLOCKED:

> RESPONSIBLE FOR PUBLISHING FIRST SPORTS VIDEO GAME WITH ONLINE COMPETITIONS (ABC'S MONDAY NIGHT FOOTBALL) IN 1996

> DEVELOPED AND LAUNCHED A NEW GLOBAL RATING SYSTEM (IARC) FOR DIGITALLY-DELIVERED GAMES AND APPS THAT IS QUICKLY BECOMING THE NEW STANDARD

> INCREASED PARENTS' AWARENESS AND USE OF ESRB RATINGS TO 84% AND 71% RESPECTIVELY

> QUADRUPLED RATE OF RETAILER ENFORCEMENT OF STORE POLICIES NOT TO SELL MATURE-RATED GAMES TO UNACCOMPANIED CHILDREN

STATS

INDUSTRY LEVEL: 25

CURRENT CLASS: PRESIDENT, CEO

CURRENT GUILD: ENTERTAINMENT SOFTWARE RATING BOARD—NEW YORK CITY, U.S.A.

SPECIAL SKILLS: MANAGEMENT, BUSINESS DEVELOPMENT, STRATEGIC PLANNING, MARKETING, CONSENSUS-BUILDING

Easter Egg

Has seen Eric Clapton play live close to 20 times.

BIO

Patricia Vance has had her head and heart in interactive entertainment for almost three decades. She has leant her extensive experience—paired with a strong interest in social responsibility—to many forms of media, and in doing so helped push the boundaries of emerging technology. Now, Vance leads the Entertainment Software Rating Board, a position important both for assisting parents in making informed choices when buying video games for their children and providing the self-regulatory framework that ensures video games remain a protected form of speech free from government interference.

With a degree in International Relations and Russian, Vance was for the most part self-taught in her rise through the ranks of media and the game industry. "Although advanced degrees are valuable if not essential in many fields, in my own career I have found that practical experience, intelligence, good interpersonal skills and a strong ethical compass can get you pretty far," she said.

LEARNING THE ABCS

Vance's career in media kicked off in cable and broadcast TV, cutting her teeth in 1980 at Warner Amex Satellite Company, as the manager of acquisition planning for The Movie Channel before moving to ABC, the broadcasting company. Leadership is in Vance's DNA; she made her way up the ABC-TV corporate ladder from sales associate in the Video Enterprises division in 1982, to vice president of ancillary marketing and sales by 1990. Throughout her career in media, she always sought opportunities to break new ground, starting out in the early days of cable, identifying different movie acquisition strategies in the new, highly competitive pay-tv landscape.

"At the start of my 18-year tenure at ABC, I worked on opening new home video markets both in the US and abroad, established a direct response video business as VCR penetration in the US exploded, and forged a partnership with one of the largest college textbook publishers in the world," said Vance. "I also developed a lucrative, recurring business providing news and sports video programing to airlines, including partnering with United Airlines to provide daily video highlights of the 1984 Olympics before airlines could receive live video entertainment via satellite."

In 1993, Vance was snapped up by ABC management as one of the founding executives of ABC's Multimedia Group. This is where she solidified her footing firmly in the interactive entertainment industry, and over the next four years she led efforts to grow a CD-ROM and interactive publishing business for consumer, educational, and institutional markets. "During this period, I helped establish two joint venture companies," shared Vance. "One was with Electronic Arts, called Creative Wonders, which published *Sesame Street*, *Madeline*, *Schoolhouse Rock*, *Inspector Gadget*, and other products targeting an under-13 audience. The second joint venture was with Microprose, a division of Spectrum Holobyte at the time, called OT Sports, to develop a line of ABC Sports-branded video games including *Monday Night Football*, *College Football*, and *Indy Racing*."

Fifteen years after she started at ABC, she was promoted to Senior Vice President and General Manager for ABC.com, responsible for launching ABC.com,

Oscar.com, Oprah.com—and later put in charge of the ABC Internet Group, which included ABCNews.com—spearheading numerous cutting-edge projects. These included record-breaking TV/online interactive events such as the 1999 April Fool's Day Drew Carey "Drewcam" episode, which brought in over 650,000 concurrent online viewers, and the *Who Wants to Be A Millionaire* online game, which boasted 5.5 million players in the first two weeks.

In 2000 Vance left Disney/ABC to run an Internet start-up. It was in 2002 that she began her full-time career in gaming, recruited to lead the ESRB as president.

ENFORCING AGE RATINGS

At the ESRB, Vance is responsible for leading the video game industry's self-regulatory body, which assigns age ratings to video games and mobile apps, enforces industry marketing guidelines, and ensures that industry members are protecting users' personal information while complying with an increasingly complex web of privacy regulations.

Shortly after joining the ESRB, it was clear to Vance that the Achilles' heel for the industry was retailers' enforcement of ratings. In 2005, she launched a partnership program with all the major game retailers in the U.S., eventually quadrupling the enforcement rate of policies to not sell Mature-rated games to children. This achievement lead to recognition by the Federal Trade Commission for significantly outpacing the self-regulatory practices of both the movie and music industries.

Under her guidance, the ESRB has evolved alongside the industry. The most notable shift being the move from boxed products to digital downloads and the transition of games to an ongoing service model with extensive post-launch downloadable content.

"I don't know if the ESRB Board of Directors fully appreciated how handy my prior experience in digital media would come into play when they hired me. I think my greatest contribution to the industry will be the way I led the transformation of its rating system to adapt to the demands of a digital world."

GOING GLOBAL

The new digital and mobile landscape necessitated an agile rating system that could scale to handle the high volume of products entering the market. Additionally, developers needed a seamless, cost-free way to obtain ratings around the world that reflect the unique cultural differences of each region. These factors led Vance to establish—and ultimately chair—the International Age Rating Coalition in 2014. IARC is governed by rating authorities from around the world. Many Americans don't realize that the First Amendment of the US Constitution protects video games as a form of speech and, as a result, prevents the government from regulating which games are published or how they are rated. Many rating authorities around the world are administered by their respective governments or established due to local regulations.

The IARC rating system is an end-to-end SaaS solution that digital and mobile storefronts license, enabling developers to complete one questionnaire to obtain ratings at no cost from from authorities around the world. The system relieves storefronts and developers of having to manually enter rating information, while ensuring the accuracy of such information through active monitoring by participating rating authorities.

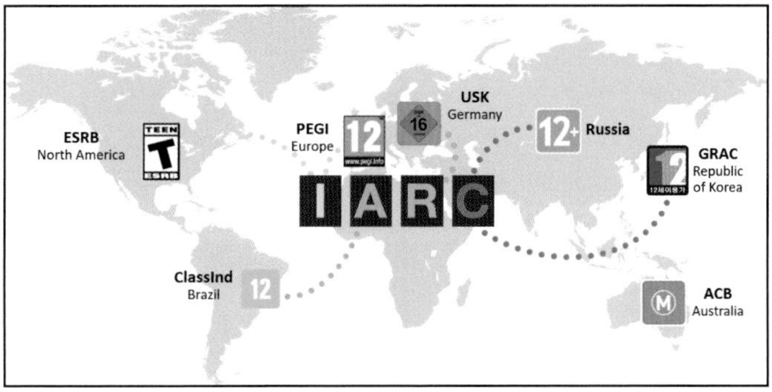

"The high volume of digital and mobile content was never contemplated when rating agencies were created, nor was the ability for a developer to publish a game globally with the click of a mouse. For me, it could not have been clearer. The digital market was an existential threat to the ESRB and game rating agencies around the world," said Vance. "Still, convincing other rating authorities from around the world to adopt an ESRB-developed process for rating mobile and digital games required years of in-person meetings, email communications, and my best persuasive skills."

Today ratings authorities throughout Europe, South America, and the Asia-Pacific are participating in IARC and the system has been deployed by Nintendo, PlayStation, Xbox, Windows, Google Play, and Facebook's Oculus with more storefronts on the way. It is quickly becoming the standard for rating mobile apps and digital games around the world.

As a voice for the industry, Vance has testified before the US Congress on multiple occasions, participated in meetings at the White House (including most recently being mis-gendered on the invitation list as Mr. Pat Vance), with Congressional leaders, state Attorneys General and legislators throughout the US. She was appointed to the Online Safety and Technology Working Group, commissioned by the Obama administration to evaluate industry efforts and make recommendations to promote online safety for children. She also is Chairman of the Board of Directors for the Family Online Safety Institute and has been a long-standing Board member of the Academy of Interactive Arts and Sciences, producer of the D.I.C.E. Awards. Vance has appeared on TV and radio nationwide to discuss how parents can effectively manage the games their kids play, on major programming such as *World News Tonight*, *Good Morning America*, and others on ABC, NBC, CBS, FOX, and CNN.

The game industry keeps Vance and her team on their toes, with new issues and concerns arising regularly. More recently, ESRB added notices about the sharing of a player's location, as well as the ability to make in-game purchases, to the rating information it assigns. One can be assured that as the industry keeps evolving, and with Vance at the helm, the ESRB will continue to fulfill its self-regulatory mission.

KATE EDWARDS

CULTURALIZATION CONSULTANT AND INDUSTRY-REFORM ADVOCATE

 geogrify  Kate Edwards

 geogrify.com

EXPERIENCE

FIRST INDUSTRY PROJECT: UNRELEASED RTS AT MICROSOFT (1993)

FAVORITE INDUSTRY PROJECT: JADE EMPIRE (2004)

PROJECTS SHIPPED: 100+ GAMES

ACHIEVEMENTS UNLOCKED:
> AWARDED CHARTERED GEOGRAPHER STATUS BY THE UK ROYAL GEOGRAPHICAL SOCIETY (2004)
> FORTUNE "10 MOST POWERFUL WOMEN IN THE GAME INDUSTRY" (2013)
> GAMESINDUSTRY.BIZ "SIX PEOPLE OF THE YEAR" (2014)
> REBOOT DEVELOP "HERO" AWARD (2018)

 STATS

INDUSTRY LEVEL: 25

CURRENT CLASS: GEOGRAPHER, CEO, PRINCIPAL CONSULTANT

CURRENT GUILD: GEOGRIFY—SEATTLE, USA

SPECIAL SKILLS: GEOPOLITICS, CARTOGRAPHY, CONTENT CULTURALIZATION WORLD BUILDING, PUBLIC SPEAKING, CORPORATE CULTURES, NEGOTIATION WITH GOVERNMENTS, CRISIS MANAGEMENT, GEOPOLITICAL & CULTURAL TRAINING, CROSS-CULTURAL COMPETENCE, ADVOCACY, POLITICAL ENGAGEMENT, NON-PROFIT MANAGEMENT

 STANDARD EQUIPMENT

FAVORITE PLATFORM: XBOX

GO-TO GENRE: FPS

MUST-HAVE GAME: HALO COMBAT EVOLVED

BIO

Kate Edwards had an end point in mind for her career at an early age: *Star Wars*. "I actually never aspired to work in the game industry. I was aiming to be a conceptual artist for Lucasfilm so I could work on anything *Star Wars*-related," she began. After a year of studying aerospace engineering and two years of industrial design, her future took an entirely different direction, and she focused on geography and cartography as her core discipline. Her master's thesis in Geography—*Virtual Worlds Technology as an Interface to Geographic Information*—was published in 1991, and she began working toward her PhD.

MICROSOFT

While pursuing her PhD, Microsoft called her university department looking for a cartographer to work on their multimedia Encarta Encyclopedia. "I ended up working on a contract basis" said Edwards. "Eventually I was offered a full-time position, so I put my PhD completion on hold and ended up working at Microsoft for 13 years total. Through this, I ended up working on nearly every game franchise at Microsoft on PC and Xbox and found my true love—doing culturalization work on video games."

Edwards became Microsoft's first geopolitical specialist in 1995, before creating the senior geopolitical strategist role to formalize her skills and experience. "I provided the initial thought leadership and vision around 'geopolitical quality' and created the Geopolitical Strategy team to serve as a centralized corporate authority on geopolitical and cultural policy, strategy, and compliance," she explained. While managing the team, she personally consulted on content releases, assessed risk across the portfolio of Microsoft products, and if needed, drafted PR and crisis-response messaging.

At the time, Edwards' work in an emergent specialty was met with slight skepticism. "It was a little bit of a challenge because the games people were initially resistant to my assertions that issues carried in game content can cause potentially huge real-world issues," she said. "But after they experienced a few major faux pas, they started listening to me."

One of those slip-ups was unknowingly using religious content in the fighting game *Kakuto Chojin*. "The team committed a faux pas of using an audio file containing chanted verses from the Islamic Qur'an, and the error was caught way too late in the process," she recalled. "To make a very long story short, the offense required me to travel to Saudi Arabia, UAE, and elsewhere to help do damage control over this serious issue which had become front-page news in the region."

Easter Egg

Can play the Scottish bagpipes, and is a true movie score geek who can often easily identify the film and composer from as little as a few notes. She is also an avid cosplayer.

> "I ended up working on nearly every game franchise at Microsoft on PC and Xbox and found my true love—doing culturalization work on video games."

After 13 years at Microsoft, Edwards' unrelenting championing of culturalization resulted in corporate-wide, mandated adoption of geopolitical compliance processes. With this major success, she decided to move on to new challenges.

GEOGRIFY

In 2005, Edwards began offering her skills industry-wide as CEO, principal consultant, and geographer at Geogrify. "In effect, I help identify risks and opportunities along the geopolitical and cultural dimensions of content and help to maximize the global reach of content," she explained. In her work, she takes both a high-level and boots-on-the-ground approach, from defining a company's overarching culturalization strategy to auditing and reviewing content for potential sensitivities. She works across mediums, and has consulted with Amazon, Facebook, Google, BioWare, National Geographic, TomTom, and Ubisoft, among many others.

Edwards' initial career aspirations came true in part when working with BioWare. "From a purely personal perspective, one of my favorite projects to work on was *Star Wars: The Old Republic* for BioWare," she said. "It fulfilled a dream I'd had since I was 12 years old to work on something *Star Wars*.

IGDA & ADVOCACY

In 2007, Edwards became increasingly involved in the industry as a whole. She founded the IGDA Game Localization Special Interest Group (SIG) within the International Game Develops Association (IGDA), creating space for localization professionals to discuss their work and establish best practices. She also became increasingly concerned about detrimental patterns that plagued the industry, but weren't being systematically addressed. After several years of running the localization SIG, as well as co-running the IGDA's Seattle chapter, she was asked to interview for the executive director position. She was subsequently offered the position, and for the next five years was responsible for the vision and growth of the global organization. Edwards knew that as leader of the IGDA, she'd have a platform to champion major industry reform, and has kept advocacy as a tenant of her career since.

As executive director, she interfaced with thousands of industry professionals all around the world, as well as governments, trade associations, and the public, which gave her an intimate understanding of the systemic issues it did—and still does—face. "I'm very active and outspoken as an advocate for changing the game industry for the better, from work/life balance issues to diversity and inclusion, and also improving the skewed public perception of our profession" said Edwards.

One key project was a collaboration between industry non-profit Take This and the IGDA, focusing on providing mental health support for games professionals. They teamed up to release a white paper called "Crunch Hurts" in 2016, which used medical data to back up the negative physical and mental impact of crunch on developers. After leaving her IGDA role, Edwards joined the board of directors of Take This.

Edwards approaches her advocacy through four areas of reform. "If I had my own Infinity Gauntlet for the game industry, I'd snap my fingers and see an industry that is fundamentally reformed around four key pillars," she said."

Perception aims to tackle the industry's PR problem. "We need a better voice for the global game industry," Edwards stated. "After decades of creation, games have become a significant cultural and economic force, yet much of the general public still believe that games are a negative force in society."

Secondly, she focuses on **wellness**. "We should value people over profits. Game creators are passionate, creative individuals," Edwards continued. "Yet all too often, their passion is exploited by their employers to the point of being detrimental to their physical and mental health." She cites excessive crunch, reminders of expendability, and other external pressures that force talent to put their self-care on hold.

Inclusion draws on the quantifiable impact of diversity, both in the workplace and the end product. "Those who create games must better reflect those who play them," she said. "A diverse workforce that earnestly builds its culture on principles of inclusion is an industry that rises above stereotypes and tropes, eliminates wage and hiring biases, and actively dispels harassment of its people both within organizations and within the public."

Lastly, **fairness**. "We should treat one another with mutual respect. From publishing contracts that take advantage of inexperienced indies to the use of unpaid interns. From ignoring reports of harassment to exploiting workers' passion. When an industry perpetually treats its own unfairly, it disrespects its own profession; the reality of that immaturity becomes all too visible to the world."

Edwards chose to express her post-IGDA advocacy efforts through her own site, GameAdvocacy.org. She works to inspire game creators to overcome their fears, stand up, and speak out to help change their profession for the better. She also advocates better forms of organized labor (e.g., unions) within the game industry to provide more leverage for professionals to secure real and lasting change. As of late 2018, her primary focus was creating and launching a legal defense fund for game creators.

One of the current issues she's championing is the growing trend of ageism. "Ageism is a rampant problem in the game industry and within the broader technology sector, and it's becoming even more so as first generations of game creators reach their traditional 'retirement years.'" Edwards conceived of and launched a peer-nominated "50-over-50 list" to help reinforce the value of experience in an industry she feels puts an emphasis on the value of youth.

"In my later years, my increased focus on advocacy work in the industry, and this is becoming more and more fulfilling because it's utlimately aimed at helping those around me," Edwards reflected. "I've been blessed with a very unique career, and I want to continue to help others succeed in this industry however I can, either by directly mentoring them, helping on their game projects, or striving to make the industry a better place for them to thrive—no matter where they may be located."

A DAY IN THE LIFE OF...

A TECHNICAL ARTIST

Technical artists use their skill sets to empower others to do their best work, communicating with the code, animation, and art teams on a game's visual presentation. Despite not putting content on-screen, technical artists influence every pixel: through scripting tools that create the art, developing exporters and pipelines to get artwork into the game efficiently, or shaders that are used to render art in the appropriate style. They must be technically minded and natural problem solvers, while also having a creative flare and strong visual eye.

Constantly at the front lines of technology, technical artists like Jodie Azhar are the first people to work with new software and try out burgeoning techniques within a game-production environment, helping artists realize the creative vision for a game. In her 10 years working in the industry—at Kuju, Rebellion, and now Creative Assembly—Azhar worked her way up the tech art ladder to director, and now works to inspire others and impart knowledge through lectures at universities, technical talks at industry events, and diversity initiatives as a woman in Games Ambassador.

JODIE AZHAR

 JodieAzhar  jodieazhar jodieazhar.com

PROFESSION: TECHNICAL ART DIRECTOR—HORSHAM, UNITED KINGDOM

YEARS IN PROFESSION: 10

ASSOCIATED WITH: TOTAL WAR: THREE KINGDOMS, TOTAL WAR: ARENA, TOTAL WAR: WARHAMMER II, TOTAL WAR: WARHAMMER, SNIPER ELITE V2, NEVERDEAD, PDC WORLD CHAMPIONSHIP DARTS PRO TOUR, GIRLS LIFE: SLEEPOVER PARTY

▶ EDUCATION

"I studied animation (a course now called Computer Animation Technical Arts) at Bournemouth University, UK. The course teaches computer programming, math for computer graphics, and 3D art and animation. I'd selected the course because it combined my interests in science, math, and art."

▶ BREAKING IN

"I got my first job in the industry after taking my CV and showreel to the careers fair at EGX. Luckily one of the studios I spoke to had a position for a junior animator open not long after the event, and they offered me the job. These days students need to be a lot more proactive. Internships and trainee positions often look for candidates before they've finished their final year of university, so it's important to be thinking not just about completing coursework, but what studios will want to see in a showreel when applying for a job."

▶ KEY QUALITIES

"To be a technical artist, you need four key skills:

- Problem solving
- Knowledge of art-creation pipelines
- Understanding of at least one scripting/programming language
- Excellent teamwork

"While the first three skills allow you to create effective solutions to art problems, the ability to work well in a team is perhaps the most important. You need great communication skills in order to work out what artists want to achieve visually, explain the requirements to programmers and collaborate to come up with solutions, train artists in how to use the solutions, as well as ongoing support and building of trust between the artists, you, and your tools."

▶ TRAINING OPPORTUNITIES

"For those wanting to find out more about technical art, there is the forum at tech-artists.org, which also has a Slack channel, allowing you to instantly ask questions and discuss things with experts from the technical art-development community."

▶ TOOLS OF THE TRADE

"As a technical artist, I work to improve the art of our games using technical solutions. This means I need to understand how to use both 3D asset creation software and various programming languages. New software is constantly being developed to improve the creation of 3D art, so it's important to be open to new ideas and how things work, so that you can come up with new solutions to problems and create amazing game art."

▶ AN AVERAGE DAY

"As a technical artist, my day consists of working on tasks to support the games I'm making. This includes writing shaders, collaborating with artists on visual problems, and writing scripted tools. I also create tools to improve long-term workflows. As a director, I also work on the long-term plans for our tools and pipelines. Working at a large studio like Creative Assembly, you may have several concurrent projects and plans for what is being worked on next. In order to remain effective as developers and ensure we are creating tools that will have longevity, we need to think about the current and future needs of the various teams."

▶ PROMOTIONAL PATH

"In many small studios, technical artists work alone, or their job may also cover creating some of the art for the game, as small studios can't afford to have too many specialized people. In larger studios you tend to be more specialized, sometimes focusing on a single area of art such as animation, characters, VFX, etc. The following are some of the roles available for technical artists in various studios:

Associate/Junior: Technical artists in this position have an understanding of the technical art role and an idea of what parts they may enjoy specializing in but require guidance for solving a wide range of problems.

Developer: This is the most common level of expertise. They are able to work autonomously and understand how to solve a range of problems, but still require some guidance in solving large and/or complex problems.

Senior: This role is for those who have a wide understanding of technical art and problem solving and need little to no guidance.

Principal/Expert: This role is for those who are experts in their field and are able to solve new and challenging problems and pass on their knowledge to other team members and provide mentorship to the rest of the team.

Lead: This position is for those who lead a team of technical artists. Their focus is on enabling their team to work efficiently and maintaining visibility over the longer-term needs of their team, to ensure they are aware of any potential future problems and how the team will tackle them."

▶ CAREER CHALLENGES

"As a Technical Art Director, I've had the challenge of looking both at what we need to work on in order to release the games we're currently developing and the long-term plan for our tools and pipelines. Sometimes you need to focus on the needs of a single project. However, we also need to think about how the tools will need to function in the future so that we don't spend every project solving the same problems or make tools that only create very specific art that won't meet the requirements of the next games we make."

▶ LIFE HACKS

"As a technical artist, you will get problems from all different areas of art, and especially working on a large team, you can get several requests every day. It's important to stay organized and know what the most important thing to work on is. That involves making sure all the tasks are logged in a place where the whole technical art team, and any artists and producers, can see it. This allows us to organize our list of tasks so that we deal with the most urgent tasks first, and everyone can see what order tasks will be completed in and if they think there will be any potential problems."

PRO TIP!

"While skills in your discipline are essential for getting a job, your ability to communicate and work with others will really make the difference in your career. This is especially important for technical artists, as we have to work with multiple disciplines to solve problems. We need to develop relationships with the people we work with and grow trust in both ourselves and the tools we create."

BONNIE ROSS

HALO'S GUARDIAN ANGEL

 PlutonForever  Bonnie Ross

EXPERIENCE

FIRST INDUSTRY PROJECT: NBA FULL COURT PRESS (1996)

FAVORITE INDUSTRY PROJECT: FOUNDING 343 INDUSTRIES

PROJECTS SHIPPED: DOZENS OF GAMES

ACHIEVEMENTS UNLOCKED:

> FORTUNE "10 POWERFUL WOMEN IN VIDEO GAMES" (2014)

> "GRACE HOPPER CELEBRATION OF WOMEN IN COMPUTING" SPEAKER (2014)

> E3 XBOX PRESS CONFERENCE OPENER (2015)

> COVER OF BLOOMBERG BUSINESSWEEK (2015)

> NEW YORK FILM ACADEMY "WOMEN TO KNOW IN THE GAMING INDUSTRY" (2017)

STATS

INDUSTRY LEVEL: 24

CURRENT CLASS: CORPORATE VICE PRESIDENT, HEAD OF 343 INDUSTRIES

CURRENT GUILD: MICROSOFT STUDIOS—SEATTLE, USA

SPECIAL SKILLS: GAME DESIGN, PRODUCTION, MANAGEMENT, SPORTS AND POP-A-SHOT HUSTLER

STANDARD EQUIPMENT

FAVORITE PLATFORM: XBOX

GO-TO GENRE: ESCAPISM

MUST-HAVE GAME: HALO FRANCHISE

BIO

In the late 1980s Bonnie Ross's future seemed destined for athletics. A background in basketball, volleyball, tennis, and softball—combined with volunteer time as a coach for youth programs—would have easily netted Ross scholarships to pursue sports as a career. Encouraged by family to look into a more practical vocation, Ross chose to study technical communications and computer science in college. After obtaining her degree, Ross reached out to tech giants NeXT, Apple, and Microsoft. Microsoft responded with interest, and the rest is history.

Ross's first job involved working on SQL Server Windows NT—a software program for operating systems and databases—at Microsoft paid the bills, but left Ross wanting for something a bit more creative. When a tailor-made opportunity came around, and Ross made sure to seize it. "I got into video games because of my love of sports," she said. "I applied for an open position as the lead producer of a PC basketball game. I got the job based on my sports and tech background."

Easter Egg

Ross had the privilege of working on a team with Alexey Pajitnov—the creator of *Tetris*—in the late '90s and early 2000s on a variety of projects such as *Pandora's Box: Game of the Year Edition*. She credits Pajitnov for making her look at gaming in a different light, as well as amazing trips to Russia and good vodka. They also became rollerblade buddies.

Microsoft Full Court Press released in 1996 and was an early title in the fledgling Microsoft Game Division. The 2D-sprite basketball title was co-developed with Australia-based Beam Software. "I couldn't have asked for a better entry into the game industry, as doing co-development meant a combination of hand-holding and leadership from Beam, and then jumping off on the deep end with development," explained Ross. "I came to Microsoft for my love of technology, but I might not have stayed if I hadn't found gaming. With gaming, I found a purpose for technology—technology empowers art, technology empowers storytelling, technology empowers creativity."

With her career path firmly cemented, Ross was in the trenches as Microsoft's games business exploded. "Much of my early career was a combination of co-development and publishing," she continued. "Microsoft—and now Xbox—has a hands-on publishing team, so for every project we would work with development partners to understand strengths and areas of need, and then we would staff up to help."

"Technology empowers art, technology empowers storytelling, technology empowers creativity."

Working in both publishing and development offered infinite learning opportunities to Ross. "In publishing, I had the opportunity to be part of a lot of games over 15-plus years, with those learnings establishing my foundation," said Ross. "I've also been honored to work and partner with a lot of amazing independent developers in the industry." Ross worked on titles in the *Zoo Tycoon* series, as well as *Fuzion Frenzy*, *Jade Empire*, *Mass Effect*, *Dungeon Siege II*, *Psychonauts*, *Gears of War*, *Gears of War 2*, *Alan Wake*, and *Crackdown*. "I worked on projects as producer, lead producer, executive producer, or studio head in co-development, publishing, or internal roles."

In the early 2000s, Microsoft was investing big in gaming, including purchasing Bungie, Inc. The industry-disrupting Xbox hit the market in 2001, along with Bungie launch title *Halo: Combat Evolved*, which drove early success of the fledgling platform. The launch of *Halo 2* in 2004, alongside the online multiplayer service Xbox Live, continued that success, transforming multiplayer gaming forever.

By 2005—the year Microsoft launched the Xbox 360—Ross was both an industry veteran and a general manager in Microsoft Game Studios. Her hard work had earned the respect and trust of her peers, as well as executive staff at Microsoft. Two years into her post as general manager, Bungie Studios decided to explore options outside the *Halo* universe and separated amicably from

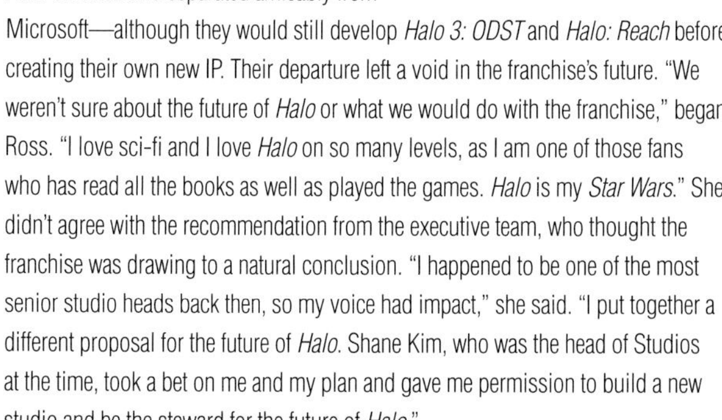

Microsoft—although they would still develop *Halo 3: ODST* and *Halo: Reach* before creating their own new IP. Their departure left a void in the franchise's future. "We weren't sure about the future of *Halo* or what we would do with the franchise," began Ross. "I love sci-fi and I love *Halo* on so many levels, as I am one of those fans who has read all the books as well as played the games. *Halo* is my *Star Wars*." She didn't agree with the recommendation from the executive team, who thought the franchise was drawing to a natural conclusion. "I happened to be one of the most senior studio heads back then, so my voice had impact," she said. "I put together a different proposal for the future of *Halo*. Shane Kim, who was the head of Studios at the time, took a bet on me and my plan and gave me permission to build a new studio and be the steward for the future of *Halo*."

"*Halo* is my *Star Wars*."

With that, Ross became *Halo*'s guardian angel. Ross's hard-earned reputation meant that people wanted to work with her. Frank O'Connor—a Bungie employee who was essential in the development of the first three *Halo* titles—followed Ross to the new studio. After a studio vote, the team was named 343 Industries—the "343" is a reference to 343 Guilty Spark, an enigmatic and intelligent Forerunner drone featured in each game of the original trilogy. 343 moved into Bungie's old office building and began building a team.

Taking the baton from Bungie was the most challenging project of Ross's career. "It was such a huge responsibility and a personal passion," she said. "Starting 343 Industries, building the incredibly talented team—hiring the amazing leaders who hired the talent—and being part of what they have created and are creating is such a cool experience."

Right off the bat Ross's presence was felt within *Halo* itself. She is credited with helping diversify and strengthen the stories of female characters in *Halo 4* and beyond. Ross planned for the *Halo* franchise to still be relevant in 30 years, and to make that happen, she argued for more diversity in characters who players could identify with.

In 2012, *Halo 4* hit the market to critical and commercial success. 343's debut game set franchise sales record in the first 24 hours. Two years later, *Halo 5: Guardians* toppled sales records in Xbox history. 343 would also experiment with different genres within the *Halo* universe, such as with the twin-stick shooter *Halo: Spartan Assault*. Opening the colossal Microsoft Xbox Press Conference at E3 2018, the studio's next project was revealed to the world—*Halo Infinite*.

The 343 team has grown to over 400 people. Ross is now a corporate vice president at Microsoft. "It is such an honor to be on this team and working in this epic universe," said Ross. "As the leader of 343 Industries, I have made mistakes over the last 11 years, and I have had successes. I'm most proud of the people, talent, and passion of the team at 343 Industries and what we have accomplished."

Those accomplishments have far-reaching effects. As stewards of a major brand ubiquitous with gaming, 343 has been in a position to make literal dreams come true. "Since we started 343 Industries in late 2007, we have had the honor of hosting more than 20 Make-a-Wish kid wishes," concluded Ross. "To see the *Halo* universe through these kids' eyes and know that they could choose any wish in the world and they chose *Halo* and 343 Industries is one of the most awe-inspiring and humbling moments. It reminds us all about why we do what we do in the gaming industry. We provide joy, escapism, awesome worlds, competition, social connections, and just plain fun. We are all so lucky to be in this industry, and we make a difference in people's lives." Ross is now actively cultivating the next generation of tech professionals in her work with the Ad Council as part of the #SheCanSTEM campaign, which launched in September 2018. The campaign showcases female role models in STEM professions, and is designed to inspire girls and young women to pursue STEM curriculum and careers."

JENNIFER HALE

VIDEO GAME'S MOST PROLIFIC FEMALE VOICE ACTOR

 JHaletweets  jenniferhale.com

EXPERIENCE

FIRST INDUSTRY PROJECT: CARMEN SANDIEGO: JUNIOR DETECTIVE (1995)

FAVORITE INDUSTRY PROJECT: "I CAN'T PICK A FAVORITE. THAT'S CRAZY TOWN."

PROJECTS SHIPPED: 170+ GAMES

ACHIEVEMENTS UNLOCKED:

> NAVGTR "OUTSTANDING PERFORMANCE IN A DRAMA, LEAD"—MASS EFFECT (2007)

> BEHIND THE VOICE ACTOR "BEST FEMALE VOCAL PERFORMANCE IN A VIDEO GAME"—MASS EFFECT 3 (2012)

> GUINNESS WORLD RECORDS "THE MOST PROLIFIC VIDEO GAME VOICE ACTOR (FEMALE)" (2013)

 STATS

INDUSTRY LEVEL: 23

CURRENT CLASS: VOICE ACTRESS

CURRENT GUILD: SBV TALENT—LOS ANGELES, USA

SPECIAL SKILLS: VOICE-ACTING, MOUNTAIN BIKING, HORSE RIDING, CONCUSSIONS

 STANDARD EQUIPMENT

FAVORITE PLATFORM: OUTDOORS

GO-TO GENRE: DIRT, TREES, AND ROCKS

MUST-HAVE GAME: ROCKET LEAGUE, TO WATCH HER NEPHEWS PLAY

BIO

Jennifer Hale's voice—however well masked with accent or inflection—is familiar to gamers around the world. Her industry contributions span over 170 games, in roles such as Alexandra Roivas from *Eternal Darkness: Sanity's Requiem*, Naomi Hunter from the *Metal Gear Solid* series, Bastila Shan from *Knights of the Old Republic*, and most famously, as Commander Shepard in the *Mass Effect* series. Hale's performances have helped elevate the standards of voice-acting across the industry, bringing a new level of emotion and impact to the screen through her nuanced portrayals.

Hale's voice-over work began at Boutwell Studios in Alabama. "I was like, 'You can make a living doing this?' So, I got the guys there—Greg and Courtney—to teach me the basics, and they were amazingly patient and wonderful to me." After her impromptu education, Hale went door-to-door with her demo tape and cold-called agencies, all while still in her teens. "I put on a little suit and organized a schedule. It made me nauseous and terrified to cold-call ad agencies to try to get voice-over work, but I knew it's what I had to do to build a business, so I did it." The hard work paid off. She began to get enough gigs to warrant a move to Atlanta for agent representation.

Easter Egg

Considers herself "gravity-prone," as she has had five concussions in her lifetime. Most of them involved horses or mountain bikes.

WHERE ON EARTH?

Hale got her start in video games through the animation industry. "The very first cartoon that I ever worked on was *Where on Earth Is Carmen Sandiego?* I was one of the series regulars on that," explained Hale. The *Carmen Sandiego* gig led to her first game. "The first game I ever did was *Carmen Sandiego: Junior Detective*. For me, working in video games was brand-new and I had no expectations going in. I was surprised at how intense the work was. It took me a couple minutes to figure out that I was completely working out of context," she continued. Hale's experience with animation was usually linear in nature—recording from the start of an episode to the finish. "When you work on a game, you're not working along the timeline from start to finish. You go back and forth, and traditional context is out the window. You have to find a way to get context for yourself, and you have to do it really fast because it's almost always cold reading. You don't get it ahead of time. I see it, I do a few takes, and then it goes to market. That's it."

The interactive nature of games is what made script-reading complicated. Hale wasn't the only one figuring out the process, though, as the shift from subtitles to voice-acting in games was only beginning to become the norm when she started. Hale learned the ropes quickly, and began getting cast in more and more complex roles.

In the late '90s she would lend her voice to Katrina from *Quest for Glory: Shadows of Darkness*, an assortment of characters in *Star Wars: X-Wing vs. TIE Fighter*, play multiple roles in *Baldur's Gate*, and secure a spot as Naomi Hunter in *Metal Gear Solid*, along with other game credits. By 2000 she had acted in nearly 20 video games, and by 2005 that number skyrocketed to over 60.

PUTTING IN THE TIME

The trajectory of Hale's career was due to her work ethic. Working in games was off-putting to some of her peers. "The game sessions were a lot more intense than most animation sessions," she explained. "In general, game sessions are basically like a four-hour, one-person show. Some of my peers were not into it, but I pretty much said yes to everything."

Often Hale would be assigned multiple roles within a project because of her constantly growing voice range. "For *EverQuest II*, I had to do 15 different voices, and they all had to be distinct," recalled Hale, explaining her process for developing a voice. "First, you start with the kind of being that you're playing. Am I playing a human being or some other being? What are the particular vocal affectations of that particular species? That's going to tell you where the voice comes from: in your chest, in your throat, or in your head. Are they going to sound small? Higher-pitched younger? Higher-pitched older? High or low pitch but with not a lot of breath because the lungs get weaker?" Hale also considers the character's personality and viewpoint on life, investigating if they are assertive and aggressive, or weak and quiet. "These are the tools that you draw on to create characters and keep them distinct. From Commander Shepard to Princess Morbucks to Cinderella: the variety of that makes me happy," Hale shared.

For that reason, it isn't possible for Hale to choose a favorite project. "My number one favorite thing is the sheer amount of variety I've had in my career. I love that," Hale explained. That being said, she does have some favorite memories. "Pissing off Fox News was really great when *Mass Effect* first came out, and they were up in arms about the same-sex relationship between Shepard and Liara. That was kind of awesome, to shake up the status quo. Recording that ending for *Mass Effect 3* was pretty moving too, and there came a time in the recording of that trilogy where it absolutely just took over. As an actress, I was riding the ride and I didn't know what was going to happen when I stepped up to the mic. I just let it happen and it was really cool." Hale won a number of performance awards for her portrayal of Commander Shepard in the *Mass Effect* series. Additionally, she cemented "FemShep" in the hearts of fans around the world with added value for female gamers who were inspired by the strength, loyalty, and tenacity of the character.

"My number one favorite thing is the sheer amount of variety I've had in my career."

In 2013 Jennifer Hale was officially recognized by the Guinness Book of World Records as "The Most Prolific Video Game Voice Actor (Female)." She now lends more than just her voice to games. "Mo-cap is one of my favorite things to do," said Hale.

THE WILD WEST

"I love that I got to be there in the early stages," reflected Hale. "I love that it was sort of the Wild West and we were all finding our way. I'm insanely grateful to have been part of that." She's also proud of helping break down barriers for diversity in gaming, both through her visibility in the industry, and the characters she portrays. "I love breaking down barriers and shaking up the status quo and helping people realize that everyone belongs. I don't believe it's a zero-sum game. There's room for everybody here."

Although not a gamer, Hale is one of the biggest advocates for what the industry can achieve. "It's been phenomenal to watch this industry blow up into a huge commercial force. It has so much potential. You have games creating empathy. You have games bringing joy. You have games breaking down barriers. You have some extraordinary things happening, and that's exciting and inspiring and I'm really hopeful," concluded Hale. "I just want to keep being a part of this incredible community and help reinvent it in new ways. I am overjoyed and honored to be able to execute my part of it."

"I love breaking down barriers and shaking up the status quo."

CHRISTA CHARTER

WORDSMITH AND COMMUNITY MANAGEMENT PIONEER

 Trixie360

 Christa Charter

 trixie360.com

EXPERIENCE

FAVORITE INDUSTRY PROJECT: XBOX 360 LAUNCH

PROJECTS SHIPPED: MICROSOFT SHIP-IT AWARDS FOR: XBOX LIVE, XBOX LIVE 3.0, XBOX LIVE NXE, XBOX 360, XBOX 360 LIVE, XBOX ONE X, ZUNE, AND XBOX.COM 7.0

ACHIEVEMENTS UNLOCKED:

> LOS ANGELES TIMES' PROFILE "A REFUGE FOR WOMEN IN A HOSTILE GAME SPACE" (2007)

> KOTAKU'S "10 MOST INFLUENTIAL WOMEN IN GAMES OF THE PAST DECADE" LIST (2010)

> INTERVIEWED ON INDUSTRY SHOWS SUCH AS X-PLAY, SPIKE TV, AND RADIO DISNEY, AS WELL AS MAINSTREAM PUBLICATIONS SUCH AS THE WASHINGTON POST AND MSNBC

> PUBLISHED FOUR BOOKS IN THE LEXY COOPER VIDEOGAME MYSTERY SERIES

STATS

INDUSTRY LEVEL: 23

CURRENT CLASS: SENIOR GLOBAL BRAND COPYWRITER & AUTHOR

CURRENT GUILD: XBOX—SEATTLE, USA

SPECIAL SKILLS: COMMUNITY MANAGEMENT, COPYWRITING, FICTION WRITING

STANDARD EQUIPMENT

FIRST INDUSTRY PROJECT: SIERRA ON-LINE'S IN-HOUSE MAGAZINE, INTERACTION

FAVORITE PLATFORM: XBOX

GO-TO GENRE: HIDDEN OBJECT & ADVENTURE GAMES

MUST-HAVE GAME: THE EMPRESS OF THE DEEP SERIES

BIO

Christa Charter found herself working in video games while looking for a position that would allow her to make money as a writer, an ambition since the third grade. After studying Literature and Journalism, she was poised for one. "I feel bad saying this, because I know people who struggle to get in, but I stumbled into the industry in 1995," said Charter. "I was just looking for a writing gig. John Williams, the brother of Sierra On-Line co-founder Ken Williams, liked my snarky style and hired me as an assistant editor for their in-house magazine."

SIERRA ONLINE

As an assistant editor for the quarterly *InterAction* magazine, which had an impressive circulation of 800,000, Charter's job was a combination of writing and editing, as well as miscellaneous tasks. She particularly enjoyed answering letters to the editor from fans. "I got a letter addressed to Roberta Williams from a 12-year-old girl who wanted to make games. I answered it and years later found out that little girl was Jenn Frank!," she recalled, speaking to a now-industry colleague. "I started doing more writing and pitching stories to the brand managers and one day my boss pulled me aside and said, 'I am so proud of you. One day you're going to be the bitch in the corner office.' That was really empowering."

Charter's responsibilities evolved further and, eventually, she managed and assigned stories to a group of 15 freelance writers, all while conducting interviews with game designers, artists, and brand managers for articles. She wrote and edited software packaging, print ads, magazine articles, press releases, and internal newsletters. Her final position at Sierra was as a Senior Copywriter, which involved writing, editing, and proofing. In addition, she established product naming and positioning, as well as researching competitive products.

TRIXIE 360

Taking her communication skills into a new direction, Charter began her journey to what would become her most public-facing role in her career. In 2002, she joined Volt Services as a contract technical writer and began writing and providing project oversite for Xbox instruction manuals across North America, Europe, Australia, and Asia. She also wrote copy for Xbox Live web articles and created content for the Xbox Live technical beta website. Her success in this role lead to a direct job with Microsoft performing many of the same responsibilities.

In her early attempts to build community at Xbox Live, she and a colleague came up with the idea for a "girl journalist" persona. She settled on the name "TriXie" with the big "X" standing for Xbox. Over time, Christa's actual personality and that of her online persona began to merge.

Easter Egg

Has written a series of murder mysteries set in the video game industry in Seattle: *Schooled, Pwned, Griefed*, and *Glitched.*

With the launch of the Xbox 360, she became Trixie360, Xbox Live's community manager. "The role was both the most fun and the most fulfilling. Community Management in video games was pretty new at that time and was a title I basically gave myself. Before that my title was Xbox.com Community Editor. I used that position and the platform I had to create a bunch of content and programs that brought people together and elevated gamers doing great stuff."

Charter produced text and video coverage of industry events such as E3 and PAX, and covered product launches for Xbox.com and Inside Xbox. Her work in community management helped pioneer programs and best practices for a field that would later become recognized as essential to the success of games development.

In her role, Charter quickly learned that passion from gamers can be expressed in positive and negative ways. "I learned that gamers are vocal and territorial and will absolutely make or break you."

XBOX GAMERCHIX

"Xbox GamerchiX is the work I'm most proud of. Around the time the Xbox 360 launched, there was a lot of talk at Microsoft about needing to broaden the audience and appeal to people other than men aged 18-35. I got the idea that women would be more likely to try multiplayer gaming if they could go with a buddy, and it would be really great if that buddy didn't hit on or insult them. So, I created a private forum in the Xbox.com forums. We called it the GamerchiX Treehouse and we eventually had over 10,000 women from 32 countries planning game nights, reporting shitty behavior, standing up for each other, and building lifelong friendships."

Additional programs she created remain relevant to this day. "Xbox Ambassadors was a seat-of-my-pants project with zero budget. This was maybe 2006 or 2007 and we were doing one of those Free Gold weekends where everyone with a Silver account could do multiplayer for the weekend. I thought, I'd hate for these people to jump into a cesspool of assholes and get scared away forever. The whole point was that they'd have so much fun they'd spend money for a Gold subscription. I thought of Tom from MySpace. When you created a MySpace account, you started with one friend, Tom. I decided to create a group of volunteer Toms to be a new Xbox Live member's friend and guide. I recruited volunteers in all time zones." The Xbox Ambassador program was a great success and continues to this day, now with program managers and a budget.

Charter wrote, produced, and hosted weekly video segments on Inside Xbox, which appeared on the Xbox 360 dashboard, and created and managed Xbox Live programming such as Ladies Night, Cross-Platform Crash, Frag Doll Friday, Co-Op Night, Xbox All-Nighter, and Family Game Night to promote new games. The most successful—Family Game Night and Xbox All-Nighter—brought in $3,000,000 in sponsorships in 2008. Contests, promotions, seasonal campaigns, sweepstakes, Game with Fame, and Game with Developer events also fell under her remit.

Direct engagement with Xbox fans came via Facebook, MySpace, and Twitter, as well as the xbox.com forums, which she managed. These interactions with fans posed problems that many public-facing industry women have encountered—being physically judged during on-camera appearances. "The most challenging project I've worked on is video hosting. I was never the cheerleader or prom queen or even what you'd call pretty, so being on camera was something I really resisted," said Charter. "The more I did it the more comfortable I got and the more I just let my personality loose. I wasn't going to be the 'hot chick', but I could be me. The people who liked me were responding to that, I think. Ego pain aside, I really enjoyed writing scripts and I'm thankful for the experiences I had, the people I met, and the places I got to visit."

There were certainly positive fan encounters to balance the negative. "There was this Marine who used to download my Community Close-up show to his Zune so he could watch it over and over at work," said Charter. "We've been married for 10 years."

"The only thing that matters to me are health, family and friends, and peace of mind."

Charter's career continued with a variety of positions including Mobile Programing Lead for Xbox Live on Windows Phone 7, Senior Account Supervisor at Edelman, CEO and founder of Missing Spoon Communications (which put all her communication skills to use), before returning to Xbox with her current position as Senior Brand copywriter at Microsoft. Personal writing projects continue to occupy Charter's free time, in addition to her *Lexy Cooper Mystery Series* of books. "I'm working on a screenplay now that I would love to see developed into an anthology series. And I'll likely write more books. Career-wise, I've come to the conclusion that I'm not my job. Beating breast cancer in 2015 clarified this for me. The only things that matter to me are health, family and friends, and peace of mind."

That being said, she recognized the importance of her work and her visibility. "It's been a very positive experience to watch young women who were just trying to get a foot in the door a decade ago become these amazing, influential, unstoppable ass-kickers."

A DAY IN THE LIFE OF...

A 3D CHARACTER ARTIST

A 3D character artist is responsible for transforming concept art into an in-game asset with as much fidelity to the original piece as possible. Character aesthetics can be widely varied—ranging from highly stylized to photorealistic. The latter requires immense attention to detail with the inclusion of scars, moles, pores, smile lines, stubble, and other small but important features.

3D character artists also branch out into modeling hair, clothing, accessories, and props. Creating digital garments is a specialty in its own right, which can be shaped and draped from 3D patterns, and then outfitted with everything from buttons and zippers to frayed threads.

Sledgehammer's Sarah McNeal has worked in gaming for 10 years, the last three as a character artist. Her background in sculpting and cosplay make her a great fit for the profession, and aid her in bringing historically accurate and believable characters to life in the *Call of Duty* franchise.

SARAH MCNEAL

 artstation.com/bats1980

PROFESSION: CHARACTER ARTIST AT SLEDGEHAMMER GAMES—FOSTER CITY, USA

YEARS IN PROFESSION: 3

WORKED ON: JUMPSTART, SCHOOL OF DRAGONS, CALL OF DUTY: ADVANCED WARFARE, CALL OF DUTY: WWII

▶ EDUCATION

"I went to Kansas State University, but I did mostly traditional work there. I was originally a sculpture major. In the end I switched to web design, but most of my 3D work is self-taught. I've also got a background in doing costumes for dolls as well as cosplay, so that feeds directly into how I make characters—especially in Marvelous Designer."

▶ BREAKING IN

"I got my job with Knowledge Adventure without too much of a problem. They were looking for someone with my skills, and I fit the niche nicely. But when I decided I wanted to move on from children's games into AAA games—that was hard. It took me a good four years of applying and reworking my portfolio over and over again to get someone to take me seriously. In that time I only had two interviews: one where I was told straight-up that I didn't have the skills they needed, and my interview with Sledge. It was really hard, but it was all worth the effort."

▶ EARLY INDUSTRY IMPRESSIONS

"I worked for a children's game company, and I honestly thought it would be more conservative. But by my first month, my cube was filled with inflatable animals, I'd been in two Nerf gun fights, and I'd helped my co-workers cover another co-worker's cube so tightly in fake spiderwebs she couldn't get into it when she came back from vacation. We work hard, but we play hard too."

▶ KEY QUALITIES

"Being calm and being able to separate your ego from your work. The thing that's important at the end of the day is the game and the quality you are turning out—not your personal artistic vision."

▶ TRAINING OPPORTUNITIES

"I've had good luck with CGWorkshops. I've learned a lot from taking classes there every now and again. Anything that will help you learn new pipelines and tech is always good. You have to stay up on it, or you'll be left behind. This industry is not kind to any veteran artist who doesn't know how to use the latest program or refuses to learn it."

▶ TOOLS OF THE TRADE

"I mostly work in Marvelous Designer, ZBrush, Maya, and Substance. I make the clothing patterns in Marvelous, which creates a draped basic garment. I take that into ZBrush and put in all the details of memory folds, buttons, zippers, seams, rips, and tears. Then I create a low poly version of that in Maya and use Substance to make the textures."

▶ HOURS & ENVIRONMENT

"I hate our open-office environment; I miss my old cube. I have ADD, although it's not pronounced, but it makes it very hard to concentrate with people rushing around me. My co-workers are all really nice family-oriented people, which surprised me coming into a *Call of Duty* studio. I was expecting a bunch of meat-heads and bro-dudes, but they're all extremely nice people. Our hours are really reasonable; our crunch is contained mostly to the last month or two before ship."

▶ AN AVERAGE DAY

"My day depends on where I am in the process. I start out with making a high poly from the concept I receive, work into low poly, then Uvs and finally textures. Once I get that finished, I have to set up the basic character skeleton, called a rig (we have a script for that), export, and set up the entries in the game. Then I run the levels to make sure the character looks right in-game. If it's a multiplayer object, I'll have to make an icon for it as well. Depending on the day, I might have a review with the lead and art director to get feedback on how the design is coming along. This whole process can be as short as three weeks to as long as three months. It all depends on the point in the development cycle."

▶ PROMOTIONAL PATH

"**Associate Character Artist:** Grunt work and piecemeal objects. Maybe integrate items in-game for the other artists. You make a lot of hats and bags.

"**Associate/Character Artist:** Full characters. You can hit the mark with a minimum of guidance. You can take direction well and work without supervision.

"**Senior Artist:** Full characters and principal characters. Match the bar set by the principal artist. Investigate new tech to make our lives easier. Teach the associates, as well as attend level meetings with the art director and environment team to get feedback and bring the notes to the lead.

"**Principal Artist/Expert Artist:** Same as the senior but you're also responsible for making the characters that everyone else will match the quality of.

"**Lead Artist:** Report to the art director, ensure that your team is working well with other teams, give feedback to other artists, as well as do some artwork. Attend meetings about the game's design and future, create schedules for how long different assets will take, review outsourcing work, and so on.

▶ PROFESSIONAL PERKS

"It's really amazing to see your work on television or as a poster in a game store. It makes me a hero to my nephews, which is always a plus. Most teenagers aren't impressed by their old aunties. Also character artists have the least amount of crunch since typically characters get written out as the game progresses, rather than written in. So there's not a lot to mess up your timeline and cause crunch."

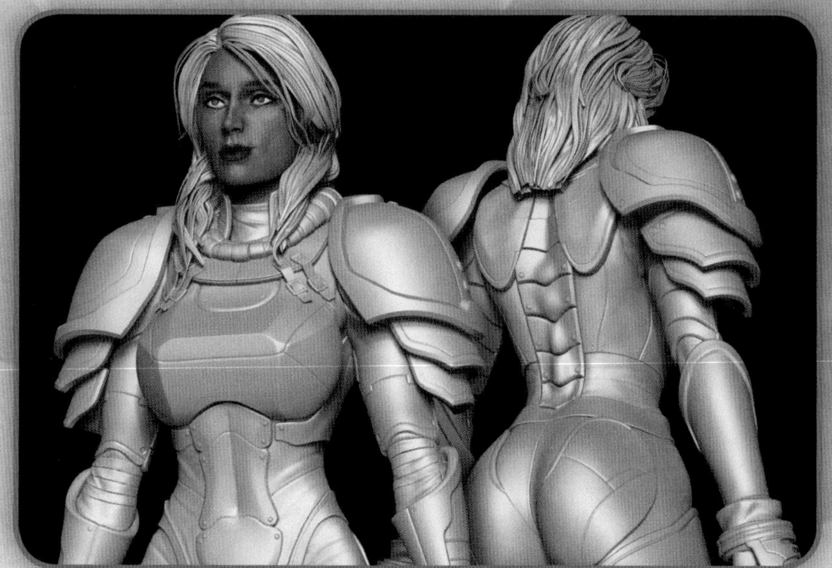

▶ CAREER CHALLENGES

"Learning new tech, sharpening my sculpting skills, being able to work in a variety of styles."

▶ LIFE HACKS

"My dad works a lot of 16-hour shifts at his power plant, and he once told me that if you're going to work long overtime hours like that, you have to pace yourself. Take lots of breaks, go for a walk, etc. I took that to heart to get me through the times I've had to crunch at work, which thankfully haven't been too many."

▶ EXCITING ADVANCEMENTS

"We're getting more and more realistic in terms of what we can do in game graphics. It's exciting, but it's also starting to veer off into uncanny valley at times when the characters start moving or speaking, or emoting. It'll be interesting to see if we can manage to make the characters look photo real when moving as well as when they're still."

PRO TIP!

"For games in general, I'd say to remember there's more good days than bad. The bad days are a punch in the gut, but the good days do make up for it. I love my job, even on the most stressful days. Specific to character art, learn how clothes are put together. Learn to sew. Learn where the seams are. Even if you're doing cartoony-style art, it'll make your work look that much better."

FRANCESCA REYES

GROUNDBREAKING REPORTER FROM THE FRONTLINES OF GAMING

 tomobiki

EXPERIENCE

FIRST INDUSTRY PROJECT: BEYOND THE BEYOND WALKTHROUGH (1996)

FAVORITE INDUSTRY PROJECT: OFFICIAL DREAMCAST MAGAZINE (1999-2001)

PROJECTS SHIPPED: 5 MAGAZINES, 8 GAMES

ACHIEVEMENTS UNLOCKED:

> FIRST FEMALE EDITOR-IN-CHIEF OF A GAMES MAGAZINE AT FUTURE US (2005)

> FIRST PERSON TO PLAY, FINISH, AND REVIEW HALO 3 (2007)

> SPIKE VGA ADVISORY COUNCIL (2006-2013)

> GAME CRITICS AWARD JUDGE (2006-2013)

 STATS

INDUSTRY LEVEL: 23

CURRENT CLASS: USER RESEARCH MANAGER

CURRENT GUILD: 2K—NOVATO, USA

SPECIAL SKILLS: WRITING, EDITING, JOURNALISM, PUBLISHING, CONTENT STRATEGY, USER RESEARCH

STANDARD EQUIPMENT

FAVORITE PLATFORM: SEGA GENESIS

GO-TO GENRE: WILL TRY ANYTHING

MUST-HAVE GAME: "JET SET RADIO, SHINING FORCE II, PHANTASY STAR IV... THE LIST GOES ON AND ON"

BIO

When a coworker handed a newspaper advertisement to Francesca Reyes—one that vaguely alluded to a job in video games—it was intended as a jest. Reyes was often teased for showing up to work half awake, having spent the night marathoning a video game. Reyes didn't see it as a joke, though. She saw it as an opportunity.

"I honestly didn't know that any sort of entry point existed for someone who was as non-technical as I was at that time," recalled Reyes. "I read game magazines and played games—that's all I knew. It was an opaque industry and there weren't any easily-categorized classes you could take to break in, outside of possibly computer science. You either had to know someone who worked in it, or you were like me—someone who applied for an entry level position."

Easter Egg

Used to call up game company hotlines for information and tips on games. As a result, she has several hand-drawn graph-paper maps sent by Sega as a guide to help get through some of the tougher *Phantasy Star III and IV* dungeons.

SCEA

Reyes applied for and was hired at Sony Computer Entertainment America (SCEA) in 1995, supporting the first PlayStation as a customer service representative. "I worked there during the day, while taking classes towards a Literature MA at night, and working at a coffee shop for extra cash," she said. "I decided to take a break from the MA program for a bit. To use an eyeroll-inducing cliché, the rest is history."

Working SCEA was not just Reyes' first job in video games, it was her first ever office job. "The fact that I could play games at my desk, talk to other people about them, and eventually write stuff about them was beyond what I could really imagine at the time," she said.

"A few months into the job, I found myself on the team responsible for writing the walkthroughs and tip sheets for all of SCEA's first party games to be referenced by the reps who manned the 900 number."

A walkthrough for the 1996 JRPG *Beyond the Beyond* was her first assignment. "Each of the guides that our team put together were usually helmed by one person, so I was the only person working on it," described Reyes. "I remember that we had to not only write the guide and any strategy advice, but also do the layout for it in Quark. I also spent countless hours taking screenshots for each quadrant of every level since dungeon maps were so important to the guides. It was tedious, but I learned so much about basic graphic design, layout, and how to write more technically than descriptively."

> "It was a very distinct moment that I was witness to—seeing the transition of dominance in console games development from Japan to the West."

A NEW FUTURE

By the time Reyes left SCEA two years later, she was a Senior Tip Member with practical experience writing about video games. She used her newfound skills to land a job at *Ultra Gameplayers* in 1997 as an Associate Editor. "Segueing into press and editorial took more learning, but knowing how to write conversationally—not just academically—and critical analysis/thinking were both skills I had picked up for my degree. It made the transition a little easier."

Parent company Future US—then known as Imagine Publishing—was quite a different environment for Reyes. "I think the most surprising thing was just how casual the office culture was," she said. "This was the mid-to-late-'90s, and the fact that you could basically just wear whatever you wanted to work, come in late, stay all night, and take breaks to do *Bomberman 64* matches wowed me at the time. You learn that it's not all good times, but at first blush, it was really exciting."

Reyes would work at Future US for a total of 17 years, split between five magazine brands. After writing for *Ultra Gameplayers*, *Next Generation*, and *PSM* over two years, she moved to the *Official Dreamcast Magazine* as Senior Editor in 1999—the year the console came to market in North America. As part of the launch team, she helped contribute ideas about the magazine mission, layout, design, and overall voice. "The Dreamcast magazine was shaped by the spirit of Sega and designed to be a very 'prestige-style' magazine with heavy paper stock and an offbeat portfolio size," she recalled.

In 2001, Reyes moved to the *Official Xbox Magazine* (OXM). Just as she had done with the Dreamcast launch, she was reporting from the frontlines of an industry-disrupting console, first as Senior Editor, then as Executive Editor. "OXM was tasked with helping to introduce Microsoft as a new competitor in the games space," she said. "It was a very distinct moment that I was witness to—seeing the transition of dominance in console games development from Japan to the West. It was such a marked shift, especially moving from covering games on the Official Dreamcast Magazine staff to the being part of the team on OXM."

In 2005, she was promoted again, becoming the first female Editor-in-Chief of a games magazine at the entirety of Imagine Publishing. The news was big enough that Reyes was making headlines—not just writing them. "As EIC, I was mainly tasked with keeping everything running and building a voice for the magazine that suited both the specific era in the Xbox 360's lifespan, as well as the culture around it," said Reyes. "I was responsible for maintaining relationships with the different publishers, developers, and readership, while also building a team, and overseeing a lot of the day-to-day and big picture stuff. I really loved a lot of my time on OXM because of the people I worked with over the years. It was never easy, I made so many mistakes, and I probably got like an average of maybe five hours of sleep a night for the entirety of my tenure, but I learned countless lessons and met so many great people."

Having earned the respect of major industry players through her knowledge and professionalism, Reyes was presented many unique opportunities in her new position as EIC. This included being the first person in the world to play and review *Halo 3* in 2007. The opportunity was so exclusive, websites flocked to interview Reyes about her impressions, authoring articles about her access such as *GamesRadar's* 2007 blog "*She's Beaten Halo 3*."

With the visibility boost from the EIC position, interview requests became regular. Mainstream press from outlets such as *Forbes*, *Rolling Stone*, and *ABC News* would reach to Reyes as a subject matter expert on pressing industry issues. Reyes was also invited to be a judge on prestigious award panels, such as the E3 Judges Awards, the Spike VGA Advisory Council, and the Game Critics' Awards Judges.

"Editorial challenged me in a way I felt was really rewarding and creatively satisfying. I thrive when juggling multiple timelines, collaborating on creative pieces with a team, and pushing myself and my coworkers to innovate and come up with new ways to present interesting concepts or ideas," said Reyes. "I think a lot of these practices carry over into other jobs I went on to do, so I appreciated getting a strong foundation in it while working in press."

Reyes left Future US after nearly two decades of helping grow and guide their best-selling magazines. She spent some time freelance game consulting, before settling in at 2K Games as a User Research Manager in 2016. "I find a way to translate feedback from players into actionable, thoughtful insights for developers to make more informed decisions," she explained. "This has been a new chapter for me where I can use my communication skills, planning, observation, and (surprisingly) empathy, in hopes of helping really smart, creative people better articulate their vision."

"Back when I was in press, I was talking to another woman who had joined the company on a different publication," closed Reyes. "This happened after I had been Editor-in-Chief for a little while. She mentioned to me that one of the main reasons she had decided to join the company was that I had been made an EIC of one of their gaming magazines. This gave her hope that she would be given the opportunity to do the same—and she did! This conversation struck a chord with me. There's something very humbling and eye-opening about someone seeing you simply doing your job as a representation of a welcoming, safe space for opportunities they didn't feel were open to them previously. That's just really cool."

KIKI WOLFKILL

SHEPHERD OF THE EVER-EXPANDING HALO UNIVERSE

 K_wolfkill

 K_wolfkill

 Kiki Wolfkill

EXPERIENCE

FIRST INDUSTRY PROJECT: MICROSOFT FLIGHT SIMULATOR FOR WINDOWS 95 (1996)

FAVORITE INDUSTRY PROJECT: PROJECT GOTHAM RACING (2000)

PROJECTS SHIPPED: 22 GAMES

ACHIEVEMENTS UNLOCKED:

> FORTUNE "10 MOST POWERFUL WOMEN IN GAMES" (2013)

> AMY POEHLER'S SMART GIRLS PROFILE (2016)

> FAST COMPANY "MOST CREATIVE PEOPLE 2017"

> SEATTLE MET "THE 50 MOST INFLUENTIAL WOMEN IN SEATTLE" (2018)

STATS

INDUSTRY LEVEL: 22

CURRENT CLASS: HEAD OF HALO TRANSMEDIA AND ENTERTAINMENT

CURRENT GUILD: 343 INDUSTRIES—SEATTLE, U.S.A.

SPECIAL SKILLS: GAME DESIGN, PRODUCTION, USER INTERFACE DESIGN, ANIMATION, RACING

STANDARD EQUIPMENT

FAVORITE PLATFORM: XBOX ONE

GO-TO GENRE: ACTION/ADVENTURE

MUST-HAVE GAME: HALO: COMBAT EVOLVED (2001)

BIO

In her 22 years working in the video game industry, Kiki Wolfkill has faithfully remained a part of the Microsoft family, contributing to major first-party game, console, and studio milestones.

"While I had always played videogames, I didn't actually realize that it was a viable career path," began Wolfkill. "I studied Chinese history and broadcast journalism in college—with a minor in art—with the intent to make documentary films. After college, I was able to leverage my experience in filmmaking just as digital video and non-linear editing were becoming more mainstream and begin working for a software company creating interactive CD-ROMs."

Easter Egg

Used to race cars professionally, including competing in the Women's Global GT Series. Still tries to push any vehicle she can find to unnatural speeds, including golf carts, foot scooters, and go-karts.

Coincidentally, this was also the time when Wolfkill got back into gaming—thanks to *7th Guest* and *Doom*. "Through a combination of opportunity and focused effort, I ended up creating digital video content for Microsoft," she explained. "I had gotten heavily into compositing and motion graphics and was inspired by what these digital tools allowed me to do creatively. At this point, I was also starting to work exclusively on game videos and cinematics." Her early multimedia production portfolio includes *Microsoft Flight Simulator* for Windows 95 and *CART Precision Racing*. Wolfkill's involvement in the latter was not a coincidence. Microsoft became aware of her talents on the track when looking for a racing expert to bring authenticity to their upcoming game and found one in Wolfkill. She would continue to contribute to racing games for years to come.

A GUIDING EYE

With several retail releases under her belt, Wolfkill took on art lead responsibilities at Microsoft, shipping *Microsoft Combat Flight Simulator: WWII Europe Series*, *Monster Truck Madness 2*, *Midtown Madness*, *Motocross Madness 2*, and *Midtown Madness 2*. She was promoted again in 1988, becoming the director of art for Microsoft Game Studios as a whole. She would hold this position for nearly a decade.

Even at the director level, Wolfkill remained entrenched in creating content. During the late 90s, gaming sat on the bleeding edge of graphics technology and entertainment. "Even if I still dealt with 8-bit RGB palettes in some cases, this energized me and I never looked back! I have watched the medium evolve and become an engine for play, story, competition, and innovation. I feel lucky to have been part of that evolution," she said.

Up until this point, Wolfkill worked exclusively on PC titles. Everything changed in 2001. Microsoft disrupted the game industry with the introduction of the Xbox, a console to challenge the established markets of PlayStation and Nintendo. Wolfkill contributed to the momentum of the Xbox launch through its launch titles, including *Project Gotham Racing*. "It was such an adventure and learning experience to think about the console player versus the PC player," said Wolfkill. "I was thrilled by our charter as first-party to deliver the best looking games in order to demonstrate the power of the platform, so it was an incredible challenge." Wolfkill would continue to help push the Xbox and its successor—the Xbox 360—to their limits. She helped ship *Fable*, *Mass Effect*, *Too Human*, and *Crackdown* among others.

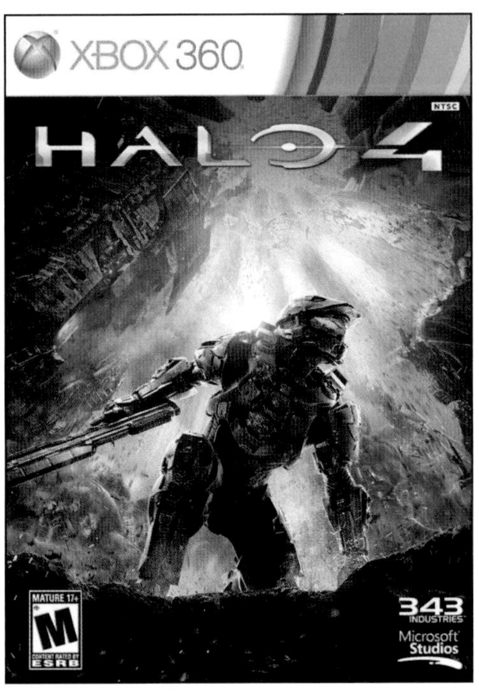

RALLYING THE TROOPS

In 2008, Wolfkill accepted the position of executive producer of the newly formed 343 Industries, working on the first non-Bungie *Halo* title—*Halo 4*. As the *Halo* visual brand owner, she drew heavily from her art background, in addition to her production role. She—along with studio head Bonnie Ross—helped build the *Halo 4* team from the ground up. This was the most personally fulfilling time in her career. "It was my first opportunity to build a game team," explained Wolfkill. "It was this extraordinary puzzle where every new piece changed the configuration of what you needed next; it was a delicate chemical formula. It was also thrilling to see such talented people come together around something they believed passionately about and make it come to life. I love building—teams, games, experiences, culture. Building the *Halo 4* team taught me so much about empathy, decisiveness, and focus. Some through success and some through failure."

Unsurprisingly, *Halo 4*s development was also exceptionally challenging. "*Halo 4* was the first *Halo* first-person shooter developed by anyone outside of Bungie and, on top of that, I was tasked with building the game while also building the team," Wolfkill continued. "It was invigorating and frightening at the same time. We as 343 needed to learn how to make a *Halo* game while also forming our own voice, all under the intense scrutiny of the enormous *Halo* fanbase and our own executive leadership team." The challenge paid off critically and commercially, as *Halo 4* set new sales records on launch day.

CREATING A WAYPOINT

With *Halo 4* successfully out the door, Wolfkill devoted herself to furthering the non-interactive arm of the franchise as executive producer on three major projects: Halo Waypoint, Halo Channel, and Halo: Nightfall. Halo Waypoint began as an application and web portal to showcase player-specific game accomplishments, but later evolved into the information hub of the entire *Halo* universe. Halo Channel is dedicated to franchise programming (official and fan made), which expands upon the rich fiction in new and exciting ways. Developed in tandem with the channel, Halo: Nightfall is a five-part, live-action digital series produced by Ridley Scott, comprising over 100 minutes of original content. All three projects were major multimedia endeavors that changed the way fans interacted with the franchise.

Returning to the home she helped build, Wolfkill still owns the ever-expanding universe of Halo Transmedia and Entertainment. The most recent addition is an upcoming Showtime and Amblin Entertainment live-action *Halo* television series, which she is leading internally. "I don't know what the future holds for me," Wolfkill concluded. "I know that how we tell stories and experience them through games and other new technologies continues to evolve and I want to be part of that change. I know that new generations of gamers are playing—and watching!—games in new ways and that will drive rapid innovation and I want to be part of that. I also know that I love building and creating and so I will always do that in some way shape or form."

MEGAN GAISER

CHAMPION OF GAMES FOR GIRLS WHO "DARE TO PLAY"

 MeganGaiser

Megan Gaiser

leadershipfordiversity.com

EXPERIENCE

FIRST INDUSTRY PROJECT: NANCY DREW: SECRETS CAN KILL (1998)

FAVORITE INDUSTRY PROJECT: HELPING TO ESTABLISH THE VIDEO GAMES MARKET FOR GIRLS

PROJECTS SHIPPED: 32 GAMES

ACHIEVEMENTS UNLOCKED:

> NEXT GENERATION "GAME INDUSTRY'S 100 MOST INFLUENTIAL WOMEN" (2006)

> MICROSOFT "WOMEN IN GAMES" AWARD (2010)

> KOTAKU "TOP 10 MOST INFLUENTIAL WOMEN OF THE DECADE" (2010)

> INDIECADE "TRAILBLAZER LIFETIME ACHIEVEMENT" AWARD (2011)

STATS

INDUSTRY LEVEL: 17

CURRENT CLASS: PRINCIPAL

CURRENT GUILD: CONTAGIOUS CREATIVITY—SEATTLE, USA

SPECIAL SKILLS: CREATIVE DIRECTOR, STORYTELLER, EXPERIENCE & CONTENT CURATOR, CREATIVE LEADERSHIP, DIVERSITY & CULTURE SPECIALIST FOR INSPIRED HUMAN EXPERIENCE

BIO

Megan Gaiser has strived to give a voice to overlooked demographics throughout her career by challenging conventional wisdom and traditional leadership behavior, systems, and practices. "I didn't intend on working in the gaming industry," began Gaiser. Her background was in educational, documentary, and corporate films and video as a producer and editor. When multimedia began to spring up in Seattle in the early nineties, it caught her attention.

With both plentiful tech opportunities and a sister in Seattle, Gaiser moved there without a job. She quickly landed a producer role at Microsoft when they were first beginning to create content for MSN. Her initial film project—showcasing personalities of university campuses across the country—was canceled shortly after she was hired, for a lack of market research. She was swiftly reassigned to CarPoint, the first online car-buying guide. "I met a lot of great people, but cars weren't my thing, and I didn't find the culture inclusive," Gaiser said. After a few years, she was ready for a change.

TAKING DREW DIGITAL

In 1996, a colleague introduced Gaiser to the CEO of local game company Her Interactive. They had recently acquired the rights to the *Nancy Drew* franchise and were in need of a creative director. "I knew nothing about the industry and wasn't an avid gamer," she said. Still, as a passionate fan of the *Drew* books, she took the job—excited by the potential to transform the iconic *Nancy Drew* adventures into inspiring, interactive experiences. "I was really interested in telling nonlinear stories that focused on the multidimensional brilliance of women, versus the limiting stereotypes the media was feeding us," she recalled. "Nancy Drew was the perfect persona to accomplish that."

Her Interactive met roadblocks at every turn and fought back. Their first challenge was unsolicited advice from publishers about the preferences of an audience they knew nothing about. "We were told, 'If you're going to make games for girls, make 'em pink and they'll come.' We made them 'unpink.' We integrated historical characters and cultural references to expand the players' worldview," explained Gaiser. They also blended entertainment and education throughout the game to broaden the players' knowledge base and world awareness.

"Her Interactive's commitment to never lower expectations is one reason we were able to create an award-winning series, a loyal fan base, and increasing revenues," said Gaiser. "We believed if we could deliver a fun and engaging experience, we would have the foundation for a successful series. The Her Interactive team fostered creativity, collaboration, respect, risk-taking, diversity, and a curiosity for what is possible. The best ideas won."

Eager to learn more about the preferences of their target demographic, Gaiser hosted one-on-one usability testing with girls ages eight to 12. "Because girls were new to games at the time, their fresh perspectives helped us improve on existing gameplay," Gaiser explained. Many girls felt that the Nancy Drew character seemed too perfect, and as a result, they didn't feel comfortable assuming her role. The company's solution was to give her character more depth and a sense of humor.

Armed with their newfound knowledge, Her Interactive presented *Nancy Drew: Secrets Can Kill* to publishers, intent on selling at retail. The response was unanimous; there was no market opportunity because girls were computer-phobic. "It felt surreal—publishers refusing to accept our game because they deemed girls 'ungameworthy'—in a medium designed for 'play.' Everyone seemed to just go along with it," recalled Gaiser. At the time, Her Interactive's tagline was "For girls who aren't afraid of a mouse."

The Her Interactive team was determined to right that wrong. Shortly after being denied entry into the brick-and-mortar retail world, the former CEO stood up and resigned at a board meeting. "The chairman looked at me and said, 'We think you can do it.' I remember thinking four things, not necessarily in this order: 1. The 'no girls allowed' rule needs to be broken. 2. We can do it. 3. I don't have traditional CEO skills. 4. Anything is possible. And then I said yes," she reflected. Gaiser began her executive education by cold-calling and meeting with CEOs. "I asked *a lot* of questions," she recalled, "and found mentors—open-minded, innovative collaborators—who valued creativity and were willing to take risks."

The first order of action Gaiser took as CEO was to address their exclusion from retail. With traditional retailers hesitant to dive into the girls' games market, the Her Interactive team became outliers. That ultimately worked to their advantage. After being stonewalled by traditional retailers, Her Interactive partnered with a tiny (at the time) e-commerce retail start-up called Amazon.

"UNBARBIE"

Game sales took off and *The New York Times* dubbed Nancy Drew the "UnBarbie" of computer games. Suddenly, retail doors opened. Gaiser soon realized that while brick-and-mortar stores brought greater visibility, they were also taking the lion's share of profits. So she and her team taught themselves to become retail publishers. Her Interactive grew from zero to nine million dollars in revenue, sold an equal number of games, and received multiple awards over the next decade. "It felt like we were kids in a candy store, playing our way to success," Gaiser recalled. They changed their tagline to "Dare to Play."

The economic crash in 2008 brought a new challenge for Gaiser—a need to reimagine the business. "The combination of the economic downturn, revised business models, price-point plunges, and platform changes brought both chaos and complexity to the situation," she reflected. The team needed additional skills and expertise to compete in the new market. Gaiser stayed on as chief creative strategist to guide the transition.

> "It felt like were kids in a candy store, playing our way to success."

CONTAGIOUS CREATIVITY

After leaving Her Interactive in 2013, Gaiser founded Contagious Creativity, a consultancy guiding the creation of enlivening and inspiring experiences across media. In addition, she's also focused on the research and development of new approaches for 21st-century leadership. She was the catalyst for the formation of the "Leadership for Diversity" initiative, supported by 300 industry leaders to champion inclusive and creative leadership practices. Gaiser also serves as an advisory board member for several entertainment, technology, and leadership organizations across industries.

When she looks back on her time at Her Interactive, feedback from loyal fans remains one of her fondest memories. "The *Nancy Drew* game series inspired thousands of girls and women—and some men and boys!—who took time to share their stories," Gaiser recalled. They handwrote letters describing how the *Nancy Drew* games inspired them to become computer scientists, engineers, technologists, cryptologists, lawyers, detectives, NASA engineers, and more.

"I am grateful to have been a part of an eclectic team who fostered a culture of creative collaboration to achieve a heartfelt mission, and also for the leadership opportunity I was given at Her Interactive. It has been one of my greatest learning experiences and has led me to the work I do now," concluded Gaiser.

Easter Egg

After she sent flowers to Mildred Benson, ghostwriter of *Nancy Drew*, the 92-year-old handwrote a letter back. Framed in her honor, it hung in the Her Interactive offices.

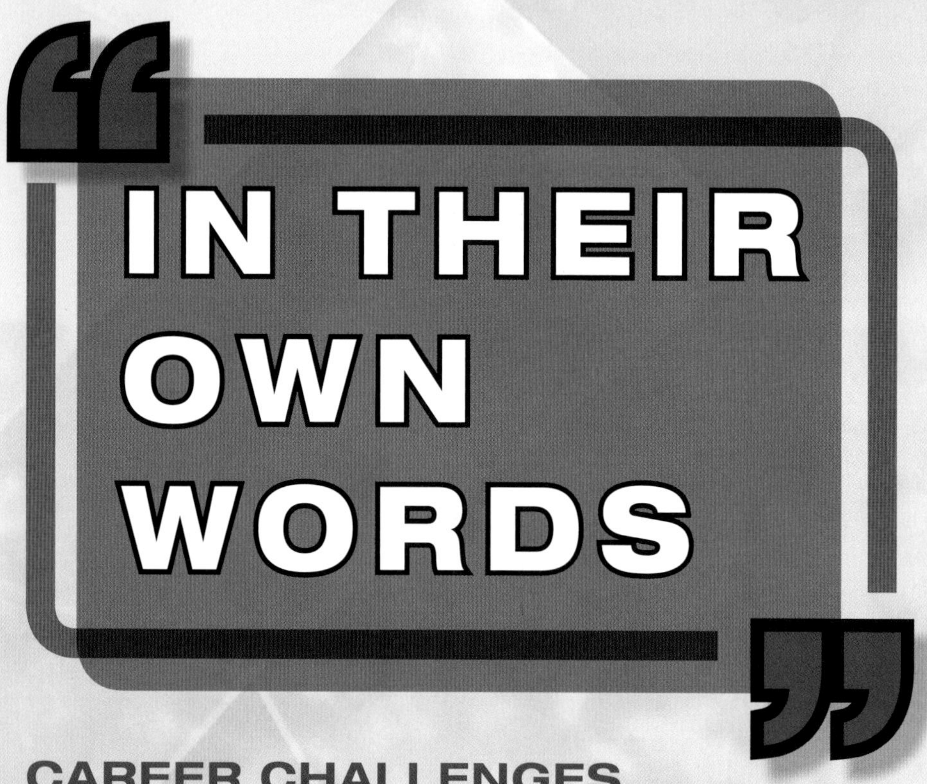

CAREER CHALLENGES

Have there been specific challenges you've faced as a game industry professional due to your gender? What progress still needs to be made in the industry to make it a more inclusive place for women?

"I've faced several challenges in my career due to my gender, but almost all of them have come back to a lack of voice. I've been in meetings of mostly men where I would say something, only to be talked over or ignored, and then minutes later, a male co-worker would say the same idea and be met with praise. I've had co-workers, and even bosses, talk to my male colleagues (even when I was their manager) about things directly related to my work. I've been interrupted, excluded, and even once had someone snap in my face (I wish I was joking). I believe there's still a 'boys club' mentality to working in games, and if we want to see progress, that needs to change. There needs to be a mutual level of respect, regardless of gender, to start creating a more inclusive workplace for women. Women need to be present in more roles throughout the pipeline and represented in leadership."

Amanda Erickson | Social Media Manager | Rooster Teeth | Austin, USA

"Yes, as most women in the games industry who joined over a decade ago, I've experienced increased scrutiny of my work compared to that of my male colleagues, harassment, insults, stalking, etc. Although by far, the worst feeling was always when someone assumed I was someone's girlfriend rather than a programmer on the game they were there to cover or celebrate. It took me much too long to realize that I didn't need to have something fully designed to bring an idea to someone who would give me a chance to realize it. Women need to be aware that they tend to undersell themselves—you don't have to be 100% qualified or have everything 100% prepared to go for an opportunity or a promotion.

"Women need more women mentors in high positions, so if you've been in the industry awhile, try to be that person for someone just starting out in her career. For people in positions to give women opportunities: give a woman a shot, even when she seems to lack confidence—she might actually be extremely good and capable but has never had a chance like the one you're offering her, before. Let her prove herself, because chances are, she will."

Anna Kipnis | Senior Gameplay Programmer | Double Fine Productions | San Francisco, USA

"I've been quite lucky in the places I've worked, having good representation and great bosses who value me, but I've also encountered a lot of the same issues that others have online. Venturing into games, forums, social media—it can all be that extra bit more daunting when you're a woman, and we'll face criticism more easily than our male counterparts. I've had people question whether I even play games, or suggest I have no place in games, as they're 'designed for men,' or that I couldn't possibly have any technical knowledge. On social media I have to be quite careful to avoid negative attention. It's a tough thing to push through, and to open yourself up to being in the spotlight. There are some great initiatives to encourage women to get into the industry, to learn coding, to meet with other women. I think that's a great step. Visible women within the industry encourage others to join. I think more can be done to retain women; it's not uncommon for burnout from dealing with harassment to take its toll."

Cat Karskens | Senior Community Manager | Square Enix Europe | London, UK

"I think I've run the same gamut as most other women in the industry, getting talked over in meetings, passed over for investment, having to decide if it's safe to go have coffee with a co-worker or if it's worth speaking up about the third time a rape joke has been used in a design meeting to describe an in-game imbalance of power. I think the real flaw in the industry comes from our rebelliousness, our inherent desire to remain agile, flexible, and disruptive. We are afraid that if we develop a set of standard 'professional' business practices, it's going to happen at the expense of our creativity, our passion. Weirdly enough, we have fallen into the same 'afraid to change' trap that our rebelliousness is supposed to be defending us against. As women, we have to be more willing to be in visible roles, not just be the silent force. We have to step up and make sure we get counted, so that people know how we are involved in making the products they love. As men, we have to accept that there's a standard of professionalism to be met. Making a game is not a contest; games are built by a team. The entire team matters; sometimes that means we have to check our dirty jokes at the door."

Kimberly Unger | Mobile/VR Producer | Playchemy | Burlingame, USA

"I have been underestimated, advised to step away from the business process, and asked to think more 'like a man' when making decisions for my company. I think it's important to keep in mind that the industry is for everyone, and the industry should be prepared to be more open to welcome new ways of doing things. Maybe business deals are not only done drinking late in bars; maybe they are done at tea salons. Maybe the face of the industry is not a shy guy with glasses; maybe the face of the industry is a beautiful mother like Maja Moldenhauer."

Laia Bee | Co-Founder | Pincer Games | Punta del Este, Uruguay

---

"I worked with someone who made a personal goal to 'beat me up to make me tough' with unrealistic work expectations, insulting words, and aggressive behavior. While he was reported for inappropriate behavior by several people, nothing happened. But his toxic presence encouraged a 'boys club' mentality in small cliques led by his attitudes; more people began to show inappropriate behavior. It only took one intoxicated person to attempt to pull my dress down at a company party. We need to prevent toxic people from influencing others as examples, and call each of them out. While one toxic example might not equate to a sexist example, a person influenced by bad examples can easily make it into one."

Lola Shiraishi | Producer | SEGA of America | Los Angeles, USA

"As long as we keep focusing on the differences and putting the genders in contrast to each other, the divisions and antagonisms will persist. By naming things, we establish the reality in which we live and operate. Standing by the oppositions, we may soon face the nightmare of the other extreme: the trap of political correctness. Of being terrorized by what can and cannot be said with or without an offense to another person only because he's a he or she's a she. Or another trap—of oversimplification and cognitive bias: demonizing the industry with preconceptions about what it's like for the girls who would consider a career in game development or those who already are developers and might start seeing each problem as a gender problem. That being said, I don't deny there's a lot of mental work to be done, shells to crack, and some soul-searching is necessary. But instead of focusing on what divides us—named as men and women in this case—I suggest we focus on what we share and care about most as human beings: having a positive and nourishing work environment, supportive of the creative work that making games is. And to us as the leaders: sharing trust and appreciation of each and every member of the crew as a valuable person and a professional, not as a mere 'human resource.'"

Magdalena Tomkowicz | "Co-Founder, Narrative Designer, Boring Documents Writer" | Reikon Games | Warsaw, Poland

---

"Fortunately, so far my experience as a female game industry professional and entrepreneur has been very positive and enriching. Even though today only about 16% of the professionals in our industry are women, the Chilean video game development sector stands out for its openness and its spirit of collaboration. It mostly comprises young professionals and entrepreneurs working to achieve their dreams. However, there's still a lot of work to be done to foster the inclusion of women in this sector. For instance, young women are still reluctant to study software engineering, even though it seems to be a very promising career path. Also, as entrepreneurs, women still face more difficulties than their male peers, because of gender inequalities, roles, and social expectations."

Maureen Berho | CEO & Producer | Niebla Games | Valparaíso, Chile

---

"I often have to work twice as hard to be heard and taken seriously. My professional achievements have often gone unnoticed and unrecognized. To combat this, I've started keeping lists of everything I do for a game to give to my managers at our meetings and reviews. Making the women who are so heavily involved in development visible still needs a lot of work. I would love to see more female spokespersons for games."

Rachel Day | Senior VFX Artist | Blizzard Entertainment | Irvine, USA

"If you asked most women, people of color, or any folks from marginalized groups what challenges they've faced in this industry, you could probably fill a whole book with only that! The truth is that marginalization happens in ways big and small, accidental and intended, subtle and overt, obscure and just plain trope-y. This industry is young, barely out of its infancy, and yet it's responsible for beginning some of the most influential technological turns and creative communities in existence. But with great power comes…the need for even greater responsibility. It's not good enough for us to look at our teams—with one woman, one Latinx, and one other—and call it a day. Much the opposite, the struggle for inclusion requires something akin to eternal vigilance—with constant study, evaluation, interrogation, and validation. The arc of the moral universe doesn't bend toward justice unless we all apply some well-placed oomph."

Shana T. Bryant | Senior Producer | Private Division, Take-Two Interactive Software, Inc. | Seattle, USA

"As a non-binary person, my barriers are the same as most binary women and different. I often say that my gender is non-binary and politically I'm a woman. I experience many of the same barriers as women, because that's the pigeon hole people see me in and that's how I grew up. At the same time, I also struggle with being addressed with she/her pronouns and generally not having my gender acknowledged at all. I have a certain amount of privilege, being white and perceived as a woman, I can get away with more masculine presentation when I want and anything outside of social binaries. Mostly, I 'just' live with internal conflict day-to-day. I do find myself reluctant to present as less feminine at events and at important meetings, and I think this is probably a fear that I'll be taken less seriously. It's a complex—or subtle—issue and one that I generally choose not to fight daily in the industry. As an advocate for accessibility and inclusion, I sadly find I don't have much energy left over to fight for my rights as a non-binary person.

"Online, I am open about my gender and that's my quiet form of protest in a way; being visible. It's in my social media profiles, it's in my streaming profiles, and I'm not quiet about it if anyone specifically asks me. This makes me vulnerable and opens me up to an entirely additional form of harassment in the shape of a very specific kind of transphobia. It's been tough to deal with at times, and it's made me question whether I should even be as open as I am, but I'm very much a person who wants to stand up for the rights of others since I have the support and social capital to do so. It's my hope that just by being visible on platforms like Twitch, Mixer, and Twitter that it makes others in the community feel welcome for who they are. I do think that the industry is becoming more welcoming to trans and non-binary people. There's a certain amount of awareness since I'm seeing pronoun ribbons at major conferences like GDC or pins available at conventions like PAX. Having said this, in the day-to-day I encounter very few people who use neutral pronouns and I unfortunately rarely feel safe or comfortable requesting people do so, whether online or in person."

Cherry Thompson | Game Accessibility Consultant | Freelance | Vancouver, Canada

---

"Specific to the game industry, the biggest challenge I faced was proving my ability and credibility as a video game personality. Unfortunately, being a woman comes with the stereotype that I don't play games, nor could I possibly know anything there is to know about games, so having to disprove that was a heavy burden I took on in my first couple of years as a host. Now that I'm a little older, my mindset has changed and I believe no one should ever have to prove anything to anyone for anything when it comes to their careers; all that matters is the work that you do. As a young and relatively new person to the industry, however, I took it upon myself to prove to them I was a gamer. It was a challenge, and a challenge that I would have never rid myself of had I never come to the realization that you can't please everybody. No matter how hard you to try to change people's minds about a stereotype, you will never win. There will always be someone who refuses to believe in you. It was one of the hardest challenges I faced but one I learned a lot from.

"To make this industry more inclusive toward women, I think more active conversations need to be had. Deliberate action needs to be taken by the leaders in our industry to make conversations about women in the workplace a focus. Workshops and company meetings where women are given a safe space to speak up about their grievances, where all voices can be heard, and where solutions can follow. Every woman has had a different experience and therefore can contribute different ideas on how we can ensure women have as much an equal chance as any man to become successful in their field and to become leaders. That they are given just as much leeway, accommodations, and recognition as men in this industry. Consistent and deliberate focus on women's issues in the workplace is the ongoing step we need to take to ensure proper change is made. We've made some progress, but we need more of it."

Naomi Kyle | Actor, Host, & Producer | Los Angeles, USA

"In my first journalism role (as one of only four women in Australia working in games media at the time), my executive producer told me I was hired to be 'eye candy' and I was instructed to 'dumb down' my knowledge of games for our television audience. Thankfully, I had a great director who went against his wishes and allowed me to be myself—but the way I was promoted put me in a position where I had to defend myself constantly to prove I deserved my job. I still see young women facing similar hurdles today, where if you are deemed attractive, you can't possibly also have a genuine interest in games. As games become universally accepted as the mainstream entertainment medium they are, I believe the stereotype of what a 'gamer' looks like will disappear. There will still be 'gatekeepers,' but they will become the minority. This is why my goal is to have games spoken about in the media just like any other form of storytelling—to have game reviews sit alongside film reviews, discussion of game trailers be right at home with talk about the latest Netflix series, and for these conversations to take place on mainstream media outlets."

Rae Johnston | Editor, TV & Radio Presenter | Junkee | Sydney, Australia

---

"One thing that bothers me a bit is some people assume that 'because you are a woman, you are motherly.' Some of my co-workers would ask me questions about how to deal with kids so they can put it in the game. As more and more woman are working in the industry, more profiles are represented. You have the feminine one, the tomboy, the shy one, the bold one—it breaks the boxes woman are often put into."

Sophie Bécam | Game & Level Designer | Dontnod Entertainment | Paris, France

---

"If anything, I would say that my age has been more of a factor than my gender. Ageism is very real in most tech verticals, and gaming is no different. It's a youth-oriented realm, and anyone 40+ has to 'prove' that they belong."

Debbi Colgin | Director of Support | Hustle | San Francisco, USA

"I think representation is still lacking. It tends to come as a surprise when people see women in male-dominated industries such as IT, let alone in the games industry. I do think it's slowly changing, but I feel you have to be extra determined and persistent to want to stay in the industry due to additional challenges. I think specific issues like being undervalued or not being taken seriously compared to your male peers can make it more difficult. I think in recent years a lot of these issues have more exposure; especially as the games industry is growing, it's getting recognition and getting called out."

Jennie Nguyen | Systems Administrator | Crystal Dynamics | Redwood City, USA

"I don't think I've experienced any specific challenges because I'm a woman, but until the late 1990s, in Japan it would be men who worked and women who looked after the household. This was common practice. As a woman, you would be expected to retire from work to get married and have a child. Even if you went back into the workforce after having a child, you'd have a long blank in your experience, which made it hard to go back. Today, that way of thinking has diminished, and women can return to the workforce. Also, men are taking time off work for child-rearing purposes and are more cooperative now. When I was at Capcom, most employees were relatively young, so even there these things were rare."

Manami Matsumae | Composer & Arranger | Freelance | Kyoto, Japan

---

THE CHAINSAW SAGA

By Jill Murray | *Lead writer for games such as Shadow of the Tomb Raider, Assassin's Creed III: Liberation, Assassin's Creed IV: Black Flag—Freedom Cry, Fated, Long Story, and Moon Hunters*

Recently my mother told me, "When you were born, you were the only girl in the nursery. Every toddler in our neighbourhood was a boy. I signed you up for music classes: boys. Gymnastics: boys. I spent your childhood trying to find you girls, wondering if you'd always be outnumbered."

I tell this story to colleagues—all men—over drinks after a long work day. They ask each other about their kids, games, sports. For me: "What's it like? The Woman in Games thing?"

If I'm to prove that I'm cool, and I'm not That Girl, I will tell them I've been lucky in my career. I'm grateful for every opportunity. This team is different.

I am not cool. I tell them it's hard to always be outnumbered.

"Why do you feel outnumbered?" they ask. "We have a lot of women at the studio." But it's been a year since I was in a creative meeting with another woman. Am I a lot?

"You have to learn to get along with men to have a career in this industry, that's for sure."

My earliest friends were David, Ross, Mark, Patrick, and Jean-Pierre. Birthday photos show a line of grinning, bare-chested boys, and me in a red, one-piece bathing suit. Our moms unleashed us every morning to play in each other's yards until sundown. I laughed and competed with them. We fought and cheered each other up. We invented games and imaginary enemies together. I loved them.

But when we started school, we were bullied. Older boys followed me and Patrick around, telling us to kiss. If I spoke back, they threatened to hit me. Mark told me to hide in a tree when he saw them approaching and I obeyed for my own safety.

Eventually the bullies won, but the more popular explanation was time and hormones. The old story goes that after a few years of taunting, you turn nine or 10 years old and boys don't want to invent games with you anymore. They don't want to race you. They want two things: not to be bullied and to talk *about* other girls, and you can't be around for either one.

"Okay, but aren't women just interested in other things? You can't blame sexism," my colleagues say. I haven't mentioned sexism, only described experiences, but they don't trust my descriptions.

Making new friends as a kid was hard. Girls found me juvenile. I didn't understand the complex rules of their friendships. It took a long time and a lot of work. Meanwhile, I buried myself in creative projects. Anything a person could make, I wanted to be the one making it.

I signed up for a coding club at lunch. There were four computers for five kids. The instructor gave me a piece of paper and told me to draw.

"We usually let the boys have computer time."

I volunteered for carpentry for a school play.

"We usually save that job for boys."

If everything good was reserved for boys and it was going to be twice as hard to get their jobs, I decided to work five times harder to protect my odds. I taught myself. I grew up and went to work. I spent years building and coding beside men who offered creepy massages and laughed and told me to go make them a sandwich. Eventually, I arrived in games.

"This industry is hard for everyone. You can't let that stop you from trying," my colleagues say. "How else are you going to change it?"

Am I going to change it?

I'm 41 now, not nine. Time runs faster every year I don't give up. Although my throat still clamps shut each time I realize I'm alone in a new room surrounded by men, I am very good at being outnumbered. The same way a street performer may juggle chainsaws, this is my act.

Chainsaw juggling must be demanding. Performing under the glare of the sun for small change from skeptics who just want you to drop one. Why do we do this? Do I find familiarity in the discomfort of being outnumbered? Does the juggler choose chainsaws simply to stand out?

After a lifetime of being outnumbered, from the nursery to middle age, here's what I know:

Standing out is not always an advantage. From career support to secret handshakes, learning how to get along with women has given me far more than knowing how to get along with men. I am a lot, all by myself. I am That Girl and I like it. You can totally blame sexism. In fact, go ahead and blame any of the "isms" that apply.

I trust your descriptions and I promise not to drown you out with what's left of my chainsaw act.

I've picked up my mother's habit of looking for women, but the difference is now I'm looking to include, not be included. I don't think women should have to work five times harder, or even twice as hard. How about half? Take a nap. I'll keep an eye on your odds.

In a future I imagine, even mediocre women enjoy the comfort of reasonable success. Like the men who no longer outnumber us, we all get by, putting in effort that is pretty good—most of the time—and then we relax and create a new handshake.

We *all* get to use the handshake. You don't have to look like me or think like me. You don't have to trust me back. I don't need creative control or a copyright on the content of the handshake.

We go off together, hand in hand, or split up our own ways, to comb every alley and intersection. We find the women who've been subject to ableism or racism or ageism or homophobia or transphobia or something else we don't even know about yet, and we invite each of them to tell us where to go next and then we do it.

I'm not going to change anything. But we are.

My mother is reading a quiz: "If you could die and come back as anything, would you come back as a woman?"

I think about it. "Yeah. What would you come back as?"

She answers right away. "A woman with a sword."

Yes. Definitely a sword. I'm hanging up my chainsaw.

A DAY IN THE LIFE OF...

A SENIOR ANIMATOR

Animators merge art and technology to bring characters, creatures, and environments to life. Nuance is key for successful animators, as they must convey mood and emotion through lifelike movement, down to the smallest ticks and gestures. Tracy Jasperson has worked for over a decade in the field of game animation, including helping to define Lara Croft's identity through scrappy combat and fledgling traversal skills in the rebooted *Tomb Raider* series.

TRACY JASPERSON

PROFESSION: SENIOR ANIMATOR AT CRYSTAL DYNAMICS—REDWOOD CITY, USA

YEARS IN PROFESSION: 10

ASSOCIATED WITH: THE SIMS 3, CHAMPIONS ONLINE, STAR TREK ONLINE, TOMB RAIDER (2013), RISE OF THE TOMB RAIDER, SHADOW OF THE TOMB RAIDER, THE AVENGERS PROJECT

▶ EDUCATION

"I earned a Bachelor of Arts degree from Cogswell Polytechnical College in Sunnyvale, California. I also completed the Animation Mentors program."

▶ BREAKING IN

"It was difficult for me to break into the industry. Most companies that I initially applied to were looking for people with some industry experience. Also, the demo reel that I had created in school was not game-specific enough. After I realized this I created a new demo reel with more game animations, like run cycles, deaths, attacks, synced fights, and I added some of the more cinematic pieces as well."

▶ KEY QUALITIES

"On all the animations teams that I have worked on, one thing has been consistent – we are a team. We work together, help each other, and give each other ideas and feedback. Being a team player is important. Realizing that we are one team working towards the same goal and that we will fail or succeed together is an important fact to consider. Also, good communication and organizational skills are very important as well. For someone trying to break into the industry I think the '3 Ps' are the most important. Passion, Perseverance, and Persistence. It is important to be passionate and show that passion in your work and in your interviews. It is imperative that you persevere through the hard times and stay motivated, and it is essential that you are persistent. These qualities served me well when I was trying to get into the industry."

▶ TRAINING OPPORTUNITIES

"I would definitely encourage animators who are new to the industry to continue to expand their animation knowledge and improve their skills. There are many different ways to do that. Online animation courses like Ianimate or Animation Mentor can be very helpful, but you can also just practice on your own. Challenging yourself with your own side projects is a great way to hone your skills. There are a lot of great, free resources online."

▶ TOOLS OF THE TRADE

"We use Maya to animate and tools within Maya that our tech art team creates for us. We also use some other proprietary tools for animation implementation."

▶ HOURS & ENVIRONMENT

"I usually work an 8-hour day, but sometimes when I get really passionate about something I choose to work more. We also do 'crunch' at certain times during a project, but that is to be expected working on AAA video games. Crunch time can consist of longer work days, up to 10 to 12 hours long, or even include weekends, but it usually doesn't continue for very long. Each company I have worked for has handled 'crunch' time differently."

▶ AN AVERAGE DAY

"On an average workday, we have morning team meetings to check work status and get everyone on the same page. Then I go over my tasks for the day with my lead and I get started on my daily tasks. Right now I am on a team that works primarily on systemic gameplay animations, so my work is a collaborative effort between designers, programmers, and myself. Each team works differently and has a varied amount of interaction with other disciplines. For example, an animator on the cinematic team may not work with a designer or programmer at all, while an animator on the systemic gameplay team works with programmers a lot."

▶ PROFESSIONAL PERKS

"The perks of being an animator in the game industry are different depending on what company you work for and what game you are working on. The perks I enjoy working at Crystal Dynamics on the Tomb Raider games are that we get some awesome Tomb Raider swag and free games, we get to perform our own motion capture, we get to work with amazing people, and sometimes even meet celebrities. For a promotional event for the Tomb Raider movie, Alicia Vikander came to our studio to meet the team and it was an exciting experience for all of us."

▶ CAREER CHALLENGES

"Balancing my overtime is the biggest challenge for me. We don't work overtime that often, but when we work long hours close to a deadline it is easy for me to over work myself and get burned out. It is important to plan carefully and balance that time so that overtime work hours are efficient and productive. Extra hours are wasted time if they are not productive. Work smart and efficient and make that extra time count."

▶ FAVORITE PROJECT

"Tomb Raider is the coolest thing I have been a part of in my career, and it is also what I am most proud of. I grew up watching my older brother play the original Tomb Raider games and I thought Lara Croft was so amazing. She was so strong and independent and kicked some major butt! When I saw the teaser trailer for the 2013 reboot game, I knew I needed to be a part of it. Working at Crystal Dynamics, I got to animate Lara Croft and I even put on the mocap suit to act out some of her movements and attacks. Working on these games has been a dream come true for me and it has been an amazing experience."

▶ LIFE HACKS

"I learned the importance of proper planning in school and it is something that I still feel very strongly about today. I was taught that the time you spend on something should be broken up into 80% planning and 20% execution. At first that sounded ridiculous to me, but after putting it into practice, it made sense and is actually extremely efficient. As far as animation goes, planning includes a clear outline of the idea, reference footage, timing layout, posing, storyboards, and so on. The execution is the implementation of that planning. With proper planning, the execution phase can be fast and easy."

▶ BIGGEST MISTAKE

"A mistake in interviews early in my career, more specifically focused on my demo reel. Now that I am someone who interviews prospective animators, I have learned the error of my ways. In the past, I did not focus my demo reels to be clear and specific to the job I was applying for. If the animation job you are applying for is systemic gameplay animation, then load your demo reel with systemic gameplay animation examples. If you are applying for a cinematic animator job, then put cinematic performance animation on your reel. It sounds simple but many people don't do this and, in the past, I didn't either. Instead, I had a mix of random student work or previous game project work. If the position is for an all-around animation job that will include many types of animation, then by all means mix it up! But if the position is specific, then your demo reel should also be more focused."

PRO TIP!

"My advice to an industry hopeful is to work hard, be passionate, and don't give up. Continue to learn and grow and collaborate with other animators. Be a friend and a mentor, share what you learn. This is a competitive industry but it is better and more beneficial to work together, share knowledge and be supportive. It is also a very small industry and the person who you help and support today could be the person interviewing you for a job in the future!"

SZE JONES

CREATING CHARACTERS THAT BLUR FANTASY AND REALITY

 Art & Jewelry of Sze Jones  szejones

 szesjones.com

EXPERIENCE

FIRST INDUSTRY PROJECT: EVERQUEST II CINEMATIC—ANTONIA BAYLE (2004)

FAVORITE INDUSTRY PROJECT: RISE OF THE TOMB RAIDER (2014)

PROJECTS SHIPPED: 30 GAMES

ACHIEVEMENTS UNLOCKED:

> GNOMON SCHOOL OF VISUAL EFFECTS HOLLYWOOD ARTIST & PRESENTER—"THE MAKING OF WARHAMMER ONLINE: AGE OF RECKONING TRAILER" (2010)

> CGSOCIETY ONLINE WORKSHOP INSTRUCTOR—"ICONIC HEROINE DESIGN AND CREATION" (2011-2015)

> LOS ANGELES ACADEMY OF FIGURATIVE ART INSTRUCTOR—"FEMALE PORTRAIT STUDY WITH ZBRUSH" (2013-2014)

> CD PROJEKT RED PROMISED LAND PRESENTER—"FEMALE PORTRAIT & HAIR SCULPTING IN ZBRUSH" (2016)

STATS

INDUSTRY LEVEL: 21

CURRENT CLASS: SENIOR CHARACTER ARTIST

CURRENT GUILD: STUDIO WILDCARD—SEATTLE, USA

SPECIAL SKILLS: ILLUSTRATION, PAINTING, 3D MODELING, TEXTURING, RIGGING, CHARACTER DESIGN, JEWELRY DESIGN

 STANDARD EQUIPMENT

FAVORITE PLATFORM: PLAYSTATION

GO-TO GENRE: CO-OP, THIRD-PERSON ADVENTURE RPGS

MUST-HAVE GAME: FINAL FANTASY VII

BIO

Celebrated character artist Sze Jones remembers being in NYC's Chinatown, visiting her favorite video game store, when she first saw the cinematic opening of *Final Fantasy VII*. "It was playing on the TV screen. My body was frozen and my breath slowed," Sze remembered. "I was deeply inspired and decided then I want to be part of a team and create such impactful experiences. I immediately used all the money from my paycheck to purchase the Japanese version of the game, and spent hours translating each line of dialogue with a pocket-sized Japanese dictionary."

Games were in Sze's blood. When she was a child, her father worked at an Atari retail shop in Hong Kong. She was allowed to play all-new releases in the back room. Additionally, a family friend ran a nearby arcade, and she was given the master key and unlimited tokens. That being said, Sze had never seen a CG cutscene before *Final Fantasy VII*. She was blown away by the realism and emotion that could be conveyed through computer graphics. "When I was in college, there were not many schools that had a gaming program," she recalled. "I first started with a graphic design program, learning to handcraft letters with a French curve and using the first version of Photoshop. In my sophomore year, I found out there was a 'Special Effects for Television and Film' class. I took it and discovered a career path for the movie and film industry. I also enrolled in several classes using the first-generation 3D computer, the IRIS Wavefront 3130. In graduate school, I had access to a computer lab full of Silicon Graphics stations. I learned how to animate, model, texture, rig, and make short films." By 1997, Sze had completed a master's of art degree, majoring in computer graphics.

Easter Egg

Is a multidisciplinary artist who also designs, sculpts, and casts her own rings and pendants. She recently trained under a fourth-generation diamond setter and intends to incorporate gemstones into future designs.

BLURRING THE LINES

In 2002, Sze found her first touchpoint to the video game industry through Blur Studio, an award-winning visual effects, animation, and design studio often utilized by game studios for promotional materials such as trailers. Sze's work at Blur would be prolific over the next eight years.

High-resolution, cinematic character creation was at the heart of her day-to-day, including developing a pipeline for best practices and quality control. She would light, composite, and render scenes for a variety of uses. "All the footage was pre-rendered and composited after with layers of effects and graphical elements to achieve a stunning visual result," said Sze. "The end product was absolutely beautiful, but the process was labor-intensive and time-consuming." Her first professional character work was preparing Antonia Bayle for an *EverQuest II* cinematic.

Female game characters were—and remain today—Sze's specialty, including rigging, cloth simulation, hair simulation, hairstyling, and digital makeup design. While at Blur, she also researched how to improve facial-expression setups and lip-sync animations for more lifelike characters. Over eight years she created in-game cinematic scenes starring Dark Elf Sorceress from *Warhammer Online: Age of Reckoning*, *Æon Flux*, *Age of Conan*'s Keira, *Dante's Inferno*'s Beatrice, *Golden Axe*'s Tyris, *Star Wars: The Old Republic*'s Eleena Daru, and *Fable II*'s Theresa. She also contributed to assets for *BioShock*, Clive Barker's *Jericho*, *Hellgate: London*, *BloodRayne*, and *Empire Earth*.

Outside of in-game assets, she worked on Satele Shan for the *Star Wars: The Old Republic*'s E3 Trailer, *Hope*, and most notably Jack and Miranda for the *Mass Effect 2* interview-styled character videos. Sze also created key pieces of art for posters or magazine covers, such as *Tomb Raider: Underworld*'s shark-infested renders.

As she became more senior at Blur, Sze would oversee character art direction and supervise a team, including managing and providing artistic feedback for outsourced assets.

TOMB RAIDERS

Toward the end of her time at Blur, Sze saw the first Unreal Engine Showcase at the annual Game Developers Conference. "I realized that making characters in real time was the future and decided that I would love to start working for a game studio and bringing the cinematic artistry to real-time characters," she explained.

In 2010, Sze landed at Naughty Dog as lead character artist, putting her on the front lines of the most impressive and lifelike in-game characters in the business. "I was able to contribute my artistry and knowledge from the cinematic world into the game engine," she recalled. "I fell deeply in love with making real-time characters." Starting with *Uncharted 3: Drake's Deception*, Sze focused on creating high-resolution character head sculpts for the trio of female characters: Chloe Frazer, Elena Fisher, and Katherine Marlowe. She also authored facial blendshapes for more realistic facial expressions, and contributed hairstyling "cards" to make the most lifelike hair possible.

"I remember when working on *Uncharted 3*, they had a 3D TV playing one of the cinematic cutscenes with water rushing out," said Sze. "I put the 3D goggles on, and the character I created was running toward me in life-size. I had never experienced my character face-to-face, so that was pretty cool!"

"Following that, I participated in *Uncharted 4*," she continued. "I teamed up with rigging lead and facial-animation experts to develop a facial pipeline for use in the game." Sze also provided pre-production character supervision on *The Last of Us*.

"I realized that making characters in real time was the future and decided that I would love to start working for a game studio and bringing the cinematic artistry to real-time characters."

After nearly three years at Naughty Dog, Sze moved to Crystal Dynamics, first working on *Lara Croft and the Temple of Osiris*, followed by *Rise of the Tomb Raider*. "I started at the company that currently made my first heroine and, in doing so, achieved my dream to be the hairstylist for Lara Croft! With all the digital styling experience I accumulated, I collaborated and developed the hair technology alongside a team of extraordinary engineers," she explained. As at Naughty Dog, she created facial blendshapes, and modeled, rigged, and textured both low-poly characters and high-quality cinematic characters, in addition to working on promotional art. After Crystal Dynamics, Sze spent two years as lead character artist on Outpost Games' *Project: SOS*, creating characters from concept to completion.

TRAINING NEW TALENT

Sze's art has evolved over the years, but more importantly, she learned how to effectively cooperate in a fast-paced, always-evolving, collaborative environment. "Besides having fun making characters, there was problem-solving, debugging, and testing for each step of production," she said. "Knowing software is not enough. In most cases the solution required knowing multiple disciplines and involved more than one department to solve the puzzles. Making video games is a team effort; it is most appreciated when each member of the team is selfless, not only making sure the components works well but also being mindful about how to make the job easier for the next person."

Armed with two decades of experience, Sze now shares her learnings with upcoming talent. "I taught a six-month online course for four years titled 'Iconic Heroine Design and Creation,' hosted by CGSociety.org," she said. "I designed the curriculum for preparing students to obtain a position in the game industry as a character artist. It is a very in-depth course that covers all the essential processes and workflows in order to perform production tasks."

Other workshops have included courses at the Los Angeles Academy of Figurative Arts, Otis College of Art and Design, Gnomon School of Visual Effects, the Art Institute of Los Angeles, Santa Monica College, and SIGGRAPH. She's also been invited to international events such as CD Projekt Red's Promised Land gathering, where she taught "Female Portrait & Hair Sculpting in ZBrush."

"I feel that it is an honor and privilege to teach and to help aspiring artists," closed Sze. "It is rewarding to share knowledge and valuable insights from years of accumulated experience. It makes me happy to see them grow, and it is inspirational to see their art become mature and polished. Till this day I hear from students from time to time and know they are doing well—those are my most fulfilling moments."

ROBIN HUNICKE

AMPLIFYING NEW VOICES & EXPERIMENTAL PLAY

 Hunicke

 Robin Hunicke

 funomena.com

EXPERIENCE

FIRST INDUSTRY PROJECT: THE SIMS 2: OPEN FOR BUSINESS (2006)

CAREER HIGHLIGHT: WORKING WITH STEVEN SPIELBERG ON BOOM BLOX (2008)

PROJECTS SHIPPED: 9 GAMES

ACHIEVEMENTS UNLOCKED:

> GAMASUTRA "TOP 20 WOMEN IN THE VIDEO GAME INDUSTRY" (2008)

> MICROSOFT "WOMEN IN GAMING AWARD FOR DESIGN" (2009)

> WINDOWS DEVELOPER "GAME CREATOR OF THE YEAR" AWARD—FUNOMENA (2017)

> PC MAGAZINE "TOP 10 MOST INFLUENTIAL WOMEN IN GAME DEVELOPMENT" (2018)

STATS

INDUSTRY LEVEL: 21

CURRENT CLASS: CEO, CHIEF CREATIVE DIRECTOR & ASSOCIATE PROFESSOR

CURRENT GUILD: FUNOMENA—SAN FRANCISCO, USA

SPECIAL SKILLS: GAME DESIGN, USER INTERFACE DESIGN, LEVEL DESIGN, PRODUCTION

STANDARD EQUIPMENT

FAVORITE PLATFORM: NINTENDO WII

GO-TO GENRE: SIMULATORS WITH CREATIVE COMPONENTS

MUST-HAVE GAME: PARAPPA THE RAPPER

BIO

Robin Hunicke was well into her computer science degree—working towards a future as a roboticist and AI programmer—when she sat in a talk on *The Sims* hosted by industry Icon Will Wright. Hunicke's curiosity wasn't fully satiated after the presentation. She approached Wright, asking question after question, trying to dissect the AI behavior and internal needs systems Sims were built on. "After a half an hour or so, he said, 'You know, you really sound like a game designer," Hunicke recalled. "And I took a step back and thought, 'Wow, I'm just a grad student. I'm just a computer scientist. I'm just a programmer.' I didn't really think of myself as a designer at the time. I laughed and replied, 'Oh, that's quite the compliment coming from you.'"

Easter Egg

Learned a lot of handcrafts as a child. She can make her own paper and baskets, and once wove a basket out of leftover telephone wire found on the street.

The conversation sparked something within Hunicke, and she came to the realization that her true interest was the systems that play was built on. "I was okay at programming systems, but I really wanted to think broadly about how games became playable," she said. "That was what gave me the first inkling that it might be a job for me."

FIRST IN CLASS

Six years later Hunicke dropped out of grad school—just before finishing her PhD—to work with Wright on *The Sims*. That six-year gap was foundational to her future career. "I wanted to build some of my own games, and I wanted to experiment with designing and make sure that I was good at it," said Hunicke. "And I realized that I could finish the dissertation and then go to games, or I could just start doing what I loved. I didn't need to wait to become a game designer. So that's what I did."

The road that led Hunicke back to *SimCity* was long and winding. "When I was studying in school, it was the late 1990s and the early 2000s. There were no college programs for video game design or video game programming," she explained. "I had to teach myself, and realized that it would be much better if there were programs that supported learning how to do this amazing and creative job."

Hunicke helped establish a community of academics interested in building programs, and together, they formalized their collective experience. "I helped design and promote the very first curriculum for video game programs at college level, along with the International Game Developers Association," Hunicke said. Over time, their work was implemented at prestigious schools such as Carnegie Mellon University, Massachusetts Institute of Technology, the University of Southern California, and eventually, the University of Santa Cruz, where Hunicke would later found and instruct a game design program as a full-time professor.

GAME JAMMING

The networking and relationship-building yielded another novel idea. "Some of the friends that I met building the program decided to do this thing called a 'game jam.' We got together for a weekend and made video games, and then put them on the Internet for free," recalled Hunicke. "I am the very first female game jammer on the planet Earth." Realizing the potential in creating rapid-iteration, experimental games, the original game jammers began to formalize and promote the activity. "It became a global phenomenon." Hunicke helped write the themes for the very first global game jam, and in doing so became a cornerstone of the international and still-thriving community.

> "I am the very first female game jammer on the planet Earth."

Six years after her first meeting with Will Wright, Hunicke joined Electronic Arts' studio Maxis, and began design work on *The Sims 2: Open for Business*, followed by *MySims*. Her third game at EA was in collaboration with one of the biggest names in entertainment—Steven Spielberg. The Hollywood giant surprised the industry when his anticipated EA collaboration turned out to be *Boom Blox* a physics-based puzzle game for the Nintendo Wii. *Boom Blox* took home game of the year awards for family and casual categories, as earned nods as an exceptional puzzle game. Hunicke led production for both the original *Boom Blox*, and the follow-up title, *Boom Blox Bash Party*.

Hunicke's resume continued stacking with innovative and experimental titles when she took up post at thatgamecompany as a producer on *Journey*. "*Journey* is a game where you walk to the top of a mountain, and maybe meet strangers along the way," she laughed. "It doesn't sound very fun, but when you have the experience, it can be quite moving. I like to work on things that are hard to describe, and genuinely delight their players." While the team knew they created something special, no one anticipated the success *Journey* would achieve, proving that an arthouse-style game could be both critically and commercially successful after sweeping the Game Developers Choice, BAFTA, and DICE Awards in 2012.

FOUNDING FUNOMENA

In 2013, Hunicke and *Journey* co-worker Martin Middleton co-founded their own game studio—Funomena. Described as a "deliberately developmental organization," they set out to recruit and retain people who thrived in uncertain and experimental environments. The studio would explore the crossroads of experimental games and new technology, starting with their first project, which built a game around data gathered from a pedometer.

Luna—described as a "VR fairytale"—was Funomena's first large-scale production. *Luna* follows the story of a bird tricked into eating part of the moon, throwing nature into disarray and ending far from home in the process. *Luna* released in late 2017 and took home a series of "Best of VR" awards, as well as landing Funomena the Windows Developer "Game Creator of the Year" Award. Funomena's next project—*Wattam*—is being developed in collaboration with Keita Takahashi, the creator and director of the fanciful *Katamari Damacy* series. Intended as a spiritual successor to *Katamari*, *Wattam* looks to be both experimental and playful in nature, hitting the design notes Hunicke has become known for.

AMPLIFYING NEW VOICES

In addition to Hunicke's personal outside-the-box contributions, she has a long history of empowering others to follow suit. "I'm really proud of the advocacy work that I've done for experimental games," she said. For the last 16 years, Hunicke has managed the annual Game Developers Conference Experimental Gameplay Workshop. "We showcase some of the best experimental designs every year," she continued. "We have 20 slots to showcase games, and we get over 250 submissions a year. We get to amplify the best and strangest and most innovative games." Many memorable games have made their debut at the Experimental Gameplay Workshop, including Valve's *Portal* and Jonathan Blow's *Braid*."

"I'm also really proud of Amplifying New Voices, which is another program I started. We fly 30 developers out to the Game Developers Conference and provide them a complimentary pass," she explained. "We give them training on how to be stronger public speakers and better advocates for diverse interests. We bring out women, people of color, differently abled developers, and people who are developers of age. And I'm really excited, because both of those programs have, in my opinion, helped create community, and amplify the number of people who are experimenting and making new things. It's so important that we enable new creators and new voices to be heard."

"What inspires my work is the desire to push the medium forward and understand what games can be, and what they aren't right now," closed Hunicke. "I like to be on the edge of what games are. I don't make games that have already been made. I will continue to develop games that are hard to describe."

LORRAINE MCLEES

20-YEAR BUNGIE GAMES VET & REYES-MCLEES SHIPYARDS FOUNDER

 Mehvechan  Lorraine McLees

EXPERIENCE

FIRST INDUSTRY PROJECT: MYTH: THE TOTAL CODEX (1999)

FAVORITE INDUSTRY PROJECT: HALO 3 (2007)

PROJECTS SHIPPED: 8 GAMES

ACHIEVEMENTS UNLOCKED:

> PATENT: BROWSER SENSITIVE WEB CONTENT DELIVERY (2005)

> PATENT: USER INTERFACE WITH VISUAL TRACKING FEATURE (2005)

> MI6 MARKETING AWARDS "BEST LIMITED EDITION/SPECIAL EDITION OR COLLECTOR'S EDITION"—HALO: REACH (2011)

STATS

INDUSTRY LEVEL: 20

CURRENT CLASS: ART LEAD, CONSUMER PRODUCTS

CURRENT GUILD: BUNGIE, INC.—BELLEVUE, USA

SPECIAL SKILLS: ILLUSTRATION, GRAPHIC DESIGN, LOGO DESIGN, 3D MODELING, TEXTURING, RIGGING

STANDARD EQUIPMENT

FAVORITE PLATFORM: XBOX ONE & PLAYSTATION 4

GO-TO GENRE: SCI-FI OR FANTASY ADVENTURE GAMES

MUST-HAVE-GAME: SECRET OF MANA

BIO

At a young age, Lorraine McLees wanted to be an archeologist. Or at least she thought she did. McLees had been infatuated with comics and illustration since her first memories of growing up in the Philippines. Eventually, she realized that she was drawn to the technical drawings that adorned the pages of archeological journals, more so than the academic insights. She was also a fan of video games, comic books, and manga—her career path in the world of art started to take shape with this personal revelation.

In her teens, after a time contributing editorial drawings to her high school newspaper, McLees was recommended for a larger gig at a citywide publication. She became the paper's graphics director shortly thereafter, working full-time while attending the American Academy of Art to further hone her skills. At age 25, she established an art department at an anime distribution company in Houston, but it wasn't long before her eye wandered back to her passions. She left to give her full attention to comics as an artist on *Elfquest*.

Soon after, one of her former classmates—Robert McLees—reached out, thinking she'd be a great addition to the art team at the then Chicago-based Bungie Software Products Corporation. Spoiler alert: she was a great fit at Bungie, and also a great fit with Robert—they eventually married.

BUNGIE SOFTWARE

McLees began her career at Bungie as a freelance illustrator and then part-time graphic designer. She was brought on to support the publishing team for their multiple releases and the anime-inspired title *Oni*, which catered perfectly to her fandom. After her first day clocked in at 12 hours, she knew the part-time status wouldn't last long. She fully left comics behind to take on the position of Art Director of Marketing at Bungie on April 12, 1999.

Aside from the logo, which had already been completed, everything visual associated with *Oni*'s identity was within McLees' scope of work. "The starring heroine had not been fleshed out," explained McLees. "I worked on key art, creating various illustrations of Konoko that served as brand identity. As the game was in its final stages, I also drew the win/loss screens, flashback screens, and the fly-in screens when characters spoke."

INTRODUCING, HALO

Her most lasting contribution in this period was finalizing the original *Halo* logo, which Bungie revealed to the world at Macworld in 1999. It has been the center of the universe's visual identity ever since. She designed one of *Halo*'s most iconic vessels—the Halcyon-class cruiser that takes the game's heroes to Halo. "It was a unique opportunity to design the Pillar of Autumn, the spaceship that you are in at the beginning of *Halo*.

Using the now iconic *Halo* assault rifle as the basis for the shape language, it was drawn up during a time when it didn't matter what team you were in (I was on the publishing team), but if you had the skill set and you weren't too terribly busy at the time, you could contribute to the company's output however you can."

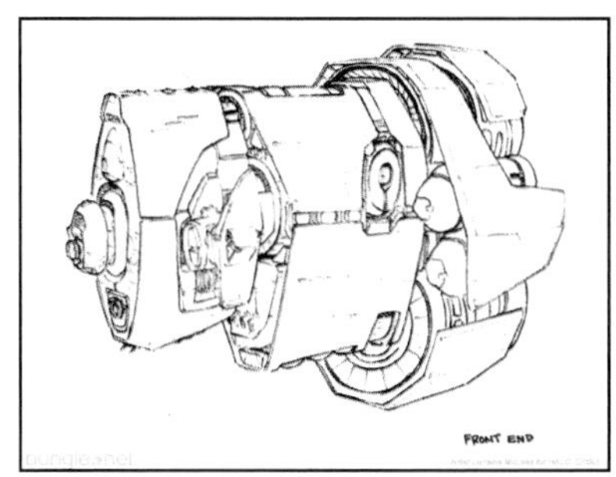

When Bungie was acquired by Microsoft in 2000, they made McLees an offer. She could choose to part ways with severance, stay with Bungie as a 3D artist, or take on a new role on the user experience team, as there wasn't an equivalent role for her in the new structure. "I had really just started bonding with my new Bungie family and didn't want to leave. I decided to join the team, which was made up of the folks who had worked on *Myth II*."

McLees chose the role of 3D artist, and her skills expanded as she learned to model, texture, and rig characters. In this role, she also provided studio brand support, such as the visual direction for Bungie's evolving website. She also aided with environment work on multiplayer levels and costume design for *Halo 2*.

She remembers *Halo 3* as her favorite project at the company. "It was the last time I would work with the Master Chief for marketing materials. But, more importantly, I was able to contribute to the creation of the Terminals," said McLees, speaking to the Forerunner machines that provide backstory to the player. "I already had a great work relationship with my husband, and working on the Terminals was one of the rare times I was able to work with him directly to put content in the game."

The work McLees led on prominent marketing materials is just as impressive as her in-game contributions. She spearheaded all of Bungie's *Halo* game covers—including the evolving logo treatments—and established the famous SMG-dual-wielding Master Chief for *Halo 2*'s "Golden" marketing campaign. "I was in a unique position where I had the line in on how art was made, had the ability to manipulate that art, create basic environments as needed to showcase those models. I could re-light a scene, pose characters, and extract printable materials—all in support for making sure that the marketing and promotional materials that accompanied the game the team was working so hard for looked great and had parity with the source material." In this capacity she also assisted in creating action figures and statues, and even supported the live-action *Halo* commercials by working with Microsoft's marketing team, the CG houses, and practical effects studios.

A NEW DESTINY

Evolving with Bungie, her work moved beyond *Halo* when the company split off from Microsoft in 2007 and entered a 10-year publishing deal with Activision Blizzard three years later. "I was the senior artist on the Visual ID and Design team during the transition to being independent again, and I designed the top secret *Destiny* pitch book that Bungie used to shop around for a good publishing partner. Once that ball was rolling, I worked with the franchise art director to establish the style guide for *Destiny* to help inform all our future graphics design endeavors," explained McLees. "Our team worked on every vidoc, every live-action commercial, every internal event and presentation, and in-game icons. On top of that, we also ran the Bungie Store and created the products we put up there. Where before, on *Halo*, we weren't in control of our own invention, our own intellectual property, and all licensing efforts went to Microsoft. With *Destiny*, it's ours."

"Championing a franchise is a never-ending task."

"It became really obvious very early on that our team had to rise to the challenge of owning our own IP. And so the Licensing team—most recently rebranded as the Consumer Products team—had to be born," she continued. "As the art lead on the consumer products team, I get the supremely fun task of developing consumer goods with like-minded partners and teammates to empower our community with the means to share their enthusiasm for *Destiny*. So if you happen to see a piece of *Destiny* product in the store shelves or on the Bungie store, I had a hand in it. And if it makes you go 'squee!' then, my friend, you have shared in my joy!"

With 20 years of perspective behind her, McLees reflected on how the studio has changed. "In 2000, I was the only female on the dev team. Until 2006 or so, I had the washrooms all to myself, and nowadays there is sometimes an actual LINE to use the washroom. We all marvel and feel great about what it implies. But for the most part, where I sit, it's pretty much the same. It is a lot of hard work, but it's also really fun work."

"Championing a franchise is a never-ending task," McLees concluded. "My kids have been enjoying *Halo* and *Destiny* for some time. We have fond memories of playing Firefight and completing raids together. I would like to think that I have created and fostered a comfortable environment for the kids to thrive in and hopefully grow into well-adjusted adults. Achievements unlocked!"

A DAY IN THE LIFE OF...

A UI/UX DESIGNER

User Interface and User Experience design are unsung heroes of game development. An interface designer must balance usability with game aesthetics, never sacrificing the player's ability to quickly process information in exchange for visual flair. When done well, most players won't notice the hard work put into on-screen text, menus, and the player HUD.

User Experience is a more nebulous and evolving field, focusing on the study of how players experience a game from start to finish. The practice involves using fundamentals of psychology and research through playtests or analytics to ensure that the end-user experience aligns with the design intention of the product. UX works to minimize player frustration and make playing the game as frictionless as possible by accounting for unconscious bias. A game designer may think an in-game mission's next step is obvious, only to be surprised by mass confusion or frustration popping up on post-launch forums.

Amrita Bharij has extensive industry experience in both UI and UX design, having worked at Electronic Arts, Playfish, Natural Motion, Space Ape Games, and Rockstar Games. She works to ensure the interface design and overall user experience seamlessly support the player though their virtual journey.

AMRITA BHARIJ

 Jamrita00  Amrita Bharij  amrita-bharij.com

PROFESSION: UI/UX DESIGNER AT ROCKSTAR GAMES—LONDON, UNITED KINGDOM

YEARS IN PROFESSION: 12

ASSOCIATED WITH: RED DEAD REDEMPTION 2, THE SIMS SOCIAL, SIM CITY SOCIAL, HARRY POTTER AND THE DEATHLY HALLOWS 2, HARRY POTTER AND THE DEATHLY HALLOWS 1, HASBRO FAMILY GAME NIGHT 2, HARRY POTTER AND THE HALF BLOOD PRINCE, HARRY POTTER AND THE ORDER OF THE PHOENIX, TRANSFORMERS: EARTH WARS, RIVAL KINGDOMS, SAMURAI SIEGE

▶ EDUCATION

"I chose to do my Honors degree in Computer Arts at Abertay, Scotland, which was a digital interactive art course back then, but has recently become tailored towards video games. At the time there wasn't too much in the way of games courses, but my passion has always been about making video games. I entered a competition called 'Dare to Be Digital' during my last year at university and took part in that after I graduated. The goal was to make a playable demo with an original idea in 10 weeks with a team of five others. We didn't win but it exposed our work to various games studios. After that, I was offered an internship as a Designer at BBC Scotland where I made web games and a role as an Interface Designer at EA, where I worked for seven years across three different studios."

▶ BREAKING IN

"Breaking into the industry took a lot of hard work while I was still studying. I tried to grab opportunities to get work experience, as well as making my portfolio and taking part in making a demo. I remember one of the obstacles was trying to have a variety of different art styles for applying to different games companies. It's impossible to cover everything when you start out.

"I definitely recommend looking out for competitions and game jams as a method of breaking into the industry. They're great because they force you to work under competitive environments and time constraints. If you can't find any of these programs, be proactive and make concept projects tailored to your desired role."

▶ EARLY INDUSTRY IMPRESSIONS

"When I first started, I was so grateful to be part of something so innovative and new, a combination of tech, art, problem solving, creativity and collaboration. I was surprised at how exciting the industry was. When I was a kid in the '80s, I had no idea I'd be making video games as a day job. I couldn't imagine going to work could be so fun!"

▶ KEY QUALITIES

"A lot of qualities and personality traits are imperative to have in this profession, like communication. Being great at collaborating with others and finding their strengths. Teamwork is the name of the game. Understanding other roles within a team. Learning what others do will help everything gel together and help you realize what can be achieved. Encouragement and positivity; be willing to help others on the team and encourage ideas. Bring new ideas to the table. Be passionate about your work and the overall product."

▶ TOOLS OF THE TRADE

"I've used different tools in every studio at which I've worked. A great skill to have is the ability to adapt to new tools and processes because different studios use different tools and software, as technology evolves all the time. As well as the obvious stuff like Adobe Creative suite, I always find it helpful to use ink and paper to rapidly explore ideas before even thinking about creating it in software."

▶ HOURS & ENVIRONMENT

"Usually in the games industry we work core hours, but when a project is ramping up it's common for game developers to go the extra mile and work longer hours. This is mainly because you're always thinking about your product all the time and having so much passion for the game!"

▶ AN AVERAGE DAY

"An average day as a UX/UI Designer varies depending on which part of the project timeline you're working on. Even though there are concept phases, building and implementing, testing and polishing, the role of a UX Designer is deeply collaborative. It entails working with the team to find solutions, so there are a lot of meetings and brainstorming even before initial designs are carried out."

▶ PROFESSIONAL PERKS

"There are so many fun things that are perks of this profession, such as having to play games as research and working with amazing people—you end up making friends along the way. Personally, the main perk of my profession is doing what I love every day, which is combining design and making people happy. For example, creating a platform for those who aren't able to play physical sports or drive in real life, video games provide an avenue to enable people to have those experiences."

▶ CAREER CHALLENGES

"The user experience of a game encapsulates some of the trickiest parts of game development because it's the glue that holds everything together. Everything has to be done just right. If it isn't carried out in the best way, it can result in frustrated players who don't know how to progress within a feature and it can potentially lose players. Designing the means of communication in every interaction type is challenging because it has to balance the usability with appropriate themes, tones, and visuals. As well as teaching or subtly guiding the player, there are many technical challenges like catering for multiple languages, resolutions, and outputs just to name a few.

▶ FAVORITE PROJECT

"One of the coolest things that I'm grateful for is the opportunity I've had to work in different countries, such as China and the US and learning about different cultures and work ethics in other parts of the world. In fact, even in the UK I've had the pleasure of working with so many people from all over the globe, it shows how diverse the games industry is!"

PRO TIP!

"Tailor your design to what the player wants or needs rather than what you personally like; always have the end user in mind. Don't be precious with your designs. They are bound to change multiple times so never get attached; go with what is right for each feature. Also, make sure your product has regular test sessions so you can act on feedback and input from the end user and work it into the game!"

JADE RAYMOND

CHAMPION FOR CREATIVELY LED AND DIVERSE DEVELOPMENT

 ibjade

Jade Raymond

EA.com/studios/motive

EXPERIENCE

FIRST INDUSTRY PROJECT: JEOPARDY! (1998)

FAVORITE INDUSTRY PROJECT: ASSASSIN'S CREED (2017)

PROJECTS SHIPPED: 12 GAMES, FOUNDED 2 STUDIOS

ACHIEVEMENTS UNLOCKED:

> FORTUNE "10 MOST POWERFUL WOMEN IN GAMING" (2013)

> CANADIAN BUSINESS "CHANGE AGENTS" (2016)

> INSPIRING 50 "INSPIRING 50: CANADA 2018"

> DEVELOP "VANGUARD AWARD" (2018)

 STATS

INDUSTRY LEVEL: 20

CURRENT CLASS: SVP & GROUP GENERAL MANAGER

CURRENT GUILD: EA MOTIVE STUDIOS—MONTRÉAL & VANCOUVER, CANADA

SPECIAL SKILLS: GAME DESIGN, TEAM BUILDING, PROGRAMMING, PRODUCTION

STANDARD EQUIPMENT

FAVORITE PLATFORM: SEGA GENESIS

GO-TO GENRE: ACTION

MUST-HAVE GAME: RESIDENT EVIL 4

BIO

The Apple II and Sega Genesis were early influences that guided Jade Raymond toward working in video games. "In grade school, I got an Apple II hand-me-down from a cousin, and became hooked on the early text-based adventure games," began Raymond. Around the same time, she participated in a trial robotics program and would often be found building and programming her creations after school.

A trip to the West Coast at 14 resulted in the moment of clarity she needed to cement her future career path. "I spent a summer living in San Francisco with my uncle Lenny, who worked in the gaming industry," said Raymond. "His Sega Genesis and huge collection of games got my attention for months and fired up my competitive nature. While challenging him, it occurred to me, 'I love video games, and someone makes video games. Why not me?'"

Several years later, Raymond enrolled in the booming computer-science program at McGill University, studying programming, with fine-art courses fit in where she could. "I filled my summers with internships at the budding consumer-interactive divisions of Microsoft and IBM. In the early days of the web as mass medium, the companies were experimenting with virtual worlds and other game-related ventures, trying to find commercial applications," she explained.

R&D AT SONY ONLINE

In 1998—three days after graduation—Raymond had a hard-earned job at Sony Online. "Over the course of my bachelor's degree, I worked hard to find game-related internships, and I saved up money working the night shift at a hospital so I could go to GDC and E3 and network," she said. Using a spreadsheet with contacts from years of networking, she reached out to 50 people at various companies, eventually securing three job offers.

Easter Egg

Moved to a remote part of Jamaica at six years old to set up a clinic with her family. With no hospitals for miles, her house became a local emergency room. She distinctly remembers encountering a man who had a huge chicken bone lodged in his throat, and another who sought treatment for a machete in his head.

Raymond quickly put her programming skills to use with a focus on online initiatives as the R&D tech lead. Her time was split between the online version of *Jeopardy!*, *Trivial Pursuit*, and the Sony Online platform as a whole. "I was the backend server programmer for Sony's parlor games," she said.

"This included about six versions of *Jeopardy!*: *Sports Jeopardy!*, *College Jeopardy!*, the PalmPilot version of *Jeopardy!*... You get the picture!"

ESTABLISHING A CREED

Moving on from Sony Online, Raymond spent a short period in 2002 at Electronic Arts, transitioning from programming to production for *The Sims Online*. Shortly after, she took a leap of faith to virtual-world start-up *There*—which eventually floundered due to lack of funds—as a senior producer.

With an already impressive track record, there were no lack of job opportunities for Raymond, and she accepted a position at Ubisoft Montréal. Though she was initially tasked with working on a next-generation *Prince of Persia*, the game evolved into something original—*Assassin's Creed*. As producer and co-creator of the premiere game in 2007, Raymond and the talented team at Ubisoft Montréal worked tirelessly to bring to life a fictional retelling of real-world events, focusing on centuries of struggles between assassins and Templars.

Assassin's Creed established a universe that would become one of the biggest in gaming—complete with a silver-screen adaptation. After the game received generally favorable reviews from critics and commercial success, Raymond would help refine the *Assassin's Creed* formula with its acclaimed sequel, which fans argue is where the franchise truly found its footing.

With the launch of *Assassin's Creed*, Raymond's public visibility skyrocketed—she often found herself in front of cameras and on major stages around the world. The exposure wasn't always easy to contend with. "When young women tell me that they decided to join the game industry because of me, that makes me proud," Raymond explained. "I think that's one of the reasons why, despite the difficulties of putting yourself out there, it's important for me personally to be a little bit more visible when I get opportunities to speak. It's my way of trying to project a positive view."

Trusting in Raymond's ability to get the new IP off the ground, she took lead on all new property. Involved in the pitch process from the very start, Raymond would validate the most promising IP proposals. Both *Watch Dogs* in 2014 and *The Mighty Quest for Epic Loot* in 2015 were greenlit under her watchful eye and benefited from her production leadership.

In 2009 Raymond helped found Ubisoft Toronto, acting as the studio's general manager. Ubisoft Toronto's first title—*Tom Clancy's Splinter Cell: Blacklist*—hit store shelves in 2013, with Raymond as executive producer.

She also helped kick-start another original IP—the fourth during her time at Ubisoft—called *Starlink: Battle for Atlas*, which launches in late 2018. Raymond's influence at Ubisoft was felt over multiple studios, across country lines, and by fans worldwide.

ENTER EA

After 10 eventful years at Ubisoft, Raymond returned to early employer EA as SVP and group general manager of Motive Studios (in both Montréal and Vancouver). Founded in 2015 in Montréal, Motive would be built from the ground up and focus on new IP.

"I love creating new IP and building new teams," said Raymond. "Neither of these things are easy, but if you get through all the hurdles and manage to create a brand that people love and a workplace where people can be happy and do their best work, then I think you can have a positive impact on people. That's what motivates me," she added, providing insight into the studio's name.

Photo credit: Alexandre De Bellefeuille

Raymond runs the studio on two mantras: creating a new process for development that is creative-led, and building teams that are truly diverse. Her ultimate goal is to ensure creativity returns to an industry that she feels can be bogged down by massive teams and formulaic approval processes. Additionally, Raymond's love for new IP is based on a belief of social responsibility in gaming. "I would like games to take their cultural impact and significance more seriously," she explained. "People are spending so much time in our game worlds and experiences, I think that developers have an obligation to make that time more enriching."

> "I would like games to take their cultural impact and significance more seriously."

FIGHTING FOR DIVERSITY

"The hardest thing I have ever tried to do is develop a new kind of creatively lead and truly diverse culture at Motive," said Raymond. "There are so many benefits to having diverse teams and I do truly believe that's how you make the best games. I have realized in the last year that it's more challenging than I thought. When you get people with different backgrounds, who make games in different ways, made games at different publishers, have different points of view, have a different way of calling things...two people may be using the same word, but it might mean different things. It's a lot more work. Everyone must be in that frame of mind to create a truly open culture that integrates what everyone has to offer."

With this in mind, Raymond has carefully curated her team at EA Motive. She's brought on people from franchises like *Portal*, *Assassin's Creed* and *GTA*, just to name a few. She hired individuals with AAA experience, indie experience, and everything in between. She's even hired from outside the games industry. And she's put in the time required to ensure that everyone is speaking the same language and is aligned on the same goals through the process.

We don't yet know what the team at Motive is cooking up, but Raymond says that the projects her team is working on are her favorite yet—a promising statement in such a landmark career.

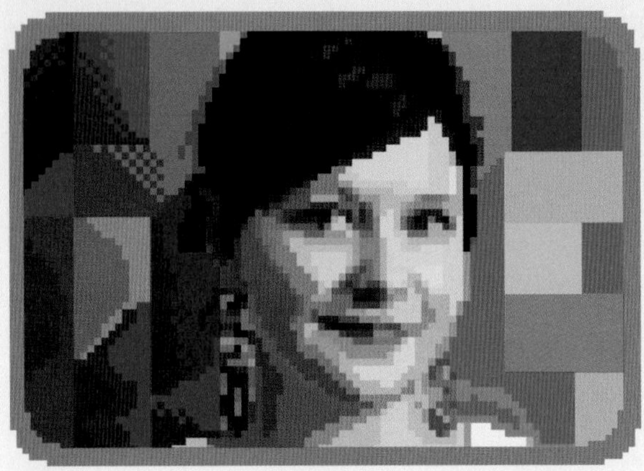

SIOBHAN REDDY

INSPIRING THE WORLD TO CREATE TOGETHER

siobhanreddy

siobhanreddy

Siobhan Reddy

EXPERIENCE

FIRST INDUSTRY PROJECT: DISCWORLD NOIR (1998)
FAVORITE INDUSTRY PROJECT: LITTLEBIGPLANET (2008)
PROJECTS SHIPPED: 8 GAMES
ACHIEVEMENTS UNLOCKED:
> MICROSOFT WOMEN IN GAMING AWARDS "PRODUCTION AWARD" (2009)
> MICROSOFT WOMEN IN GAMING AWARDS "INNOVATOR AWARD" (2014)
> QANTAS "AUSTRALIAN WOMAN OF THE YEAR" (2013)
> FORTUNE "10 POWERFUL WOMEN IN GAMING" (2014)

STATS

INDUSTRY LEVEL: 20
CURRENT CLASS: STUDIO DIRECTOR
CURRENT GUILD: MEDIA MOLECULE—GUILDFORD, UNITED KINGDOM
SPECIAL SKILLS: GAME DESIGN, COMMUNICATION, PRODUCTION, LEADERSHIP, THEATER

STANDARD EQUIPMENT

FAVORITE PLATFORM: PLAYSTATION
GO-TO GENRE: HORROR
MUST-HAVE GAME: RESIDENT EVIL

BIO

Born in South Africa and raised in Australia, Siobhan Reddy describes herself as an eclectic youth. Her interests were so varied and unique that for much of her formative years she was unsure how they could be funneled into a career. She spent her time championing unknown bands—and writing about them in her own fanzine—performing in theater, working for an indie record label, and eventually toying with the idea of working in film. Reddy loved all mediums of storytelling, and was equally fascinated by technology. Still in her teens, she wasn't yet aware of career options at the intersection of art and tech.

At the age of 18—still unsure of what to pursue in her adult life—Reddy picked up and moved to the United Kingdom. She got a job to keep a roof over her head, and was contemplating a return to theater until a friend called her attention to the realm of video games.

Easter Egg
Talks to trees.

Reddy wasn't a big gamer but, like most of her generation, had played games. She recalled *Donkey Kong* and *Monkey Island* growing up and had recently picked up the brand-new Sony PlayStation. "I was 19. Playing games like *Heart of Darkness* and *Resident Evil* on the PlayStation were the moments that I realized games were going to go to places way beyond film or theater," said Reddy. "They brought together my love of technology, theater, film, music, and dress-up all under one roof!"

A PERFECT OPPORTUNITY

Armed with this information, Reddy applied and was hired by Perfect Entertainment, working on *Discworld* games based on the Terry Pratchett novels. "My first project was *Discworld Noir*, and I mostly made Luci Black cups of tea and wrote meeting notes!" said Reddy. "I also did some localization, but I was so green it was mostly learning and doing administrative jobs whilst I learned." Black, the producer who hired Reddy at Perfect Entertainment, would later have the favor returned at Media Molecule. Black was the first of many strong relationships Reddy formed with women in the industry—a second being Perfect Entertainment's co-founder Angela Sutherland.

> "I realized that games were going to go places way beyond film or theater."

"I was surprised by how vibrant it was," Reddy continued, speaking to her initial impressions of the game industry. "I had worked at a web and graphic design company in Sydney and so knew what creative companies were like, but games had something else. It was electric as walking through a busy dance studio that has different forms of dance/music blasting out of every studio. I immediately fell in love with the creative chaos!"

LIFE IN THE FAST LANE

Reddy moved to Criterion Games in 1999, another studio with a woman co-founder—Fiona Sperry. "I arrived late in the dev process of *Trickstyle*, and I helped with the localization of it," she said. "I really enjoyed that, as I got to know the full game very quickly." As senior development manager, she helped bring the popular *Burnout* franchise to market in 2001, followed by work on *AirBlade*, *Burnout 3: Takedown*, and *Burnout 4: Revenge*.

"It was on-the-job training for me. I often think of my role at Criterion being almost like an apprenticeship," she said. "I learned so much from Fiona Sperry, and she gave me so much of her own time and I benefited massively from that approach."

"I was given some advice 'to always stay in the trenches with the troops' and not become one of 'those producers who looks on but isn't involved,'" she continued. "That really stayed with me; I don't know if I exactly knew what it meant until a bit later, as those first years were totally in the trenches. I learned that you bond with people for life when shipping—the first experience of starting with an idea and then going to buy the result of that idea from a shop en masse with your whole team is quite amazing." That lesson would be taken forward with Reddy to her next big endeavor.

MAKING A LITTLE BIG DIFFERENCE

In 2006, Reddy made a big leap of faith and left Criterion—alongside other industry veterans—to co-found Media Molecule in Guilford. In her role as executive producer, Reddy was pivotal in bringing Media Molecule's debut title—and runaway success—*LittleBigPlanet* to market. Players controlled an adorable avatar named Sackboy in a sandbox full of toys meant to encourage their imaginations to run wild; *LittleBigPlanet* was developed to facilitate user-generated content. In that regard, it seemed as if Reddy's life experiences had been building up to the game—a cacophony of eclectic images, items, sounds, and actions allowing players to create and share on a global stage.

LittleBigPlanet hit store shelves in 2008 and would become one of the most critically successful games in industry history. It went on to win eight out of 10 award categories at the AIAS Interactive Achievement Awards, including Game of the Year. It took home a BAFTA for "Artistic Achievement" and won four Game Developers Choice Awards, including the Innovation Award. "Shipping *LittleBigPlanet* and drinking a beautiful bottle of champagne with the team remains one of my favorite memories," recalled Reddy.

In 2009 Reddy took over Media Molecule as studio director, helping transition the team through their purchase by Sony Computer Entertainment that next year. A sequel of *LittleBigPlanet* kept the team busy through 2011.

"Shipping LittleBigPlanet and drinking a beautiful bottle of champagne with the team remains one of my favorite memories."

THE LIMELIGHT

That same year, at the age of 34, Reddy received a lot of attention herself. She was named one of the 100 most powerful women in the UK by the BBC and, not long after, was named "Australian Woman of the Year in the United Kingdom" by Qantas. The then-prime minster of Australia, Julia Gillard, even sent Reddy a congratulations video.

For someone who once thought she's find her home in theater, Reddy isn't fond of being in the limelight—as herself, at least. After receiving two high-visibility awards in a single year, it was hard not to be considered a public persona and a person of influence.

Until this point, Reddy had remained so focused on work—and had the good fortune of working at many female-friendly studios—that the issues surrounding gender bias and discrimination in the gaming industry hadn't personally affected her. As the topics began bubbling to the top of public discourse, Reddy made a point to ensure that their next new IP—*Tearaway*—featured male and female playable characters and began looking for other ways to use her newfound visibility for good.

A platform adventure told in a paper craft-inspired world, *Tearaway* released for the PlayStation Vita in 2013 and took full advantage of the unique features of the handheld system. Well received by critics for its stunning art style and creative play, *Tearaway* won three BAFTA awards across Handheld, Artistic Achievement.

Now, 13 years after starting the studio, Media Molecule is finishing up an ambitious new title. *Dreams* returns to the realm of user-generated content. Players must solve their way through levels, called dreams, and are encouraged to create their own to share and play online. "Every project has taught me something, and I love them all, but I am going to say *Dreams* has been the most challenging," said Reddy. "It's been the hardest by far in terms of pushing ourselves as a studio. We've had to learn so much, and the entire studio cares about it in a way that is unique to every other project I have worked on."

"I'd really like to think that I have helped some people along in their careers, and hopefully a couple of the teenagers who have come into the studio might be inspired to make video games in the future," concluded Reddy. "I love the act of making games and expressing myself in creative ways. I love the people who make games, and I am endlessly motivated to support people bringing their ideas to life. I love Media Molecule and hope to continue working with that bunch of brilliant people on the most mad and creative projects and get the world creating together."

MICHELLE HINN

ADVOCATING GAMES FOR ALL

 Vrgrrl

 Michelle Hinn

EXPERIENCE

FIRST INDUSTRY PROJECT: HALO (2001)

FAVORITE INDUSTRY PROJECT: IGDA GAME ACCESSIBILITY SPECIAL INTEREST GROUP (2004)

ACHIEVEMENTS UNLOCKED:

> NEXTGEN MAGAZINE "GAME INDUSTRY'S 100 MOST INFLUENTIAL WOMEN" (2006)

> IGDA "MOST VALUABLE PLAYER AWARD" (2006)

STATS

INDUSTRY LEVEL: 20

CURRENT CLASS: CO-CHAIR

CURRENT GUILD: IGDA GAME ACCESSIBILITY SPECIAL INTEREST GROUP—NEW YORK CITY, USA

SPECIAL SKILLS: GAME ACCESSIBILITY, USER RESEARCH

STANDARD EQUIPMENT

FAVORITE PLATFORM: IPAD

MUST-HAVE GAME: ODDWORLD: MUNCH'S ODDYSEE

BIO

Game-accessibility advocate Michelle Hinn believes that access to fun is a right, not a luxury. "In the video game industry, we often talk about quality-of-life issues from an employee standpoint, but we rarely stop and think about the positive impact games can have on life itself," she began. "I believe there is a 'right to fun' that we all have, because leisure activities such as video games can be healthy for us."

Hinn has spent nearly 15 years challenging able-bodied developers to imagine a different reality. "What would you do if you suddenly lost your hearing? Or your sight? Or your mobility?" she questioned. "Would you take issue with not being able to play games—the activity that led you to your profession? Chances are, you would."

Easter Egg
Is also a professional flute player.

ACADEMICS

Michelle Hinn knows what it's like to contend with challenges on a daily basis—she's dyslexic, and so the fight for accessibility is personal for her.

Hinn earned a bachelor's degree for music performance, and a second in psychology, followed shortly by a master's in multimedia design. No finished yet, she returned to school to earn a PhD in human-computer interaction, specializing in accessible game design.

While a PhD student in 1997, she spent time working at the National Center of Supercomputing Application—the home of the first graphical web browser, Mosaic, which popularized the use of the Internet. "At the time it was hard to get time slots in the CAVE—cave automatic virtual environment; think room-sized VR—to do work on my thesis," she explained. "I then got a graduate internship at Microsoft Games and I was hooked. I realized that console games were more accessible than VR at the time."

USER RESEARCH

As a user researcher at Microsoft Game Studios in 2001, Hinn's work focused on running usability tests for Xbox multiplayer titles such as the soon-to-be released *Halo: Combat Evolved*, as well as single-player experiences like *Fuzion Frenzy* and *Oddworld: Munch's Oddysee*.

User-research sessions for *Halo* hold a special place in her heart. "I loved conducting usability studies and hearing the players compare it to other games like *Golden Eye*," said Hinn. "There was so much secrecy about the game, and to see such joy from participants who had been waiting for the game to come out was unforgettable!"

Her time as a user researcher gave Hinn insight into what it would be like to work in video games, and additionally introduced her to the diverse pool of people who were eager to play them.

A SPECIAL INTEREST

After Microsoft, Hinn joined the International Game Developers Association's Game Accessibility Special Interest Group as a chairperson, and has remained entrenched since 2004. The SIG's primary focus is to advocate developing games with a wider audience in mind, making them accessible to players with a range of disabilities. Over the years, the SIG would conduct large awareness campaigns, host dozens of panels and workshops for game creators, and offer more personal services such as one-on-one mentorship to aspiring developers with disabilities. "Working with the SIG has been the most fulfilling part of my career," said Hinn, who is now starting to see the fruits of their labor over a decade later. It's been a long haul for her and other accessibility advocates.

While one would hope empathy alone would be enough to encourage able-bodied individuals to champion accessibility causes, that isn't always the case. As such, Hinn and her fellow SIG members have often put accessibility in more universal terms—the great equalizer being age.

Still, for years it was an uphill battle to get attention for a cause often written off as too small a demographic to make financial sense. Hinn challenged this notion.

> "Working with [the IGDA's special interest group] has been the most fulfilling part of my career."

"We used to make presentations at conferences for years, trying to get out awareness of gamers with disabilities, but we'd get maybe a handful of participants," said Hinn. "We'd plan for these sessions about a year out and invited as many as we could via email, handed out session flyers, but we still couldn't get a room filled no matter what we did." Panels covered everything from the basics to more nuanced discussions—"Game Accessibility 101" to "Dynamic Closed-Captioning for Your Game."

At one point, this hard reality nearly broke the SIG apart. "I spent a year organizing and planning a session where participants would present their accessible game designs," Hinn explained. "We had judges from the Game Accessibility SIG and called it 'Accessibility Idol.' The day of, we barely had an audience, and we felt terrible because we'd put in so much work to make it a big smash. The participants were all famous game designers, and afterward they acknowledged that this was the smallest audience turnout that they'd ever seen. I felt really rejected, and the SIG almost fell apart. I learned to just keep on pushing, hoping that one day we'd get large audiences—and we did!"

While the SIG regularly hosted programming at important industry events such as the annual Game Developers Conference, they couldn't rely on that to get the word out. Hinn began consulting work and would take the fight straight to developers, contacting them directly to set up best-practice workshops.

While executing her accessibility work, Hinn also advocated from an academic level, working as a game design instructor at the University of Illinois, and in her current position as an adjunct professor at Valdosta State University. She and other SIG members collaborated on academic papers speaking to universal accessibility, and won awards for the work, recognized by the American Evaluation Association and the International Visual Literacy Association. Published papers included "Game Not Over: Accessibility Issues in Video Games" and "Advances in Game Accessibility from 2005 to 2010." She is in the process of writing a book on game accessibility with the help of the SIG.

VICTORIES BIG & SMALL

Recent victories in accessibility include the 2013 addition of an "Accessibility Award" in the Game Developers Association of Australia's annual ceremony—she and her colleagues have championed for a long time, and hope it spreads throughout the industry.

"With regard to accessibility, there are now a large number of companies making strides," added Hinn. "Games have especially become more accessible for people with disabilities since President Obama signed the Communications and Video Accessibility Act (CVAA) into law in 2010. So now we're seeing things like Xbox's new controller for people with disabilities, and many more games with subtitles, color-blind mode, and much more. Our panels are routinely bringing in much larger audiences. It's an exciting time consulting with companies who are looking for assistance in making their games more accessible!"

There's still much work to be done. Key topics for the future include standardizing an industry accessibility ratings system and more.

Hinn is proud of the work she and the other SIG members have done over the years, knowing it's starting to pay off. "It was difficult keeping the game-accessibility movement going during all the early years where we had to fight to get on conference schedules, where few people would attend, and nobody wanted to talk about it. Today, the movement is very strong and there are now long-fought-for laws. Now we see greater audiences, participation by an amazing number of companies. Giving voice to those game players that have been shut out of playing many video games inspires me to keep moving."

A DAY IN THE LIFE OF...

AN AUDIO DESIGNER

Audio Designers are just that—designers. They don't simply implement sounds into a game; they craft interactive worlds that are as immersive to the ears as they are to the eyes. Soundscapes in modern games feature layer upon layer of nuanced work ensuring the player's footsteps change when stepping from grass onto concrete, or tweaking the sound of gunfire to match a specific firearm. Oftentimes this means capturing sounds in the real world, or heavily modifying an existing audio asset. Once in the game, these sounds are never in isolation. An Audio Designer must balance a cacophony of noises at one time to truly bring a world to life. Nikki Myers earned a Master of Fine Arts in Sound Design and paired it with her love of video games on titles such as *Radical Heights* and *LawBreakers*.

NIKKI MYERS

TheNikkiMyers Nikki Myers nikkimyerssound.com

PROFESSION: FREELANCE AUDIO DESIGNER AT NIKKI MYERS SOUND—RALEIGH, USA

YEARS IN PROFESSION: 7

WORKED ON: RADICAL HEIGHTS, LAWBREAKERS, ASSORTED SHORT FILMS

▶ EDUCATION

"I earned a B.A. in Film Studies and a B.A. in Music from UNC-Wilmington, then went on to get my M.F.A. in Sound Design from the Savannah College of Art and Design. However, the curriculum for these degree programs focuses on sound for linear media with the exception of a game audio implementation class at SCAD. They helped lay a foundation for my career and the time spent in school gave me an outlet to find my unique 'voice' as a sound designer. That being said, the bulk of the technology I use in game audio is either self-taught in my spare time, or absorbed through immersion while at work when a specific tool is an integral part of a project."

▶ BREAKING IN

"I was offered a job from a company to which I sent a speculative application. They didn't necessarily need any additional audio personnel, so I'll admit that I did get somewhat lucky. However, the reason I was hired was partly because I had written a Master's thesis on software that the company was gearing up to use, and partly because I exhibited my organization skills in the design of my website, résumé, and portfolio. You could say that breaking into the industry was 'easy' for me because 'the stars aligned,' but at the same time, the reasons why I was hired were things that took me months to refine."

▶ KEY QUALITIES

"Just be an overall good person. Your current coworker may end up being a future reference. If people like working with you now, they'll likely want to keep working with you on other projects at other studios. You'll also need to be able to handle criticism and work collaboratively in order to produce a game that everyone is proud of.

"Specifically for game professionals, you really have to learn to be comfortable communicating with people from all departments and you'll need to be okay with receiving feedback on your audio from people outside the audio department. Working collaboratively across all departments is vital to ensuring that your audio truly fits in the game."

▶ TRAINING OPPORTUNITIES

"Conference talks are great training opportunities! They can provide a huge advantage not just to newcomers, but to everyone working in the industry. Attending talks is a good way to expand your skillset and learn new tips and tricks, and they are led also led—and attended—by other industry professionals. They provide a great networking opportunity.

"For further networking, I recommend Women in Games International (WIGI), the Women in Audio slack channel, the Game Audio Network Guild (GANG), and any game industry and audio conferences. There are also some really great Facebook groups that deal specifically with game audio, such as Game Audio Denizens and Wwise Wwizards & Wwitches."

▶ TOOLS OF THE TRADE

"I use Perforce for source control, which allows me to sync all of the necessary game files to my computer so I'm not working on anything that someone else may have revised, making the file out-of-date. I use Jira for bug- and task-tracking. "For sound editing and design, I'll alternate between Pro Tools and Reaper, depending on the project. If any audio restoration or cleanup is required, I'll generally do this in Adobe Audition or iZotope RX.

"For audio middleware, I currently use Wwise, but what middleware you use really depends on the studio. Wwise is a specialized program that helps me have greater control over how the sound should perform in the game.

"The Unreal Engine 4 is the game engine I'm currently working in. As is the case with audio middleware, the game engine you end up working with will depend on the studio."

▶ HOURS & ENVIRONMENT

"It depends on the day. Some days I may work a normal eight hours in a regular work environment, while other days I may have to work longer hours because of an approaching deadline that may be stressing us all out.

"I use a dual-monitor setup that consists of two computer screens. One is rotated vertically and is my default screen for Wwise, while the other—my main screen—is set to the normal landscape orientation and is the screen that I will run the game on. I have a 5.1 speaker system and two sets of headphones, a set of professional studio headphones and a pair of gaming headphones that I alternate between. I have sound-dampening panels on my walls to cut down on the room's sound reflectivity.

"Most of my work is done at my desk, but occasionally I'll spend a day or two out in the field recording sounds for particular things I might be working on. If I need to record any dialogue, I'll usually record myself at my desk first so I can have placeholder audio ready immediately, then we'll book a recording studio to record the actual actor while the director and/or I monitor the session over Skype or Source-Connect from my own office."

▶ AN AVERAGE DAY

"First, and most importantly, coffee! After that, I'll take care of administrative tasks, which usually includes checking and responding to emails, checking Jira to see if I have any new bugs/tasks and noting what priority they've been assigned, and syncing source control so I have the most up-to-date version of the game files. The lion's share of my day will be spent on editing, hooking up audio and/or music cues into the game, testing the audio in-game to make sure it's working as intended, and debugging any issues that come up.

"If I'm working on asset creation, this can range from going out in the field to record my own sounds to pulling sounds from an existing library, and then taking those elements into my digital audio workstation to process and design a unique sound effect. Occasionally, co-workers will stop by my office if I'm working on-site or will send me a Slack message if I'm working remotely to discuss something."

▶ PROFESSIONAL PERKS

"The technology is always changing and improving, so it's exciting to take part in that evolution. That being said, my favorite part of the job is when I get to work with voice actors. It's amazing to watch a character come to life in the collaboration between director, writer, and actor."

▶ CAREER CHALLENGES

"It's easy for people to forget just how important audio is, so you really need to learn how to advocate for yourself. If you don't, you could end up with not enough time to meet a deadline, feature creep, last-minute changes, and so on."

▶ LIFE HACKS

"I've been using the 50/10 Rule since college. The 50/10 Rule means you work for 50 minutes and rest for 10 minutes. This helps with productivity and helps fight burnout because 50 minutes of work is a more manageable amount of time than eight hours."

▶ EXCITING ADVANCEMENTS

"I'm actually quite enjoying the emergence of audio-only interactive adventure stories. These are voice-controlled and are usually played using devices like Amazon Echo or Google Home. I enjoy listening to radioplays and audiobooks—I love hearing how other audio professionals approach the challenge of developing rich aural environments with no supporting visuals, and it's cool to hear this applied in an interactive format. I also appreciate the fact that, since these interactive adventure stories are completely audio-based, they are accessible not just to those with visual impairments, but also to young children who may not have reading fluency yet. Check out *Baker Street Experience* for the Echo."

"To be a good content creator, you need to be a great content consumer. Take the time to play and listen to video games. Don't just pay attention to the things that work, but also take note of what doesn't work. This observation will help you make wise design choices in your own work."

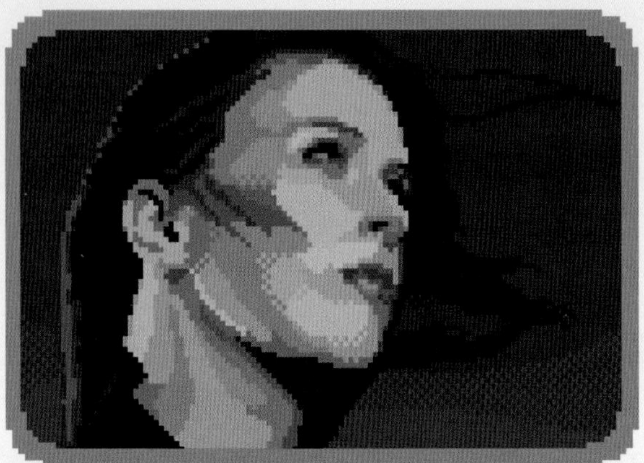

RHIANNA PRATCHETT

GAMES WRITER MOVING BEYOND THE "STRONG FEMALE PROTAGONIST"

 RhiPratchett  rhiannapratchett.com

EXPERIENCE

FIRST INDUSTRY PROJECT: JOURNALISM: MINX MAGAZINE (1998), GAME: BEYOND DIVINITY (2004)

FAVORITE INDUSTRY PROJECT: OVERLORD (2007)

PROJECTS SHIPPED: 22 GAMES

ACHIEVEMENTS UNLOCKED:
> BAFTA "STORY AND CHARACTER" NOMINATION—HEAVENLY SWORD (2007)
> WRITERS' GUILD OF GREAT BRITAIN "BEST VIDEO GAME SCRIPT"—OVERLORD (2008)
> WRITERS' GUILD OF AMERICA "OUTSTANDING ACHIEVEMENT IN VIDEO GAME WRITING"—RISE OF THE TOMB RAIDER (2015)
> MCV WOMEN IN GAMES "CREATIVE IMPACT" AWARD (2017)

 STATS

INDUSTRY LEVEL: 20

CURRENT CLASS: WRITER

CURRENT GUILD: FREELANCE—LONDON, UNITED KINGDOM

SPECIAL SKILLS: NARRATIVE DESIGN, SCRIPT WRITING, EDITING, AUDIO DIRECTING, CONSULTANCY

 STANDARD EQUIPMENT

FAVORITE PLATFORM: PLAYSTATION 4

GO-TO GENRE: WILDERNESS SURVIVAL GAMES

MUST-HAVE GAME: DUNGEON KEEPER 2, DON'T STARVE

BIO

Writer and narrative designer Rhianna Pratchett lists *Frankenstein* scribe Mary Shelley as a source of inspiration, and it's easy to see why; they're kindred spirits separated by centuries.

"We both had writer fathers and both went on to embrace writing ourselves," began Pratchett. "She was someone who was incessantly fascinated by life and human advancement. She traveled widely and attended public science experiences, which was rare for a woman at the time. She found a way to flourish whilst surrounded by famously difficult men."

Pratchett's story is in many ways parallel. The daughter of famed fantasy author Sir Terry Pratchett, her interest in the intersection of entertainment and technology led to work as a games journalist in the late '90s. Throughout her career she has traveled the world, expanding her knowledge of an advancing medium, pushing the boundaries of industry expectations, and eventually, leaving a unique mark on a male-dominated field.

Easter Egg
Doesn't consider herself to be particularly musically talented, but likes to dabble in learning instruments, including the keyboard, recorder, guitar, tenor saxophone, and violin.

DIVINITY

"I did my degree in journalism, but since then I've pretty much been self-taught and learned on the job," said Pratchett, who graduated with honors from the London College of Communication in 1998.

Monthly UK magazine *Minx* was the forum for Pratchett's first published works, followed closely by *PC Zone* and *The Guardian*. "There weren't very many women working in games journalism back in the late '90s, so I was a bit of a curiosity," she said. "I'd also been playing PC games for many years, so I definitely knew my stuff."

Games journalism offered educational opportunities at every turn. "I've played games since I was tiny, but I didn't get to understand development until I became a writer and started to travel around the world visiting developers and seeing how games were created," she explained.

That knowledge bore fruit in 2003, when Larian Studios approached Pratchett to work on the sequel to their 2002 title *Divine Divinity*. "They were looking for a story editor for their next game and knew I was a fan," said Pratchett. "I'd never seen a game writer in all the time I was visiting development studios. There were people writing the narrative—if the games had one—but it was usually designers, or literally anyone who had the time or inclination to do it." Pratchett used her editing eye to help rewrite existing text for *Beyond Divinity*, providing original content to fill gaps where needed, and also authored a companion novella.

A TASTE FOR NARRATIVE

Working for Larian resulted in a desire to move past critiquing games, and instead, help create them. "I decided to utilize the contacts I'd made as a journalist to get more narrative work," said Pratchett. "Doing so allowed me to slowly start hacking my way through the narrative wilderness and carving out a career path."

Narrative wasn't something widely recognized within the industry at the time—there weren't breakout panels or category-specific awards in the early 2000s. "I was surprised at how low the general narrative literacy was in games," said Pratchett. "In the early days, I was often the only person on the team working on the narrative and one of the few who cared about it."

Pratchett contributed to an array of games in quick succession, gaining valuable insights and experience. She worked as a communications consultant for Nevrax's *The Saga of Ryzom*, wrote level and NPC dialogue for *Pac-Man World 3*, and provided story design and in-game mission scripts for Firefly Studios' *Stronghold Legends*, among others.

One of Pratchett's first big gigs was the 2007 action-RPG *Overlord*. She laid the groundwork for the story and character design before writing the script in its entirety. Additionally, Pratchett co-directed *Overlord*'s audio, ensuring the performance matched the intent of her work. *Overlord* won the Writers' Guild of Great Britain "Best Video Game Script Award" in 2008 and was short-listed in the "Best New IP" category of the Develop Awards. Pratchett was asked back as writer, story designer, and audio director of *Overlord 2*, which she rolled directly into after finishing the first game.

BEYOND STRONG

Over a period of three years, Pratchett contributed to five games as a freelancer, working on most of them simultaneously. While writing *Overlord*, she was also collaborating with developer Ninja Theory to help flesh out their newest IP, *Heavenly Sword*, as the co-story designer and primary writer. She worked closely with actor and director Andy Serkis on the game's narrative.

Heavenly Sword followed the story of Nariko, a long-prophesized warrior shunned by her tribe at birth when her gender was seen as a mockery of the legend. This was the first in a trio of major works where Pratchett made an intentional point to move beyond one-dimensional depictions of physical strength at the core pillar of a heroine's character. Both Nariko and her erratic friend Kai were unique and nuanced characters who elevated the game overall.

Heavenly Sword released in 2007 and was nominated for a BAFTA award for story and character, additionally short-listed for "Best New IP" in the 2008 Develop Awards, and "Best Video Game Script" for the Writers' Guild of Great Britain Awards.

FAITH & FEAR

DICE's innovative first-person action-adventure game *Mirror's Edge* was Pratchett's next key project. As the main writer, she crafted the storyline and helped establish characters and themes, before writing the full script and dialogue. She also helped cast voice actors, was on-set to direct performances, and wrote a tie-in miniseries for DC Comics.

The story followed protagonist Faith Connors, a "runner" tasked with transporting important intel to revolutionaries rallying against a totalitarian government. Connors—a combination of strength, intelligence, and perseverance—bucked tradition in everything from her appearance to personality, landing her a spot on many "top female character in gaming" lists. *Mirror's Edge* won best new IP at E3 2009, and best adventure game at the Interactive Achievement Awards.

Through connections made while writing Eidos Montreal's game *Thief*, Pratchett was introduced to the team at Crystal Dynamics, which was in the process of rebooting one of the most iconic characters in the history of gaming.

In 2010, Pratchett joined the team as lead writer for *Tomb Raider*, a reimagining of Lara Croft's origin story. She collaborated closely with the creative director and narrative designer for nearly three years, establishing Croft as a relatable, complex, and flawed young woman who would push her way past fear to realize her untapped potential. Released in 2013, *Tomb Raider* was short-listed for the Writers' Guild of Great Britain "Best Video Game Script."

"I've got great memories of fans' feedback on *Tomb Raider*, particularly when Lara's grit and determination in the game helped them get out of their own difficulties in real life," said Pratchett. She reprised her role in 2015's *Rise of the Tomb Raider*, and the game took home the "Outstanding Achievement in Video Game Writing" award from the Writers' Guild of America, and was recognized for "Outstanding Achievement in Character" at the annual DICE Awards.

> "I've got great memories of fans' feedback on *Tomb Raider*, particularly when Lara's grit and determination in the game helped them get out of their own difficulties in real life."

A LASTING LEGACY

Pratchett's freelance career continues to flourish—already spanning two decades and 22 shipped games—and has expanded outside of video games. "I'm doing a lot of work in film and TV at the moment, so I hope the skills I gain there will strengthen me as a storyteller for whatever medium I choose to work in," she said.

"Narrative is taken more seriously now. Publishers, developers and players are all focusing on it more. Professional game writers are becoming a lot more common, as are narrative designers and narrative directors," reflected Pratchett. "We have summits on game narrative, awards, and generally a lot more recognition. However, we still have a ways to go. Writers often aren't hired early enough in the process and struggle to get hard power on a team. Narrative often gets rinsed through committees of people who have no real storytelling experience. We still have a lot of teething problems to deal with."

Pratchett has directly influenced this positive change, both through her body of work and through continued discourse. "I believe I've helped open up the field of games writing and pushed it forward as a viable career," she closed. "Hopefully I've also encouraged developers to look harder at the way they construct their narratives and engage with writers."

THE 2000s: A NEW CENTURY CONTENDER

2000: THE PLAYSTATION 2 IS RELEASED

Sony's sophomore outing would become the best-selling game console of all-time, with over 150M units sold globally[1]. The PlayStation 2 featured cutting-edge audio/visual capabilities, as well as backwards compatibility with PSOne titles and accessories. Released at $299 and reduced to $199 in 2002 to more aggressively compete with the GameCube and Xbox, the PlayStation 2 benefited from being one of the most affordable consoles on the market.

Throughout its lengthy life cycle, the PlayStation 2 was continuously bolstered by numerous high profile franchises and sequels, including *Final Fantasy*, *Gran Turismo*, *Grand Theft Auto*, *Tekken*, *Metal Gear Solid*, *God of War*, *Kingdom Hearts*, and *Ratchet & Clank*.

2000

2001

2001: ANGELINA JOLIE STARS IN TOMB RAIDER

Following the box office failure of *Super Mario Bros.* (1993) and *Street Fighter* (1994), and the success of *Mortal Kombat* (1995), *Tomb Raider* was the next major game franchise to receive a film adaptation. Although *Lara Croft: Tomb Raider* received a low approval rating by critics, the film was a commercial success, spawning a sequel in 2003.

2001: MICROSOFT AND MASTER CHIEF ENTER THE CONSOLE WARS

Years after working with Sega to feature its Windows CE operating system on the Dreamcast, Microsoft entered the home console market full-force with its own system. The Xbox (a contraction of "DirectX Box") was a massive contraption—with an equally clunky controller—that would make most multi-deck VHS players blush. However, the console's large size allowed it to pack more impressive hardware, outperforming all other sixth generation rivals in the visual department. In addition, it included the first built-in hard drive of any home console. The system's first-party launch title, *Halo*, was largely responsible for making the Xbox a true competitor to Sony and Nintendo. Halo was a breakout success and helped establish the modern gaming blockbuster.

2001: THE NINTENDO GAMECUBE IS RELEASED

The GameCube was Nintendo's first foray into disc-based consoles, using a proprietary mini-DVD format. Unfortunately, the system could not play audio CDs or DVDs and the mini-DVD format had a reduced storage capacity of 1.5GB compared to the Xbox and PlayStation 2, which both used 8.5GB dual-layer DVDs. The GameCube sold 21.74M units worldwide, putting it in third place behind the Xbox and PlayStation 2[2].

Nintendo's 32-bit Game Boy Advance, also released in 2001, fared much better, surpassing 81M lifetime units, and preceding the Nintendo DS (2004), which sold an astounding 150M units[3].

2001: GRAND THEFT AUTO III IS RELEASED

Developed by DMA Design and published by Rockstar Games, *Grand Theft Auto III* took the world by storm in 2001. Although the fifth title in the *GTA* series, *Grand Theft Auto III* was the first to introduce 3D graphics, giving new life to the franchise's patented open-world, crime-oriented gameplay. While open-world games had existed in many forms prior, *Grand Theft Auto III* featured an unparalleled living, breathing city, complete with living breathing civilians. Just as avant-garde titles in other genres spurred a lifetime of imitators, open-world games would become a staple in modern video games. *Grand Theft Auto III* remains one of the most impactful games in video gaming history.

2002

2003

2004

2003: DEFENSE OF THE ANCIENTS POPULARIZES MOBAS

Blizzard's highly successful RTS series, *Warcraft*, completed its trilogy in 2002 with the release of *Warcraft III: Reign of Chaos*. The *Warcraft III* World Editor allowed players to create custom maps with special rules, one of which was known as *Defense of the Ancients* (DOTA). DOTA popularized the multiplayer online battle arena (MOBA) genre, which would eventually give birth to *League of Legends* (2009), *Heroes of Newerth* (2010), *Smite* (2014), and *DOTA 2* (2013).

2003: STEAM LAUNCHES

In 2003, Valve, the company behind the award-winning *Half-Life*, launched its own digital distribution platform. Steam didn't pick up momentum until it became a requirement for Valve's highly-anticipated *Half-Life 2* in 2004. In late 2005, third-party titles became available on Steam, with an exponential increase in both users and publishers pushing digital distribution (and digital rights management, a.k.a. DRM) into the mainstream alongside Xbox Live.

2004: WORLD OF WARCRAFT IS RELEASED

Blizzard released *World of Warcraft* in 2004, an MMO based on its best-selling fantasy universe. It was designed to be more accessible than typical MMOs up to that point. This approach, combined with the game's colorful, stylized graphics, quickly made *World of Warcraft* the best-selling game of its time, and the most successful MMORPG ever. At its peak, the game had 12 million monthly subscribers[5].

2005: THE XBOX 360 AND THE 7TH GENERATION OF HOME CONSOLES

While the original Xbox had an uphill battle against Sony and Nintendo, its successor, the Xbox 360, was notably more successful. Microsoft amped up its first- and third-party support for its second console outing, with top-notch games and exclusives like *Halo*, *Gears of War*, and *Forza*, as well as a notable push in the JRPG genre, although the Xbox 360 failed to gain traction in Japan.

Microsoft doubled down on its Xbox Live platform, streamlining now-ubiquitous console game features such as matchmaking, voice chat, online leaderboards, achievements, and downloadable games and content. This coincided with the industry's overall push towards consoles as multimedia boxes, rather than being dedicated exclusively to gaming.

2005: GUITAR HERO LAUNCHES

Inspired by games like *PaRappa the Rapper* and *Guitar Freaks*, *Guitar Hero*, developed by Red Octane and Harmonix, was a breakout success, launching the music rhythm genre, which had previously been dominated mostly by Japanese-centric arcade titles like *Beatmania* (*Dance Dance Revolution*) and *Taiko: Drum Master*, into the mainstream. The instrument-based gameplay and music featured in the game made *Guitar Hero* accessible to gamers and non-gamers alike.

The music rhythm genre became so popular it helped drive console sales, with music games representing approximately 18% of the video game market and 53% of that player base being women[5]. Once the genre exploded, notable entries included Harmonix's *Rock Band* and *Dance Central*, Konami's *Just Dance*, and Activision's *DJ Hero*.

2005

2006

2007

2006: PLAYSTATION 3 AND NINTENDO WII

The PlayStation 3 initially struggled to reclaim its position as the industry leader due to a high price tag and an initial lack of must-have titles, partially due to an overly complicated chipset that made the PS3 more difficult to develop for compared to the Xbox 360. The PS3's biggest advantage was that it included a Blu-ray drive, and as Blu-ray became the dominant form of entertainment media over the system's lifespan, the PS3 was able to cash in on this feature.

The Nintendo Wii, which also released in 2006, opted not to compete directly with the Xbox 360 and PlayStation 3, instead focusing on an affordable, family-friendly console utilizing a new motion control scheme for its games. Bundled with *Wii Sports*, the Wii was a smash hit, surpassing 100M units sold worldwide[4]. However, the Wii's technical shortcomings (such as a lack of HD video support) and lack of third-party support led the console to have a much shorter lifespan than its competitors.

2007: CALL OF DUTY 4: MODERN WARFARE IS RELEASED

Infinity Ward's acclaimed *Call of Duty* series left behind World War II for its fourth outing, a decision that would contribute to the game's universal acclaim and the franchise's blockbuster status. *Modern Warfare* didn't just reinvigorate first-person shooters, it established the standard in storytelling, atmosphere, and multiplayer that countless others would attempt to match throughout the following decade.

2008: APPLE LAUNCHES THE APP STORE

Apple launched the App Store in 2008, which gave rise to the Western mobile market. Highly visible, early successes such as *Angry Birds*, *Doodle Jump*, and *iShoot* led to a gold rush on the App Store. With little barrier to entry, virtually anyone could publish an app—gaming or otherwise—to the App Store, something Apple actively encouraged and celebrated through its marketing. With 500 total applications available at launch, the App Store currently features over 2 million, with $38.5B in revenue recorded in 2017 (compared to almost $60B across all platforms)[6].

2008: THE RISE OF INDIE GAMING

Alongside the App Store making game development and distribution accessible to a much broader spectrum of content creators, indie gaming on PC and consoles was experiencing a renaissance of its own. Up that point, indie games generally existed as Flash-based freeware on web portals such as Kongregate and Newgrounds. In the late 2000s, indie gaming was pushed into the mainstream with the Summer of Arcade event for Xbox Live, which saw the release of highly successful indie darlings *Braid* and *Castle Crashers*. Similar events would go on to promote games like *Limbo*, *Bastion*, *Super Meat Boy*, and *Dust: An Elysian Tail*.

Meanwhile, *World of Goo* (PC and Wii) was sweeping awards and critical acclaim, leading to a greater prestige associated with well-made indie games. Indie games would flourish on PC and home console platforms, with Sony deeply embracing experimental titles such as those from thatgamecompany, including *Flower* and *Journey*. *Half-Life* developer Valve hired a team of DigiPen Institute of Technology alumni who had developed a freeware game called *Narbacular Drop*, which formed the basis for their next game, *Portal*.

The rise of indie gaming led to an increase in available tools for creators—Unity, RPG Maker, GameMaker, etc. Steam would become a stronghold of indie games throughout the next decade, being home to massively successful titles such as *Five Nights at Freddy's*, *Spelunky*, *Stardew Valley*, and and many others. The accessibility of these tools was a democratizing force on the industry. The accessibility of indie development helped marginalized voices—including women—and create and share games that may not have otherwise been possible.

2008

2009

2008: THE RISE OF INDIE GAMING

Alongside the App Store making game development and distribution accessible to a much broader spectrum of content creators, indie gaming on PC and consoles was experiencing a renaissance of its own. Up that point, indie games generally existed as Flash-based freeware on web portals such as Kongregate and Newgrounds. In the late 2000s, indie gaming was pushed into the mainstream with the Summer of Arcade event for Xbox Live, which saw the release of highly successful indie darlings *Braid* and *Castle Crashers*. Similar events would go on to promote games like *Limbo*, *Bastion*, *Super Meat Boy*, and *Dust: An Elysian Tail*.

Meanwhile, *World of Goo* (PC and Wii) was sweeping awards and critical acclaim, leading to a greater prestige associated with well-made indie games. Indie games would flourish on PC and home console platforms, with Sony deeply embracing experimental titles such as those from thatgamecompany, including *Flower* and *Journey*. *Half-Life* developer Valve hired a team of DigiPen Institute of Technology alumni who had developed a freeware game called *Narbacular Drop*, which formed the basis for their next game, *Portal*.

The rise of indie gaming led to an increase in available tools for creators—Unity, RPG Maker, GameMaker, etc. Steam would become a stronghold of indie games throughout the next decade, being home to massively successful titles such as *Five Nights at Freddy's*, *Spelunky*, *Stardew Valley*, and many others. The accessibility of these tools was a democratizing force on the industry. The accessibility of indie development helped marginalized voices, including women, to create and share games that may not have otherwise been possible.

1. "PLAYSTATION2 Sales Reach 150 Million Units Worldwide." Sony Computer Entertainment. February 14, 2011.
2. "Consolidated Sales Transition by Region" (PDF). Nintendo. June 2011.
3. "Consolidated Sales Transition by Region" (PDF). Nintendo. June 2011.
4. IR Information: "Sales Data—Hardware and Software Sales Units." Nintendo Co., Ltd.
5. Crossley, Rob (2008-10-21). "Music Overtakes Sports Genre." *Edge Magazine*. Next-gen.biz.
6. "App Revenue Climbed 35 Percent to $60 Billion in 2017." TechCrunch. January 05, 2018.

LISETTE TITRE-MONTGOMERY

CHAMPIONING STEM STUDIES IN MARGINALIZED COMMUNITIES

Zette16 — Lisette Titre

Lisette Titre-Montgomery — lisettetitre.com

EXPERIENCE

FIRST INDUSTRY PROJECT: FREEKSTYLE (2002)

FAVORITE INDUSTRY PROJECT: PSYCHONAUTS 2 (PENDING RELEASE)

PROJECTS SHIPPED: 13 GAMES

ACHIEVEMENTS UNLOCKED:

> BLACK ENTERPRISE MAGAZINE COVER FEATURE (2012)

> BUSINESS INSIDER "23 OF THE MOST POWERFUL WOMEN ENGINEERS IN THE WORLD" (2015)

> ESA FUNDING AND GOVERNOR JERRY BROWN RECOGNITION FOR PROJECT A GAME (2013)

> MEMBER OF THE UNITED STATES EMBASSY SPEAKERS BUREAU

STATS

INDUSTRY LEVEL: 18

CURRENT CLASS: ART DIRECTOR

CURRENT GUILD: DOUBLE FINE PRODUCTIONS—SAN FRANCISCO, USA

SPECIAL SKILLS: ART DIRECTION, INTERNATIONAL ART TEAM MANAGEMENT, ART PIPELINE DEVELOPMENT, MILESTONE PLANNING, CONCEPT ART, 3D MODELING, UV MAPPING, TEXTURING

STANDARD EQUIPMENT

FAVORITE PLATFORM: PLAYSTATION 2

GO-TO GENRE: PUZZLE AND EXPLORATION

MUST-HAVE GAME: SUPER MARIO BROS. (NES)

BIO

Self-reliance is a trait highly valued by Lisette Titre. Unwilling to accept sub-standard status quos, she doesn't wait for someone else to make change; she gets the job done herself.

"I got a BA in computer animation from art school," explained Titre. "We were the first batch of students in the program. After my first year, I realized my professors where not teaching me everything I wanted to know, so my last two years I was self-training after I completed my coursework. This really taught me not to rely on others to advance my skills, and just dive headfirst into learning what intrigued me. The extra work I did during that time is what got me my first game job."

Titre first put her animation skills to use in 2001 as a character modeler on Page 44 Studios' *Freekstyle*. "I was responsible for modeling the likenesses for several of the named riders in the game," she explained. "When I wasn't modeling, I did a few costume designs for the female riders."

During her first years in the industry, Titre proactively sought out opportunities to get hands-on experience with a variety of art disciplines. "I am naturally curious and wanted to get things working without a ton of support," she continued. "I learned rigging and skinning, prop modeling, lighting, and VFX. I even did concept art when needed. Anything that could be considered part of the art pipeline, I studied. Learning all of these techniques really helped me down the road when I became an art lead and needed to plan pipelines and schedules."

OUTSOURCING INFERNO

That diverse skill set earned Titre a position at EA as a senior character and special effects artist and eventually additional responsibilities managing the art-outsourcing pipeline. *Tiger Woods PGA Tour 2007* was her first project at EA, followed by *The Simpsons Game*, *The Godfather II*, and *Dante's Inferno*.

"The most challenging project of my career was *Dante's Inferno*," began Titre. "I was one of the first six people on the project. It was the first time I got to be involved during the conception phase of a project and watched the concept evolve as it passed through the lens of executive producers, marketing, and focus testing." An aggressive production schedule and the introduction of outsourcing added to the challenge of the project.

"My team of character artists went from 10 to two people in just a few projects," she continued. "I had to balance being a content creator and learning how to provide effective art direction and feedback to off-site artists. This was the first time I had to work with overseas partners directly, and quickly learned about cultural and language barriers in relation to situational reference and vision setting. It was the game that prepared me for being an art director."

After six years at EA, Titre left in 2011 to seek out new opportunities. Over the next several years she lent her talents to a variety of Bay-area studios, shipping titles such as *Dance Central 3*, *The Sims 4*, and *Transformers: Age of Extinction* on mobile. At Double Fine Productions since 2017, Titre is now the art manager working on the sequel to a cult-classic Tim Schafer title. "*Psychonauts 2* is shaping up to be my favorite game to make so far," expressed Titre. "Meaningful content, creative freedom, and an amazingly talented yet humble team."

ENCOURAGING BLACK ENTERPRISE

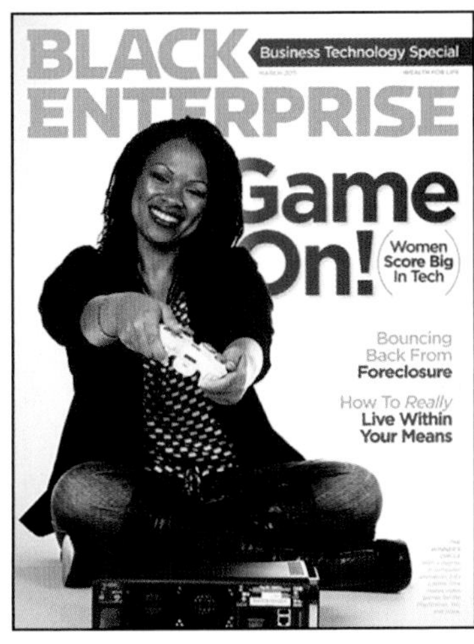

While making her mark on AAA titles, Titre began to grow tired of feeling out of place in the industry. "After many years of feeling like a unicorn, being one of the few (and often the only) African American female game developers on teams left me searching for answers," she explained. "I started looking into why I was often the only one. My journey started with social media. An editor, Marcia Talbert, found me on LinkedIn. She was working on an article about black women in STEM and offered to include me." Titre jumped at the chance to increase awareness of black women working in video games, and to her surprise, the interview became a 2012 cover feature on nationwide magazine *Black Enterprise*.

"After the article, I began to get hundreds of letters from parents and students who were interested in game development, and they were excited that there was someone who looked like them making games," recalled Titre. "Due to the volume of responses, I knew I touched on something badly needed: a pipeline to expose black and brown kids to STEM by capturing their interest in gaming."

Inspired to make change, Titre helped start two non-profit game-development programs in Oakland, California. The first one—Project A Game—was formed in partnership with outreach program Youth Uprising. Together, they created an eight-week curriculum to teach kids basic coding, game design, and analytical skills to jump-start their career in video games.

The second program—Gameheads Oakland—is another youth program that helps train low-income youth and youth of color in tech fields. "Gameheads is very successful, and our students are getting into the top game schools in the country," said Titre.

REACHING OUT

Outreach is now an integral part of her career, and an impressive list of milestones is added to Titre's résumé each year. Kimberly Bryant, the founder of Black Girls Code, asked her to speak to the program's first-ever class of students. Titre presented at NASA's Ames Research Center, sharing how a game-based curriculum could drive youth toward STEM fields. She was a guest speaker at Intel's Girls in Tech Day, was interviewed by NPR, has written an op-ed for *The New York Times*, spoke at Yale Women's Leadership Conference, and in 2016, made her way to the White House.

"I was honored to be chosen out of 3500 applicants to attend the White House LGBTQ Tech and Innovation briefing," said Titre. "Over 300 lesbian, gay, bisexual, transgender, and queer people gathered to address some of our nation's biggest issues. The goal was to bring together some of the best LGBTQ minds to help provide insights to improve government policy and process."

More recently, Titre was invited by the US State Department Speakers Bureau to travel to Hong Kong and share her experiences as part of a *Hidden Figures* tour. "I spoke at several colleges and high schools about my experience in the games industry and some of the design problems I helped to solve," said Titre. "We also discussed some of the roles in the game industry, current trends, and challenges. It's an honor to be requested by two nation states to advocate for an industry I feel so passionately about."

> "My hope is that more brown women and girls will read [the *Essence* article] and realize a career in games I possible."

One of Titre's more personal points of pride came this year, when she was featured in the February 2018 issue of *Essence*, in an article focusing on women paving the way in STEM studies. "I have been an avid reader of *Essence* all of my life," she explained. "I got a subscription so my daughter would have positive black females to read about and see every month. To be sharing this issue with Oprah Winfrey, Ava DuVernay, and Kimberly Bryant just makes it even more humbling. My hope is that more brown women and girls will read this and realize a career in games is possible."

NEW EXPERIENCES

"The focus on creating emergent stories is going to continue to evolve along with technology," said Titre, looking to the future. "I think the stories that we tell are going to drastically change because who gets to tell our stories is changing. There are 1.2 billion new people coming online by 2020, mostly from Latin America, South Pacific Asia, and African countries. Our current player base is 1.8 billion. Most people will access the Internet via a smartphone. The first thing people download is a chat app. The second thing people download is a game. These new players want to tell their own stories in new mediums. These new players will want to make games. These new players will create new experiences we haven't even imagined. I think the best games haven't even been played yet. I can't wait to see what they do."

Easter Egg

Used to run a pop-up jerk chicken stand called Evil Jerk Cart in her free time. She would tweet her location and fans would flock to her for no-holds-barred spicy jerk chicken. Her food won awards and is requested at every Double Fine family picnic.

STEPHANIE JOHNSON

BUILDING GAME BRANDS BRICK BY BRICK

 Stephanie Johnson

EXPERIENCE

FIRST INDUSTRY PROJECT: ROBOTECH: BATTLECRY (2002)

FAVORITE INDUSTRY PROJECT: PAMOJIA MATANI (2008)

PROJECTS SHIPPED: 75 GAMES

ACHIEVEMENTS UNLOCKED:

> AMERICAN ADVERTISING AWARDS "GOLD ADDY WINNER AND JUDGES CHOICE AWARD"—LEGO BATMAN VIDEO GAME WEBSITE (2009)

> 8TH ANNUAL GAME MARKETING AWARDS "OUTSTANDING OVERALL MARKETING CAMPAIGN FINALIST—FAMILY GAMES—LEGO BATMAN 2: DC SUPER HEROES (2013)

> THE SHORTY AWARDS "BEST USE OF VIDEO GAME CONTENT IN SOCIAL MEDIA"—LEGO MARVEL SUPER HEROES (2014)

> CLIO AWARDS "BEST GAME SHORT FORM CONTENT" BRONZE WINNER—LEGO DIMENSIONS (2015)

STATS

INDUSTRY LEVEL: 17

CURRENT CLASS: HEAD OF GLOBAL MARKETING FOR GEFORCE NOW AND SHIELD

CURRENT GUILD: NVIDIA—SAN FRANCISCO, USA

SPECIAL SKILLS: MARKETING, BRAND DEVELOPMENT, SOCIAL MEDIA, STRATEGIC PARTNERSHIPS

STANDARD EQUIPMENT

FAVORITE PLATFORM: NES

GO-TO GENRE: MUSIC/PARTY GAMES

MUST-HAVE GAME: WII BOWLING

BIO

"I started in television and movies," began longtime marketing professional Stephanie Johnson. "Great storytelling has always been my love. One of the early movies I worked on was *Final Fantasy*. While I had played games, I never really saw the beauty in their stories and the artform until I worked on that film, which came from the rich game universe created by Hironobu Sakaguchi."

Johnson earned her degree in television communications in 2000, and worked in news media at the start of her career. "Whether it was interviewing someone in a moment of happiness or despair, a great reporter can relate to the person to capture the moment—to be the advocate for that person's story," she explained. "I'd say that has prepared me very well for my career in marketing, where I try to tell a story that people can relate to, in order to bring a product to life for the audience personally. I also feel like it's my job to advocate for the customer in everything we do."

Easter Egg

When working on a live-action commercial for the Guinness Book of World Records game, Johnson was on set with the world's most flexible man, the woman with the longest fingernails, and a 6-time record holder for breaking stuff. She bounced between disbelief and laughter all day.

TAKE-TWO INTERACTIVE

In 2002, when an opportunity came up to work in marketing at a game company, Johnson jumped at it. "I probably wouldn't have considered the game industry, had it not been for *Final Fantasy: The Spirits Within*, and understanding the exciting storylines, characters, and unique content I would have to work with in my career," she said.

Johnson started out as a junior brand manager at TDK Mediactive, which was later purchased by Take-Two Interactive. "I supported a variety of licensed brands—Shrek, No Rules, Dinotopia, and Robotech, to name a few. Very quickly after I started, when the original brand manager of Robotech left, I was given the task to bring the product to market. It was sink-or-swim time! I suppose I was a little surprised people entrusted me with characters that I saw as so rich and special," she admitted. "So I made it my mission to be their 'protector.' I wanted to make their creators proud by producing marketing materials that would ensure the world saw the outstanding stories they created and remained true to the experience they were delivering."

Over the next three years, Johnson would grow into a senior brand manager, working on campaigns for a variety of audiences, collaborating closely with licensors, organizing brand presence at shows like E3, and working closely with hardware manufacturers Microsoft, Sony, and Nintendo to maximize product exposure across their customer ecosystems.

WB GAMES

In 2004, ready to try something new, Johnson accepted a job as senior brand manager for the Warner Bros. Entertainment group. She quickly moved through the ranks until being promoted to vice president of brand marketing for kids, casual, and new markets at WB. Her focus was supporting their budding video game branch—the “WB Games” label was created a year after she joined. “I felt my career really start to grow at Warner Bros.,” she said. “The organization was looking to move outside the games-licensing business and to launch their own self-published games. They wanted to bring in folks from the games industry to help do that. I was marketing employee number one, and built up the marketing department at WB Games. I worked alongside a scrappy team intent on building and launching great game franchises. We felt like a little start-up under a great big umbrella.”

The year Johnson joined the team, WB acquired their first development house, Monolith Productions. Over the next decade, they would acquire many other studios, such as NetherRealm, Rocksteady Studios, TT Games, and Turbine. With these acquisitions, they would publish major hits such as *Mortal Kombat*, *Injustice*, *Middle-Earth: Shadow of Mordor*, a run of uber-successful LEGO games, and the genre-redefining *Batman: Arkham* series. Johnson helped WB’s interactive arm grow from a licensing-led organization to the #3 game publisher in 2015. “I’m incredibly proud of what that has grown into, and the brands we were able to nurture and grow into blockbuster game franchises.”

LEGO

One of those blockbuster brands was LEGO. Over the past decade, Warner has published nearly 20 LEGO games in the Batman, Harry Potter, Lord of the Rings, Marvel Super Heroes, Star Wars, and Jurassic Park universes. The 2015 release *LEGO Dimensions* was the most ambitious, though, as it combined gaming with the beloved brick-building play of LEGO and spanned across 30 unique franchises.

“I’ve had many great partnerships over the years, but being able to work with Jon Burton, founder of TT Games, and the outstanding front-end innovation team at LEGO to bring *LEGO Dimensions* to life was a highlight in gaming for me,” said Johnson. “We were able to do things no one thought could ever be done—hello!—*The Simpsons*, *Portal*, *DC Comics*, *Scooby-Doo* and *The Goonies* all in one game! I loved that I was able to work on parts of the business beyond just marketing and really dive into product and business-development discussions with this unique team from many different sides. Having that level of collaboration on the product side made the marketing campaign and the overall experience incredibly rich.”

As a whole, Johnson recalls her work on the LEGO brand as a major point of pride. “We gave the LEGO games a consumer identity, drove anticipation for the unique flavor of storytelling that only LEGO could achieve, and ultimately introduced an opportunity for parents and kids to share their favorite lore in a way they both could enjoy and relate to,” she continued. “In my time with the brand, we sold over 160 million copies of LEGO games, so I’m quite proud to be part of a brand that really reached the masses.” Many of the WB Games’ LEGO titles took home awards for their marketing assets and campaigns, thanks to the team Johnson built from the ground up.

PAMOJIA MATANI

While at WB, Johnson worked on some of the biggest franchises in the world, but it’s a little game published in 2008 that’s distinguished as her career favorite. “Pamojia Matani was made as part of a public-private partnership between WB and the US government (PEPFAR) to educate Kenyan youth about AIDS prevention,” she said. “It was a PC-LAN game placed in youth centers in the slums of Nairobi. When we launched the game in each of the centers, we hosted events where we literally handed the PCs and games to the community in huge celebration. It was a chance for them to have fun, but also learn important life skills they might not have ever had the opportunity to hear about otherwise. It was incredibly moving and wonderful to be part of a project that could truly make a difference. I was forever changed by the experience.”

NVIDIA

In 2016, after 12 years at WB, Johnson took her career in a new direction and is now the head of global marketing for GeForce NOW and SHIELD at NVIDIA. Johnson’s work is to oversee the consumer marketing efforts behind their streaming line of products, composed of NVIDIA SHIELD and the upcoming game-streaming service GeForce NOW, which is currently in beta. “We are building something really exciting with the future of gaming in GeForce NOW,” she said. “Clearly I believe the future is in the cloud. I believe it can be the center of gaming—access to high-performance gaming in the cloud, cloud saves to pick-up-and-play wherever/whenever, playing your gaming library across multiple-devices, and more. I’m extremely excited to educate and champion new developments in gaming, allowing customers to game in enhanced and expanded ways.””

Through a storied career, Johnson has many achievements to be gratified of. “If I am doing my job well, you will never know who I am. It’s the stories I weave and the customer’s connection to the product that they walk away knowing. This book was an incredible opportunity for my girls to hear what their mom has done in her career—and all those hours away from home. I hope this book shows them that doing what you love can take many forms, so just go with it! I didn’t set out for a career in the game industry, but I am so incredibly grateful this is where I landed.”

“If I am doing my job well, you will never know who I am. It’s the stories I weave and the customer’s connection to the product that they walk away knowing.”

A DAY IN THE LIFE OF...

LOCALIZATION

Localization is a profession that, when done masterfully, often goes unnoticed. This is an unfortunate reality, because best-in-class localization helps players feel at home, making localization professionals some of the unsung heroes of game development.

Localizing a game is about much more than translating text. In regions with large language markets, full voice-over dubbing is commonplace. Smaller markets receive subtitles, with accuracy and spot-on timing making or breaking the experience. Additionally, in-game user interfaces, packaging, and manuals all must be translated. Cultural considerations are also taken into account. Will an American fan understand a pop-culture reference written by a French designer? Not necessarily. When dialogue misses the mark, it pulls the player out of the game.

Ammie Puckett has worked at Naughty Dog for 18 years, and is one of the most veteran localization professionals in video games. She works hard to ensure that every fan who plays one of the studio's games—no matter where they are in the world—enjoys the same high-quality experience.

AMMIE PUCKETT

**The opinions expressed are my own and are not representative of PlayStation or Naughty Dog.*

PROFESSION: LOCALIZATION MANAGER AT NAUGHTY DOG—SANTA MONICA, USA

YEARS IN PROFESSION: 18

WORKED ON: JAK & DAXTER SERIES, UNCHARTED SERIES, THE LAST OF US SERIES

▶ EDUCATION

"I was hired as the office assistant. The team was in the middle of development for the first *Jak & Daxter* game. Eventually, they realized that they needed someone to go through and create scripts as read for the cinematics, along with tracking all the dialogue audio files going out for localization and foreign files being returned. I was tasked with that to help keep things organized. After *Jak 2*, I was officially given the title of localization manager at Naughty Dog.

"While I had no formal localization training beforehand, I learned more and more about the process with each game. I do think that my education degree in sociology (with an emphasis on organizations) and media arts (with an emphasis on research) has helped me understand working in video game development over the years."

▶ BREAKING IN

"I was not expecting to go into video game development. I sort of fell into it."

▶ EARLY INDUSTRY IMPRESSIONS

"When I started at Naughty Dog in 2000, *Space Invaders* had been the last game I played. The biggest surprise was how far games had come since I had last played. My first E3 was about two months after I had started working, and I'd never been to anything like that before. It was crazy! I also had no idea how popular the company I had just started working for was until being at that E3 and I was approached multiple times while wearing my Naughty Dog T-shirt. I had no idea that the video game world had gotten so big, and that was 18 years ago!"

▶ KEY QUALITIES

"Being organized is the top skill to have. You never know when someone is going to ask you about what files were sent, or how many changes in a cinematic, etc. Being able to have an answer quickly is essential."

▶ TRAINING OPPORTUNITIES

"Project-management training is helpful. Since localization is one of the very last steps completed before the game is released, it can be nearly impossible to organize and schedule. There also do seem to be a lot more organizations for localization in the last few years than when I began in the industry. Various game conferences usually have a few seminars on localization specific to games as well."

▶ TOOLS OF THE TRADE

"The majority of dealing with localization for a game is keeping track of all the assets. These are audio files, text strings, etc. Creating a good tracking schedule and spreadsheets is a must. Having a robust dialogue and localization database tool is essential. A familiarity with widely used audio tools (like Pro Tools or Reaper) is also helpful so that you can make any quick and easy edits needed."

▶ HOURS & ENVIRONMENT

"The hours depend on where we are in the development cycle. As the project gets closer to the end, localization really starts to get busier and busier. The hours get longer as you move toward the gold master date."

▶ AN AVERAGE DAY

"When you're in the thick of things during crunch, a typical day includes answering a lot of emails. Territories all over the globe simultaneously send similar files, and these emails contain questions ranging from when things will be delivered, which languages will be included, tracking changes in text and audio files that will need to be redelivered. The more context and visuals you can send about what you need translated and recorded, the better. Once the overnight emails have been answered, it's time to track what has come in, changed, etc. Add some checking what bugs are in the queue, watching subtitles to make sure timing is okay."

Photo credit: Almudena Soria

▶ PROFESSIONAL PERKS

"Being able to meet some of the actors who work in the game. Over the years, our company has had some opportunities to go to console launch parties and some other industry events, which were really cool. But the best perk was when my nephews were younger and I was the cool aunt because I worked in video games. Specifically, because of *Jak & Daxter.*"

▶ CAREER CHALLENGES

"Helping everyone realize that localization must be considered part of the overall development cycle. Localization is sometimes treated as an afterthought, but as our games have become more complex, while also gaining popularity internationally, it's important to give each territory a chance to put their regional stamp on a game through the localization process."

▶ BIGGEST MISTAKE

"It's always hard to have to acknowledge that you can't do everything alone. There wasn't a localization department at Naughty Dog. I was it and it has been hard to learn to ask for help and realize the need for an extra person to get all the work done. You want to be able to say that you did it alone, but as the games become bigger, a team is needed. But once I did acknowledge that, we hired a localization coordinator. Not only was it great to help balance the workload, but I also had a new appreciation for having another person as part of my team."

▶ EXCITING ADVANCEMENTS

"It is fantastic to see the steady growth in the amount of games being localized into various languages. When I started in the industry 18 years ago, video games only seemed to focus on EFIGS (English, French, Italian, German, Spanish) and Japanese. But now, there are so many languages with audio and text, or just text only. We currently localize our games in over 20 languages with text, and there are about a dozen unique audio dialogue tracks."

"Go to the localization or video game conferences and just start meeting people."

JANE NG

THE PRACTICAL DREAMER

 ThatJaneNg  janeng.com

EXPERIENCE

FIRST INDUSTRY PROJECT: LORD OF THE RINGS: RETURN OF THE KING (2003)

FAVORITE INDUSTRY PROJECT: FIREWATCH (2016)

PROJECTS SHIPPED: 8 GAMES

ACHIEVEMENTS UNLOCKED:

> BAFTA "BEST DEBUT GAME"—FIREWATCH (2017)

> GAME DEVELOPERS CHOICE "BEST NARRATIVE"—FIREWATCH (2017)

> GOLDEN JOYSTICK AWARDS "BEST INDIE GAME"—FIREWATCH (2016)

> UNITY AWARDS "BEST 3D VISUAL EXPERIENCE"—FIREWATCH (2016)

STATS

INDUSTRY LEVEL: 17

CURRENT CLASS: ARTIST

CURRENT GUILD: VALVE CORPORATION—BELLEVUE, USA

SPECIAL SKILLS: ENVIRONMENT ART, ZBRUSH, MAYA, MODELING, TEXTURING, RIGGING, LIGHTING, PRODUCTION WORKFLOW, ART ASSET MANAGEMENT AND OPTIMIZATION

STANDARD EQUIPMENT

PLATFORM: PC

GO-TO GENRE: CITY/BASE BUILDING

MUST-HAVE GAME: DRAGON AGE: INQUISITION

Easter Egg

Competed in the Club Crew World Championships in Penang, Malaysia

BIO

Jane Ng is a veteran game artist who creates out of necessity—it's fundamental to her well-being. "I don't really get inspired as much as I literally don't know what else to do work-wise if I'm not making game art," she explained. That being said, Ng does find inspiration from time to time, just not from behind gallery glass. Life experiences are what fuel her work: cooking, traveling, hiking, and gathering a robust portfolio of human experiences.

"She's the realistic, practical side of the dreamer," described *Kill Screen's* Caty McCarthy in a profile on Ng, noting that her work parallels that of a craftsman executing the vision of an architect, taking two-dimensional concepts and translating them into spaces ripe for exploration.

Ng began her career in video games at age 20. "I fell into the industry by chance, but the first company I worked for shut down within two years. I got my 'real start' at my second job, which was Electronic Arts." Her time at EA involved work on global franchises. "I was an environment artist on *Lord of the Rings: The Return of the King*. Being a junior artist was basically like being in an apprenticeship," she recalled.

Although there weren't official game art curricula available at this point in her career, Jane's formal education in fine art and engineering at a liberal arts college proved transferable. "All my 'work skills' are self-taught on the job, but I believe my education gave me a really good foundation in critical thinking and problem-solving; two skills that are essential to what I do now."

This mixture of left and right brain undertakings—both analytical and imaginative—helped define Ng's career of blending art and implementation. Asset management, optimization, and improving production pipelines are as fulfilling to her as creating worlds.

DOWNSIZING

After working on franchises such as *The Lord of the Rings* and *The Godfather*, Ng transitioned into a Senior Artist role at Maxis, lending her talents to the studio's galactically ambitious title *Spore*. Eventually, a conscious desire to move away from industry behemoths surfaced. She found herself at Double Fine Productions in 2007 and worked on fan-favorite titles such as *Brutal Legend*, *Costume Quest*, *Stacking*, *Broken Age*, and *The Cave*. The smaller team sizes required her to wear many hats, contributing to environment modeling, climate and lighting systems, and diagnosing and resolving performance issues. As lead artist on *The Cave*, Ng established the production workflow for all environment art and created the principal level art for half of the game.

Ng now has 17 years of industry work behind her and a spot on the 12-person team at *Firewatch* developer Campo Santo, which was acquired by Valve in April 2018. Working on such a small team is an opportunity she feels wasn't sustainable at the start of her career. "Indie development was not really viable because there were no off-the-shelf engines for a studio to use. Nowadays a lot more people can make games; even folks with very limited programming knowledge."

Firewatch, a game which Ng describes as adult in nature due to heavy themes of grief and isolation, is where she feels her full potential was finally met. As the only full-time 3D environment artist on the then 10-person development team, Ng was pushed to her limits. With that responsibility came a sense of truly significant contribution. "I had 100% ownership on this game. It was the first project I felt like really represented what I could achieve as a game artist."

LIFE IMITATES ART

That sense of pride is amplified when interacting with fans, who connect with Campo Santo's work on a deep level. The most endearing story is that of a 14-year-old who fell in love with the world Ng carefully crafted and was inspired to join the Forest Fire Lookout Association, an organization that works to preserve old fire tower sites, even though they are functionally obsolete. He directly thanks the Campo Santo team for inspiring his future career path in forest fire control.

The indie life isn't always easy, but it's where Ng's heart lives. Additionally, she believes there can be added benefits for women in working with small and scrappy teams. "I had to deal with my fair share of implicit bias. The problem with implicit bias is that the examples are never obvious, and, if detailed, would always sound petty and dubious," Ng explained. "I've experienced plenty of macroaggressions at the workplace such as being told I had 'attitude' when I was being assertive. There were times when my technical advice as a lead was ignored in favor of recent hires who were men. I now choose to work at a small company where I'm treated with unquestioned respect, so it doesn't happen to me anymore."

Ng intends to funnel the adversity she's faced in a positive direction. "I was lucky to have started my career on a team with an above-average ratio of women. I want to spend more of my energy on mentoring up-and-coming talent and also to promote more inclusion and diversity in the industry."

Now focused on *In the Valley of the Gods*—a game that could easily go toe-to-toe with *Firewatch* with its stunning, stylized graphics—Ng is using her technological prowess and desire for diversity to improve representation in nuanced but weighty issues such as identity through hair. "As an immigrant woman of Chinese descent with atypically frizzy, wavy hair, my hair is, to an extent, an outward expression of my struggle with who I am and where I belong. I want to love my hair the way it naturally is, but it's never quite as simple as that."

A single-player, first-person game set in 1920s Egypt, *In the Valley of the Gods* co-stars a woman of color named Zora. Ng recognized that creating Zora's hair would be a challenge for both cultural and technical reasons. The team would need to provide proper representation of Zara's "type 4" hair by ensuring it moves accurately, reacts to light properly, and is generally believable.

"None of us has type 4 hair, characterized by tight coils and common among black women. In fact, none of us has even made video game hair before, but we are committed to giving Zora the hair she loves, the way she chooses to wear it, with all the care and effort we can."

The detailed blog that delved into the art and engineering of Zora's hair on the Campo Santo development Tumblr resulted in over 30K notes, illustrating that Ng's career-spanning attention to detail and drive for diversity is both needed and noticed more than ever.

"I want to spend more of my energy on mentoring up-and-coming talent and also promote more inclusion and diversity in the industry."

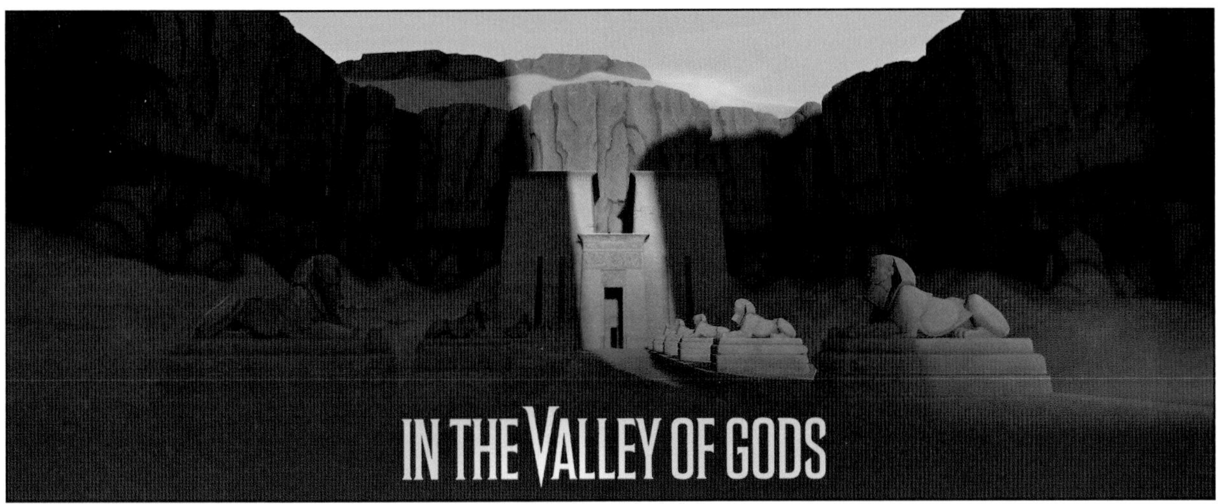

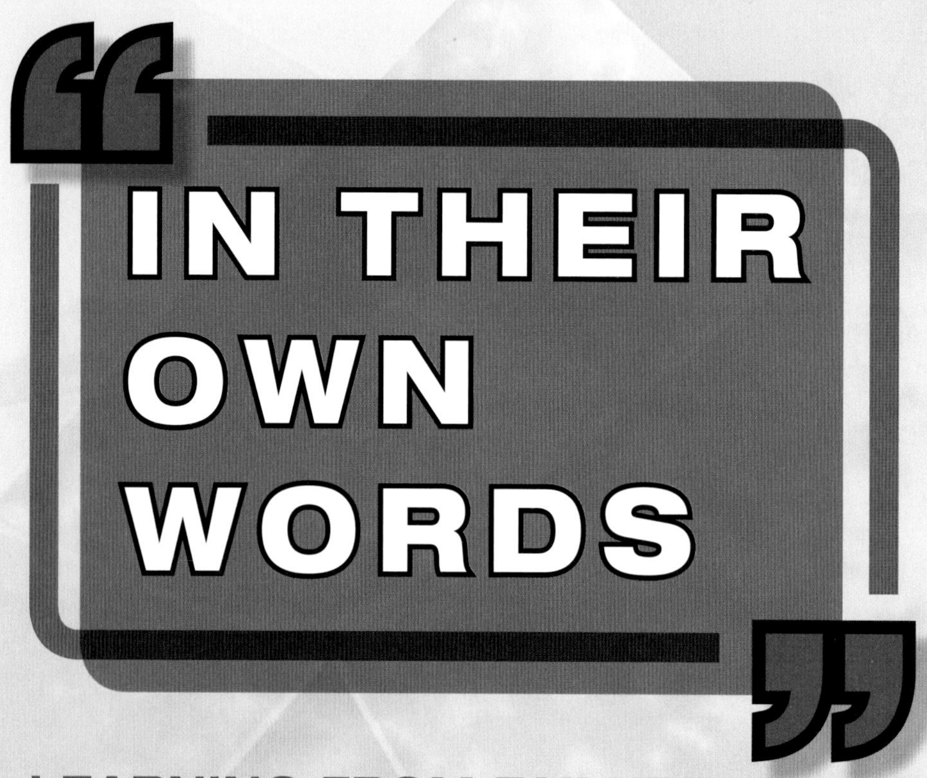

IN THEIR OWN WORDS

LEARNING FROM FAILURE

What is a mistake you made in your profession, and how did you learn from it?

"In my six-plus years working in games media, I've certainly gotten too caught up in what people thought. When I first started out, I was told I didn't belong; I was told I was only being helped by men in the industry because they wanted to sleep with me (which is not only a discredit to me, but also to the incredibly supportive men I have the pleasure of working alongside!). I was told I should dress a certain way and act a certain way. I'm sure a lot of that has still stuck with me, but I've absolutely learned that I shouldn't constantly feel like I have to prove myself to people I might never even meet. I got where I am today because I worked hard, I have the experience, and I've always been incredibly passionate about games. It was hard to break through that first wave of self-doubt, but I'm glad I overcame it."

Alanah Pearce | Writer/Producer | Rooster Teeth | Los Angeles, USA

"I think one of my first mistakes was to believe that as a game designer, I should be the one who made the most decisions about the game. I had learned that position during my studies in film direction in the previous years. The direction and the script, to which I dedicated myself especially in my training, are very important roles, from which the vision of the work is constructed. Upon entering the video game industry later, I discovered over time that I had an attitude that was not very flexible with the proposals of other team members. When I realized that, I tried the opposite: take into account many ideas from others to apply to the game. But that was not all that good either, because a game designer really has to take charge of key decisions. It took me a while to learn to balance the two things in me: to be open to the ideas of everyone—the team, the client—and at the same time, to take responsibility for taking and polishing the best ones to apply to the product, no matter who they come from."

Alejandra Bruno | Narrative & Game Designer | QB9 | Buenos Aires, Argentina

---

"The first game I ever worked on as a programmer was *Psychonauts*, a wonderfully written game (by Tim Schafer and Erik Wolpaw), with lots and lots of dialogue. The grievous mistake: we put that dialogue directly into the code we were writing, with not a care about how sound was going to play, or the fact that the game needed to ship in four other languages, or what would happen if changes to the script had to be made, or how in the world a localization producer was going to track which audio file belonged to which text line, or how to fix the text when the actor in the studio said the line totally differently than how it was originally written, or what to do when the actor did multiple takes and they were all great, but the code only had the one line, and about a gazillion other problems. The amount of crunch it took for 10+ people to fix this was obscene. Needless to say, we have never made the same mistake again. I give a talk about the solutions to this, and it's available to watch for free on YouTube: 'Dialog Systems in Double Fine Games.'"

Anna Kipnis | Senior Gameplay Programmer | Double Fine Productions | San Francisco, USA

"It's constant learning each day, every day. We strive to do better and learn from our mistakes. Being on the distribution side, marketing has to constantly work hand in hand with the sales and distribution team. When I first joined the industry six years ago from an aviation background, I had implemented a campaign and later was told that the title was not approved by the censorship authorities. That's where I learned how important communication with the team is, and how intricately woven together each division is."

Divya Sharma | Marketing Manager | Shooting Stars | Dubai, UAE

"Self-doubt and giving others who are said to know better the power to negatively affect my performance—without following my gut. I never studied economics or business management; everything I do is by self-studying and constant practice, making mistakes and learning from them. At the end, I realized that not everything comes from a textbook and top universities. At times, a business runs and lives by experience, as its daily needs rule change to achieve its goals. Don't ever allow an external person who hasn't seen your growth and fought next to you in achieving them make you doubt. Use their knowledge, hear from them, and take pieces of their experience to evolve, but never forget your own experience in the making and how you got where you are today. In this same matter, we need to know how to support ourselves and back up our ideas with knowledge, facts, goals, and strategies."

Fernanda Contreras Stange | CFO | Gamaga, Inc. | Santiago, Chile

---

"Oh, there are so many to choose from. The thing is, most mistakes can be corrected or kludged or worked around. Those are the easy ones—you still have to deal with the fallout of the mistake, but there's a path to a solution. I think my biggest one, the one that was hardest to fix, was allowing myself to become jaded. I'd reached a point in this industry where I was seeing people reinvent the wheel; game mechanics were being retooled and presented as new and nifty. I needed to take a little time to look through the eyes of a player, rather than a designer, so I could see what was so enticing about these old ideas made new. I figured out that I had fallen out of the habit of playing games for fun and had been playing them for analysis. Now I play a lot more broadly than the first-person shooters and third-person adventure games that had been my preference before."

Kimberly Unger | Mobile/VR Producer | Playchemy | Burlingame, USA

"I used to care too much what people thought—I thought I had to please everyone. I learned very early on that not everyone will like you, and that's okay. I can't remember now who it was that told me, 'If everyone likes you, you're doing it wrong.'"

Pippa Tshabalala | Video Game Reviewer/Presenter | Glitched | Johannesburg, South Africa

---

"There was a point in my career where I became apathetic to a project. My passion for what we were making was just gone for a number of reasons. Unfortunately, that earned me a stigma on the team that took two years to turn around. I learned from this that keeping your passion alive for a project and being a good teammate by uplifting those around you are incredibly important."

Rachel Day | Senior VFX Artist | Blizzard Entertainment | Irvine, USA

"Before I was in the game industry, I did everything from waiting tables to managing the register at a hardware store. I had never worked a salary job or in an office, and my idea of my own personal value as a staff member hadn't fully developed yet. I wouldn't describe it as a mistake, but rather an oversight, that I didn't take time to acknowledge the value in the work that I did and my value as an employee sooner. Perhaps this is something you learn in business school, but in my first few years as a video producer, it never occurred to me that as a company employee, my opinions mattered and my work contributions were as important as anyone else's. I always thought I was simply there to do what I was hired to do, that my work wasn't as valuable as, for example, an editor's, and that I had no say or control in what I did at the company. It took me years to find my confidence and voice in meetings with my peers and to come to that realization. Through observation I learned to take pride in my work, I saw that everyone at the company had a small but important role in the big picture, and instead of worrying about my role, I adopted a sense of community and camaraderie with the people I worked with. That perception changed everything and made me a happier person both in my work and personal life."

Naomi Kyle | Actor, Host, & Producer | Los Angeles, USA

"Having players from all over the world means that your community never sleeps, but that doesn't mean that you shouldn't either. When I started out, I always wanted to be there for the community, at any time of the day. If someone posted a cool new cosplay or fan art in the middle of the night, I wanted to be up to see it. If anyone had a question on the forums, I wanted to be online to help. Even on weekends I was constantly checking our mentions and hashtags for updates. Being 'on' all the time takes a toll on you at some point. That is definitely something I had to keep reminding myself of in the beginning."

Anne van der Zanden | Community Manager | Guerrilla Games | Amsterdam, The Netherlands

---

"After almost 30 years, there are as many failures as successes. My takeaway would be: trust your gut no matter what. After you make a successful game, there are a lot of stakeholders in the franchise—your publisher, the media, your teammates, your critics, your fans. There will be a lot of opinions—mostly conflicting—clamoring for your attention. Be open to input, criticism, and new ideas, but don't let them drown out the inner voice that guided you to success in the first place."

Amy Hennig | Senior Creative Director & Writer | Independent | San Carlos, USA

"When I first started working in a marketing role, no one trained me; I was just kind of thrown into the role. The mistake I made was not asking enough questions or seeking out information. I guess I assumed that people would tell me things that were important or relevant, but that's not always the case. Everyone is focused on their own work and isn't necessarily going to remember to tell you things you need to know. This is when I learned to meet with anyone who might have anything to do with my role or who might just have some good advice or insight, and ask lots of questions!"

Kirsten Duvall | VP of Business Strategy | Blueprint Reality, Inc. | San Francisco, USA

"I don't toot my own horn, and I am still failing at it personally. Basically, when nobody else on the team knows what my contributions are, then as far as the rest of the team knows, I do nothing. After the work that I put in for *Halo* and *Halo 2*, I thought I might be moving up in the world. But with my boss leaving and the work I had done never really being socialized, I remained 'artist' for another few years. I went away on maternity leave and came back to find that I didn't really have a job anymore. Everyone else was too busy making games to really pay attention. But Bungie being Bungie, I was able to build myself back up. But I would attribute that ability to my managers these last eight years or so being much better about making the work that my team and I do be more visible to the rest of the studio."

Lorraine McLees | Consumer Products | Bungie, Inc. | Bellevue, USA

"I lost influence in a transmedia project that went forward with aspects that I did not have the opportunity to review since I had only officially worked on one component. It was a situation where my name was associated with the wider intellectual property despite the fact that I hadn't been included in all branches. I have learned to look for similar patterns and address that dynamic directly, although it has taken years of experience and building confidence in order to get to this point. Even though it is unfortunate that this process is necessary, I focus on the valuable lessons and insights, such as contractually ensuring I am able to see and comment on all aspects of any IP I am affiliated with."

Elizabeth LaPensée | Designer, Artist, & Assistant Professor | Michigan State University | Lansing, USA

"When developing *Uncharted 4*, I redesigned *Uncharted*'s climbing system. I had a lot of really cool ideas for it, like how we could make Nathan Drake's climbing play and feel more like real rock climbing. We spent tons of time and resources throughout the game's production trying new things. We visited a rock-climbing gym to research the look and feel of actual climbing. I was really focused on the goal of traversal being a more fully-featured game on its own. But as we got further into production, the new features weren't really catching on or fitting into the game's levels. The deeper the climbing mechanics, the harder traversal blended with other types of gameplay, specifically combat. So, we ended up cutting way back and going with something a lot more basic than I had been dreaming of. The climbing system looks a lot better than it did in *Uncharted 3*, but I don't think we were able to make an equivalent leap forward with the systems themselves.

"What I learned from this is something I should have known already—system design must go hand-in-hand with level design. I was so caught up in getting the proposed systems and features implemented, I should have been spending just as much, or more, time creating level setups, proving the systems worked in real scenarios, and adding new features only when I felt I didn't have enough depth in the gameplay that already existed. If I had, maybe I would have developed a better understanding for the place traversal played in the game as a whole and tailored my efforts to what was really necessary. I also neglected one of my main roles as a designer—selling my ideas to the team, getting them invested, and building on my ideas with their own."

Emilia Schatz | Lead Game Designer | Naughty Dog | Santa Monica, USA

"After Dante's my lead left the company. I thought that since I worked so hard and helped to ship the game on time I would be a natural choice for promotion. I am direct but sincere. I also have a reputation for having a low tolerance for bullshit. Because of my personality I largely try to avoid politics and focus on the task at hand. Unfortunately, politics meant dealing with the boys club of producers. At that time, I believed that working hard was enough. Being a good artist was enough. Being a loyal employee was enough. So, I let my lead deal with the politics so I could focus on my job of being a senior artist. Sadly, when my lead left he did not recommend me and instead picked someone from the boys club. That was the last time I let anyone speak for me or my hard work. I will elbow my way into the room and take a seat at the table before I let anyone represent my work or my skills ever again."

Lisette Titre | Art Director | Double Fine Productions | San Francisco, USA

"I think my most notable failure happened early on in my career. I didn't always speak up for what I believed. I was worried how I was perceived and tried to make sure I was always 'one of the guys.' I think challenging that status quo is important, but it's scary. It changes how people perceive you. I'm glad I've grown, started to stand up for what I believe in, but still maintain my compassion for others to hopefully be my guiding force. I've learned that if I don't speak up or don't participate, how can I truly initiate change? And often I've found if I state my case or opinion, I have helped to give voice to others who were too afraid to speak or felt confident enough to speak once I spoke up."

Stephanie Bayer | Manager, Community Development | Blizzard Entertainment | Irvine, USA

"Ruining my health and having to leave work for six months. This was during a project kick-off stage, so with help from my boss and the game director, I somehow managed to start the project. Since then, I listen to my doctor and do not work excessively. I feel grateful that the reason I can work on projects as both producer and director today is because everyone at SEGA is supporting me."

Rieko Kodama | Producer & Director | SEGA | Tokyo, Japan

"I gave my first solo talk at GDC in 2015 and it was also the first time I had presented any part of my doctoral research outside of my university. I felt like I bombed it and it gave me a lot of anxiety about ever trying to give that kind of talk at GDC again. The format for this solo presentation was different than many of the other casual talks I had given about gender and gaming in the past, but I did not adjust my preparations to account for this different, more formal format. I learned that I could not wing it with a complex academic topic like I could when telling the stories of women gamers. I developed a new appreciation for the preparation needed while giving a formalized presentation and applied this new perspective to the preparations for my 2016 talk. It took a lot of courage and positive self-talk to get back up on that stage, but my preparation paid off. For 2016 my talk, 'Running a Women's esports Tournament,' got me rated as one of the Top 50 Speakers at GDC 2016.

Morgan Romine | Director of Initiatives | AnyKey | San Diego, USA

NPC:

On Being Unseen in the Game Dev Community

By Ari Green | *Co-Founder of Couple Six Inc.*

I asked my friends at what age they knew the story wasn't about them. That the protagonists in the stories that were ostensibly made for them would never feature people that looked like them. That they were "NPCs." Someone told me it was age seven when they started associating "the black kid" with "the weird kid." For someone else it was around eight years old, a gradual realization calcifying into the certainty that being gay meant being invisible.

I think for girls it happens at a younger age. Watch enough Saturday morning cartoons and eventually you'll figure out you'll never be a Red Ranger. Being any kind of outsider or minority means you have your own version of this epiphany. The black person always dies in the horror movies. Action heroes are never colourblind. You should never fall in love if you're queer. You take these things as a given. Or you begin to seek your stories elsewhere.

As an "NPC" you cobble together representation from bits of different media. The background tomboy from one comic, the queer-coded villain from another show, a handful of anthropomorphic characters that could be read as POC if you squint.

Piece by piece you craft a little homunculus-you.

For many of us, games are where we found our ultimate retreats. RPGs let us pretend to be the heroes for once, even if the pronouns were wrong. Character creators let us sculpt heroes who we could see ourselves in, even if the features were off or the hair wasn't quite right. The homunculus was made real for the first time. For many of us, this wasn't and isn't enough.

We became creators out of necessity. Growing up and realizing the story isn't about you means you craft a new story, compose a new song. Build a new game.

We found in ourselves narratives that had never been voiced aloud and sang them into being. This was the whole reason my best friend and I founded our game studio, Couple Six.

But the game industry often acts like these narratives are side-quests, the purview of smaller indie titles or bonus content for AAA games, and never the main experience. The industry is saturated with coverage of AAA games and the studios that make them. Games that primarily feature handsome, straight, white males as their protagonists. This sends a message: it reflects a warped view of reality where only one demographic gets to be the hero. Which isn't just wrong, it's boring.

I was able to attend the Game Developer's Conference in San Francisco one year through a scholarship offered by an organization called I Need Diverse Games. I attended two nearly identical game design workshops on two separate days where I was grouped up with five or six other people I'd never met before. In each workshop, we were tasked with coming up with a paper prototype of a video game.

I had a blast in the first workshop. The majority of us in the group were women. Everyone was encouraged to contribute their ideas and it felt like we were collaborating. Nobody was left out and every voice was valued. We ended up with a game that asked the players—"patients"—to explain to the main player—"the doctor"—why their real-life mothers deserved to be saved. A brutally successful way of getting a protagonist to care about some "NPCs."

In the second group, I felt immediately uncomfortable as the only woman. One guy dominated the conversation, making off-colour jokes about US politics and bragging about how, as a producer, he had to cajole the programmers on his team into working. The same guy also ended up insulting the favourite game of another man at the table. The game our group came up with was an uninspired "Werewolf" clone I had little interest in working on. I didn't bother to come back after the lunch break because I figured if I was going to be spending a limited amount of time at the biggest game developer conference in the world, I might as well be spending it on something I actually enjoyed.

The first group's game was unique. The product of collaboration, but also the result of a team willing to let empathy be a driving mechanic. The male-dominated group created a boring clone. The same experience as so many other games. Telling the same type of story. Too comfortable, or perhaps too afraid, to incorporate new ideas and create something new and exciting.

In that moment it became suddenly, viscerally clear to me why so many women and minorities leave the game dev industry. It's not because of a lack of fortitude or skill. It's because no one wants to be in an environment that is unwelcoming to them.

The games industry isn't an RPG.

It's not that some people are the heroes of the story and others are NPCs. The truth is the world is filled with protagonists and our experiences are only enriched when we fully embrace this reality. The Dictionary of Obscure Sorrows, a website of made-up words, describes this feeling as "sonder," or "the realization that each random passerby is living a life as vivid and complex as your own." Far from being a sorrowful realization, I see this as a beautiful thing.

Everyone in the industry—from developers to journalists —understands the power games have to uplift, delight, and represent. The escape that they offer and the fantasy that they provide shouldn't be exclusive to a particular group of people. If you're someone in a position to give a voice to the voiceless, or to champion those who have been unseen for too long, you must lend a hand. Hire them in your studios, consult them for your narratives, cover the work they're doing.

And for anyone reading this who is used to being the NPC, I want to say this: We're going to make games about you. We're going to tell everyone your story. We see you.

SOFIA BATTEGAZZORE

GROWING THE GAME INDUSTRY IN URUGUAY FROM THE GROUND UP

 sofiabatte  Sofia Battegazzore

EXPERIENCE

FIRST INDUSTRY PROJECT: ROBOTIC BIRTHDAY (2002)

FAVORITE INDUSTRY PROJECT: BIG FAT AWESOME HOUSE PARTY (2005-2007)

PROJECTS SHIPPED: 50+ GAMES

ACHIEVEMENTS UNLOCKED:

> CO-FOUNDED THE FIRST GAME STUDIO IN URUGUAY (2002)

> GAMES FOR CHANGE AWARD—SEPTEMBER 12TH: A TOY WORLD (2003)

> 13 MILLION REGISTERED ACCOUNTS FOR BIG FAT AWESOME HOUSE PARTY IN ONE YEAR (2006)

> GAMES FOR CHANGE "LIFETIME ACHIEVEMENT AWARD"—SEPTEMBER 12TH: A TOY WORLD (2009)

STATS

INDUSTRY LEVEL: 16

CURRENT CLASS: VIDEO GAME & SOFTWARE PRODUCER

CURRENT GUILD: PAYANA GAMES—CIUDAD DE LA COSTA, URUGUAY

SPECIAL SKILLS: GRAPHIC DESIGN, GAME DEVELOPMENT, GAME PRODUCTION, ART DIRECTION

STANDARD EQUIPMENT

PLATFORM: NINTENDO DS

GO-TO GENRE: ANYTHING EXCEPT HORROR GAMES

MUST-HAVE GAME: THE SIMS (2000)

BIO

Sofia Battegazzore was a successful graphic designer at a Montevideo-based advertising agency in Uruguay during the late '90s. "After eight years I wanted to try different things," she said. "I started doing game localization for the Cartoon Network, and I loved it. That's when I realized that I'd been working for the dark side up until then, and that I didn't want to work in advertising ever again. Working and learning from the video games industry was like a breath of fresh air for me."

Prior to her advertising career, Battegazzore let her curiosity guide her future. She was criticized at times for starting to study a new field and then being lured away by a new and exciting venture before finishing the last. "I didn't know why I did so many things, like study a couple of years in architecture, one year of industrial design, another year of interior design, a year of music, one year of cinema school, and then painting and sculpture," she admitted. "I would go and do a scriptwriting class, and after that I would start working in scenography. I learned a lot working in advertising, too. It all came together when I started working in games, and everything made sense. I was using all the skills I had learned!"

Easter Egg

Buckminster Fuller's design ideology made such a large impact on Battegazzore that she built a geodesic, dome-shaped greenhouse in her backyard, where she grows her own vegetables.

POWERFUL ROBOT

In 2002, she and game researcher Gonzalo Frasca founded Powerful Robot, where Battegazzore would serve as CEO, art director, and producer for 10 years. Powerful Robot gained visibility through licensed works for companies such as Pixar, Lucasfilm, Disney, Warner Bros., and most prolifically, the Cartoon Network.

They chose a difficult time to launch a start-up, but were undeterred by the challenging path ahead. "When we founded Powerful Robot in 2002, there was a huge economic crisis in Uruguay," she explained. "It was difficult because there was no gaming industry in Uruguay, so we had to create it and learn along the way. I didn't know what to expect, really, but despite the difficulties, I was surprised by how much fun I was having."

When setting up the studio, Battegazzore made a point to hire with diversity in mind from the very start. "At the time I would ask myself, am I the only woman interested in video games? Not having an industry in Uruguay yet, I realized it depended on me, since I was the one doing the hiring," she recalled. "I knew I was doing something right when, in the future, other studios started asking advice on how to find women to work in their studios, too."

The studio's first game project was *Robotic Birthday*, developed in partnership with the Cartoon Network. "It was the first game we did as a studio, and with the money earned, we would be able to rent office space, buy equipment, and hire

"I knew I was doing something right when, in the future, other studios started asking advice on how to find women to work in their studios, too."

more people," she shared. Battegazzore was in charge of the overall art direction of the game.

"At Powerful Robot, we used to create mostly online Flash games, and projects would take usually three to six months of production," she continued. "So when we started working in 2006 on *Big Fat Awesome House Party* for the IP *Foster's Home for Imaginary Friends*, we didn't even know if we were going to be able to pull that kind of project off. But we knew it was going to be huge for an online game. It took a year of production, plus another year and a half creating monthly content. I loved the challenge, and the result was a very successful game that led to other projects, and episodic games based on different shows."

House Party generated over 13 million registered accounts in its first year. It was intended to only run for a year as part of a campaign tied to the television show, but due to its success, Cartoon Network extended its online life for another six months.

Future licensed games Powerful Robot developed included *Path of the Jedi*, a 2009 *Star Wars: The Clone Wars* tie-in, an episodic *Torchwood* game and *Green Lantern Battle Cards* in 2011, *Adventure Time—Legends of Ooo: Big Hollow Princess* in 2012, and many more—over 50 in total.

NEWS GAMES

"When we were not working in commercial games, we would develop political games, which we created under the brand Newsgaming," Battegazzore revealed. The goal was to make timely games about political events as a new way of civic engagement and expression. "In 2003 we created *September 12th: A Toy World*, one game I feel really proud about." The game was based on stories emerging from coverage of the War on Terror, and the civilian casualties resulting from it.

"It was certainly a subject that had not been treated in video games yet. Set in a small Middle East-like town, the player is given a missile launcher and told who civilians are and who terrorists are," she explained. "If you try to kill the terrorists, you will always kill civilians as collateral damage. Other civilians will mourn their dead and turn into terrorists. After a couple of minutes of play, the screen is full of terrorists and the town is in ruins."

The intent was to force players to think critically about violence. "It went viral very quickly and it was really controversial at the time, but since then up until recently, it has been in exhibitions in various museums or used to debate about war in many universities all over the world."

Later that year Powerful Robot developed the first-ever commissioned video game for a presidential campaign, created for Howard Dean. The flash title aimed to help his supporters understand the importance of their grassroots outreach, and try to increase participation numbers in pre-caucus campaigning. Subsequently, their studio developed *Cambiemos* in 2004, a game for the Uruguayan presidential campaign.

The Flash game *Madrid* was released only two days after the 2004 train bombings in the Spanish capital. The player would click on vigil candles that illuminated mourners from various terror attacks around the world. The goal was to help them collectively shine as bright as possible by clicking each in rapid succession. With the volume of mourners on-screen, several would always fade before completing the circuit. When the timer ran out, simple text read, "You have to keep trying," an emotional appeal to continue fighting what can sometimes feel like unwinnable battles.

In 2008, as with much of the world, Powerful Robot took a huge hit from the global financial crisis. "We were working mainly for clients in the United States, so we almost went bankrupt," she said. "We had to let a lot of people go, and even though I don't think we could have done things differently, it was a really tough experience. We had to get smaller and learn to adapt and find creative ways to do the same quality projects with a lot fewer resources."

"Running a studio for about 10 years makes you use many different hats," said Battegazzore. "I started as graphic designer, worked in HR and PR, but I most loved working on production. Being able to see the big picture and seeing a project taking shape is really rewarding. Also, I like to think that I can speak fluent programmer-artist/artist-programmer and help them understand each other."

The studio closed down in 2012, at which time Battegazzore began as a professor of game production at ORT University in Uruguay, and a freelance game developer under her personal brand, Payana Games.

"Payana Games is an independent development studio based in Ciudad de la Costa, Uruguay," explained Battegazzore. "We believe in building bridges between video games and other disciplines, helping create new experiences. We create games mostly for mobile, like *el juego de Buscaespecies* for Plan Ceibal, which teaches about the native and endangered animals of Uruguay." Another project Payana is collaborating on is *The Loog App*, which makes the experience of learning music easier through interactive peripherals such as a children's guitar with only three strings.

"The most challenging project of my career was helping create a video game industry in a small country, in the middle of an economic crisis," she reflected. "Starting from scratch about 20 years ago and now working side by side with government and institutions to help the industry thrive seems like a great accomplishment."

When they opened Powerful Robot, it was the first game studio in Uruguay and one of the only in Latin America. "Now there are around 20 in Uruguay alone," she closed.

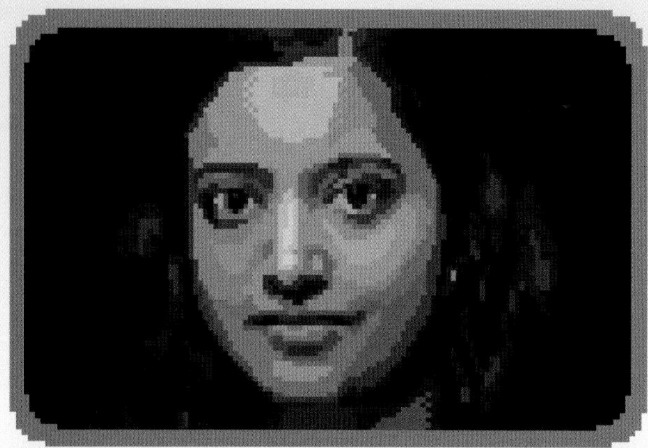

SHILPA BHAT

BRINGING FREEMIUM TO THE FOREFRONT IN INDIA

 shilpabhat_

 Shilpa Bhat

 Shilpa Bhat

 99games.in

EXPERIENCE

FIRST INDUSTRY PROJECT: IMPERIAL GLORY PORT TO MAC OS X (2005)

FAVORITE INDUSTRY PROJECT: STAR CHEF (2013)

PROJECTS SHIPPED: 24 GAMES

ACHIEVEMENTS UNLOCKED:

> LEAD PRODUCER ON STAR CHEF, THE HIGHEST MONETIZED GAME FROM INDIA

> STAR CHEF, BEST OF APPSTORE 2014, FICCI BAF 2015 MOBILE AND TABLET GAMES (INTERNATIONAL) AND IAMAI 6TH INDIA DIGITAL AWARDS – BEST MOBILE GAMES.

> PRODUCER ON DHOOM: 3 THE GAME, FASTEST TO 10 MILLION DOWNLOADS IN INDIA

> SPEAKER AND MENTOR AT GOOGLE INDIE GAMES ACCELERATOR PROGRAM FOR APAC REGION FROM INDIA (2018)

STATS

INDUSTRY LEVEL: 16

CURRENT CLASS: VP OF GAMES

CURRENT GUILD: 99GAMES—UDUPI, INDIA

SPECIAL SKILLS: PROGRAMMING, PRODUCTION, MONETIZATION, PRODUCT MANAGEMENT, LIVEOPS

STANDARD EQUIPMENT

FAVORITE PLATFORM: MOBILE

GO-TO GENRE: SIMULATION

MUST-HAVE GAME: HAY DAY

BIO

"While India is an emerging gaming market at the moment, gaming in India was very different when I grew up, or even when I joined the software and game-development industry," said 99Games VP Shilpa Bhat. "Except for a few privileged-class families, children wouldn't get easy access to PC or video games. Gaming arcades were very few and limited to large cities in the country. Gaming was generally thought of as a distraction for children, something for which kids needed permission from parents, and adults wouldn't play as a hobby or entertainment."

Bhat wasn't an exception to this reality. "I gained access to a personal computer only after high school, and I would play *Dangerous Dave*, *Prince of Persia*-styled retro games, and a few racing games," she continued. "As was common back then in Indian households, I was stereotypically encouraged to pursue medicine and was well on my way to doing so! I feel karma had other plans for me, and I stumbled upon a brief computer course."

None of her family was yet aware of her keen interest in computer graphics and programming, although fortunately when they found out, they were supportive. Bhat joined the Manipal Institute of Technology in 1998, and earned her bachelor's of engineering and computer science. "I immersed myself in logic designs and programming—this was when I realized my interests lay more in artificial intelligence and computer graphics—my first step towards game development."

ROBOSOFT

In 2002, Bhat began her first post-graduation job at computer software company Robosoft Technologies. "It was an emerging software services company back then, in my hometown Udupi," she explained. "Having worked here with some of the brightest minds on the Macintosh platform, the first two years in Robosoft strengthened my fundamentals in design and coding."

Bhat began as a software engineer and, over a period of 10 years, worked her way into a leadership position. Her first official project was a software application called Swift 3D, which allows users to create or import 3D models, animate or manipulate them, and export them for use in Adobe Flash animations.

Easter Egg

Loves cooking and experimenting with Chinese, North-Indian, and Thai recipes.

"By now, game tech enthusiasts noticed a spike in the developing market of gaming," recalled Bhat. "With a nod from our CEO Rohith Bhat, a passionate lot of developers, including myself, began porting PC games to Mac, followed by a few game-development services for Robosoft clients. As a team lead by that point, I acquired a deeper understanding of game engine tech and monetization models, including freemium and data analysis."

When Robosoft started exploring the possibility of developing video games, the focus was on consoles and PC. "At one point we were seriously considering becoming a console developer," Bhat shared. "Game publishing was limited to well-established companies with a publishing track record. The growth opportunities of a potential indie company were limited. Later, smartphones and App Store/Play Store evolution changed the entire picture, giving indie companies a fair chance to sell their innovative games directly to end users, cutting all barriers, thus opening up avenues to study player data, iterate, and improve their games."

99GAMES

With the rise of smartphones, Robosoft decided to more actively pursue the opportunities in gaming, and established a game-focused subsidiary in 2011, 99Games. "With my interest and experience in game development, I naturally transitioned to 99Games as senior project manager to develop our IP games," she said. "My first original IP game-development project at 99Games was a time-management casual game for women—*Nightclub Mayhem*." During this period, 99Games was experimenting with premium titles for iPhones and iPads.

One of their first big hits was the movie tie-in to Bollywood hit *Dhoom 3*. The endless runner they developed was the first game to reach more than one million downloads in the Indian Windows phone store. As senior producer at the time, the game's success remains one of Bhat's favorite memories. "One month post-launch period of *Dhoom 3: The Game*, our team had their fanboy moment meeting the Bollywood superstar Aamir Khan. The whole team had worked on a very short schedule to pull this game off to coincide with the movie release, and the success that followed made every moment of pain extremely worthwhile and rewarding."

STAR CHEF

After a year of experimenting with premium games in the time-management and puzzle genres, Bhat realized it wasn't their path to success. They conceptualized their first hit freemium title *Star Chef*, which released in 2014 to global success. It became the highest monetized game in all of India. "*Star Chef* has been downloaded over 20 million times and generated positive ROI since the game's launch date," shared Bhat.

After the game's release, she was promoted to VP of games, and is now focusing on scaling the teams to handle multiple production lines in parallel. Their 2018 title *Fantastic Chefs*, just released worldwide. "Rather than a project or event, the most challenging part in my career so far was to put together a good game-development team in India," she explained. "Having roots in a software development company, Robosoft, our first tech and design team was easier to put together. However, scaling the team was a challenge, as good gaming talent is sparse in India. At times we had to follow unconventional routes, recognize talent from other industries, and transition them to gaming art and tech. As *Star Chef* scaled globally, we had to strengthen our analytics, UA, and community teams, and again most of the learning had to be self-taught."

Star Chef has become one of Bhat's favorite projects. "Being a cooking enthusiast myself, I thoroughly enjoyed leading the design of this game. We gave much attention to detail to every culinary item in this game. The end result was very rewarding, as the game went on to become the first globally successful monetized game from India, and the growing fan base response was heartwarming."

GROWING INDIAN GAMES

The Indian game industry was nascent when 99Games started developing their portfolio—existing Indian gaming companies either provided outsourcing services for global IPs, or focused on card/casino games. As a pivotal member of the studio, at an important time in the local industry, Bhat's influence is far-felt.

"Developing a globally successful monetized game out of India has demonstrated the potential of Indian studios and encouraged several indie developers here to follow a similar path," said Bhat. "It was a much-needed success for the Indian gaming ecosystem. The fact that we are based out of Udupi, a small town in the southern part of India known more for its cuisine, and that we are placing it on the world map of gaming inspires and motivates me every day. I, along with our team at 99Games, dream of being the number one gaming studio in India."

"While my career is more focused on achieving this goal and I hope to achieve the same with support of my brilliant team, I am personally aiming to gain more knowledge of game design, emotion engineering, and the science behind audience engagement," she concluded. "This is my message to all young gaming aspirants, especially women in India: Every person is born with a natural talent, something he or she is really good at. It could be teaching, crafting, being a homemaker, or even game development. Identify your passion and pour your heart and soul into it. Your life will thrive and become a fun and satisfying journey."

A DAY IN THE LIFE OF...

A USER RESEARCH ANALYST

User research has become a vital part of development, ensuring that the player is part of the development process from preproduction stages all the way until the game has gone gold.

Drawing heavily on anthropology, psychology, and human-computer interaction, user research is the science behind the art of making games. UR analysts are responsible for authoring targeted surveys, executing playtest sessions, and condensing findings into a digestible format that has clear, actionable feedback for the team. Information gathered through user research allows publishers and developers to make decisions with confidence, providing data on the reception of in-game features, systems, plot points, and more.

Bethesda's Elizabeth Zelle studied marine biology and, after stumbling into a career in gaming, found that the scientific foundation of her studies translated well into user research. Zelle now lends her expertise to teams across Bethesda's portfolio to ensure games hit the mark with the intended audience.

ELIZABETH ZELLE

PROFESSION: USER RESEARCH ANALYST AT THE BETHESDA SOFTWORKS RESEARCH LAB, LOCATED AT ID SOFTWARE—RICHARDSON, TX USA

YEARS IN PROFESSION: 6

ASSOCIATED WITH: SAINTS ROW SERIES, RED FACTION SERIES, HOMEFRONT: THE REVOLUTION, AGENTS OF MAYHEM, WOLFENSTEIN SERIES, DOOM SERIES, QUAKE CHAMPIONS, ELDER SCROLLS ONLINE, ELDER SCROLLS: LEGENDS, PREY: MOONCRASH, AND A HANDFUL OF UNRELEASED TITLES

▶ EDUCATION

"Most people looking to break into games user research are coming in with a strong education in psychology, human-computer interaction, or games media studies, often with at least a master's degree in one of those fields. I went to school for marine biology, so I definitely came into games from a non-traditional route! However, my education is useful in my day-to-day job a lot more than most people think. How to design a good test, how to execute a study, how to analyze data and look for trends, and how to report upon my findings are all things I originally learned to apply to fishes and algae, but are the cornerstone of being a user researcher. When I came into games, I did have to ramp up quickly on subjects related to psychology so I could apply the skills I already had to games and gamers; I accomplished this through a lot of reading/study on my own time, as well as watching talks and presentations from members of the games user research community."

▶ KEY QUALITIES

"You have to love games and love science to be a great user researcher, because this field is a blending of both. Being adaptable is also a personality trait that is highly valuable, because my work is never the same from one day to the next!

▶ TRAINING OPPORTUNITIES

"If anyone is interested in pursuing a career in user research, I'd recommend getting involved with the research community early to find a mentor and talks aimed at junior researchers. The IGDA GRUX SIG—Games Research and User Experience Special Interest Group—is the place to be for games user research. We have a very active and friendly community on Twitter and Discord, along with annual summits in both the USA and Europe."

▶ TOOLS OF THE TRADE

"The tools I most often use day to day as a researcher are survey tools like SurveyMonkey, SurveyGizmo, and Qualtrics. Surveys are an extremely adaptable research method, and I utilize them in almost every study I design. Tools for interacting with and visualizing large datasets like Tableau and SPSS are also common in user research, as are video-capture tools like XSplit or OBS, since you often need to record playtest sessions. Being able to design readable reports is also highly valuable, which is something most often done in some combination of Word/PowerPoint, so make sure you can whip up a pretty presentation on a moment's notice!"

▶ HOURS & ENVIRONMENT

"My standard day is the typical eight hours in the office, but as a researcher I need to be flexible. Sometimes we schedule tests in the evenings or on weekends in order to bring in a different group of people, though our standard tests are during normal business hours. I work on a small research team, so we're highly collaborative and I'm always bouncing between a wide variety of responsibilities from day to day. We have a dedicated lab space, with a setup to run up to 12 playtesters simultaneously, along with support for VR testing and a room for group discussions."

▶ AN AVERAGE DAY

"In user research we generally don't have an 'average day,' but instead more of an 'average test cycle' as we go through the lifespan of a game test. We spend a week or two prepping for a test (getting the build, playing through content ourselves, developing our test methodology, recruiting testers), then spend one to five days running the actual test with playtesters in the lab, followed by a two-to-five-day period of analyzing results and writing the report. The exact length of this 'average test cycle' varies depending on the needs of the project, but the general rhythm of prep-execute-report is always the same. Often parts of the cycle overlap with one another (already starting prep while wrapping up a report from a previous test), which is why adaptability is so important!"

▶ PROMOTIONAL PATH

"At the junior level you're mostly executing a test designed by someone else. You will probably be doing a lot of the screening and recruiting of playtesters for the research lab, moderating of participants during tests, taking notes, and general lab work like moving builds and prepping stations for the next round of testing. During this time you'll be learning from the more senior members of the department their standard test methodologies and tools, and be introduced to the generation of test plans.

"As you move into mid- and senior-level roles, you will start taking on more and more independence and ownership over the projects in your lab. You'll interact more directly with the development teams to assess their needs, start developing your own test plans, and take point on analysis of data and report writing. At some companies, researchers start specializing depending on their areas of expertise, though at other companies their positions are more generalist."

▶ PROFESSIONAL PERKS

"Getting early hands-on with games from franchises I love as a fan will never grow old! Plus, I get to say I work in a lab, which just sounds really cool."

▶ CAREER CHALLENGES

"We all have subconscious biases we carry with us, but as a researcher you have to train yourself to recognize your own and work toward counteracting them in your professional role. The reports I deliver need to be an accurate reflection of the data and feedback I collect, so maintaining a professional and unbiased mindset (to the best of my ability) is required to do my job well. However, I also need to account for potential biases in the readers of my reports and make sure my findings are presented in an easy-to-read way that doesn't leave room for misinterpretation. It sounds like it should be easy, but it's actually quite mentally taxing!"

PRO TIP!

"People skills, or being able to comfortably interact with a wide variety of other people on a regular basis is often overlooked when talking about what skills to develop as a user researcher, but they are some of the most vital. In this role you interact daily with diverse groups of people from a multitude of different backgrounds. You'll bring in people you don't know to participate in playtests—you need to be relaxed and friendly with them, while also being confidently in charge when giving instructions and moderating tests. You have a team of research colleagues that you need to have strong communication lines with in order to track progress on shared tasks and design new studies. Then you have the development and publisher teams you deliver reports to; you must be able to clearly discuss their needs and desires from the test and also explain the results of your reports to a non-researcher audience. The ability to clearly and effectively juggle all of these different relationships is critical to being a good researcher, but often overlooked."

JUDE OWER

ENABLING GAMES TO HAVE A POSITIVE IMPACT ON LIFE

PlayInTheCloud
 Jude Ower
 Jude Ower
 playmob.com

EXPERIENCE

FIRST INDUSTRY PROJECT: INFINITEAMS (2002)
FAVORITE INDUSTRY PROJECT: DUMB WAYS TO KILL OCEANS (2018)
PROJECTS SHIPPED: 50+ GAMES & CAMPAIGNS
ACHIEVEMENTS UNLOCKED:
> GIRLS IN TECH "TOP 100 WOMEN IN TECH IN EUROPE" (2012)
> TALENT UNLEASHED "THE ONE TO WATCH" (2015)
> COMPUTER WEEKLY "MOST INFLUENTIAL WOMEN IN TECH (2018)
> MASERATI 100 (2018)

STATS

INDUSTRY LEVEL: 16
CURRENT CLASS: FOUNDER & CEO
CURRENT GUILD: PLAYMOB—LONDON, UNITED KINGDOM
SPECIAL SKILLS: MARKETING, PRODUCT MANAGEMENT, DEPLOYMENT, PITCHING AND PRESENTING, GAMES DESIGN, REQUIREMENTS GATHERING, INNOVATION, START-UPS, ENTREPRENEURSHIP, BUSINESS, SOCIAL BUSINESS, CAUSES, CHARITIES, CAUSE-MARKETING

STANDARD EQUIPMENT

FAVORITE PLATFORM: MOBILE
GO-TO GENRE: PUZZLE
MUST-HAVE GAME: DUMB WAYS TO DIE (2013)

BIO

Since her very first industry project, Jude Ower has been trying to make the world a better place through play. "I had always loved gaming even as a young child, playing the Commodore 64 and the Spectrum," said Ower. "Playing was a family activity; we all huddled around the console on a Friday night and played together. I continued my love for gaming through my teenage years and when I reached university."

Ower began studying marketing at Abertay University in 1997—the first university in the world to offer a computer games degree. The groundbreaking curriculum attracted like-minded students. "I met two coders and a behavioural scientist who were developing a game for corporate team building," explained Ower. "I loved this; combining the fun of gaming with the education and training. To me, this was really exciting and innovative!"

The four founded a company together—TPLD—focusing on the crossroads of education, training, and video games. This would be the first of many entrepreneurial endeavors for Ower. Their debut game was *Infiniteams*, a multiplayer team-building game for corporate training. The follow-up—*Eduteams*—had the same premise, but for schools. "I joined the start-up as a marketing person, and my job was really to test the product/market fit—running sessions with companies and schools, gathering feedback, requirements gathering, feeding back to the product teams, testing."

> "I loved this [coding for corporate team building]; combining the fun of gaming with the education and training. To me, this was reallying exciting and innovative."

"This helped me break into gaming," continued Ower, "and subsequently, when I branched into working with entertainment games to make impact, I had quite a few connections within the entertainment space already." Her first start-up had affirmed the value in games as a source for good, specifically with awareness, education, and adjusting behaviors in a positive way. "I always thought I would end up in the travel industry. Little did I know the travel I would be involved in would be transporting people to digital worlds, to make the real world a better place!"

In 2006 Ower became a senior consultant for NMP, a company that focused on digital media and her role was specifically within serious games and virtual worlds. Working with companies such as BP, Shell, and RBS, her group focused on projects aimed to train staff in how to learn new tasks and techniques through games. The direction Ower's career would follow was now cemented.

'Games for Good' was starting to gain traction elsewhere too. Inspired by developer Mark Pincus and author/designer Jane McGonigal, Ower experienced a moment of clarity when Zynga began selling virtual goods to raise money for survivors of the 2010 earthquake in Haiti. She began formulating a plan that would allow her to pursue both her passions.

PLAYMOB

Initially, Ower played with the idea of developing games directly for charity, but ultimately decided that creating a platform that would facilitate collaboration between brands to vetted charitable causes had more potential. Playmob would connect brands to millions of already engaged gamers and encourage them to help deliver a tangible social impact through playing branded mini-games and interactive ads. In addition to the engagement and awareness, a percentage of campaign costs would go back to the cause, generating funds for the charity in the process.

Ower took a year to formalize and develop her learnings, training at a tech accelerator boot camp in Cambridge. As the company formalized on paper, she began to show the potential to NGOs and other social-conscious brands, and in her words, the reaction was "phenomenal."

> "I feel that showing how games can be a force for good has been my biggest contribution."

Two million pounds were raised to build a team and get Playmob off the ground. Not long after Playmob debuted, the company—and its founder—was garnering global attention. Ower was named *Growing Business*'s "Young Gun" in 2012, and named Talent Unleashed's "One to Watch" in 2015, nominated by Sir Richard Branson and Steve Wozniak. Playmob took home recognitions as *The Launch Conference*'s "Best Start-Up" in 2012, "BBAA Social Investment of the Year" in 2013, and a Maserati 100 in 2018. Perhaps most impressively, Ower was awarded an MBE by the queen—Member of the Most Excellent Order of the British Empire—for her services to entrepreneurship.

Playmob has raised awareness and funds for important issues such as mental health, cyber-bullying, and climate change. The company has collaborated with the World Wildlife Fund for Nature, Oxfam, Save the Children, and with the Duke and Duchess of Cambridge and Prince Harry's Royal Foundation to bring light to the dire circumstances of the rhino. Environmental causes are often a focus for Playmob, including repeated collaborations to create games raising awareness of looming ecological threats. One of these games was *Dumb Ways to Kill Oceans*, where the player would complete mini-levels doing a variety of tasks that involved ocean issues. Over 160,000 pledges were made as a result along with 60 million actions taken from Playmob's platform.

Perhaps best of all, the good Playmob has done is easily quantifiable. "We can see how many trees have been planted, how many families will get fresh water, how many children will receive an education, and how many CO2 emissions are offset," said Ower.

The return on investment isn't only illustrated in numbers. "Being able to raise over $300K for a small cyber-bullying charity with Pixelberry and hear stories of impacting young people's lives as they were able to find a way to get help through the game and call a helpline that the donation funded. That was a real magical moment, seeing how games can truly impact lives," said Ower.

"A few years back, a player emailed to say he felt useless and wanted to do more good in the world, but he was still young—age 12—and didn't have money to give back," she continued. "And the fact he could give back while he played made him feel good and like he could make a difference. He was thanking us for making campaigns happen in-game and making it simple and easy for all to participate!"

POSITIVE SOCIAL IMPACT

To date, Playmob has helped raise 1.5 million pounds for various causes through play and, in doing so, link gaming to positive social impact. "I feel that showing how games can be a force for good has been my biggest contribution," said Ower. "Changing the negative perception of the industry to one of being able to solve the world's greatest problems is no small feat!"

PLAYMOB.

Ower hopes to extend the opportunities provided to her to a new generation of entrepreneurs. Her visibility as a BAFTA games judge, member of the UK Interactive Entertainment company, and speaker at various events such as MADE Festival, SXSW, Women in Games, Browser Games Forum, Games for Brands, London Games Conference, Social Games Summit, and Tech@State means she's constantly imparting her hard-earned lessons to others. "I hope to become an investor and invest in start-ups. I would love to support and mentor more women and join boards, especially within gaming and impact."

Easter Egg

Used to make physical games with rubbish from around the house, including egg cartons, elastic bands, and cake decorations.

REINE ABBAS

TRANSFORMING ARAB CONSUMERS INTO CREATORS

reineabbas

reineabbas

Reine Abbas

wixelstudios.com/reineabbas

EXPERIENCE

FIRST INDUSTRY PROJECT: PROJECT FUN (2002)

FAVORITE INDUSTRY PROJECT: SURVIVAL RACE (2013), ANTURA AND THE LETTERS (2018)

PROJECTS SHIPPED: 10 GAMES

ACHIEVEMENTS UNLOCKED:

> WIT "WOMEN IN TECHNOLOGY AWARD" (2010)

> INC.COM "5 MOST POWERFUL WOMEN IN GAMING"

> ARABIAN BUSINESS "THE WORLD'S MOST POWERFUL ARAB WOMEN (2014, 2015)

> MIT ENTERPRISE FORUM "PANARAB REGION COMPETITION" WINNER (2017)

STATS

INDUSTRY LEVEL: 16

CURRENT CLASS: FOUNDER/CEO

CURRENT GUILD: WIXEL STUDIOS—KASLIK, LEBANON

SPECIAL SKILLS: ANIMATION, DESIGN, GAMING, SINGING, SURFING

STANDARD EQUIPMENT

FAVORITE PLATFORM: PLAYSTATION 3 & GAME BOY

GO-TO GENRE: ACTION

MUST-HAVE GAME: HALF-LIFE 2

BIO

Artist and designer Reine Abbas is a gamer, a serial entrepreneur, a mom, and an advocate for young women, who is making change in Lebanon.

"I always created video games to take control of my own destiny," she explained.

Abbas achieved her masters in visual arts in 2000, after which, she used her skills to found the art department at the DigiPen Institute of Technology in Lebanon. Over the next five years, she taught everything from 2D and 3D game production to illustration, character design modeling, and focused on passing her knowledge along to game development hopefuls.

Easter Egg
Collects action figures, and has an entire room dedicated to them in her house. The room is off limits to her three children.

WIXEL STUDIOS

In 2008, Abbas co-founded Wixel Studios in Kasliks, Lebanon, with Karim Abi Saleh and Ziad Feghali. They decided to open the studio after the success of their politically-charged game *Duoma*.

During a political protest in Lebanon, Abbas and her husband witnessed a street brawl between opposing parties break out. It was a shock to see such young people committing violent acts in public. As a form of political commentary, they designed a game that turned the tables. Tired of feeling like the people were puppets of the government, *Duoma* gave the populous power. "Duoma is an online street fighting game, where the player can choose one politician to fight the other," explained Abbas. "Based on a live scoring system, the politician with the highest score wins." The game spread like wildfire, and currently sits at over three million plays.

Wixel stands for weird pixel, a name Abbas considers relevant. As the only game company in the region at the time with no established video-game industry to support their studio, founding Wixel was considered a 'weird' move.

The studio's goal is to create games with an Arabic focus, featuring local talent, and telling local stories. Early on the also prioritized educational gaming in addition to more games as a form of political commentary.

"'Wixel' stands for 'weird pixel,'' as being the only video game company in the region, where no industry existed to support it, it was considered a 'weird' move."

SURVIVAL RACE

One of their early successes games is called *Survival Race: Life or Power Plants*, released for iOS and Android in 2013. Developed by a team of six, the game explored the ramifications of global warming on the Middle East, told through the adventures of a Saudi stunt man and a middle-age botanist as they tried to protect the world from man-eating mutant plants that had devastated humankind. The player's goal was to safely transport DNA strands back to a lab for analysis, so to learn the weaknesses of their enemy.

"Survial Race was highly anticipated by fans, and we had over 2 million downloads across Android and Apple stores," said Abbas. "We won many prizes, and most importantly, the game was featured in Preapps latest ebook: *App Success Stories*."

The 2013 game *Little Heroes* had a slightly more serious approach to an equally important issue, training children in essential safety skills. Facilitated through 29 minigames, *Little Heroes* taught children to be aware of safety risks big and small, be it putting on sunscreen, or how to avoid causing a fire hazard. The game was made in conjunction with the Ministry of the Interior.

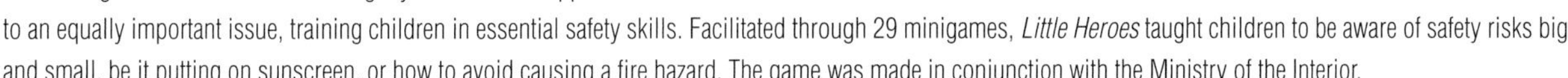

Wixel's newest project continues the trend of educational entertainment. *Antura and the Letter* was funded through a partnership with the Cologne Game Lab and Video Games without Borders. A free smartphone and computer game, *Antura* helps teach Arabic literacy though minigames and quizzes, with a vocabulary of over 400 words. One of the primary goals of the game is to make resources available to Syrian children in refugee camps, so that they are able to navigate the world as adults. "*Antura and the Letters* reunited Syrian refugee children who lost the opportunity of education with their native Arabic language," said Abbas. "It was selected as one of the 2018 #EduApp4syria competition winners!"

SPICATECH

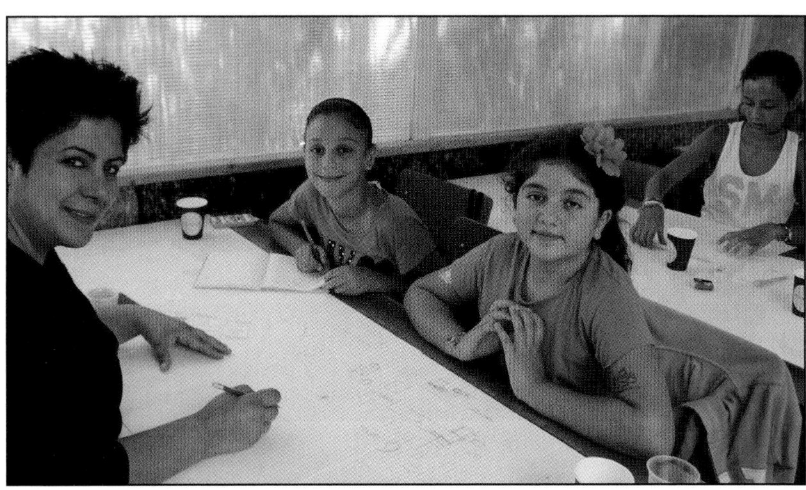

In 2014, Abbas founded another venture, a game academy for children age eight and up. She explained that while the Arab world plays games, they consume them rather than produce them. Abbas wants to help train the next generation of producers.

We started offering physical 20 hours courses in various locations and with different ages," she said. "The main tested courses were in subjects of game design, programing methodologies, visual coding, arts and product implementation (creating the game). We solidified our info delivery methodology and we are now taking what we've learned online through Spica web platform that will host pre-recorded and life gaming sessions in basic, intermediate and advanced gaming education. As a parent, gaming entrepreneur and a hard core gamer, I experienced both worlds. I know the complexity of creating a video game and I want to use kids' passion for games to motivate them to create their games."

Abbas is also working hard to change the gender ratio for the future video game talent pool. She feels the girls are trained to disengage from education at an early age; instead, they are groomed to get married and have children. Abbas dreams of more girls stepping forward and taking charge of their futures.

Part of this achieved through her personal visibility. Abbas eagerly takes on media opportunities to work towards change the image of what a woman is expected to be. Abbas is also a two-time TED talk speaker, and was selected by the US government for business management and entrepreneurship training for three weeks the US.

Abbas offers free 20-hour workshops to girls around the country, traveling to their schools, local meeting centers, and even homes. She frequently works with Syrian refugee girls, who convey their desire to move away from traditional norms like early marriage, and establish their own identities. The games they create together are then published online, to boost their voice beyond geographical borders. Recently Abbas has expandedthrough school partnerships acrossthe Middle East and North Africa.

CONSTANCE STEINKUEHLER

ACADEMIC AND RESEARCHER OF GAMES FOR LEARNING

constances

Constance Steinkuehler

c0nstances

Constance Steinkuehler

bit.ly/uci_informatics_constance_steinkuehler

STATS

INDUSTRY LEVEL: 16

CURRENT CLASS: PROFESSOR OF INFORMATICS

CURRENT GUILD: UNIVERSITY OF CALIFORNIA—IRVINE, USA

SPECIAL SKILLS: MIXED METHOD RESEARCH, CURRICULUM DEVELOPMENT, ACADEMIC WRITING, DATA ANALYSIS, EDUCATIONAL TECHNOLOGY, UNIVERSITY TEACHING

EXPERIENCE

FIRST INDUSTRY PROJECT: RESEARCHING LINEAGE (2002)

FAVORITE INDUSTRY PROJECT: "WHATEVER GAME I'M CURRENTLY STUDYING"

PROJECTS SHIPPED: 2 BOOKS, 30 ACADEMIC ARTICLES IN PEER-REVIEWED JOURNALS

ACHIEVEMENTS UNLOCKED:

> OUTSTANDING ADVISOR, C&I UNIVERSITY OF WISCONSIN-MADISON (2012)

> NATIONAL SCIENCE FOUNDATION IDEAS WORKSHOP INVITED PARTICIPANT (2013)

> HIGHER EDUCATION VIDEO GAME ALLIANCE (HEVGA) FOUNDING FELLOW (2016)

> GAMES FOR CHANGE VANGUARD AWARD (2017)

STANDARD EQUIPMENT

FAVORITE PLATFORM: PC

GO-TO GENRE: MULTIPLAYER COLLABORATIVE

MUST-HAVE GAME: LINEAGE

BIO

Academic Constance Steinkuehler remembers hanging at arcades as a young teen in the 1980s, but left them behind a few years later. "I became a 'kill your television' person when I was 17, eschewing all pop culture for 'high culture,'" explained Steinkuehler. "I didn't game again until I was in graduate school studying cognition in online chatrooms, looking at social interaction and learning."

During her university research, Steinkuehler had grown tired of studying online environments in labs and wanted to view it "in the wild." "My advisor, James Paul Gee, told me to investigate massively multiplayer online games, and though I thought it was a pretty silly place to study, I downloaded one—*Lineage*—and logged in," she recalled. "I was so wrongheaded about games and pop culture! I was immediately overwhelmed with the sophistication of social interaction and cognition happening in such game titles, all under the rubric of 'play,' so I changed my focus, moved departments, and took my career in a whole new path that didn't even exist at that time."

BA, MA, & PHD

An intense academic workload is what led Steinkuehler to video games. She earned three bachelor's degrees by 1993, in mathematics, literature, and religious studies. In 1998, she registered at the University of Wisconsin-Madison to work toward her master's of science in cognitive sciences applied to education, simultaneously earning her PhD in literacy studies.

After discovering *Lineage*, she dove into the community. "My first research project was a 2.5-year ethnography of a *Lineage* community back in the early 2000s," she explained. Her doctoral thesis, *Cognition & Learning in Massively Multiplayer Online Games: A Critical Approach*, formalized the findings of her research.

GAMES & LEARNING

After finishing her PhD in 2005, Steinkuehler remained at the University of Wisconsin-Madison as a professor, and faculty at the Wisconsin Institute for Discovery. She would stay there for over 11 years, teaching classes on video game research methods, and running a research lab. The lab was home to both undergraduate and doctoral students, and focused on cognition and cultural practices related to gameplay and learning, pulling most research from online game communities.

Easter Egg

Helped stash a *Portal 2* gun on a shelf with space equipment in the White House Administration office. No one noticed.

One specific research project ran for two years beginning in 2007. The participant pool comprised at-risk teen boys who were failing at school. They were provided game-based training on literacy, which offered insights into how an interest in games could have productive academic applications. In 2010, the work resulted in a $350,000 grant from the MacArthur Foundation to continue studying "adolescent online games and reading."

In 2012 Steinkuehler became co-director of the Games+Learning+Society Conference (GLS) at UW-Madison, homing in on how games could enrich lives of children and youth, and designing games based on her research.

"My favorite project to work on was a collaborative project with the Center for Investigating Healthy Minds with Dr. Richard Davidson, PI," she said. "We developed two game titles together, one to promote self-regulation of attention and one to promote social acuity. It was my favorite project because the partners were so diverse—neuroscientists, mediation scholars, Buddhist monks, game designers, emotion experts, artists, data analysts, and game dev folks. I love working with experts in topical areas I know little about. I love working with people who are smarter than myself. Also, artists always make everything better."

THE WHITE HOUSE

In the midst of her research at UW-Madison, Steinkuehler was appointed to the White House Office of Science and Technology Policy as a senior policy analyst. "I advised on national initiatives related to video games," she explained. "Policy work there included the coordination of cross-agency efforts to leverage games toward national priority areas such as childhood obesity, early literacy, and STEM education; and the creation of new partnerships to support an ecosystem for more diversified innovation in commercial and non-commercial games."

While her work focused on championing the potential of video games for good, she also found herself having to defend them after the tragic 2012 Sandy Hook Elementary School shooting. In the wake of the incident, Steinkuehler was granted a one-on-one meeting with Vice President Joe Biden prior to a "games and gun violence" meeting that was organized in response to the event. "I convinced Vice President Biden that while the games industry has a PR problem, a decade of research has shown that games do not cause violence," said Steinkuehler.

"We know what causes gun violence in the lives of youth—poverty, exposure to real-world violence, mental-health issues, access to guns—and games are not the cause," she continued. "My brief with Vice President Biden was a 45-minute bloodletting debate between one of the most brilliant minds in politics and me, a politically inexperienced White House staffer who was called in to help organize the administration's response to the Sandy Hook national tragedy. I'm pretty sure I burned whatever political capital I had in that discussion by refuting his staff's stereotypes and unfounded causal claims, but I did it nonetheless."

The meetings that followed included game-industry CEOs from the industry, the attorney general, and the head of HHS. According to Steinkuehler, they focused on how the video game industry could be part of the solution, instead of being pinned as the source of the problem.

"...While the games industry has a PR problem, a decade of research has shown that games do not cause violence."

A HIGHER ALLIANCE

In 2014 Steinkuehler returned to Washington as the founder and president of the Higher Education Video Game Alliance (HEVGA). The non-profit aims to create a platform from which higher-education leaders can raise awareness of the cultural, scientific, and economic importance of video game programs as part of university curriculum. "Our goal is to create a robust network of resources—including unified advocacy, policymaker engagement, media coverage, and external funding—in order to incubate and harness the impact of this community in a 21st-century learning environment," she said. "As president, I supervise and have charge of HEVGA's affairs under the direction and oversight of the board of directors, preside at board meetings, manage employees and contractors, and champion the cause of the organization as defined by its broad membership."

In addition to her work at HEVGA, Steinkuehler is now a professor of informatics at the University of California, Irvine. "I research cognition and learning in commercial entertainment games and, more recently, games designed for impact in areas including literacy, scientific reasoning, attention, and emotional well-being," she detailed. "I am actively involved in field-building efforts in game design and game studies programs in the United States and abroad, including advising federal agencies and foundations on their game-based investments, enabling partnerships across academics and industry, and better educating the public about games as an intervention and, perhaps most importantly, a new art form."

The academic study of video games has evolved greatly since Steinkuehler began her research efforts in 2005. "There's a broad range of scholarly work that simply didn't exist when we first started studying games: critical game studies, game data analytics, social sciences applied to games, games for impact, game design and development, and more," said Steinkuehler.

"The people I study inspire and motivate my work, and the designers who create interactive media," she shared in closing. "Games give players first-person experiences, and social sciences applied to empirical data is how I come to understand, however partially, what sense others make of those experiences. I am very lucky here. It is difficult to be cynical or lose your faith in humans when you study them at play."

A DAY IN THE LIFE OF...

A QUALITY ASSURANCE MANAGER

Quality-assurance professionals fight on the front lines of development to ensure the games you buy are as polished as possible when they hit store shelves. They review content and catalog bugs on a daily basis, ensure quality is on track at each development milestone, and give the final sign-off on a product, testing and retesting until the game is taken out of their hands. Despite popular belief, QA is not only about finding bugs—as 2K QA Manager Casey DeWitt accounts—it's about recognizing trends of quality within an entire project, and effectively communicating them to colleagues. With over a decade of work in video game QA, DeWitt knows what it takes to make a great game, and a great game-tester.

CASEY DEWITT

PROFESSION: QUALITY ASSURANCE & PROJECT MANAGER AT 2K—NOVATO, USA

YEARS IN PROFESSION: 12

ASSOCIATED WITH: MLB/NHL/NBA 2K7 AND 2K8, THE BIGS, ALL-PRO FOOTBALL 2K8, BIOSHOCK, BIOSHOCK 2, THE BUREAU: XCOM DECLASSIFIED, SKYLANDERS: GIANTS, BATTLE PIRATES, KIXEYE.COM, THE SIMPSONS: TAPPED OUT

▶ EDUCATION

"I fall into the self-taught category. The most formal education I had ever received before entering the industry was going to Technology High School on Sonoma State University's campus. It was high school, but they emphasized group learning, computer science, and engineering to a higher degree than any other school I had gone to. For what it's worth, I have attempted to attend college a few times. I found most classes taught at these colleges were a bit outdated when it comes to applying something practically to my work."

▶ KEY QUALITIES

"Without perseverance, someone in QA could never hope to argue the importance of fixing an issue even in the face of business decisions to ignore it as an acceptable risk. Without critical thinking, one can never hope to fully appreciate the connectivity of defects between these complex systems that make up a game, nor can one ever hope to develop new and more efficient methods of bringing the best game they can to the living room of millions. Without a commitment to excellence, QA can become the data entry of game development. If you are not living and breathing the standard to which you hold your game accountable to, then your ability to make judgments will be sub-standard, predictable. The games you make will reflect that."

▶ AN AVERAGE DAY

"There is no average day, but there are trends. Developers need something stable to build off—the sooner we can complete our morning tests and determine how stable the engine and game are, the sooner they can get to work and the more efficient the day will go. As games and game engines become more complex, they stop working in unpredictable ways, usually to the tune of multiple times per day. Investigating what is going on so someone can fix it promptly has to happen immediately, and shifting priorities must be accounted for in every tester's day. Game is broken? Find out why. Going to take a few hours for a fix? Go help troubleshoot issues for various developers. No problems at all in the whole team? Go back to the last stable build and see what you missed (because there are always more bugs). If all else fails, analyze and build new procedures and tools to ensure days like this are mitigated in the future."

▶ TOOLS OF THE TRADE

"If there's ever been a database tool, or task-tracking software, or data-entry product that hasn't been used at some point by QA, I'd be taken aback. Because of the nature of our profession and how we are involved with every discipline all the time, I could rattle off everything from JIRA to 3DS Max to Unity to Android XDK and still not even cover the basics. What's more, one of the coolest aspects of a great QA team is that we ultimately wind up building our own tools for things like automation or streamlining bug entry for common issues the developers run into."

▶ PROMOTIONAL PATH

"I like to structure my teams in tracks and have seen a lot of success with this model, as have other QA managers. I use multiple tracks. The Analyst track is designed to function as the technically instructive and well-versed group who do not manage people but rather tools and methods of test, always reviewing how we're doing and getting a leg up on emerging technology to translate it for the rest of the QA team's efforts.

"The Engineering track is all about building tools and automating tests using technology vetted by the Analysts. They are effectively full-fledged programmers, only instead of building the game, they build systems on top of the game to increase efficiency and ease of development.

"The Management track handles the mentoring and development of all people within the QA department. They exist as a dotted-line reporting structure to all these personnel in tandem with the senior-most members of their track, so they can learn the soft skills of working as a team alongside the technical skills of their role."

▶ PROFESSIONAL PERKS

"Working in QA, you will learn everything there is to know about making a game—period. There is no better holistic approach to learning the craft, as the best perk of the job is being involved with every department every step of the way, from concept to shelf and beyond. What's more, you learn how to appreciate the interconnected nature of development teams, so that if you were to move into a different department, your ability to work with other upstream and downstream efforts would improve effortlessly."

▶ CAREER CHALLENGES

"There is a well-known diagram that's been out there for many years, a triangle with the points: Time, Cost, and Scope. At the bottom of the triangle there is a caption stating, 'You can only pick two' and the word QUALITY is in the exact middle of the three points.

"The challenge is not with the three points; they do indeed combat each other and keep each other in check. The challenge is rather that you really don't have to pick just two and quality is not the nexus between the compromises made within the chart. The nexus is rather the product itself, while the quality is what transcends all points of the diagram and elevates the product to be more than the sum of its parts. I would say most of my career has been about arguing this point and proving that you can indeed make something that stands the test of time regardless of how much time it takes, how broad the scope, and how much it costs.

"Unfortunately, this same problem also lends itself to the other major challenge of being in QA—convincing other people of the importance of a defect. It's one thing to find bugs; it's quite another to communicate the details about the bug so that swift action can be taken to address it, and to ensure people want to act against it because they trust your quality judgement. This is fundamentally a challenge with human perception.

"Every day, in every action big or small, the biggest challenge about working in QA is that you alone will often be the first and last measure of setting the quality bar for a game. This challenge never goes away and, if ignored, will manifest itself in a myriad of ways—all to the detriment of the player."

▶ LIFE HACKS

"Think long-term and pad everything you do by 20%. It doesn't matter if everything around you is working perfectly and everyone is happy. It's a constant battle to attain perfection, and the entropy of development will always creep in. If you apply these two simple-to-say-but-difficult-to-master concepts to your work, your project, and yourself, your efficiency will never be a problem."

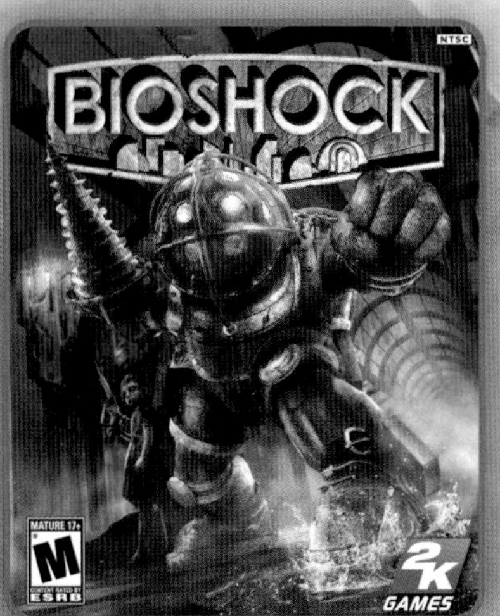

PRO TIP!

"Never stop asking what makes a game tick. If you find something you like, investigate why you like it and how well it fits the methodology behind its creation. If you find something you don't like, do the same. Like the building blocks of life itself, there is always a new layer more fundamental than the one before it, so what may appear to be a broken game may in fact be a masterpiece save for one issue. Never stop asking questions, never stop learning."

EMILIA SCHATZ

DESIGNING VIRTUAL PLAYGROUNDS FOR LARGER-THAN-LIFE ADVENTURES

 thegreatbluebit

EXPERIENCE

FIRST INDUSTRY PROJECT: RE-MISSION (2006)

FAVORITE INDUSTRY PROJECT: UNCHARTED 3: DRAKE'S DECEPTION (2011)

PROJECTS SHIPPED: 17 GAMES

ACHIEVEMENTS UNLOCKED:

> AIAS, DICE, & BAFTA "GAME OF THE YEAR"—THE LAST OF US (2014)

> BAFTA "GAME OF THE YEAR"—UNCHARTED 4 (2017)

> AIAS & DICE "ADVENTURE GAME OF THE YEAR"—UNCHARTED 4 (2017)

> FAST COMPANY MAGAZINE "100 MOST CREATIVE PEOPLE IN BUSINESS" (2017)

STATS

INDUSTRY LEVEL: 16

CURRENT CLASS: LEAD GAME DESIGNER

WGUILD: NAUGHTY DOG—LOS ANGELES, USA

SKILLS: LEVEL DESIGN, LAYOUT, SCRIPTING, GAMEPLAY SYSTEMS, USER INTERFACE DESIGN

STANDARD EQUIPMENT

FAVORITE PLATFORM: NINTENDO SWITCH

GO-TO GENRE: THIRD-PERSON ACTION/ADVENTURE

MUST-HAVE GAME: LEGEND OF ZELDA: BREATH OF THE WILD

**The opinions expressed are my own and are not representative of PlayStation or Naughty Dog.*

BIO

"I remember when I was in college, I played Ico, and there's a moment toward the end of the game where you and Yorda are running across a bridge to finally escape the castle," recalled Naughty Dog Lead Game Designer Emilia Schatz. "As you cross the halfway point, a gap opens up as the two sides of the bridge begin to retract, separating the characters. I was compelled to turn around and jump back over the gap—I couldn't leave without her." In that moment, Schatz wasn't just empathizing with the fate of an on-screen heroic character. She was the hero, willing to sacrifice whatever the stakes required to save a character she cared for. "For me, that idea was fascinating, and it demonstrated a potential in games that I didn't see in other creative mediums."

Games had been a constant in Schatz's life since her youth; she began exploring the idea of creating games in high school, when she learned how to program RPGs on her calculator. Her interest led to studying computer science, visual arts, and English at university. "In order to pay for school, I had a work-study job where I made web pages for professors," Schatz explained. "Eventually that turned into making simple educational games and interactions using Macromedia Flash. And then I started making my own games and animations in Flash."

Easter Egg

The movie *Grandma's Boy* showcases game footage from a project the main character is developing as part of the narrative. In reality, the footage is from a canceled Terminal Reality game called *Demonik*, and the level in the final showdown was designed by Schatz.

TERMINAL REALITY

Schatz first got her foot in the door at a game studio as a level designer in 2002. "I applied to a bunch of game companies in the Dallas area," she said. "Terminal Reality was making an educational game called *Re-Mission*, and that sort of aligned with my experience in educational Flash games."

Re-Mission had a noble purpose—to help kids with cancer understand the fundamentals of their disease and their treatment regime. "I designed several levels," she said. "I remember one of my first was to teach kids why it was important to take stool softeners. The player flew at high speed along the surface of stool and fired medicine at sharp protrusions before they could tear at the inside of the large intestine."

While her first game gig was unusual, it had a meaningful purpose that Schatz valued. Transitioning from an educational game catered to children with cancer to laying out levels for *BloodRayne*'s sequel was jarring.

"When I began my career, pretty much everything was made and marketed directly to 18-25-year-old men, and although that is still a dominating trend today, it was so much worse then," said Schatz. "After *Re-Mission*, we went on to *BloodRayne 2* and the canceled title *Demonik*. The lead character Rayne was an overly sexualized half-vampire who straddled enemies as she sucked their blood to gain back health. I remember we had a character physics system that simulated things like the bounce of her hair, but was named the 'JUG sim' because it was primarily designed to simulate her breasts jiggling."

Schatz began to question if she wanted to continue making games. "I grew up loving cartoony and fun games like *Mario* and *Zelda*. I wondered when or if I'd ever make a game that I wanted to play," she questioned.

Before departing Terminal Reality in 2009, Schatz had the opportunity to work on *Kinect: Star Wars* and *Ghostbusters: The Video Game* as senior game designer. After working on both titles, she felt there was enough high-profile work on her résumé to apply to her dream studios. Naughty Dog was one of them.

NAUGHTY DOG

Naughty Dog flew Schatz out for an interview, and extended an offer that same day. She relocated to Los Angeles and began her work as a game designer. Schatz started at the studio the first day of production on *Uncharted 3: Drake's Deception*, tasked primarily with level and puzzle design for Drake's third adventure. "It was unreal, me being such a fan of the studio and the *Uncharted* games, and then being given a chance to actually create levels for them," recalled Schatz.

"I began *Uncharted 3* terrified that someone would realize it had been an awful mistake to hire me," she continued. "And by the time development concluded, I had helped design some of the most iconic moments in the game. I made so many wonderful friends at the studio and discovered talent in myself that I didn't realize was there." Those moments—which she designed layout and puzzles, scripted, and aided with initial level art animation—included the French Chateau, the Talbot foot chase, and what they internally referred to as the "Sandlantis" escape level at the very end of the game. The latter became an outlet for Schatz to express her love of platforming games.

Over the course of developing *Uncharted 3*, Schatz says she grew leaps and bounds as a designer, in great part due to Naughty Dog's commitment to playtesting. "At Naughty Dog, we take playtesting very seriously, running them throughout the production of each game," she explained. "It's one of the most rewarding parts of what I do. I love the process of iterating on my level spaces and then seeing how it improves player experiences in the next playtest."

Naughty Dog's playtesting pool diversified greatly during development of *Uncharted 4: A Thief's End*. "A handful of us made a real effort on *Uncharted 4* to include help for people with a variety of disabilities," she began. "And with help from Sony, we put together an accessibility focus test to see how well a lot of the features we included would work."

It was a struggle to gain traction at the studio at first, but by the end of *Uncharted 4*, we had a ton of support." Now as we move forward to new projects, accessibility is a consideration from the start of development. I'm incredibly proud to help bring that about, and to work for a studio that cares about including these features in our games.

"I grew up loving cartoony and fun games like *Mario* and *Zelda*. I wondered when or if I'd ever make a game that I wanted to play."

Embracing diversity wasn't only a public-facing initiative at Naughty Dog—it began with fostering an inclusive community internally. In 2014 Schatz came out as transgender to her colleagues, and began living all aspects of her life as a woman. Having coordinated the effort with HR beforehand, the studio supported her in every aspect. Before the announcement went out, a new email account was activated with her chosen name, freshly printed business cards had been delivered, and her picture was swapped out across the company databases. Schatz was overwhelmed with the support from her colleagues, and living as her true self allowed for a greater focus on her work.

After shipping *Uncharted 4*, Schatz joined the team creating a sequel to one of the most critically acclaimed games in industry history, which she contributed to after finishing *Uncharted 3*. "Right now I'm working on *The Last of Us Part II*, and there is an incredible amount of pressure to live up to and possibly exceed the success of the first game," she said.

CG MASTER ACADEMY

In 2018, Schatz began teaching level design through CG Master Academy, and in doing so discovered one of the most rewarding experiences of her career. "I wrote my own lectures and assignments, answered student questions, and gave them feedback on their work," she explained. "I learned a lot about how I designed games and levels, as it forced me to break down my process into understandable chunks for the lectures. But most of all, it was incredibly rewarding to see how much students could improve over the length of the course, and how I had affected that."

Balancing life as a new mom, Schatz plans on continuing to build worlds through her design work at Naughty Dog, and supplemental teaching opportunities that allow her to guide aspiring game developers. "I've known so many wonderful people in my life who are teachers," she said in closing. "My mom is an elementary school art teacher. I really believe teaching to be one of the most admirable professions you could do, tangibly improving the world by inspiring others to improve themselves. I love kids, too. Though I'd be happy teaching at any level, I think. Maybe that's what I'll do someday when I get tired of this whole games thing."

LUNA JAVIER

KICK-STARTED THE PHILIPPINE GAME INDUSTRY

 Luna Cruz Javier  lunajavier.com

EXPERIENCE

FIRST INDUSTRY PROJECT: ANITO: DEFEND A LAND ENRAGED (2003)

FAVORITE INDUSTRY PROJECT: AWAKENING: THE DREAMLESS CASTLE (2010)

PROJECTS SHIPPED: 18+ GAMES

ACHIEVEMENTS UNLOCKED:

> FIRST FEMALE GAME DESIGNER IN THE PHILIPPINES

> INDEPENDENT GAMES FESTIVAL "INNOVATION IN AUDIO" AWARD—ANITO: DEFEND A LAND ENRAGED (2004)

> CREATOR OF THE AWAKENING SERIES, DOWNLOADED OVER 17 MILLION TIMES

> ANDROID EXCELLENCE AWARD—DREAM DEFENSE (2017)

STATS

INDUSTRY LEVEL: 16

CURRENT CLASS: CREATIVE DIRECTOR, CO-FOUNDER

CURRENT GUILD: ALTITUDE GAMES—MANILA, PHILIPPINES

SPECIAL SKILLS: GAME DESIGN, GAME WRITING, PRODUCTION, KRAV MAGA

STANDARD EQUIPMENT

FAVORITE PLATFORM: MOBILE

GO-TO GENRE: ROLE-PLAYING GAMES

MUST-HAVE GAME: MASS EFFECT SERIES

BIO

In 2002, only a few weeks into her first gaming gig, Luna Javier realized creating 3D art wasn't the right fit for her. Luckily, Javier's boss saw potential in the recent graduate, and a new career path opened in the process.

"I had just graduated from college, and wanted to be a screenwriter for film," Javier explained. "I saw an ad in the paper for a 3D artist in a gaming company. I had taken a 3D animation elective in school and thought I could use the job as a stepping stone to work at Pixar."

Javier's lack of experience in 3D art ultimately landed her a spot as head writer for the studio's debut game. "I found that writing for games was much more fun than writing for film," Javier said. "Dialogue choices, branching storylines, the works! I fell in love with it and never looked back."

Easter Egg

Is a certified Krav Maga instructor with the International Krav Maga Federation and teaches self-defense classes a few times a week.

PAVING THE WAY AT ANINO ENTERTAINMENT

The studio was Anino Entertainment, and it wasn't only Javier who was green when it came to making games. Anino was the first game studio in the whole of the Philippines, and by that measure, their debut title was the first-ever Filipino-made game. "We were all self-taught," remembers Javier. "We made our own engine and learned how to make games on the job. I used my writing background and the RPG games I'd played as basis for my work. There was no one around to teach us, or let us know how good—or bad—we were doing!"

Their ambitious debut title was the PC role-playing game *Anito: Defend a Land Enraged*. "We had two playable characters: Maya and Agila, siblings with intertwining stories but completely separate gameplay," she explained. "I wrote the part of Maya, including designing quests and puzzles."

The studio earned the indie title, most illustrated as they ramped up to launching *Anito.* "There were less than 10 of us on the dev team, and the night before launch, we were sticking CD keys and sticker seals on the retail boxes ourselves," recalled Javier. "We released it in 2003, and it won Innovation in Audio at the 2004 Independent Games Festival."

If Javier could have seen the future, she would have known that the foundation laid by Anino would be far-reaching. "I had no idea the game would give birth to the Philippine gaming industry, and I'm glad I didn't know at the time," she said. "We were just an indie team making a game. It snowballed into something much bigger than us. It put the Philippines on the map."

Anito: Defend a Land Enraged wasn't a financial success, but it was a milestone. "I've met several people who said they became game developers because they played *Anito: Defend a Land Enraged,*" said Javier. "To meet people whose lives were changed because of it—it's still unreal to me."

"[Anito] snowballed into something much bigger than us. It put the Phillipines on the map."

PUTTING THE PHILIPPINES ON THE MAP

Within two years of *Anito*'s debut, other studios began to form. Subsequently, industry organizations were founded, including the Game Developers Association of the Philippines, and the Manila chapters of the Global Game Jam and the International Game Developers Association, the latter of which Javier supported as a board member. Conferences were created to facilitate networking and visibility in the burgeoning industry. "Being one of the 'oldies,' I was active in the organizations, spoke at conferences and schools, and became very visible in the early days," said Javier.

Javier worked at Anino for several more years, transitioning into a producer role to lead end-to-end game development and outsourcing processes. She eventually departed for newly formed studio Boomzap Entertainment. There she would work as senior game designer and writer for nearly six years.

"In 2009 my boss at Boomzap asked me to pitch a casual adventure game to Big Fish Games," recalled Javier. "We had never made a game like that before. I noticed that most of the hit adventure games back then were dark and scary, such as *Mystery Case Files*, which was the gold standard at the time." She decided to go the opposite route and pitched a bright and colorful fantasy world where everyone could use magic—except, surprisingly, the player character. "Because of that, the character had to do things the old-fashioned way, such as pick locks and build contraptions, which fit right in with adventure games."

"I was just enjoying building the fantasy world and wasn't worried about the market or profitability."

Big Fish Games greenlit the pitch, which became *Awakening: The Dreamless Castle.* "*Awakening* went on to become an eight-game series with over 17 million downloads," said Javier. "Back then, I was just enjoying building the fantasy world, and wasn't worried about the market or profitability. The experience felt very pure." She would design and produce other franchises for Boomzap, including *Dana Knightstone*, *Otherworld*, and *Botanica.*

THE NEXT GENERATION

While Javier was breathing life into new franchises, she was also splitting her time as a professor of game design—and later, interactive narrative for games—at De La Salle University in Manila. She was more directly than ever teaching the next generation of game developers, using the skills and knowledge she earned to help kick-start the local industry.

In 2014 Javier left Boomzap and founded Altitude Games, where she currently works as creative director. The studio—which is staffed by 40% women—focuses on original mobile free-to-play games. Since opening their doors, Altitude has developed *Run Run Super V*, *Zodiac Pop!*, *Kung Fu Clicker*, and *Dream Defense*, which took home an Android Excellence award in 2017.

Javier and her team are eager to maintain their spot ahead of the innovation curve, but this time in both the local and global industry. Javier is one of 300 individuals who form Experimental Community, a group of blockchain professionals and enthusiasts who advise on blockchain-based games. "The most exciting gaming platform for me right now is the blockchain," she explained. "Cryptogaming—games that use blockchain technology—is only a year old. Designing for the blockchain is very different. The limitations of the network, UX, decentralized information… It's a whole new world of game design. We've started studying it at Altitude, and I'm excited to see where it goes."

With such extensive industry experience, Javier has been asked to speak at global conferences, including Google's Women Techmakers, Casual Connect, the IGDA Leadership Forum, the Global Mobile Game Confederation, and blockchain gathering NIFTY Conference. Her presentation for Casual Connect—"Designing a Studio for Game Designers"—illustrated Javier's continued trend of transparency, sharing the lessons learned in running a design team, which has aided other game studios around the world.

Looking back, Javier distinctly remembers a specific moment of clarity within her career. "Someone asked me, 'What does it feel like to be the first female game developer in the country?' I didn't even realize it until it was pointed out," she concluded. "Being a pioneer means I helped pave the way for others. If my being onstage helped a female student in the audience realize that she, too, could be a game developer, then the hard work was worth it."

ELIZABETH LAPENSÉE

CHALLENGING COLONIALISM AND EMPOWERING INDIGENOUS SELF-DETERMINATION

 odaminowin  elizabethlapensee

 Elizabeth LaPensée  elizabethlapensee.com

EXPERIENCE

FIRST INDUSTRY PROJECT: AMERICA ONLINE TEXT ROLE-PLAYING COMMUNITY

FAVORITE INDUSTRY PROJECT: THUNDERBIRD STRIKE (2017)

PROJECTS SHIPPED: 19 GAMES

ACHIEVEMENTS UNLOCKED:

> INTERNATIONAL GAME DEVELOPERS ASSOCIATION MVP (2015)

> SERIOUS GAMES COMMUNITY LEADERSHIP AWARD (2017)

> IMAGINENATIVE FILM & MEDIA ARTS DIGITAL MEDIA (2017)

> GUGGENHEIM FOUNDATION FELLOW (2018)

STATS

INDUSTRY LEVEL: 15

CURRENT CLASS: DESIGNER, ARTIST, & ASSISTANT PROFESSOR

GUILD: MICHIGAN STATE UNIVERSITY—LANSING, USA

SKILLS: WRITING, STORYTELLING, GAME DESIGN, LEVEL DESIGN, ILLUSTRATION, ADVOCACY, TEACHING, MENTORSHIP

STANDARD EQUIPMENT

FAVORITE PLATFORM: NINTENDO SWITCH

GO-TO GENRE: ACTION RPG

MUST-HAVE GAME: ULTIMA ONLINE

BIO

Designer and educator Elizabeth LaPensée took her first steps into the video game industry at an exceptionally young age. "I started off running a text role-playing community on America Online somewhere around 12 years old," began LaPensée. "I was given a formal position, and free Internet! I just kept playing games, sketching, and writing anywhere I could, including coordinating an Orc guild in *Ultima Online*. Game development has been ingrained in me since the first joyful moment of creating."

LaPensée's family has been the foundation of her work since youth. She is Anishinaabe from Baawaating (the Place of the Rapids), with family at Bay Mills Indian community, and also Métis. Both her aesthetics and aspirations have centered on her culture. "My art style, which is a merging of both Anishinaabeg and Michif aesthetics, has grown since I was a kid sketching in school," she said. As an adult she studied graphic design, technical writing, and pieced together a minor in indigenous studies at Portland State University in Oregon before it was a formal program.

After her initial graduation in 2004, LaPensée would achieve her master's in writing, and subsequently her PhD in interactive arts and technology. "Self-determination and self-expression are vital to creating a path that will lead to your ideal life, and that means learning in every moment you can in any possible way you can."

VENTURING FORTH

"I made my way into the industry by networking as an events journalist who interviewed developers and covered talks," she continued. "Not only was I learning from amazing developers with insights, but I made connections while building up a portfolio."

The very first game in LaPensée's portfolio was a 2006 eco-sim, on which she was both writer and cultural researcher. "I was fortunate to work for Andy Schatz from Pocketwatch Games on *Venture Arctic*, which challenges the player to act as the force of nature amidst oil extraction," she explained. "He was very receptive to my input about cultural expression. The experience exemplified the best possible scenario."

The next several years of her career would be prolific. In 2007, LaPensée was a game writer and designer for Aboriginal History Media Arts, where she created an alternate-reality game to share knowledge on traditional medicines with Squamish elder and artist Cease Wyss. She simultaneously worked as a research assistant for Aboriginal Territories in Cyberspace, as a researcher, curriculum writer, and visiting designer for game development workshops for indigenous youth.

Easter Egg

Coined the term "storyline role-playing" used in America Online's text role-playing community, in order to distinguish writing with ongoing stories.

LaPensée's body of work began to make waves after only a couple of years. The 2011 indigenous social-impact game *Survivance* would become the focus of her dissertation, was shown at imagineNATIVE Film & Media Arts Festival 2013, and nominated at IndieCade 2016. In 2013 she spent time as a co-game designer and researcher at the Oregon Museum of Science and Industry, and released *Gathering Native Foods*, a series of touchscreen mini-games focused on traditional and sustainable food-gathering. The same year she wrote and designed the cooperative board game *The Gift of Food* for the Northwest Indian College. In 2015 she moved to the University of Minnesota as a postdoctoral associate for the Research for Indigenous Community Health Center, where she worked on *Honour Water*, a singing game for iOS designed to pass on teachings about water, exhibited at festivals and museums.

INVADERS

LaPensée's 2015 title *Invaders*—a parody of the retro classic *Space Invaders* with colonizers in lieu of aliens—marked a turning point in her career. "I struggled with how often companies wanted to use me as a token and just put my name on a game but not actually listen to my input."

After LaPensée lost most of her belongings in a fire, she decided there was nothing else to lose. "The only person who could give me complete autonomy in a game was myself," she shared. "Invaders set the tone for the games that are truest to my voice." *Invaders* released for web and mobile in 2016, with design and programming by LaPensée, art by Steven Paul Judd, and music by Trevino L. Brings Plenty, and was also showcased at multiple festivals.

LaPensée now resides at Michigan State University as an assistant professor. Her focus is providing research and teaching through the Games for Entertainment & Learning Lab, and the American Indian & Indigenous Studies program.

"I struggled with how often companies wanted to use me as a token and just put my name on a game but not actually listen to my input."

STRIKING BACK

LaPensée's most ambitious, and arguably most impactful, game was released in 2017. Funded with a fellowship from the Arrowhead Regional Arts Council, *Thunderbird Strike* is a 2D side-scroller where the player embodies the foundational figure and flies across Turtle Island to protect it from its most dangerous foe—oil pipeline development.

"I worked on *Thunderbird Strike* very gradually over weekends and breaks for a long while," she recalled. "It turned out to be the longest development cycle but also garnered the most attention yet."

That attention came in the form of a proposed Minnesota State bill aimed to put grant awards under government approval, spearheaded by the pipeline advocacy group Energy Builders, who argued that *Thunderbird Strike*'s primary objective was to encourage eco-terrorism.

"The bill threatened to shut down freedom of speech in art by putting grant awards under government approval, which was counteracted by many people stepping forward in support of my work and future work," said LaPensée. "Although there were intense moments of harassment, games were recognized as art thanks to many voices coming together in support."

Thunderbird Strike was awarded Best Digital Media at imagineNATIVE in 2017, awarded runner-up at EarthGames on Tap in 2018, and exhibited at multiple venues.

LaPensée's newest game, *When Rivers Were Trails*, is described as *Oregon Trail* told from an indigenous perspective. "Working on a game for the Indian Land Tenure Foundation has been an incredible process," she said. "Including over 24 indigenous writers, the gameplay aims to bring awareness to the impact of 1890 allotment acts—a government effort to divide indigenous lands. My greatest hope is to generate more game development opportunities for indigenous collaborators."

TEACHING NEW GENERATIONS

Outside of her development work, LaPensée has made an active effort throughout her career to help build the future of indigenous-led game development, be it through establishing curriculums, offering workshops, or one-on-one mentorship. "I went to Algoma University in Sault Ste. Marie, Ontario in Canada to run a game-development workshop for Anishinaabeg youth right before starting my PhD program in 2007," she said. "It was important to me then, and still is now, that indigenous youth are given the opportunity to make any kind of game they want without requiring cultural content. A game is a contribution to indigenous expression because the developer is indigenous."

LaPensée's educational efforts have made a tangible difference across many mediums, including this book. After calling attention to the problematic origins of the word "pioneer" within the context of the Americas, we changed our original title from "Pioneers of Play" to "Professionals of Play" in solidarity with our indigenous contributors.

"My greatest hope is to see more capacity and structural support for indigenous community members to develop games of their own choosing. I advocate for not just including indigenous people as consultants on games, but genuinely providing ongoing support through training and access to technology."

A DAY IN THE LIFE OF...

A SYSTEMS ADMINISTRATOR

Systems administration—part of the broader category of information technology—is the foundation upon which game development is built. Without the technically trained staff to keep production, communication, and collaboration pipelines flowing efficiently, many games wouldn't make it to market. Systems administrators are on the floor just as long as developers, ensuring hardware and software are updated as needed and known issues are resolved, performing emergency maintenance when needed, and executing many other vital tasks.

The role of IT has expended further in more recent years, with systems administrators often responsible for keeping sensitive intellectual property safe by eliminating weak points from a corporate network, training employees to spot scams, and investigating requested tools to ensure they meet safety standards. Crystal Dynamics' Jennie Nguyen started in the industry as a concept artist, but found her passion in the ever-changing landscape of technology.

JENNIE NGUYEN

PROFESSION: SYSTEMS ADMINISTRATOR AT CRYSTAL DYNAMICS—REDWOOD CITY, USA

YEARS IN PROFESSION: 4

ASSOCIATED WITH: LARA CROFT AND THE TEMPLE OF OSIRIS, RISE OF THE TOMB RAIDER, THE AVENGERS PROJECT (WORKING TITLE)

▶ EDUCATION

"I'm self-taught. I originally studied art and animation and got my Bachelor of Fine Arts in it, and I intended to keep on an artistic path. I did concept art at a game studio for a while, and then ended up taking a really different turn. When I first started in IT, I worked at my college. It was a part-time job to pay off bills. I was learning on the fly. After a few years using my degree, I decided to go back to IT and give that a shot. I kept learning by reading books, forums, getting certification, and by mentorship from the people I worked with."

▶ EARLY INDUSTRY IMPRESSIONS

"The culture and the pacing was familiar to me, as I had pretty much always worked in games. It's what I've grown up in career-wise. I think what surprised me was how closely I ended up working with the development teams. IT falls under the Operations branch at Crystal Dynamics, but to me, it feels like we're a direct support for the devs. Our hours follow their hours, and we also have to work around that to ensure minimal disruption to production."

▶ KEY QUALITIES

"In my opinion, I think it's important to have a good work ethic. Willingness and drive to keep learning and adapt. Being able to take feedback well and utilize it to better yourself and your work."

▶ TRAINING OPPORTUNITIES

"Generally in IT, training is dependent on the path you want to go down. Some paths are vendor-specific and, depending on what companies use that vendor's products or software, it can be desirable to have official certification or training. If someone is going down a really specific path, it might even be required. It always varies by what companies are looking for. If your company provides official training and classes, definitely get as much of that as you can. I've also taken classes through Global Knowledge.

"Outside of official courses, there are a lot of resources to study for certification exams. I've utilized online training courses and videos from Udemy.com and similar websites at reasonable prices. There's honestly a lot of online resources that are great to jump off from. Even if you're starting out and you're not sure which path you want to go down, you can easily obtain more knowledge and test out the waters this way."

▶ TOOLS OF THE TRADE

"All things Windows Active Directory related, DHCP (dynamics host configuration protcol), DNS (domain name system), Group Policy, LDAP (lightweight directory access protocol), VMware/Vsphere, Google, Powershell, Solar Winds (monitoring), Exchange, and Confluence for documentation are a good start to name a few. These tools range from software and services, down to the physical hardware such as our blade system for virtualization, back-up systems, standalone physical servers, and our enterprise storage system.

"These tools are what's used to create and maintain the environment that users work from. Active Directory, DNS, DHCP, and LDAP protocols are what allow you to have a network, to authenticate, and to have enterprise domain environment. This includes ensuring best practice regarding security and maintaining a consistent environment.

"I use VMware to create and maintain virtualized servers. These servers will host production-critical services like Perforce, various licensing services like Autodesk, Foundry, Atlassian, and other developer-related services. I use PowerShell to automate tasks and run commands. I'll use it to generate audits or reports. There's tons of other tools, but these are the basics."

▶ HOURS & ENVIRONMENT

"I work a lot of hours. Aside from core hours to support a site, there's always odd hours, weekends, late nights or even all-nighters to do necessary patching, maintenance, rollouts, support for critical services that break or if there's an incident. Special or major events like a site move or major project will require lots of attention and time. It's a very fast-paced environment where there are a lot of moving pieces."

▶ AN AVERAGE DAY

"An average day will consist of me starting off with a physical walk through of the server room, working on day-to-day tasks, putting out fires, pending tickets, and then working on longer-term projects. The day-to-day can shift a lot, from one high-priority task to another, depending on the development team's priorities. Then there's projects that are purely IT, submitting CABS (change advisory board/change management tracking) for maintenance or upgrades. Managing and prioritizing your projects and tasks becomes a time puzzle and slotting in what you can do in between your tasks. I'll get tickets escalated to me from our service desk and spend time helping them out. I'll also help train and mentor."

▶ PROMOTIONAL PATH

"The higher you go, the more you are responsible for, and the more you become a point person to solve bigger and more technical problems. You'll take lead on driving projects and be responsible for getting key stakeholders to buy in. You will need to be able to mentor and pass down knowledge to the rest of the team."

▶ CAREER CHALLENGES

"Everything is constantly changing at such a rapid pace in IT. Huge shifts in technology, such as everything becoming a service and going to cloud, have really shaped where things are going. Keeping up and staying ahead of what is shaping the environment provides a lot of interesting challenges. Learning to adapt to these things and gracefully integrate them into your environment can be tough.

"I think another main challenge of this profession is visibility and value. One of my coworkers summed it up pretty well: 'IT is like the road you drive on.' You're used to it being there and it's key infrastructure you need to go about your lives. You don't think about it until you're having problems with it. If you get noticed, it usually means something has gone wrong! People can get the impression you're not busy or doing anything when it's working, but that's when you're doing the most work to keep it running seamlessly and provide the best service."

▶ LIFE HACKS

"I keep a cheat sheet of useful commands or scripts I've created or used in a Notepad++ doc for reference. It comes in handy for things you don't want to type up when it's long or complex. I use Rainmeter to organize my UI."

"Keep up-to-date as much as you can, and never stop learning."

MORGAN ROMINE

FRAG DOLL FOUNDER AND INCLUSION IN ESPORTS ADVOCATE

 Rhoulette  Morgan Romine

anykey.org
morganromine.com

EXPERIENCE

FIRST INDUSTRY PROJECT: SPLINTER CELL: PANDORA TOMORROW (2004)

FAVORITE INDUSTRY PROJECT: FRAG DOLLS

PROJECTS SHIPPED: 8+ GAMES

ACHIEVEMENTS UNLOCKED:

> NEXTGEN "GAME INDUSTRY'S 100 MOST INFLUENTIAL WOMEN" (2006)

> FRAG DOLLS BECAME THE FIRST ALL-WOMEN'S TEAM TO ACHIEVE SEMI-PRO STATUS IN A MLG CIRCUIT (2006)

> FASTCOMPANY.COM "THE MOST INFLUENTIAL WOMEN IN TECH: THE GAMERS" (2009)

> TOP 50 RANKED SPEAKER AT GDC FOR TALK "RUNNING A WOMEN'S ESPORTS TOURNAMENT" (2016)

STATS

INDUSTRY LEVEL: 15

CURRENT CLASS: DIRECTOR OF INITIATIVES

CURRENT GUILD: ANYKEY—SAN DIEGO, USA

SPECIAL SKILLS: DIVERSITY & INCLUSION, ESPORTS, COMMUNITY MANAGEMENT, COMMUNICATIONS, PUBLIC RELATIONS, SOCIAL MEDIA, DIGITAL MARKETING, ETHNOGRAPHY, PUBLIC SPEAKING, WRITING, EDITING

STANDARD EQUIPMENT

FAVORITE PLATFORM: PC

GO-TO GENRE: RPG/FPS

MUST-HAVE GAME: EVERQUEST

BIO

Morgan "Rhoulette" Romine describes *EverQuest* as her second major in college. Joking aside, she did feel that the skills she developed as a guild leader would serve her well as a community manager for a video game company; during her senior year, she'd even taught a class on anthropology of online gaming communities.

"When I graduated, I was playing *Shadowbane*, an MMO published by Ubisoft, so I made an effort to make connections there," began Romine. "I didn't get hired the first time I applied for a community-management position there; they felt that I didn't have enough experience. But I followed up with the people I had met and convinced them that my lack of experience would be made up for by my passion and hard work." The team at Ubisoft gave Romine contract work in 2003, and when a full-time community-management role became available, she was first in line to interview. "It took me almost a full year to get hired, but my patience and persistence paid off."

Romine was thrown into the deep end at Ubisoft as community and online marketing manager on one of their biggest franchises—*Splinter Cell: Pandora Tomorrow*. "This was the first *Splinter Cell* to feature a multiplayer mode, so the community became more socially integrated than ever before," she explained. "It was a fun challenge to manage that transition, and also to step in as community manager for a community of gamers that was already well established." Romine was a natural at the role, and continued on to manage community and online marketing initiatives for *King Kong* and the original *Assassin's Creed*.

THE FRAG DOLLS

In 2004, Romine helped found the highest-profile community initiative of her time at Ubisoft—the Frag Dolls. The Frag Dolls were an all-women team of professional gamers sponsored by Ubisoft. They promoted Ubisoft titles, competed in tournaments, and gave visibility to the increasing number of women gamers.

"Before entering the game industry, I knew no other women who loved playing games the way I did," she said. "When I helped to found the Frag Dolls team in 2004, I got to meet a whole group of women who shared my interests, and it was like finding a tribe of long-lost sisters. Ever since that life-changing experience, I have wanted to share that feeling with other women gamers and grow our supportive network so that women who are new to the game industry can have guidance while navigating the challenges of working in a male-dominated industry."

Known as "Rhoulette" on the team roster, Romine was responsible for directly managing up to eight recruits at a time as team captain. Behind closed doors, she helped establish the team brand strategy, managed budgets, and organized events and appearances. Her public responsibilities included participating in high-profile interviews, representing the team at speaking engagements, and keeping her gaming skills sharp for competitive play—in 2006 the Frag Dolls became the first women's team to reach semi-pro status in a Major League Gaming circuit.

"Managing the Frag Dolls team has been the most fulfilling role of my career because of the way our all-women's competitive team turned into a pipeline program for women gamers to get into the game industry," said Romine. "Beyond the seven to nine members of the official Frag Doll team in any given year, we also had 12-15 new 'cadettes' every six months who, like paid interns, got to work Ubisoft events, contribute to projects, and make content. Many of these cadettes were able to leverage their experience within our program to get jobs in the game industry. Founding and managing this program made me feel like I was able to make a positive, long-term contribution to the industry I love."

Running with the Frag Dolls also cemented Romine as a visible face for women in gaming, which she would go on to embrace in her future advocacy. The Frag Dolls retired in 2015, after a successful 11-year run.

FIREFALL

In 2011 Romine left her home at Ubisoft to pursue a new venture, joining Red 5 Studios as their esports director. Using her extensive experience leading the Frag Dolls, she managed tournament strategy and PR for their new open-world shooter, *Firefall.*

"It was an ambitious project undertaken by a start-up company with a team of outstanding developers," explained Romine. "As with all start-ups, much of the challenge is that everyone in the company has to wear multiple hats and fill multiple roles to help get the game finished."

Red 5 was committed to developing the game with active participation from the community, complicating things further for the team. "Interpreting and processing all of the community feedback during an already extremely large and complex development process was another contributing factor to the overall challenge," she said. "But the quality of the team and sense of camaraderie that grew over the course of development made the community-driven start-up challenge feel worthwhile." Romine departed Red 5 in 2013.

Easter Egg

Lives with an 18-year-old Colombian red-tailed boa constrictor named Max that's over eight feet in length. Max has been a model for CGI artists in the past, providing lifelike animations for snakes in movies.

PRESS ANY KEY TO CONTINUE...

For the next two years Romine would focus on her PhD and prepare for her subsequent professional endeavor. Romine finished her doctorate in cultural anthropology in 2016. Her dissertation—"Fractured Imaginaries: An Ethnography of Game Design"—examined the local cultures of game development.

In 2015 Romine founded AnyKey, an outlet for the summation of her extensive career in esports. An advocacy and research initiative, AnyKey was established through a partnership with Intel and the Electronic Sports League.

AnyKey focuses on the cultural aspects of gaming. Romine serves that cause as a consultant and advocate with an emphasis on fostering healthy esports communities. "My current advocacy work in diversity and inclusion is inspired and motivated by the dream that games can be a positive social equalizer, where people from around the world can play and compete together and develop meaningful relationships," she explained. "But in order to achieve that dream, we must address some of the cultural barriers that currently make gaming spaces seem unwelcoming or inaccessible to many."

The research arm of AnyKey is focused on examining the causes of that inaccessibility, looking at the limitations women, LGBTQ players, players of color, and disabled or developmentally challenged gamers face when engaging in competitive play.

As the director of initiatives, Romine focuses on creating actionable strategies and programs from that research.

"My career has been built on esports, so I have a lot of visibility into the exploding growth in the popularity of esports and competitive gaming," said Romine. "My hope for the future is to see the entire esports ecosystem—from grassroots tournaments to global mainstage championships—become more diverse, so that the entire rainbow of humanity can be represented."

On a personal front, Romine hopes to continue contributing to an environment of growth and support for women professionals and consumers in gaming. "I didn't enter this industry with the goal of advocating for other women, but I've been lucky to find myself in various roles where I could make a difference in the lives of aspiring game industry professionals by paying forward my own experience and access. Diversity benefits the industry as a whole, not only for those women, but for everyone who loves how games allow us to tell stories in new ways. Greater diversity among players and creators will lead to greater diversity in the games themselves."

BRIE CODE

BEFRIENDING THE FORGOTTEN 50 PERCENT

 briecode

 briecode

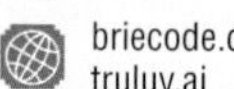 briecode.com
truluv.ai

EXPERIENCE

FIRST INDUSTRY PROJECT: COMPANY OF HEROES (2006)
FAVORITE INDUSTRY PROJECT: #SELFCARE (2018)
PROJECTS SHIPPED: 8 GAMES
ACHIEVEMENTS UNLOCKED:
> EUROPEAN WOMEN IN GAMES CONFERENCE—KEYNOTE SPEAKER (2017)
> MINDTREK—KEYNOTE SPEAKER (2017)
> INDIECADE EUROPE—KEYNOTE SPEAKER (2017)
> VIDEO GAMES ARE BORING, GAMESINDUSTRY.BIZ (2016)

STATS

INDUSTRY LEVEL: 16
CURRENT CLASS: CEO, CREATIVE DIRECTOR
CURRENT GUILD: TRU LUV—TORONTO, CANADA
SPECIAL SKILLS: AI, PROGRAMMING, & GAME DESIGN

STANDARD EQUIPMENT

FAVORITE PLATFORM: MOBILE
GO-TO GENRE: RPG
MUST-HAVE GAME: THE ELDER SCROLLS V: SKYRIM

BIO

After graduating from university, Brie Code was struck with a severe case of wanderlust. She'd worked hard to earn a degree in computer science with a focus on artificial intelligence and psychology, but lacked direction on where the education would take her. "I knew I wanted to do something creative that helped people, but had no idea what that could be," said Code. "I didn't want to work at a bank." She hoped to find answers on the road. After a few months away, Code returned home with a maxed-out credit card and no more focus than when she departed. She resigned to finding any programming job she could.

"And then I found a job that I didn't realize existed—I found a job at Relic Entertainment, a games studio," said Code. "It was such good timing. They had decided to hire their first two junior programmers right when I had started looking for work. I heard that I was the first programmer to ace their programming test. I started writing gameplay and user interface code and progressed to writing AI code. *Company of Heroes* was the first RTS to have squad-level AI, where units not only act as individuals but also coordinate with each other, and I helped write that. I also wrote half of the player AI: if you play *Company of Heroes* against the AI, you are playing against my colleague Shelby Hubick and me."

Code found the answers she had been looking for at Relic. "I had amazing role models," she shared. "The team was smart, creative, collaborative, and generous with their knowledge and ideas. My love for games deepened, and I realized I would make my career in this industry."

> "If you play *Company of Heroes* against the AI, you are playing against my colleague Shelby Hubik and me."

After four years at Relic, Code spent some time at Pandemic Studios, followed by Ubisoft Montréal, lending her talents to a series of AAA games. Discontent was beginning to stir within her, though. Neither the environment nor the products were fulfilling her as they once had. She would soon be able to articulate why.

TEND-AND-BEFRIEND

"I read Sheri Graner Ray's book *Gender Inclusive Game Design*, and her chapter on stimulation resonated with me," explained Code. "She said that some women tend to enjoy 'mutually beneficial outcomes to socially significant situations,' and I was like, 'Yes, I sure do.' It seemed like a key to some arguments I was having with my colleagues at the time."

As Code dug further, she found a theory from the UCLA Social Neuroscience lab that challenged the underlying framework of every game design book she'd read. "This theory, called tend-and-befriend, provides a succinct explanation for why about half of people find games boring," she said. "It suggests a framework for how we could make games about care and connection to engage and inspire those people. I wondered if we could make games differently, and if we did, would I (and many of my non-game-playing friends) want to play them?"

Easter Egg

Has spectacularly failed her driving test three times, and still doesn't have a license.

Code points out that the tend-and-befriend theory was identified as recently as 2000, after the UCLA Social Neuroscience lab noticed that early stress research had been done almost exclusively on male rats. "Tend-and-befriend is largely linked to female, not male, rats," she explained. "In humans it seems to be more mixed, but still may be linked people we might describe as having more feminine traits. Game designers tend to be one kind of person, stimulated by frustration and mastery, and have repeatedly ignored the intuitions, desires, and opinions of their more feminine colleagues."

WANDERLUST: THE SEQUEL

Code continued to study the theory, developing a framework around it. The more she learned, the more dissatisfied she became with her station in the industry. "In 2015, after 12 years of devoted, conscientious work in the industry, I quit my job spontaneously, dramatically, in the middle of a meeting, with no plan," said Code. "I had never done anything like that before. It was deeply satisfying, but it was also impulsive and ridiculous."

Code considered her options: apply at another studio, work toward a PhD, teach, found her own studio, or start over in a new field. "I wanted to take time to make the decision," said Code. "Then I got an invitation to do the opening keynote for a conference in Australia. I said yes. Some old friends who happen to have a house in the woods invited me to come stay with them after. It was perfect."

On the second day of her Australian getaway, Code's host asked what caused her to quit. "I talked with her about my frustrations with the industry," began Code. "I talked to her about 3-5% of game programmers being women. I talked with her about how one of my bosses had decreed that women want only *Vogue* magazine and not deep, rich experiences. I talked with her about a theory in the field of stress psychology that challenged the underlying assumptions of game design, provided a clear explanation for why about half of people find video games boring, and suggested how we could double the market."

"I quit my job spontaneously, dramatically, in the middle of a meeting, with no plan."

Later that evening, Code's host said she'd seen a vision of her future. Code would travel the world, make games with people who traditionally don't find them interesting, and find a new community. "I woke up the next morning and I knew I would do it." She returned home, packed up her belongings, and left. Code prototyped six games with six friends, experimenting with the tend-and-befriend framework along the way. "While I was traveling, I built a speaking career to pay for the trip," explained Code. "I spoke with game developers in places such as Tunis, Casablanca, Beirut, Berlin, Utrecht, Kuala Lumpur, and ended the trip in Melbourne where I started."

Code wasn't ready to stand still when the year was up. "I felt a sense of urgency. I felt a great sense of unfairness in how the games industry has ignored so many people," said Code. "So I traveled for another year, building up my consulting business to help games studios around the world reach wider audiences, and I ramped up my own studio with a distributed team around the world to develop our first product. And now I've just settled back down in Canada, in Toronto, and released *#SelfCare*."

FINDING LUV

#SelfCare is the first release from Code's start-up, TRU LUV. What TRU LUV creates aren't quite games, nor are they apps. Code calls them companions. "A companion is an autonomous friend who is along with you for your adventures," she elaborated. "They have their own needs and tastes and interests and goals, and you have yours. And you help each other. Each experience is about care and connection. In TRU LUV's framework, you don't tell your phone what you need, and your phone doesn't tell you what you need. Instead, you work together towards shared goals. You help each other. The game design curve inside a companion app is designed with tend-and-befriend rather than fight-or-flight in mind, so we go from awkward to orderly rather than from easy to hard."

#SelfCare launched on the App Store in mid-2018. "We had to keep going and keep trusting our intuitions in the face of my games industry colleagues telling us repeatedly our work was boring or that what we were making wasn't a game or wasn't marketable," shared Code. "It's very early to draw any conclusions about how we're doing. But without spending anything on advertising, we made it into the top 100 apps in seven countries, and we were #9 in the Games Store in Australia. We don't prompt the player to rate or review the app at all, but we have a 4.7 star rating from over 1000 ratings. The reviews are directly confirming some of our theses about how to do things differently."

While TRU LUV's first companion app focuses on relaxation and self-care, Code sees a future where they design companions for studying, cooking, motherhood, fitness, and more. "We already live in mixed reality through the little window in our phones. Eventually we'll have glasses or contact lens or implants. I am very motivated to provide different kinds of experiences created by and for new audiences as we move into this new, highly connected, cyberpunk world."

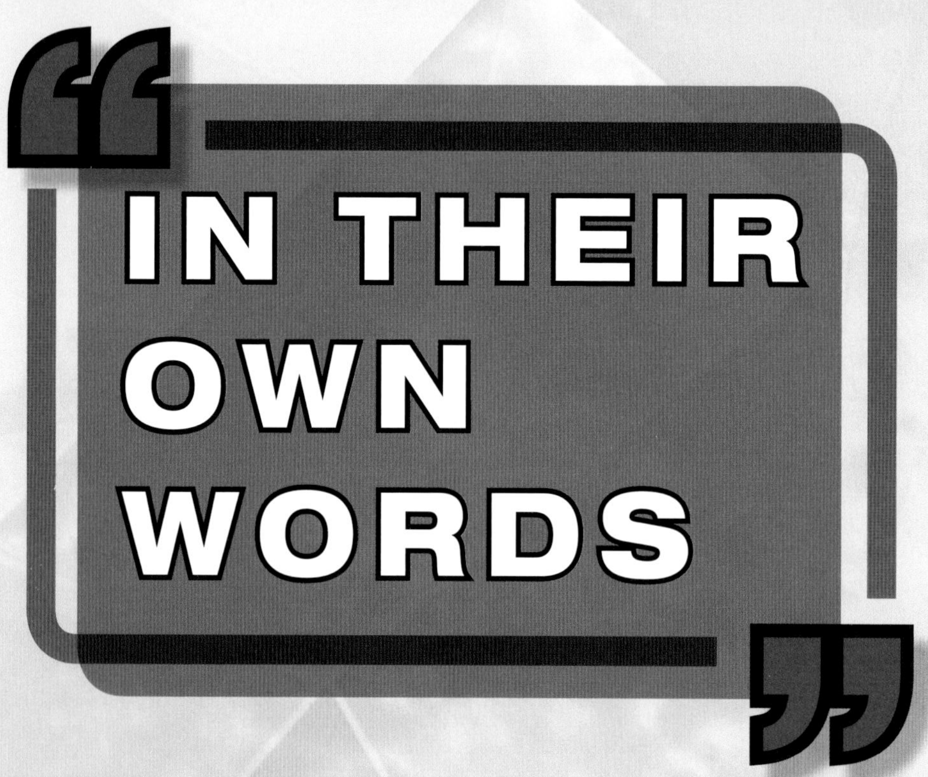

FAVORITE FEMALE CHARACTER

Who is your favorite female character in video games, and why is she important or meaningful to you?

"One of my favorite female video game characters is Yennefer from the *Witcher* series because she helped me better understand myself. My personality type, INTJ, is incredibly rare in women and aspects of it made me very self-conscious. It was often portrayed in fiction by villains, and to me, felt like the worst parts of my personality were on display. During my test, it said that Yennefer was a fictional character with the same personality type. I took a closer look at her as a character and, as I began see more and more of the good parts of Yennefer, I started to appreciate those aspects in my personality."

Amanda Erickson | Social Media Manager | Rooster Teeth | Austin, USA

"Tess from *The Last of Us* is one of my favorite female characters in games. Because she's not a player character, the developers were able to make her much more distinct. She becomes so much more than a helpful NPC or a way to push the story forward. Her forthright attitude and skillfulness makes her an equal partner, if not leader, to Joel, the protagonist. Her death, perhaps the most trope-like aspect of Tess, is also something rare and wonderful. Across the spectrum of entertainment, female characters are sheltered from this kind of violence—violence by choice with the ability to meet it head on. Going down fighting is an acceptable way to sacrifice male characters, but female characters are meant to be kept both protected and helpless. Only in recent years have we begun seeing physically capable female characters with the freedom and knowledge to decide their own fate. Tess dies for a cause she believes in and it is because of Tess' sacrifice and her final request that Joel ultimately continues on her crusade, which becomes the story of *The Last of Us*."

Robyn Tong Gray | Co-Founder & Chief Creative Officer | Otherworld Interactive | Los Angeles, USA

"Jade from *Beyond Good and Evil*. I appreciate her for the authenticity of her friendships and chosen family, and the fact that she was designed to be appealing but not exploitative."

Heather Kelley | Kokoromi Member & Assistant Teaching Professor | Carnegie Mellon University | Pittsburgh, USA

"There are so many incredibly strong, powerful, and quirky women in games and I love many of them. Perhaps my favorite, and the one for whom I have the most admiration and awe, is Yeesha from the *Myst* series of games. Yeesha is Atrus' and Catherine's daughter, who you meet for the first time in *Myst III* as an infant, see again in *Myst IV* as an 11-year-old girl, and as a grown woman in *Myst V*. She's also in *Uru: Ages Beyond Myst*. *Myst* was one of the first PC games I played and it has had a huge impact on my life, but more than that, Yeesha embodies who I hope all women (and men) would aspire to be: peaceful, kind, adventurous, and willing to teach others with her wisdom."

Katherine Postma | Community Manager | Stoic | London, Canada

---

"My favorite female video game character is, without a doubt, Joanna Dark from *Perfect Dark*. She showed up at a time when I was just starting to question why there couldn't be a smart, sophisticated female version of James Bond, and with a game that was even better than *Goldeneye* to boot! Joanna is well respected, tactical, and—above all—independent. I'm positive that playing through the first *Perfect Dark* as her has had a lasting impact on me."

Alanah Pearce | Writer/Producer | Rooster Teeth | Los Angeles, USA

"*Parasite Eve*'s Aya Brea stuck with me far more than any of her other contemporaries. In the opening opera scene, she takes control of the situation, pushing her date out of the way and seeking the source of the trouble. I didn't really see many take-charge female characters when I was young, so this was inspiring. It helped to see a woman who was not only confident in her abilities, but who was also willing to stand up for herself and what she believed in. I look at her as a turning point for female characters in video games, representing a push for leaders who'd never been considered damsels in distress. Not only was Aya strong, she was relatable. She didn't initially have superpowers and did her job as a New York City detective well, something any woman could do."

Kimberley Wallace | Features Editor | *Game Informer* | Minneapolis, USA

"Rinoa Heartilly from *Final Fantasy XIII* was definitely the first heroine who showed me that you should pursue what you want in life. If she wanted to do something, she just did it. She was sincere with her feelings toward Squall right from the start even though she was a girl. Everything she did happened with an amazing confidence. She made me feel it was okay to speak my mind, and that it was okay to do things my way."

Laia Bee | Co-Founder | Pincer Games | Punta del Este, Uruguay

---

"I'm currently in love with Ellie from *The Last of Us*, in part because kids are far more capable than we give them credit for and we need to be reminded of that. I love the way she was written and the way she has grown up over the various installments."

Kimberly Unger | Mobile/VR Producer | Playchemy | Burlingame, USA

"A character whose appeal has helped build one of Nintendo's long-lasting franchises is Samus. At a time when the trope of damsels in distress ran rampant, Samus burst onto the scene as a woman whose strength was being a bounty hunter and badass."

Morrigan Johnen | Community & Social Media Manager | Crystal Dynamics | Redwood City, USA

"Widowmaker from *Overwatch* has become my favorite character from a video game over the past few years. She has depth and purpose to her. She knows what she is and how to use her talents to get what she wants. But there is also a beautiful tragedy to her story. She is an over-the-top fantasy character, but she is so much more than that in the nuance of her story and background. I appreciate how she was handled."

Rachel Day | Senior VFX Artist | Blizzard Entertainment | Irvine, USA

"Kreia in *Star Wars Knights of the Old Republic II: The Sith Lords*. Without going into too much detail (to avoid spoilers), Kreia is a complicated character and very nuanced. At first she feels like a fairly baseline RPG character intended to present you with questions and choices that make her more of a sounding board or someone who helps drive the narrative along, but she takes on more and more of an important role as you progress through the game. You make assumptions about her when you start and almost write her off for a while until you really start to see the depth behind the writing. She's intelligent, mysterious, and forces you to think and question the world around you. She's manipulative and charismatic, cold yet maternal, intelligent and deeply flawed. And an absolute badass to boot."

Cat Karskens | Senior Community Manager | Square Enix Europe | London, UK

"Kate Walker from the *Syberia* game series. She is significant for being the protagonist of a graphic adventure in which she shows a strong and empathetic temperament. The story is extraordinary and—thanks to Kate—I understood how games were capable of narrating complex, deep events, and of transmitting subtle sensations, such as nostalgia. In addition, it is a character who has a well-resolved transformation arc through action, which also interested me from the point of view of the script."

Alejandra Bruno | Narrative Game Designer | QB9 | Buenos Aires, Argentina

---

"It may be obvious, but Lara Croft will forever be my favorite video game character. I was a young girl when *Tomb Raider* was first released 1996, and I was immediately drawn to Lara's independence, wittiness, smarts and physical strength. This was at a time when it was hard to find all of these traits represented in one female character, let alone one who was gainfully self-employed. She was a role model for my younger self in regards to being self-sufficient and following your own path. The fact I've had the opportunity to work on the *Tomb Raider* franchise actually feels like this path has come full circle, and I know Lara Croft will continue to inspire future generations to come!"

Katie Swindlhurst | Brand Manager | Crystal Dynamics | Redwood City, USA

"I'd have to say Lara Croft or Alyx Vance. Lara because she was a prominent, aspirational heroine when there weren't many female characters like that in games, and Alyx because *Half Life 2* demonstrated that female game characters could be realistic, layered, and believable at a time when many were one-dimensional."

Amy Hennig | Sr. Creative Director & Writer | Independent | San Carlos, USA

"Elena Fisher, from the *Uncharted* series. She doesn't follow the conventions of a female sidekick as present in most video games, or even the conventions of video game heroines. She is a more nuanced character and you get the sense from the very beginning that she is already the star of her own action-adventure that just happens to intersect with Nathan Drake's, and I love that dynamic."

Kellee Santiago | Partnerships Development Lead | Google Entertainment | San Francisco, USA

"Tetra in *The Legend of Zelda: The Wind Waker.* When I was a little kid, I used to pretend Link was a girl when I was playing. When Tetra came along, I no longer needed to invent an awesome female character for the Zelda games; she was right there."

Keza MacDonald | Video Games Editor | *The Guardian* | London, UK

"Faith Connors from *Mirror's Edge*. First, she's the epitome of grace under pressure. She fights tirelessly for her cause and, as someone terrified of heights, just playing those games as Faith makes me feel like the badass that I certainly am not!"

Kayse Sondreal-Nene | Sr. Merchant, Video Games | Best Buy Co., Inc. | Minneapolis, USA

"Playing *Mass Effect* as female Commander Shepard was one of my biggest inspirations for becoming a game writer. She was strong, smart, and brave—and exactly as capable as her male counterpart. No one treated her like she was somehow worth less than a man, or offered her anything less than the respect of a hero. It made me feel like I could do anything. And after experiencing that, all I wanted was to make other women feel the same way."

Samantha Wallschlaeger | Writer | ArenaNet LLC | Seattle, USA

"My favourite characters in video games are often those who evolve throughout the game and have to make difficult choices, or where the player's perception of them changes through the game experience. Tifa Lockhart from *Final Fantasy VII* and 2B from *Nier: Automata* are both characters who care deeply for other characters in their games, but their complexity is only revealed as their stories progress."

Jodie Azhar | Technical Art Director | Redhill, UK

"For me, one of my favorites is Sarah Kerrigan from the *StarCraft* universe. Along with Lara Croft, she's one of the more iconic female characters I came across growing up. She goes from being tossed aside and left to die to commanding the entirety of the Zerg to get her revenge. She's aggressive, cunning, and determined."

Jennie Nguyen | Systems Administrator | Crystal Dynamics | Redwood City, USA

"It would have to be GLaDOS, from *Portal*. To be fair, I think that everything about *Portal* is fantastic, but I think the way the character of GLaDOS was written is absolutely exceptional. It starts out as a guiding voice and quickly becomes a villain you can't help loving while she victimizes you. I love that there is nothing stereotypical about this character. She is not sexy; she doesn't even have a body and doesn't need saving. The whole goal of the game is to defeat her, and she is deliciously sinister and dangerous. And I think I listened to *Still Alive* maybe one too many times."

Simona Tassinari | Lead Programmer Snowdrop | Massive (Ubisoft) | Malmö, Sweden

---

"Susan Ashworth from *The Cat Lady*, a surrealist horror game about depression. Susan is a flawed hero whose experiences kicked me right in the gut. It's a dark game about fear, feelings of worthlessness, and recovery. I highly recommend it for folks looking for an emotionally intense story."

Soha El-Sabaawi | Manager of Diversity & Inclusion Programs | Riot Games | Los Angeles, USA

CREATIVITY:

Source Code for the Human Operating System

By Megan Gaiser | *Principal, Contagious Creativity LLC*

HIDDEN IN PLAIN SIGHT

For much of its existence, the game industry has been exclusive and homogeneous. Gamergate—the controversy centered on issues of sexism and progressivism in video game culture—brought the issue of abuse toward women to the forefront, but it didn't move the needle. The ongoing harassment against women went unchallenged by the industry leadership.

As a result, women had to go it alone, speaking out amidst regular online harassment and vitriolic language. For many, this toxic environment ranged from moments of chaos, hopelessness, depression, rage, anxiety, and fear. At one point, threats of rape, and even death, caused a few women to flee their homes. The FBI got involved. I asked some senior game colleagues why they weren't speaking out in support of these women.

Some believed doing so would hurt their brand and their bottom line. Others didn't think it had anything to do with them. Still others were afraid of being targeted themselves. One courageous leader, Dean Takahashi, brought the issue forward in his opening GamesBeat keynote in 2015, stating "I would not recommend the game industry to my daughters." These events brought to light just how warped our moral compass had become. The game industry would never be the same.

2017 ushered in the #MeToo movement, catalyzing a worldwide revolt against the longstanding subjugation and objectification of women. Who knew that most women across industries have been sexually assaulted or harassed at one time or another? It was the best-kept secret until Pandora's box busted wide open.

REDEFINING LEADERSHIP BY UPGRADING OURSELVES

Reflecting on the last century's atrocities—or at least, the disclosure of them—their sheer volume and frequency seems to lull us into the acceptance of bad behavior as part of the "human condition." Yet this ongoing climate of hostility and disconnection provides the perfect opportunity to reexamine the culture we have unwittingly agreed to.

Business was designed for humans, yet profit is often valued over people, data over wisdom and money over meaning. On a monetary, technological, and intellectual scale, progress has increased dramatically. However, the mastery of heart intelligence has advanced very little over the ages. It's time for that to change.

If we agree that business as usual no longer works to lead today's diverse populace, the logical place to start is to redefine what it takes to become a 21st century leader. We have been told that leadership equals the right to authority. It doesn't.

Leadership isn't just about roles or titles. This new way of being, leading for the diversity of humanity, demands we replace the flawed belief in leadership as authority, with leadership as sage and benevolent behavior.

The opportunity before us is to break the conditioning of homogenized expression to become more finely tuned versions of ourselves. Encouraging what is possible for the greater good begins with the courage to embrace curiosity—the gateway to creativity.

This is a radical departure from the longstanding authority that tends to dismiss the more intuitive sides of the brain. It's not simply about implementing tactics or integrating diverse personalities, ethnicities, age, or gender. Becoming a leader for diversity is an inside job. It requires that we reject habitual mental, emotional and behavioral patterns to choose our thoughts—rather than being ruled by them.

Relearning how to access *all* of our intelligence is the path to adopt more wholesome behaviors. We upgrade computers when they are not operating at their maximum capacity. Why wouldn't we upgrade ourselves?

21ST CENTURY LEADERSHIP FOR DIVERSITY

Many emboldened leaders within the game industry viewed this climate of chaos and dysfunction as an opportunity to catalyze positive leadership change. Organizations like The IGDA Foundation, Women in Games International, Games for Change, Global Game Jam, Girls Behind the Games, iThrive Games, Amplifying New Voices, Microsoft's 'Gaming for Everyone', Carnegie Mellon's Entertainment Technology Center, Feminist Frequency, and The Venture Reality Fund, have stepped up to help create a climate of inclusivity, diversity and opportunity.

While we celebrate these inspired initiatives, we are also reminded that there are no quick fixes. More importantly, there is something far bigger going on. Before we can begin to realign our moral compass, it is necessary to understand the root causes for this less than humane state of consciousness, often passing as leadership.

HOW DID WE GET HERE?

As children, we used pure, sensory information to access *all* of our senses. We lived in the moment, reveling in the act of play. We were empowered by an unbiased, open heart and mind. Unfortunately, the influences of social, cultural, religious, political, educational and/or governmental systems condition us to accept prescribed behaviors at an early age—limiting creative freedom.

Boys are taught 'to be a man', to essentially shut down their hearts by the age of ten. Conversely, girls are taught to defer to and please in a system designed without them in mind. Girls 'pretty up.' Boys 'soldier on.' All of our psyches—girls, boys, women, and men—eventually become damaged; short-circuited in the process. The result is the adoption of an artificial set of biases in favor of or against certain people or groups, their behaviors and/or beliefs.

Bias stems from a disconnection from the heart, resulting in fear-based thinking. Conscious bias is intentional. Unconscious bias however, is not. It is a blind spot, a bad habit we all suffer from. Because it is unconscious, we often don't even realize that it festers within us. It fosters a sense of entitlement, arrogance, superiority, and judgment on one end; and blame, shame, inferiority and guilt on the other.

Despite the smokescreens, a lack of consciousness perpetuates bias—a major source of human *dis-ease.* It is so deceptive that both genders have been unwittingly set up to become perpetrators or victims of bias—or in my case, a combination of both.

As a female and a creative leader in an environment that deemed girls less than game worthy, I experienced the feeling of being dismissed, placated, and unwelcomed. What had eluded me is how many times I was unconsciously doing the same thing in my life. Once one blind spot revealed itself, it opened the floodgates.

In retrospect, the most dangerous bias I suffered from was the assumption that I didn't have any. I realized that my biases had one thing in common: fear. Accepting my role as a victim of bias *also* set me up to be a perpetrator. It was the perfect wakeup call.

On a positive note, the experience led me to conduct multidisciplinary research, coursework, meditation and yoga for six years with two questions in mind: (1) Why aren't we leading with our heart in partnership with our brain and (2) How do we stay in our truth when consumed with fear? I learned more about creativity, unconscious bias, ethics, consciousness, heart and emotional intelligence, neuroscience, history, mysticism, psychology, and quantum physics. The research served to bridge the gaps between science and spirituality. This wisdom—coupled with a determination to overcome the invisible enemy of bias—put a kink in my programming. It broke the spell of amnesia. Slowly, surely, and sometimes painfully, I've been reassembling the remnants ever since.

The research also compelled me to initiate many conversations with diverse thought leaders. I came to better understand the historical context and strategies designed to create social division and self-isolation—the illusion of duality. I've heard that earth is the school for late bloomers, a euphemism for slow learners. If so, then one thing is true. I'm in the right school.

COMING BACK INTO ALL OF OUR SENSES: UNEARTHING BIAS

What I learned is that a large part of our human intelligence remains untapped. Out of three billion base pair chemicals in the human gene code, only sixty million are active. Our subconscious mind is one million times more powerful than our conscious mind. It governs 95% of our behavior. It works through habit by repetition, running much of the show without our explicit conscious awareness.

It is like an immersive, mixed reality (MR) adventure experience, a massively multiplayer video game, designed to look real. This adventure game mirrors our own fragmented consciousness, preventing manifestation of the player's DNA—their unique soul blueprint.

Fear is the game mechanic of this programmed reality, the trigger to keep us off balance—out of touch with our inner guidance. This steady control system clouds the ability to sense the truth at the core of our experience, creating abbreviated versions of our selves. The player is unaware of their true origin and the power of who they really are. That is the set up.

It resembles a computer program coded to distort all sense of unity, connection and belonging, to one of disharmony, disconnection and fear. It is achieved in part by the distribution of scarcity and hate through "fear porn." It takes form through the dehumanizing systems of gender/racial inequality, addiction, economic disasters, predictive programming, bio/geo-engineering, poverty, war, pedophilia, homelessness, human trafficking, and more.

The goal of this game? Reconnect with the motherboard that runs our pure operating system—genetically sequenced, unique in expression and purpose. The rules of the game unfold as awareness expands. The challenge? Players hooked to the drip feed of fear rely on pre-programmed thoughts, resulting in biased behaviors. Though this energy is within us, it is not who we truly are. To be what we are not in any moment, no longer self-steering, is to live the conditioning.

This deception hologram feeds and breeds the *dis-ease* of bias. Under these conditions, it is not possible to genuinely welcome diverse people and perspectives. We have been told that this is 'how the world works', to accept these things as 'human nature.' 'That it's just the way it is.' Except it isn't.

We have become so disempowered by the inescapable presence of fear we are unable to evolve as a species. We have put our trust into an untrustworthy system of authority at the expense of our innate power(s). The purity of our consciousness has been hacked. We've all been played. So how do we move forward?

Traditional leadership tends to primarily value our 'thinking'; analytical intelligence, (literal, logical and linear) as the primary driver, which may or may not include heart (creative) intelligence, our 'knowing.' And while our brain serves an important role, we also need our intuitive and sensory powers to function optimally.

Creativity enables us to transcend traditional rules, behaviors, and systems in favor of fresh ideas, meaningful approaches and progressive interpretations. This creative intelligence (perception, intuition, sensing, feeling and imagination) is the body's most sophisticated navigational system. So why aren't we leading with it?

Historically, creativity has been relegated to making art or creating products. It has been underestimated because the value it brings wasn't adequately quantified. That's no longer the case. The science of creativity has been proven. The value of creative intelligence as a force for leadership that inspires the collective is undeniable. The good news? It's teachable.

Word of this *game* is spreading fast via walkthroughs, cheat codes, Easter eggs, and social media. Once critical mass levels up, it will end. Though it served as a longstanding distraction with a debilitating hold on human consciousness, the game will ultimately be remembered as a futile attempt to inhibit the powerful diversity of humanity.

RADICAL CREATIVITY

Creativity is the most valuable leadership skill of the 21st century. It represents the most radical act of freedom. If human evolution has been hindered by our inability to access full sensory intelligence, consider what's possible when we reconnect our creative and analytical intelligence—to make the business of life, fully human.

- Imagine starting with a clean slate—learning to experience life more authentically—instead of picking up where we left off.
- Imagine leadership teams as wisdom keepers, inspiring us to reach for what is possible and in doing so, serving the greater good.
- Imagine using our creativity to intentionally eradicate the pervasive psychological warfare within and around us.
- Imagine reshaping the role of HR to become HIR (Human Inspiration Resources).
- Imagine a game industry where men and women feel safe enough to bring their entire selves to truly collaborate.
- Imagine the primary purpose of products and services geared toward human evolution instead of productivity alone.

This evolution happens from the inside out. It shifts the very core of our being, forever altering our psyche for the better. There is nothing about a caterpillar that tells you it's going to become a butterfly. And yet within the cocoon hides the promise. At some point, the caterpillar realizes it has a much more powerful purpose. In that moment, dormant cells biologists had the genius to call "imaginal cells," begin to transform. Once the shape shifting is completed, a butterfly emerges in all its glory.

Human imaginal cells are at least as powerful. The uncomfortable act of shedding our skin seems more than worth the investment. Revealing our best selves beneath the conditioned veneer inspires others to level up. Achieving this state of presence defines both the path and mark of true leadership. It's like coming home.

WE ARE THE TECHNOLOGY—THE HUMAN RE-BOOT

Human evolution is not industry specific. It is a worldwide event unfolding in real time. While the veil is being lifted for bad behavior globally, it is also exposing the unexamined sides of our own beliefs and biases, still hidden from us. The fight we are fighting is not out there. It never has been.

The consciousness cleansing game is in full swing. Though not formally invited, we are all participants in the greatest reality show on earth—hidden in plain sight. As androgynous, sentient, creator-beings playing a role and a gender, we are here to experience the distortions of consciousness to break free from bias.

We are at a crossroads, witnessing the unprecedented implosion of a longstanding paradigm, and the creation of a new one—*unity in diversity*. Collective intelligence is the only acceptable reality to catapult the collective forward.

It is not possible to create an inclusive reality on top of a toxic one. We must reimagine it. The obsolete socio-economic and cultural approaches, systems, rhetoric, and practices designed with only half of the population in mind, are ripe for redesign.

Therefore, *we can't wait* for the game industry, or any industry, to reimagine itself—because *we are* the industry. We are being called to become consciousness catalysts—architects redesigning business as a human enterprise, in a fully conscious reality. What better moment to summon heartfelt intent to positively transform ourselves.

Whether victims or perpetrators of bias, or both, we can reject the deception of fear to take control for the full rendition of ourselves. No one is guilty, just reawakening.

We are the technology we've been waiting for. Our subtle, sacred senses are surfacing. Like city lights switching on at sunset, we are self-activating—retuning our human instruments from one way of knowing, to another.

Some call it flow. Some call it light. Some call it source. I call it creativity, the human operating system.

It's time to reunite our creative and analytical intelligence to lead for the diversity of humanity—stepping into innate wisdom as authority, to reclaim our true identity.

The power is within us *and* it *will* take all of us.

Let's go home.

Excerpt from an upcoming book "The Human Re-Boot"—©2018.

STEPHANIE BAYER

"THE SASSIEST, REDHEADEDEST, ROCKABILLIEST, PROUD LATINX VIDEO GAME PROFESSIONAL AROUND!"

NSSteph

Stephervescent

Stephanie Bayer

stephervescent.tumblr.com

EXPERIENCE

FIRST INDUSTRY PROJECT: SCOOBY-DOO! MYSTERY MAYHEM (2004)

FAVORITE INDUSTRY PROJECT: SUNSET OVERDRIVE (2013), GUITAR HERO PROJECTS (2008-2010), PLANTS VS. ZOMBIES: GARDEN WARFARE (2012)

PROJECTS SHIPPED: 16 GAMES

ACHIEVEMENTS UNLOCKED:

> HAS BEEN AN OFFICIAL GDC SPEAKER FOUR TIMES AND GAVE A MASTER CLASS ON COMMUNITY MANAGEMENT

> HAS APPEARED IN THE GDC SPEAKER CARD DECK TWICE BECAUSE OF HIGHLY RATED PANELS

> COMPLETED ONE FULL MARATHON AND 15 HALF-MARATHONS

> ONSTAGE AT EA E3 PRESS CONFERENCE, DEMOING PLANTS VS. ZOMBIES: GARDEN WARFARE (2013)

STATS

INDUSTRY LEVEL: 15

CURRENT CLASS: MANAGER, COMMUNITY DEVELOPMENT

CURRENT GUILD: BLIZZARD ENTERTAINMENT—IRVINE, USA

SPECIAL SKILLS: SOCIAL INTERACTIVITY, SOCIAL MEDIA, COMMUNITY MANAGEMENT, CONTENT STRATEGY, SOCIAL ANALYTICS, INFLUENCER RELATIONS

STANDARD EQUIPMENT

FAVORITE PLATFORM: XBOX ONE

GO-TO GENRE: FPS, SURVIVAL HORROR

MUST-HAVE GAME: BIOSHOCK

BIO

When Stephanie Bayer was three years old, she ran away from home with 11 cents in her pocket, and headed for a liquor store more than two miles away to play *Pac-Man*. "My neighbors found me walking alone, took me home, and my mother bought me an Atari 2600 because she figured it'd be a lot safer than not having one in the house," laughed Bayer. She also remembers playing games on the NES and Genesis growing up, and then as an adult, spending her first paycheck on a PlayStation. "I played *PaRappa the Rappa*, *Tony Hawk*, *Tomb Raider*... I bought an N64 and kept my game collection going, and it's never stopped. Games were escape, fun, anger, joy, frustration, elation, and everything in between. It felt like a natural fit."

It isn't a surprise, then, that Bayer always intended to work in video games. The trick was figuring out in what capacity. "When I went to college, I focused on technology and engineering. I was in hardware programming when I started my first job in video games as QA at THQ in 2003." Her time at THQ provided a deeper understanding of the various roles at a game studio. While she would eventually land in community and social media, Bayer doesn't regret her tech background. "It's come in handy so often in my career—every job I've had since that first job has honed my skills further."

ROAD TO COMMUNITY

After THQ, Bayer's next stop was the Walt Disney Internet Group as an associate producer, and subsequently Neversoft Entertainment in 2008. "I had a really great time working on *Guitar Hero*," said Bayer. "The studio culture was one of the strangest, most hilarious, and sometimes craziest of any studio I've worked at. I launched five titles that year! So, it was busy!" She had accepted her first community management job in the midst of the *Guitar Hero* craze, and helped bring *Guitar Hero World Tour*, *Guitar Hero: Metallica*, *Guitar Hero: Van Halen*, *Guitar Hero 5*, and *Band Hero* to market. "I can genuinely say I made a lot of friends during that time," she recalled. "Between my co-workers, running community events, interacting with the *Guitar Hero* community at large, and getting the chance to meet so many others while working on one of the most popular game franchises at the time, I'm super humbled I had that experience period."

Having established herself as a strong community manager, Bayer lent her talent to a series of impressive studios over the next several years. As assistant community manager at BioWare, she worked on *Star Wars: The Old Republic*, followed by a contract position running all social media for Xbox in 2010. The total social presence she was responsible for included three Facebook pages, three Twitter accounts, a YouTube channel, and a Myspace page, resulting in daily communications with over four million fans around the world. During her five-month contract position, she helped grow the Xbox fan base an additional 30% by posting carefully curated content.

"I was also the trained zombie handler [for Plants Vs. Zombies] and traveled around the world. And I wouldn't have traded that experience for anything!"

POPCAP

Bayer was hired to PopCap Games in 2011, where she would leave one of her most enduring impacts on a video game franchise. She began as a customer engagement leader for the mega-successful *Bejeweled* series, which she helped grow to over five million fans across social media, before taking over as community marketing manager for the *Plants vs. Zombies* franchise. Bayer devised the overall community and social strategy for game releases, created content, executed social plans, and engaged with the community online wherever they were. She launched the first official forums for PopCap, and reported bugs to the development team. During her time at PopCap, Bayer helped grow the *Plants vs. Zombies* Facebook fan page to nearly 11 million fans.

"Some of my favorite memories are the fun activations I've had the chance to do at PopCap," said Bayer. "Launching *Plants vs. Zombies 2* on iOS and Android were some of the most memorable campaigns I've ever worked on. I got to ride in a helicopter and take video of the namesake browncoat costumed zombie on top of the Space Needle. For the Android launch, our zombie appeared in the crowd during a taping of *Good Morning America*, and then he visited NYC landmarks with a food truck. It all culminated in the zombie working a day at the NYC Google offices, where I filmed him making coffee, playing pool, doing desk work, and so on. Besides managing social media, community management, and social content creation for the *Plants vs. Zombies* franchise, I was also the trained zombie handler and literally traveled around the world capturing content of a costumed zombie. And I wouldn't have traded that experience for anything!"

Managing two major franchises was rewarding, but also demanding. "I had to really consider my work/life balance when I was on *Plants vs. Zombies*. It was such a huge franchise, and I was the only person managing social and community for multiple games across PC, mobile, and consoles," she said. "It was hard because I could feel burnout creeping up on me—I was creating all the reports, trying to maintain documentation, deciding on the strategies for the channels and for content releases, doing all the copywriting for posts on social, figuring out new ways to engage the community, all on my own... It was exhausting. I realized at that point my entire life was work and I didn't want it to be like that anymore. I knew it was time for a change. I loved the thrill of it all, learned so much in that role, and loved so many of the people I worked with, but knew it just wasn't sustainable. I also knew I was ready to lead a team and help them grow. I miss working on the property, but I don't regret my decision to grow in my career."

BLIZZARD

Bayer moved back home to Southern California, working at major studios such as Insomniac Games, Disney Interactive, and Skydance Interactive before settling in at Blizzard Entertainment as the manager of community development in 2017. There, she focuses on *Heroes of the Storm* and *Diablo*, creating programs for social media, community activations, influencer relations, and esports activities.

"I really love my current role at Blizzard," said Bayer. "I still maintain a foothold in community and social media, but I also get to help shape and manage the careers of my team. Helping my team figure out their next steps, work out large-scale programs and projects, and help them go farther in their careers is really rewarding for me. I feel incredibly proud of the projects we've launched so far at Blizzard, and the best is yet to come. That makes me excited to come into work every day."

With such a storied career in community management behind her already, Bayer has made a point to share her best practices with others through lectures and online discourse. "My goal for the future is for me to be the sassiest, redheadedest, rockabilliest, proud LatinX video game professional around," said Bayer. "I don't consider myself a role model, but I've had many people come up to me and tell me I've inspired them to be more creative, to go further in their career, and to go outside of their comfort zone. That truly surprises me. I didn't have anyone to look up to when I started in the industry. There wasn't someone like me already here. I was lucky enough to find some great mentors, but I had to be my own role model. Am I perfect? Hell no. But if seeing a loudmouthed, hardworking lady out there asking questions, encouraging others to be better, striving to be a good listener, and pushing for results inspires others, then so bet it!"

Easter Egg

Met an impressive number of celebrity musicians as a kid due to her uncle being a tour bus driver, including Queen Latifah, Santana, Ziggy Marley, L7, Offspring, Stone Temple Pilots, The Vandals, and other musical acts.

A DAY IN THE LIFE OF...

A CUSTOMER SUPPORT DIRECTOR

No product is perfect. Despite the time, energy, and passion poured into development, games are not an exception to this rule. Furthermore, as video games get more and more advanced—especially those moving into a constantly updated online service model—there are exponentially more opportunities for customers to be in need of support. Their difficulties can range from issues with the physical disk or download code, online account access and security, in-game bugs, and an array of other complex scenarios.

Timely, friendly, and professional customer support is a measure of a company's integrity. Debbi Colgin has worked as a customer support professional for 13 years, guiding teams of representatives to ensure that when a player escalates an issue, it is resolved as quickly as possible. At the director level, she moves beyond the reactive resolution of support tickets, using data to tell a story, tracking performance over time, supporting suppositions, and predicting future events based on past player behavior. Through her team's hard work, they ensure players feel heard, respected, and most importantly, that their money was well spent.

DEBBI COLGIN

PROFESSION: DIRECTOR OF SUPPORT AT HUSTLE—SAN FRANCISCO, USA

YEARS IN PROFESSION: 13

WORKED ON: VIRTUAL MAGIC KINGDOM, HABBO HOTEL US & HABBO HOTEL CANADA, FIESTA ONLINE, SECRET OF THE SOLSTICE, LUVINIA, FISTS OF FU, DIVINE SOULS, SECOND LIFE

▶ EDUCATION & BREAKING IN

"I am definitely self-taught, having come from working for AOL for over seven years as a Community and Program Manager. In regards to working in video games, while it was never 'easy,' I don't really feel that I faced many obstacles in breaking in. I was fortunate to have a connection from AOL who eased my intro to Sulake, a terrific mentor in Susan Choe at Outspark who fed my curiosity about the business aspects of gaming and encouraged me to trust my instincts, and several coworkers across departments at Linden Lab who fostered a sense of comradery, mutual respect and trust. Obstacles were more cross-departmental. For example, heads of engineering at all three companies discounted my 'intuition' about anything from UX to bugs to fraud, despite me being proved right on a consistent basis. I think it was less about me being female than it was about me NOT being a member of their department."

▶ KEY QUALITIES

"For me, curiosity and optimism are the two most critical traits to have. Gaming can be stressful, hectic and—if we are honest—at times soul-sucking. Gamers tend to be highly invested and passionate, which can result in some heated exchanges across support tickets, forums, and social media. You need a thick skin, but mostly you need to be able to shrug it off and get back to business as well as life. At the same time, gaming is not an exact science. Changes to one aspect of gameplay can have an unplanned impact elsewhere; having a strong sense of curiosity helps to understand cause-and-effect. It can also help embolden game design, with the foundational courage to ask 'what happens if we do X.'"

▶ TOOLS OF THE TRADE

"So many tools! Some for communication—such as slack, Gmail, social media, salesforce, zendesk—and others for productivity and analytics, like spreadsheets, Google docs, Looker, and Periscope. Some are bespoke tools that allowed us insight into everything from a player's inventory items (where they came from, what the properties are, etc.) and chat events (some monitored chat in real time, some were logs of past chats; the best could do both). There are also internal tools that gather data on everything from user activities within the game and on the site, to what people are searching for in Help/FAQs, how long we take to answer support tickets, how many tickets we get and what they're about, and so on. These help deliver a better support experience by making sure we have Help articles that answer the right questions and ensuring agents are doing their best."

▶ HOURS & ENVIRONMENT

"Days in gaming are long, especially when you're supporting a product that never closes. Days generally start late (9-10 am) but can go well past 7 pm and often flow over into the weekend. 'Just checking for fires' is a thing. The companies I have worked for have been high energy, congenial, and collaborative. Since most people who work for gaming companies are gamers themselves, there has been a shared culture and language. Not only do my coworkers share my love of games, they usually also have the same general taste in pop culture. Nerd references abound!"

▶ AN AVERAGE DAY

"An average day usually starts with checking email, slack, and tickets for anything pressing; I deal with those first. I check my calendar and prepare for meetings. Then I check in with my team. From there the day varies in terms of order, throughout the day I check on metrics such as:

- How many tickets (and/or calls, chats) are coming in? Is that high or low based on the norm? If higher, is there something specific driving it? If we find that something is broken, I collect info and reach out to the appropriate team.
- How busy is the site/game? Are we running any sort of promos or events that are impacting usage?

"Next, I start on my inbox, working through a variety of automated reports, cross-team info, meeting requests, and so on. I also examine the dashboard in the customer relationship management tool that provides an overview of the team's metrics for the day, week, and month. Later in the day, I'll check again on the ticket queue to make sure we're clearing it and that nothing is languishing. Throughout the day I keep an eye on conversations in various slack channels, including my own team's"

▶ PROMOTIONAL PATH

"In general, it goes like this:

Tier 1: Is generally familiar with product, responds to general "how do I" or "where do I" questions, and triages tickets for the rest of the team.

Tier 2: Is very familiar with product, responds to more specialized questions, and basic technical and product troubleshooting.

Tier 3: Has detailed understanding of product, responds to highly technical questions—including bug tracking and resolution—and creates documentation.

Team Lead: Can be tier 2 or 3; helps monitor team workload, makes general task assignments, some reporting, takes on the more demanding support requests, and creates Help articles (FAQs) as needed

Supervisor: Can be tier 2 or 3; can include the same tasks as Lead plus: some direct supervision of others; scheduling and attendance tracking; monitoring work quality and providing regular feedback; conducting one-on-ones with direct reports; and is involved in the hiring process

Manager: Same as the Team Lead plus: attend interdepartmental meetings; metrics gathering and presentation. Depending on the size of the organization, can usually serve as "head of support" for some time, making hiring decisions and working directly with upper management and other stakeholders until a director is needed.

Director: Same as the Manager, plus: sets policy, strategy and direction for department, distributes regular company-wide reporting on support volume, key concerns and trends, and achievement. Oftentimes speaks on behalf of support both internally and externally."

▶ CAREER CHALLENGES

"Support is very much an interrupt-driven workload. It's difficult to plan or set goals because any of them could be derailed by a site outage, bug regression, game glitch, class imbalance, or—heaven forbid—a security incident. Support teams tend to only hear what is broken and most of the users we interact with are unhappy. So being able to get into the game (as civilians) to see and hear users excited about the game is a big and important shift."

▶ LIFE HACKS

"Lists. I live by lists. I keep a 4x6 lined sticky note stuck to my desk labeled 'To Do.' It helps me keep focused. I've been known to have one for each day of the week and stack them. A few years ago, I was constantly getting to the end of the day and seeing that less than half of the list was crossed off. I felt frustrated that I had gotten so little done and wondered where the day went. That's when I started leaving a section called 'Done' and I added all those little tasks that crept in during the day. Having that bit of clarity at the end of the day helped me realize what the ad hoc demands on my time were and allowed me to develop a plan to better manage them."

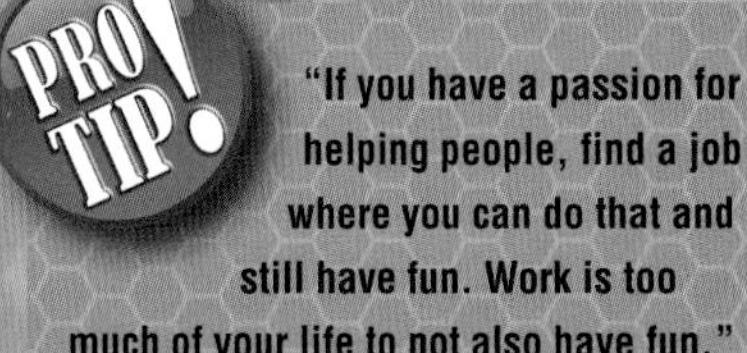

"If you have a passion for helping people, find a job where you can do that and still have fun. Work is too much of your life to not also have fun."

STEPHANIE HARVEY

GAME DESIGNER AND COUNTER-STRIKE WORLD CHAMPION

 misshearvey

 harvinator

stepharvey

twitch.tv/missharvey

EXPERIENCE

FIRST INDUSTRY PROJECT: PRINCE OF PERSIA: THE FORGOTTEN SANDS (2010)

FAVORITE INDUSTRY PROJECT: UNRELEASED UBISOFT TITLE

PROJECTS SHIPPED: 3 GAMES, 100+ TOURNAMENTS

ACHIEVEMENTS UNLOCKED:

> FORBES "30 UNDER 30: GAMES" (2014)

> CANADA'S SMARTEST PERSON WINNER—SEASON 3 (2016)

> BBC 100 WOMEN (2016)

> FIVE-TIME FEMALE COUNTER-STRIKE WORLD CHAMPION (2007, 2010, 2011, 2012, 2015)

STATS

INDUSTRY LEVEL: 15

CURRENT CLASS: PROFESSIONAL GAMER & INFLUENCER

CURRENT GUILD: FREELANCE—MONTRÉAL, CANADA

SPECIAL SKILLS: COMPETITIVE GAMING, GAME DESIGN, PUBLIC SPEAKING, ARCHITECTURE, FOODIE, DOG MAMA

STANDARD EQUIPMENT

FAVORITE PLATFORM: PC

GO-TO GENRE: ACTION-ADVENTURE, MULTIPLAYER, FIRST-PERSON SHOOTER

MUST-HAVE GAME: COUNTER-STRIKE: GLOBAL OFFENSIVE

BIO

While Stephanie Harvey was at university studying architecture, her professor asked a poignant question: why wasn't she investing her future into video games? By his logic, if she invested as much passion into architecture as she did into her already impressive competitive gaming career, she would be a great architect. So, he suggested she choose one or the other. "I was super insulted and wanted to prove him wrong," recalled Harvey. "At the time, I already had one world cup win in my pocket, but I still wanted to be an architect."

"It was only a year later, when I moved to France to complete my bachelor's degree, that I realized life was a lot more flexible than I thought, and it was okay for me to switch my master's and follow my heart to study gaming," she continued. And so, Harvey finished her bachelor's degree in architecture, and pursued a post-graduate diploma in video game design.

PRO GAMING

The foundation of her career began in fandom, however. "I've played *Counter-Strike* daily for the past 15 years," said Harvey. "I really think it is one of the best all-around multiplayer games, with simple core mechanics yet so much depth in the strategies and playstyles."

Easter Egg

Won a game show called *Canada's Smartest Person* in 2016, which tested for six different kinds of intelligence: musical, physical, social, logical, visual, and linguistic.

Recognized for her exceptional talent in competitive *Counter-Strike*, in 2006 Harvey was signed by leading esports organization SK Gaming as a professional player. Over the next five years, she would compete under their banner at major international tournaments, taking home two world-championship titles in 2007 and 2010.

"Winning competitions have to be the best memories I have in gaming," said Harvey. "The rush is incredible and the sense of accomplishment is strongest then. Winning a tournament is so damn relieving and satisfying; it is not possible to compare it to anything else I have ever felt before."

When not competing, she represented SK Gaming and their sponsors at events through interviews for websites, TV shows, magazines, and other mediums. She'd engage with community, write blogs, and post in the forums, all of which helped build her personal "missharvey" brand.

"...Coming to work every day was about building my dream game with my dream team."

Looking for self-determination in her career, in 2011 Harvey co-founded an independent all-female *Counter-Strike* team UBINITED. That independence meant more responsibility, though. In addition to competitive play, Harvey was in charge of the team's brand, securing press coverage, finding sponsors, running social media, and everything that was involved in keeping a competitive team on top of their game. UBINITED won two video game world championships together. In 2011, they took home the top title playing *Counter-Strike*, and in 2012, *Counter-Strike: Global Offensive*. In 2015, she joined the ranks of Counter Logic Gaming Red and won another world championship, completing her five world title set.

JUNIOR DESIGNER, UBISOFT

As Harvey was playing in top-ranked tournaments worldwide, she was also starting her career as a video game designer. In 2009, she joined Ubisoft as a game design intern, working on an assortment of undisclosed projects. Harvey left an impression and was hired on as a full-time dev tester. By late 2010, she was promoted to a junior game designer, and occasionally a company-wide consultant when her competitive multiplayer expertise was needed.

The first project she contributed to was *Prince of Persia: The Forgotten Sands*. "I was a development tester on the prince's acrobatics," she explained. "I supported the design team with the implementation of the acrobatics features with the level designers, the programmers, and the animators to make sure that the prince's movements and gameplay were smooth and also fun." She also designed open-world quests and implemented the hunter vision for *Far Cry Primal*.

Harvey's favorite project is one that, sadly, the world may never know about. "I cannot talk about the project in detail, but what I can tell you that I felt so challenged and honored to be working with this specific team, and that coming to work every day was about building my dream game with my dream team."

While Harvey is now at peace with the project, it was difficult to digest initially. "It was one of the toughest pieces of news I have ever had to learn," she said. "It took me a couple of years to get over the bitterness of never being able to finish this game. I assume it is one of the downsides of being so passionate about your work. If you work in game dev, you might not have control of everything and need to come to peace and make the best out of someone else's decision."

At the end of 2015, Harvey jumped to professional gaming full-time. Although a 15-year veteran at this point, she feels keeping competitive gets more difficult with time. "Every time I have to get ready for a major competition, it is both the most amazing time of my life and the hardest," she said. "It actually becomes harder every time because I now know what's at stake and how awful it is to lose. Being scared to lose instead of being hungry to win is a big problem in my community; you have to be able to break that mental barrier, or else it can lead to your downfall."

Harvey has also been hard at work growing her personal brand. She currently works as an esports collaborator for broadcast channel RDS, is the brand ambassador for Omen by HP in Canada, and the spokesperson for DreamHack Montréal, Canada's biggest video game festival. Harvey also creates regular content for YouTube, Twitch, and her other social media channels.

MISSCLIKS

As a woman in esports, Harvey often had to prove her skills to be taken seriously, and as such, she's made a concerted effort to break down barriers through visibility and advocacy. "Most people who never saw me play would instantly say I am probably terrible at the game, and got to where I am only because I was one of the few women doing it," she said. "Where I am today has nothing to do with my gender but my hard work, talent, and passion."

In 2013 she co-founded the non-profit Misscliks with fellow game-industry women as a means of combating the ingrained sexism they often faced, and to increase the visibility of female role models in geek culture. "I actually love when women support each other. I think a woman is so strong when she pushes someone's success and shines a light on another woman. In this extremely competitive and self-oriented world, it takes a lot of humility and maturity to do something like that. It brings me joy to do it myself as well."

"Where I am today has nothing to do with gender but my hard work, talent, and passion."

Harvey has become one of these role models; she travels the world to break barriers in gaming and hopes to shape the image of a healthy gamer lifestyle. She's been featured in international spotlights for her breadth of game-industry contributions, including the BBC's 100 Women list and *Forbes'* "30 under 30." "I am not your 'stereotypical' gamer," she explained. "I have post-graduate diplomas both in architecture and game design, have worked in game dev before going full-time as a pro gamer, and also try to have a healthy, balanced life. I do a lot of media appearances and attend a lot of local community events with the mainstream public to push gaming as a legitimate career and inspire others to pursue this career. I want to make a difference in every way I can and help our society tackle important issues like cyberdependance, cyberbullying, our education system, and the role of the internet, etc."

That inspiration is a fact, not speculation, as evidenced by an interaction she had with a past Ubisoft colleague. "When I was a couple of years into my Ubisoft work, a colleague told me she started her video game studies because of a show I was on in my early gaming career," said Harvey. "I was the only girl on the show, and she said it was definitely a game-changer for her life and future. This was the first time someone came to me to talk to me about their experience and how my life affected them. This has been the first but not the last; still today, I get these kinds of interactions often. It helps me push myself, knowing that maybe I am not only doing this for me, but for others out there."

MARINA GONCHAROVA

RAISED THE BAR FOR LOCALIZATION IN RUSSIA

 Marina Goncharova  Marina Goncharova

EXPERIENCE

FIRST INDUSTRY PROJECT: LEGO STAR WARS (2005)

FAVORITE INDUSTRY PROJECT: THE WITCHER (2007)

PROJECTS SHIPPED: 100+ GAMES

ACHIEVEMENTS UNLOCKED:

> GAMELAND "BEST PC LOCALIZATION" AWARD—THE WITCHER (2008)

> RUSSIAN GAME DEVELOPERS CONFERENCE "BEST LOCALIZATION COMPANY" AWARD—NOVIY DISK (2008)

> OK.RU "BEST ROLE-PLAY GAME" AWARD—LEAGUE OF ANGELS (2015)

> GAMEGURU "BEST MMORPG"—BLESS (2016)

 STATS

INDUSTRY LEVEL: 14

CURRENT CLASS: HEAD OF PARTNERSHIP PROJECTS

CURRENT GUILD: MAIL.RU GROUP—MOSCOW, RUSSIA

SPECIAL SKILLS: LOCALIZATION, PRODUCTION, PROJECT MANAGEMENT, GAME DESIGN, MONETIZATION

STANDARD EQUIPMENT

FAVORITE PLATFORM: NINTENDO SWITCH

GO-TO GENRE: RPG

MUST-HAVE GAME: THE WITCHER

BIO

Marina Goncharova was never one to be rescued. From a young age, she wanted to do the rescuing. "It was 1988. My mother was a teacher in school, and she invited me to her computer class, where I played my first computer game ever," explained Goncharova. "Unfortunately, I can't remember the title as I was young, but it was an arcade game where you should save a princess. It was then I decided that would be the business of my life. Saving damsels in distress, I mean." While not saving players directly from distress, throughout her career, Goncharova certainly would rescue them from the practice of low-quality localization that plagued the Russian games industry.

Marina put her passion for games and proactive disposition to use right out of university. After graduating in 2003 with a master's in economics, she found quick employment. The wonder that captured her attention from a young age hadn't lessened with time. "I always considered computer games as some kind of magic," she recalled. "That making games was very special and only the best of the best would work there. I worried it was like a dream that would never come true. But once I sent my first résumé to one game-publishing company, I immediately received an invitation to the interview. That same evening, I started my dream."

Easter Egg
Trained and earned a karate belt when she was a child and can still kick ass.

The dream began at one of the largest distributors of PC games in Russia, Russobit-M. As advertising manager, Marina worked directly with printing houses and gaming magazines to get the word out about their titles. On the side, Marina opted to return to her studies to give herself a greater edge in gaming. "I started my career in the game industry, and I decided to continue my education and receive a degree in computer science," she said. "It helped me a lot."

In 2005, new doors opened to Marina as the head of localization at Noviy Disk. In the massive Russian market, localization was big business. She created the localization department from scratch, preparing publishing plans that would allow the company to meet tight turnarounds in order to simultaneously launch localized AAA games with their native-language counterparts. Her work entailed everything from subtitles to full voice-acting, as well as translation of in-game interfaces and quality control. Marina and her team would compile feedback on builds, submit bug reports, and more. Translations were not often one-to-one. The work required a strong understanding of the Russian market to avoid cultural concerns and translate country-specific references, colloquial language, or idioms from foreign IPs in a way that was relatable to fans in Russia.

The team of 25 worked for major clients such as Activition, Eidos (Square Enix), Warner Bros., Codemasters, Deep Silver, CD Projekt Red, Disney, and dozens more.

The job kept Goncharova on the go—she worked in London for the localization of *LEGO Star Wars*, *Project: Snowblind*, and *Imperial Glory*. She traveled to Warsaw for the localization of *The Witcher*, and temporarily lived in Dublin for the localization of *Call of Duty 4: Modern Warfare* and its follow-up *World at War*.

> "I worried [working in the games industry] was like a dream that would never come true."

The Witcher remains her favorite project to this day. "It was a huge game," began Goncharova. "There were gigabytes of text for translation, and a huge number of files for voice recording. We did voice casting with the help of Andrzej Sapkowski fans. Our goal was to release a Russian version simultaneously with the other versions. There were many sleepless nights, but my team and I did it eventually."

The game was also the most challenging project in her career, involving a huge localization pack, strict timeline, and the pressure of working on a top-tier project. Russian fans weren't alone in being impressed with the finished project—the team's work on *The Witcher* won several localization awards, and her team took home a "Best Localization Company" award in 2008.

Moving up the ladder at Noviy Disk, Marina was soon head of the web division and a digital producer for social and online games. She managed her time between production, licensing, porting, localization, and marketing.

PORTALS FOR PLAY

Marina Goncharova has worn many hats in her time in the industry, including PR, localization, community management, HR, and production. The latter has been the most personally rewarding. In 2011—as a senior game producer at Moscow-based Game Insight—she led several titles from conception to release. Success at Game Insight led to increased responsibility at the popular Russian casual and mobile games publisher 101XP.

As VP of Publishing and Operations, Marina managed a team of over 100 people, and took the lead on marketing, production, operations, QA, customer support, IT, and community. Over five years her team helped ship 30 games, including award-winning titles like *Bless* and *League of Angels*. In her opinion, their greatest accomplishment was the launch of multi-lingual game portal 101XP.com—a platform to showcase their products and keep fans within the publisher's ecosystem.

As a self-described workaholic, Marina hasn't slowed down in the course of her career; she even chose to forgo maternity leave after each of her two children was born. Now at the Mail.Ru Group—an internet communication and entertainment company—her focus is publishing browser games on Russian social networks such as OK.ru and VK.com, as well as Facebook and proprietary portal My.com. As head of Partnership Projects, she once again built a department from the ground up, this time a game studio. Marina launched 3i Games Studio in 2016 and she oversees complete production and workflow on their titles. Since founding the studio, they have launched nine games. Drawing on past experience, they also launched a successful online game portal to showcase them.

Working directly with game-development teams has been very rewarding to Marina. "Since I was young, I always dreamed of developing games," she said. "However, in the first years of work, my destiny took me to publishing and localization." That being said, Marina's work making online games accessible and improving the quality of Russian-localized games can't be overstated. "In the Russian game industry, piracy was very common, especially in the early 2000s," she explained. "People bought low-quality, pirated games, often without translation, or translated into Russian using poor-quality dictionaries." By bringing high-quality translations and voice-acting to games published in Russia, Marina Goncharova not only gives players the authentic experience they deserve, but works to curb piracy and further legitimize the market.

JANE MCGONIGAL

CHAMPIONING GAMES TO CHANGE THE WORLD

 Avantgame  janemcgonigal.com

EXPERIENCE

FIRST INDUSTRY PROJECT: THE GO GAME (2001)

FAVORITE INDUSTRY PROJECT: SUPERBETTER (2012)

PROJECTS SHIPPED: 25+ GAMES

ACHIEVEMENTS UNLOCKED:

> GAME DEVELOPERS ASSOCIATION "INNOVATION AWARD"—HALO 2'S I LOVE BEES (2005)

> MIT TECHNOLOGY REVIEW "WORLD'S TOP INNOVATORS UNDER 35" (2006)

> SOUTH BY SOUTHWEST INTERACTIVE "ACTIVISM AWARD"—WORLD WITHOUT OIL (2008)

> O, THE OPRAH MAGAZINE'S "20 IMPORTANT WOMEN OF 2010" (2010)

STATS

INDUSTRY LEVEL: 19

CURRENT CLASS: DIRECTOR OF GAME RESEARCH & DEVELOPMENT

CURRENT GUILD: INSTITUTE FOR THE FUTURE—PALO ALTO, USA

SPECIAL SKILLS: GAME DESIGN, ARG DESIGN, FUTURE FORECASTING, PUBLIC SPEAKING, WRITING

BIO

Jane wants to make the world a better place through games. She knows it's possible from personal experience. Video games saved her life, and she's dedicated to helping others get "*SuperBetter*" too.

POSITIVE PSYCHOLOGY

McGonigal sees games as much more than a form of entertainment; she argues in their potential to harness collective intelligence for the betterment of all. She argues that game designers have a humanitarian mission to help improve lives and solve real problems, and her top goal in life is to witness a game developer win a Nobel Peace Prize.

Much of McGonigal's work focuses on alternate-reality games, location-based games, and massively multiplayer online gaming. The biggest influence on her work is the science behind positive psychology, followed closely by Buddhist philosophy. When starting to design a game, she first asks, "How can this game lead to real and positive impacts? How can it be in service to something bigger than ourselves?" Such goals include encouraging positive emotions and engagement, reinforcing stronger social relationships, and improving resilience in the face of challenges. The real-world problems she wants to help fix are impressive in scale—poverty, hunger, and climate change. She knows this can only be achieved through "planetary-scale collaboration."

After finishing her bachelor's degree in English in 1999, McGonigal returned to school to earn a PhD in performance studies, with a focus on video games—a first for her department. While studying, she taught undergraduate writing and research courses such as Theater and Games, Performance and Play.

All the while, McGonigal was experimenting in new forms of games, including *Tele Twister*, which had her and an opponent battling with their flexibility, at the mercy of online audiences who chose how they would contort themselves on camera. Another concept tested what would happen if gamers had free control of the Whitney Art Museum's plaza-facing webcam.

OUTSIDE THE BOX

As lead designer at marketing company 42 Entertainment, McGonigal took lead on the award-winning *Halo* alternate-reality game *I Love Bees*. The game took home a 2005 Innovation Award from the International Game Developers Association. She also worked with Ian Bogost in 2006 on "benevolent assassination game" *Cruel 2 B Kind*.

Easter Egg

Started a personal game in 2005 called "Cookie Rolling" to help with the anxiety, depression, and loneliness associated with writing a dissertation. To play she would "install" the essay "The Myth of Sisyphus" one word at a time in various cities, spelled out with local cookies, and documented in photographs.

By this point, McGonigal had found her unique voice within gaming, and began working as a creative director and consultant. Through this work, she helped to design gaming events and alternate-reality campaigns for big business, including Nike, the International Olympics Committee, and McDonald's, as well as organizations such as the American Heart Association and New York Public Library.

Always looking forward, in 2008 McGonigal took up position as the Director of Game Research and Development for the Institute for the Future, where she remains today. Her work and research continued to center on how video games are transforming our lives, and the potential they have to improve resilience and well-being.

Several of her projects during this time made major waves in serious games circles. McGonigal led a team as creative director on 2010's *EVOKE*, developed for the World Bank Institute. Billed as a "crash course in changing the world," *EVOKE* focused on empowering people across Africa to make local change through 10 weekly challenges. Real-life good deeds would be rewarded with points in the online community.

Created for the Independent Television Service, with funding by the Corporation for Public Broadcasting, *World Without Oil* took home a South by Southwest Interactive Award for Activism in 2008. McGonigal was both participation architect and game designer, working with a team to create a framework for what a realistic oil crisis would look like. Players would sign up and create believable character profiles, then begin documenting what their lives looked like under those conditions via blogs, photos, and videos.

Most projects McGonigal designs have a real-world component to them and, as such, can't be played on demand. They're often live events mixed with online play, and once finished, she provides documentation in a public archive should others want to run their own gameplay sessions.

GETTING SUPERBETTER

McGonigal's life took an unexpected turn in 2009, when a severe concussion didn't heal properly and resulted in debilitating symptoms. She found herself in a dark place, in physical pain, as well as anxious, depressed, and questioning if her life would ever get back to normal. It made sense for her to funnel the darkness into something positive, and so her game design instincts took over, resulting in *Jane the Concussion Slayer*, later renamed *SuperBetter*. She set an epic win for herself—a full recovery—and began to map out the quests—daily goals—needed to get her there. She made note of the "bad guys" who could throw obstacles in her way, and detailed daily "power-ups" she could perform that would provide positive reinforcement toward her goal. By turning her recovery into a game, she felt she came back a stronger, more capable version of herself —hence the name *SuperBetter*.

After recovering, McGonigal created SuperBetter Labs, and as creative director she raised a million dollars to fund an expanded version of the game to share with others. Since its launch in 2012, *SuperBetter* has been played by a million people, helping them through a variety of ailments including depression, anxiety, chronic pain, and traumatic brain injuries. McGonigal reports that the game has been integrated into college coursework, recommended to patients by therapists, and integrated into workplaces by HR as a wellbeing resource for employees. In recent years, SuperBetter has been the subject of multiple clinical trials and randomized controlled studies by various medical groups, including The Ohio State University Medical Research Center, Cincinnati Children's Hospital, and University of Pennsylvania. Studies published in scientific journals (such as *Brain Injury* and *World Psychiatry*) show that SuperBetter effectively reduces symptoms of depression and anxiety. Additionally, it has shown to help young individuals with concussions recover faster. These studies and more are available to read on her website.

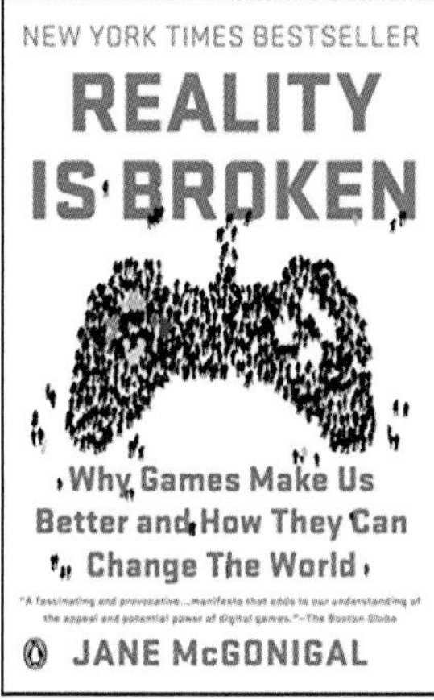

REPAIRING REALITY

In 2011, McGonigal released her first book called *Reality Is Broken: Why Games Make Us Better and How They Can Change the World*. She once again drew from positive psychology, as well as cognitive science and sociology, to argue that games can be used in meaningful ways to positively affect the world, from facilitating happiness and motivation, to instilling meaning and helping develop community. McGonigal formalized and shared the methodologies behind *SuperBetter* in a 2015 *New York Times* bestselling book by the same name.

McGonigal continues to travel and share her philosophies around the world as a frequent tech conference headliner, with impressive outlier speaking opportunities such as TED Talks—of which she's done two—and an invitation to lecture at the annual World Economic Forum in Davos. Her primary speaking topics include games and education, games and healthcare, the engagement economy, and games to change the world. She also passes her mantra of making changes for change onto new generations of game developers though her work teaching game design and game theory at UC Berkeley, Stanford, and the San Francisco Art Institute.

A DAY IN THE LIFE OF...

A BRAND MANAGER

A brand is synonymous with reputation—it reflects the quality and integrity of not only a product, but the people who work tirelessly to bring it to market. Ultimately, everything public-facing falls under the brand umbrella, including social media, community, marketing, events, merchandising, and PR. As such, understanding and properly managing a brand is imperative. Brand managers collaborate with teams across every discipline in development and publishing, and this visibility and guidance ensures that a game is being positioned, promoted, and sold in a way that is genuine to the product while achieving awareness and revenue goals.

Annette Gonzalez has worked in a variety of roles over the past eight years, including editorial, community, product management, partner management, and now brand management. The work requires her to be both analytical and creative, and for Gonzalez, this is the best of both worlds.

ANNETTE GONZALEZ

 Annette Gonzalez

PROFESSION: ASSOCIATE BRAND MANAGER AT PLAYSTATION—SAN MATEO, USA
YEARS IN PROFESSION: 1
ASSOCIATED WITH: GAME INFORMER, HARMONIX, PLAYSTATION

▶ EDUCATION

"My career in the games industry began in editorial. There was a pivotal moment in my childhood where I received a free issue of *Nintendo Power* and became obsessed with reading any and all game coverage. I studied journalism in college and worked at our campus magazine, where I introduced video game coverage to the publication. This experience is what ultimately led me to working at *Game Informer*. I'd spent a lot of time and care building my portfolio so I'd be prepared when the right opportunity came through.

"Of course, I'm no longer in editorial. I've explored different roles in the communications and marketing space over the last few years, each time taking learnings from my last job and applying them to the next. While education is important to build a foundation for your career and identify your interests, hands-on experience is where the bulk of learning and skill building will take place."

▶ BREAKING IN

"My entrance into the industry wasn't easy. I held office jobs and contract marketing gigs by day, while spending my evenings improving my writing and getting published. During lunch breaks I conducted interviews for my pieces. It was a lot of hustle and very little sleep. I never expected it to be easy, but I was hungry. Working in the games industry in some capacity was my dream and I didn't stop until it became a reality. Thankfully, I lucked out!"

▶ KEY QUALITIES

"Here are a few key qualities that I've seen embodied by successful colleagues:

"Being an extrovert is surprisingly not a hard requirement. If you're not already someone comfortable speaking in public or speaking up, it's worth finding opportunities to practice. Volunteer to present in a meeting, do a game demo for a group, or lead a call. Be sure to express to your manager that this is a growth area for you—any manager will be happy to help you reach your professional goals.

"**Organized:** Be your own project manager. A big part of this is not only tracking your tasks, but prioritizing them. This is especially critical if you manage a lot of project deliverables, such as game assets. Do the legwork to organize and prioritize at the start of a major task or project.

"**Collaborative:** Working with a variety of different groups within and outside your organization requires a lot of collaboration. Be open to ideas, be willing to explore new concepts, and support other groups' initiatives wherever it makes sense."

▶ TRAINING OPPORTUNITIES

"Read. A lot. I spend a lot of my spare time reading sites like *Inc.*, *Business Insider*, *Harvard Business Review*, *Fast Company*, and *AdWeek* to learn critical skills for the workplace and review trends (these are solid for professions in any industry).

"Another resource that has yielded great results for friends in their career development—General Assembly (there are locations around the country). They offer intro classes across many disciplines, weekend boot camps, as well as extended courses (part-time and full-time) if you're looking to learn or refresh skills across things such as project and product management, design, marketing analytics—the list goes on."

▶ TOOLS OF THE TRADE

"**Powerpoint.** I spend a pretty significant amount of time preparing decks for pitches, stakeholder meetings, metric reporting, major product presentations—everything. Coming from a communications background (with design experience), this is thankfully right in my wheelhouse. The ability to communicate ideas, concepts, an overall vision, or results is critical regardless of what gaming field you go into. Practice! Otherwise, I use standard Office software and Google Drive to keep organized and maintain project trackers."

▶ AN AVERAGE DAY

"An average day for someone in brand is often spent either in face-to-face meetings or on calls with internal and external teams. A lot of these discussions typically entail planning for upcoming campaign pulse points, briefing teams on brand initiatives, creative reviews or reviewing campaign metrics, and coming up with recommendations and next steps based on results. When not in meetings, there's a steady flow of email throughout the day to read and respond to."

▶ PROMOTIONAL PATH

"Every organization handles this very differently, but here's what I've seen across a few publishers/game companies:

"**Level 1: Coordinator or Specialist.** Assists in day-to-day campaign work (e.g., organizes assets and files, routes content for approvals, captures meeting notes and action items, etc.).

"**Level 2: Associate.** Assembles tactical plans for pulse points within a larger campaign, executes on campaign tactics, provides brand checks on creative, occasionally manages brand for smaller titles in portfolio.

"**Level 3: Manager.** Develops campaign strategy and oversees tactical planning and execution of campaign on global level. Manages campaign budget.

"**Level 4: Senior Manager.** Manages team L1-3, oversees group efforts on brand portfolio level."

▶ CAREER CHALLENGES

"The games business is constantly evolving, which can be challenging, but also makes it an exciting business to work in. We're seeing a boom in games breaking the mold of traditional digital business practices, which are having great success (and in some cases reaching world domination). Keeping up with trends as you're planning campaigns a year (and in some cases years) in advance can be tough, as the marketplace can look completely different once the game launches. Getting ahead of trends and being prepared to adapt, while a challenging part of the job, is part of what makes it fun."

▶ BIGGEST MISTAKE

"Not negotiating when receiving a job offer. Landing a job in games feels like you hit the lottery. It's something you want so badly that you're afraid if you ask for too much, it'll get taken away. I've never heard of anyone negotiating an offer and then the offer getting revoked. Do the research and know your worth. Setting yourself up for success early in your career will pay off for years to come. There are lots of resources available online to help guide these types of conversations with recruiters and hiring managers. Use them!"

PRO TIP!

"Do the work: Identify your career interests, figure out the experience required by reviewing job listings across the industry, and build up your portfolio via internships, volunteer projects, school or personal projects, and so on. You don't want your dream job to come along and not be prepared to submit an application. These jobs are competitive. Be prepared.

"Network: Put yourself out there and meet people in the games industry, either at a convention or regional meetups (or even seek out other hopefuls in college). Referrals in this business are critical."

SHRUTI VERMA

HELPED ESTABLISH AN INDIAN GAMES INFRASTRUCTURE

Shruti_verma

Shruti Verma

Shruti Verma

EXPERIENCE

FIRST INDUSTRY PROJECT: NASSCOM ANIMATION & GAMING SUMMIT (2003)

FAVORITE INDUSTRY PROJECT: GAME JAM TITANS PROJECT (2015)

PROJECTS SHIPPED: ORGANIZED 8 NASSCOM GAME DEVELOPER CONFERENCES, 4 EXTERNAL CONFERENCES, AND PARTICIPATED IN 10 PANEL DISCUSSIONS

ACHIEVEMENTS UNLOCKED:

> DUBBED THE "BOSS GIRL" OF THE INDIAN GAMING INDUSTRY

> HELPED GROW THE NASSCOM GAME DEVELOPERS CONFERENCE FROM 150 TO 2500 ATTENDEES IN FIVE YEARS

> ORGANIZER OF FIRST UNITE INDIA CONFERENCE, ATTENDED BY 1200 INDUSTRY PROFESSIONALS (2017)

STATS

INDUSTRY LEVEL: 14

CURRENT CLASS: HEAD OF MARKETING INDIAN SUBCONTINENT

CURRENT GUILD: UNITY TECHNOLOGIES—NEW DELHI, INDIA

SPECIAL SKILLS: PROGRAM MANAGEMENT, CORPORATE RELATIONS, GAME DEVELOPMENT, START-UPS, NON-PROFITS, BUSINESS DEVELOPMENT, EVENT MANAGEMENT, DANCING

STANDARD EQUIPMENT

FAVORITE PLATFORM: MOBILE

GO-TO GENRE: ACTION, PUZZLES

MUST-HAVE GAME: ANYTHING MARIO

BIO

"In India, getting access to a Game Boy or a console while growing up in the '90s was a novelty," said Unity Technologies' Shruti Verma. "As a kid and teen, I played video games at home; at that time I never thought I would get into the games industry." Much of that was due to a prevalent perception that video games were not a serious career option at the time. "Since the industry was so small, there was no awareness of video games as an industry and parents never thought that children should join the industry that may not pay as well as a technology job."

NASSCOM

In 2003, however, a chance summer internship at non-profit NASSCOM—the top-tier industry body for tech in India, similar to the IGDA in the US—gave Verma a glimpse of what could be. "NASSCOM, unlike other associations, is research-driven," she explained. "NASSCOM was the first body that released a research paper on the animation and gaming industry landscape in India in 2003."

Verma came from business administration and didn't have any training or ties to video games, aside from a personal interest. Intrigued, she volunteered to help with the first Animation & Gaming Summit hosted by NASSCOM in 2003, aiding with registration and delegate marketing. "Everyone was inclusive and helped me learn the ropes of game development," she said. "My first years were all about understanding how the industry worked and how, as an industry association, we could strengthen the community to encourage the spirit of collaboration."

In 2005 Verma joined NASSCOM as a full-time associate, and started to engage closely with leaders in the emerging field. "I talked to industry members like Rajesh Rao, CEO, Dhruva Interactive; Vishal Gondal, ex-founder, Indiagames; Manavendra Shukul, CEO, Lakshya Digital; and many more," she listed. "I think my willingness to listen and learn enabled me to connect with founders, indies, and everyone in the industry. The more I got to know the industry, and what a labor of love a video game is, the more I got hooked on helping to grow it within India."

Easter Egg

Is passionate about reading when not involved in community building. She has a personal library of more than 500 books and counting.

Identifying market opportunities for the Indian game-development community was one of her first priorities, as well as supporting the internal research team with their efforts. "Every initiative that we did was learning because there was no precedence; we were sailing on unchartered water," remembered Verma. "Industry research was the most challenging project; assembling data and coming out with factual findings and staying true to the growth story. We always wanted the reports to be inspiring and grounded in reality," she said. Report topics included deep dives into the evolution of mobile within the Indian games industry, as well as growth drivers within the area of serious games. Verma also began talking to international companies, pitching them on bringing business to the Indian market, and would act as liaison with various country trade offices looking for partnership opportunities for existing companies.

DIVERSITY FIRST

Verma's efforts were recognized by promotion after promotion within NASSCOM, until she eventually became the head of developer relations for the entire organization. Over the years, her contributions expanded from trying to grow the industry to diversifying the talent pool. She started a mentorship program for middle- to senior-management women, and facilitated shared-services childcare for NASSCOM members.

Looking to inspire the next generation of game developers, Verma also helped create programming aimed at youth. "The Game Jam Titans is a project that we do with the school children aged 10-16 years old," she explained. "It is a program to let students learn via creating experimental video games. Over four years, we have impacted more than 3000 students. It's incredible to see how kids perceive a theme and build a game." When an all-girls team won the city round of Game Jam Titans in 2016, it was a special point of pride for Verma. "One of the girls from the team came up to me to say that I have inspired her to enter the gaming industry."

Over a period of 12 years at NASSCOM, Verma evangelized the Indian development community at every opportunity, including heading the Developer Program Start-Ups initiative, which helped provide start-ups in the gaming sector access to the technology needed to build their businesses. "In these 12 years, I developed the NASSCOM Game Developer Conference from a 150-delegate half-day summit to 2500 delegates spread over three days, organized game jams, took Indian game studio delegations to international conferences, advised international studios while they were exploring setting up offices in India, and researching the Indian games industry," she summarized. The contributions she made to helping India get its foothold in the global games market cannot be understated.

"The more I got to know the industry, and what a labor of love a video game is, the more I got hooked on helping to grow it within Indian."

UNITY THROUGH TECHNOLOGY

After years of championing the Indian game industry at NASSCOM, in 2017 Verma accepted a new position as head of marketing for the Indian subcontinent at Unity Technologies. Through her new post, she leads online subscriptions and license sales, continues to organize events and Unity user groups, and manages relationships with partners. As Unity's technology is used heavily in the mobile-first game industry in India, she helps devs understand how to use the latest Unity tech, listens to their product feedback, and champions them internally. In 2017, she organized the debut Unite India conference, which was attended by 1200 industry professionals.

"When I entered the industry, I had no idea what to expect. It was all new to me," said Shruti. "I grew with the industry in India, so I trumpeted when there was a successful game from India, and I felt sad for them when the industry had a low. Change is constant. When I started, Indian game developers were following the services path. Slowly, as they moved to make their own games, the quality of the games has improved, and the narratives have matured. We have come a long way."

Helping establish an infrastructure and community for game developers in India is part of the legacy Verma leaves in her wake. She doesn't intend to stop her efforts. "I want to meet new people and work on initiatives and programs that serve a larger good. And I want to continue to contribute to making the Indian gaming industry stronger and enable an ecosystem for creators to create beautiful content and be commercially successful at the same time."

"I grew with the industry in India, so I trumpeted when there was a successful game from India, and I felt sad for them when the industry had a low."

EMILY RIDGWAY

EXPERT IN THE ART AND TECH OF AUDIO DESIGN

 R1dgw4y 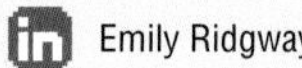 Emily Ridgway

EXPERIENCE

FIRST INDUSTRY PROJECT: DESTROY ALL HUMANS! (2005)

FAVORITE INDUSTRY PROJECT: BRÜTAL LEGEND (2009), CS:GO (CURRENT)

PROJECTS SHIPPED: 7 GAMES

ACHIEVEMENTS UNLOCKED:

> AUSTRALIAN GAME CONFERENCE "BEST AUDIO AWARD"—DESTROY ALL HUMANS! (2005)

> GAME DEVELOPERS CHOICE "BEST AUDIO" & "BEST WRITING" AWARDS— (2008)

> AIAS "OUTSTANDING ACHIEVEMENT IN SOUND DESIGN"—BIOSHOCK (2008)

> AIAS "OUTSTANDING ACHIEVEMENT IN SOUNDTRACK"— BRÜTAL LEGEND (2010)

 STATS

INDUSTRY LEVEL: 13

CURRENT CLASS: AUDIO

CURRENT GUILD: VALVE CORPORATION—BELLEVUE, USA

SPECIAL SKILLS: SOUND DESIGN, WRITING, MUSIC DIRECTION, VOICE DIRECTION, GAME DESIGN, HARDWARE DESIGN, PROGRAMMING

STANDARD EQUIPMENT

FAVORITE PLATFORM: ARCADE MACHINES

GO-TO GENRE: RPGS, SHMUPS, ADVENTURE GAMES

MUST-HAVE GAME: PORTAL, WORLD OF WARCRAFT, PHOENIX WRIGHT: ACE ATTORNEY

BIO

Born and raised in Newcastle, Australia, Emily Ridgway has always been guided by diverse interests and an insatiable desire to learn about the world around her. It is fitting, then, that she would seek out a career creating virtual worlds, allowing her to coordinate an extraterrestrial attack, explore an underwater dystopia, and rock out with musical legends.

"I started out wanting to be a National Parks ranger, then a fighter pilot," began Ridgway. "In my final year of high school, my three choices for study at university were political science, maritime engineering, and music performance."

Of the three, Ridgway pursued a degree in music and sound for film, TV, and multimedia at Queensland University of Technology. "During that time I deemed the amount of time required to be a successful professional musician was too high, too competitive, and not rewarding financially enough for the amount of effort required," she explained. "So I started looking at other areas to apply my education. While playing *Morrowind* on PC late one night, it dawned on me that games need music and sound, and I liked games, and I liked music and sound, so perhaps that might be an area of work I could happily do."

Ridgway wasn't aware of anyone else in her local community doing full-time audio work for video games, so she figured the competition would be naturally low. Brisbane was starting to grow as a hub of game development in Australia, so she set to work. "I contacted all the local game companies in my home city and pitched myself as someone who had a formal education in sound who wanted to help them with their game audio," said Ridgway. "I asked if I could hang out at their studio, learn what they do, and score a trailer or do a demo for them." She was willing to make coffee, run errands—whatever it would take to be in and around game development so she could observe and learn.

A few unpaid gigs were what yielded from her intense networking. "Nothing solid seemed to come of it," recalled Ridgway. "However, six months later, I had just about abandoned that career plan when I got an email from Pandemic Studios in Brisbane, Australia asking if I'd like to come in for an interview as a junior sound designer."

TRIAL BY FIRE

Ridgway landed a job as junior sound designer at Pandemic Studios and started work on the 2005 alien-invasion title *Destroy All Humans!* She was eager to start working and learn the formal process of game audio design through collaboration with an experienced team. "I assumed by my title that there would be a senior sound designer or a lead sound designer overseeing my work," said Ridgway. "But there wasn't, and I quickly realized I was actually the only sound person on the project."

"You can completely change the mood, feel, and meaning of any visual with sound."

The task laid before Ridgway was daunting, but she rose to the occasion. She created and implemented sound effects game-wide; interviewed, hired, and managed an external composer; and designed and implemented all the resulting in-game music. She also mixed and implemented voice-overs, designed custom audio tools, and managed the audio budget.

"Leading all sound efforts for an AAA project…was stressful," she admitted. "On the other hand, I discovered a deep love for marrying sound and image and the power that comes along with that. You can completely change the mood, feel, and meaning of any visual with sound, and so I felt like people in general had very much underestimated the effect of sound, including myself. I threw myself at the job, knowing the credit and experience would be worth it on my résumé and in the future. With some help and support from designers and programmers on the team, we ended up making the audio on *Destroy All Humans!* consistently the highest-rated component of that title." Later that year, the game won an Australian Game Conference Award for "Best Audio," which, as she was the only audio person on the team, was a recognition that fell firmly in Ridgway's lap, and led to even greater opportunities.

RATIONAL SOUND DESIGN

"My work on *Destroy All Humans!* provided me an opportunity to create and submit a demo for an audio director role at Irrational Games," continued Ridgway. "Working on *BioShock* was my second job in the games industry."

In 2005, after landing the job at Irrational, she packed up and moved across the world to work on what would become a landmark title of the decade. Many of Ridgway's responsibilities stayed the same as audio director, since she had already been doing senior-level work at her first job. This time, a mastery of the processes and tools allowed her to focus on the artistry in the work.

Audio was a major element in bringing to life the underwater dystopia that was Rapture. One of the main focuses for Ridgway was to create an audio experience that mirrored the setting—stunning, but also disconcerting.

The decision to focus on linear rather than dynamic audio design allowed for a greater control of emotion. Ridgway could cue music to trigger exactly when and where she wanted, to support the scenario.

Ridgway also had the opportunity to expand her skills further in *BioShock*—writing, directing, and implementing game voice-over for AI. The soundscape of *BioShock* was lauded as an invaluable part of the player's journey to Rapture, and as such, it took home a variety of audio honors, including "Best Audio" from the 2008 Game Developers Choice Awards.

CREATING A LEGEND

After making her mark on *BioShock*, Ridgway joined Double Fine Productions to work on heavy-metal rock game *Brütal Legend*, starring comedian and musician Jack Black. As lead sound designer, all things audio continued to be under Ridgway's remit—music, sound design, technical audio feature design, audio tools and pipeline design, managing both internal and external talent, and more.

Ridgway took a unique, holistic approach to *Brütal Legend*, ensuring heavy-metal music was never far from them, consciously, or subconsciously.

"Much of the background ambience in *Brütal Legend* is re-constructed snippets of original heavy metal tracks," she shared. "They're not recognizable, but when sculpted and processed into a different form they still retained the attitude and grit of the original performance. For instance, I used the opening snare hits of Def Leppard's 'Rock Of Ages' as a core element in creating the sound of a rhythmic, grinding stone gyre powered by the fuel of headbanger muscle."

Brütal Legend nabbed a nomination for "Best Audio" at the Game Developers Choice Awards in 2009. While at Double Fine, Ridgway also worked on *Stacking, Costume Quest, and Sesame Street: Once Upon a Monster.*

LANDING AT VALVE

Originally intending to work remotely for Double Fine, Ridgway returned home to Australia in 2010 for some familiar scenery. It wasn't long before she decided to branch out on her own as Emily Industries Audio Production and try her hand at freelance. She also went back to school, working toward a bachelor's degree in civil engineering, and certification in graphic design. After a couple of years of freelance, Ridgway began to miss the constant exchange of ideas and energy inherent to working in-house at a development studio.

So in 2013, Ridgway joined Valve Corporation as an…employee—the studio famously doesn't use titles internally or externally. She's contributed to *Counter-Strike: Global Offensive* and *The Lab* since starting, as well as some unannounced projects she's especially excited for. Since joining Valve, Ridgway has expanded her skills to include programming, hardware prototyping, and game design. She regularly contributes to both hardware and software VR projects, *CS:GO,* and Steam Audio.

Ridgway knows that today, asking to hang out at a games studio and observe people likely isn't going to play out the same way it did for her back in 2005, but she still has wisdom to impart. "Being a professional game developer is about being able to summon the passion you need to do good work, regardless of the context of the work. There is something to love and learn from in every project. My advice would be to just start doing the work you want to do, and eventually people will pay you to do it. Grab a copy of Unity, create a project yourself, or find a team to help, and keep working until you end up at Valve," she said with a laugh.

Easter Egg
Competed in the 42nd Annual World Bodysurfing Championships in San Diego.

CHIPZEL

HACKING TOYS TO HARNESS NOSTALGIA

 Chipzel  Chipzel

 Chipzel  chipzel.co.uk

EXPERIENCE

FIRST INDUSTRY PROJECT: SUPER HEXAGON (2012)
FAVORITE INDUSTRY PROJECT: INTERSTELLARIA (2015)
PROJECTS SHIPPED: 11 GAMES, 12 ALBUMS
ACHIEVEMENTS UNLOCKED:

> BAFTA "BRITISH GAME OF THE YEAR" NOMINATION—SUPER HEXAGON (2013)
> VGMO'S "BEST INDEPENDENT COMPOSER" AWARD—INTERSTELLARIA (2015)
> XBLA FANS "BEST SOUND" AWARD—SPECTRA (2015)
> TEDXWANDSWORTH TALK "WE ARE ALL HACKERS" (2016)

STATS

INDUSTRY LEVEL: 6
CURRENT CLASS: COMPOSER, PRODUCER, & PERFORMER
CURRENT GUILD: FREELANCE—LIVERPOOL, UNITED KINGDOM
SPECIAL SKILLS: COMPOSITION, SOUND DESIGN, AUDIO ENGINEER

STANDARD EQUIPMENT

FAVORITE PLATFORM: PC, PS4, NINTENDO SWITCH
GO-TO GENRE: STRATEGY, SIMULATION, SURVIVAL
MUST-HAVE GAME: THE ELDER SCROLLS: OBLIVION

BIO

Niamh Houston describes herself as "one of those confusing millennials who found a way to make a living through a weird hobby." The pastime Houston has transformed into a full-time career is composing and performing music on a Nintendo Game Boy—a style of music known as chiptune. Her upbeat, melodic creations transport listeners back to a simpler time, triggering waves of nostalgia through the bleeps and bloops native to the hardware.

Now a chiptune ambassador, Houston describes it as the first musical movement to come directly from Internet culture. "Chiptune is a style of music that is composed and sequenced with retro consoles—machines such as the Commodore 64, Atari, Amiga, for example, or the Nintendo Game Boy, which I use for my own chip compositions," she explained. "The art form is defined by its technology rather than its form and every artist within the community draws from their own musical influences."

> "[Chip music] is an art form defined by its technology rather than its structure."

Born and raised in Northern Ireland, Houston—now known by her stage name Chipzel—first began making chiptune music over a decade ago, while still in her teens. "Throughout school I was motivated to work in a creative field," she said. "I was pushing towards something in the arts industry. I remember thinking it would be amazing to be an artist or animator for video games, but it was seen as an 'unrealistic goal' at the time."

INSPIRATION THROUGH LIMITATION

Houston found her way into chip music in 2005 when searching for a sound to feed her eclectic taste in music. When she stumbled upon underground community sites like 8BitCollective and 8BitPeoples, everything changed. These sites acted as a central hub for musicians, artists, and hackers withe a passion for all things retro. "I immediately fell in love," she explained. "I had discovered new lands of the Internet that were completely alien to me—a worldwide community with forums full of art and people from all around the globe who never lost their love of the computers and consoles of the past. Instead they looked at these machines and though, 'what can I do with this?'"

Houston fell in love with chip music, and immediately began researching how it was created. She wanted in, and quickly dug out her old Nintendo Game Boy and got herself a copy of LSDJ, software for the Nintendo Game Boy that provided the tools to treat it like a basic sequencer and synthesizer.

"I was a teenager fascinated with electronic music, but a license for a DAW (Digital Audio Workstation), like Cubase or Logic, is expensive; in contrast, LSDJ is very accessible. It took me over 10 years of learning the ins and outs of electronic music production to actually pay attention to and fully understand the manual that came with it, but that didn't stop me. Once I had the basics covered, I was eagerly making some noise. In a very unique way and at my own pace, I could write full songs and upload them to 8BitCollective for feedback." she recalled.

Easter Egg
Featured in the 2019 *Guinness World Records: Gamer's Edition* under "First Video Game Created to Showcase a Chiptune Artist's Songs" for her work on *Spectra*.

The choice to write music with retro consoles comes with extreme limitations, but these constraints aren't seen as a negative to chiptune creators. Chiptune is in fact *inspired* by those limitations. With only four sound channels available in the Game Boy's sound chip, it forced Houston to approach composition from a unique angle. "To me, it inspires creativity because you don't have endless possibilities of what you can do. If I have the option to polish a creative work indefinitely, I find that it's easy to lose the original meaning or the core view. With LSDJ, you have to find ways around the lack of space available, which will usually result in some happy accidents or something that sounds much more interesting. Even after six years of writing in a DAW, I still find myself to be much more creative when I write in LSDJ."

Within several months of picking up her Game Boy, Houston was booked for her first show. At one year, she was flying abroad to perform. In 2009, she released her first EP, *Judgement Day*, and her first full album, *Disconnected*, launched in 2010. In 2011—at the age of 19—Houston traveled to New York to perform in front of a thousand-person crowd at Blip Festival.

"The beauty of chiptune, for me, was the ability to create music without expectation or standards."

Houston's success encouraged her to study music formally. "I didn't study music seriously until university," she explained. "It felt like the right path to take." Houston had already proven an innate ability for original composition, and as such, she chose to study music technology. "At a compositional level, I am totally self-taught and everything is done by ear," said Houston. "University gave me a greater knowledge and guidance in subjects where I could improve my understanding of what it meant to be an audio engineer and the fundamentals of music technology as a whole; and since graduating, I have continued to teach myself in these fields, notably: sound design, synthesis, and production."

GOING FREELANCE

Once established in the chiptune scene, Houston started to be courted for collaborations. After a few offers, she decided to go freelance. "Deciding to go freelance was a monumental step for me and really forced me to mature. I learn something new about myself with every project," she shared. "Working freelance is not easy, especially in the first few years. It's easy to get carried away with other people's projections for a project and ultimately sell yourself short. Make smart deals that cover you, and always value that you have something to bring to the table."

Houston wasn't yet out of university when she was approached by Terry Cavangh to work on the frenetic rhythm-based arcade game *Super Hexagon*, the title that would pivot her onto the path of a video game composer. "I had always been striving towards something in music, but I was never sure of what exactly I was pushing for," she said. "I figured it would all make a lot more sense after I left university. Terry Cavanagh's *Super Hexagon* reached a ridiculous audience, featuring my work right at the start of my final year, and so I was almost thrown into this world. It was incredibly overwhelming, and although I had been making music, playing shows, self-publishing for nearly five years prior to this, I felt totally unprepared. Since then, it's been a journey of trial and error, self-teaching and self-learning. You really have to face yourself when you go freelance."

Super Hexagon was nominated for a BAFTA in 2013, recognized as one of the top British games of the year. Work offers began to pour in. "*Interstellaria* was the first game that I worked on from start to finish," she explained, speaking to her next big project. "I made a point of trying something completely new, moving away from the Game Boy—my comfort zone at the time—and writing the soundtrack entirely in a DAW—putting everything I learned to the test. I poured every bit of my being into that project, and I'm so proud of the results."

In 2015, her music was the inspiration for retro racing game *Spectra*. In an unusual reversal of roles, the game was inspired by Houston's original album by the same name, released in 2013. *Spectra* was developed to showcase the music—earning her a Guinness World Record for the first video game to be designed from the ground up around original music.

Since then, Houston has contributed to nearly a dozen other games adding to her unique musical lens to each. This includes the 2014 action game *Size DOES Matter*, which won a BAFTA as "The One to Watch" in 2014. In addition, she worked on licensed title *Adventure Time: Secrets of the Nameless Kingdom*, a remixed OST *Chipped of the Necrodancer*, *Pixelgrams*, *Octahedron*, and *Just Shapes and Beats*. Recently she has joined forces again with Terry Cavanagh, along with artist Marlowe Dobbe, on the upcoming title *Dicey Dungeons*. Anticipated for a late 2018/early 2019 release, *Dicey Dungeons* is a turn-based, dice-rolling, rougelike where you balance the luck of your roll against long-term strategies. Creating the dynamic, reactive, and energetic soundtrack for the game, Houston is excited to bring the collaboration and chemistry between the team to life, and grow the loyal community of fans.

Houston has made incredible memories over the years, including playing live at international festivals and collaborating with artists who inspired her. One moment in particular stands out, though. "I once performed *Super Hexagon's* 'Focus' with an orchestra at the Edinburgh Game Symposium with Mantra Collective. That was incredibly surreal and brilliant. A Game Boy with a live ensemble! Everything about that makes me smile."

KIM SWIFT

TOPPED THE CHARTS WITH A VIOLENCE-FREE FIRST-PERSON SHOOTER

K2theSwift  K2theSwift

Kim Swift

EXPERIENCE

FIRST INDUSTRY PROJECT: PORTAL (2007)

FAVORITE INDUSTRY PROJECT: QUANTUM CONUNDRUM (2012)

PROJECTS SHIPPED: 6 GAMES

ACHIEVEMENTS UNLOCKED:

> GAMASUTRA "WOMEN IN GAMES: THE GAMASUTRA 20" (2008)

> GAME DEVELOPER CHOICE AWARDS "GAME OF THE YEAR, INNOVATION AWARD, AND BEST GAME DESIGN AWARD"—PORTAL (2008)

> FORBES "30 UNDER 30" (2012)

> GEEK.COM "11 WOMEN WHO SHAPED THE WORLD OF GAMING" (2018)

STATS

INDUSTRY LEVEL: 13

CURRENT CLASS: STUDIO DESIGN DIRECTOR

CURRENT GUILD: EA MOTIVE STUDIOS—MONTRÉAL, CANADA

SPECIAL SKILLS: GAME DESIGN, GAME ART, UNITY, UNREAL ENGINE, LEVEL DESIGN

STANDARD EQUIPMENT

FAVORITE PLATFORM: SUPER NINTENDO, SWITCH

GO-TO GENRE: RPG

MUST-HAVE GAME: LEGEND OF ZELDA: LINK TO THE PAST

BIO

Kim Swift's story has become a fairy tale of sorts within the industry, after her innovative senior project at university was picked up by a major name in gaming and became a runaway success. That game was *Narbacular Drop*, which evolved into the beloved teleportation puzzle title *Portal* after Swift and her team were hired by Valve Software.

Easter Egg
Owns a pet parrot named Rocki, which she has had for over 20 years.

DEBUTING NARBACULAR DROP

Swift had known she wanted to make games since the age of eight. As an adult, she enrolled at the DigiPen Institute of Technology, working toward a bachelor's degree in computer science called Real-Time Interactive Simulation. "It was a really difficult school, but I felt that it really prepared me for being in the game industry," said Swift. "Each year, there is a projects class where teams of students create games to suit specific requirements, which means that coming out of school, I already had a portfolio of games that I worked on."

Her final year in the program—2005—was when Swift's career accelerated in an unanticipated way. "My senior year of college at DigiPen Institute of Technology, our game project team created a game called *Narbacular Drop*," she began. "We showed the game off at the school's job fair, and a couple employees from Valve were there to check out prospective students. Our team was invited to come to the Valve offices to show the game to folks and, to our surprise, Gabe Newell." It only took 20 minutes before the head of Valve offered the entire team jobs on the spot, tasking them with re-creating their student project as full-time employees.

THINKING WITH PORTALS

The team was kept lean—around 10 people total were committed to bringing *Portal* to market. "Everyone worked on a bit of everything," said Swift. "I was our project lead, lead designer, an environment artist, our PR representative, and I even designed our merchandise with another teammate."

"I think one of my favorite memories of working in gaming was having my morning meetings with Erik Wolpaw on *Portal*," continued Swift. "Both of us are morning people, and every day before everyone else came into the office, we would sit and have coffee and go over the game's story and dialog.

I'd show him the level that I worked on the previous day, and we'd talk about what we'd want GLaDOS to say and what we needed for gameplay. It was this perfect collaborative moment."

Portal shipped to great acclaim, going on to be named one of the top 100 games of all time by *Time*, one of the most influential games of the decade by *Wired*, and the best game of all time by *GamesRadar*. Swift stayed at Valve post-*Portal*, working as an environment artist and level designer for the mega-popular 2008 zombie shooter *Left 4 Dead*, as well as the sequel. After nearly five years at Valve, Swift moved on to a new endeavor at Airtight Games as creative director.

AIRTIGHT GAMES CONUNDRUM

"I think my favorite project to work on was *Quantum Conundrum* while I was at Airtight Games," said Swift, speaking to the studio's 2012 puzzle-platformer. "Getting the project funded took a lot of work and it was really scary, but eventually we were able to get a publishing deal with Square Enix. Once we had secured money to create the project, it was just a really fun project to work on, with an amazing team of passionate people. We got to take interesting risks and were able to create a lot in a short amount of time with a relatively small budget."

While working on *Quantum Conundrum*, Swift proved that inspiration is everywhere. "I think everything in life motivates and inspires me," she explained. "There's so much to appreciate, and you'll never know how inspiration might strike you. The dimension-shifting idea in *Quantum Conundrum* actually came from me watching a toilet paper commercial, of all things. The commercial had this woman in a 'plush' world with extra-fluffy robes and slippers, and everything was so cushy. I thought to myself, 'Huh, I wish I could live in that fluffy world and I could just change everything around me.' One of the first dimensions we prototyped in *Quantum Conundrum* was Fluffy Dimension."

> "I think everything in life motivates and inspires me."

Swift left the studio in 2014, at the end of what proved to be a very difficult year. The studio was nearing the end of its lifetime, and Swift felt personally responsible for not being able to keep it afloat by securing funding for the next round of games.

"Getting funding is a really difficult thing to do in the game industry as an independent studio," said Swift, who explained that she was the best candidate to campaign for funding because her name is attached to *Portal*'s success, but it wasn't a position she desired to be in. After months of trying to secure funding, and nearly five years at Airtight total, Swift left. "I knew I had to leave for my own health. It was something truly devastating that I'll never forget." From that struggle came valuable learnings that Swift would take forward in her career as she accepted leadership positions at other studios.

Amazon Games Studio was the next stop for Swift, where she started as a senior design manager. She transitioned to Senior Product Manager of Broadcaster Success in 2016, the year that Twitch Prime launched—a premium service that provides exclusive perks to those with an active Amazon Prime subscription. Swift helped define the program parameters and announce it.

A NEW MOTIVE

Recruited by industry veteran Jade Raymond, Kim is now the studio design director at EA's Motive Studios in Montréal. "My current position as Motive's studio design director is extremely rewarding. I feel like I've been fortunate in my career. Overseeing a design department and having the responsibility to help others grow their careers and skills feels like giving back," she said. "Seeing others succeed is satisfying."

As a designer, Swift also wants to see more diversity in games—concepts that challenge the traditional conventions of gaming. Swift feels her most meaningful career achievement so far did just that. "With *Portal*, I helped create a successful first-person shooter where you as the player don't commit any violent acts," she said. "I think we constantly underestimate that the fun in games can come from other things besides violence."

"If I could change something about the game industry, I would want to create more opportunities for AA or smaller games to try something new or different," she continued. "Games are an extremely risky business. It's like betting money on horses; even if you know the genealogy of the horse or even what it ate that morning for breakfast, you still have no idea if the horse will win the race. As games only seem to get bigger, you'll likely see aversions to risks and innovation. I want to see more games from diverse creators with a decent amount of money at their disposal. I want to see those games."

> "I want to see more games from diverse creators with a decent amount of money at their disposal."

Motive brands itself as "a start-up with big-time support," and it seems the studio vision aligns with Swift's aspirations. Although Motive's new projects haven't yet been announced, EA's resources combined with Swift's history of innovation, are promising. "At the end of the day, I just want to keep creating interesting games, solving problems, and helping others achieve what they want to see in their careers."

A DAY IN THE LIFE OF...

A PR MANAGER

A public relations manager is a conduit between the hard-working developers who create a game and the outside world. A good PR manager can look at a product and distill three key elements: what to share, how to share it, and where to share it. What features in the game are most important to highlight? What specific language should be used to discuss these features? What medium (i.e., a press release, interview, or developer diary) will convey the message most clearly?

As Freaks 4U Gaming PR Manager Christina Kaiser knows, PR is a social business that requires great interpersonal, organizational, and communication skills. Collaborating daily with press and influencers, Kaiser works to ensure key messaging gets out to fans and that they are as excited about the games as she is.

CHRISTINA KAISER

 C0kaiser  Christina Kaiser

PROFESSION: PR MANAGER AT FREAKS 4U GAMING—BERLIN, GERMANY

YEARS IN PROFESSION: 6

WORKED ON: DEPONIA 1-3, MEMORIA, BLACKGUARDS 1 AND 2, EU LAUNCH OF ARENA OF VALOR

▶ EDUCATION

"While part of my studies of media sciences and economics included specific topics, such as writing press texts and developing strategies, for the most part I'm self-taught and learned most of my skills on the job. A huge part of my work in games PR relies on experience. I need to know what sort of stories work for specific target groups, which gaming topics are relevant for journalists, and what kind of news won't work at all. These details can only be learned on the job."

▶ BREAKING IN

"Here in Germany, getting an entry-level paid internship was relatively easy in 2012, even though that also meant cutting back regarding income for several months. The most challenging part is probably coping with the structure of young gaming businesses. That means not really having established training structures, having to handle a lot of responsibilities quite early in your career. It really requires a lot of dedication to not be discouraged by these sometimes less-than-ideal circumstances."

▶ EARLY INDUSTRY IMPRESSIONS

"For the most part, the industry was what I expected. What made me go into games was a desire to work with creative people on story-based products. To this day, I very much enjoy the working atmosphere among creative colleagues. I appreciate the closeness of the industry. When you have a problem, there's always a network or a forum with people willing to give advice and help you out. However, as the work was my first 'real' job, fresh out of university, the lack of structures and quickly changing environment was a bit surprising at first and I had to grow accustomed to it."

▶ KEY QUALITIES

"I personally see PR as the contact point between a company and the outside world, mostly the press. It's my job to 'channel' information coming from both sides and mainly provide journalists all the necessary information and help so they can do their jobs and write interesting content about my 'products'.

"Considering all these things, as a PR Manager you should be well organized as on most days a lot of information is coming your way and you'll need to do a lot of prioritization, while still keeping track of things.

"Also, of course, you need to be outgoing to a certain extent and not shy of social contact. Overall, a positive and solution-oriented attitude is required, as your main task is to find a solution to other people's questions and problems. You don't need to know all the answers yourself, but you'll need to coordinate the flow of information between many different stakeholders."

▶ TOOLS OF THE TRADE

"One of the main tasks of PR is to stay in contact with people and mold provided information into an appealing and easy to share form. For this we require good contact and content managements systems.

"At Freaks 4U Gaming we are using Prezly, a CMS that offers a specifically designed newsroom where all the press releases and information are bundled. It also gives you the opportunity to manage your contacts, sorting them into target groups, and keep all the relevant contact data up to date and easy to share with your team members."

▶ HOURS & ENVIRONMENT

"At an agency, the work very much depends on our customers' needs, current projects and workload. On most days, I work at the office from around 9 am to 6 pm. Most of my work could also be done from home, but I prefer to be where my colleagues are. It makes communication with the team a lot easier."

▶ PROMOTIONAL PATH

"Usually you move from Junior PR Manager or Associate to PR Manager and later to Head of or PR Director. The responsibilities move upwards from basics such as clippings and text writing to more strategy-oriented tasks and team managing processes."

▶ PROFESSIONAL PERKS

"One of the most exciting parts for me is to introduce people to new games and their features. Also, being able to talk to experienced journalists, who very often have decades of experiences in gaming and a whole different perspective on a product, as well as the industry, and thus broadening my own horizon.

"As an extra perk, there's the opportunity to follow the production of a game from its early beginnings to the final product. It's incredibly exciting to see how everything evolves from a first idea to the final complex product."

▶ CAREER CHALLENGES

"I think the main challenge is to stay organized and keep track of all the information and tasks that are coming your way. You need to prioritize and swiftly decide which task should be tackled first and which one can wait until later.

"In an agency environment, it is also important to manage the expectations of your customers. Sometimes clients come to us with an idea that we know will most likely not work. Instead of trying to realize it no matter what, it's better to show our customers better solutions to meet their goals. Occasionally, it will also mean to direct them to other departments at our agency, such as marketing or community management."

▶ LIFE HACKS

"I'm an absolute Post-It! addict! If you're a more digital person, Post-Its! are basically organizers for your phone such as One Note. They work like a storage for ideas and thoughts that cross my mind during the daily business and that I don't want to forget, but that are also distracting me from my current work.

"I made a habit of writing a quick to-do list at the end of every day and every week. These basically work like a golden thread that helps me to stay on track with my tasks, even though I might have been distracted by important requests and little questions coming in throughout the day."

▶ EXCITING ADVANCEMENTS

"It's not so much on the horizon, but we're already in the middle of it. The influencer movement and with it the huge shift of focus from earned media content to paid media content to reach our target audience.

"After some humble beginnings, influencers are becoming more and more professional, developing formats that rely more on information and professional production environments, closer to traditional media formats.

"As the main focus of PR – other than marketing – has always been generating earned media content, the question is, how do we still reach influencers as multipliers of our messages? What new formats can develop from this merging of traditional media and influencers?"

PRO TIP!

"Make a habit of going to industry events. PR is a peoples' business and it's important to keep in contact with people. Even when you don't have a specific request or just don't feel like attending industry events, it's important to show your face once in a while to stay in mind."

JANET HSU

LOCALIZING FAN-FAVORITE FRANCHISES FOR GLOBAL PLAY

 capcom-unity.com/zeroobjections

EXPERIENCE

FIRST INDUSTRY PROJECT: MEGA MAN POWERED UP (2006)

FAVORITE INDUSTRY PROJECT: GHOST TRICK: PHANTOM DETECTIVE (2010)

PROJECTS SHIPPED: 15 GAMES

ACHIEVEMENTS UNLOCKED:

> FIRST EVER LOCALIZATION PLANNER TURNED LOCALIZATION DIRECTOR AT CAPCOM

> ENGLISH AND FRENCH VOICE ACTRESS FOR ACE ATTORNEY CHARACTER FRANZISKA VON KARMA

> ASSORTED ENGLISH VOICES FOR RESIDENT EVIL 7 DLC

STATS

INDUSTRY LEVEL: 13

CURRENT CLASS: LOCALIZATION DIRECTOR

CURRENT GUILD: CAPCOM—OSAKA, JAPAN

SPECIAL SKILLS: LOCALIZATION, TRANSLATION, OPERATIC SINGING, PLAYING THE SHAMISEN

STANDARD EQUIPMENT

FAVORITE PLATFORM: NINTENDO DS

GO-TO GENRE: STORY-DRIVEN

MUST-HAVE GAME: PHOENIX WRIGHT: ACE ATTORNEY

BIO

Localization is one of those underappreciated jobs that most people only notice when done poorly. As Capcom Localization Director Janet Hsu has exhibited throughout 13 years of industry experience, localization can make or break one's enjoyment of a game.

"I've wanted to work in gaming since I was in middle school," she began. "I remember seeing an ad for QA playtesters in an issue of *Nintendo Power* and thinking how great it would be to play games all day, only to read the ad and find out that you had to live in the state of Washington." Hsu was born in Taiwan, but relocated to New Jersey at a very young age. A cross-country move wasn't in the cards for a teenager.

Putting video games on hold for the time being, Hsu explored her other passion at university, where she majored in music. After graduating, she set off on an adventure to Japan and began teaching English. "Eventually, I had the dawning realization that I was not suited to teaching as a profession," said Hsu. Not wanting her overseas journey to end prematurely, she decided against returning stateside and becoming a music teacher—her initial career plan. "I had to figure out what I wanted to do."

Hsu's hobbies at the time involved singing, writing, and translating. Dabbling in other areas of study, she had also spent some time in pharmacy school and taken half a year of programming. These skills added up to a unique offering. "I realized that I had the logical mind and training to comprehend the technical side of making games, while my creative output centered on things that dealt in empathy and interpretation," said Hsu. "Combine that with living in the 'land of games,' and I took a shot at reviving my childhood dream of working in games by applying to a number of companies as a translator."

Easter Egg

Considers herself a humongous music nerd. She is a music major, and operatic singing is her go-to stress reliever.

POWERING UP

Capcom's Osaka headquarters became Hsu's new home in 2005, a place she's stayed ever since. The first game on which Hsu left her localization mark was the 2006 PSP title *Mega Man Powered Up*. "I translated the voice script for the cutscenes, which was a unique challenge, since in addition to *Mega Man*, you could play as any of the robot masters," she explained. "I had to make sure all of the lines the characters said to each other made sense for every possible combination in each cutscene."

Being in-house was a huge help in Hsu learning the nuances of localization, and improved the quality of the final work. "I quickly learned from those around me to take advantage of that fact and ask the Japanese scenario writers for clarification whenever I wasn't sure about something," she said. "It could be about something as simple as, 'How many power-ups is the player picking up?' to 'What's the nuance you intended to convey here?'" Being of a curious nature, she asked about anything and everything.

ACE ATTORNEY

Localizing an action game turned out to be a completely different experience from her next major project. In 2006 she began what would become a long-running relationship with the *Ace Attorney* series, which had only been introduced outside of Japan the year before. As a text adventure game with context-heavy scenarios, strong localization was imperative to the success of the final product.

Her work began by being the lead translator for *Phoenix Wright: Ace Attorney—Justice for All*, and she would continue to work on all six main-series entries in the franchise, with responsibilities increasing each iteration. As she began a project, Hsu would first play through the game and then ask herself, "How can I recreate the feeling and experience—not just the language—in a way that would be understandable to Western audiences?"

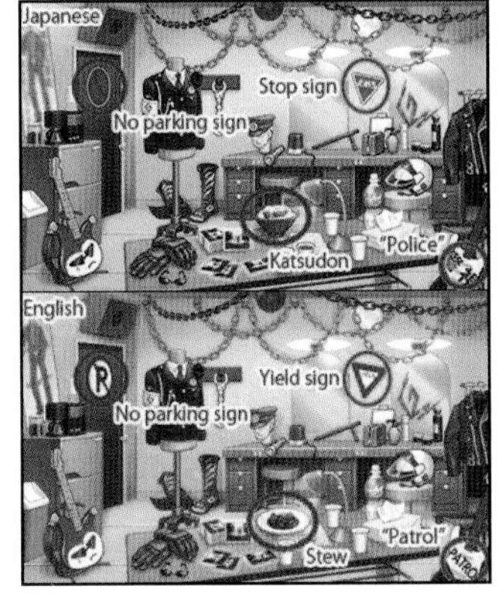

This involved translating in-game dialogue, reworking culture-specific jokes, modifying in-game art assets such as signs or newspapers, and even taking time to consider the snacking habits of characters. One franchise character's favorite snack is a Japanese treat called Karintou, which isn't visually recognizable to Western audiences. As such, Hsu had to explain what the food tasted like through the game's dialogue and localized it by giving it a more familiar-sounding name: Snackoos.

TAKING THE STAND

As the *Ace Attorney* franchise became a global success, the most challenging project Hsu tackled was leveling up Capcom's localization practices. She realized that in order to continue improving the localization quality of their games, the team needed to grow. "When I joined in 2005, we only had translators, which was fine for most of the action games we worked on at the time," she explained. With text adventures like *Ace Attorney*, she needed to be more involved during the development process. "The text and the gameplay were one and the same—unlike most games, it wasn't just about how easy it would be to implement the translated text, it was about the very quality of the overseas version," she continued. "Details like how the characters moved and when sound effects played could affect how a sentence was read and interpreted by the player, and the amount of usable space I had on-screen affected how simple or complex the text could be. Since a number of key puzzles involved language and/or cultural references, the slightest detail could affect a player's gameplay experience."

Hsu drafted a "localization planner" proposal, which detailed all the roles and responsibilities she knew needed oversight. "There were many steps between the proposal and the creation of a whole new position," she said. "After my boss at the time got the ball rolling with upper management, I led and attended meeting after meeting with representatives of different sections from throughout the company, from game designers to sound team members and UI leads, to hammer out the finer details of what a localization director would do." She formally took the role of localization director in 2010, and while her role continues to evolve with each game, the core vision of what she proposed is still at the heart of her work.

"Being a localization director has been a great experience, and I love the challenge of dealing with each title on its own terms," said Hsu. "I've also been especially fortunate to work on a series that puts all of my knowledge and skills to the test, so it might be writing and singing some lyrics for a song one day, or directing a trailer the next, in addition to the in-game localization."

ZERO OBJECTIONS!

Outside of the *Ace Attorney* series, Hsu has led localization on an array of games, including titles in the *Monster Hunter* and *Lost Planet* series, as well as *Ghost Trick: Phantom Detective* and *Dragon's Dogma: Dark Arisen*.

Hsu makes a point to bring transparency to the field of localization. Her personal blog on the Capcom Unity portal is called "Zero Objections," and allows her to share insight into the world of her work. "I try to demystify the game-creation and localization processes as much as I can, and it appears that my blogs have been used as a springboard for discussions on localization in games," she said.

She also makes a point to highlight fan works on her blog, an official recognition that they greatly appreciate and, in turn, reciprocate. "At Anime Expo one year, a cosplayer came running up to me and began to excitedly talk about *Ace Attorney*. I was really touched by the story she had to share about how the series had affected her life," recalled Hsu. "Seeing fans—especially female, trans, and non-binary fans—empower themselves through the games we make and the fan works they create is simply the best. Fan works have always been a safe haven of sorts for socialization and self-exploration, so I'm always thrilled to find a thriving fandom for any game or series."

When Hsu started her industry journey in 2005, she didn't know what to expect. She was told, however, that even the most exciting industries lose their luster once the curtain is pulled back. "So far, it's been the opposite for me," she concluded. "I think it's made me appreciate the games I play even more. I feel so fortunate to work in an industry that produces so many wonderful and unique experiences no matter where you look. Even if your idea of fun is something that's super niche, there's someone making a game that will scratch that itch. It's amazing."

"Fan works have always been a safe haven of sorts for socialization and self-exploration, so I'm always thrilled when I find a thriving fandom for any game or series."

KELLEE SANTIAGO

GAMES AS ART ACTIVIST

 KelleeSan  Kellee Santiago

 kelleesantiago.com

EXPERIENCE

FIRST INDUSTRY PROJECT: flOw (2007)

FAVORITE INDUSTRY PROJECT: FLOWER (2009)

PROJECTS SHIPPED: DEVELOPED 4 GAMES, PUBLISHED 90+

ACHIEVEMENTS UNLOCKED:

> VARIETY "TOP 10 INNOVATORS TO WATCH" (2008)
> KOTAKU "TEN MOST INFLUENTIAL WOMEN IN GAMES OF THE PAST DECADE" (2010)
> MICROSOFT "WOMEN IN GAMING LIFETIME ACHIEVEMENT AWARD" NOMINEE (2012)
> LOS ANGELES BUSINESS JOURNAL INNOVATION AWARD (2011)

 STATS

INDUSTRY LEVEL: 12

CURRENT CLASS: PRODUCT DEVELOPMENT LEAD

CURRENT GUILD: GOOGLE ENTERTAINMENT, VR/AR/XR—SAN FRANCISCO, USA

SPECIAL SKILLS: GAME DESIGN, PRODUCTION, INVESTMENT, START-UPS, ARTISTICALLY-CRAFTED GAMES

STANDARD EQUIPMENT

FAVORITE PLATFORM: NINTENDO WII

GO-TO GENRE: MULTIPLAYER PARTY & CO-OP GAMES

MUST-HAVE GAME: "REJECTS THIS QUESTION!"

BIO

In 2003, Kellee Santiago was on the fast-track for a career in theater. She'd enrolled at the University of Southern California to pursue her master's in live performance and digital media after earning her bachelor's in theater from New York University.

When Santiago was introduced to Tracy Fullerton—then professor, now Chair of the Interactive Media & Games Division—through a class exploring the history of game design throughout humanity, her commitment to theater began to waver. "It opened my eyes to two things," said Santiago. "First, design in video games had only scratched the surface of what was possible when it came to implementing known interaction vocabulary; and second, game-making was this wide-open field with little definition of how you go about making one, or who is supposed to do what." The nebulous nature of game development was appealing to Santiago, and she shifted her focus at USC, transitioning to game design, art, storytelling, and the business of games.

Under Fullerton's guidance, Santiago and six other students began collaborating on a class-agnostic project to showcase their skills. Led by Jenova Chen, Santiago took the role of producer, organized the team, maintained the budget and schedule, as well as collaborated on design. *Cloud*—which was told through the dreams of a boy confined to his hospital bed—won the annual game-innovation grant from the USC, as well as the Student Showcase Award at the 2006 Independent Games Festival. As a result, *Cloud's* visibility skyrocketed and caught the eye of PlayStation.

Easter Egg

Sparred online with renowned film critic Roger Ebert in 2010, discussing the topic of video games as art.

GOING WITH THE flOw

Between internships and *Cloud*, Santiago was armed with considerable industry experience upon graduation. She evaluated industry options, and couldn't find a place fully dedicated to innovation and experimentation. "I pursued the opportunity to start my own studio quite aggressively, because it did seem like the only way I was going to be able to work in games the way I wanted to," Santiago explained.

Teaming up with Jenova Chen a second time, the pair founded thatgamecompany, LLC in 2006, with Santiago at the helm as president. The success of *Cloud* earned the studio a three-game deal with Sony Santa Monica to develop digital games for their new PlayStation Network.

Their first project was *flOw*, based on a flash game from Chen's master thesis on dynamic difficulty adjustment. Santiago led a team of four in bringing Chen's prototype to the PlayStation as a fully-downloadable title. "I also interfaced with our Sony counterparts on reporting progress, preparing materials to show at conferences, and on the sound effects, which had to fit with the soundtrack so that it behaved as an interactive score," she said. "Basically, I got to work with a lot of different people and different disciplines, so it was a great learning experience, but also an extremely stressful one, as I was doing so many things I had never done before."

A stylistic life-simulation title with no menus or guidelines, *flOw* put thatgamecompany on the map with recognitions such as *Gamasutra's* "20 Breakthrough Developers" of 2006. *flOw* took home the Game Developer's Choice "Best Downloadable Game Award," as well as nominations from AIAS and BAFTA.

Drafting off the success of *flOw*, thatgamecompany released their next experimental title, *Flower*, in 2009. A game in which the player guides a flower petal through a variety of dreamy landscapes by controlling the wind, *Flower* was even more critically and commercially successful than its predecessor. It took home the AIAS Casual Game of the Year Award, a BAFTA for "Artistic Achievement," "Best Interactive Score" from the Game Audio Network Guild, and a variety of top independent game and innovation awards. *Time* magazine went so far as to name it one of the 100 greatest video games of all time. *Flower* was selected for the 2012 Smithsonian exhibit *The Art of Video Games*, and acquired for the permanent collection in 2013.

GAMES AS ART

Flower was often referred to as an "art game," and the "games as art" argument is one that Santiago finds deeply personal—for good reason. In 2009, Santiago contested film critic Roger Ebert's stance that video games could not be art through a TED Talk hosted at USC. To her surprise, Ebert responded online. "I warmed to Santiago immediately," Ebert said in his 2010 blog. "She is bright, confident, and persuasive. But she is mistaken."

"Art is in the eye of both the creator and the beholder."

Critiquing Santiago directly, he doubled down on his stance, igniting industry-wide debate and a firestorm of comments from devoted gamers. Santiago would engage him once more through a follow-up on Kotaku.com, highlighting that Ebert admittedly didn't play games, and offering to send him a PlayStation loaded with a copy of *Flower*. "Art is in the eye of both the creator and the beholder," she concluded. "And as those two groups of people grow and change, so will the definition and perception of art."

ENJOYING THE JOURNEY

Closing out the PlayStation deal, Santiago brought on industry veteran Robin Hunicke as producer for their 2012 adventure-art game, *Journey*. As thatgamecompany's trajectory would indicate, *Journey* was a colossal success, both critically and commercially. *Journey* took home Game of the Year wins from IGN and GameSpot and swept the DICE Awards with eight wins out of 11 nominations, including Game of the Year. It also took home five BAFTA awards, six Game Developer Choice awards, and was nominated for a Grammy, the first game to be recognized for "Best Score Soundtrack" for a visual media.

"Winning Game of the Year at the Game Developers Choice Awards for *Journey* was such an incredible moment for me," said Santiago. "In many ways the game itself felt like the conclusion of an arc that began when Jenova and I graduated from school. Having all of that work culminate in a game that resonated with so many people is, of course, an all-time high moment in the life of any game developer. I remember sitting in the audience at the GDC Awards as a student with Jenova and Tracy, and dreaming that we might be on that stage one day, accepting an award from the developer community we respected so much. I feel so very, very lucky to have that memory."

A NEW REALITY

In 2012, Santiago left thatgamecompany and took up a position as head of developer relations at Android-based microconsole OUYA, eager to help indie developers with unique ideas make their home on the new system. "Building the OUYA developer ecosystem was a complete delight," said Santiago. "I worked with an amazing team of producers, and the developers themselves were so passionate and supportive of each other and of us." Although the company dissolved in 2015, Santiago took pride in creating a developer-first ecosystem and hopes to do it again someday.

Now at Google, Santiago is diving into the worlds of augmented and virtual reality as the partnerships development lead for VR/AR/XR entertainment at Google. Helping build a library of Daydream-compatible apps—Google's mobile VR platform—as well as for ARCore, she's on the front line of innovation at Google.

For the time being, *Flower* still resonates as Santiago's personal favorite project, although great things are expected of her new post at Google. "*Flower* is still such a completely unique video game experience, and took a lot of guts to make," Santiago concluded. "The fact that it was both commercially very successful and also went on to be one of the first two games in the permanent collection of the Smithsonian American Art Museum hit the core of my mission as a game developer—to show that games can be both deeply meaningful and wildly entertaining —and that they can be an art."

JESSICA CHOBOT

HOST, WRITER, AND PROUD VIDEO GAMING MOM

JessicaChobot

Jessica Chobot

Jessica Chobot

EXPERIENCE

FIRST INDUSTRY PROJECT: IGN

FAVORITE INDUSTRY PROJECT: HOSTING THE D.I.C.E. AWARDS

PROJECTS SHIPPED: CREATOR AND HOST OF BIZARRE STATES (PODCAST AND SHOW), HOST OF NERDIST NEWS, SIDELINE REPORTER FOR BATTLEBOTS ON DISCOVERY/THE SCIENCE CHANNEL, AND CO-WRITER FOR THE COMIC BOOK FIREBRAND ON WEBTOONS.

ACHIEVEMENTS UNLOCKED

> VOICE AND MODEL FOR DIANA ALLERS, MASS EFFECT 3 (2012)

> VOICE OF HOUSE OF SOVEREIGNS GEAR, GEARS OF WAR 4 (2016)

> CO-WRITER FOR FIREBRAND COMIC (2017, 2018)

> HOST, D.I.C.E. AWARDS (2017, 2018)

STATS

INDUSTRY LEVEL: 12

CURRENT CLASS: HOST

CURRENT GUILD: NERDIST INDUSTRIES—BURBANK, USA

SPECIAL SKILLS: HOSTING, WRITING, PODCASTING

STANDARD EQUIPMENT

FAVORITE PLATFORM: DREAMCAST, NINTENDO 64

GO-TO GENRE: ACTION/ADVENTURE, SANDBOX RPGS

MUST-HAVE GAME: LEGEND OF ZELDA: BREATH OF THE WILD

BIO

Jessica Chobot's career skyrocketed at a time when there were few public-facing women in the industry. "I started making specific moves to work in the video games industry shortly after college," said Chobot. "It all came about when I had a 'quarter-life crisis,' where I realized that nothing I was doing was very satisfying or leading me to a future that I wanted." She quit her job to become a keyholder at EB Games. "I'd always loved video games, and even that small bit of time at EB helped me realize that a career within the field was possible."

ON-CAMERA TALENT

"My original goal was to be part of editorial as a games reviewer, but I botched my chance at one of those positions. I actually never wanted or had planned to be on-camera because I have uncontrollable stage-fright," confessed Chobot. "But when IGN offered me a hosting job, I said 'yes' without a moment of hesitation. I was not going to toss away another opportunity to get involved within the games industry just because of my own personal fears." She moved to Los Angeles, determined to make the most of the opportunity.

In the mid-2000s, the industry wasn't as saturated with video content as it is now. "I was incredibly lucky to start hosting on-camera content during a time when video was just starting to become popular and accessible via the Internet," she explained. "Being able to learn and grow alongside that aspect of the industry was incredibly helpful, and fortunate for me as I was able to get some serious 'sink or swim' on-the-job experience, as well as being helped and supported by incredible, talented writers and crew."

The waters she plunged into were relatively uncharted, however, and nothing could truly prepare her for taking such a high-profile position. One of Chobot's first industry gigs was covering the Consumer Electronics Show. Here she cut her teeth with show floor reports and interviews. "I would say 'survival' was what I learned the first few years of being in the industry," recalled Chobot. "I was WAY out of my depth and struggled to fake it till I made it. I eventually did get to a place where I was comfortable with what I doing, although that doesn't stop me from still getting nervous from time to time."

Working full-time at IGN as on-camera talent, Chobot kept gamers up-to-date with breaking news as host of the *Daily Fix*, live on-location show floor reports from events like the Tokyo Game Show, E3 and Gamescom, and provided gaming tips and tricks on *IGN Strategize*.

"There was a lot of travel and excitement. It was an industry full of young adults doing new things within a creative atmosphere surrounded by new tech that was blossoming," said Chobot. "Everything had a sense of adventure." As one would expect, the rapid industry evolution likewise resulted in some fairly public

Easter Egg

Has a limited-edition powder-blue Hello Kitty Dreamcast imported from Japan.

growing pains. Debates began over who was—and more importantly, wasn't—a gamer: the "casual vs. core" divide. "In hindsight," said Chobot, "maybe that's what surprised me the most about working within the industry: How many arguments and debates there were at any given moment. I naively came into it at the start thinking, 'Yay! We all love games! We're all going to be friends!' While that was the case with most folks, others were having none of it."

TRANSITIONING TO TV

Making a move into broadcast media, Chobot worked part-time as a field reporter and host for G4TV from 2010 to 2014. She stepped into the studio as a field reporter for *Attack of the Show*, *X-Play*, and *Proving Ground*, as well as traveling for on-location correspondence gigs at CES, E3, and San Diego Comic Con.

Being co-host of the original television series *Proving Ground* was a big career step for Chobot. Alongside *Jackass* cast member Ryan Dunn, the duo tested pop-culture concepts in the real world, including a venture to determine if a banana peel could really cause a go-kart to spin out, as *Mario Kart* would lead us to believe. It was a challenging time in her career on multiple levels. "G4's *Proving Ground* was probably the most stressful and challenging. It was a physically grueling shoot: lots of dirt, lots of heat, and a lot of painful stunts. Then there was the emotional heartbreak when Ryan Dunn passed away shortly after we wrapped the shoot," she said, speaking to the car crash that killed Dunn in 2011. "All in all, a very difficult time."

Leaving the familiar behind, Chobot made a career change in 2014, moving to the Nerdist network. At Nerdist she hosts a slew of programming, including *Nerdist News*, *Nerdist Presents*, and her own podcast, *Bizarre States*. Although regularly in the studio, she still attends and covers a busy roster of industry events.

Chobot's long list of achievements don't stop with hosting work; she's lent her voice to several video games, starred in fan films, and created her own IP with Bizarre States. Chobot's less visible work is something to be equally proud of. She joined her friend and writer, Erika Lewis, in 2017 to help co-write the comic book series, *FIREBRAND*. Since then, she's been a season judge and sideline reporter on *BattleBots*, and co-hosted prestigious industry awards two years in a row.

"I think my most meaningful contribution to the video game industry is proving that being a gamer doesn't end when you become an older adult."

Despite the high-profile on-camera work on her résumé, it wasn't until 2015 that Chobot fully received recognition she'd long deserved. "Despite having worked as an on-camera host since 2006, it wasn't until 2015 during the 2015 *Halo 5* Live Event that I was billed as a proper 'host' alongside my male counterparts instead of a 'co-host,'" said Chobot, noting that there is a meaningful difference between the two. "I don't think this ever was something that was done on purpose or mean-spiritedly. I think it just never occurred to those making the decisions that you could have a woman in a standalone host position with or without additional male hosts for that demographic."

Chobot has made significant contributions to the industry, but coyly answers that her most significant contribution is sticking around. "Currently, I think my most meaningful contribution to the video game industry is proving that being a gamer doesn't end when you become an older adult. I am a 41-year-old working mom and I'm still involved in gaming as both a career and as a lifestyle and hobby, and I don't see that changing anytime soon. It is my personal goal to still be involved in the industry, on some level, for as long as I possibly can. If I can reach 75+ years old and continue to be hired to report on new consoles and titles, I will feel like I truly accomplished something."

INSPIRATIONAL WOMEN

Who is a woman in the game industry that inspires you and why?

"There are countless women in games who inspire me. In fact, I'd probably say all of them do—all for different reasons. I've always looked up to people like Bonnie Ross, Jade Raymond, and Amy Hennig who are leading studios and making incredible, world-renowned games. I'm proud to have them as leaders in our industry, working behind the scenes to create experiences we love, often for people who don't even realize the contribution they had."

Alanah Pearce | Writer/Producer | Rooster Teeth | Los Angeles, USA

"When I was deciding what to do with my life after high school, I knew I wanted to work in games. I had no idea what I needed to do or study to become a developer, because there were no game schools or courses at the time. But I knew it was possible for me to become a game developer, because I had played the *King's Quest* games, and was aware that they were designed by Roberta Williams. Because Roberta was so prominent and respected, I assumed that this was an industry where women belonged. I am so grateful to all the women pioneers in the field who gave me that impression. That list would also include Brenda Romero, Rieko Kodama, Carol Shaw, Jane Jensen, Sheri Graner Ray, Dona Bailey, and others who made it possible for me to follow in their footsteps, simply by finding their way into the industry and doing such great work. I owe them so much."

Anna Kipnis | Senior Gameplay Programmer | Double Fine Productions | San Francisco, USA

"All the women who work and contribute in Gamaga. I get to see their passion, skills, and constant efforts to grow and be better. These women don't see themselves just as a gender in the gaming industry, but their skills and impact in achieving the best games in the best work environment in South America. They give me, and Gamaga, their full trust and support in what we believe as a company. They push us and their teams to be better, to achieve our goals, and to always exceed expectations. I cannot select just one woman who inspires me when I'm surrounded by these incredible people showing what they are capable of and their constant will to make a difference. If I fail to them, I will fail too many others who deserve the same opportunity to grow this industry to make an impact and do what they love. It's because of them that I know I can—and must—do everything in my power to take this company and industry to the next level."

Fernanda Contreras Stange | CFO | Gamaga Inc. | Santiago, Chile

---

"That would be Louis Van Baarle, also known by her artistic name, Loish. I began to follow her work back in 2012 and was immediately drawn to her cartoonish style and her skill in using colors. Then, in 2017, I learned that she had worked as a concept artist for the character Aloy from the game *Horizon Zero Dawn* by Guerrilla Games. That's when I realized maybe my cartoonish style might be cool to enter in games or animated movies. To some, seeing other artists creating 'better' art than you might be a downer and sometimes I do feel that way. But the thing is, they wouldn't be as good as they are now if they didn't train and keep doing their best to surpass themselves and see themselves evolving. Even if that evolution is slow, if you keep trying, you will definitely see the results. My goal is to use my reference artist as Loish, deconstruct their work, and learn from it."

Ines Borges | UI Designer and Game Artist | Elifoot 18 & GameNest | Lisbon, Portugal

---

"My biggest influence to get into games writing was Francesca Reyes, who was editor-in-chief of the *Official Xbox Magazine* at the time. Not many women held leadership positions, especially the key role of editor-in-chief. I always looked at Fran as paving the way for other women like me. I think it said a lot that she was visible and active, so up-and-comers could look and say, 'I can be there some day.' I also just loved her passion for video games, which always shined through in her writing."

Kimberley Wallace | Features Editor | *Game Informer* | Minneapolis, USA

"I'll be honest, until recently there were not many women in the spotlight so most of my inspirations are industry figures I've only come to know recently. Women like Amy Jo Kim, Brenda Romero, Elizabeth LaPensée, and Kate Edwards all do things I find inspiring, whether it be in the actual game design process itself, or their interactions with—and examples they set for—the game development community."

Kimberly Unger | Mobile/VR Producer | Playchemy | Burlingame, USA

"Maja Moldenhauer from Studio MDHR. She wears many hats in the company in a formidable way, combining work and family. Also, there's no way someone would guess she's a game developer by looking at her— and that's awesome. We need different faces in front of our industry. Another woman who inspires me is Martina Santoro from Argentina. When I started focusing on the business side of our studio, I felt quite alienated since there where not many women in visible business roles out there, and the image in my head was of boring men in suits. Martina showed me you can be passionate and involved in the industry and was a fresh role model for me."

Laia Bee | Co-Founder | Pincer Games | Punta del Este, Uruguay

---

"Bronwen Grimes of Valve. When I was just a student, she took the time to help mentor me. It is something that I will always be grateful for and I truly feel it helped me to push my own career down the right path. Not only that but she is a brilliant technical artist. Finding creative solutions to solving games' visual problems."

Rachel Day | Senior VFX Artist | Blizzard Entertainment | Irvine, USA

"Before I started showing up to gaming events, esports were a focus of my college papers. I wrote about women making an impact at the time: TossGirl competing in *StarCraft*; VAN3SSA and Kat Gunn playing *Dead or Alive* in the Championship Gaming Series; and Athena and AthenaTwin, the twin sisters who founded PMS Clan. When I got the chance to interview Amy (Athena) and Amber (AthenaTwin) about their clan, they asked me to join it. When I finally met Vanessa and Kat, it was as fellow competitors on the show WCG Ultimate Gamer. One day, when I meet TossGirl, I plan to say the same thing to her that I said to the others: 'Thank you! I followed you here and I'm trying to bring as many with me as I can.'"

Rachel "Seltzer" Quirico | esports Host | CSA | Irvine, USA

"There are a lot of them, but the one who made me want to join the industry as a professional is beyond a doubt Jane Pinckard. After five years of university, I wasn't too sure where to go. At the time, Jane was an editor on 1up.com and host on the 1Up Show. She also had a blog called 'Game Girl Advance,' which I read avidly. Her take on video game culture and history, as the way she made it accessible for someone who had missed out on the latest generation of consoles, was unprecedented to me. She was showcasing videogames as a culture and an art, and I found myself wanting to take part in that."

Catherine Vandier | Marketing & Communications Manager | Electronic Arts | Guildford, UK

"Ally McLean is a constant source of inspiration for me. She sees a problem that needs to be addressed and takes practical steps to address it. By launching The Working Lunch mentorship program (which I am grateful to be a part of), she has been able to directly provide entry-level women with skills, contacts, and confidence to enter the games industry and, at the same time, assure a future where they won't be the only women in the room. Ally works tirelessly so the next generation won't have to experience what we have. I'm lucky to have her as a colleague and a friend."

Rae Johnston | Editor, TV & Radio Presenter | Junkee | Sydney, Australia

---

"One of my video game developer heroes is Brie Code, the CEO and creative director of TRU LUV and former programming lead at Ubisoft. One of the things that inspires me about her is her interest in making games for people who don't like games, and her work on games where the mechanics are not driven by the player getting an adrenaline rush. Instead she promotes tend-and-befriend, a concept similar to fight-or-flight, where under stress instead of wanting to fight or flee, a person becomes more aware, fearless, and protective due to the release of oxytocin instead of adrenaline. It's important to explore these different human responses through games, as they allow us to create experiences that appeal to different audiences. A lot of the most well-known games are still seen as aimed at the male population, but by incorporating different methods of interaction and play, we can create games that other large demographics identify with and enjoy playing."

Jodie Azhar | Technical Art Director | Creative Assembly | Redhill, UK

"At the end of my first year of study in game art and design, one of my favorite games at the time came out—*Assassin's Creed*. For a long time, I loved the game and the sequels that followed. I loved the vast world it created, the unique story, characters, the gameplay—everything. One of the producers and major contributors of the franchise was Jade Raymond. The game industry has always been a male-dominated industry, and at the time, her role in that franchise really inspired me. For her to be part of something for so long and help it grow into the success that it is many sequels later is so impressive. Then, for her to move on to become the founder of Ubisoft Toronto is incredibly inspiring. It's so great to see strong women leave their mark and create something big."

Daryl Hanna Tancinco | Senior Artist | Infinity Ward | Los Angeles, USA

"Bonnie Ross. She's the head of 343 Industries. The higher up you go, the harder it gets. Seeing another woman at the top of a great studio and franchise is inspiring. I respect and admire what she represents in this industry, especially for pushing for more female representation in this industry. I think enacting changes from the top goes a long way to bringing in more women to game development."

Jennie Nguyen | Systems Administrator | Crystal Dynamics | Redwood City, USA

"Jessica Chobot is a huge inspiration for me. Seeing her when she hosted for IGN is what made me want to be a host in the video game industry in the first place."

Melonie Mac | Streamer & Host | Freelance | Los Angeles, USA

"Laura Fryer is one of the most amazing women in the industry I've met. I feel fortunate to have worked for her, to have been mentored by her, and to be able to call her a friend. Laura exudes sincerity and passion for everything she does, whether it's inventing new technology, making games, or forging new paths for people to share knowledge and innovate together. "

Dana Cowley | Senior Marketing Manager | Epic Games | Raleigh, USA

"Laila Shabir, the founder of Girls Make Games, is a woman in the industry who inspires me. She's made such an impact on so many young women's lives. And, in turn, when those women go out and get jobs in the game industry, they impact the teams they work on, the games that are made, the companies they work for. All of us benefit from Laila's efforts. She's really created something remarkable."

Kirsten Duvall | VP of Business Strategy | BlueprintReality Inc. | San Francisco, USA

"Lucy Bradshaw. Lucy is the kind of low-key leader who understood the value of a diverse team and actually hired a diverse dev team long before there were any hashtags."

Jane Ng | Artist | Valve | Bellevue, USA

"Keza MacDonald is one of the most inspirational women in our industry. I'm lucky enough to call her a friend, but I am constantly inspired by her intelligence, wit, work ethic, dedication, passion, and humor. She has an incredible way with words and I love reading her work. She is able to express herself and stand by her words and work while rising above harassment and negativity in a most inspirational way. She really is something special."

Hollie Bennett | Channel Manager | PlayStation Access | London, UK

"There are three women I really like in the game industry and I look at them as wonder women and as models in the industry: Brenda Romero, for being one of the first woman to earn a role in the industry, thanks to her technical skills, also by contributing to creating the industry itself; Debbie Bestwick, for her strong approach to business at Team17 and the ability to follow her passion since she was a young girl and make a satisfying job out of it; and Kiki Wolfkill, as I really admire her tenacious attitude and how she arrived to cover her actual role, starting from an artistic background."

Giulia Zamboni | Producer | Gamera Interactive | Padua, Italy

---

"It would be hard to just say one woman. There are multiple women in the game industry who inspire me. The strength of Lei Baustista-Lo; the adaptive programmer, Michelle Chen; the grace of Pamela Ann Puen, who can take on any client and task; the immensely creative game designer, Luna Javier; the talented artist, Patsy Lascano; and Abigail dela Cruz. Women are celebrated and well respected in the local industry."

Gwendelyn Foster | Game Developer | Imayon Studios | Manila, Philippines

---

"Sheri Graner Ray. She literally wrote the book on gender-inclusive game design. She was a voice for women in games from the very beginning, created the first professional association dedicated to women in games, and has fought tirelessly for diversity. She's a legend."

Brenda Romero | Game Designer & CEO | Romero Games | Galway, Ireland

---

HOW MOTHERHOOD CAN HELP —NOT HURT— WORKING WOMEN

By Patricia E. Vance | *President of the ESRB and Founder/Chairperson of IARC*

The other day I was waiting for a yoga class to begin and overheard a conversation between two women in their 20s expressing disdain for a female work colleague who had three children at home. "How could she be a good mother spending so much time at work?" one of them asked the other. Having been a working mother for the past 30+ years, I was aghast. I can understand how young women early in their careers cannot fathom how "having it all" is achievable, let alone desirable. The fact is, I think being a mother has enhanced—not hurt—both my career and the lives of my children.

Driven by unconditional love, a mother spends virtually all of her family time giving to others, putting herself last, without expecting to get much, if anything, in return. Conversely, work is primarily a selfish pursuit where she can accomplish tasks, set goals for herself, meet deadlines, challenge herself, and hopefully build confidence. Work is also about getting something in return beyond just monetary compensation—to be treated fairly, to be respected, and to gain experience and knowledge. The point is that there are numerous benefits that mothers receive from working and, assuming they have good child care (unfortunately, not a given), children's lives can be demonstrably enhanced by having a mother who gains a different kind of personal satisfaction through work outside of the home.

When I had my first (of three) daughters in 1985, I was determined to set an example for my work colleagues (especially my male colleagues) that indeed a woman can take maternity leave and return to work full-time. So, as proscribed in the company's short-term disability policy, I took two weeks off in advance of my due date and returned precisely six weeks after having given birth. I did virtually the same with my other two children. Would I have enjoyed a few more weeks or months at home? Of course, but I didn't have the luxury of that choice, nor could I afford forgoing the income, as is the case with so many other working women in the U.S. And, although I won't sugarcoat the frequent waves of guilt that overcame me spending so much time away from home, the reality is my children adjusted well to the schedule throughout the various stages of their childhood and have grown up to be independent, confident young women in their own right.

One of the most vivid and unusual examples of the beneficial symbiosis of motherhood and work for me occurred with my second child, who was diagnosed with leukemia at a very young age. Over the course of my daughter's 18 months of treatment, I spent a significant amount of time in doctor's offices and hospitals (including living in isolation for 8-10 weeks during her bone marrow transplant) but continued to work.

This may seem strange or even horrifying to many, but during those darkest moments in my life I feel fortunate for the welcome diversion of work. And it was during that period when ABC promoted me to vice president, not because of the hardships I had endured outside of the office, but because of the material contributions I had made at work regardless of my frequent absences.

Throughout my career, I have found that mothers bring a unique perspective to the workplace. Although broadly generalizing, it's fairly common knowledge that mothers tend to be empathetic, can multi-task, are detail-oriented, and don't typically sweat the small stuff. Having children, at least for me, shuffled around my priorities and, although still important, work became less about who I am and more about something I do. As a result, I find that being a mother has made me less fearful at work and more confident to take risks. Motherhood taught me to be less concerned about workplace politics and more focused on the work itself. As a manager, I think being a mother has made me more empathetic to the needs of working parents and generally increased my "EQ," or ability to recognize and understand the emotions of those around me, as well as my own, and apply this awareness to manage my own behavior and relationships with others. It also goes without saying that being a mother has given me a leg up in my current role as president of the ESRB, whose primary objective is to inform parents—especially mothers, who tend to be more proactive than fathers—when it comes to choosing appropriate video games for their families.

I hope that one day those two women in my yoga class gain a first-hand understanding of the power of combining motherhood and work, two life endeavors filled with equal parts of challenge and fulfillment. I would be lying if I said it was always easy, because it wasn't, but I can confidently say that I'm better for it, my children are better for it, and I'm proud to have had both in my life without regrets.

A DAY IN THE LIFE OF...

A COMMUNITY MANAGER

While the industry is home to community veterans with over 25 years of experience, only in the last decade has the role been formalized. Still, community management remains a nebulous profession to many. At its core, community managers are the liaisons between a studio—or publisher, distributor, manufacturer, etc.—and their audience. They facilitate two-way communication between companies and fans, providing the public information on new products and reciprocally condensing feedback in a digestible way for internal stakeholders.

While this may sound a bit sterile, the job is anything but. Community managers also create programs to reward brand evangelists, plan and host in-person events, showcase user-generated content, answer questions on forums, and even at times take on customer-service roles. Additionally, many companies roll social media management into the job description, even though it is an entirely different specialty that utilizes distinct tools and measures in unique key performance indicators.

As a community manager at Guerrilla Games, Anne van der Zanden had the rewarding opportunity of helping build a community around a new IP. She interacts with passionate fans on a daily basis, ensuring their feedback makes it to the development team, as well as showing appreciation through unique programs and fan spotlights.

ANNE VAN DER ZANDEN

WLF359

Anne van der Zanden

PROFESSION: COMMUNITY MANAGER AT GUERRILLA GAMES—AMSTERDAM, THE NETHERLANDS

YEARS IN PROFESSION: 3

WORKED ON: HORIZON ZERO DAWN

▶ EDUCATION

"I have a Bachelor's degree in Communication Science at the University of Amsterdam. This mostly involved marketing and PR, but I also took classes focusing on conducting user-experience research and designing entertainment products aimed at children and young adults. I never really considered I would be able to work in the games industry with my educational background, until we sat in on a guest lecture from a historian who worked at a game studio to make sure the games they developed were historically accurate. Seeing someone with a somewhat unconventional background work in games was that final push for me to pursue a career in this industry."

▶ EARLY INDUSTRY IMPRESSIONS

"What I like best about my experience with the industry so far is that everyone is super eager to help each other out. All other community managers I've met online and during events are extremely passionate about their jobs, and it's so inspiring to hear them talk about how they manage their communities and handle situations that I run into on a daily basis."

▶ KEY QUALITIES

"Good communication skills are key. I serve as a bridge between our development team and the people who play our game. I can show the fans what cool new things our team has been working on, and at the same time I can show our developers what the fans in our community created: their own projects, stories, cosplays, fan art, films—all inspired by what we created in the studio.

You have to be a great listener, too. You can learn a lot from the feedback that your community gives you."

▶ TOOLS OF THE TRADE

"Social media makes it so easy to connect with people all over the world. You do have to keep in mind that different people in your community use different social media channels and for different reasons. You need to understand how each of these platforms works, what their strengths and weaknesses are to develop your strategy for each. We use tools like Tweetdeck and Spredfast to monitor engagement on our posts and hastags on Twitter, Instagram, and Facebook."

▶ HOURS & ENVIRONMENT

"Guerrilla is a pretty laid-back studio and a great environment to work in. We have 40-hour workweeks, and every Friday we serve drinks downstairs in our cantina. Our office is located in the center of Amsterdam, which is really nice because you're right near all the cinemas and bars when you get off from work."

▶ AN AVERAGE DAY

"An average day for me starts with checking social media for new content and questions. We don't have our own forums, so I try to be everywhere our community is. At the end of every month, our team reports on the topics that the community discussed with our management team.

"I'm also responsible for the day-to-day communication with our brand ambassadors. We keep track of the most passionate fans and try to keep in touch for their feedback—for our own community strategy development, but also for our developers and marketing teams. It's really helpful to understand what kind of people your most passionate players are when you're developing new features and projects.

"My favorite thing is when I get to jump in the game to take screenshots of all the intricate outfits for cosplayers. We have a cosplay guide for Aloy, but not for the rest of the cast of characters. I received mail from someone who wanted to cosplay as one of our main character's allies, but couldn't quite make out all the details. Even though we have a photo mode in our game, it can be challenging to get a good look at the outfits worn by other characters when you're playing. I love when I get to finish my day by jumping in and grabbing some renders, especially since I always discover something interesting in the designs that our character art team came up with!"

▶ PROFESSIONAL PERKS

"Going to events to meet fans in person has to be one of the coolest things that comes with the job! It's so amazing to hear their stories and experiences with the game."

▶ CAREER CHALLENGES

"I only just started out in my career, but finding out what I really wanted to do was challenging. Going from marketing to community management might not seem like a big leap, but to me it was. I feel like my current role is a way better fit for me than when I was studying marketing. The key is to find something you're really passionate about."

▶ FAVORITE PROJECT

"My favorite project was the first fan meetup we organized for Gamescom 2017! *Horizon Zero Dawn* had been out for half a year, and there weren't really any concrete plans for Guerrilla to attend the event. Nevertheless, one of the German Aloy cosplayers, a PR manager from the German PlayStation team, and myself decided to organize a cosplay meetup. It was surreal to meet everyone and see so many Aloys and other characters from the game up on that big stage!"

▶ LIFE HACKS

"Try to always be in the know on everything that is going on in your studio and in the game. We were really lucky that our QA team kept very detailed documentation, even before the game was released. This made it so much easier to anticipate things that I thought the community would be interested in. It can sometimes be challenging to work with other teams in the studio, since we work on completely different schedules, but make sure you stay in the loop during the whole development process."

▶ BIGGEST MISTAKE

"Having players from all over the world means that your community never sleeps, but that doesn't mean that you shouldn't either. When I started out, I always wanted to be there for the community, at any time of the day. If someone posted a cool new cosplay or fan art in the middle of the night, I wanted to be up to see it. If anyone had a question on the forums, I wanted to be online to help. Even on weekends I was constantly checking our mentions and hashtags for updates. Being 'on' all the time takes a toll on you at some point. That is definitely something I had to keep reminding myself of in the beginning."

▶ EXCITING ADVANCEMENTS

"When I started, *Horizon Zero Dawn* was almost finished already. The marketing and community strategies were already determined, and it was up to me to make sure that they were executed. I'm really excited to work on new projects and be able to experience the process of developing the community strategy from start to finish."

PRO TIP!

"You don't need to be an artist or a programmer to be a game developer. The games industry continues to professionalize; there is need for your skill. Don't be afraid to bring something unique to the table."

SHANNON SYMONDS

PRESERVER OF THE PAST

 Smsymonds

 International Center for the History of Electronic Games

 Shannon Symonds

 museumofplay.org

EXPERIENCE

FIRST INDUSTRY PROJECT: EGAMEREVOLUTION EXHIBIT (2008)

FAVORITE INDUSTRY PROJECT: WOMEN IN VIDEO GAMES (2018)

PROJECTS SHIPPED: CATALOGED MORE THAN 45,000 MUSEUM OBJECTS

ACHIEVEMENTS UNLOCKED:

> CURATOR "WOMEN IN VIDEO GAMES" EXHIBIT (2018)

> FACILITATED MORE THAN 300 VIDEO GAME DONATIONS

> OFFICIALLY ACCESSIONED LANDFILL DIRT FROM EXHUMED ATARI CARTIDGES IN NEW MEXICO INTO THE MUSEUM'S COLLECTION

STATS

INDUSTRY LEVEL: 12

CURRENT CLASS: CURATOR OF ELECTRONIC GAMES

CURRENT GUILD: THE STRONG NATIONAL MUSEUM OF PLAY—ROCHESTER, NEW YORK, USA

SPECIAL SKILLS: WORLD HISTORY, JAPANESE STUDIES, BOOK HOARDING, STAR TREK TRIVIA

STANDARD EQUIPMENT

FAVORITE PLATFORM: NINTENDO DS

GO-TO GENRE: PUZZLE AND PLATFORMERS

MUST-HAVE GAME: FINAL FANTASY XI

BIO

Shannon Symonds is a preserver of history. At her most recent museum posting, she happens to focus on preserving a key piece of modern entertainment history—video games. "I want there to be an accurate record of the industry and the amazing work it produced, and I want to educate others on the care and preservation of this unique medium," said Symonds. "And most importantly, I want to preserve the stories of the people who made it so successful."

While her lifelong goal has always been to preserve and interpret history, she never envisioned herself working with video games. "I originally went to college to study journalism, but I eventually turned my history minor into a double-major and realized my real future was in studying the past," Symonds explained. "I graduated with a master's in World History and a concentration on Asian studies, with a thesis on the intersection of religion and politics in Japanese history. I assumed I'd be continuing on to a PhD program to become a professor, but I quickly found out teaching was a calling best left to others blessed with more patience. Instead, I interned at two local museums and, before I knew it, I was on the road to public history."

THE STRONG MUSEUM

Before long, Symonds found a place at The Strong Museum, which houses the world's largest public collection of artifacts related to play and is the only museum dedicated to the history and study of play. "It was a far cry from the type of traditional history museum I'd originally envisioned myself working in," said Symonds, noting she expected to work with large collections of antique Japanese artifacts. "But the museum business is about as difficult to break into as the game industry, so I was not about to complain."

Photo credit: The Strong Museum

Easter Egg

Has no problem eating sushi but refuses to eat any other kind of meat that isn't cooked well-done.

Symonds worked her way up the hierarchy at The Strong, beginning as a gallery host, and then joining the collections team as an artifact cataloger, which involved performing data entry on items donated to the museum. "It so happened that when I joined the team, we'd just begun intensely collecting video and electronic games, as it was a form of play we hadn't focused on documenting in the past," she recalled. "As I entered information for thousands of games into our database, I found myself doing more and more research on the industry to help inform my cataloging." Symonds had little knowledge of the game industry at the time, especially from a historical perspective, as she was primarily interested in the ancient world. "But the more I learned, the more I became fascinated. Before I knew it, I ended up as a curator responsible for a collection of 60,000 video game-related artifacts!"

Photo credit: The Strong Museum

The first exhibit under her belt at the Strong—eGameRevolution—opened in 2008 as a permanent showcase of the history of the gaming industry. "It was the first major exhibit I helped to physically set up. Other members of the team did the initial layout, but I learned a lot about how to put together an exhibit space, especially one with a huge interactive component."

Amusingly to Symonds, she did end up working with Japanese artifacts, albeit modern ones. "We currently have the most comprehensive public collection of Japanese video games anywhere in the world, including Japan!"

HISTORICALLY SIGNIFICANT

As a historian, Symonds' primary motivation is preservation of the past. She is often asked why her museum has a huge focus on video games, because it is a relatively new form of art and entertainment. "We have a saying here: 'Museums don't collect something because it's old, they collect something because it is historically significant.' For a museum focused on the history of play, it becomes easy to understand why we consider video games so important. And believe it or not, we're actually running out of time already," said Symonds. "Magnetic media, such as old floppy disks, are already past their originally calculated life spam. We've been very lucky thus far when it comes to migrating data, but if we'd waited until they were considered 'old,' we would have surely missed our chance."

From time to time, however, objects do slip through the museum's grasp. "It seems like such a simple concept, but it's one I'll never be able to completely, fully accept: We can't save everything. It's impossible. We lose eBay auctions to private collectors with more money. We approach companies to ask for records only to find that they were thrown out decades ago. We acquire a unique prototype only to discover it's beyond salvaging and the data is lost. We know this going in and, quite frankly, I have it a lot easier than historians who are still fighting for Picasso's art and Roman pottery shards. But it's still hard not to take it personally when something just barely slips out of our grasp."

"I would never want to stand in the way of progress, but I could wish that things were going to remain physical for longer than I anticipate."

The industry's shift towards a digital landscape has also complicated her role. "In some ways, the future of gaming is going to make my job a lot more difficult! While we're moving forward at a steady pace, digital preservation on this large of a scale is not only difficult, but also extremely expensive," she enlightened. "When someone donates a physical game, we have concrete, time-tested ways of preserving it. Digital migration is another ball of wax, with each console, computer, and mobile device providing unique quirks. I would never want to stand in the way of progress, but I could wish that things were going to remain physical for longer than I anticipate."

WOMEN IN GAMING

The Strong's upcoming video-game related exhibit is a passion project for Symonds. "I'm currently working on an exhibit that focuses on the history of women in gaming, slated to open in November 2018. My excitement is two-fold. On one hand, this is a topic I've been wanting to focus on for a very, very long time," she said. "There are so many amazing women in all aspects of the gaming industry, from development and programming to voice acting and graphic design, and I'm thrilled to be creating an experience that allows gaming fans to really delve deeply into this history. I'm a storyteller at heart and this is one of the most inspiring tales I've ever had the privilege of telling." This is also the first major exhibit Symonds has led and the first time she is creating an online component to complement the physical one. "It's challenging and demanding, and I'm learning more about exhibit design and planning than I ever have."

Through her work, Symonds hopes to make an impact on future generations. "I want to make sure gamers never forget their roots. Even if they've never played an Atari 2600, I want there to forever be video captures and emulations available so that they can see how the industry came to be. I want classic arcade games to remain playable for as long as possible. And I want to ensure corporate records, design documents, and interviews with developers remain preserved. Perhaps most importantly, I want to ensure all these things are available publicly and not hidden in someone's basement. I love working with the collecting community because of the amazing care fans lavish on their items, but at the end of the day, I hope to see such treasures on display for everyone to appreciate. In the words of Indiana Jones, 'It belongs in a museum!'"

EMILY GREER

KONGREGATE'S ARCHITECT OF ECONOMY

 EmilyG  kongregate.com

EXPERIENCE

FIRST INDUSTRY PROJECT: KONGAI (2008)

FAVORITE INDUSTRY PROJECT: KONGREGATE GAMING PLATFORM

PROJECTS SHIPPED: 1 GAME DEVELOPED, 60 GAMES PUBLISHED, 1 PLATFORM LAUNCHED

ACHIEVEMENTS UNLOCKED:

> W2.0 "FEMALE FOUNDER TO WATCH IN SOCIAL GAMING" (2010)

> GAMEINDUSTRY.BIZ "PEOPLE OF THE YEAR: EMILY GREER" (2017)

STATS

INDUSTRY LEVEL: 12

CURRENT CLASS: CEO

CURRENT GUILD: KONGREGATE—SAN FRANCISCO, USA

SPECIAL SKILLS: MONETIZATION, ANALYTICS, E-COMMERCE, GAME DESIGN, PRODUCT MANAGEMENT, FIGURE SKATING

STANDARD EQUIPMENT

FAVORITE PLATFORM: MOBILE

GO-TO GENRE: TOWER DEFENSE

MUST-HAVE GAME: BLOONS TOWER DEFENSE SERIES

BIO

Emily Greer worked in book publishing after graduating from university. "I majored in Eastern European studies in college and wrote my thesis on 16th-century Transylvanian history—not relevant to anything outside of academia," joked Greer. Unfortunately, she found that working professionally in publishing took away from her love of reading. She wanted a job more analytical in nature. Through her search, she stumbled into direct marketing and e-commerce, working on the leading edge of data science before it was defined as such.

"Once I realized how much I liked it, I took some courses in stats and math to get more theory," said Greer. "My work was very flexible about it, even though it wasn't really needed for what I was doing. I also self-taught SQL (structured query language) because I hated waiting for the IT group to pull things for me."

"After about seven years of doing that, I gradually got a little bored, and concerned about the environmental impact of catalogs, and started thinking of doing something a little more meaningful to me," continued Greer. She almost returned to school for economics, but her brother Jim—a games programmer for some time—had an idea. He pitched her on a web-based publisher and gaming portal with a focus on Flash and free-to-play games. The hope was to help grow indie game developers and their communities, offering an alternative to the "core" gamer.

"I almost went to grad school for economics, but my brother had the idea for Kongregate," said Greer. "I had no experience in the industry, but I liked playing games, and because I knew quite a bit about business generally, I volunteered to be his co-founder. It turned out that my data, analytics, marketing, and finance background was very relevant and helpful."

With a business plan put together, the next step for the duo was securing funding. "I struggled to be taken seriously by venture capitalists and other investors," explained Greer. "I was asked to give up my COO title and seat on the board as a condition of investment. We compromised—I kept the board seat—and the VC later admitted that they had funded my brother and considered me a negative on the deal. It was a pleasant surprise to them that I turned out to be competent and smart."

Greer is unquestionably both competent and smart. She led the initial product development of Kongregate—from establishing the first wireframes to launching the final website—including fleshing out her brother's initial idea for a level and points system that their massive community has assembled around. "I helped select vendors and was the daily producer, product manager, QA, and was making all sorts of design decisions including points values and level progression," explained Greer. "I was also the producer on a collectible card game, *Kongai*, which was tied into the site through a card-collection system."

For the past 12 years, Greer has been involved in the day-to-day of Kongregate, and her self-taught skills have become increasingly relevant as the industry grows more data-oriented. From 2006 until 2014, she was the acting COO, overseeing the day-to-day operations of the company, including product development, marketing, analytics, advertising, community-management finance, and accounting. Since 2014, she has taken the mantle and responsibilities of CEO.

Kongregate.com was a clear success. The web portal hosts over 100,000 free games played by tens of millions of gamers monthly. In order to keep up with the evolving tastes of gamers on the go, Kongregate opened a mobile publishing business in 2013. Mobile has become the bigger business arm of the company under Greer's leadership as CEO. Kongregate's mobile portfolio includes 30+ games that boast 100 million downloads collectively. The company now employees over 100 staff in two locations, with a new Montréal branch underway. Greer also navigated the company though the purchase of two game studios. Allowing Kongregate to develop proprietary games, Ultrabit was acquired in 2016 and Synapse in 2017.

Kongregate attracted so much attention, it was bought by industry giant GameStop in 2010, and then acquired by Modern Times Group in 2017. "Taking Kongregate through a sales process was challenging, first to Gamestop in 2010, then to Swedish media group MTG in 2017," said Greer. "It's incredibly high stakes: you're deciding the future of your company, convincing a buyer that your company is valuable, and wading through an intense amount of legal and financial minutiae in a relatively short period of time."

The focus on community is a major aspect of Kongregate's success. Greer's economy of points, unlockable badges, and medals encourages players to stay in their ecosystem and earn collectibles to show off in their profiles. Players can even unlock unique daily "Kongpanions"—cute animated creatures—to decorate their profile pages.

"I once had a Lyft driver who had every Kongregate Kongpanion in Shiny going back years, meaning that he'd logged on every single day for years to collect our achievement of the day," explained Greer. "I can't even imagine how many thousands of hours it represents. We had a great chat and I was able to send him some gifts."

Kongregate's success is global, too. "I went back to Hungary recently to visit my host family from when I was a teenager," said Greer. "I hadn't seen them since I started Kongregate and they didn't really know about it, but I found one of our games, *Burrito Bison: Launcha Libre*, installed on my host mother's phone by her grandson. I love that something I worked on reached into their lives and brought joy even when we'd fallen out of touch."

In the summer of 2018, Kongregate introduced Kartridge, a new PC gaming platform dedicated to indie developer success. Kartridge expands the platform beyond just browser and free or free-to-play games, as the indie scene is now often native, downloadable, and/or premium in nature. It offers developers of all sizes full control over their games—including determining their own pricing model and customizing the user experience within the framework. Kartridge continues the trend of social and community-rich features within Kongregate, and illustrates the staying power of a company continually evolving within a rapidly changing industry.

Although this isn't where Greer expected her life to take her, she's more involved in gaming now than ever before. As a visible leader and example of women in games and tech, she regularly speaks at conferences and on topics related to free-to-play game design and in-game economics. She is also a board member of the International Game Developer's Association.

> "I love that something I worked on [*Burrito Bison: Launcha Libre*] reached into their lives and brought joy even when we'd fallen out of touch."

With the video game landscape shifting to digital distribution and development becoming more accessible, Greer knows Kongregate has helped move the needle. "As a platform, Kongregate had a big impact on improving the treatment and expectations of Flash developers. Helping small independent developers all over the world succeed is great—I love sending small teams big checks."

Easter Egg

Started figure skating at age 30, and now competes at national competitions.

LAURA SHIGIHARA

FAN-FAVORITE COMPOSER, SONGWRITER, SINGER, AND GAME DEVELOPER

 supershigi

 projectrakuen.com
youtube.com/user/supershigi

EXPERIENCE

FIRST INDUSTRY PROJECT: WOBBLY BOBBLY (2007)

FAVORITE INDUSTRY PROJECT: RAKUEN (2017)

PROJECTS SHIPPED: 30+ GAMES

ACHIEVEMENTS UNLOCKED:

> GAME AUDIO NETWORK GUILD "BEST ORIGINAL VOCAL: POP" AWARD—PLANTS VS. ZOMBIES (2009)

> ROCK PAPER SHOTGUN "BEST GAMES OF 2017"—RAKUEN (2017)

> GAMESTAR.DE "GOLD STAR & STORY" AWARDS—RAKUEN (2017)

> INDEPENDENT GAMES FESTIVAL "EXCELLENCE IN NARRATIVE" HONORABLE MENTION—RAKUEN (2018)

STATS

INDUSTRY LEVEL: 11

CURRENT CLASS: FOUNDER & DEVELOPER

CURRENT GUILD: LEEBLE FOREST—USA

SPECIAL SKILLS: COMPOSING, SONGWRITING, SINGING, AUDIO DESIGN, GAME DESIGN, STORY WRITING

STANDARD EQUIPMENT

FAVORITE PLATFORM: SNES

GO-TO GENRE: STORY-DRIVEN GAMES

MUST-HAVE GAME: CHRONO TRIGGER

BIO

Laura Shigihara loved *Mega Man* growing up. Like, really, *really* loved *Mega Man*. "I would draw new boss robots and design different levels," began Shigihara. "I subscribed to the Capcom newsletter, and expanded on their short *Mega Man* comic by illustrating my own. I would also procrastinate my classical piano assignments in favor of either playing music from the game or composing alternative level themes!"

It was in these formative years that her love of video games and music converged, igniting a desire to work as a composer within the industry. "My parents were gracious enough to let me take piano lessons for most of my childhood. I was also able to take computer science classes in college," she explained. "Any music software I use for composing, arranging, or production, I learned by just diving into it and figuring it out by trial and error. I taught myself how to compose music and write songs. I've found that when you have a vision, and you really want to see it through, you become more resourceful and learn what you need to learn in order to get by."

Easter Egg
Was offered contracts as a singer-songwriter from two major record labels in Japan before working in video games.

Shigihara has spent the large majority of her career as a video game composer, primarily as an independent contractor. "Though I mostly created video game soundtracks, I became known for writing and performing songs for video games," she said. "My biggest challenge at the time was finding enough work to be able to make a living off of what I was doing. I supplemented my contract work with things like teaching piano to elementary school children. I took whatever video game composing jobs I could find in order to build my portfolio."

Her first official game gig was lead composer on TikGames' *Wobbly Bobbly* in 2007. She also began to regularly collaborate with Big Fish Games, contributing soundtracks and audio design to an assortment of their games such as *Mahjong Tales: Ancient Wisdom* and *Flower Shop: Big City Break*.

ZOMBIES ON YOUR LAWN

Shigihara got her own big break when working on PopCap's 2009 release of *Plants vs. Zombies*. She composed the entire soundtrack, doing both sound design and foley work for the wildly popular game. "I also wrote, produced, and performed the ending theme song 'Zombies on Your Lawn,' which was used to market the game," she shared. After the debut of her first vocal track, Shigihara became a hot commodity. She paid tribute to her *Plants vs. Zombies* character in 2010 as the voice of *World of Warcraft*'s singing sunflower pet.

In 2011, Shigihara wrote, produced, and performed the theme song "Everything's Alright" for Freebird Game's *To the Moon*. She also wrote, produced, and performed the theme song "First Day" for *High School Story* and, in 2012, co-created the ending theme song for the official *Minecraft* documentary.

Shigihara was selected to participate in a major anniversary event in 2015—the official Square Enix 20th Anniversary *Chrono Trigger* & *Chrono Cross* Arrangement album. "Also known as *Haruka Naru Toki no Kanata E*, this album was a joint effort between the original composer Yasunori Mitsuda and Square Enix to celebrate the 20th anniversary of these games," she explained. "For this album, I wrote lyrics, performed, and co-arranged three of the songs. The album peaked at #5 on the Oricon charts—the Japanese version of Billboard!" In total, Shigihara has worked on over 30 games and written 29 original songs.

Shigihara's enduring relationship with her fans has provided a stable foundation for her freelance work. She runs a YouTube channel where she posts original music, remixes, and covers of well-known video game songs. Her channel currently sits at nearly 120,000 subscribers, and is approaching 16 million views.

While Shigihara has enjoyed collaborating with developers on their visions, years of freelancing illustrated the inherent difficulty of the position. "It's definitely a challenge getting to a point where you can make a living as a video game composer; I noticed that I usually had to work extra hard in order to prove myself," she recalled. "Folks were pretty quick to dismiss what I had to say when I chimed in about audio software, production advice, or video game music in general. I had to actually make and ship my very own game before people would treat me as if I had any game design sense."

RAKUEN

That game would be her 2017 release, *Rakuen*. In 2012 Shigihara opened her own game studio, Leeble Forest. "When I set out to make *Rakuen*, I had several hopes for my little game," she explained. "I wanted to highlight the importance of empathy. I wanted to show that sometimes you can be a hero by just being there for someone, by listening to them, caring for them, and trying to understand them. I also saw a distinct lack of mothers in games, so I wanted 'Mom' to have a unique and important role in my game. Like so many other moms, she hides her own fears and struggles in order to make the world feel safe, whimsical, and full of warmth and joy for her hospitalized child."

Rakuen was the culmination of nearly a decade of work and learning through collaboration with companies big and small. Shigihara wrote the story, designed and programmed the game, contributed some of the in-game art, organized testing, wrote press releases, and of course, composed the soundtrack, implemented audio effects, and recorded voice tracks. "Without a doubt, making my own game was the most fulfilling thing I've done within the game industry," she said. "Besides wanting to make a game ever since I was a child, I was also very excited to tell this particular story. Prior to this, my role was always to bring someone else's vision to life, but for *Rakuen* I actually got to tell the story."

Total ownership goes hand-in-hand with high levels of responsibility, as Shigihara learned. "*Rakuen* was also the most difficult thing I've done in the industry. In a given day, I'd switch from coding a puzzle, to working on pixel art, to composing a character's theme, to writing a press release, to reading through spreadsheets where beta testers posted bugs," she detailed.

"I've found that when you have a vision, and you really want to see it through, you become more resourceful."

"Even though I tried to maintain a good work-life balance, during crunch time my health suffered a lot—my stress level was so high for an extended period of time, which eventually led to me getting an ulcer."

Looking back on this period, Shigihara said she'd definitely do it again, but this time armed with better tools to take care of her health. "I had no idea whether or not people would relate to the story, so I was very nervous putting it out there. But when folks wrote me talking about things like how the game made them want to be a better person, or how they were going through a time of depression and the game allowed them to feel things again... All that was so fulfilling. I still am truly thankful for the chance to make something like this."

Rakuen was extremely well-received. It made the "Best Games of 2017" list from *Rock Paper Shotgun*, received a 9.5/10 from *Polygon*, and has "overwhelmingly positive" reviews on Steam. It also nabbed an honorable mention for "Excellence in Narrative" from the 2018 Independent Games Festival.

Shigihara's emphasis on empathy in *Rakuen* is a culmination of her experiences getting to know others, both in person as well as through her online community. "I feel like these days, when it comes to human connection, the Internet is a double-edged sword. It helps us connect with others all around the world in ways we never could before, but I feel that at the same time, it's also making us feel more isolated," she said. "I've met a lot of people who feel cut off, and are lonely as a result of that isolation. I want to help enable people to experience connection with others, and to feel like they're a part of something. I wrote the dialogue and developed all the different stories within the game with the hope that players would walk away feeling inspired to be kind to others, and that they'd want to be the best people they could be."

A DAY IN THE LIFE OF...

A MARKETING MANAGER

Like many game-industry professions, marketing is both a science and an art. Effective marketers must be able to pull actionable insights from data gathered through business-intelligence channels, including industry and competitive trends, target-market research, and customer behavioral data.

Marketers use this information to craft informed and creative campaigns aimed to grow their brand awareness and reach potential new customers—referred to as user acquisition. This is done through paid advertisements; owned media such as websites, blogs, and social media; and organic word of mouth, called earned media. Marketers work closely with brand, public relations, and community-management stakeholders, as they all feed back into the same ecosystem.

With nearly two decades of marketing experience under her belt, Dana Cowley has called Epic Games home for over half her career. Cowley's primary focus is supporting Unreal Engine initiatives, but she's also been at Epic during the making of *Gears of War*, *Unreal Tournament*, *Shadow Complex*, *Paragon*, *SPYJINX*, *Battle Breakers*, and the international-phenomenon *Fortnite*.

DANA COWLEY

DanaCowley

Dana Cowley

PROFESSION: SENIOR MARKETING MANAGER AT EPIC GAMES—RALEIGH, USA

YEARS IN PROFESSION: 18

ASSOCIATED WITH: OCTAGON ENTERTAINMENT, MERSCOM, CLEARIMAGE, EPIC GAMES

▶ EDUCATION

"I earned my bachelor's degree in journalism and mass communication at the University of North Carolina at Chapel Hill. Although advertising was my degree concentration, my favorite class was newswriting. As I learned about the constructs of effective business writing and was taught how to fact-check and deliver on accuracy, I became hooked. Although I had no formal PR training, I was forced to think like a reporter, and that helped me when I took on a marketing and PR internship at a games company."

▶ KEY QUALITIES

"The top qualities I value in terms of marketing and communications include: the ability to intelligently articulate ideas and messages through written, verbal, and visual communications; an astute attention to detail and quality; and a temperament that can adapt to a wide range of social settings, e.g., being able to read a situation and knowing when to ask a question, when to be assertive with a thought, and when to sit back, observe, and learn from others."

▶ TOOLS OF THE TRADE

"At Epic, we use Google's enterprise suite, so that includes everything from Gmail to Google Drive, Docs, Sheets, Slides, and Hangouts. But not everyone uses Google products, so I'm often switching over to Microsoft Word, Excel, and PowerPoint in order to review and edit content. While we lean most heavily on Google Hangouts for calls and video conferencing, Skype is critical to have as well, as many journalists prefer to use it for recording capabilities during interviews.

"The engine marketing team uses Trello for tracking our content calendar, and more broadly, the engine team uses it to share the Unreal Engine 4 features roadmap with the development community. Slack is also useful for team and cross-team communications, especially when we're working on a release and coordinating to flip many switches at the same time as other people in the company.

"Lastly, we can't forget about social media. I'm frequently on Twitter, Facebook, and Instagram for work, and we're currently using a tool called Oktopost for publishing social content and reporting performance metrics."

▶ HOURS & ENVIRONMENT

"In terms of company culture, my observation is that Epic hires people who are really passionate about the types of products we build and how they can contribute to them. While we're all very devoted to what we do, the hours are flexible, and there's no cap on vacation or sick time. I'm usually in the office eight or nine hours a day in order to work with colleagues and to attend meetings, and am online some in the mornings and evenings. As for the physical workspace, our studios are nicely furnished, with many types of meeting spaces and kitchens that are stocked to the gills with popular food and beverages. We enjoy pizza and beer at company meetings and cater meals for lunch meetings and for those working during evening hours. Epic also provides a ton of employee perks, like an annual company picnic with all the bells and whistles, discounted tickets for sporting events, as well as stylish team apparel and merchandise."

▶ AN AVERAGE DAY

"My average day consists of checking email, attending meetings, communicating internally and externally, and overseeing content. A significant part of my time goes toward editorial and brand management, e.g., reviewing, editing, and approving written communications for tone and style, and checking over creative imagery to ensure it meets our visual standards."

▶ PROFESSIONAL PERKS

"What I find to be most rewarding is being able to see new projects, new technologies, and new paradigms take shape behind the scenes. I thrive on watching our team create what doesn't yet exist, and being able to help tell that story, and to help others understand how they can benefit from what we're making. For example, we offer Unreal Engine as a free download, and thousands of games have been made with it. We also build *Fortnite* and the improvements we make for the game go back into the engine for the 6.5 million people and counting who've chosen to license the engine. Beyond games, though, people use Unreal to train autonomous vehicles, to prepare astronauts for space, and even develop new pharmaceutical drugs using virtual reality."

▶ CAREER CHALLENGES

"There's a high signal-to-noise ratio in marketing, especially when you're in management in a busy company. Planning and prioritization require great focus because it's easy to slip into reactive mode when you're on the front lines of communication."

▶ FAVORITE PROJECT

"At Epic, just before we released Unreal Engine 4 for free in 2015, we launched a program called Unreal Dev Grants. It's a $5 million fund designed to reward outstanding work in and around Unreal. Individual grants range from $5000 to $50,000 with no strings attached. The funds are meant to give people in the Unreal community the means to achieve even more success. We've awarded grants to all sorts of individuals and teams, from independent game developers to filmmakers. Our earliest rounds of grants went toward projects that were fairly unheard of at the time but are now widely recognized and critically acclaimed or highly anticipated for release. A few independent games we've awarded Unreal Dev Grants to include *Astroneer*, *Planet Alpha*, *Moss*, *Dead Static Drive*, and *The Artful Escape*. It's hard to describe how humbling and rewarding it feels to be in a position to give back to our community."

▶ LIFE HACKS

"Be protective of time. I regularly schedule appointments in my work calendar for specific tasks and deadlines, because otherwise those precious little windows may get booked. In addition, I avoid holding meetings for the sake of holding meetings. When syncs happen, an agenda and a defined output should be shared in advance so that everyone can be prepared and make the most of time together. Time is money and a lot of people want a bite of your time, so it's important to consciously decide how to spend it every day."

PRO TIP!

"When it comes to marketing a game or technology, there's no such thing as a one-size-fits-all approach. Get to know your product and the team behind it. Learn how to be an active listener and ask thoughtful, open-ended questions. Be able to articulate the value of the product and what makes it stand out. Do your competitive research and validate where it fits in the market—again and again—because the games industry moves fast, and change is the one constant you can count on.

"Validate your target audience and understand where they go to consume content and make buying decisions. Solicit feedback in channels where your users want to engage with you, whether it be over social media, Twitch, Discord, forums, email, and other messaging platforms or even in person at events. Document the phrases and takeaways that stick or are repeated—both positive and negative—and work with your team to strengthen your product and its reputation based on that feedback. Test ideas for marketing your product early with small audiences and lean into the content that yields the most positive results."

GISELLE ROSMAN

"AUNTY" TO THE AUSTRALIAN GAMES INDUSTRY

 jazzrozz

 IGDA Melbourne (Group)
Global Game Jam

 Giselle Rosman

EXPERIENCE

FIRST INDUSTRY PROJECT: MELBOURNE GLOBAL GAME JAM (2011)

FAVORITE INDUSTRY PROJECT: CROSSY ROAD (2014)

PROJECTS SHIPPED: 2 GAMES, 8 LOCAL GAME JAMS, 60 REGIONAL GAME JAMS, AND 1331 GLOBAL GAME JAMS

ACHIEVEMENTS UNLOCKED:

> MICROSOFT WOMEN IN GAMING "PIONEER AWARD" NOMINEE (2014)

> MCV PACIFIC "WOMAN OF THE YEAR" AWARD (2015)

> MCV PACIFIC "WOMAN OF THE YEAR" AWARD (2016)

> XBOX AUSTRALIA "SHINING STAR" AWARD (2017)

STATS

INDUSTRY LEVEL: 11

CURRENT CLASS: CHAPTER LEAD, REGIONAL ORGANIZER & BUSINESS ADMINISTRATOR

CURRENT GUILD: IGDA MELBOURNE, GLOBAL GAME JAM, HIPSTER WHALE—MELBOURNE, AUSTRALIA

SPECIAL SKILLS: EVENT MANAGEMENT, GAME DEVELOPMENT, PUBLIC RELATIONS, PUBLIC SPEAKING, COMMUNITY MANAGEMENT, PROJECT MANAGEMENT

STANDARD EQUIPMENT

FAVORITE PLATFORM: PLAYSTATION

GO-TO GENRE: PARTY GAMES

MUST-HAVE GAME: JOURNEY

BIO

Giselle Rosman has facilitated the creation of somewhere between two and 14,000 games, give or take. Through her coordination of the Global Game Jam on a local, regional, and eventually worldwide stage, she has provided the framework and resources for thousands of developers—both veteran and aspiring—to collaborate, educate, and innovate.

"I started out in games as an over-30 mother of two young children, looking to get out of the house and get back into working," began Rosman. "A good friend was the head of school at a local games college. I started as the receptionist, and became the marketing manager when the role was vacated. This was 2008. Things were not good for the Australian games industry then."

Rosman remembers how the global financial crisis gutted the Australian games industry, which she recounts as having shrunk to 30% of what it once was. "During that time I, along with some colleagues, rebooted the Melbourne chapter of the International Game Developers Association (IGDA)," she continued. "As a college marketing manager, I'd spent time building relationships with the 'industry.' That industry was broken and hurting. The first meetup we ran, in November 2009, was more like a wake than a celebration."

"The timing of the release of the iPhone was a life raft for local game development," she recalled. "It allowed developers to pivot into smaller teams on a new platform. Had those two elements not coincided, I have no idea what the local games industry would look like, or even if we'd still have anything worth mentioning." Rosman has continued to run monthly meetups since 2009 and says that's how she became known as "Melbourne's gamedev aunty."

"The timing of the release of the iPhone was a life raft for local game development."

IGDA MELBOURNE

While the moniker "aunty" conveys the affinity that the Australian game-developer community feels for Rosman, her actual titles are a bit more formal. Rosman became the director of the IGDA Melbourne chapter in 2009, and over the past nine years has championed the local development community at every opportunity. She has worked to expand business prospects, develop the communication and networking infrastructure through social media, and facilitate relationships with internal and external stakeholders. The latter has included government branches and Film Victoria, which she advised on their independent game-developer financial-support model. She has also arranged networking and social events to help with the morale of local talent after major studio closures.

In 2011, Rosman began the Melbourne Global Game Jam, an annual, collaborative game design event that enables small groups to rapidly develop experimental games. Coordinating her first jam required attention from top to bottom, securing sponsorships, volunteers, catering, and organizing all other logistics needed to host dozens of people for 48 hours straight. "For our first jam we had 70 game developers who created 23 games in 48 hours," she explained. "In 2012, it grew to 107 participants and 30 games. By 2018, this had ballooned to 309 jammers making 94 games."

Easter Egg

Died as a baby after being born premature with severe complications. After resuscitation, she lived in and out of hospitals for the first few years of life. Coming from a family of nurses, she was later told that survival rates for premature babies are higher among girls than boys, instilling the strongly held belief that her gender is a strength, not a weakness.

After her first successful jam, Rosman moved up to regional organizer for the 2013 Global Game Jam, responsible for assessing and approving game jam sites across Australia and New Zealand, and providing them all the information and support they needed to be successful. She also accepted a position as an executive committee member and a board member the following year.

Rosman's regional influence continued throughout 2013 as event manager for the multi-day industry event Game Connect Asia Pacific. She was tasked with coordinating speakers, sponsors, and curating the event to fit the most pressing needs of the local game-development community. Part of this duty involved arranging the Australian Game Developer Awards from inception, all the way through judging.

GOING GLOBAL

After her successful run of local and regional events, Rosman accepted the role of executive producer for the entire Global Game Jam organization in 2015. "I coordinated over 630 sites across 93 countries and managed a 750-person Slack team to ensure a successful event," she said. "The Global Game Jam 2016 was the largest event ever of its kind and saw substantial growth on previous years, including being held in 12 countries for the first time." According to Rosman, the participant count came in at over 30,000 individuals worldwide.

The event was not only demanding from a time and organizational standpoint, but a physical one as well. "Running a game jam in 93 countries simultaneously takes the cake," she joked. "A 48-hour game jam becomes about 80 hours when they all start at 5 pm local time Friday and finish 5 pm Sunday. Rocking that weekend with an amazing executive team and a legion of helpers is a frightening and glorious thing."

As a unique occasion to make an impact on a truly global scale, Rosman notes the global role as one of the most memorable experiences of her life. "When working as the executive producer, I had the opportunity to 'meet' people from all over the world, all passionate about game creation," she said. "It's given me mad respect for the importance of localization, along with an appreciation of game mechanics being a universal language."

HIPSTER WHALE

Simultaneous to her work with the Global Game Jam, Rosman sought an opportunity to get her hands dirty in a more direct way within the Australian games scene. In 2015 she took the role of business administrator at Melbourne-based game studio Hipster Whale, creators of the retro-inspired, endless runner *Crossy Road*.

"I joined the team at Hipster Whale about three months after *Crossy Road*'s release," explained Rosman. "With 10 million downloads in the first three months, it was like jumping onto a moving train. The highlights definitely include the letters from young players. The suggestions for characters are always wonderful, and the handwritten letters and drawings sent all the way to Australia from all over the world are inspiring."

The success of *Crossy Road* resulted in a collaboration with Disney Interactive Studios on the spin-off game *Disney Crossy Road*. It launched in 2016, and now includes over 440 Disney characters. "As a massive Pixar fan, working with Disney and Pixar on *Disney Crossy Road* was... Well, I entered the fangirl realm when on a video conference call with Pixar artists, tweaking the work we'd done and making their magic," she laughed. "They make it look all so easy! I also had the chance to visit Pixar and make my children very jealous."

With a run of extremely successful years behind her, Rosman's work has been recognized in a big way. She won *MCV Pacific*'s "Woman of the Year Award" in 2015, and was a finalist in every other award category. She took home the same award in 2016, and earned Xbox Australia's "Shining Star" award in 2017.

Rosman is proud to see how much the Australian game industry has grown since the financial crisis. "There's been a lot of changes over the last decade. We've gone from siloed studios creating largely mid-level games to a very indie industry, with several bigger players." Rosman's work centralizing and championing the game-development industry throughout Australia has undoubtedly helped facilitate its success.

KARISMA WILLIAMS

USER EXPERIENCE & USABILITY ADVOCATE

 Matimeo

 matimeo.com

EXPERIENCE

FIRST INDUSTRY PROJECT: CHARLIE AND THE CHOCOLATE FACTORY (2005)

FAVORITE INDUSTRY PROJECT: FORZA MOTORSPORT 6 (2016)

PROJECTS SHIPPED: 3 PLATFORMS, 1 OPERATING SYSTEM, 16 GAMES

ACHIEVEMENTS UNLOCKED:

> GUINNESS WORLD RECORD FOR "MOST CONTESTANTS IN A GAME SHOW"—1 VS. 100 (2009)

> GUINNESS WORLD RECORD FOR "FASTEST-SELLING CONSUMER ELECTRONICS DEVICE"—KINECT (2010)

> BAFTA AWARD NOMINATION "BEST FAMILY GAME"—KINECT ADVENTURES (2011)

> BAFTA AWARD NOMINATION "BEST SPORTS GAME"—FORZA MOTORSPORT 6 (2016)

STATS

INDUSTRY LEVEL: 10

CURRENT CLASS: PRODUCT UI/UX DESIGNER & TECHNICAL PROGRAM MANAGER

CURRENT GUILD: MICROSOFT

SPECIAL SKILLS: RESPONSIVE DESIGN, AUGMENTED REALITY INTERFACE RESEARCH, USER INTERFACE DESIGN, PRODUCTION, USABILITY, DEVELOPING UI TOOLS

STANDARD EQUIPMENT

FAVORITE PLATFORM: PC

GO-TO GENRE: RACING & FIGHTING GAMES

MUST-HAVE GAME: SUPER MARIO BROS.

BIO

Karisma Williams is one of those lucky few who knew almost instinctually what she wanted to do when she grew up—work in video games. "I think this was largely subconscious from the time I was around eight years old, and became much more of a focused goal by the time I was in college," said Williams. Having taught herself web programming and the fundamental principles of design in high school, she enrolled in college as a dual major in graphic design and multimedia. Williams didn't know where she would fit in the industry and initially thought that designing marketing materials would be the best use of her skills. Once she discovered user interface design, however, she had found her true calling.

Although she was qualified and driven, breaking into the industry was difficult for Williams. "The industry is very insular, and back then there was no LinkedIn. The industry also has the caveat of wanting to hire people who have shipped a product; however, everyone at some point has never shipped anything," she said, highlighting the paradox.

Williams' skill set and persistence eventually led to a job, and she quickly realized that the ability to adapt was a valuable trait in what could be an unpredictable industry. "I was initially hired to be a web designer and developer at my first game industry job. Within weeks that changed to motion-capture artist, which I had no knowledge of even existing prior to joining the team," she said, speaking to her work on *BioShock* and *Stubbs the Zombie*. Williams learned to help run the motion-capture equipment during shoots, as well help clean up motion-capture data, which was then sent to animators for polish.

In 2008, after some time at High Voltage Software, THQ, and Valve, Williams made the jump to Microsoft. Brought on as a technical UI/UX designer, she collaborated with the Xbox Live Prime Time team on the console's user experience, user interface, and visuals, as the platform didn't have a design in place to support scheduled entertainment.

"[1 vs. 100] really helped redefine how the industry viewed 'gamers.'"

The scheduled entertainment that needed support was *1 vs. 100*, a live game show that showcased the potential in the Xbox Live platform to bring people together. Williams was integral to the game's creation. "It's meaningful because it was something that had never been done before. The North American version of the game surpassed the Guinness World Record for 'most contestants in a game show,' with over 114,000 simultaneous players," she explained. "It had the ability to reach both core and non-gamers, making it a rare product for its time of release. It really impacted those who played and is still talked about today by gamers in various online forums. It was a project that really helped redefine how the industry viewed 'gamers' and what type of experiences they would be open to."

KINECT ADVENTURES

An exciting new challenge was just over the horizon for Williams, in the form of entirely new technology—the Kinect. Designed for the Xbox 360, the device tracked players' body movement with a special camera, allowing them to interact with games in a new way. Williams was part of the team that worked on launch titles for the peripheral, as well as the Kinect Fun Labs platform.

"Having to design around a new interaction model with no fallback to controller was incredibly challenging," said Williams, speaking to her work on *Kinect Adventures*. "The project also had huge dependencies on the platform team, who we hoped to follow as far as interaction design, with a tight schedule aligned with new hardware. It also was the first time many people on the team had worked on a game that was less focused on core and more focused on 'family timers,' a new market segment Microsoft was interested in tapping into post-Nintendo's success with the Wii."

That technology—although challenging to successfully develop for—had the ability to engage often overlooked audiences. "A participant noted that they probably could not play due to their physical impairment," recalled Williams, recounting one of *Kinect Adventures'* playtesting sessions. "The excitement shown when the first participant realized they could control the game with their hands was magical and is something I will never forget. Many of us take for granted holding a controller, often forgetting it's not physically possible for everyone, but that doesn't mean we can't build meaningful experiences for them as well. I imagine many times the first participant had been told they couldn't do things, and I hoped the moment was also life-changing for them to never stop trying."

Easter Egg

Is a huge fan of game manuals, and was featured in the manual for Kinect Adventures, playing the Kinect.

FORZA

Outside of *1 vs. 100* and the Kinect's industry impact, Williams found her most personally fulfilling work on a mega-popular racing franchise—*Forza*. The series boasts loads of unlocks and customization, and as such, required extensive work on its menus and a careful eye on the in-game HUD to keep the player's focus on the road. "I had a rare opportunity to do everything from design to development of the UI, which allowed me to utilize my entire skill set I have been developing over the years," said Williams. "I was also proud to be part of bringing the franchise to PC for the first time. Forza is also a series I enjoy playing, and it is rare to get to work on a product you also enjoy as a consumer."

Williams now additionally develops tools and applications that help to streamline the production of products. Branching out from gaming, she assisted Microsoft as a senior experience developer on the Windows Phone 8.1 OS and on Microsoft's mixed reality "smartglasses," HoloLens.

It was during this short break from gaming that Williams was able to take a step back and reflect on the nature of the industry. Her mother passed away when she was quite young, and as such, she and her brothers were raised by her father. "The industry felt comfortable to me, as I was used to being the 'only woman' most of my life. My perception has changed mostly due to awareness over time," reflected Williams. "Not until much later in my career—during a break from gaming while working on the Windows Phone, which had a very balanced team of men and women of various backgrounds—did I realize how odd the gaming industry tended to be."

"I know that by allowing myself to be somewhat visible, I am inspiring others like me."

Although she often prefers to stay low-key and avoid public events, Williams knows that in addition to her design work, being visible also makes an impact. "I know that by allowing myself to be somewhat visible, I am inspiring others like me," she said. "I hope other young women see me and can see themselves and know that there is a place for them in the industry as well."

With nearly 15 years of industry work behind her, Williams is motivated by the desire to inspire others the way she was inspired when she was little—she understands the rarity of living out a childhood dream. "It really is amazing to help contribute to products that are like the games I enjoyed as a kid. Games had a positive impact on me, and I know that games I have worked on have had a positive impact on many others."

ASHLY BURCH

ANTAGONISTIC SIBLING & EMMY WINNER

Ashly_Burch

AshlyBurch

ashlyburch.com

EXPERIENCE

FIRST INDUSTRY PROJECT: HEY ASH, WHATCHA PLAYIN'? (2008)

FAVORITE INDUSTRY PROJECT: CHLOE—LIFE IS STRANGE (2015) & ALOY—HORIZON ZERO DAWN (2017)

PROJECTS SHIPPED: 125 HAWP EPISODES & 33 GAMES

ACHIEVEMENTS UNLOCKED:

> GOLDEN JOYSTICK AWARDS "PERFORMANCE OF THE YEAR"—CHLOE, LIFE IS STRANGE (2015)

> PRIMETIME EMMY AWARDS "OUTSTANDING SHORT FORM ANIMATED PROGRAM"—ADVENTURE TIME (2016)

> GOLDEN JOYSTICK AWARDS "BEST GAMING PERFORMANCE" AND "BREAKOUT PERFORMANCE"—ALOY, HORIZON ZERO DAWN (2017)

> PLAYSTATION BLOG GAME OF THE YEAR AWARDS "BEST PERFORMANCE"—ALOY, HORIZON ZERO DAWN (2018)

STATS

CURRENT CLASS: VOICE ACTOR & WRITER

INDUSTRY LEVEL: 10

GUILD: UNION TALENT—LOS ANGELES, CA

SKILLS: WRITING, VOICE ACTING, BAKING, ROGUELIKES

STANDARD EQUIPMENT

FAVORITE PLATFORM: NINTENDO SWITCH & PLAYSTATION 4

GO-TO GENRE: VIDEO GAMES

MUST-HAVE GAME: MASS EFFECT 2, SPELUNKY, & HARVEST MOON 64

BIO

"I poured apple juice on my head while re-enacting one of my brother's real-life memories," said award-winning voice actress Ashly Burch, recalling her early industry work. "I was wearing a fake beard from Party City. It was weird." All of that "weirdness" kick-started a career for Burch, in which she would be inundated with "Best Performance" awards for bringing to life a cast of complex and nuanced characters.

Burch first became aware of voice-acting as a potential career path after spotting something unusual in the 1998 title *Metal Gear Solid*. "The text would have the character's name—i.e.: Solid Snake—and then another name underneath it. In this case, David Hayter." At the time, she didn't understand the significance of the second name. "I researched David Hayter and discovered that he was, of course, the actor that provided Snake's voice. It suddenly hit me that putting your voice in games and cartoons was an actual job that I could have! From that point on, I decided I wanted to be a voice actor."

HAWP

Before establishing herself in the world of voice-over work, Burch detoured into a long and successful run creating episodic online content. In 2008—before the web experienced an avalanche of original programming—Burch and her brother Anthony debuted *Hey Ash, Whatcha Playin'?* The low-budget comedy series about video games quickly gained popularity. "We actually started making HAWP because my brother wanted to learn how to use a camera," explained Burch. "His original goal was to make a documentary about independent game developers, but he didn't have much experience with filmmaking, so he wanted to use HAWP as a fun exercise so that he could learn. Unexpectedly, HAWP became our focus and sent us both off on our respective career paths."

Burch played a dramatically exaggerated version of herself in HAWP, embracing prevalent gamer stereotypes and antagonizing her brother for entertainment, and occasionally for social commentary.

> "It suddenly hit me that putting your voice in games and cartons was an actual job that I could have!"

The series was picked up by GameTrailers TV in 2009, and the large built-in audience skyrocketed their success even further. Over the period of 125 episodes, the show acted as informal training for Burch's current career. "If starting a web series wherein I down a bottle of fiber and then poop in my brother's bed can be considered formal training, then yes. If you have actual standards, then no—I haven't had any formal training," said Burch, discussing her transition to voice-acting. "It definitely helped me get over some of the self-consciousness of performing and having my work received by an audience. We created so many episodes and were immediately treated to unfiltered, often brutal responses to our content from thousands of people. You learn at a certain point that about five of those critical comments are worth listening to, and you filter out the rest."

Easter Egg
Once confused Hideo Kojima by trying to tell him she loved *Metal Gear Solid* in broken and awkward Japanese.

CHLOE PRICE

Burch's investment in comedy paid off with one of her first major voice-acting gigs—Tiny Tina, *Borderlands 2*'s explosives-obsessed teenager. Although she got her foot in the industry through bizarre and often self-deprecating humor, before long Burch was taking on more emotional and mature roles. She brought believable angst to Chloe Price from *Life is Strange*, in a game that explored grief, depression, and even suicide. Her portrayal earned her untold accolades but, more importantly, gave an authentic voice to youth who could relate to the trials Chloe faced.

"Strangely, I didn't find that transition very challenging. Well, maybe it's not so strange. I've heard before that comedy is harder to do than drama, so if you can do the latter, then you can definitely do the former," explained Burch, noting the difficulty of honing comedic timing and voice. "It's also much more subjective, so it's harder to teach. It's more of a personal craft. Whereas, in my experience, drama tends to tap into the universal. Even if I don't express sadness the exact same way as someone else, they can identify it and feel it in a performance. Comedy takes you more by surprise."

A NEW HORIZON

More recently, Burch brought *Horizon Zero Dawn*'s Aloy to life with equal commitment to her craft. "Creating Aloy in *Horizon Zero Dawn* was a deeply collaborative process between myself, the team, and my director Jamie Mortellaro. It was important to me—as it was, of course, to the entire team—that Aloy was a compelling and memorable character. So I found myself voicing my opinion, asking questions, and disagreeing with my director more than I had with any other character I voiced." Burch worried that her intensity would position her as "difficult to work with," but the end result benefited from her strong perspective on the character.

"It was hard for me to advocate for my viewpoints without feeling like I was overstepping my bounds. But again, that concern was entirely in my head," she said. "The team was absolutely supportive of my contributions and my viewpoints, and the result is a character that we're all tremendously proud of. The process of finding Aloy turned out to also be a process of me finding my own confidence and security in my craft."

Burch has now lent her voice to over 30 video games, including Ray in *Fortnite*, Nebula in *Guardians of the Galaxy*, Cassie Cage in *Mortal Kombat X*, and Chun-Li in *Marvel vs. Capcom: Infinite*. Her work outside of voice-acting is equally celebrated. Burch was part of the writing team that took home an Emmy in 2016 for their work on *Adventure Time*.

"I think Chloe has made many folks feel seen and Aloy has made many of them feel strong."

Burch's defining roles thus far have helped the video game industry move away from the altruistic but one-dimensional "strong female protagonist" roles, to real-world representations of complex human characters—a trend she hopes will continue. "Chloe and Aloy are both extremely rich female characters that have a depth and nuance that is sometimes rarely seen in games. I think Chloe has made many folks feel seen and Aloy has made many of them feel strong."

A DAY IN THE LIFE OF...

CONSUMER PRODUCTS & E-COMMERCE

Consumer products and e-commerce are big business in video games, providing players the opportunity to showcase their fandom while creating additional revenue streams to augment game sales. Wearable gaming gear, toys, art, and other geek goods have gone mainstream in the past decade. Creating high-quality products, maintaining intuitive commerce portals, and ensuring customer support is responsive requires the commitment of dedicated teams.

Before interning at Blizzard Entertainment, Monika Lee already had an understanding of the fundamentals of e-commerce through her successful cosplay brand. Now working with some of the biggest franchises in gaming, Lee has helped redesign and launch the new Blizzard Gear Store, assists with daily maintenance and upkeep of the site, and supports marketing for all consumer products launch campaigns.

MONIKA LEE

MnikaLee

Monika Lee
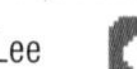
London2191

Monika Lee

PROFESSION: ASSOCIATE E-COMMERCE MERCHANDISER FOR CONSUMER PRODUCTS AT BLIZZARD ENTERTAINMENT—IRVINE, USA

YEARS IN PROFESSION: 5

ASSOCIATED WITH/WORKED ON: BLIZZARD ENTERTAINMENT

▶ EDUCATION

"I went to Georgia Tech for industrial design, which is essentially product design. A lot of my education involved the entire product process from conception, research, manufacturing to marketing and market research. Two of my summers at Georgia Tech were spent doing internships for my current team at Blizzard, which was then known as Licensing and Business Development. I didn't learn much about licensing in school, but my internships were definitely a crash course in this.

"It wasn't until I started full-time that I worked more in e-commerce, which is my current focus at work. However, I had some prior experience with e-commerce running my own small business online and at events for my cosplay."

▶ BREAKING IN

"To be honest, I didn't have that much trouble. I feel really fortunate to have gotten my internships, and from those, I was able to make meaningful relationships with my team. I think without my internships, I wouldn't be where I am now. The biggest thing I find people have a hard time capturing is fitting in with company culture, and with video games there's another layer of culture to relate to. Culture fit is really important in terms of work ethic and overall personality. In any job, it's the kind of thing that elevates you above other applicants who are able to perform a job, but can't quite fit in as well."

▶ EARLY INDUSTRY IMPRESSIONS

"I think it was all that I expected and more. I was most surprised at how easy it was to fit in, though I think part of this is just the Blizzard culture and how accepting and welcoming the employees are here. It's really awesome being able to mingle with other people in the industry, though, because everyone seems to have a similar hardworking work ethic and a huge passion for games and whatever projects they work on. It's rare to come across someone in the industry who dislikes what they're doing or is apathetic about their work."

▶ KEY QUALITIES

"Since licensing and the consumer products business are very front-facing—serving customers, working with licensees, retail partners, and others—it's definitely important to be able to socialize professionally, and be mindful of the culture fit I mentioned previously. My work environment is very casual, while being pretty motivated and focused on the task at hand. We're especially collaborative since everyone on our team has a role in the product-development process."

▶ TRAINING OPPORTUNITIES

"For licensing, there's a huge show called the Licensing Show in Vegas every year where licensors and licensees gather for business meetings and to learn about new and upcoming IPs. It's pretty insane how big that world is. For e-commerce, there are a variety of conferences depending on what platforms you use, and even within those platforms, there are tons of help guides and tutorials for optimizing your work."

▶ TOOLS OF THE TRADE

"Since I'm in e-commerce, I'm usually computer-bound and typically on the digital backend of our store, managing things."

▶ HOURS & ENVIRONMENT

"I work pretty typical office hours: 9am to 5pm, five days a week. Because the nature of my work is public-facing, I'm always 'on-call' for any incidents. From my experience, the Blizzard work culture is pretty relaxed, but it can also be 'work hard, play hard.'"

▶ AN AVERAGE DAY

"An average day for me usually involves a few meetings to sync with our franchise publishing teams or to kick off upcoming promotions we have planned. I do a lot of planning for upcoming product launches, managing our calendar and monitoring or performing daily maintenance on our Gear Store."

▶ PROMOTIONAL PATH

"Our team is a bit unique in that we're a consumer products business within the overall Blizzard business. This means we have a manufacturing team, e-commerce, events, designers, category managers, among others. On our e-commerce team, there are a few of us with roles/responsibilities that overlap. Like most businesses, responsibilities and direct reports increase as you get promoted."

"Get really familiar with trends in both pop culture and overall consumer products. Understanding what properties or types of brands are popular can help a lot with marketing your brand and understanding your consumer and what they like."

▶ PROFESSIONAL PERKS

"Getting to work various events, interacting with customers, and just making cool swag in general is the best part of what I do. The majority of people on our team are huge fans of all our games, so we always nerd out when we get to make cool things. Personal favorites of mine from last year were the Murloc kigurumi and Overwatch Rikimaru ramen bowl."

▶ CAREER CHALLENGES

"We're constantly striving to be the best within the consumer products business in entertainment, not just video games. This means staying up-to-date with business and entertainment trends, as well as understanding your key audience. It fluctuates a lot, and you have to be able to react accordingly."

▶ FAVORITE PROJECT

"I'd say most of our team is really into BlizzCon. It's where we really get to engage with our fan base, and a lot of our passion projects in consumer products get to debut there. It's a massive effort between our team in setting up the event, getting product delivered, supporting from an e-commerce/online point—for those who can't be there physically—and creating fun activities for our fans."

▶ LIFE HACKS

"I try to be really diligent about tracking through calendars what I need to get done. For me, establishing processes for all my work really ensures I don't miss a beat, and ensures that the result is quality every time. On top of that, visibility is a major thing here. I want to make sure my coworkers get eyeballs on the things I'm doing, and that there are proper approvals for everything so that nothing comes as a surprise."

ANNA ANTHROPY

DESIGNER OF PLAY

Adult_Witch 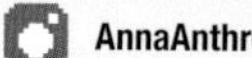 AnnaAnthropy

 w.itch.io

EXPERIENCE

FIRST INDUSTRY PROJECT: ZZT GAMES (1990s)

FAVORITE INDUSTRY PROJECT: LESBIAN SPIDER-QUEENS OF MARS (2011)

PROJECTS SHIPPED: 100 GAMES

ACHIEVEMENTS UNLOCKED:

> INDIECADE "GAME CHANGER AWARD" (2013)

> VGA GALLERY'S "GLOBAL ILLUMINATION AWARD" (2017)

> IGF "EXCELLENCE IN NARRATIVE" FINALIST (2013)

STATS

INDUSTRY LEVEL: 10

CURRENT CLASS: GAME DESIGNER IN RESIDENCE & AUTHOR

GUILD: DEPAUL'S COLLEGE OF COMPUTING AND DIGITAL MEDIA—CHICAGO, USA

SPECIAL SKILLS: DESIGN, CREATIVE WRITING, CASTING HEXES

STANDARD EQUIPMENT

FAVORITE PLATFORM: PAPER

GO-TO GENRE: TABLETOP ROLE-PLAYING

MUST-HAVE GAME: COCKROACH POKER

BIO

"I think that making a hundred tiny, horrible games is probably the best game design education you can have," began experimental game designer Anna Anthropy. "Everything I know about game design is self-taught."

Anthropy's informal education and career trajectory were established at a young age. "When I was little, I used to buy game magazines and cut the characters out into little paper dolls so I could play game designer." The discovery of *ZZT*—a 1991 MS-DOS title that included a game editor—allowed her imagination to expand in a new way. *ZZT* provided Anthropy, without extensive technical knowledge, the building blocks she needed to bring her games to life. After discovering a similar tool in 2003—*Game Maker*—her future as an experimental game designer solidified.

Anthropy's first game—*Jaywalker: The Game of Pedestrian Revenge*—encouraged chaos by walking blindly into busy intersections. Over 100 games later, Anthropy's body of work is nearly impossible to describe because it is so varied in themes, genres, and mechanics. If anything provides insight into Anthropy's work, it's the views she holds on the AAA industry. Her work—intentionally the antithesis of big-budget, mass-market games—is fueled by "anger and resentment at what games have been tortured into becoming."

Even with triple-digit games under her belt, Anthropy feels she hasn't broken into the industry in a traditional sense. "I did a lot of weird experimental work that I was occasionally able to leverage into freelance projects and book deals," she explained. One of her first freelance projects explored the idea of being "always on." "Giant Robot's Eric Nakamura's San Francisco-based art gallery wanted to pair independent game designers with some of their artists to create playable works to run alongside *Game Over / Continue*, a video game-themed art show," she explained. "I was paired with Saelee Oh, who does a lot of really beautiful cutout art, especially of nature and sea life."

Easter Egg
Has a cat who draws Tarot cards for her.

Designing for the 2009 exhibit, Anthropy expected players to ebb and flow through the space, handing off controllers in the process. The resulting game was *Octopounce*. "If someone put down their controller, their character—a cute floral octopus, based on Saelee's character design—would just fall asleep and start drifting with the currents," she said.

> "As a marginalized person, people will talk endlessly about what an important voice you are in games, how your work is pushing the medium forward, but will rarely want to pay money for that work."

"Other players could bounce off their heads to catch fish and birds. Designing for a venue is so much more interesting than designing for the home: there's so many facets of the experience to consider."

Anthropy designed her largest commercial project for a popular adult-oriented cartoon block in 2011. "My biggest industry break was selling my gonzo B-movie pulp arcade game, *Lesbian Spider-Queens of Mars*, to Adult Swim in 2011. They pushed back on a lot of things. The game featured tits, themes of kink and consensual power exchange, and, scandalously, had the word 'lesbian' in the title. That was the one thing I wouldn't budge on—I wouldn't let them change it."

GETTING PERSONAL

Relationships, romance, and sex are common themes in Anthropy's work. The short puzzle game *Triad* tasks the player with fitting three lovers in a bed in a way that lets them all sleep comfortably. The added challenge comes from catering to each participant's unique sleeping requirements. *Duck Duck Poison*—another exhibit-based experiment—is playable with controllers embedded in oversized bras by pressing on mechanical nipples.

Queers in Love at the End of the World is an experience that ends in 10 seconds. The player attempts to convey the love they feel for their partner through selecting hyperlink choices in a wall of text. With the seconds ticking down until "everything is wiped away," they can choose to kiss or hold their partner, take her hand, or tell her something. Each option branches out into new choices, but the world ends before they can truly say goodbye. Replaying the game results in further progression, but trades deliberate, meaningful choices for furious clicking.

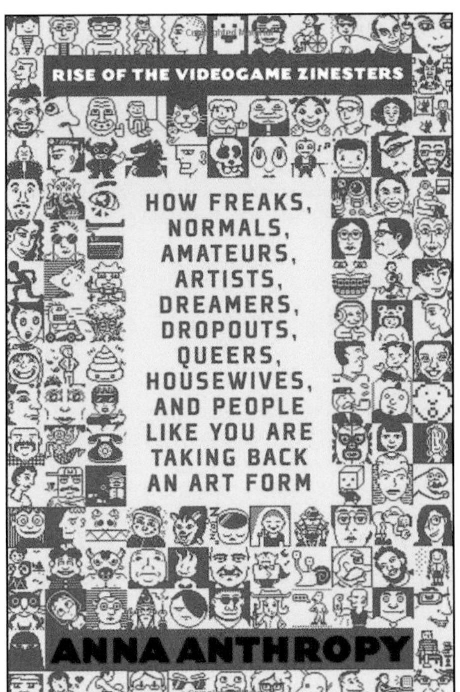
RISE OF THE VIDEOGAME ZINESTERS
HOW FREAKS, NORMALS, AMATEURS, ARTISTS, DREAMERS, DROPOUTS, QUEERS, HOUSEWIVES, AND PEOPLE LIKE YOU ARE TAKING BACK AN ART FORM
ANNA ANTHROPY

ZINESTERS

Anthropy's 2012 book, *Rise of the Videogame Zinesters: How Freaks, Normals, Amateurs, Artists, Dreamers, Drop-outs, Queers, Housewives, and People Like You Are Taking Back an Art Form,* explores her vision of the future. "The only real change and growth in the industry can come from non-professionals, people outside of games culture and without backgrounds in technology and programming, making their own personal games with accessible tools."

Shortly after *Rise of the Videogame Zinesters* was published, one of these accessible tools—Twine, the open-source software that allows for the easy creation of interactive fiction—hit peak popularity. Indie distribution site itch.io wasn't far behind, and Anthropy believes there are now more small games made by hobbyist authors than ever before.

Rewarding as this influx of experimental and intimate games may be, Anthropy argues that it hasn't actually become any easier to make money in experimental game design. She frequently feels the value placed on her voice as a marginalized designer doesn't translate to money in the bank. "When I was young, I thought celebrity and notoriety implied financial success, or at least stability. Working in games dispelled that illusion for me," said Anthropy. "Bodies need food and shelter, not 'voices.'"

DESIGNING PLAY

In recent years, Anthropy has begun to move away from the title of game designer entirely, embracing the mantle of "play designer." "The discourse around play—especially in academic spaces—privileges games, and particularly video games," explained Anthropy in a GamesCritisism.org interview titled "Liberating Play." "It embraces the idea of play as a product and not the broad range of ways that we interact with people through play. In this turn, we lose both the expressiveness of play, and a rich cultural and ritual history that predates game technology."

Instead of a form of commercial media, Anthropy prefers to think of games as experiences. "We worship games; we talk endlessly about the game itself and ignore the play that's going on," she continued. "Sometimes, playing includes constructing communities, or performing. The culture here is what's interesting, not the thing that produces it. It is interesting how we can design things that will encourage playful experiences. Without players, a game is just a set of rules—it requires engagement."

Anthropy is beyond the point of worrying if something she's created is formally considered a game and continues moving toward less digital, less formal, and less structured creations. "If my work is 'not really a game, just interactive art,' I'm okay with making art."

LEIGH ALEXANDER

FEARLESS FREELANCE JOURNALIST TURNED NARRATIVE DESIGNER

 leighalexander  Leigh Alexander

 leighalexander.net

EXPERIENCE

FIRST INDUSTRY PROJECT: DESTRUCTOID WRITER (2007)

FAVORITE INDUSTRY PROJECT: REIGNS: HER MAJESTY (2017)

PROJECTS SHIPPED: 8 GAMES

ACHIEVEMENTS UNLOCKED:

> GDC "BEST MOBILE GAME" NOMINATION—REIGNS: HER MAJESTY (2017)
> BAFTA "BEST BRITISH GAME" NOMINATION—REIGNS: HER MAJESTY (2018)
> DEVELOP "BEST WRITING OR NARRATIVE DESIGN" NOMINATION—REIGNS: HER MAJESTY (2018)
> GDC QUEENS OF THE PHONE AGE: THE NARRATIVE DESIGN OF REIGNS: HER MAJESTY TALK RANKED 28TH OF 400+ PANELS BY PEERS (2018)

 STATS

INDUSTRY LEVEL: 10

CURRENT CLASS: NARRATIVE DESIGNER, CONSULTANT, MULTIDISCIPLINARY WRITER

CURRENT GUILD: INDEPENDENT—LONDON, UNITED KINGDOM

SPECIAL SKILLS: GAMES WRITING, FICTION WRITING, NARRATIVE DESIGN, PODCASTING

STANDARD EQUIPMENT

FAVORITE PLATFORM: TURBO GRAFX 16

GO-TO GENRE: ROGUELIKES

MUST-HAVE GAME: METAL GEAR SOLID 3

BIO

"I've played games since I was small, and the early parser-based computer text games became the language I dreamed in," began writer and designer Leigh Alexander. "But even though I spent most of my time on games, I never expected I'd end up working in the industry."

Alexander was studying theater in the mid-2000s, anticipating writing to be a short stop on her way to the stage. Standard 9-5 jobs didn't work for an aspiring actor, but the flexibility of freelance writing would allow her to make daytime auditions and keep a roof over her head. Games journalism was the obvious choice for Alexander. Not only could she write about a passion, but doing so would help fill a void in representation. In 2006, there weren't many public-facing women speaking candidly about feminism and diversity in games.

The more articles Alexander published, the more doors opened for her. Within 10 years, she'd be delivering story bibles and narrative docs to indie developers, sitting in writing rooms for AAA projects, taking the helm as narrative director on a popular mobile title, and having published a world-building novella for Fantasy Flight's *Netrunner* card game universe—*Monitor*.

Easter Egg
Went to school for theater and draws on learned skills through regular presenting and voice work, including writing and hosting a documentary for BBC Radio 4.

A FRESH PERSPECTIVE

Taking a step back to the beginning of her career, Alexander began contributing to a number of rising gaming websites, including *Destructoid*, *Kotaku*, *Game Informer*, and *Gamasutra*. "My articles about games, often from a feminist perspective, became really popular—and frequently controversial," explained Alexander. "During this time I was also a featured columnist in *Edge Magazine* and had mainstream features published in the *Guardian*, *Slate*, the *New Statesman*, the *Atlantic*, and others."

Alexander soaked up new subjects like a sponge during her freelance years. "I learned about the industry by writing about it, studying games, critiquing designs, and interviewing developers," she said. By 2013, Alexander knew the DNA of games both good and bad and, more importantly, could communicate her critiques clearly. She began consulting with teams on their games during development. To formalize the feedback, Alexander and Ste Curran founded Agency for Games, a consultancy service focused on helping indie games reach their full potential.

"I learned about the industry by writing about it, studying games, critiquing designs, and interviewing developers."

All the while Alexander continued her freelance writing career. The important and often divisive topics that she explored increased her visibility in what proved to be a turbulent time in video games. "When I started, there were so few women game journalists that we all knew each other," recalled Alexander. "I experienced a lot of sexism and double standards, and struggled to make sense of them. I just wanted to be able to do what everyone else did, and be bold and silly around my work, but for years industry women had very few options for how to be visible and succeed without facing cruelty or creepiness."

GAMASUTRA & GAMERGATE

These challenges came to a boiling point in 2014, when Alexander nearly walked away from games entirely. After heavily criticizing the culture around mainstream gaming in an editorial piece for *Gamasutra*, Alexander became the target of Gamergate's collective reach. In addition to threats and harassment on a personal level, a campaign was organized to flood a *Gamasutra* advertiser with messages encouraging them to pull their ads from the industry website.

Unfortunately, the tech giant did just that, giving in to the volume rather than the context of the complaints. They would later publicly apologize, walk back their apparent allegiance with the troublesome campaign, and resume advertising with *Gamasutra*. The exact culture Alexander took to task in her editorial used her as a rallying point and illustrated how badly industry change was needed.

"The 'Gamergate' events of 2014 were a real low point," said Alexander. "Friends and colleagues were giving up hope left and right that our field could be a happy place to work for everybody, not just certain kinds of dudes. I really wanted to leave the industry, and for a while I did, focusing on fiction and journalism work." She didn't give up, however; she stayed visible, including hosting the first #1ReasonToBe panel at GDC in 2015. The forum focused on providing a place for women and other minorities to share their stories about working in the game industry.

Alexander also took a step back to focus on passion projects that would reignite her love for gaming. Firstly, she co-founded games website *Offworld* with industry colleague Laura Hudson. *Offworld* focused on indie game coverage published by women and people of color. She also returned to her adventure roots by creating and hosting *Lo-Fi Let's Play*, a "soft-voiced" playthrough of 20+ retro adventure games.

TAKING THE REIGNS

By late 2015, Alexander had become known for her love of quirky indie titles and narrative-heavy adventure games, in tandem with her literacy of game design and mechanics. Nerial's François Alliot contacted Alexander and asked her to write the follow-up game to popular mobile title *Reigns*—*Reigns: Her Majesty*.

Alexander eagerly accepted. Right away, she made the decision to shift the expected power dynamic. Rather than simply swapping the monarch's gender,

Reigns: Her Majesty tells the story of the king's wife. This forces the player to wield power through back channels, resulting in indirect—but no less important—influence on the kingdom. The queen's limitations

were both a fresh distinction between the games, and a commentary on gender. *Reigns: Her Majesty* was nominated for an array of awards, including nods for best writing, best narrative design, and best British game.

"The team made it what it is," said Alexander. "They respected me and gave me a lot of room to express my ideas. They hired me to create the experience of a queen, and hopefully to say interesting things about women and power, and they showed respect for my values."

Although change is slow, Alexander feels the industry is moving toward a more widespread acceptance of diverse values. "In some ways I think it's gotten so much better: the industry has gotten the message that games are for everyone, and that new kinds of characters and experiences are very much in demand," she shared. "I never used to see myself reflected in the games I would buy; now I see people who represent my experiences a lot more, and I think it just makes the space more unique, a wider range of fun options for everyone. That really inspires me."

In turn, Alexander inspires others. Whether she's sparking dialogue on important industry topics without compromising her voice or values, or creating content that moves the needle of women's representation in games, her work has resonated across the industry.

"The industry has gotten the message that games are for everyone."

Alexander is happy to have made a difference on a more personal scale, too. "I like knowing there are people out there who think like I do, who might memorize some weird and broken little game world and love it forever. As a child I used to buy crummy tie-in novels from card and tabletop universes I would never play and then act them out with my Barbies," she concluded. "As an adult I wonder if some kid bought my crummy tie-in *Netrunner* novel, *Monitor*, and loved it in the same weird way."

JESS ONG

EXPLORING THE DIVERSE APPLICATIONS OF GAME DESIGN

 Jessedeke

 Jess Ong

 jesse-ong.com

EXPERIENCE

FIRST INDUSTRY PROJECT: PICOPOKE (2008)

FAVORITE INDUSTRY PROJECT: CANCELED STAR WARS TITLE (2010)

PROJECTS SHIPPED: 8 GAMES

ACHIEVEMENTS UNLOCKED:

> MICROSOFT "DREAM.BUILD.PLAY" WINNER—CARNEYVALE: SHOWTIME (2008)

> INDEPENDENT GAMES FESTIVAL "SEUMAS MCNALLY GRAND PRIZE" FINALIST—CARNEYVALE: SHOWTIME (2008)

> INDEPENDENT GAMES FESTIVAL "BEST MOBILE GAME" FINALIST—BACKFLOW (2008)

> INDEPENDENT GAMES FESTIVAL "NEXT GREAT MOBILE GAME" FINALIST—PICOPOKE (2009)

STATS

INDUSTRY LEVEL: 10

CURRENT CLASS: SENIOR GAME DESIGNER

CURRENT GUILD: PIKPOK—WELLINGTON, NEW ZEALAND

SPECIAL SKILLS: GAME DESIGN, LEVEL DESIGN, GAME WRITING, QUALITY ASSURANCE

STANDARD EQUIPMENT

FAVORITE PLATFORM: PC

GO-TO GENRE: MOBAS

MUST-HAVE GAME: DOTA 2

BIO

Game designer Jess Ong got her start in the Singapore game industry a decade ago, when it was first starting to flourish. "I took an 'Introduction to Game Design' class my last year at university, and that's when I seriously considered it as a career option," she explained.

Ong's love for game design was fueled in part by a love for MOBA games. "I didn't really enjoy the original *DotA*, as I didn't understand it when I was younger," she said. "But when I first played *DotA 2*, I knew it was the one for me. As a designer, the depth and complexity are endlessly fascinating—there's always something to learn and improve on."

Focusing all her energy into game design, Ong landed a spot in an internship program at Massachusetts Institute of Technology. "My nine-week internship at Singapore-MIT GAMBIT Game Lab was the best education I had to prepare me for my career," she shared. "We had to make an experimental, research-based game prototype in a multidisciplinary team, mentored by amazing industry veterans who helped shape my perspective on my career in games!"

Easter Egg

Really, *really* loves cats. She volunteers with a cat-rescue group called Love Kuching Project in her spare time, helping to rescue and rehabilitate sick strays and abandoned kittens. They also started the first feline therapy program in Singapore, bringing therapy cats to visit the elderly and disabled.

SINGAPORE-MIT GAMBIT GAME RESEARCH LAB

After finishing her two-month internship at Singapore-MIT, Ong was offered a return position working in QA. Over the next three years, she would hone her understanding of the game-development process, cement QA methodologies, and learn the essentials of systems design that would serve her in her future.

Providing QA support—and eventually leading QA efforts—Ong worked on a run of celebrated games at the GAMBIT Game Lab. *Backflow* was nominated as a 2008 IGF finalist for mobile. *CarneyVale: Showtime*—an early "Xbox Live Community Games" release—won Microsoft's "Dream.Build.Play" competition in 2008, became an IGF finalist that same year, and was selected for showcase at the 2010 Penny Arcade Expo. Social game *Picopoke* was nominated in the "Next Great Mobile Game" category of the 2009 IGF awards. *Monsters in My Backyard* was her first official design credit.

Ong was simultaneously working for Singapore-based studio Playtiva, exploring the world of games writing. Her work focused on developing narratives with branching and systemic game design that would afford the player a unique storyline based on their decisions. She worked on several titles at Playtiva, including *21:15*, *The Break-Up Game*, and *Blind Date*.

A GALAXY FAR, FAR AWAY

Ong left GAMBIT and Playtiva in 2011 to apply her knowledge as a game designer at LucasArts Singapore. Her responsibilities expanded to encompass prototyping with Unity and HTML5, game systems design, economy balancing, and quest and level design. She would learn a great deal at LucasArts before all international development was ceased in 2013 after their acquisition by the Walt Disney Company.

"My first 'commercial' industry project did not ship," explained Ong. "It was an ambitious *Star Wars* title. I contributed to it by balancing the game's economy and designing minor systems and features. At that time, it was the golden age of Facebook social games and MMORPGs. This project was a combination of both and even more." Details on LucasArts' global portfolio later leaked to *Kotaku*, and it was revealed that the project was a social Facebook game referred to as *Outpost*.

Unfortunately, Ong's second project was also ill-fated, although it was completely finished. A mobile strategy game referred to as *Deathstar* in the same *Kotaku* article—she designed and balanced 40 levels of the game in Unity. "That team was truly amazing," Ong said. "I learned so much from my great leads and the team's dynamic is really special to me, despite it being the smallest 'ragtag' team in the studio. I am also really proud of that game, even though it would never see the light of day."

This was Ong's first chance to show what she was capable of through complete ownership over a set of level designs. "One of the studio heads at LucasArts was playing the game, and commenting on how he loved the later levels as they provided the right amount of challenge and thrill," she recalled. "It was my first experience fully crafting the entire progression of a game and was incredibly validating." It remains Ong's favorite project to this day.

The closure of LucasArts shook up the local game industry, but Ong landed on her feet at nearby Ubisoft Singapore. As a junior game designer, she was tasked with prototyping, systems design, and exploring procedural content generation in the early stages of *Skull & Bones*' development—the first Ubisoft title led by their Singapore team. Ong utilized their newly developed procedural content generation tools to supply work that would usually require dozens of level designers.

TAKING THE LEAD

Ong accepted her first lead designer role at Touch Dimensions in 2013. "I joined Touch Dimensions from referral to learn more about strategy games, starting with creating additional content for a post-launch update to *Autumn Dynasty: Warlords*," she said. "We then worked on several prototypes, including a freemium variation of *Autumn Dynasty* for a publisher deal. At the time, it was the age of freemium games, with premium games losing appeal due to piracy and shift in audience."

Accepting a request from her lecturer to fill in as a game design teaching assistant at the National University of Singapore, Ong's leadership extended into academia. "I focused on guiding students to systemic solutions, rather than providing the answers," she said. She also trained them on commonly used tools, and provided qualitative feedback for students with specific insights into areas of improvement.

After teaching, Ong explored the world of advertising games at Ksubaka as lead designer. She left her mark on the company by contributing to over 40 games in 14 months. Her game design talents resulted in much more engaging games, improving completion rates from 60-70% to 80%+, and leading to a 10% increase in revenue. Ong also introduced a game model that could be reskinned and rebalanced to fit the needs of new clients, which fundamentally changed the company's business direction.

"I focused on guiding students to systemic solutions, rather than providing the answers."

LIFELONG LEARNER

Ong's decade of industry experience has been carefully curated to provide her a well-rounded portfolio with insights into all major facets and genres in the industry—something that makes her a major asset to future employers. "It was quite deliberate for me to pick jobs that were quite different from each other," she explained. "So though I started out with research-based indie games, I also wanted to work in AAA, and get a bit of mobile experience. Every single one of these jobs has shaped my perspective to see a wider or different perspective when it comes to game design."

Ong is now a senior game designer at PikPok, having recently relocated to Wellington, New Zealand. "At this point in time my current project is the most challenging of my career so far," said Ong. "I tend to push myself into areas where I am not fully comfortable so I will grow. In my current unannounced project, the scope is pretty ambitious and provides interesting challenges. I enjoy what I'm doing. I enjoy the process. I would like to continue learning and growing."

"We have a saying in the rescue community," said Ong in closing. "'Saving one animal won't change the world, but it will change the world for that one animal.' I think increasingly my career is taking me towards the route of being able to pay it forward and do the same for others like what my mentors did for me. I hope to achieve that."

"I tend to push myself into areas where I am not fully comfortable so I will grow."

A DAY IN THE LIFE OF...

A GAMES RECRUITER

Video game recruiters ensure that studios are staffed up with the top talent available on the market, narrowing down candidates with surgical precision based on education, job experience, specialties, portfolio reviews, and other measures of compatibility. Top games recruiters aren't generalists; they are authorities within their select recruiting fields. In order to know what a skilled 3D artist candidate looks like, the recruiter needs to know what modeling tools are on trend and anticipate the future by understanding what emerging skills will give their studio an edge.

Katie Nelson got her start in the game industry in 1996, and has worked in games recruiting for over a decade. Her foundational knowledge of how studios work is imperative to being a successful recruiter. Although trends in recruiting have to do with automation technology, she takes an "artisanal approach" to her job, looking at every résumé by hand, and screening all applicants herself before setting up interviews with internal stakeholders.

KATIE NELSON

KatieRaeNelson | Katie Nelson

PROFESSION: SENIOR RECRUITER AT INSPIRED HIRES—NOVATO, USA

YEARS IN PROFESSION: 10

ASSOCIATED WITH: 2K GAMES, HANGAR 13, VISUAL CONCEPTS, ILLFONIC, GUN MEDIA, TURTLE ROCK STUDIOS

▶ EDUCATION

"I find that very few people end up doing what they intended to do when they went to college. For that reason, I'm a big believer in a strong liberal arts education, especially if you don't know what you want to be when you grow up. It gives people the tools to lead well-educated lives: communication skills, problem-solving skills, critical thinking. I went to USC wanting to go into the film industry. I ended up graduating with a degree in creative writing. I have zero regrets."

▶ BREAKING IN

"I never set out to work in games. An opportunity presented itself, and there I was. I was offered a job as the front desk person at Shiny Entertainment in Laguna Beach, CA. I was young and capable, and it was a small company, so they started giving me more and more duties. I started doing a little customer service, recruiting, and facilities work. I was also a gamer, so that helped. Good communication skills, experience in doing admin work, and an outgoing personality really helped me in that job."

▶ EARLY INDUSTRY IMPRESSIONS

"I expected it to be fun, and it was. I wasn't really expecting it to be run like an actual business, which it was. There were so many more details and people working behind the scenes that I never thought about. I had no idea that games companies needed a publisher. I mean, it makes sense when you think about it, but back then I was young and hadn't really put the pieces together. I started meeting people from Interplay, Shiny Entertainment's publisher, and that was an eye-opener."

▶ KEY QUALITIES

"Patience, organization, and intuition."

▶ TRAINING OPPORTUNITIES

"Keeping up-to-date on hiring trends and fluctuations in the industry is imperative. I mainly hire art and design candidates, so I like to know what the newest, latest, and greatest tools and software updates are.

"And games. Knowing, and hopefully playing, the newest games is always a good idea. It's important for me, when talking to an artist, that I understand the job they're applying for, and what skills and tools they need to know. It helps if I understand all of that and can speak their language."

▶ TOOLS OF THE TRADE

"Most of what I do is web-based. We use Taleo as our applicant tracking system, and I spend a LOT of time on LinkedIn. And email. I am emailing constantly. We've recently added Slack to our communication pipeline, and at first I was reluctant to add one more form of access to me, but I really like being able to have quick conversations with people and groups. It's been a good add. And, of course, the telephone. I spend a lot of time on the phone talking to candidates, hiring managers, and other recruiters. I have permanent ridge in my hair from my headset."

▶ HOURS & ENVIRONMENT

"I generally work from about 9am to 6pm. Sometimes that shifts depending on what project I'm recruiting for, and which time zone my candidates are in. I have the luxury, as a consultant, to work from my home office. It can be isolating, which is why Slack and Skype are great communication tools. I also go into the studio I'm recruiting for at least once a week to meet with other recruiters and my hiring managers to stay in touch, and sane. Connecting with my hiring managers is critical to understanding the kind of person they want to hire. A job description can only say so much. Sitting down with them and talking about the job is good for both of us in defining the role."

▶ AN AVERAGE DAY

"An average day starts by checking my email, then the swirling miasma of recruiting starts, as long as there aren't any fires to put out. I'll run through my open requisitions to see if any new candidates have applied. I'll do this off and on during the day around any phone interviews I have scheduled. I spend most of my day reviewing résumés and portfolios, submitting candidates to hiring managers, setting up phone interviews for me or for a hiring manager, tracking feedback on candidates, negotiating offers, and hopefully extending offers. If a role is proving difficult to fill, I'll also do some sourcing, looking on LinkedIn for candidates, and Art Station. The hardest part, or maybe my least favorite part of recruiting, is scheduling on-site interviews. Luckily, I have two great coordinators who book on-site interviews and travel for me; otherwise I'd go insane."

▶ PROMOTIONAL PATH

"Duties will vary from company to company, but normally the higher up you get, the less actual recruiting you do and the more managing of processes, procedures, and big picture recruiting directives. There's also an aspect of recruiting that comes into play when a company is deciding how to grow their business. It's vital for recruiting to be involved in that process since we have our ear to the ground, so to speak."

▶ PROFESSIONAL PERKS

"Working with great people. I know that sounds trite, but it's true. I work with a really wonderful group of recruiters, and we have a lot of fun. Also, I get to work in video games! I work with massively talented people in a creative atmosphere, and I get to meet so many interesting people in my day-to-day duties as a recruiter."

▶ CAREER CHALLENGES

"Finding talent and competing for talent. We want to hire the best of the best, and so does everyone else. We need to find out what makes us different, or better, and why people should work here instead of somewhere else. It sounds simple, but it isn't always easy. Convincing hiring managers to take a risk on a candidate is challenging too. Sometimes it pays off, which is very rewarding, and sometimes, not so much. But we always learn something from it."

▶ LIFE HACKS

"I'm always changing up my organizational strategy to keep me interested and focused. From time to time I'll keep track of everything I'm doing, candidate statuses, and open jobs in an Excel spreadsheet. Then I'll switch to a pencil and notebook, then maybe go back to digital or ATS (Applicant Tracking System) only. I find that if I keep changing how I'm tracking my to-do list, I stay fresh and on top of things. Taleo plug-ins don't hurt either."

▶ BIGGEST MISTAKE

"I've made a few bad hires. Generally it was because I was rushing to fill a position, or desperate for lack of a better candidate. In every case I didn't listen to that little voice inside me that said something was up. Always trust your gut! In the end, it only means that I have to rehire for that position a few months down the road, so I'm always better off taking my time and finding the perfect candidate."

PRO TIP!

"Be willing to start at the bottom, and have the enthusiasm to move up. Be passionate. Always ask for more, keep your eyes open, learn everything you can, and be passionate about it. Doing things outside of normal work hours that show what you do is meaningful to you makes others take notice. Be nice. Recruiters have a bad rap. I can't tell you how many times people have told me I'm the nicest recruiter they've ever worked with."

THAIS WEILLER

FACING PERSONAL DEMONS THROUGH PLAY

 ThaisWeiller
 ThaisWeiller
Thais Weiller
ThaisWeiller.com

EXPERIENCE

FIRST INDUSTRY PROJECT: ONIKEN (2012)
FAVORITE INDUSTRY PROJECT: RAINY DAY (2016)
PROJECTS SHIPPED: 40 GAMES
ACHIEVEMENTS UNLOCKED:

> FODINHA DE OURO "BEST GAME OF 2012 MADE IN BRAZIL"—ONIKEN (2012)

> DROPS DE JOGOS "BRAZILIAN DEVELOPER OF 2015"—THAIS WEILLER

> GLITCH MUNDO INDIE FESTIVAL ORGANIZER

> SPEAKER, TEHRAN GAMES CONVENTION (2018)

STATS

INDUSTRY LEVEL: 10
CURRENT CLASS: CO-FOUNDER
CURRENT GUILD: JOYMASHER—PARANÁ, BRAZIL
SPECIAL SKILLS: GAME DESIGN, LEVEL DESIGN, USER INTERFACE DESIGN, UNITY3D, PRODUCTION

STANDARD EQUIPMENT

FAVORITE PLATFORM: SNES
GO-TO GENRE: GENRE-FLUID
MUST-HAVE GAME: DIFFERENT GAMES FOR DIFFERENT REASONS!

BIO

At GDC 2017's #1ReasonToBe panel, Brazilian game developer Thais Weiller asked the room full of industry veterans a simple question: Why did they make games? She challenged them to stop and really think about what motivated them to create—not simply paying bills or being attached to a prestigious AAA project. What sparked their interest in the first place?

For Weiller, creation and emotion go hand in hand, and she believes that no powerful experience can be made of thin air; all great pieces of art and knowledge draw from something deeper, including suffering. So she asked, "Why not make a game about that shitty moment in your life? That nasty breakup, that awful boss, or an ongoing health condition? Why not direct your unhappiness into something good?"

Weiller knows how hard it is to face your demons. She did exactly that with *Rainy Day*, a game that explores the endless struggle of living with social anxiety and depression. As a game designer, Weiller isn't interested only in fun and positive emotions. "My job is to make change," she said. "My goal is to create experiences that put players in situations uncomfortable enough that they may change their outlook."

> "My goal is to create experiences that put players in situations uncomfortable enough that they may change their outlook."

COURSE CORRECTION

Weiller had already earned a bachelor's degree in both fashion and journalism before realizing she wanted nothing to do with either industry. Video games had been a part of her life since youth, when she binged on Atari 2600 titles and played *Doom* and *Wolfenstein 3D* with her father. Weiller returned to school in 2010, working toward a communication master's in video games and human cognition. She augmented her master's work with online courses and boot camps, studying everything from UX to AI—logging hundreds of hours against Stanford University online classes.

Easter Egg

Lives with an 11-year-old bunny named Odin, and believes he is plotting her death in order to take sole custody of the apartment.

Still in school, Weiller got her first gaming gig in 2011, working as a game designer for Facebook social games in São Paulo. She was responsible for game design, game balancing, project management, coordinating the art and programming teams, and more. "It was a horrible experience. I was overworked, overstressed, and getting underpaid," said Weiller. The company went bankrupt before any of the games she was working on were published. "I learned to always have a plan B, to always try to land on my feet."

Things were better at Best, Cool & Fun Games, where she contributed concept and level design to *Bunny Shooter Christmas*, *Pet Dash*, *Road Trip*, and canceled title *SkyCastle*. It was at Black River Studios, though, where she hit her stride and found stability, working in both design and production on multiple titles, including VR titles *Jake & Tes' Finding Monsters Adventure*, and her first original game pitch, *Rococo VR*.

PROFESSOR WEILLER

Before finishing her master's, Weiller was already finding ways to widen the door for the next generation of Brazilian game developers, with a particular emphasis on helping women and minorities find a safe space to learn their craft and counter what she describes as an institutionalized "machismo" culture in the local industry. She became a public figure in this fight in 2015, after publishing a piece on the place of women in games on a major entertainment website.

She first worked as a game design professor at technology centers Alpha channel & PUCPR, teaching Game Design 1010 and helping students with their personal game prototypes. As students grew in the curriculum, she would introduce systemic thinking, and mentor them on larger university projects. "Since I became a professor, I have been able to reach young female and queer developers in the making, reassuring them that they have a safe space in here," said Weiller.

Weiller used her writing as a more accessible form of education for those without the resources to attend classes. In 2015 she formalized her master's work into a Portuguese-language book, helping to demystify the game-development process. *Game Start Lesson: Game Design Lessons for Your Video Game* is available to download for free from her website, published under creative commons, which allows others to localize and share her findings. She opened a blog of the same name shortly after publication, sharing short articles about her personal views on game development, including *Games Are Not Art*, and *Designing Anguish*.

Small Think: Finish Your First Video Game was published in 2017. "When we are in the middle of this hurricane of creativity and hard work, it is very easy to lose focus," explained Weiller. "*Small Think* exists to help put your attention where it is most needed at every moment of development." Again, the publication is available free of charge on her website.

ODE TO RETRO

Balancing teaching and full-time development at Black River Studios, Weiller and industry colleague Danilo Dias formed indie game studio JoyMasher in 2012. JoyMasher's projects are love letters to retro gaming, and Weiller shifted her focus between growing the company and creating games.

"JoyMasher is the sole most challenging project I have ever taken part in," she confessed. "It is pretty weird being in charge of so many things as I am, such as finance, PR, management, and commercial affairs, but hey, here I am doing those and also working on making a game! <send help>"

JoyMasher's first commercial game, the 8-bit action platformer *Oniken*, was released in 2012 on the now-defunct Desura distribution platform. "After two and a half years of hard work, it sold an amazing $200," said Weiller. Luckily, its 2014 release on Steam was another story entirely, but it took two years until the game became profitable. A successful 2013 crowdfunding campaign for their next title, *Odallus: The Dark Call*, in 2013 provided a bit more security for the team, and the founders were able to quit their day jobs and focus entirely on JoyMasher. They are currently working on run-and-gun game *Blazing Chrome*.

PASSION PROJECTS

Personal games are still a big part of Weiller's life and allow her to push the boundaries of what games can convey. *Rainy Day* came about after a prolonged bout of depression on Weiller's part, and aside from the art, it was a one-person project. "There is some sort of peace in being the only person responsible for making a whole game work, and also in being the only culprit in [screwing] it up." *Rainy Day* beautifully illustrates how—when rife with anxiety and depression—a simple act such as getting out of bed can be debilitating.

Players who have also struggled with depression have come forward to share how much they identified with Weiller's work, and those who hadn't shared how the game helped them better understand the condition of a loved one. Reflecting, Weiller was surprised by how many people were brought to tears when playing *Rainy Day*. "I didn't know whether to feel good, or feel bad. So I felt both."

For her next project, Weiller intends to tackle another complex subject matter: abusive relationships. "A lot of the victims cannot see themselves in this situation," she said. "I want to make a game where you interact with someone who goes through this, which will help lessen stigma and taboo. By playing like a woman, you understand what it's like to be a woman."

A CHANGE IN PERSPECTIVE

Weiller hopes that through her studio projects, personal projects, and teaching, she can influence the direction of the industry in the future, even if on a small scale. "I think we need to stop thinking of games and 'gaming' as something else and start seeing it as part of human expression. Any new formats or medium of expression will end up having games on it. That's just how we are—we are playful by nature."

"How it handles different voices. I believe this is changing but I'm not sure it is changing fast enough. I also would love less FOMO driving developers to crystallizing genres and provoking homogeneity in production. Our industry is every day less daring and more trying to replicate the same success format of previous best-sellers. This stagnates creativity and development." Weiller is doing her best to avoid homogeneity in gaming through her work. "I hope I can help in the arduous task of making game development a safer place for dissident voices and that I can contribute in making games weird."

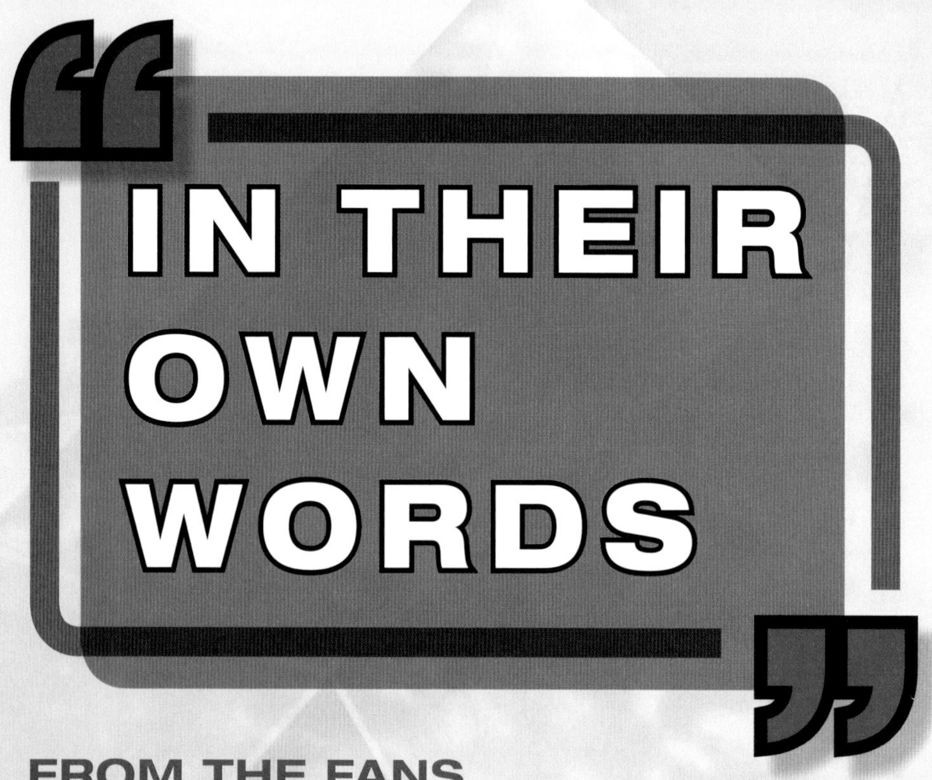

FROM THE FANS

Do you have a favorite moment with a fan of your work?

"A few times a week we have people emailing us telling us about how much they cried playing *Rumu*, which is always lovely. Eliciting a strong emotional response with our stories is so important to me."

Ally McLean | Director | The Working Lunch | Sydney, Australia

---

"I've worked with people who have gotten the wrist tattoo from *BioShock*. It's incredibly humbling to have worked on a game that people felt that strong of a connection to. (And then I get to tell them how the chain tattoo was a quick fix to the problem of making sure that it was clear that it was always Jack's hands between the opening, the game, and the ending videos.)"

Alyssa Finley | Executive Producer | San Rafael, USA

"So many! I've been really touched by the kindness and generosity of the fans—it really sustains game developers to hear how much our work has meant to someone. I've had letters from women in their fifties telling me how much they enjoyed *Uncharted*. Parents who bonded with their children while playing *Uncharted* together. Grown children who played *Uncharted* with a terminally ill parent, saying how much the game brightened their final days. I'm profoundly grateful to have been in a position to reach so many people with our games."

Amy Hennig | Senior Creative Director & Writer | Independent | San Carlos, USA

"The first time we showcased our game at AnimeKon in Barbados, there was this one kid who kept coming back to our booth to play the prototype again and again. It was incredible to see how much fun he had playing it even though it was so rough. He started timing himself and kept repeating the build to try to beat his time. Our first major fan was also our first speedrunner!"

Ari Green | Studio Co-Founder & Programmer | Couple Six | Barbados

---

"At the Game Devs of Color Expo in 2018, one of the young women who played my game asked if she could hug me after playing *after HOURS*. It felt like my heart was simultaneously contracting and expanding—I was so flooded with emotions. I couldn't believe how a video game could connect people."

Bahiyya Khan | Experimental Narrative Master's Student & Tutor | University of the Witwatersrand | Johannesburg, South Africa

---

"There was a man playing *Train* who kept playing even after everyone else had stopped. It's normal for people to stop playing, but it's not normal for people to keep playing, particularly by themselves. It took him maybe 20 minutes. I approached him after it was over, and asked him what he was doing. 'I wanted to set everyone free.' It was a beautiful expression. He was unaware he was being watched. That moment will stay with me forever."

Brenda Romero | Game Designer & CEO | Romero Games | Galway, Ireland

---

"While riding on a bus, a young man waited for me and shook my hands. He was from Maatcha Games and he wanted to thank me for the work I do in the local game community scene. At that moment, I needed that."

Gwendelyn Foster | Game Developer | Imayon Studios | Manila, Philippines

---

"As a YouTube channel, we are lucky to receive kind and encouraging comments, tweets, emails, and interactions every single day from people who are part of our community. It's sometimes overwhelming when we read some of their messages; to think we have impacted their lives in a positive way is incredibly humbling. From a single tweet to handwritten letters and gifts, it's hard to sum up just how much those mean and how I appreciate every single one of them."

Hollie Bennett | Channel Manager | PlayStation Access | London, UK

"Hearing from players who tell us our game means a lot to them. One time I was introduced to a random stranger, and as I was about to describe what *Firewatch* is, he pulls up his sleeve to reveal a full-color tattoo of our key art on his arm as he says, 'I know.'"

Jane Ng | Artist | Valve | Bellevue, USA

"Every time someone emails me, writes me, or comes up to me randomly somewhere and tells me I made something that affected them is a gift. I can't possibly rank them."

Kellee Santiago | Partnerships Development Lead | Google Entertainment | San Francisco, USA

"My husband and I have one personal project that we do every year at Emerald City Comic Con. An attendee saw Robert, saw his name on a sign, and looked at me and asked if I was Lorraine, and the look of amazement and expression of gratitude took us by surprise. He told us we met over a decade previously, at Gen Con in Indianapolis, where his dad brought him over to us while we were doing the *Halo* PC demo. His dad asked for advice on his behalf (because he was a bit too shy to speak)—his son who loved to draw, who loved to game—what should he do? We had just started a family, so we knew where the man was coming from, and we gave the best advice we could, and that kid was the adult standing in front of us. The kid who took our advice to heart and was inspired to pursue a career in games. And got there—and was making a living doing so."

Lorraine McLees | Consumer Products | Bungie, Inc. | Bellevue, USA

"One time while I was demoing *Keys to Success*, a fan praised the game and told me to keep at it and so forth. After a few minutes, I left for the restroom, and when I got back, I saw that same fan surrounded by a lot of people—his friends, as it turned out—as he showed off his acquired skills in the game, and they kept sort of wrestling for the controllers. I think game makers live for moments like these, and it's one moment I will never forget."

Nourhan ElSherief | Game Designer & Developer | Instinct Games | Cairo, Egypt

---

"I would play *Star Wars Galaxies* with a group that didn't know I was a developer…that is until I was 'outed' by the company! They did a 'meet the dev' column in our online forums and decided to feature me. However, in that column they used my in-game name, which my guildmates saw. When I logged in that night, my guild was absolutely agog at the idea they'd been playing with a dev all this time, but one member was actually stammering! Seriously! He was so shocked he couldn't even finish a complete sentence. We've since become good friends and laugh about the memory."

Sheri Graner Ray | Senior Designer | Electronic Arts | Austin, USA

"Anytime that someone approaches me in cosplay of a character I've given voice to, it blows my mind."

Ashly Burch | Voice Actor & Writer | Union Talent | Los Angeles, USA

"I once had a very sweet person present me with a piece of art, inspired by my release *Spectra*, made with Hama Beads. It totally floored me. I have it hung in my studio!"

Chipzel | Composer, Producer, & Performer | Freelance | Northern Ireland

---

"I attended an event with ESL Intel Extreme Masters in Oakland. The analyst desk and caster desk were placed in the crowd with little separation, so the audience could walk right up to us for a chat between segments. This young woman approached the desk and had a card for me—I still have it! It was such a kind and genuine gesture. We chatted briefly about her favorite team, champion, and her time at the event. She was rather shy and quickly shuffled off, but the memory of that interaction sits on the corner of my desk, and I make sure to bring that card to every international event I attend alongside my prep. Thank you, Scarlet."

Indiana "Froskurinn" Black | *League of Legends* Shoutcaster | Riot Games | Shanghai, China

---

"After *Portal* shipped, someone made these amazing, metal Companion Cubes in their garage and gave them to the team. I still have mine, and it's one of my prized possessions!"

Kim Swift | Studio Design Director | EA Motive Studios | Montréal, Canada

---

"My first major speaking event in the industry was just at the beginning of this year, and I was most afraid that I was the last presentation of the entire conference and people would leave, bored of me halfway through. Instead, I got a standing ovation and a whole bunch of the developers in the audience cried. A few came up to me after to tell me they were my number one fan, including Jenny Lay-Flurrie, Microsoft's head of accessibility, who I look up to greatly. I still can't believe she came to another one of my talks later in the year to show me support."

Cherry Thompson | Game Accessibility Consultant | Freelance | Vancouver, Canada

---

"I love meeting fans after concerts and hearing comments like 'I listened to your music and the sadness saved me,' or 'I listened to your music and aspired to become a composer,' or 'I've listened to and studied your music for a year, which helped me get accepted into my desired university.' Hearing such comments makes me happy. I think each conversation like this is important."

Yoko Shimomura | Composer | Freelance | Tokyo, Japan

"Every now and then I'll receive really kind, heartfelt messages from people in the industry and the larger gaming community about the D&I initiatives I lead at Riot. It's difficult for me to accept a compliment, so I get pretty weepy and my heart grows three times larger! My favorite moment comes from my biggest fan—my mom—who once texted me to say that she rereads my first article in gaming criticism about being a Palestinian woman who plays and loves games. Since there's a pretty big age gap between my parents and me, I never thought they'd 'get' what I do or why I do it. That was an incredibly touching moment."

Soha El-Sabaawi | Manager of Diversity & Inclusion Programs | Riot Games | Los Angeles, USA

"Hearing a kid laugh and knowing that I was part of the team that delivered that joy. Having worked on LEGO games for years, I can say watching kids try our games, having fun, and laughing is just the best. My favorite fans are my kids. As they get older, it's incredibly special to watch them experience all the games I worked. It was also a fun moment when a close friend's son called excitedly to say he'd seen my name in the credits. He thought I was famous!"

Stephanie Johnson | Head of Global Marketing for GeForce NOW & SHIELD | Nvidia | San Francisco, USA

"Our global titles like *Star Chef* and *Fantastic Chefs* are targeted at women aged 20-55, and we received several heartwarming fan mail and messages. I particularly remember one Australian fan who was very encouraging and taking the time to write us very detailed emails on nitty-gritties of the game; what she liked and didn't like and the improvement suggestions. Very grateful to such fans."

Shilpa Bhat | VP-Games | 99Games | Udupi, India

"I've got loads. But one of the most recent was when a mum and her son came up to me in a signing queue at the Emirates Literary Festival. The son gave me some comics to sign and his mum started asking me questions about getting into the games industry. I quickly realized that these were the son's questions and he was shy about speaking to me. So, I listened politely to the mum, then turned to the son and addressed my answers directly to him. This seemed to work, as he slowly started to engage with me and even joked when I apologized for my hand writing that his was worse. The mum looked delighted and I later found out she'd spoken to the organizers about that interaction and how happy it had made her son, who happened to be autistic."

Rhianna Pratchett | Writer | Freelance | London, UK

"It used to be hearing from fans that my adventures gave them hours of entertainment, and then later that my work inspired them to become game developers. Now, it's that my life changes and visibility have inspired them to step out, make similar changes in their own lives, and take a risk that could find their way back to happiness as well."

Jennell Jaquays | Designer & Artist | Dragongirl Studios | Seattle, USA

"In 2013, we got a call from Make A Wish Foundation. One of our longtime fans named Rachel had terminal cancer. Her final wish was to meet the Her Interactive team. We rented a car and drove a few hours to meet her. Rachel was hunched over, semi-conscious in her living room surrounded by her family. We played a voice recording of a Nancy Drew character saying Rachel's name, and telling her how special she was. I touched her shoulder gently. I could literally feel her feeling love from us. About an hour after we left, we received a call from her mother. She told us that Rachel had just passed away, and that she got her wish. We dedicated our next game to her."

Megan Gaiser | Principal | Contagious Creativity | Seattle, USA

"I have so many. One of the coolest moments was when I was approached by a woman who had a bad stroke at like 32 years old. Her physical therapist said, 'Go get a game console and start playing a game to help you get your fine motor skills back.' So, she picked Mass Effect and went after it. She had it all back when I saw her. She was incredible. She went from limited mobility to fully recovered using Mass Effect to help get her fine motor skills back."

Jennifer Hale | Voice Actress | SBV Talent | Los Angeles, USA

"A moment of absolute awe that will always stay with me happened in my comics rather than games. A fan sent photos of her cosplaying as the lead character from the web comic *The West Was Lost*. I was blown away by her effort, but even more so by her email in which she expressed how thankful she was for a Native woman comic book character she could identify with. It reminded me of why I got into games to begin with, when I was just a kid looking desperately for characters that represented me in any kind of way, and all I had were characters like Nightwolf, Wolf Hawkfield, and Turok. We can do better and it begins with being true to ourselves."

Elizabeth LaPensée | Designer, Artist, & Assistant Professor | Michigan State University | Lansing, USA

FEMINISM: The Rules of the Game

By Muriel Tramis | *CEO of Sensastic Prod*

Prior to my first year of high school, my schooling was not mixed. I knew what "boys" were—I climbed trees with some of them in my neighborhood—but I didn't come into contact with them every day. Their attendance on the same school benches, at the age of adolescent hormonal upheaval, led me to discover a new distribution of powers: the empire of seduction.

From then on, in my studies as in my professional environment, I have always been in the minority in a world of men. This did not displease me; it was actually good to be an exception.

Parity did not exist in the profession I had chosen—computer science. With this imbalance came an automatic mission for anyone with the slightest sense of responsibility. I discovered myself to have a feminist temperament.

My first job took place in an environment charged with testosterone. My duties consisted of training military personnel in the use of my maintenance software for drones. On the walls of the workshop where I taught, women with few clothes, from so-called "masculine" magazines or calendars, were pinned like trophies.

I had a small glass room in the middle of the workshop. It came to me, I don't know why, to line the glass panels with pictures of men in a similar state of shameless undress. It was my first feminist victory, a silent fight—but effective. In the end, the workshop walls were redecorated with pictures of cute little cats.

I quickly became aware that my incursion into the world of weapons systems would not allow me to express the intense creativity I felt bubbling inside me.

I started designing video games and educational software in the Coktel Vision studio. There, I found a passion for point-and-click adventure games.

I naturally questioned the place of women, in front of and on the screen. There, too, was a terrible imbalance on both sides. The player audience was mostly male, and among my fellow programmers and game designers, there were hardly any women. Only the graphic field was beginning to recruit "small hands."

So I asked myself, in what role should I showcase women? I had no desire to make them passive like cartoon princesses who wait for Prince Charming. Why not expose my own fantasies?

First came the game *Emmanuelle* (1989), that was at the time in Europe, the symbol of the liberated women who expresses her desires and claims her right to please. I convinced my boss to buy the exploitation rights to the game, and there I was, inventing a story that takes place in Brazil, a country with very free customs, par excellence. The pictures were very chaste, nothing pornographic. Symbolism was everything. You had to find erotic statuettes to increase your seductive power and practice seducing randomly met women. This scenario is typically aimed toward men as an initiatory journey to the heart of female desire. Isn't Brazil home to a rather humid forest, still little-explored?

Then, in the same vein, there was *Geisha* (1990), another symbol of eroticism, if a bit more refined. But Japan is also a symbol of modernity, and I am quite proud to have invented the first virtual-sex machine. In the game, you had to caress a female hologram to the point of ecstasy. It was a technological advancement for the studio because, for the first time, real images were used in a drawn setting. We used a topless model for this purpose, who took suggestive poses in panties, to the great pleasure of my male colleagues. They were, of course, delighted to participate in such an avant-garde project.

Other phases of the game were even crazier, like the Pac-Man-type, phallus-shaped vessel that had to avoid mouths full of teeth by protecting itself with condoms.

For these two titles, my publisher considered it prudent to create a distinct brand, Tomahawk, to differentiate my erotic content from the educational stories for children I created elsewhere. Now I wonder how these two titles, quite unique in their kind, would be received if I produced remakes of them today.

After this experimental breakthrough, I started thinking again. I needed a real female hero, one who wouldn't simply be there to flatter the male libido. She had to be active without using direct confrontation or aggression—only cunning, logic, and intuition. Probably a rejection of my early armament career, my shrink would say.

This is how Doralice Prunelier was born. She appears as an airline pilot in Miami-based thriller *Fascination* (1991), and a science-fiction adventurer in *Lost in Time* (1993), where she finds herself propelled from Brittany, France, into her own past on a Caribbean island.

I received some letters from women who explained that I had saved their relationships because, finally, they could share this incomprehensible passion of their boyfriends, addicted to video games, by solving the puzzles in my games together.

I was quite satisfied to have won that battle, to interest women in video games, but I had not won the war.

Had I been right not to choose violence and fighting? Likely not, because Lara Croft arrived shortly afterward, with her arsenal of weapons and her physical fighting spirit. In addition, I had fallen into ease and cliché by mixing exoticism and eroticism.

My editor ended my turpitude by asking me to choose a male hero from now on. This was the case for my next title, *Urban Runner* (1996), totally shot in real images, which starts with a shootout chase on the rooftops of a disused factory. There, Max, the hero, barely escapes a guy more stupid than nasty, who shoots very badly. Anyway, the fact remains that Max doesn't like weapons and uses logic and cunning rather than strength.

MARÍA MARTINA SANTORO

A CATALYST FOR GROWTH IN ARGENTINA'S VIDEO GAME INDUSTRY

SantoroMartina  mmartinasantoro

 Martina Santoro  okamgames.com

EXPERIENCE

FIRST INDUSTRY PROJECT: FOOSBALL: GOAL CRUSADERS (2012)

FAVORITE INDUSTRY PROJECT: ÚLTIMO CARNAVAL (2014)

PROJECTS SHIPPED: 15 GAMES

ACHIEVEMENTS UNLOCKED:

> FIRST FEMALE PRESIDENT OF THE ARGENTINE VIDEO GAME DEVELOPERS ASSOCIATION (2017-2018)

> HELPED GROW THE LATAM VIDEO GAMES FEDERATION

> "ÚLTIMO CARNAVAL" REPRESENTS THE FIRST PARTNERSHIP BETWEEN JAPANESE SQUARE ENIX & A LATIN STUDIO

> SUCCESSFUL "THE INTERACTIVE ADVENTURES OF DOG MENDONÇA AND PIZZABOY" KICKSTARTER CAMPAIGN

STATS

INDUSTRY LEVEL: 10

CURRENT CLASS: CEO, CO-FOUNDER, & PRESIDENT

CURRENT GUILD: OKAM STUDIO & VIDEO GAME DEVELOPER'S ASSOCIATION

SPECIAL SKILLS: GAME PRODUCTION, ANIMATION PRODUCTION, SOCIAL MEDIA, START-UPS, STORYTELLING, BUSINESS DEVELOPMENT

STANDARD EQUIPMENT

FAVORITE PLATFORM: MOBILE

GO-TO GENRE: PUZZLE GAMES

MUST-HAVE GAME: DONKEY KONG COUNTRY 2, MONUMENT VALLEY

BIO

María Martina Santoro is a people person, who, by her own description, never stops talking, loves meeting interesting individuals, and fosters connections through her network. "Growing up, I loved film and animation and storytelling, playing games, listening to music, reading books and comic books, and was always very curious about new technology," she began. "I always thought I would end up in a government office, working behind a desk." She never imagined working in video games. Her reasons were twofold: she wasn't aware that there *was* a games industry in Argentina, and she was convinced that you needed to be a math genius to make games.

"I couldn't have been more wrong," admitted Santoro. She decided to attend the annual EVA expo—a local equivalent of the Game Developers Conference—on a whim. "What I saw there lit up something that changed me forever: there were thousands of people making games in my country. And not only that; this amazing industry brings together people with all kinds of backgrounds. There were programmers and artists, writers and animators, designers and musicians, lawyers, accountants, actresses, and all sorts of different talents who were needed to make a game. I found out that there was also room for someone who could make things happen as a connector. Someone like me."

Easter Egg

Is immortalized as an Easter egg in *The Interactive Adventures of Dog Mendonça & Pizzaboy.*

OKAM STUDIO

In 2010 Santoro founded Buenos Aires-based OKAM Studio with friends Lucas Gondolo and Santiago R. Villa, where she works as the CEO and business developer. "We specialize in high-quality video games for PC, console, and mobile," she explained. "Our portfolio includes international hit titles such as *Foosball: Goal Crusaders* and *Último Carnaval.*"

The studio's foundational goal was to create and share new IPs with the world, but that required funding. They found a source of income through pitching their services to the local film and TV industry. "Back then it wasn't common for independent film or TV producers and directors to work on a game," Santoro said. "They didn't know how to reach the gamers, how to monetize, or how to distribute them. But we did. Our first jobs came from these amazing studios. They didn't spend a dime on our original IPs, but they did invest in our original way of developing content."

OKAM's first industry project was *Foosball: Goal Crusaders*, a mobile game based on Academy Award-winning director Juan José Campanella's animated feature film *Underdogs*. The free-to-play mobile game released with the film internationally. Santoro was in charge of the business development, administration, and production. "It was a big deal in Argentina," she remembers. "We had the city covered with gigantic ads, and we even made it on one of the main TV shows!"

PUPS & PIZZA

Soon after their initial success, OKAM secured the rights to develop a game based on *The Interactive Adventures of Dog Mendonça and Pizzaboy*. "The game expanded the world of the critically acclaimed comic book by Filipe Melo, Juan Cavia, and Santiago R. Villa," shared Santoro. "As my partner Lucas likes to say, it was the game that made us a team. At first it was a two-hour-long prototype, but it was our first project where we had creative freedom, and ended up opening the doors to lots of opportunities and helped us build our reputation."

Impressed with the project's potential, the Argentine Video Game Developers Association and Buenos Aires government sponsored the development team to fly out to Gamescom in Germany to pursue business opportunities. "For the first time ever, we were talking with people from the games industry," she recalled. "People who spoke the same language as we did and that loved the team's original humor and art style. To help fund it, we created a Kickstarter campaign, and thanks to the support of industry titans like Tim Schafer, Robin Hunicke, and Charles Cecil—and many others—we were successfully funded in 2014. Running the campaign was super fun, and its success with the community and the press got us a big distribution deal with one of Europe's main publishers: Koch Media."

Santoro believes the team's biggest break came in the form of a collaboration with Square Enix on one of their first original IPs. "*Último Carnaval* (the Last Carnival) was one of our most ambitious projects ever. It was a collectible card game for mobile that was released in 2014, based on Latin American myths and folklore. It was the first collaboration between Square Enix and a Latin studio, and was the result of a vision Fukushima-san himself—the founder and honorary chairman of Square Enix—had for the Latin region."

Collaborating with such a big company presented new challenges to the team, for more reasons than cultural differences. "First of all, they are based on the other side of the world, and secondly, they had a very high standard for the production process, so we learned a lot about how to organize the team, how to communicate and deliver content, proper documentation, and so on. We also had to develop a game that would meet the challenges of 2014 Latin America: poor Internet connection, lack of payment methods, and low mobile phone adoption. This experience helped us learn not only how to develop a game professionally with international industry standards, but also understand the importance of having a very clear plan of monetization, retention, and communication while developing a game."

OKAM has released 12 games since 2010, including *Realms of the Void*, *Ship Ahoy*, *Spellart*, *Black Velvet Bandit*, and *Mr. Bean Around the World*—a co-production with Endemol that resulted in over 25 million downloads around the world. "We also collaborated with companies from all over the world, like Cartoon Network, Disney, Versus Evil, Daedalic, Miniclip, and Kongregate, among many others."

CONNECTING THE DOTS

In addition to making games, Santoro continued connecting dots through networking and creating opportunities for others to succeed in the local industry. For three years, she was the editor-in-chief of Inside Games LATAM, a primary resource for industry news in the region.

Currently, she is the head of animation and interactivity careers at the Universidad Del Cine. "We created the first Latin scholarship for the region's talent to grow," Santoro explained. "I tutor several projects for many education institutions like Universidad Nacional de San Martin as well. I have also collaborated with the Inter-American Development Bank on several education projects in different countries in Latin America. Thanks to the IDB, I had the recent pleasure of working with Juan Pablo Pison and Phill Penix-Tadsen on a book about the past, present, and future of the Latin games industry and its main players."

Santoro has also attended an incalculable number of events, both locally and internationally, as a speaker, judge, and workshop instructor to mentor new talent. She is most proud to have been a part of Rami Ismail's #1REASONTOBE panel at GDC 2017.

"It took me years to understand who I am. I am the *catalyst*. I start the reaction. I start change. And I love it."

ADVA

Since 2016, Santoro has been the president of the Argentine Video Game Developers Association. Founded in 2000, the non-profit represents over 110 game-development studios. "As the first female president, I've worked hard with a team of colleagues from all over Argentina to help promote the industry and make it grow in each corner of the country," she said. "I have helped organize several game industry events in Argentina, from conferences and business roundtables, to workshops and special activities like the EVA expo, the Game Business Summit, the Education and Games Summit, Zona Videojuegos, and Conferencias VJ. We are now working hard on different activities and actions to help bring more diversity into our local industry, like the Girls and Games Workshop in collaboration with the Goethe-Institut and the EVA Scholarship with IBM Argentina."

"I realize it's hard to define my position in the industry," summarized Santoro. "I work in a game-development company, but I am not a designer, programmer, or artist. I work with schools and universities, yet I don't teach. I'm involved with events and promotion activities, but I am not a producer or a journalist. It was only a short while ago that a friend from Microsoft helped me realize that even though I am not those things, these games, conferences, courses, and scholarships wouldn't exist as they are without me. It took me years to understand who I am. I am the *catalyst*. I start the reaction. I start change. And I love it."

ANNA PROSSER

BUILDING UP, NEVER TEARING DOWN

 AnnaProsser  Anna Prosser

 annaprosser.com
twitch.tv/annaprosser

EXPERIENCE

FIRST INDUSTRY PROJECT: WORLD CYBER GAMES USA (2009)

FAVORITE INDUSTRY PROJECT: BLIZZCON & TWITCHCON

PROJECTS SHIPPED: 100+ TOURNAMENTS/EVENTS HOSTED

ACHIEVEMENTS UNLOCKED:

> OREGON STATE UNIVERSITY "MAGNA CUM LAUDE" (2007)
> MISS OREGON USA (2011)
> WHITE HOUSE ROUND TABLE ON WOMEN IN GAMING (2015)
> KEYNOTE SPEAKER AT THE CENTER FOR DEMOCRACY AND TECHNOLOGY (2017)

STATS

INDUSTRY LEVEL: 9

CURRENT CLASS: LEAD PRODUCER

CURRENT GUILD: TWITCH STUDIOS—SAN FRANCISCO, USA

SPECIAL SKILLS: VIDEO AND STAGE PRODUCTION, COMMUNICATION, HOSTING, LIVE STREAMING, MARKETING, PUBLIC SPEAKING

 STANDARD EQUIPMENT

FAVORITE PLATFORM: "DEPENDS ON THE DAY OF THE WEEK"

GO-TO GENRE: RPG

MUST-HAVE GAME: HORIZON: ZERO DAWN (2017)

BIO

"I don't fit in the boxes people want to put me in," said Twitch Studios Producer Anna Prosser. "'Gamer' has a box, 'pageant girl' has a box, 'intellectual' has a box, 'tech professional' has a box; people try to put me into just one. I think what's so important right now in the industry is to recognize that women are not monolithic, and that humans are inherently multifaceted and hard to define."

By refusing to be easily categorized, Prosser is championing for women who feel pressure to conform to easy-to-read, non-threatening archetypes in order to find industry work. Throughout her on-camera career, she's been there, and done that. Now Prosser uses her position of power to ensure that in the future, complexity of character is seen as an asset, not a liability.

Prosser earned dual bachelors of art in speech, communication, and international studies in 2007, graduating magna cum laude. While at university, she honed her pubic-speaking skills as captain of the speech and debate team, winning numerous regional speaking awards in the process. She studied abroad in Spain, performed in a dance group, worked as a lifeguard, and participated in pageants, taking the title of Miss Oregon USA in 2011. All the while, she was an avid gamer with a keen eye on esports.

Easter Egg

Won the Miss Oregon USA beauty pageant in 2011, which makes people assume a lot of things about her.

EVIL GENIUSES & TWITCH

"I was in college when I started getting involved in the esports scene," said Prosser. She knew her educational background and extracurricular activities would lend well to on-camera work. After becoming a regular on the official forums of esports organization Team Liquid, Prosser began conducting interviews for them. They asked her to fly out to the World Cyber Games in 2009 and provide event coverage."They compensated me by covering my flight," she recalled. "I was so excited!"

In 2011, Prosser started to actively pursue a job providing video coverage for esports events. She began picking up contract work for a pro-gaming team Evil Geniuses. "I kept trying to convince them that I would bring value to the company by creating video content full-time, and that they should hire me to do it."

After championing herself within the organization, Prosser was hired full-time to create content and cover the team. "I made a few videos, which became two of the most highly viewed videos on their entire channel," she explained. "They were shot with my little crappy point-and-shoot, and I edited in Windows Movie Maker. I had no idea what I was doing; I just wanted to make video content so bad. Over time, the success of videos like that finally convinced Evil Geniuses to invest in more media. I like to believe that I was part of their shift from pro-gaming team to media agency, because of my dogged belief that those things were worthwhile."

Since 2015, Prosser has been lead producer at Twitch Studios in San Francisco. She produces and hosts live video content for internal use, and for major industry events such as E3 and PAX. "Anything that Twitch makes to broadcast on its own platform, that's what I touch," she said. "I'm usually project managing and conceptualizing, coming up with creative ideas, and I do a lot of script writing. For TwitchCon, I'm responsible for most of the content on the main stage. I also produce original shows, such as our streamer competition game show, *Stream On*, and I talk directly to the community through *Twitch Weekly*."

HOSTING

In addition to her day job, Prosser has been an independent communication consultant and freelance host for nearly 10 years. Prosser's first time hosting a major, high-budget esports event was the 2011 IGN ProLeague. "I was the main emcee and interviewer," she recalled. "It remains special to me not only because it marked a major stepping stone in my hosting career, but because of the amazing, passionate people I worked with there who believed in me and in the value of the esports community."

"In 2014, I got my first official hosting job at Blizzcon on the *Heroes of the Storm* stage, and since last year I've been one of the hosts of the BlizzCon digital ticket," she continued. "That big job has been a goal of mine since I started hosting, and achieving it feels amazing."

Having hosted well over 100 events and tournaments to this day, Prosser is open about struggles she faced while establishing herself, and notes that the way she dresses has been a reflection of that struggle. "I used to be a spokesmodel, and so sometimes at the beginning of my career, that's how I would get work in the industry. A lot of times when I was hired by companies to do interviews, like Monster Energy, for example, they would put me in a leather bustier with their logo on it. I didn't mind the outfit so much, I like dressing sexy sometimes! But dressing that way often invited the unfounded "not a real gamer" stereotype, and my credibility was often questioned just because of my appearance."

"Because of that, I went through a huge swing once I started on the management side of Evil Geniuses, where I was extremely wary of being feminine. I intentionally dressed very masculine because I felt like if I didn't, I would be undercut, underpaid, and my opinion wouldn't be taken seriously. Already, a lot of times my male colleagues would be credited for my ideas."

One day, while looking through her closet and realizing nothing represented who she really was, something clicked. "It was around the time that I made the transition to working at Twitch, when I was a little less in danger professionally, and I had a little more independence to be accepted for who I was and express myself outwardly the way I wanted to—which is with variety and freedom!"

> "The 'always build up, never tear down' mentality was that we believed it's really, really important to condemn mistreatment, but we also want to focus on uplifting others who are doing the right things."

MISSCLIKS

Prosser and several friends founded online community Misscliks in 2013. Their goal was to create content that provided positive visibility to female role models in geek and gaming culture, and to create a safe space for discussing the gendered bias they encountered.

"While we believed it's really, really important to condemn mistreatment, the 'always build up, never tear down' mentality meant that we also wanted to focus on uplifting others who are doing the right things; identifying good behavior and celebrating it," said Prosser.

Misscliks became a network of solidarity and support. "All four of our founders at one point or another, felt like, 'You know what, this isn't worth it. I'm not wanted in this industry, and it hurts too much, and I should just do something else.' Having women around us who would say, 'No. I need you here, and I appreciate you, and you're doing good work,' was the only reason that we all stayed. I think that the more women who do stay, the more women who do support, and the more opportunities that are afforded without being tokenized, the better it will get."

It was through this advocacy that Prosser was invited to the White House in 2015 for a roundtable focused on women in video games. "It was a surreal experience that left me feeling empowered," she recalled. "We got to meet in the Roosevelt room, just a few steps from the Oval Office! I met and still stay in touch with what I consider to be some of the greatest minds and big movers and shakers in the industry there. We still collaborate often."

Prosser hopes her visibility and positivity will help people find their sense of belonging and purpose. "If you want to work in this industry—or, for that matter, in any particular industry—start by knowing yourself well," she said. "Identify your mission, your strengths, and your particular brand of awesome, and then look for where that can be most useful. If you try to become someone else in order to fit into a career or community, sure, you may climb, but you will never experience the fullness of fulfillment that comes from knowing it was because you truly brought yourself to the table."

A DAY IN THE LIFE OF...

HUMAN RESOURCES

Human resources is all about ensuring employees are set up for success and get as much fulfillment out of their jobs as possible. Many specialties fall under the human resources umbrella, including diversity leads, relocation specialists, and recruiting. That being said, HR generalists tend to have shared responsibilities and skills. An HR generalist needs to be motivated, creative, and most importantly, adaptable. Standard HR duties often include new employee orientation, establishing team benefits, creating and enforcing workplace policies, running yearly reviews and promotions, and anything related to payroll.

HR also provides training programs to help employees reach their full potential, lend an ear and provide resources for troubled times, and work to resolve interpersonal workplace conflicts. They are often also culture activists—making sure staff feel valuable and engaged by organizing family picnics, team outings, holiday celebrations, and more.

Agnieszka Szamalek-Michalska found her home at CD PROJEKT RED, a studio that was required to quickly staff up after achieving massive success with *The Witcher* franchise. With a huge team of people from around the world—all with unique backgrounds and sensibilities—the service Szamalek-Michalska provides is pivotal for success.

AGNIESZKA SZAMALEK-MICHALSKA

 Agnieszka Szamalek-Michalska

PROFESSION: INTERNAL COMMUNICATION & CULTURE MANAGER AT CD PROJEKT RED—WARSAW, POLAND

YEARS IN PROFESSION: 12

ASSOCIATED WITH: CD PROJEKT RED

▶ EDUCATION

"I studied international law at Warsaw University. After I graduated, I tried my luck with a career in diplomacy, but shortly after realized it's not what I really want to do. I switched to the private sector, organizing business conferences, where I was given the chance to fulfill new professional goals—work in HR. I started with recruitment. After a few months, I signed up for postgraduate studies in HR management. I liked it so much that after finishing it, I also started studying business psychology."

▶ BREAKING IN

"It wasn't difficult for me to break into video games, but I must say it took two attempts to land a job at CD PROJEKT RED. The first time I succeeded in getting to the final stage of the recruitment process, but someone else was chosen. I hate to lose, so when I saw another job advert similar to the first one, I wrote a letter directly to the HR director explaining how I was the perfect candidate for the position of relocation specialist. When I think about what helped me adapt so quickly, I guess it is my flexibility, being open to new situations and changing environment, and my passion for getting to know new people."

▶ EARLY INDUSTRY IMPRESSIONS

"I was greeted into a young team full of people with amazing talents and passion, open and tolerant. When I started, though, there were not that many women in the company. However, after almost six years, I can say we made huge improvements in this area."

▶ KEY QUALITIES

"Open-mindedness, creativity, persistence, flexibility, sense of humor, the ability to self-start."

▶ TRAINING OPPORTUNITIES

"Grow as a person. Read books, watch TED Talks, paint, and write—I don't know, whatever you fancy. And do a lot of it. I always had a dream to study psychology, so I did. And it helps a lot."

▶ TOOLS OF THE TRADE

"My eyes and ears are the most important tools I use. I am not even joking. I personally believe that no amount of software or magic big-business workflow procedures can substitute for talking with people and observing what they communicate beyond the spoken word.

For me, a good HR rep is a person who's there to fight for the team. I might not know much about programming or the intricacies of level design, but I do know a lot about how to create a safe and balanced work environment for people who do. Like I said, eyes and ears, not email and spreadsheets."

▶ HOURS & ENVIRONMENT

"I am a mum of two kids, so I work from 9am to 5pm. There are days when I need to come in early or stay longer, but it's nothing that would seriously disrupt my work-life balance.

"As for what the environment is like, our gamedev is about keeping things fun and professional; never uptight. Our goal is to fulfill the dreams of gamers from around the world. Even though HR isn't directly involved in making the games, we are working closely with the people who are. We put a lot of effort into providing them with what they need, so that they can continue to grow professionally and stay motivated.

"Culture-wise, at RED, we have a no bull$%&@ policy. Quality, no compromises, huge ambitions, and hard work—we want to make the best games the world has seen, ones we would like to play ourselves. There's no dress code, we have flexible hours, it's a dog-friendly office. Every now and again we do social Fridays, allowing everyone to wind down and enjoy tasty food and beverages.

"Our team consists of people who love games and are the best at what they do. It's our job in HR to make sure things stay this way."

▶ AN AVERAGE DAY

"This is one of the most difficult questions for me. At the risk of sounding cliché, no day is really average. I mean, I come into the office, I get my morning coffee fix, and that's about it. Thirty minutes into the day, sometimes earlier, people come and share their thoughts and problems, and you just go with the flow. This can range from 'Why didn't I get the email that we're doing a pet calendar?' to 'We could use some more opportunities to talk with C-level execs."

So I look at the issue from every angle and try to address it as best I can. There's over 600 people at RED, which creates an infinite stream of stuff to do!"

▶ PROFESSIONAL PERKS

"Working in a creative environment and being part of something 'big.'

"There are plenty of opportunities to get goodies that have to do with our games. Each time we release a game, everyone at the studio gets a copy for the platform of their choice.

"We organize cool parties, too, with amazing attractions: fire shows, ice sculpting, quads, climbing, and sports tournaments just to name a few. We go to the cinema to watch movies, get together during social Fridays, where we play board and video games, and have barbecues in the summer.

"We also engage in charity events on a regular basis. We build houses for homeless animals and do bake-offs and fundraisers for a variety of causes. For example, last year we published an internal "Dogs of RED Calendar" featuring pictures of our employees' dogs, the proceeds from which were donated to an animal shelter. More recently, we organized a trip to the biggest fun park in Poland for kids from one of the children's home in Warsaw.

"I don't know if these are perks specific to working in games or games HR, but for me, these are definitely perks that make RED a great place to work."

▶ CAREER CHALLENGES

"A constantly changing environment and the self-induced pressure for the highest quality in every aspect of my work.

"Good is never good enough. You have to constantly challenge yourself, look for ways to be innovative, and think outside the box. It's not easy and requires a lot of determination, patience, and flexibility."

▶ FAVORITE PROJECT

"In terms of 'big and visible,' it was organizing the release party of *The Witcher 3: Wild Hunt* for our employees. Tons of prep work, talking with the venue—which was an old fort—coming up with activities based on people's suggestions, and so on. In terms of 'big, but hard to quantify,' I am really proud of how we've grown from an initially small crew of passionate people to a friggin' big multinational team of passionate people without losing our soul. Communication and internal culture are big parts of that, and I'm proud I had—and still have—some say in how this happened."

▶ LIFE HACKS

"Nobody sees rum in your coffee. Seriously, though, you need to find a good way to decompress. Read a book, dance, or go to the shooting range and kill some cardboard zombies—as long as you have your own way to unwind, you'll always be efficient."

▶ BIGGEST MISTAKE

"I think studying law for five years was kind of a failure, because I knew from the beginning it's not my thing, but I was too scared to drop it. Still, I am proud of myself that I finally found my way and hopped onto my current career path."

▶ EXCITING ADVANCEMENTS

"I love the shift in perspective of how the 'R' part of 'HR' stops being a 'resource' and starts being a person. A person with feelings, emotions, strengths, and weaknesses. I also love that making mistakes has started to be perceived as an opportunity to grow, not as an excuse to let someone go."

"Learn to listen and identify blockers in listening. In HR, you are there for people. You're a conduit. If you focus on 'transmitting' instead of 'receiving,' problems occur."

HOLLIE BENNETT

COMMUNITY MANAGER AND CONTENT CREATOR

HollieB

PhoenixB

Hollie Bennett

twitch.tv/hollieb

EXPERIENCE

FIRST INDUSTRY PROJECT: EUROPEAN COMMUNITY MANAGER, DESTRUCTOID (2010)

FAVORITE INDUSTRY PROJECT: PLAYSTATION ACCESS

PROJECTS SHIPPED: 40 GAMES, 1800 PLAYSTATION ACCESS VIDEOS

ACHIEVEMENTS UNLOCKED:

> GAMES MEDIA AWARD "RISING STAR" NOMINATION (2011)

> MCV 30 UNDER 30 (2012)

> MCV'S TOP 100 WOMEN IN GAMES (2015)

> WOMEN IN GAMES "INFLUENCER OF THE YEAR" AWARD (2018)

STATS

INDUSTRY LEVEL: 8

CURRENT CLASS: PLAYSTATION UK CHANNEL MANAGER

CURRENT GUILD: SONY INTERACTIVE ENTERTAINMENT EUROPE—LONDON, UNITED KINGDOM

SPECIAL SKILLS: COMMUNITY MANAGEMENT, SOCIAL MEDIA, VIDEO ON DEMAND PRODUCTION, LIVESTREAMING, INTERVIEWING, HOSTING

STANDARD EQUIPMENT

FAVORITE PLATFORM: PLAYSTATION 4

GO-TO GENRE: JRPG/RPG

MUST-HAVE GAME: FINAL FANTASY VIII

Easter Egg

Was a midwife before working in the gaming industry. In her career she assisted on hundreds of births, delivered nearly 150 babies, and had three newborns named after her.

BIO

To say that Hollie Bennett's career did a 180 in her mid-20s is an understatement. After graduating from Bournemouth University in 2009, Bennett put her education to work as a midwife. In the downtime between her demanding job, Bennett fed her passion for video games as the European community manager for Destructiod.com, a website she had been an active member of since 2006. "At the time, it felt like the best of both worlds," she recalled. "I had my grown-up 'real job' and now I was in a position where, thanks to Destructoid, I was given unprecedented access to a world I loved. I never considered it getting much better than that."

BANDAI NAMCO

Only a few years into her midwife career, Bennett found herself burning out. "The National Health Service in the U.K. is a demanding world and working long hours as a midwife was both mentally and physically draining," she explained. "Meanwhile, all my spare time was now spent talking about games instead of actually playing them." Juggling her profession and passion, Bennett took some time off to cover Gamescom, a major European gaming convention. "Bandai Namco asked me to take a look at an upcoming and unannounced new IP," she recalled. The new IP was Ninja Theory's *Enslaved: Odyssey to the West*. Bennett fell in love. "The presentation by Ninja Theory co-founder and designer Tameem Antoniades ignited a spark within me. That's when I knew that I wanted to make this my career. I fell back in love with games, more madly and deeply than ever before."

Aside from having a passion for people and working well under pressure, Bennett knew her midwife experience wouldn't translate into industry experience. Instead, she formalized all the hobbyist work she'd done over the years in her CV and started applying. "Without realizing it, I had gathered a great deal of experience already. Enough experience that companies were replying to my applications!" After a few false starts, Bennett put her networking skills to use. "While attending an event for Bandai Namco, I bumped into the European VP and decided to give him my business card, stating that I was trying to make a move into the industry full time. I explained why Namco was the perfect place for me."

They agreed. The next morning, Bennett woke up to a job offer to be the Consumer and Community PR executive for Bandai Namco games. "It was hard work but I have never regretted my decision to keep trying and I never looked back."

TELLING NEW TALES

Bennett worked at Namco Bandai Partners for two years, learning the ropes of the industry in a four-part role that involved digital communication, community management, consumer PR, and customer service. Her first professional project—working on the *Tales* franchise—was a challenge rife with opportunity. Although very popular in Japan, the series never quite garnered the same level of success in the States. "It was, however, incredibly clear when I started that there was a loyal, passionate and rather loving community of fans in the West who were starting to feel rather unloved," she recalled. "*Tales of Graces* originally saw its launch in 2009 in Japan. In March 2013, it finally launched in the United States while European fans were left waiting until August 2013." Bennett and her colleagues didn't just want to push the game, they wanted to rally the community together.

"We started a community project called 'My Tales of,' which included a dedicated Twitter account for *Tales* news, thus opening direct dialogue between us and the community," Bennett detailed. "We also created a special Day One Edition of the game which, at no extra cost to the community, included additional physical and digital items and a free magazine. The magazine was packed full of community creations; poems, short stories, fan-art, and cosplay."

Through these programs, the community was ignited and given a voice. "We saw huge changes. Not only did we exceed our day one sales targets, but the Japanese development team wanted to get more involved. They actively wanted to travel to European events to meet and thank their fans," said Bennett. "We were also able to open up an internal dialogue within the company to request assistance like never before and the company moved towards global release dates for subsequent launches, a first for the series!"

PLAYSTATION ACCESS

Her success at Namco Bandai opened new doors for Bennett. She found a position at PlayStation UK in 2013, working as the UK Social Media and Community Manager. Bennett found another way to connect directly with the community through her most influential project—a YouTube channel called PlayStation Access. She developed the channel and maintained the brand internally and externally, and it eventually became a pillar of PlayStation UK's marketing and promotion plans. "PlayStation Access has been my favorite project. I've spent the last five years working with an incredible team to help it grow into what it's become today," she recalled. Under Bennett's guidance, she helped develop licensed PlayStation Access products, console themes, apps, and more. The channel and its genuine, passionate staff who are viewed as experts by fans, had a direct and positive impact on sales and pre-orders of PlayStation products.

> "The community aspect of what I do is what I find most fulfilling. I like to build things; brands, community or channels."

The success of the channel—which currently sits at 1.6 million subscribers—led her to take over as the PlayStation Access Channel Manager in 2017, developing and maintaining content schedules for editorial and marketing teams, introducing livestreaming to a traditionally video-on-demand oriented channel, running live event programming in the UK, and continuing to work with first- and third-parties to secure coverage that fans are interested in.

COMMUNITY

Although much has changed over the years as Bennett's career has evolved, she still fundamentally focuses on community. "The community aspect of what I do is what I find most fulfilling. I like to build things; brands, community or channels. Places where people can go and find those of a like mind. To share in something together and to feel welcomed and a sense of belonging. PlayStation Access has allowed us to create personality-driven content, something people can connect and relate to. We receive numerous letters, emails, comments, and direct messages from fans thanking us, telling us how we've made them laugh or even helped them through some of the darker moments in their lives. These messages make everything worth it; the long hours, the work, the stress, and the occasional tears."

Now one of the most recognizable women in gaming in the United Kingdom, Bennett was featured on the cover of *GamesTM* magazine in 2017 and included in an article that provided advice on how to be successful on YouTube. More recently, she took home "Influencer of the Year" at the 2018 Women in Games Awards. "The room was filled with women who have I looked up to and worshipped for years and I was on stage in front of them. It was pretty magical," said Bennett. "I've spent a good deal of my career with imposter syndrome. I almost constantly question both myself and whether I deserve the success I've found in my career. Am I doing enough? Do I deserve the kindness, the love, and support I receive from my community? Am I really any good at what I do, or have I just gotten lucky? I think that night and winning the award just meant so much to me. It grounded me and was a reminder that you know what? I might just be doing ok."

Photo credit: games™ and Future Publishing.

ANITA SARKEESIAN

AN AGENT OF CHANGE THROUGH POP-CULTURE CRITIQUE

 anitasarkeesian

 Feminist Frequency

 femfreq

 anitasarkeesian.com
feministfrequency.com

EXPERIENCE

FIRST INDUSTRY PROJECT: FEMINIST FREQUENCY (2009)

FAVORITE INDUSTRY PROJECT: TROPES VS. WOMEN IN VIDEO GAMES SERIES (2012)

PROJECTS SHIPPED: 239 FEMINIST FREQUENCY VIDEOS

ACHIEVEMENTS UNLOCKED

> NAVGTR HONORARY AWARD—DAMSEL IN DISTRESS VIDEO SERIES (2013)

> GAME DEVELOPERS CHOICE "AMBASSADOR AWARD" (2014)

> TIME "THE 100 MOST INFLUENTIAL PEOPLE" (2014)

> THE NEW SCHOOL HONORARY PHD RECIPIENT (2016)

 STATS

INDUSTRY LEVEL: 9

CURRENT CLASS: EXECUTIVE DIRECTOR

CURRENT GUILD: FEMINIST FREQUENCY—CALIFORNIA, USA

SPECIAL SKILLS: VIDEO PRODUCTION, PUBLIC SPEAKING, ACTIVISM

STANDARD EQUIPMENT

FAVORITE PLATFORM: NINTENDO SWITCH, SNES

GO-TO GENRE: PLATFORMERS, METROIDVANIA

MUST-HAVE GAME: GONE HOME

BIO

"It is really important to me that we fight for the liberation of all people," began feminist media critic Anita Sarkeesian. "I think that one of the ways we create change is through the media, because the media can work to reinforce particular values. And so the question is, are they going to reinforce oppressive, dangerous, harmful values? Or are they going to reinforce positive, liberating, and world-changing values?"

FEMINIST FREQUENCY

Sarkeesian first began deconstructing pop culture in 2009, while finishing her master's degree in social and political thought from York University. "I fell into being a media critic," she said. "I saw that there was a much-needed space for an accessible and engaging mainstream conversation about feminism, and realized it would be more easily facilitated through the lens of popular culture. As someone who has always been a bit geeky, there was a really nice synergy there."

When Sarkeesian first began creating videos in her living room, she wasn't looking to break into gaming. "I just started making videos on YouTube," she said. "It wasn't necessarily 'This is going to be my career.'" She applied her feminist lens to a wide array of pop-culture content: movies, TV, video games, toys, and more. Her work began to attract attention, and in 2011 she partnered with Bitch Media to create *Tropes vs. Women*, a series of videos exploring commonly used character archetypes and plot points in film.

Easter Egg

Learned how to design websites by creating GeoCities fan pages, mostly about Courtney Love.

In 2012, after producing a video series on LEGO's transition from gender-neutral to heavily gendered toys, Sarkeesian's work blipped on Bungie Studio's radar. "Someone who worked there thought it was really interesting," she explained. "They have an internal speaker series, and invited me to come and talk. I developed a presentation specifically for them about women's representations in games, and that is one of the reasons *Tropes vs. Women in Video Games* came to be."

TACKLING TROPES

In early 2012, Sarkeesian launched a Kickstarter campaign to help realize *Tropes vs. Women in Video Games*, a series of videos that would explore limiting roles female game characters were often relegated to, such as the Damsel in Distress, the Sexy Sidekick, and Background Decoration. Her goal was to raise $6000, which would help offset the costs of production and allow her to upgrade equipment to produce higher-quality videos.

"They said, 'You talked about one of my games. I realized that using that trope... is harmful, and I'm not going to do it again, so thank you.' It blew my mind."

> "The point was never to shame creators for what they've done, but to educate and offer tools to make better, more inclusive games."

Shortly after her Kickstarter went live, a demographic of gamers—who would, two years later, be unified under the "Gamergate" banner—felt the series was a personal attack on their favorite pastime. "When my work became higher-profile—specifically my videos about video games—that's when everything became more complicated," she said. "I had an extreme, vicious backlash that took the form of a massive hate mob that is still active to this day. I didn't expect to be threatened out of my house and at my public appearances. The environment of doing this work was way more vitriolic than I ever could have imagined. But I also got support from a lot of people who were really excited about my work and wanted to see a more inclusive games industry."

When the ongoing harassment against Sarkeesian received widespread news coverage, her campaign was overfunded to the tune of $158K as a sign of solidarity from nearly 7000 backers. The additional funding allowed Sarkeesian to expand the initial scope of her video series and bring on a second staff member. The first *Tropes* video was released in March of 2013.

"The process of making a *Tropes* episode required an enormous amount of research and assessment," explained Sarkeesian. "We had to determine what examples were relevant, and part of a larger reoccurring pattern throughout gaming history. Then distill it down into specific examples, and take feminist theory to weave it all together. The process of writing the scripts took two to three months per episode. There was also the enormously grueling process of capturing gameplay, because you'd be playing a game for hours just to get 10 seconds of footage. It was a production to put all of it together."

The first season of *Tropes vs. Women in Video Games* included 10 videos clocking in at over 200 minutes of thoroughly researched critiques. The series garnered nearly 11 million views on YouTube alone. Each release was reported on industry-wide and would spark new debate about the current culture of video games.

As Feminist Frequency's influence expanded, they leveled up their productions. "We did a series called *Ordinary Women Daring to Defy History*, which had a full crew on an actual studio set," she said. "The scripts were all pre-written and recorded in one day." Feminist Frequency is soon starting a new series called *Queer Tropes*, with Sarkeesian taking a role exclusively behind the camera. "We partnered with Adrienne Shaw of Temple University and the database that she's put together of queer representations in games," she shared.

Feminist Frequency is now a registered non-profit with several full-time staff members. While they continue to highlight issues of representation for women in pop culture, content has expanded to be a voice for many types of marginalized people, discussing not only gender, but race, sexuality, and the intersection of all three.

COUNTERING THE MOB

With her video production work at Feminist Frequency, it was impossible—dangerous, even—for Sarkeesian to ignore the ongoing attacks from Internet mobs. So she began to speak out and raise awareness of how prevalent attacks against women online are. She was a guest on *The Colbert Report* in 2014. She gave a TEDxWomen Talk, presented at the XOXO Festival, and accepted guest invitations to dozens of conferences around the world. In 2015, Sarkeesian was invited to speak at the United Nations for their Broadband Working Group on Gender, which aimed to find ways to combat gendered cyber harassment.

While online mobs would try to paint Sarkeesian as a villain destroying their hobby, mainstream media would swing the pendulum the other way, often representing her as a one-dimensional victim, overshadowing her numerous accomplishments as a critic and an advocate. And those accomplishments are many. *Rolling Stone* named Sarkeesian "pop culture's most valuable critic." *Time* ranked her as one of the 100 most influential people of 2014. She was profiled in *The New Yorker*, *Bloomberg Businessweek*, *The Guardian*, *The Wall Street Journal*, *The New York Times*, and other leading publications worldwide. Additionally, Sarkeesian was the recipient of the 2014 Game Developers Choice Ambassador Award, and received an honorary PhD from the New School in New York City.

CATALYZING THE CONVERSATION

Sarkeesian's impact on the video game industry is immeasurable, be it through the discourse she sparks, the content she creates, or through personal acts of courage in the face of endless adversity. "Relatively early on, when I began releasing the *Tropes* episodes, I started hearing from developers," said Sarkeesian. "They said, 'You talked about one of my games. I realized that using that trope or that characterization is harmful, and I'm not going to do it again, so thank you.' It blew my mind, because that was the whole point. The point was never to shame creators for what they've done, but to educate and offer tools to make better, more inclusive games. It was really motivating."

"I think the conversation has changed dramatically since I started doing this work," she continued. "The industry isn't a perfect bastion of feminism by any stretch of the imagination, but back then developers were not bringing in speakers to come talk about diversity and inclusion in their studios. The press wasn't asking questions about representation, or even acknowledging those aspects in their game reviews."

Sarkeesian regularly has women approach her at public appearances and share that they joined or stayed in the industry as a result of her work. "And I always laugh and ask, 'How did my experience of being viciously attacked make you want to stay in this industry?' But I also get that they're here and they're ready to fight, and they refuse to be sidelined. And if my speaking up inspired them, that's amazing."

THE 2010s: CONTROVERSY, COMMUNITY, & COMPETITION

2011: U.S. SUPREME COURT RULING

In a landmark moment for video games, the US Supreme Court ruled that video games were entitled to the same protection of free speech as film, music, and literature. The ruling came decades after the video game industry found itself in the hot seat during the early 1990s, and again in 2005 when the "Hot Coffee" mini-game in *Grand Theft Auto: San Andreas* led to substantial controversy and an attempt led by U.S. Senators Hillary Clinton, Joe Lieberman, and Evan Bayh to heavily regulate video game sales.

2011: NINTENDO 3DS IS RELEASED

Throughout the 2000s, 3D film became a popular way to boost Hollywood revenues. 3D gaming soon followed, and in 2011, Nintendo released the 3DS. Unlike 3D glasses used for film and comparable gaming accessories for consoles and PCs, the 3DS achieved a stereoscopic 3D effect without additional peripherals. Although it initially got off to a slow start, the 3DS would go on to sell over 72M units worldwide, with the larger 3DS XL and 2DS models helping the platform thrive throughout the decade[1].

2011: TWITCH.TV LAUNCHES

Twitch.tv was originally a gaming-centric spin-off of Justin.tv, the all-purpose streaming platform that had popularized livestreaming. Over the next few years, Twitch would slowly supersede Justin.tv, with JTV abruptly shutting down in 2014. That same year, the Twitch Plays *Pokémon* stream went viral, substantially boosting Twitch's prominence. It was later reported that Google intended to acquire Twitch in a deal worth approximately $1B. However, it was Amazon that ultimately closed the deal for $970M[2].

2011: MINECRAFT POPULARIZES THE EARLY ACCESS BUSINESS MODEL

Indie blockbuster *Minecraft* was first made available to the public via a paid alpha, which enabled early adopters to play the game in an unfinished state and provide feedback on the game's official forums. *Minecraft* was immensely successful and influenced many other developers to embrace the same business model. "Alphafunding" went full tilt when it was officially introduced to the Steam digital distribution platform in 2013 under the name Early Access. Other platforms, such as Xbox Live, have also adopted early access models.

Minecraft is the second best-selling game of all-time (after *Tetris*), and its success led to the IP being acquired by Microsoft in 2014 as part of an unprecedented $2.5B deal.[3]

2010 2011 2012 2013 2014

2012: KICKSTARTER REVOLUTIONIZES GAME FUNDING

Double Fine Productions launched a project on the crowdfunding site Kickstarter. The record-breaking campaign raised over $3.4M on a goal of $400K, initiating a Kickstarter gold rush similar to what the App Store experienced a few years prior.

Often combined with an Early Access release, crowdfunded games allowed developers of any size and experience level to—theoretically—circumvent the need for publishers, who had largely become a contentious part of the development process. For this reason, indie gaming in particular received a massive boost.

Eventually, the quantity of projects on Kickstarter drastically shot up while the quality fluctuated greatly. Crowdfunded games, along with Early Access, became a slippery slope for both developers and customers alike. In both cases, many projects were abandoned before being finished, leading to consumer concerns, crowdfunding fatigue, and a wildly unpredictable marketplace.

2012-20XX: THE NEXT GENERATION

Nintendo launched the eighth generation of home consoles with the release of the Wii U in 2012. Utilizing a tablet-inspired controller, the Wii U attempted to be more competitive with the core gaming audience than the Wii while still innovating, but failed to achieve its predecessor's success. The Wii U was discontinued in early 2017. Nintendo followed the Wii U with the Nintendo Switch in 2017, which gained popularity thanks in part to two highly anticipated and critically acclaimed titles: *Super Mario Odyssey* and *The Legend of Zelda: Breath of the Wild.*

Sony and Microsoft entered the eighth generation one week apart in November 2013, with the PlayStation 4 and Xbox One, respectively. Facing stiff competition from the mobile gaming and PC markets, the PlayStation 4 managed to secure a formidable 81 million+ global unit sales by mid-2018, compared to the Xbox One's estimated 39 million, and the Switch's 19 million[4]. Both consoles received iterative redesigns, the PlayStation Pro, the Xbox One S, and Xbox One X, enabling them to better support the emerging Ultra-HD display market.

2012: OCULUS RIFT REVIVES VR

Oculus VR utilized Kickstarter for the Oculus Rift in late 2012, receiving $2.4M in funding[5]. Once a failed gimmick, VR gained better traction this time around, receiving major support from companies like Valve and Sony. In 2014, shortly after the initial wave of VR titles were released, Facebook acquired Oculus VR for $2B[6]. The library of available VR games ballooned in April 2016, when the HTC Vive—developed by Valve and electronics manufacturer HTC—was released for its Steam platform.

While the expensive entry point and lack of killer apps haven't led to mainstream market penetration yet, the possibilities of VR give many developers hope that as costs decrease and technology improves, VR will pave the way for the next generation of gaming and non-gaming apps alike.

2018: BATTLE ROYALE GAMES DOMINATE THE MARKET

The Battle Royale genre, inspired by the Japanese manga/films of the same name, began as user-created modes in *Minecraft* and mods in *ARMA 2* before being popularized by *DayZ* and *H1Z1*. In early 2017, *PlayerUnknown's Battlegrounds* launched in Steam Early Access and sold over 50 million units across all platforms, rocketing it into the top five best-selling games of all-time[7].

In late 2017, Epic Games released a free-to-play Battle Royale mode for its Early Access PvE title, *Fortnite*. Pieced together in roughly two months, *Fortnite* became a worldwide phenomenon, achieving 125M players across all platforms by mid 2018 and surpassing $1B in revenues during that same milestone[8].

#1REASONWHY

In late 2012, Kickstarter's Head of Games, Luke Crane, tweeted the question, "Why are there so few lady game creators?" Over the next several hours, he received thousands of responses using the hashtag #1ReasonWhy. Women from all corners of the game industry shared personal stories of sexism and harassment, sparking a #metoo movement long before Hollywood. While the hashtag raised awareness of systemic issues, meaningful change was still years in the making. The event culminated in a second hashtag introduced by video game writer Rhianna Pratchett: #1ReasonToBe. "#1ReasonWhy is important, but I'm creating #1ReasonToBe because I'd like female devs to share why they're in games and what they get from it," she said on Twitter. Women spoke out about the reasons they persist through gender-based challenges and the rewards of working in the video game industry. The hashtag was adopted into a yearly panel at the annual Game Developers Conference (GDC)highlighting the work of industry women, which has since expanded to welcome the voices from all types of marginalized game creators.

2015 2016 2017 2018 2019

THE GAMERGATE CONTROVERSY BEGINS

Gamergate is a broad term used for a series of events focusing around the harassment of several women in the game industry. The catalyst was an inflammatory blog post written in 2014 by a man who falsely alleged his ex-girlfriend had an intimate relationship with a game journalist in exchange for positive media coverage. While "Gamergaters" continually argued that the controversy centered on a long-running discussion around ethics in games journalism, Gamergate is primarily known as an industry-wide, anti-feminist harassment campaign, resulting in rape and death threats, doxxing, and other forms of intimidation aimed at women and their allies. Gamergate is often cited as the boiling point of a culture war over traditional and progressive views of the gamer identity. Gamergate was covered by the mainstream media, fictionalized on television shows, and recounted first-hand in Zoë Quinn's 2017 book, *Crash Override*. The Crash Override Network was established in 2015 as a support group for victims of online abuse.

ESPORTS EXPLOSION

Thanks in large part to the popularity of Twitch, competitive gaming experienced a meteoric rise in visibility and economic significance. Organized tournaments around the world matched those of professional sports, with world championships and multi-million-dollar sponsorships and prize pools on the line. In 2008, *Fortnite* streamer Tyler "Ninja" Blevins became the first professional gamer to be featured on the cover of *ESPN The Magazine*, further validating the increasingly blurred line between esports and sports.

ONLINE COMMUNITIES

While social media, online forums, and chat programs like TeamSpeak and Ventrilo have always played a role in the discourse surrounding the game industry's many facets, the rising importance of online communities became much more apparent in the 2010s. Sites like NeoGaf and Reddit helped steer the dialogue between gamers and game makers, while influencers on Twitch and YouTube built their own empowered communities. Social media also facilitated ongoing communication directly from fans and industry professionals, which has had both positive and negative ramifications.

1. Nintendo Hardware Sales. Nintendo of Japan. June 2018.
2. "Amazon to Buy Video Site Twitch for $970 Million." *The Wall Street Journal*. 25 August 2014.
3. Bogart, Nicole. Updated: September 15, 2014 8:35 pm. "Microsoft Acquires 'Minecraft' Maker for $2.5 Billion." Shaw Media. Global News.
4. IR Information: "Sales Data—Dedicated Video Game Sales Units." Nintendo Co., Ltd.
5. "Oculus Rift: Step Into the Game." Kickstarter. August 2012.
6. "Facebook to Acquire Oculus." Facebook Newsroom. Facebook. March 25, 2014.
7. McWhertor, Michael. "PUBG Reaches 50M Copies Sold, 400M Total Players." Polygon.
8. Valentine, Rebekah. July 17, 2018. "Fortnite Has Earned $1 Billion From In-Game Purchases alone." GamesIndustry.biz.

JENNY XU

COMPUTER SCIENCE ADVOCATE
& JUMP SCARE ENTHUSIAST

Xujennyc
Jennycxu
Xuoot
jcsoft.com

EXPERIENCE

FIRST INDUSTRY PROJECT: CLICK ON A BALL AS MANY TIMES AS POSSIBLE IN 60 SECONDS (2009)

FAVORITE INDUSTRY PROJECT: CAN YOU ESCAPE FATE (2017)

PROJECTS SHIPPED: 60 GAMES

ACHIEVEMENTS UNLOCKED:

> MICROSOFT XBOX "GAME CHANGER AWARD" (2016)

> INTERNATIONAL GAME DEVELOPERS ASSOCIATION "WOMEN IN GAMES AMBASSADOR" (2016)

> MIT "OUTSTANDING NEW LEADER" AWARD (2017)

> FORBES "30 UNDER 30: GAMES" (2018)

STATS

INDUSTRY LEVEL: 8

CURRENT CLASS: STUDIO FOUNDER & SOFTWARE ENGINEER

CURRENT GUILD: JCSOFT INC.—SAN FRANCISCO, USA

SPECIAL SKILLS: PROGRAMMING, ART, ANIMATION, SOUND DESIGN, FARMING, RUNNING

STANDARD EQUIPMENT

FAVORITE PLATFORM: NINTENDO WII

GO-TO GENRE: HORROR-COMEDY

MUST-HAVE-GAME: SUPER SMASH BROS. BRAWL

Easter Egg

Became a trained fly assassin after the unwelcome guests became serial harassers of her six pet chickens.

BIO

While many internet denizens find joy and distraction in cats, Jenny Xu found career inspiration in one. "In 7th grade I used Adobe Flash to design and animate a cat," began Xu. "After hitting 'run animation' the cat burst into motion, legs churning. I was delighted. Until I realized I couldn't stop it." If she hadn't intervened, her creation would have been doomed to a life in perpetual motion. "My mission was clear: I needed to code a 'stop' button." An additional three lines allowed her to freeze the feline mid-sprint and she became captivated by what code could do.

A FOUNDATION OF FRIGHT

Her 2009 experiment was the catalyst to a longtime relationship with Flash games. At the age of 15, Xu founded her own company as an umbrella to brand her growing list of Flash titles. *Animatronic Jumpscare Factory* was her first large undertaking and first large success. A free-to-play mobile app inspired by horror sensation *Five Nights at Freddy's*, Xu tackled the art, animation, sound design, coding, and promotion of the title. The app encouraged the creation of custom creepy characters used to frighten unwitting friends and family.

Early after release, she got her own scare while working on *Animatronic Jumpscare Factory* and learned a valuable lesson in the process. "I was surprised when over 10,000 players picked up the game in the first week," she began. "But I was confused when I started receiving a wave of one-star reviews mere minutes after an early update went live on the Android market. A deeper investigation revealed that she'd overridden the save data of tens of thousands of users.

To Xu, the episode illustrated her responsibility as a developer and the importance of safe coding practices. "Even now, I make sure that my code takes on several use cases and I make sure to check all the edge cases. And I make sure that I always have an eye out for one-star reviews in case it's time for me to take action again. This time, I'm ready." Three years later she continues to update *Animatronic Jumpscare Factory*, which boasts over 2.5 million downloads on the Google Play App Store.

Despite the success, Xu—still in her teens at the time—was plagued by fear for her body of work. "I was afraid that the games I was making weren't good enough to be considered acceptable in the industry. I was young and anything I made was almost embarrassing to me to put out in the world," she began. "However, I found that once I started, I couldn't get enough of the industry. I loved seeing people comment on my games, create YouTube videos of them, and tell me that they were inspired by my games. It was a relief that people actually liked what I made." Dozens of games later, Xu has created a community around her work.

DEFINING GAME DEVELOPER

Xu kept creating, but had another hurdle to overcome—she didn't believe herself to be a proper game developer. It took reassurance from industry veteran Kate Edwards, Former Executive Director of the International Game Developers Association, to make her recognize her own hard-earned success. "Kate told me the five most powerful words I've ever heard: 'You are a game developer'. I realized then that it's not like you hit 1,000,000 million downloads and suddenly you're a game developer. It's in the process of coding, of designing a level, or in the middle of mixing a game track that you truly become a game developer. So, in that moment, I realized that instead of trying to become something with all my energy, I'd embrace who I already was."

Now 21 years old—and one of Forbes' 30-under-30 for 2018—Xu's success is undisputable. She's published a total of 60 Flash games and 10 mobile games, resulting in more than 4,500,000 cumulative downloads between Apple, Google, and Amazon app stores. She presented her game *Hungry Trash,* aimed at teaching elementary students how to properly sort rubbish, to the Department of Energy at the White House. She also spoke in front of 400 industry colleagues at the Women in Games Luncheon presented by Microsoft at the Game Developers Conference in 2017.

In her fourth year at the Massachusetts Institute of Technology, pursuing a computer science and comparative media studies degree (and with internships at PlayStation and publishing giant EA under her belt) Xu is already taking steps to encourage the next generation of game developers. "I think the gaming industry seems like a gigantic monolith to those who aren't in the industry right now. I know that as a female software developer, I can inspire other girls to start learning computer science."

"I'd like it to be easier for newcomers to join the market and feel like their games will be noticed and seen. "

Her goal is to help establish game programs for those who don't have them readily accessible, and to hold workshops for aspiring professionals. She's already established game development workshops at MIT, hosting dozens of young girls to teach them the basics of coding in Unity. "I think from that, I was able to help some girls get a kick-start in the industry, and I hope they take that away for life."

Xu also intends to inspire change through play, on topics as varied as education on global warming, to mental health, and the gender gap in the game industry. "I want to show that games can also be used to improve lives and perform research on issues such as depression. It is fascinating how children with autism can convey their feelings and emotions through video games, and I hope that I can contribute to this kind of research."

"Sometimes I still think about that poor cat I made when I was 12," reflected Xu. "Now, I'm the one in constant motion. But unlike my cat, I hope I never find my 'stop' button. There's way too much to do. "

ELOISE

THE #1 SHADOW PRIEST OF CHINA TURNED HEARTHSTONE CHALLENGER

 TempoEloise  Tempoeloise

 twitch.tv/eloise

EXPERIENCE

FIRST INDUSTRY PROJECT: CHINA VS NA S1—HEARTHSTONE (2013)

FAVORITE INDUSTRY PROJECT: WORLD CHAMPIONSHIP QUALIFIER (2014)

ACHIEVEMENTS UNLOCKED:

> DRAGON SOUL SPEED-RUN CHALLENGE—WORLD OF WARCRAFT, WORLD 1ST (2012)

> HEROIC 25 MAN LICH KING RAID—WORLD OF WARCRAFT, WORLD 6TH (2011)

> CHINA VS. NORTH AMERICA—HEARTHSTONE, TOP 4 (2013)

> GOLD LEAGUE GRAND FINAL, CHINA—HEARTHSTONE, TOP 8 (2014)

STATS

INDUSTRY LEVEL: 8

CURRENT CLASS: PROFESSIONAL HEARTHSTONE PLAYER

CURRENT GUILD: TEMPO/STORM—USA

SPECIAL SKILLS: NO.1 SHADOW PRIEST IN CHINA, MOST FAMOUS COMPETITIVE FEMALE HEARTHSTONE PLAYER, EXPERT ON DPS

STANDARD EQUIPMENT

FAVORITE PLATFORM: PC

GO-TO GENRE: MMO

MUST-HAVE GAME: WORLD OF WARCRAFT

BIO

Professional gamer Haiyun Tang—better known as Eloise—says she spent the best six years of her life in *World of Warcraft*. "I learned a lot about life from *World of Warcraft*," began Eloise. "I started playing *WoW* when I was in college. I found I was very good at it—my role was as a Shadow Priest—and I was able to make incredibly large DPS (damage per second). So, people suggested I join a really good team, which I did."

In 2010, Eloise joined the top raiding guild in China—the Stars. Her skills were honed even further during practice sessions with her top-ranked teammates, and Eloise quickly became a breakout competitive *WoW* player, known as "The #1 Shadow Priest of China." "It only took me about one and a half years to reach the top ranks, but I was able to stay on the top for a few years," said Eloise. "I played *WoW* competitively for about four years."

> "I learned a lot about life from *World of Warcraft*."

REACHING FOR THE STARS

Although it may seem strange to an outsider, professional gaming can be grueling, and Eloise found this out early on in her career. "When I first joined the top-ranked team of *WoW* in China, my captain was very strict and tough. Many female candidates left the team because they couldn't take harsh criticism. Also, as team members, we normally practiced for 16 hours a day. I was on a team with all boys, and sometimes I felt as if I was having trouble keeping up physically, but I had no choice."

She pushed past these hurdles, and during her time on the team, the Stars completed raid instances on the highest difficulty:

- Heroic 25-person Lich King raid—World 6th
- Heroic 25-person Magmaw raid—World 5th
- Heroic 25-person Cho'gall raid—World 5th
- Heroic 25-person Sinestra raid—World 5th
- Heroic 25-person Omnotron Defense System raid—World 4th
- Heroic 25-person Spine of Deathwing raid—World 2nd
- Heroic 25-person Madness of Deathwing raid—World 2nd
- Heroic 25-person Garrosh Hellscream raid—World 2nd
- Dragon Soul speed-run challenge—World 1st.

Easter Egg

Has three iPads on at all times: one to practice *Hearthstone*, one to watch *Hearthstone* streaming videos, and a third for playing around.

Despite Eloise's great success in *World of Warcraft*, she found her eye wandering to a new game in 2013—*Hearthstone*. She decided to give it a try and ended up switching her competitive career path. Considering the taxing training it took to achieve success in *WoW*, it was not an easy decision. "The career switch took me a considerable amount of time and effort to adjust to," explained Eloise.

A NEW GAME

With tens of millions of other players discovering *Hearthstone* at the same time, Eloise once again started rising in the ranks. Soon she found herself competing professionally on an international scale. "My first *Hearthstone* tournament, I was a member of a Chinese team competing against a team from the United States for a place in the quarterfinals," said Eloise. "Although we lost, it was my first large, international game as a *Hearthstone* player representing my country. I have been a professional *Hearthstone* player ever since."

Around the same time she picked up *Hearthstone*, Eloise began streaming her practice sessions as well. "When I was playing *WoW*, I didn't stream. In fact, I didn't even like talking or interacting with other people—I just wanted to play the game and enjoy myself," explained Eloise. "This was changed after I started playing *Hearthstone*. I joined DouYu—a streaming video platform in China—as one of the first video game streamers. I started to learn how to interact and talk with others. Streaming changed my personality—I found it was actually fun to be able to interact and share my experience with others instead of only focusing on playing games." Streaming opened Eloise up to the world, and she began to learn English and Western pop-culture references from her interactions on Twitch. She now streams daily, has posted 1500 videos to the platform in the past five years, and 200,000 followers tune in to watch her play, hoping to improve their skills in the process.

Eloise's *Hearthstone* achievements continued as she trained. In 2014, she was in the top eight of the Gold League Grand Final, the biggest *Hearthstone* tournament in China. Eloise also earned a top-five World Championship qualifier spot in China that same year. In 2015, she was one of eight Chinese players to compete against Europe.

TEAMING UP WITH TEMPO STORM

Out of the European tournament came an offer from a professional gaming team. "Because of the China vs. EU tournament, Tempo Storm contacted me to try to get me on the team," said Eloise. "I wanted to compete against more people from outside of China. I wanted to compete on a bigger stage, so I joined Tempo Storm." Tempo Storm—founded in 2014—is currently composed of nine players from the United States, Germany, Iceland, and China.

The achievements continued for Eloise after joining the team—she placed third in the second season of GEICO Brawl, third in the HS Arena Grand Opening Invitational, second in the Gang Wars Major Tournament, fourth in the Kinguin for Charity Tournament, fifth in the ONOG Pax East Major Tournament, and fourth in the NSL 2017 Invitational.

Competing on a global scale has given her a unique perspective on being a woman in esports. "In the West I feel like people respect me as a woman, but they don't respect me as a player. But in China, people respect me as a player but don't respect me as a woman," shared Eloise. On her home turf, she often faced disparaging comments about her appearance, but no one questioned her gaming skills. In the West, she was considered cute, but not a strong player. Despite the inherent difficulties, Eloise feels there are benefits to being in the minority. "As for esports, female professional players often actually make more money than male players even in this male-dominated industry, because female professionals are rare. It's as simple as that."

Despite her high skill level, Eloise has felt the sting of defeat before. "During the 2015 *Hearthstone* World Championship held at BlizzCon, I lost my position before entering the top four players ranking in China, and that experience hit me hard," shared Eloise. "I was feeling depressed and wasn't able to pick myself up during the competitions. Instead, I'd spend a large amount of my time streaming." Luckily, support was there around the corner. "My mother helped and gave me all the support and courage to continue my gaming career. She is very proud of me."

Picking herself back up, Eloise placed in the top eight in the Summer Mansion Tournament, Titanar Invitational, and Sydney *Hearthstone* Invitational, all in 2017. She's also taken top 16 in the HCT Sydney Global Qualifier, top 16 in the Gold League Suzhou, and second in the NUTSBET Streamer Cup.

Whatever the placement, Eloise has become known not only for her skill, but for her sportsmanlike behavior and sense of humor. She's tweeted smiley faces after a loss, sharing excitement over being able to sit back and enjoy the rest of the tournament as a spectator. Her followers appreciate that she doesn't take herself too seriously on stream—"Best of Eloise" supercuts have over 300,000 views on YouTube.

Eloise's visibility and perseverance as a professional player are certainly inspiring. Her work ethic and drive led her to become one of the most successful female competitive gamers in the world in a short window of time. Eloise hopes to instill this passion in her female followers. "Many of my female followers who look up to me want to reach a higher player level, and my experience encouraged them to join esports," Eloise concluded. "I am happy about this contribution."

A DAY IN THE LIFE OF...

A VOICE-OVER & PERFORMANCE CAPTURE ACTRESS

The game industry has come a long way since the days when pixelated characters could only communicate through subtitles and intentionally exaggerated animations. Now technology has advanced and become accessible to game developers big and small, allowing them to bring characters to life on motion-capture stages that simultaneously record voice, movement, and expressions. Called "performance-capture artists" when offering this combination of skills, these professionals enable game characters to convey genuine emotion in a way not previously possible. Stephanie Panisello came to Los Angeles on vacation... and never left. Deciding to pursue her dream as an actress, she worked her way through production and small NPC (non-playable character) roles. Now Stephanie is lending her talents as the lead in a major AAA game franchise.

STEPHANIE PANISELLO

 StephaniePanisello  StephaniePanisello  Stephanie Panisello  stephaniepanisello.com

PROFESSION: VOICE-OVER AND MOTION-CAPTURE ARTIST—LOS ANGELES, USA

YEARS IN PROFESSION: 5

WORKED ON: SHADOW OF THE TOMB RAIDER, DOOM, THE EVIL WITHIN 2, FINAL FANTASY XV, BLADE 2, MOBIUS FINAL FANTASY, LIGHTNING RETURNS: FINAL FANTASY XIII

▶ EDUCATION

"I was born with a love for performing. Ever since I could remember I was always acting in plays and hosting my own 'talk shows' as a young kid. When I decided I wanted to be a professional actress, I knew I had to perfect my craft, so I started taking acting, stunt training, voice-over, fight choreography, and gun-training classes."

▶ KEY QUALITIES

"One of the best personality traits you can have is a good sense of humor and thick skin, because this business can be tough. Laughter is the best thing to keep a fun, creative environment and it will come in handy when you don't land the role you really wanted or you need to do multiple versions of a line until you land it right. Also, being a great listener will help you take better direction so you can give different and honest performances."

▶ TRAINING OPPORTUNITIES

"I'd recommend anyone looking to get into full performance capture to take acting classes as well as voice-over classes. One part of my job is the body performance of the character, and this is where training the acting muscle is a must. To get yourself really comfortable with this, I suggest you perform on-camera in front of a crew and in live theater performances. The second part is the voice aspect of my work, for which voice-over classes can help you gain technique behind the mic. Voice-over is very unique, in that you'll want to be able to hear the story your 'face' would normally tell. The key is to consistently work out your voice and body, because they are your tools."

▶ TOOLS OF THE TRADE

"On a regular basis I use Pro Tools, a condenser mic, a mic interface, a computer, and my recording booth. For facial-capture auditions I use a camera, lights, backdrop, and edit with Adobe Premiere Pro. I also like using YouTube, Twitch, and video games in general as a resource. The more I know about the medium I'm acting in, the better an understanding I have of the game and the type of performance the directors want."

▶ HOURS & ENVIRONMENT

"There is no real average day in the acting world. During a voice-over session I work in a sound-recording studio booth, anywhere from 20 minutes to four hours. When I'm on a motion-capture job, I'll typically work up to eight hours or more in the volume, depending on how many scenes we have to cover that day.

"A 'volume' is a huge padded room with cameras everywhere that pick up the data from the little white shiny balls on the suit and the face cam I wear. These studios are where adults get to play make-believe with their friends and call it work."

▶ PROFESSIONAL PERKS

"A voice-over acting perk is having the ability to work barefoot or strolling into work in your pajamas. However, the best perk of being an actress in games is getting the opportunity to 'play' for a living. And the most humbling and encouraging perk is getting to work with legends in the business. It's amazing to meet them, but learning from them is invaluable."

▶ CAREER CHALLENGES

"The biggest challenge of my profession is having to keep my mouth shut when all I want to do is scream at the top of my lungs about the new cool project I'm working on, but unfortunately, the NDA (non-disclosure agreement) I signed prevents me from doing so. This is hard because you can't ever share with your friends and family what you're doing, which kind of makes you feel like some sort of spy or CIA agent, even in real life."

▶ FAVORITE PROJECT

"One project that really stands out was getting to play Lara Croft for *Shadow of the Tomb Raider*'s cinematic trailer. If I could go back in time and tell little kid Stephanie she'd get to be Lara Croft, I'm not sure she'd even believe me -- DREAM COME TRUE! The other project, and my favorite role to date, is as the lead for a major video game franchise that I can't talk about just yet—like I said, NDAs are tough."

▶ LIFE HACKS

"Vocal warm-ups while I drive, picking up new hobbies, rock climbing, and staying physically active have been the best life hacks to staying agile for any role thrown my way."

▶ EXCITING ADVANCEMENTS

"I love that we are seeing a trend of stronger, empowered female characters. Which is a long way from where games started. The biggest advancement I've seen is how women are being depicted through the actual camera lens itself. Slowly but surely we are straying away from 'butt and boob shots' and camera focus is starting to emphasize more on the characters' abilities rather than on their 'assets.' This subtle but impactful change is enhancing our respect for females in games."

PRO TIP!

"Practice every day! Do vocal warm-ups regularly and imitate characters within your wheelhouse until you gain enough instinct to create your own. I learned through trial and error that there were certain character voices I could keep for up to four hours and some I couldn't. The ones that I struggled with, I chose to practice, until I was able to master them and add them to my repertoire. My final tip is to watch what the pros do and understand your medium by playing video games."

GISELA VAQUERO

GIVING VOICE AND VISIBILITY TO SPAIN'S WOMEN GAME PROFESSIONALS

 gisvaq
mujeresenjuegos

 giselavaquero

 Gisela Vaquero

 jellyworld.es

EXPERIENCE

FIRST INDUSTRY PROJECT: HOVER CABS (2014)

FAVORITE INDUSTRY PROJECT: WITCHES (2015)

PROJECTS SHIPPED: 16 GAMES

ACHIEVEMENTS UNLOCKED:

> VI ASPASIA "IN DEFENSE OF GENDER EQUALITY AWARD" FINALIST (2018)

> WOMEN IN GAMES "HALL OF FAME AWARD" NOMINATION (2018)

STATS

INDUSTRY LEVEL: 8

CURRENT CLASS: GAME DESIGNER, FOUNDER, & PRESIDENT

CURRENT GUILD: JELLYWORLD INTERACTIVE, WOMEN IN GAMES ESPANA—BARCELONA, SPAIN

SPECIAL SKILLS: GAME DEVELOPMENT, SYSTEMS DESIGN, NARRATIVE DESIGN, LEVEL DESIGN, GAME BALANCING, SCREENWRITING

STANDARD EQUIPMENT

FAVORITE PLATFORM: PC

GO-TO GENRE: RPG

MUST-HAVE-GAME: ULTIMA ONLINE

Easter Egg

The room she played in as a little girl was an old attic, which could have easily been a set from a '90s horror film.

BIO

While studying film at university with the intent of being a scriptwriter, Gisela Vaquero was inspired by a bad game to pursue a different career. "One day, when I was at the apartment complex where I lived, I saw a colleague playing a console video game," she began. "I sat down to watch, and I noticed that the script was very little taken care of; it was not realistic nor had any depth. At that moment, I realized that I would like to dedicate myself to designing and making scripts for video games, although I had no idea where to start."

For family and friends, this course correction wasn't a surprise. She had been playing video games from a very young age. "We bought many consoles: Atari 2600, Game Gear, Master System II, Game Boy," Vaquero recalled. "When I was a little girl, I 'designed' games and drew 'labyrinths' on a sheet of graph paper."

As soon as she set her mind to correcting the injustices of poor narrative design, she took to the Internet and began researching how to become a game designer. "I learned different programs, but I also had to spend the day at my job," she said. "It was difficult; I was working during the day and learning and practicing during the remaining time available: programming languages, game design theory, game engines, and other programs." Squeezing in time where she could, she finished her first two personal projects as a test of her skills, *Broken Night* and *Strawberry Basket*—the former a puzzle game, the latter a platformer.

When she later discovered a master's program in design and programming for video games, she enrolled. But before even finishing the degree, all her hard work and late nights paid off with an offer for her first job as a game designer.

CODIWANS

In 2012, Vaquero was hired as a level designer to Codiwans in Barcelona. "The first video game I professionally designed was *Hover Cabs*. My initial role was level designer, and my tasks were to design and build the game levels and the missions in those levels," she explained. "But in the end, I also designed the whole narrative and characters."

As her first official industry job, working at Codiwans provided valuable training for her future career. "I had been working on my own, and did not have much knowledge of how to work with a team of people," she said. "This was my first true test as a designer: communication and being sure that they really understood the internal aspects of the design!"

Additionally, Vaquero had to push beyond her nearly paralyzing sense of shyness. "My shyness was so great that I could not call to order a pizza," she shared, "and that affected me a lot during the first years. I decided to face it, and with time, it is no longer a problem. To be as little nervous as possible, I would prepare and study a lot for meetings. Sometimes I recorded myself preparing the meeting, and analyzed the communication errors I had made. That helped me to learn and improve my communication skills."

A TRAINED EYE

In 2014, Vaquero moved on to serious games studio Davalor Salud as lead game designer, where she stayed for two years. "*Witches* is, for now, my favorite project," she explained. "It was a video game in which the user helped to make a potion for a spell for two sister witches who had very different personalities."

"I liked the idea of creating and designing a puzzle game aimed at women that featured witches with magic powers," Vaquero continued. "My approach for this game was that women were looking for new types of video games with strong and determined female characters. During the development of the video game, the fact that it was a game aimed at women and that the protagonists were witches was cause for mockery for some people in the office, but despite the contempt, I was happy with the project and the end result was highly praised."

Uniquely, the game was designed not just for entertainment. It integrated optometric tests into the 3D game to help diagnose eye conditions and assign type parameters if needed.

"My approach for [*Witches*] was that women were looking for new types of video games with strong and determined characters."

JELLYWORLD INTERACTIVE

Wanting to finally be in control of the type of content she created, Vaquero founded Jellyworld Interactive in 2016. She funneled all her skills and passions into their first project, *Trainpunk Run*. A World War II steampunk mash-up, *Trainpunk Run* stars military messenger Ryana, whose work is imperative to saving the world. To deliver her message, the player must guide Ryana through side-scrolling levels rife with enemies and obstacles.

"One of my favorite memories is when I presented my first personal project, *Trainpunk Run*," she shared. "It was at a stand during the Madrid Games Experience. I dressed like Ryana, the character I had created. It was a few days of hard work presenting the game in costume, but it was worth it, and for me, it held great personal satisfaction."

WOMEN IN GAMES EVENT

Often one of the only women on her various development teams, a year after founding Jellyworld, Vaquero set out to connect with women game developers in Spain. She began organizing the first Women in Games conference in Spain. "It was something completely new," she said. "I wanted to give voice, make visible, and make known the women of the video game industry. I had no idea the effect in the industry and in the media that an event like this would cause. It began a 'small' revolution in the Spanish video game industry that transcended our borders."

With the event held at the Mobile World Center in Barcelona in 2017, professional women from across the country attended to share their knowledge and network with one another. "It was the first time I organized an event," said Vaquero. "I did not know where to start; all I had was great enthusiasm. Organizing the event was hard work. I didn't even know how to find professional women in video games, because at that time, women who worked in video games were not known. We were neither visible nor valued."

After announcing the event, Vaquero began to receive complaints across social media from individuals who thought the event was exclusionary, or a waste of time. "The event was very successful, however," she said. "It had more than 150 attendees and they were all very happy. For me, it came with great personal satisfaction to hear people saying that it was one of the best events they had ever attended and that the content given by the speakers was really interesting."

Equally important, as the first of its kind, the conference brought in an impressive amount of media and social network coverage. "We have managed to raise awareness of the situation of the women working in video games and the women players, especially around the issue of harassment."

#WIGES

With the success of Spain's first Women in Games event, Vaquero used the momentum and founded Women in Games ES with three other industry professionals. "The activities of Women in Games ES have helped make a radical change," she explained. "We have helped, advised, and encouraged many women to develop video games. We have also encouraged girls through video game programming courses, created a physical and virtual community of support, and organized events in which these professional women can make their work known." The latter is achieved through the annual Women Make Games event, which showcases projects developed by women.

For her advocacy these past several years, Vaquero has been recognized with nominations for the Women in Games "Hall of Fame" and, most recently, as a finalist for the VI Aspasia "In Defense of Gender Equality Award."

"Now, organizers are taking care that there are more women at video game events as speakers or jury members, and are offering content that is also interesting for women," summarized Vaquero. "This year, the Spanish government publicly expressed interest in promoting the role of women in video games as a fundamental part of its policy of support for the technology sector. We have given visibility and voice to professional women in the video game industry."

NIDHI AJWANI

PAVING THE WAY FOR WOMEN GAME PROGRAMMERS IN INDIA

 nidhi_ajwani  Nidhi Ajwani

EXPERIENCE

FIRST INDUSTRY PROJECT: CHILLINGHAM MANOR (2011)
FAVORITE INDUSTRY PROJECT: IT'S DICEY (2017)
PROJECTS SHIPPED: 17 GAMES
ACHIEVEMENTS UNLOCKED:
> FICCI-BAF INDIA "BEST PC GAME" AWARD—SCRIBBLED ARENA (2017)

STATS

INDUSTRY LEVEL: 8
CURRENT CLASS: UNITY TEAM LEAD
CURRENT GUILD: SQUARE PANDA INDIA—MUMBAI, INDIA
SPECIAL SKILLS: PROGRAMMING, DATABASE MANAGEMENT, GAME DESIGN

STANDARD EQUIPMENT

FAVORITE PLATFORM: PLAYSTATION
GO-TO GENRE: RPGS
MUST-HAVE GAME: GOD OF WAR (PS2)

Easter Egg

Is an amateur numismatist (the study and collection of currency), although she hasn't been active for quite some time.

BIO

"I loved playing games since I was a kid, and it was a dream to get paid to play games," began programmer Nidhi Ajwani. "As I was completing my undergraduate degree, I had no knowledge of how the industry worked, or what the scope of it was in India. Like all other engineering undergraduates, I sat in on the campus recruitment drive with all the IT leaders in the Indian industry and got placed with two of them."

"Indians generally place a lot of importance on a graduating with a professional degree, and being a doctor or engineer tops the list," she continued, providing additional context. "As an engineer, it is considered very prestigious to land a job via campus recruitment, especially with one of the leading IT companies. Gaming is still not considered as a serious business and neither is it considered as a serious job. Application development, on the other hand, is considered to be a part of IT."

As with many other countries around the world, when Ajwani graduated in 2009, India was feeling the impact of the world economic crisis. As a result, formal campus placement offers were delayed. So she set out job-hunting on her own. "I found a gaming start-up, and that was my first stint in gaming," Ajwani explained. "It didn't last very long, though, as my campus placement came through four months later. As soon as I worked in the IT industry, I realized this was not what I could do for the rest of my life. I came back to the game industry in less than a year."

SYNQUA GAMES

While on track to begin one of her childhood dreams, Ajwani still had hurdles to clear. "My degree in computer science helped prepare me for my career in the gaming industry. Having said that, there is a very wide gap between what we learn academically and what is expected in the real world, and that gap was even larger for working in games," she said. "I worked my way through various resources on the Internet to teach myself more about the programming required in game development."

Ajwani started at Synqua Games in 2011 and worked the first year as an iPhone game-development specialist, after which she was promoted to a senior game developer. "My responsibilities included working closely with the game design team to ideate and validate the game logic and feasibility, developing the game code from scratch, and leading other team members," she explained. "My first project was *Chillingham Manor*. I was the only developer on the project, so my duties started right from the prototype stage to designing the architecture until the final game was released."

The tile-matching puzzle game released in 2011 for the iPhone, featuring 45 levels of scaling difficulty. "The day my first game was released—that feeling of having something that I worked on being out there for people to play was something that can't be put into words," Ajwani recalled. After departing Synqua, she spent a year at Playcaso in Mumbai as senior game developer, before finding her way to longtime home Apar Games.

> "There is a very wide gap between what we learn academically and what is expected in the real world, and that gap was even larger for working in games."

APAR GAMES

Ajwani was hired on to Apar as a senior game developer and, within two years, was promoted to lead game developer. Apar is one or the biggest game-development studios in the whole of India, with over 100 games released for an array of platforms since their founding in 2007. At Apar, she collaborated on games for large global companies, including Big Fish Games, Addicting Games, National Geographic, Mattel, and a diverse portfolio of industry and non-industry clients.

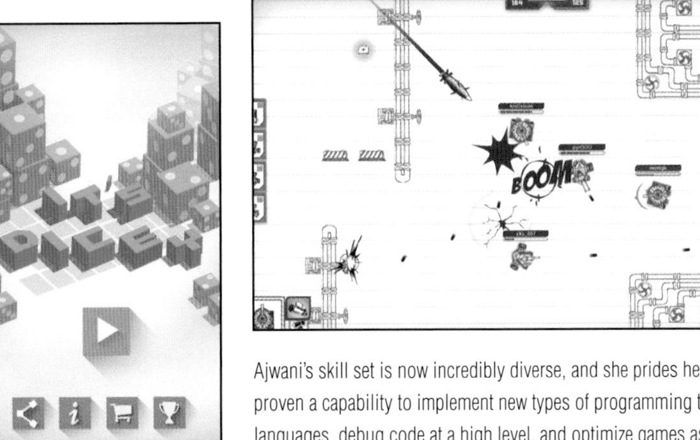

As lead game developer, Ajwani was in charge of handling the mobile development team, and brought more transparency and reduced turnaround times to them through implementing sprint-based, project-management methodology.

"My favorite project from working at Apar Games is *It's Dicey*," she recalled. "That was one of the smoothest projects I've ever worked on. The designer and I collaborated to get the game out in three months. It was a lot of fun because the designer was very clear about what he wanted in the project right from the beginning. Also, I had created a level designer for him to use so that we could add more levels as and when required." Her level designer allowed them to add upwards of 200 levels to the game at launch.

Throughout the past eight years of work, Ajwani has made a point to always keep on top of technology. "The programming field is such that it changes very quickly, and to keep up one has to constantly keep reinventing themselves and keep learning new technologies," she explained. "The day you stop learning is the day you are going to be left behind. The most challenging project that I worked on was *My Mini MixieQ's* for Mattel, as it was my first project on Unity 3D and the timeframe was really short. It was also during this project that my boss was traveling frequently and was out of communication, and hence I had to also coordinate with the client and take management calls. At the end, we delivered the project on time and the client was impressed." If Ajwani hadn't been self-motivated to test the waters of Unity 3D prior to the project, that success wouldn't have been guaranteed.

Another game she programmed has become a point of pride for the studio. "*Scribbled Arena* for PC won the Best PC Game Award in FICCI-BAF India in 2017," she said. The game brings nostalgic arcade tank battles into a hand-drawn landscape, allowing for up to 10-person competitive multiplayer. In addition to the award, *Scribbled Arena* was showcased at various expos throughout Asia and the US.

Ajwani's skill set is now incredibly diverse, and she prides herself in having proven a capability to implement new types of programming techniques and languages, debug code at a high level, and optimize games as needed.

"I would love to work on a game that would actually impact people out there—not just in terms of entertainment but actually teach something too," she said. Very recently, she accepted a position at e-learning company Square Panda's Indian branch as unity team lead and will be getting that chance to do social good. Square Panda focuses on helping children reach their education potential through phonic-based playsets in a game-based curriculum.

> "The day you stop learning is the day you are going to be left behind."

A GROWING INDUSTRY

"I think the industry has grown in India a lot in the last eight years, and it is way more accessible than earlier. In India, gaming companies can be found even in the non-metro cities, and that's a huge leap," Ajwani explained. One thing that hasn't changed, though, is a lack of women programmers in her local development community. "Most of the women I have come across are artists, and they then move on to management roles. I would love to see more women enter the programming stream. I have been fighting to change the way women are perceived here in India, even within in my own extended family. I think the biggest notion that needs to change is that games are played only by men or boys and hence men or boys make them the best. Both parts of that thinking are wrong—women do play games and are equally well-adapted to work on them."

"I think the fact that game development brings stories and designs to life is what keeps me going," she said in closing. "The fact that games can be used for entertainment or to deliver a serious message or to teach something in a fun manner makes them so diverse. The application of games is endless, and that's what makes each game unique—just like every person who plays them."

GWENDELYN FOSTER

GRASSROOTS COMMUNITY BUILDER

ifnotnowgwen

ifnotnowgwen

Gwendelyn Foster

ifnotnowgwen.com

EXPERIENCE

FIRST INDUSTRY PROJECT: ORDER AND CHAOS (2011)

FAVORITE INDUSTRY PROJECT: FIND THE EMOJI (2017)

PROJECTS SHIPPED: 12 GAMES

ACHIEVEMENTS UNLOCKED:

> IDEASPACE "BEST STARTUP IDEA" FINALIST, SUPERSET STUDIOS (2015)
> BOARD MEMBER OF INTERNATIONAL GAME DEVELOPMENT ASSOCIATION—MANILA CHAPTER
> JUDGE OF PHILIPPINE INDUSTRY GAME ON AWARDS FOR PROFESSIONAL AND STUDENT SUBMISSIONS (2016)
> GLOBAL GAME JAM SCHOLAR (2016)

STATS

INDUSTRY LEVEL: 7

CURRENT CLASS: GAME DEVELOPER

CURRENT GUILD: IMAYON STUDIOS—MANILA, PHILIPPINES

SPECIAL SKILLS: GAME DESIGN, PROGRAMMING, RELATIONSHIP BUILDING, CREATIVITY

STANDARD EQUIPMENT

FAVORITE PLATFORM: PC

GO-TO GENRE: POINT AND CLICK ADVENTURE/PUZZLE GAMES

MUST-HAVE GAME: SECRET OF MONKEY ISLAND

BIO

Gwen Foster is a Philippine game industry advocate who has an inexhaustible passion for advancing her local development community through organizing events, volunteering at local chapters of industry associations, and sharing her hard-earned knowledge with industry hopefuls.

While growing up, resources that were commonplace in international gaming hubs were inaccessible in the Philippines, so she made the best of what was available. "Multiple screenings of *Indie Game: The Movie*, reading *Gamasutra*, lurking at TIGSource, and asking questions in engine forums were the closest to formal training I had about game development," explained Foster, speaking to her start in gaming. "People would hand over pirated PDFs of books about video games. I would beg my stepfather to buy me books whenever I visited Kinokuniya in Bangkok. Those same books have travelled to different aspiring game developers and some of them have failed to come home, said Foster. "Nowadays, game development courses are available in local universities, the internet has a lot of tutorials and resources, and social media has made it easier to connect with people from across the world."

CRACKING QA

Introduced to the inner workings of the industry via a friend and programmer, Foster found her enthusiasm for video games contagious. "Dropping out of college and the exhaustion of over 14 years of education led me to take a QA Position at Gameloft," she began. "Since there were no producer or trainee positions available, the closest position I could apply for was Quality Assurance. Being part of the QA team showed me how important attention to detail is."

At that time, the game industry in the Philippines was growing, but focused on the business of outsourcing, and there was a distinct lack of studios bringing to life their own visions. "Knowing what I know now, there is a good reason people did not take the risk," she explained. Digital distribution platforms were not as accessible as they are today, and Foster believes it is now the perfect time for independent game developers in the Philippines to take risks and reap the rewards.

Working in QA was a good opportunity to learn about the business of games, which led to a freelance consultant gig for various companies in the Philippines. She took on roles in design, business development, marketing and publishing, programming, and account management. Not long after, she transitioned to production at Quickfire Studio and Dreamlords Digital before moving on to Ritmo Learning Lab as Director of Technology.

Easter Egg

Is an actual Easter egg in more than one game developed in the Philippines and can be killed in a mission from Chryse's *Shots Fired*.

Foster found her sweet spot in production. "As someone who has worked a variety of positions, the most fulfilling role was becoming a game producer," said Foster. "My co-Producer and COO, Harry Cabamalan, had a way with people. Focusing on production allowed the view of both the forest and the trees. Quickfire Games was filled with a talented group of young and passionate game creators who either worked too hard or played too much. Harry's leadership gave people the freedom of their own time, as long as milestones were met. There was always room for failure and his firmness with decisions after looking at all possible angles is something I aspire to do. The production role felt a lot like checks and balances."

Speaking to her own games, Gwen is driven to tell stories through simplified game mechanics with attention to detail. "*Dugas* is a game heavily inspired by *Where's Waldo* and *Hidden Folks*, but the innovation came from the fact that a lot of people disappeared during the Marcos Regime. It has been a hard game to make since I wanted to stay as close to the facts and tell their stories as best as I could. Hopefully, people will experience the emotions I have right now."

"At the end of the day... What matters most is the drive and willingness to learn and grow from the mistakes people are bound to make along the way"

Foster is also motivated by her love for her country and the industry as a whole. "Game developers in the Philippines need more courage and trust in themselves. They are capable of creating beautiful and amazing games. It is always hard when someone leaves the industry because it is not sustainable. The dream is to have an ecosystem and to be at a level where we are known for creating quality games that allow people to live a comfortable life."

The emerging Philippine game industry is driven by passion from people who are ambitious, resourceful, and accepting, says Foster. "The Philippine Game Industry does not judge based on which university, what gender, and where people came from. At the end of the day, it does not matter how talented a person may be. What matters the most is the drive and the willingness to learn and grow from the mistakes people are bound to make along the way."

Speaking specifically to gender in the industry, Foster expanded further. "The Philippines is an inclusive environment that supports people across the gender spectrum. Many video game studios in the Philippines are run by powerful, strong-willed women." She notes that despite the welcoming mindset, there is proactive work to be done to work towards gender parity. "The lack of women in the game industry stems from the perception that it is a 'boys club.' Universities, both locally and internationally, have a lower ratio of women enrolling in game courses. Michelle Chen, a Filipina-Chinese, is a Women in Games Ambassador who wants to mirror the program from the UK in the Philippines. They go to all girls' high schools and educational institutions to talk about women in the games industry and how it is a viable career for women to take."

BUILDING A COMMUNITY

After firmly establishing her own career path, Foster began working to ensure other aspiring industry professionals had the resources to take their own shot. She volunteers with the Game Developers Association of the Philippines, the International Game Developers Association's Manila Chapter, is the director of ESports and Gaming Summit Indie Fiesta and works as the Global Game Jam's regional organizer. She also judges in regional gaming competitions and is a Casual Connect Asia Advisor.

"Grassroots community building is a thankless job. It is a job, notoriously unpaid, and highly motivated by the individuals who paved the way, which is why I am where I am today," explained Foster. "The work is always excruciating and the very definition of blood, sweat, and tears. The necessity for these programs to exist in both the local and the Southeast Asian industry is greater than any ego or fatigue I feel in my body."

Foster has numerous examples of additional passion and progress she sees within the community. Industry colleagues offer advice to people on how they should design their qualifications exams, help others find jobs when a studio closes down, present panels at student capstone projects, organize game jams, and connect people from across the globe to make collaboration possible. "And my inbox is always open," she said.

Foster's activism achieved global awareness recently when she made headlines by speaking up about pervasive roadblocks that keep developers in emerging markets from seizing educational and networking opportunities such as the annual Game Developer's Conference. In an article for Gamasutra called "#ThirdWorldProblems: How to Not Get a Visa for GDC," she discussed how despite being an invited speaker to the annual industry gathering with fully sponsored flights, hotels, and an industry pass, she—like many other devs from the Philippines before her—was denied a visa to enter the states multiple times. She isn't letting the hurdle stop her or the progress that continues to be made in her local community.

Foster has big plans for the future. She intends to first write a book about the Philippine game industry, as well as finish a bachelor's degree in game development, execute four games in 10 years, improve Filipino game developers' access to resources, and own 72 cats.

A DAY IN THE LIFE OF...

A PROFESSIONAL GAMER

While a career in esports may be the closest thing to the idealized notion that industry professionals play games all day, there is a reason "sport" is in the job description. Esports have exploded in the past several years, rising to—and in some cases surpassing—the popularity of traditional sports like soccer and football. The intense training regime needed to perform at a professional level has even led to talks with the International Olympic Committee for consideration as a future official activity. While integration may still be a while off, five professional *League of Legends* players carried the Olympic torch at the 2018 Winter Games in South Korea. Watching competitive play has also become a worldwide phenomenon, with events such as the Intel Extreme Masters World Championship drawing a crowd of 173,000 live spectators and—more staggering—over 45 million unique viewers online. Prize pools at major tournaments have started creeping over the million-dollar mark.

Anna "ant1ka" Ananikova has been a pro *Counter-Strike: Global Offensive* player for four years now, taking first with her team in the women's bracket at major tournaments such as the 2017 World Electronic Sports Games, ESU Masters, and the Intel Challenge Katowice. She's also a popular streamer in the Russian-speaking community, offering her subscribers a chance to watch her daily training regime and learn from a pro.

ANNA "ANT1KA" ANANIKOVA

PROFESSION: PROFESSIONAL COUNTER-STRIKE PLAYER—MOSCOW, RUSSIA

YEARS IN PROFESSION: 4

ASSOCIATED WITH: REASON GAMING, TEAM SECRET, DYNASTY GAMING, RES GAMING, ALPHA REPUBLIC OF ESPORT GAMING

▶ EDUCATION

"To become who I am now, I spent a lot of time teaching myself. When I started, there were no schools or boot camps like we have now. Esports is growing with an unreal speed, so there are a lot of new eSport opportunities. I was a big fan of *Counter-Strike*, so I spent half of my day practicing, and each day it made me want to continue getting better and better."

▶ BREAKING IN

"The most difficult thing was finding a team and adapting to the playstyle of each person. But that is only true of games like *Counter-Strike*, *DOTA*, *League of Legends*, and other games where you play with four other people. It was also very challenging for me to enter into the international team, where I was required to speak English, and people there have a different mentality."

▶ EARLY INDUSTRY IMPRESSIONS

"I was really hyped to be in esports, to be a part of big tournaments, to compete with other girls, and to show what I could do. I wanted to meet every girl we played against in real life!"

▶ KEY QUALITIES

"First of all, a pro gamer must be calm and coldhearted, because first and foremost, it is your job. Of course, if you play with a team for a long time, you become close, sometimes even best friends. But you need to remember that sometimes things change, and you need to be able to make a hard decision to continue advancing your career.

"Pro gamers should be diligent and purposeful. You need to have passion to be a part of competitive esports. I think it's the first thing people should think about. Nowadays young guys and girls think that they can become the best with little effort, and become rich. It doesn't work like that. You need to spend a lot of time training yourself, or in esports schools, or boot camps—it doesn't matter. The most important thing is to be respectful of other players, be open, and work at getting better and better."

▶ TOOLS OF THE TRADE

"My gear is:

Keyboard: QPAD MK90.

Mouse: ZOWIE FK2

Headset: Elite Pro

Video Card: GeForce 1080

Processor: Intel Core i7-6700K"

▶ TRAINING OPPORTUNITIES

"Everyone should visit conventions or festivals like Epicenter, Intel Extreme Masters, DreamHack, and esports portals like StarLadder, as they feature really high-level prepared tournaments. If you want to focus on *Counter-Strike* after achieving a high skill level, start playing on the competitive gaming platform FACEIT."

▶ HOURS & ENVIRONMENT

"We play from 7pm until midnight with our team, and one girl is on multiple teams, so it is hard for her to stick to this regimen. We play online—I play from my home, and other girls do the same. Sometimes if we are traveling, we play in PC clubs or we ask someone if we can use their PC. We always bring our gaming stuff with us, because we can't play without our comfort items; it's really important."

▶ PROMOTIONAL PATH

"If we find a good structured esports organization, the most common thing is to sign a contract that commits us to play under their name. We have responsibilities that are specified in our contracts and we need to follow them; otherwise the organization can fine us. For example, practicing five days a week, meeting with sponsors, putting a sponsor's logo on our shirts, and having a sponsor's logos on our Twich/YouTube channels. We need to boost our media and be a social person, give interviews, and be respectful with other eSport players; if not, it may give our organization a bad reputation. Sponsors are responsbile for travel support, boosting media, management, and salary (if it's in our contracts), and so on. The most needed thing is travel support."

▶ PROFESSIONAL PERKS

"When you are a pro gamer, you travel a lot. I've been playing for years, and I've already traveled to countries such as Sweden, Denmark, Poland, Germany, the USA, Emirates, Spain, France, China, and more. It is one of the best things. Also, if you are part of a competitive esport team, sometimes you can meet esports stars, and it's really cool!"

▶ CAREER CHALLENGES

"It's really hard for Russian girls to travel around the world for a tournament. They need visas and spend lots of money and time, and sometimes the visa request is rejected. I think it's one of the biggest problems. Also, there can be conflicts on teams because of personalities and playstyles. When you have a lot of conflicts and you can't fix them, it's one of the main problems in esports."

▶ FAVORITE PROJECT

"A charity tournament in the USA was really cool! They had 15 big play places and about 2000 gamers. We played on stacking chairs against male pro gamers, and it was really funny. Then we mixed our teams and played against each other."

▶ LIFE HACKS

"You need to be calm while you are playing against opponents. To be honest, I'm a really emotional player and it's hard for me to be coldhearted in the game. But if you want to stay calm and be confident in your game, the best thing is to believe that nothing will change even if you lose, because it's an experience that you will learn from. It only becomes a problem if you don't evolve from your mistakes."

▶ EXCITING ADVANCEMENTS

"I think the biggest advancements coming from games are *Fortnite* and *PUBG*, and in the future I believe people will use VR worlds to compete with each other!"

PRO TIP!

"If you want to become better in your esports profession, you need to find one of the best players in the sphere and try to learn from them. It is one of the most effective ways to improve."

ANA RIBEIRO

FROM BAKING PIES TO RIPPING PIXELS

AnaGameDev

AnaGameDeveloper

Ana Ribeiro

pixelripped.com

EXPERIENCE

FIRST INDUSTRY PROJECT: SHEO (2012)
FAVORITE INDUSTRY PROJECT: PIXEL RIPPED 1989 (2018)
PROJECTS SHIPPED: 1 GAME
ACHIEVEMENTS UNLOCKED:
> INTEL "BEST DEMO PITCH"—PIXEL RIPPED 1989 (2014)
> INDIECADE "OFFICIAL SELECTION"—PIXEL RIPPED 1989 (2015 & 2018)
> RIO OLYMPIC GAMES TORCH CARRIER (2017)
> TOM'S GUIDE "BEST VR GAME—GDC" (2018)

STATS

INDUSTRY LEVEL: 7
CURRENT CLASS: CREATOR
CURRENT GUILD: ARVORE IMMERSIVE EXPERIENCES—SÃO PAULO, BRAZIL
SPECIAL SKILLS: VR GAME DEVELOPMENT, GAME DESIGN, PIE MAKING

STANDARD EQUIPMENT

FAVORITE PLATFORM: PHANTOM SYSTEM
GO-TO GENRE: PLATFORMING
MUST-HAVE GAME: MEGA MAN 2

BIO

Government jobs are sought-after positions in Brazil because of the stability they provide, explained Ana Ribeiro. "Seven years ago I used to work at the justice council after graduating with a degree in psychology. It was super bureaucratic work. Most Brazilians wish to get a stable job and spend the rest of their lives doing the same thing until retirement. For me, working there was a prison for my creativity."

SURPRISE PIES

Needing a creative outlet, Ribeiro began baking pies and selling them at work. "As the pie smell reached down the corridor, colleagues from other departments started to ask me to bring some for them too," she explained. "Within a few months, I was selling more than 4000 pies a month." Ribeiro had inadvertently found herself operating a small and successful business. Inspired to use the opportunity as a springboard for a new career path, she took a course on small-business start-ups. She soon realized that she was investing in the wrong industry. Pies were profitable, but not her passion. That distinction belonged to video games.

After establishing a sizable savings from her pie business, Ribeiro sold her car, left her government job, and flew to England to start a new life as a game developer. "My family and friends all thought I was going crazy," she remembers. "But for the first time I felt like I was making the right decision for myself." Ribeiro studied game programming at SAE Expression College in London before earning her master's in game design and development at the National Film & Television School. "I didn't know anything about programming, or the engines and software I would use to make games. It was a new fresh start of a life: new country, new language, and a new career."

RIPPED FROM A DREAM

Ribeiro's thesis project at NFTS was a VR game-within-a-game, a nostalgic homage to industry classics. "The idea for *Pixel Ripped 1989* came from a dream," began Ribeiro. "I dreamed that I was in my room playing a 16-bit console. As I played, the graphics in the game began to evolve, and the room around me started to look like the game. I realized how weird and powerful it felt to be inside a pixelated world. When I woke up, I immediately knew I had to do something with this idea, and that virtual reality was the only way to experience what I had seen in that dream."

"At first I set the game in the late 1980s, in the portable 8-bit console era, when you would have to hide your games in class from the teacher," she continued. "Even though it was a nice idea, I was having trouble making the story come together. I had automatically made the association that a gamer kid in the '80s was by default a boy." Pieces began to fall into place when she channeled her own story for inspiration. "I changed the video game character to Dot, and the human who controls her into Nicola. The stories and ideas began to flow because it became my story."

"I immediately knew I had to do something with this [dream] and that virtual reality was the only way to experience what I had seen in that dream."

Surprisingly, the biggest and most innovative aspect of *Pixel Ripped* resulted from a bug. "I was working on a level, and the game rendered Dot—the main 2D character—on top of the classroom desk in the 3D world. I could move her around the real world, and it was mind-blowing. I changed every level, and the entire narrative, to fit this experience. The evil Cyblin Lord would steal the Pixel Stone, which allowed him to bring the 2D and 3D worlds crashing together."

To call it a promising student project would be an understatement. "After posting the demo online on a worldwide platform for sharing virtual reality apps and games, *Pixel Ripped* achieved the first place in the whole world," said Ribeiro. "It was a big achievement for a student project at the time." Media attention followed shortly after, and Ribeiro found herself on the receiving end of offers from investors—including a VR headset brand. She decided to focus on polishing her student project for a commercial release.

Although *Pixel Ripped*'s origin story sounds charmed from the get-go, the entire experience was a whirlwind for Ribeiro. "I had some ups and downs: a failed Kickstarter, a co-founder that left, and an accelerator in Silicon Valley which eventually gave a little investment," she recalled. "Three years had passed, and I was working alone at home, self-funding the project with the help of freelancers and friends helping when they could."

One of the biggest challenges she faced was the constantly shifting landscape of the VR market. "Not only were the headsets and controllers changing, but also the engine itself. I was constantly adapting to new technology. The challenges and the lessons learned were the worst and the best parts of working with such new technology."

HOMETOWN HERO

After four years, the project seemed stuck in purgatory, until Ribeiro returned to her roots and partnered with a virtual reality company from Brazil. "The ARVORE partnership gave the game the last push it needed to be released in 2018," she explained. "*Pixel Ripped* was our first release, and it achieved top sales in Steam VR, the Oculus Store, and PlayStation VR market."

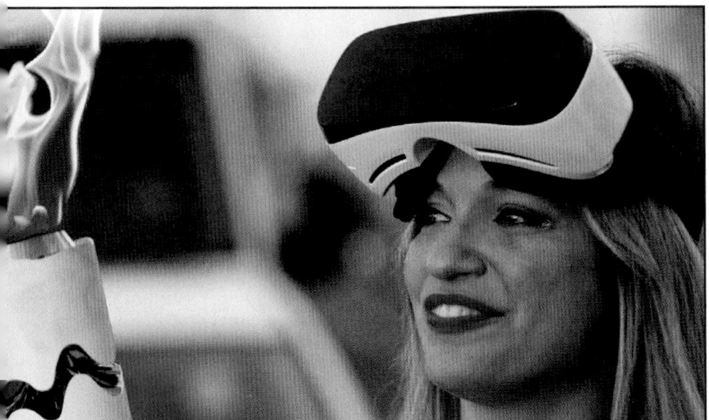

Reflecting on the project, Ribeiro would do things differently, despite the eventual triumph. "I designed a too-ambitious game for an indie developer, without great funding. It was a big mistake," she admitted. "I should have released a smaller version of the project sold for less. I could have then used the profits to release the full version. I made the classic mistake of underestimating the amount of work I had ahead of me."

"I designed a too-ambitious game [*Pixel Ripped*] for an indie developer, without great funding. It was a big mistake."

Despite the difficulties, *Pixel Ripped* was ultimately a success story, and a particularly meaningful one back home in Brazil. "I am considered a pioneer in my country, and have been told that I inspired early adopters to start developing for VR," shared Ribeiro. "I still today receive messages from developers who started working with VR after they played my game. Most say it was the first time they understood the potential of the medium."

For her innovative efforts, Ribeiro was chosen as an official torchbearer at the 2016 Rio Summer Olympic Games. "I wore a VR headset to represent not just game developers, but women in games, and developers from the North of Brazil, the poorest area of our country. It was an honor to be selected, and I never imagined that making games would lead me to represent my country in such an important event as the Olympics."

"I am considered a pioneer in my country and have been told that I inspired early adopters to start developing for VR."

"Seeing people playing my work is the biggest inspiration to keep making games," said Ribeiro. "There is nothing more rewarding to me than seeing a smile on the face of someone after playing your game. I want to be able to leave something to remember, an experience that players can take with them for life."

Easter Egg

At the age of 11, she vaulted over the three-meter-high perimeter walls of her school and ran to freedom. Although she was eventually caught and assigned detention, it remains a point of pride that she was the first girl in the school to successfully clear the barrier.

JENNIFER SCHEURLE

DESIGNING INTERSTELLAR EXPERIENCES

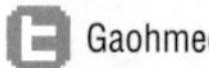 Gaohmee  Jennifer Scheurle  gaohmee.com

EXPERIENCE

FIRST INDUSTRY PROJECT: TWINKOMPLEX (2011)

FAVORITE INDUSTRY PROJECT: EARTHLIGHT SPACEWALK (2017)

PROJECTS SHIPPED: 10+ GAMES

ACHIEVEMENTS UNLOCKED:

> MCV PACIFIC "30 UNDER 30" (2017)

> IGF FINALIST "ALT.CTRL.GDC AWARDS" (2017)

> PAX AUSTRALIA "INDIE SHOWCASE WINNER"—OBJECTS IN SPACE (2016)

> AUSTRALIAN GAME DEVELOPER AWARDS "GAME OF THE YEAR"—EARTHLIGHT SPACEWALK (2017)

STATS

INDUSTRY LEVEL: 7

CURRENT CLASS: GAME DESIGN LEAD

CURRENT GUILD: OPAQUE SPACE—MELBOURNE, AUSTRALIA

SPECIAL SKILLS: GAME THEORY, GAME DESIGN, NARRATIVE DESIGN, DIGITAL ILLUSTRATION, MENTORING, PUBLIC SPEAKING

STANDARD EQUIPMENT

FAVORITE PLATFORM: PC

GO-TO GENRE: NARRATIVE-DRIVEN GAMES

MUST-HAVE GAME: THE BEGINNER'S GUIDE

BIO

The saying "You don't know if you don't try" was particularly true for Jennifer Scheurle when, at the age of 20, she started her long-anticipated career as a curator and artist. "I grew up with everybody believing that was my calling—and as soon as I actually did it, I hated it," Scheurle began. "Sometimes life just doesn't go in a straight line. It felt wrong, and the community was not mine." A fan of video games since youth, Scheurle shifted her attention toward the industry after spotting a game design course advertised in a local magazine. "Games have everything I love about art —except all of it has a common, very practical purpose," she continued. In 2009 Scheurle signed up for a game design program in Berlin—the first of its kind in Germany—and started down her newfound path.

Scheurle would spend the first part of her career testing the water at various companies, across a variety of genres and platforms. She started in QA and quickly transitioned into game design, expanding her skills through narrative design and game balancing, supporting service- and browser-based titles, creating storyboards and concept art, and leading monetization planning across multiple products. The experiences were broad in scope and practical in experience, but weren't passion projects.

By 2015, Scheurle was ready for a change and moved to Sydney to take up a post as lead game design tutor for the Academy of Interactive Entertainment's Sydney campus. She taught the basics to first- and second-year students, focusing on narrative design, UX psychology, and production. She also aided in developing the curriculum itself, which would be outsourced as teaching material across Australia.

Easter Egg

Traveled Japan for a couple of months during her last year of university, writing her bachelor's thesis and performing as a rope-bondage artist.

ENTERING ORBIT

In tandem with her teaching, Scheurle joined Flat Earth Games as part of their four-person core team; her focus was concept art and ship design for *Objects in Space*. Scheurle also built a physical and fully functional control system in the form of a cockpit for the game, which was described as a "modempunk space trading game." "*Objects in Space* was a very personal and long experience, a game in development for 4 1/2 years and that I poured a lot of time and sweat and ultimately burnout into," she said. "It was amazing and very exhausting at the same time." *Objects in Space* won PAX Australia's Indie Showcase in 2016, and Scheurle's work on the physical controller set was nominated for the Alt. Ctrl.GDC award in 2017.

Once in space, Scheurle never returned from orbit. In 2017, she was one of four founding members of Opaque Space, a company that specializes in emerging technology and VR content for both education and entertainment. Scheurle was brought on as game design lead, taking charge of studio design efforts for collaborations with companies such as Boeing and NASA.

The 2017 VR title *Earthlight: Spacewalk* became a landmark moment in her career by allowing players to step into the weightless shoes of modern-day explorers. Created in collaboration with NASA, *Earthlight Spacewalk* was

celebrated across the industry. "It was the first game for me as a game design lead, and I had waited so long to spread my wings as a designer and truly work on a game and make all design decisions," said Scheurle. "To receive an Australian Game Developer Game of the Year award was the most overwhelming thing that had ever happened to me. It equally humbled me, as it gave me confidence, and I'm grateful for that."

The *Earthlight* experience expanded to multiplayer with *Earthlight: Lunar Mission*, a six-player VR experience unfolding in a future settlement on the moon. "We had international guests from all over the world in the office, mainly diplomats and other representatives," Scheurle explained. "We had them play the experience, and one of them came out of the headset with tears in her eyes. She walked up to me, grabbed my hands, and told me how she vividly remembered watching the moon landing when she was a child. She said our experience felt so real and was one of the best things she had ever done. It was beautiful and moving, and I will never forget it."

In the realm of education, Scheurle left an even bigger impact by helping reach an industry milestone. "Through Opaque Space, we are one of the first game companies to work with NASA on games for training," she said. "It has been a life-changing experience to work on something that will matter beyond our own lifetime, which contributes to the advancement of our entire species, and I have been humbled by NASA's incredible work ethics. I am determined to bring those learnings to the larger games industry over time and intertwine our talents more with other industries in the future."

> "It has been a life-changing experience to work on [*Earthlight: Spacewalk*] that will matter beyond our own lifetime."

HIDDEN GAME DESIGN

Scheurle hopes to share her hard-earned knowledge with more than industry professionals, though. One of her personal missions is to lift the curtain on game design and close the gap between designers and their audience. "I believe that being as removed as we are from the people who experience our work is a missed opportunity for connection and exchange," she explained. "I want to expose our work more, our processes and the way we work and function, to foster empathy among our audiences as well as build better and healthier connections between them and our work."

In 2017, Scheurle made a big leap forward in this mission by encouraging her peers to expose hidden game design mechanics on Twitter. She kicked off the conversation by revealing how popular shooters would make the last few player hit points go further than the rest, to facilitate a feeling of "just surviving" a firefight. Others weighed in, sharing insider stories such as decreasing NPC accuracy with proximity to the player to make them feel more powerful.

The thread went viral among both game developers and game consumers. "In essence, my work on hidden game design is an exploration of the techniques game designers use to make their players feel certain things such as empowerment, loss, engagement, and more; guide them in certain directions; and lead them on to have surprising, new, and compelling experiences. It definitely has been controversial in a way, as some developers don't think we should share our techniques so openly, and because some of our players were very confused and hurt by some of the revelations," she said, likening it to killing Santa or exposing the Matrix. "I, however, believe that sharing our craft has some of the untapped potential this industry has still to explore." Since igniting the hidden game design discourse, Scheurle has given several talks on the subject matter, and is currently working on a book with CRC Press.

CHANGING THE GAME

Arguably of equal import as her game design and educational outreach, Scheurle uses her voice as an agent of advocacy and change within the industry. That voice becomes more confident and powerful every year. "I was not prepared for the hostility I would face as a woman within the industry," she began, recalling her early impressions of working in gaming. As illustrated by her already successful career, opposition didn't slow Scheurle down. Rather, it fueled her, and led her to seek out like-minded communities for support and to strengthen their voices through solidary.

Scheurle works to facilitate change through honest online discourse, speaking engagements, and writing. "We have so much work to do on change within this industry. I want diversity, more accessibility, better creator-audience relationships, unions, no crunch culture, and generally better regard for the craft we do. I could list things forever here; as much as I love working in this industry, we are still young and there is a lot to work through," she said.

"The industry is incredibly complex in its community, politics, and processes, but I often feel like we make impossible things happen every day," concluded Scheurle. "My main motivation and drive comes from the chance of being part of a revolution within the games industry. This is what drives and inspires me and my work every day."

> "As much as I love working in this industry, we are still young and there is a lot to work through."

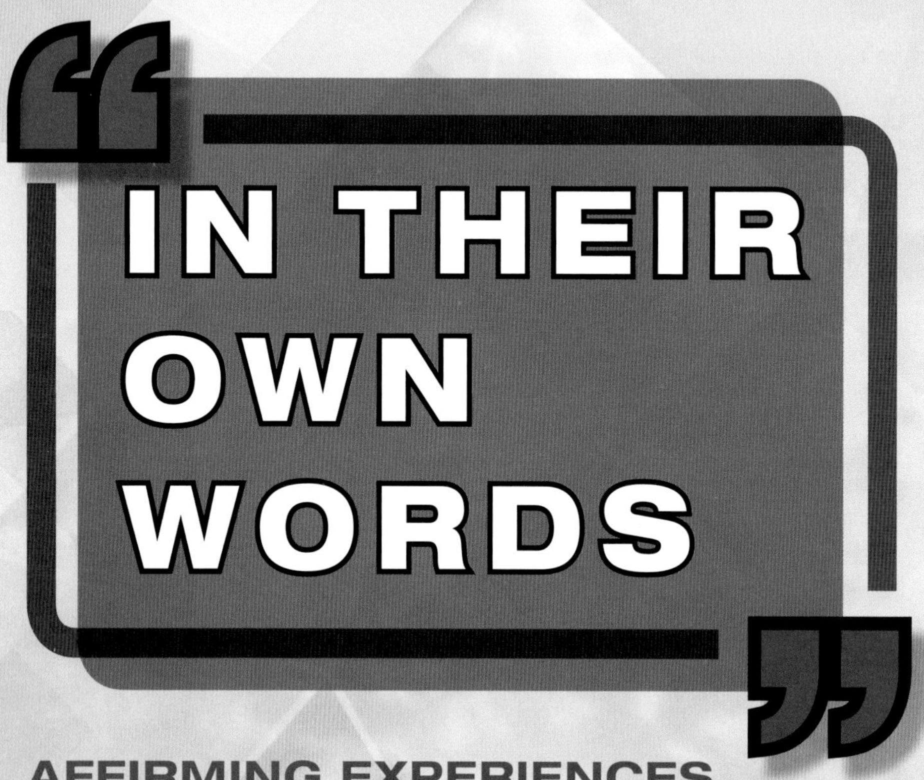

AFFIRMING EXPERIENCES

What has been the most positive, or affirming, experience for you related to women in gaming?

"The moment we are experiencing right now in 2018! I have been developing videogames for 10 years and it was only recently that it became clear that women are having a larger presence in this medium. It is a sign of a worldwide movement, so being part of this historical moment is a powerful experience. This book, which features 100 women in video games, is in itself a significant experience for the industry and for me."

Alejandra Bruno | Narrative Game Designer | QB9 | Buenos Aires, Argentina

---

"During 2018, Chile's sexist culture was directly confronted by a powerful feminist movement, which placed the issue of gender equality at the center of a public debate. In this scenario, it's very heartwarming and inspiring to see the emergence of the Chilean Association of Women in Video Games, an organization that seeks to create a more inclusive gaming industry in our country."

Maureen Berho | CEO & Producer | Niebla Games | Valparaíso, Chile

---

"I'm currently writing the Working Lunch Handbook, which is a resource for the students of our mentorship program. The process of writing this book has involved reaching out to some of my personal industry idols like Brenda Romero, Robin Hunicke, and Rhianna Pratchett. Experiencing their enthusiasm and willingness to support and encourage the next wave of women entering games was extremely affirming for me. There is a powerful support network for us here."

Ally McLean | Director | The Working Lunch | Sydney, Australia

---

"In 2018, there was a line at GDC for the women's room. That wasn't the case 15 years ago and, despite the inconvenience, I'm glad for the change."

Alyssa Finley | Executive Producer | San Rafael, USA

"Whenever a young woman comes up to me at an event and tells me that my work influenced her to join the industry, that's the best. As women in the industry, we're often so busy and focused on the task at hand that it's great to be reminded how much our voices matter, and how important it is for us to be visible role models for young women and girls who may aspire to a career in game development."

Amy Hennig | Sr. Creative Director & Writer | Independent | San Carlos, USA

"In 2017, I was raising money to fund my travel and stay in San Francisco for GDC and, after helping my cause, Nina Freeman sent me an email saying she would love to hang out and was available if I had any questions related to games. When I was fortunate enough to have made the trip, she took me out for some cream puffs and was incredibly kind and accommodating to the arsenal of questions I had. After GDC, she remained a friend, whether through swapping poetry with me, or by ensuring that I meet other nice people through my travels. Having a friend like Nina definitely makes being a woman in video games more inhabitable. On that note, I would also like to mention that I've received wonderful care from other women in gaming, such as Ana Jelicic, Sithe Ncube, and Marie Claire LeBlanc Flanagan."

Bahiyya Khan | Experimental Narrative Masters Student & Tutor | University of the Witwatersrand | Johannesburg, South Africa

---

"I think it is how far we have come. We still have a long way to go, but we are making progress by attracting more women into gaming. When I started in the game industry in 1994, there were so few women in the industry. We started our first Microsoft Women in Gaming (WIG) cocktail networking event at GDC, around '96 or '97, and there were maybe 25-35 women. The last GDC WIG event had over 1,500. This is just an event at a gaming conference, but the growth in women attendees over the last few years has been good to see."

Bonnie Ross | Corporate Vice President, Head of 343 Industries | Microsoft Studios | Seattle, USA

"It's been a very positive experience to watch young women who were just trying to get a foot in the door a decade ago become these amazing, influential, unstoppable asskickers."

Christa Charter | Senior Global Brand Copywriter & Author | Xbox | Seattle, USA

"Seeing young women I have mentored succeed. It's genuinely the best thing."

Brenda Romero | Game Designer & CEO | Romero Games | Galway, Ireland

---

"When I won the Influencer of the Year Award at the Women in Games Awards earlier this year, I think that might have been one of the most affirming experiences I have ever had. The room was filled with women who I have looked up to and worshipped for years and I was on stage in front of them. It was pretty magical. I've spent a good deal of my career with imposter syndrome; I almost constantly question both myself and whether I deserve the success I've found in my career. Am I doing enough? Do I deserve the kindness, the love, and support I receive from my community? Am I really any good at what I do, or have I just gotten lucky? I think that night and winning the award just meant so much to me. It grounded me and was a reminder that, you know what? I might just be doing ok."

Hollie Bennett | Channel Manager | PlayStation Access | London, UK

"I think many of the events that are constantly organized by Women in Gaming and Women in Games/Tech associations all around the world are always very positive and stimulating experiences for every woman who works in the industry. Being a speaker, or a contributor, or just being there is something that is helpful to other women, because you realize you're not alone and there are so many women working hard in this crazy gaming world. They're achieving amazing results despite the obstacles and the difficulties coming from 'being a woman' in a publicly recognized, male-only industry. I hope the number of these events will grow more and more in the future."

Giulia Zamboni | Producer | Gamera Interactive | Padua, Italy

---

"People investing in my business because it was a good idea, not just because I am female. I think this can give hope and inspire more women to set up their own companies within gaming, which will mean more women on boards, in teams, and a much more diverse industry!"

Jude Ower | Founder & CEO | Playmob | London, UK

"It has been gratifying to see women using their courage to rise up, speak truth to power, and unite in meaningful ways. I've also been heartened by the many men in support. We are all in transition. The opportunity to shed the cultural conditioning to embody our authentic power, multifaceted gifts, and unique voices is the future we are in the process of creating."

Megan Gaiser | Principal | Contagious Creativity | Seattle, USA

"I'm a life-long learner and putting together this exhibit on women in games has been one of the best learning experiences in my museum career. I love highlighting pieces of history that most people haven't heard before. I love bringing people's experiences out of the shadows and into the light. Knowing that I'm making all this information available on a large, public stage is simply thrilling!"

Shannon Symonds | Curator of Electronic Games | The Strong National Museum of Play | Rochester, USA

"When I get to meet people who tell me that I inspire them to be themselves. Sitting alone in my hotel room while I prep and stress over an event can take its toll on the road but seeing messages from people in the community who feel surer about themselves because they see themselves in me on-screen can get me through any homesick stretch."

Indiana "Froskurinn" Black | *League of Legends* Shoutcaster | Riot Games | Shanghai, China

---

"I think the top affirming experience for me has been seeing former female students of mine enter and thrive in the game industry!"

Michelle Hinn | Co-Chair | IGDA Game Accessibility Special Interest Group | New York City, USA

"Seeing more women and non-binary people speaking openly and honestly about their experiences, both negative and positive, on panels and at conferences has been so powerful. It's what gave me the courage to get up and speak on inclusion and accessibility in the first place. Marginalized people as a whole went through some horrendous times on the Internet with one of the worst being around 2014, so seeing so many women—including many of my friends—come out of that experience stronger and more determined kept me going, too. Other than that, seeing women and non-binary people make the games they want to make and talking about the process alongside their peers has been a beautiful thing. I recently saw a panel on coziness in games and how that's achieved and why those developers want to make those games. The majority of the panel were women and it was just really lovely in the truest sense of the word."

Cherry Thompson | Game Accessibility Consultant, Speaker & Streamer | Independent | Vancouver, Canada

---

"At one point at WB Games, the president had an inspiring, women-led leadership team. The heads of production, marketing, business development, and the general counsel were all women. I had never seen an executive board made up of such strong and dynamic women. I was honored to work alongside them, as well as all the phenomenally smart men leading the company to success."

Stephanie Johnson | Head of Global Marketing for GeForce NOW & SHIELD | Nvidia | San Francisco, USA

"I was blown away by having an opportunity this year at the ESA Awards dinner. This is an event run by the Entertainment Software Association, which this year recognized girls in games champion Laila Shabir. It was the first time a woman had been awarded this prestigious award in its 20-year history. Kiki Wolfkill, Shannon Loftis and company from Microsoft decided this called for having a table—front and center—filled with 'incredible women from the games industry.' I received an invite and couldn't quite believe it. Games is a very young industry. It's been around for decades, but attracts young employees and has difficulty retaining its talent beyond a certain age. I am considered an ancient person in games in Australia. To have been possibly the second youngest at a table filled with women kicking arse across the industry… well, that couldn't happen in my home country, or it would be a very intimate dinner."

Giselle Rosman | Chapter Lead | IGDA Melbourne | Melbourne, Australia

---

"Finally seeing female characters portrayed as complex people in games, not just as objects intended to satisfy the male gaze, as quest goals, or victims, or tired storyline tropes, or described only in relation to male game characters."

Jennell Jaquays | Content Designer & Artist | Dragongirl Studios | Seattle, USA

"I've participated in countless 'women in games' events, talks, meet-ups, etc., but I have to say that while many of us yearn for the day when we don't need to be specifically called out for our gender in this industry, it's always been vastly rewarding and inspiring to be able to gather with women who have a common passion for games and just talk shop. One of the most positive experiences was just recently in Tehran, when I met with a group of women working, or aspiring to work, on games and just being able to instantly bond through our common challenges was moving."

Kate Edwards | Geographer, CEO, & Principal Consultant | Geogrify | Seattle, USA

"The most affirming experience for me related to women in gaming has been my time with the Frag Doll team and the sisterhood within our community of women gamers. Seeing the power of a supportive network of people, all dealing with many of the same challenges, has helped me to envision a future for the game industry where we have outgrown many of the problems that plague us today."

Morgan Romine | Director of Initiatives | AnyKey | San Diego, USA

"To be able to successfully navigate this industry and stay in it as my career path. To be able to mentor youth and encourage, teach, and hire them. To be a key part of Amplifying Voices boot camp, built solely to train individuals from diverse backgrounds from all over the world. It is a super meaningful effort because there is so much talent out there, but few are trained on how to present and sell themselves. We need a whole new generation of that. To be comfortable with your decisions and not let others rock your boat. I know what I am doing in my field of expertise and I am sticking to it!"

Perrin Kaplan | Principal | Zebra Partners | Seattle, USA

"The community of women in gaming is very colorful, passionate, and supportive. Whether it's giving opportunities to speak, work, financially supporting other women, or generally giving life tips or exposure to each other's work. I have never been in a more supportive community and it makes me hopeful that we can overcome the issues that remain to be addressed within our community."

Sithe Ncube | Founder & Director | Ubongo Game Lab | Lusaka, Zambia

---

"The most positive experience that I already have related to the topic of women in games is the community that we have created with Women in Games ES (WIGES). It is a physical and online community made up of all WIGES members. In this community we support each other, talk, and help solve the problems that arise. Things like how and what to study to develop videogames, how to access studies in videogames, what roles there are and what can be the most attractive for each of us, how to make a good curriculum, and personal problems that some members find or suffer at all levels during their studies, in collaborations, at work, interviews, etc. Above all, we inform each other how the situation of the videogame industry is different in other parts of the world (we have many members from outside of Spain. like Mexico and Argentina), and we also provide solutions to the gender problems that arise."

Gisela Vaquero | Founder & President | Women in Games ES | Barcelona, Spain

---

"It is incredible the number of women who support one another every day on social media and forums. Watching other women offer résumé advice, portfolio critiques, surveys about their work, spending time discussing how to negotiate for better salaries, how to fight imposter syndrome… it's just wonderful to see support networks like these on the rise and growing! There wasn't anything like that when I started, or at least it was a lot harder to discover and join, and now there are so many ways and opportunities to connect, it's just rad to see it happen."

Stephanie Bayer | Manager, Community Development | Blizzard Entertainment | Irvine, USA

VIRTUAL REALITY:

Worlds within the Wardrobe

By Robyn Tong Gray | *Co-Founder, Otherworld Interactive*

I grew up devouring books like *The Lion, the Witch, and the Wardrobe*, stories about ordinary people stumbling into extraordinary worlds and gaining new destinies and identities in the process. That fantasy—uncovering other worlds and trying on new identities—is something that I've carried with me as a creator. It's a large part of what sparked my interest in virtual reality. In VR (virtual reality), players stop being players and become part of the world. Just as the children emerge into Narnia as kings and queens, VR players shed their identities and don new ones. In VR, this is known as embodiment.

Virtual reality is all about presence. Presence is defined as a visceral feeling of being in a virtual world. Players are no longer looking at a window into your game via a 2D screen—they're in it. The world is all around them. VR experiences create spatial memories. After an experience, players can close their eyes and remember the dimensions and atmosphere of VR environments in the same detail as they would a genuine environment. The human brain is much better at remembering things in space than on a screen. As a result, VR experiences can leave a longer-lasting, more detailed impression on players compared to experiences confined to 2D media.

Embodiment is unique to VR. It's an opportunity for people to become someone else without placing the burden of acting or imagination on them. This makes it more accessible as an interactive storytelling medium than traditional roleplaying. Embodiment is successful when a player's new virtual body responds naturally to the motions of their physical body, further grounding their belief in this new reality. The most basic version of VR embodiment provides players with virtual representations of their controllers, such as the controllers themselves or "virtual hands." In VR, these virtual representations track a player's physical hand motions, allowing he or she to interact in a seemingly physical manner with the virtual world. As it relates to storytelling, embodiment can be a powerful tool for entertainment, evoking empathy or simply being somewhere else—as someone else—for a little while.

In traditional games, players are privy to a small window into other worlds. Their character represents their presence in that world and players can exude influence through that character. In a game with heavily authored characters, this influence is about guiding the character through a predetermined story. In games like *Fallout 3* or *Dragon Age: Inquisition*, in which the character is more of a blank slate (or tabula rasa), there is the opportunity to roleplay and influence the story based on player preference. But characters in traditional games are mostly a one-way street; the player guides and commands from a distance, driving the story but rarely being influenced in return.

In virtual reality, players *are* the character. The complete blocking out of reality through a VR headset also means the erasure of players' physical forms. In VR, we no longer view the over-the-top muscular male or hypersexualized female protagonist from afar—we become them. Therefore, thoughtful design of characters and stories is all the more critical.

In recent years, there's been a huge push for diversity of characters in games. The year 2017 saw an unprecedented number of female game protagonists in spectacularly practical, ass-kicking attire. We've also witnessed a rise in the number of games whose stories are rooted not in grand, sweeping adventures, but stories about family, relationships, and mental health. And to no one's surprise, this new and diverse content has been met with an eager and positive audience.

Now consider embodiment and the implications it—and the power of VR—can have on an audience. The most comfortable and immersive embodiment option is to feel like yourself in VR, perhaps a more idealized version, but not something completely different (assuming the representation is literal and not abstract). For example, if you're a woman entering a VR experience, looking down to see a male body can be bizarre and immersion breaking. By creating content that can support a range of genders, ethnicities, and body types we can encourage and welcome a diverse audience and increase the immersive power of the worlds we create and the impact they can have.

It's important to note, however, that having a player assume an identity not their own is not necessarily an immersion breaker when done deliberately. When it is a deliberate choice (and when there is enough diverse content to provide alternative options as desired), creating opportunities to become someone else is a creative decision.

VR is an empathetic medium. It can have a very real and powerful emotional impact on its users. Beyond entertainment, VR has successfully been used to help treat PTSD and been utilized for exposure therapy among other therapeutic applications. Creating opportunities for players to become someone else means introducing them to new perspectives. VR's blocking out of reality and creation of spatial memories means experiences are more visceral and evocative. There are wonderful experiences in which players can take on different genders, ethnicities, capabilities, and actually "walk a mile" in that character's shoes. VR might be the only way to truly experience a different perspective and can, therefore, potentially impart experiences that help us relate to one another.

The games industry has finally started shifting towards diverse content so that everyone might have the opportunity to play as a character reflective of himself or herself. This also means players have more opportunities to experience different perspectives. The possibilities and power of embodiment makes providing this diversity of characters and experiences in VR not optional, but vital. Diversity of content is necessary for the success of VR as a medium and—arguably—to help contribute toward a more empathetic society as a whole.

VR is a young medium. There are no set rules about how to create content and no notion of limits as to what can or cannot be done. There are also no set expectations about who can make—or play—VR experiences. Now is the time to explore, include, and expand ideas, people, and stories to provide experiences that are as new and fresh as the medium. Who knows what worlds are waiting at the back of the wardrobe!

LAUREN CASON

INDIE GAME ARTIST AND INCARCERATED YOUTH VOLUNTEER

 Miss_lady_pants  Lauren Cason

 laurencason.com

EXPERIENCE

FIRST INDUSTRY PROJECT: PROJECT COPERNICUS (2012, CANCELED)

FAVORITE INDUSTRY PROJECT: MONUMENT VALLEY 2 (2017)

PROJECTS SHIPPED: 5 GAMES

ACHIEVEMENTS UNLOCKED:

> IGN "BEST MOBILE GAME"—MONUMENT VALLEY 2 (2017)

> THE GAME AWARDS "BEST MOBILE GAME"—MONUMENT VALLEY 2 (2017)

> WEBBY AWARDS "BEST PUZZLE GAME"—MONUMENT VALLEY 2 (2018)

> FORBES "30 UNDER 30" (2018)

STATS

INDUSTRY LEVEL: 7

CURRENT CLASS: SENIOR ARTIST

CURRENT GUILD: USTWO GAMES—LONDON, UNITED KINGDOM

SPECIAL SKILLS: ILLUSTRATION, DIGITAL PAINTING, ANIMATION, 3D MODELING, CONCEPT ART, CHARACTER DESIGN, SWING DANCING

STANDARD EQUIPMENT

FAVORITE PLATFORM: MOBILE

GO-TO GENRE: SURVIVAL HORROR

MUST-HAVE GAMES: PORTAL, DIABLO II, SHADOW OF THE COLOSSUS

BIO

Lauren Cason realized her heart wasn't in editorial art the third year of her illustration degree. With that realization came an existential crisis about what to do with her education. While looking for guidance, she signed up for a 3D modeling class; it was the only elective that fit into her schedule. "I'm so glad it did, because it blew my mind," said Cason. "I built this couch and I felt like I was playing *The Sims* but now I had control of *every slider*. I don't think it had ever occurred to me that it was a job, that people were behind the 3D worlds you run around in." She pivoted her portfolio and decided to study 3D art the last few months of her degree. She'd have to learn the rest on her own.

Cason put her newfound skills to use on a research project at the nearby MIT Game Lab, helping develop a demo to showcase new tech. "This brilliant programmer, Mark Sullivan, had been working on a soft-body physics engine, and myself and one other artist were helping to create a demo for it," explained Cason. "The Game Lab was such an amazing experience; the things I learned there really laid the foundation for me." She contributed concept art level design, modeling, texturing, and engine integration—testing her knowledge in a real-world environment for the first time.

Easter Egg

Is an obsessive swing dancer and seeks out teams whenever she moves to a new city. She has competed for the past five years and hopes to start teaching swing soon.

TRY AND TRY AGAIN

While she looked for her first full-time industry job, persistence and a thick skin eventually earned Cason a well-deserved spot at an indie studio. "I took my portfolio to a bunch of portfolio reviews. I probably spoke to 30 studios, and no one was interested in hiring me," she said. "One art director looked at my stuff and said, 'Look, straight-up, games might not be for you. Your stuff isn't very good.'" Undeterred, Cason asked for specific feedback, which he provided. She continued asking for detailed feedback and areas of improvement with every rejection, and spent the summer working to lift the weak points in her 3D art.

With an updated portfolio, Cason returned to many of the same studios months later. "That same art director who told me games wasn't for me recognized me, and said he'd never seen someone improve so quickly," she recalled. "He gave me my first industry job after graduation. Trying to turn any failure or rejection into an opportunity for feedback has served me well. Feedback is a gift."

Resilience would still be required in Cason's early career. "My first industry project was *Project Copernicus* with 38 Studios. I did weapon sculpting and armor refitting," explained Cason. "The early years were hard. I went through two studio shutdowns—38 Studios and Zynga Boston—within the first year of graduation, and then narrowly avoided layoff rounds at the next stop. My place in the industry felt extremely precarious. This was obviously very stressful. But if I could talk to my younger self, I'd say, 'This period is going to be scary, but you'll learn so much.'"

Over the next several years, Cason would lend her artistic talents to an array of companies and games. She worked as a concept and 3D artist at Harmonix on *Fantasia: Music Evolved*, followed by an artist position at Proletariat, Inc. on *Zombination*. Cason found a home at Funomena in 2014, moving cross-country to San Francisco as a senior 3D artist on their narrative VR game, *Luna*. After the launch of *Luna*, she worked as a 3D production artist at Dim Bulb Games, on their "bleak American folktale" *Where the Water Tastes Like Wine*.

> "Trying to turn any failure or rejection into an opportunity for feedback has served me well."

USTWO

In 2016, Cason was presented with an opportunity she couldn't refuse—a position as senior artist on *Monument Valley 2* at UsTwo Games' studio in London. For this sequel to the critically and commercially successful *Monument Valley*, the team found their own voice within the beautiful isometric puzzle game, told through a mother-and-daughter narrative. Cason was responsible for designing the visuals for a variety of levels, and ensuring the art aligned with both puzzle mechanics and story beats within the game.

"I loved *Monument Valley*, so getting to add to that world was so incredibly special," said Cason. "Our tools were amazing, I had a lot of creative freedom, the team was great, and it was just such a pleasure." The high stakes made *Monument Valley 2* the most challenging project of her career as well. "It's very hard to try to add to something that you love—it felt like such a responsibility; we didn't want to ruin it! But we also wanted to make it our own. It also was such a short turnaround from when I joined to when it shipped—about nine months—and so much changed during that time. We changed the entire UI system two weeks before content lock. Our willingness to change constantly made for a better game, but man, it was hard!"

The team's dedication bore fruit; *Monument Valley 2* was a success, overtaking its predecessor in sales. It won Best Mobile Game from both IGN and the Game Awards, and Best Puzzle Game during the 2018 Webby Awards.

"When *Monument Valley 2* came out, UsTwo did an amazing thing and flew all of our parents out to London for the launch party, as the game was about motherhood and family legacy," shared Cason. "One of the attendees brought their little girl, probably about seven years old, with them, who had a print of one of the levels I worked on. I got to talk with her about why we designed the level that way, the relationship between the mother and the daughter in the game, stuff like that, and sign the print for her. My mother was sitting with me while I talked to her, and it was just such an affirming moment—talking to this little girl about a game about relationships between women, and getting to share that with my mother, it was so special. We all had a place at that party, on that couch. Every generation. I'll never forget that."

GIVING BACK

No matter where Cason has lived, she's made a point to keep volunteering a part of her life. She has spent time teaching incarcerated youths to make games, mentored young women via the Girls Make Games program, and has a long-running relationship with Intel's Computer Clubhouse Network.

Through Intel, Cason works as a technology mentor with youths from underserved communities in the Bay area. "My focus is on teaching video game art and design, specifically with young women," explained Cason.

Cason has found immense satisfaction in giving back. "I was a mentor at the Intel Computer Clubhouse in Boston for a while, and being there always lifted my heart," she said. "I'd come in and an 11-year-old girl would be super excited to show me a game she'd made in Scratch where you are a terrifying all-powerful ice witch who has to destroy demons or something like that, and another girl made a piano out of marshmallows with her raspberry pie. Every time I walked in there, I'd be excited for the future of games."

A DAY IN THE LIFE OF...

A STREAMER & HOST

Streamers, YouTubers, brand ambassadors, online personalities, web hosts, influencers—whatever you call them, individuals who make a living through creating content and cultivating a following need skills as diverse as the titles that attempt to define them. These professionals have become significantly influential in the industry and, in doing so, have disrupted both games journalism and marketing by connecting with fans on a more personal level. Melonie Mac built her audience from the ground up in a time before video monetization made it a viable career. Years of hard work later, she now has hundreds of thousands of followers who crave her content.

MELONIE MAC

PROFESSION: FREELANCE STREAMER & HOST—LOS ANGELES, USA

YEARS IN PROFESSION: 9

ASSOCIATED WITH: GAMESTOP, DISNEYXD TV, RIOT GAMES, UBISOFT, RAZER, NICKELODEON, FUTURE SHOP, WALMART GAMECENTER

▶ EDUCATION

"I have no formal training. I earned a degree in Web Development and was working as a bank teller when I first started my YouTube channel. That was before video monetization and I had no idea my career would stem from it. I did have dreams of hosting for gaming though; Jessica Chobot and the Frag Dolls were big inspirations of mine, and I hoped that making YouTube videos would help me be more comfortable on camera. It certainly helped a lot!"

▶ BREAKING INTO THE INDUSTRY

"It was very difficult. I first applied to be a Frag Doll back in early 2006. My application got me to the next stage of phone interviews, but I was so shy and nervous that I bombed it. That was very discouraging, but I picked myself up. I was in my late teens and had room to grow and, sure enough, I got my chance again. I finally made it as one of the spring 2010 Cadettes."

▶ FIRST ASSIGNMENT

"My first industry assignment was promoting Splinter Cell Conviction at PAX East. I discovered that a lot of gaming industry work is just like regular work. It felt much like what I did in retail. It was more fun because I got to talk about a game I loved, but it was still hard work with long hours, hectic scheduling, and coordinating with coworkers."

▶ KEY QUALITIES

"I think the most important qualities to have for hosting especially are work ethic, optimism, and an easygoing attitude. This kind of work is challenging and, at times, extremely exhausting.

"Charisma is also important as a host and streamer. You always want to be true to yourself, but it's important to keep your energy up. I find that when I give myself rest days, put a little time into fitness, surround myself with positive people, and allow some offline gaming, I am much happier and perform at my best."

▶ TRAINING OPPORTUNITIES

"I'm a big fan of self-teaching through experience. Get that practice in, even if no one sees it. Twitch also has a hosting workshop that is really great for those who are seeking training."

▶ TOOLS OF THE TRADE

"For streaming I use OBS broadcasting software and, regarding hardware, I use a Logitech Brio webcam, Audio Technica 2020 mic, Brookstone Cat Ear Headphones, two Asus monitors, and a souped-up Xidax PC rig. It's nice to have fancy gear, but when I first started streaming I used an outdated laptop with its integrated webcam and a cheap headset with a mic. Don't ever let your limitations keep you from getting started."

▶ AN AVERAGE DAY

Streaming: "For streaming I set my own schedule, but it's something I am constantly adjusting as I find what works best for my viewers. I wake up, eat breakfast, check and reply to emails, and engage fans/ post on social media. I also need to prepare any sponsored content, ensuring the balance of the client's key points are mentioned while still retaining my voice and opinions. I then prep myself, clean my stream room, take pictures to promote the stream, eat, and test my streaming software. Then I go live and share the stream on social media!"

Hosting: "Most shoots are very early, so usually I wake up at 4:30 AM and do a run-through of the script. I arrive on set for call time, eat breakfast, get my makeup done, choose an outfit with the stylist, and get mic'd up! Then I go over content and flow with the producer and read the prompter or host conversationally depending on the segment. After, I go backstage and eat or study while they arrange the set for the next scene.

"I repeat this throughout the day until we finish and go back to the hotel or hop on a plane. I'm always happy but extremely exhausted by the end of a shoot."

▶ PROFESSIONAL PERKS

"Being around video games (especially playing them early) and traveling a lot are my favorite perks! "

▶ CAREER CHALLENGES

"The biggest challenge is staying relevant, both in streaming and in hosting. It is a constant grind. You have to figure out what makes people enjoy your streams, pay attention to the numbers keep up with different streaming platforms because this space is constantly growing.

"In regards to hosting, it's nice to have ongoing gigs, but when you don't have one steady job you have to constantly look for and negotiate work."

▶ BIGGEST MISTAKE

"The biggest mistake I made was overloading myself. Once I accepted a hosting job for a day shoot in New York when I already had an early shoot in California the day before. I woke up at 4:30 am, drove to the set, filmed for approximately 12 hours, went straight to the airport, flew to New York, got to my hotel and had an hour before call time for the next shoot. I was jet lagged and exhausted and didn't perform nearly as well as I usually do."

PRO TIP!

"Make a name for yourself and open your own doors. Don't wait for others to do it for you. The beauty of this industry is that you can start now! Want to be a streamer? Just do it! You may stream for one viewer, but get in the practice. Make your own shows to host. Talk about your favorite games, or shoutcast a stream. Keep working through the discouragement and don't give up."

MICAELA ROMANINI

CELEBRATING VIDEO GAMES AS CULTURE ON AN INTERNATIONAL SCALE

MicaelaRomanini   MicaelaRomanini

Micaela Romanini    womeningamesitalia.org

EXPERIENCE

FIRST INDUSTRY PROJECT: VIGAMUS MUSEUM PROMOTION (2012)

FAVORITE INDUSTRY PROJECT: GAMEROME DEVELOPERS CONFERENCE (2017)

PROJECTS SHIPPED: 8 EXHIBITIONS, 9 EVENTS, 10+ CONTRIBUTIONS TO GAME STUDIES' PUBLICATIONS

ACHIEVEMENTS UNLOCKED:

> GREW MONTHLY VISITORS TO THE VIGAMUS (THE VIDEO GAME MUSEUM OF ROME) BY 40% IN ONE YEAR (2014)

> CURATOR OF THE GLOBALLY COVERED "E.T. THE FALL: ATARI'S BURIED TREASURES" EXHIBIT (2014)

> CHOSEN ITALIAN REPRESENTATIVE BY INTEL AND ESL AT THE GLOBAL ESPORTS FORUM IN KATOWICE (2018)

> FOUNDED WOMEN IN GAMES ITALIA, THE LOCAL CHAPTER OF WOMEN IN GAMES WIGJ (2018)

STATS

INDUSTRY LEVEL: 7

CURRENT CLASS: VICE DIRECTOR

CURRENT GUILD: VIGAMUS FOUNDATION—ROME, ITALY

SPECIAL SKILLS: COMMUNICATION & DIGITAL MARKETING, CONTENT CREATION, COMMUNITY MANAGEMENT, SOCIAL MEDIA MARKETING, BRAND MANAGEMENT, INTERNATIONAL BUSINESS RELATIONS, EVENT MANAGEMENT

STANDARD EQUIPMENT

FAVORITE PLATFORM: XBOX

GO-TO GENRE: ADVENTURE GAMES

MUST-HAVE GAME: OMIKRON: THE NOMAD SOUL

BIO

While Micaela Romanini enjoys video games as a consumer in their current form, from a career standpoint, there was something about the industry's *past* that gripped her and wouldn't let go. As such, she tailored her university education toward a very specific and niche vocation. "I loved games and I was very interested in the use of technology in museums and culture in general," said Romanini, who earned her bachelor's degree in communication sciences and journalism in 2005. Quickly thereafter she returned for a master's in library and information science, writing her master's thesis on the work of David Cage at Quantic Dream.

While still in school, Romanini freelanced as a games journalist, reporting for a variety of online and print publications, including *PS Mania* and *Game Republic*. She also taught "Video Games History and Journalism" at the University of Rome as a graduate teaching assistant.

Easter Egg
Her official first day of work in the games industry took place on a plane headed to E3, in Los Angeles.

HIGHLIGHTING VIDEO GAME HISTORY

After graduating with her master's in 2012, Romanini knew exactly where she was going to apply—the nearby Video Game Museum of Rome, abbreviated VIGAMUS. "I was very lucky to meet my manager, who saw I had potential since the very beginning and advocated for me," she said. Romanini was hired to lead local and online promotion of the museum by planning out and managing campaigns with the goal of increasing visitors. Romanini kicked off multifaceted campaigns that utilized social media marketing, SEO, email marketing, Google AdWords, and other marketing tools to get the word out. As a direct result of her efforts, the museum's weekly visitor rate increased by 30% within one year, and monthly visitor numbers increased 40% during the same window of time.

"I also was responsible for the planning and management of exhibitions and events, including the *Pixels: The Movie* launch event, and shows for the *Space Invaders* 35th anniversary and the *Pac-Man* 35th anniversary," explained Romanini. "And I created content and managed the European Federation of Game Archives, Museums, and Preservation Projects online presence. The Federation was launched by the Computerspielemuseum (Video Game Museum of Berlin) director, the VIGAMUS museum director, and MO5 director (France) to promote the preservation of games as part of our heritage and now counts over 11 members in Europe and international partners from all over the world.

DIGGING UP THE PAST

One of Romanini's favorite exhibitions involved actual video game archeology. "I was responsible for the exhibition 'E.T. The Fall: Atari's Buried Treasures,'" she said. "The VIGAMUS Museum secured a worldwide premiere exclusive to the Atari buried findings in Alamogordo, items received in permanent donation on October 20, 2014. I managed the exhibition's planning and promotion: the event received international press coverage, including reports from industry leader website Polygon. A few relevant museums displayed the findings in special exhibitions later that year."

The exhibit received praise from the operations manager of the Alamogordo excavation, Joe Lewandowski, and the lead archaeologist, Andrew Reinhard. "When they visited the Atari items exhibition displayed at our museum, they told us it was their best display ever," shared Romanini. "They showed it off when talking at events and conferences all over the world. They were so moved when they saw the items finally belonging to a museum, and it was so inspiring to give visitors the opportunity to see the only example of archaeology in video games. That moment really paid off and made me really happy and proud of the work achieved with the entire team."

In 2016, Romanini moved to the UK and was selected for a role as international coordinator on the integrated marketing team supporting Xbox.com. "I took care of over 44 markets across Europe, the Asia-Pacific, China, and Latin America." She learned a great deal working in an international environment.

After returning to VIGAMUS, Romanini worked her way up the promotional ladder, and is now the vice director of the VIGAMUS Foundation. "In this role, I take care of new business strategies and development for the foundation's activities and products," she explained. "I also working with local and global institutions to execute international projects. Among them, I was responsible for the VIGAMUS Foundation and EFGAMP panels at the European Youth Event in Strasbourg and the European Culture Forum in Milan, organized in collaboration with the European Parliament and European Commission."

> "[Vice director of VIGAMUS] is absolutely the most fulfilling and compelling in my career so far."

"This role is absolutely the most fulfilling and compelling in my career so far, as I have a broad range of tasks and responsibilities, and it allows me to work with many international partners, giving me the chance to travel a lot." She also recognizes the greater good her work achieves. "Working with cultural projects allows me to advocate for video games in general, explaining the benefits and the opportunities this amazing medium offers to cultural institutions, especially in the areas of VR and AR."

EXTRACURRICULAR ADVOCACY

While she's still full-time at the museum, in 2017 Romanini accepted the position as event director at the annual Game Developers Conference Gamerome. "One of my best memories is the director of the VIGAMUS Foundation, Marco Accordi Rickards, and Frank Sliwka, former director of the GDC Europe, asking me to become Gamerome's event director."

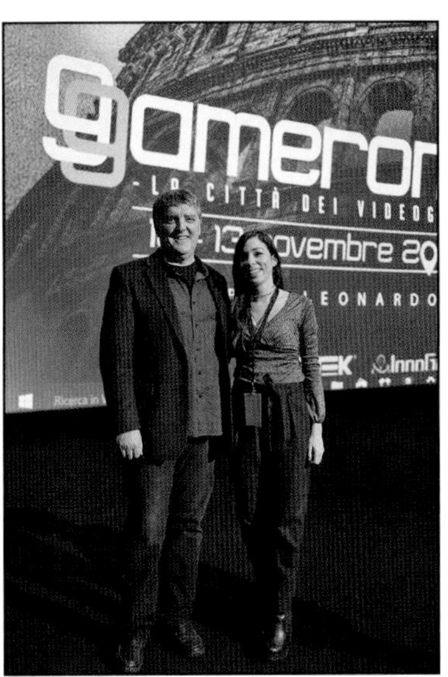

As event director, she manages the show from top to bottom. "I plan the contents of the talks, the speakers list, the developer showcase, and take care of the international partnerships," Romanini detailed. "Working on Gamerome gives me the chance to learn new skills and to meet many experienced professionals. When you're finally there, opening the conference with your team, it's kind of magic to see everything in place."

The next year Romanini also founded the Italian chapter of non-profit Women in Games (WIGJ). "I was selected by the Women in Games organization and its founder David W. Smith and CEO Marie-Claire Isaaman to launch the Italian network, Women in Games Italia. I represent the organization and take care of its mission in Italy," said Romanini. Founding the local WIGJ chapter was a natural evolution of her previous advocacy. She's an associate at the organization Women & Technologies and was selected by Intel and the Electronic Sports League as the Italian representative at the Global esports Forum in Katowice, Poland. While there, she participated in workshops on the inclusion of women in esports.

"Being an advocate for video games in Italy and also a mentor for many students and young women motivates my work," said Romanini. "I was very lucky to find professionals who helped me in my professional growth, and I feel responsible to support and empower the young girls and boys who are the next generation."

REGINA LUKI KGATLE

PROVIDING UNDERPRIVILEGED CHILDREN ENTERTAINMENT AND EDUCATION

 RrrEeGina

 Regina Kgatle

educade.co.za
67games.org

EXPERIENCE

FIRST INDUSTRY PROJECT: EDUCADE (2011)

FAVORITE INDUSTRY PROJECT: THERE'S A MONSTER FOR EVERYONE (2016)

PROJECTS SHIPPED: 6 GAMES

ACHIEVEMENTS UNLOCKED:

> YOUNG PEOPLE INTERNATIONAL AFFAIRS "35 UNDER-35 AFRICAN LEADERS" (2012)
> UNITED NATIONS "AFRICAN ALLIANCE AWARD" NOMINATION (2015)
> OCULUS "AMPLIFYING NEW VOICES" AWARD (2016)
> FACEBOOK "20 TECH CHANGEMAKERS" AWARD (2014)

STATS

INDUSTRY LEVEL: 7

CURRENT CLASS: MANAGING DIRECTOR

CURRENT GUILD: EDUCADE & 67GAMES—CAPE TOWN, SOUTH AFRICA

SPECIAL SKILLS: EDUTAINMENT, PUBLIC SPEAKING, LEADERSHIP, TEACHING, PROGRAMMING, GAME DESIGN

STANDARD EQUIPMENT

FAVORITE PLATFORM: MOBILE

GO-TO GENRE: ONE TOUCH GAMES

MUST-HAVE GAME: PAC-MAN

BIO

Regina Kgatle comes from a family of entrepreneurs. "My family owns entertainment garages throughout Johannesburg," she began. "I used to go to them and play the arcades when I was young. I would watch people spend a coin and play a game until they lost." Kgatle developed a fascination not just with the games, but also with the technology that powered them. She made it a personal mission to build one herself someday to help expand the family business.

Kgatle began to realize that arcades had a really bad rap, however. Parents would come to vent their frustrations. "We had a lot of people complaining that kids were playing games and not doing their homework or advancing their educational level," she recalled. "That is when I first had the idea that I could make games that were educational."

Easter Egg

Facebook COO Sheryl Sandberg mentioned Kgatle's work in a statement about women around the world facilitating change.

EDUCADE

"I went to the University of Cape Town to study electrical and computer engineering," continued Kgatle. "I did a lot of coding, and that's when I realized I was actually good at it. I knew this is what I wanted to do for the rest of my life."

One day, while eating lunch at her university, she noticed a poster rallying young change-makers for ideas that were both innovative and social. Kgatle had recently learned that out of all the children worldwide who would never receive a primary education, half were from Africa. Given that she'd grown up in an underserved township—a remnant of segregation from apartheid—the statistic hit close to home.

Kgatle founded Educade in 2011. Repurposing old arcade cabinets, she began to design and program a series of games that would reinforce foundational elements of the current South African primary school curriculum. "This is inclusive," said Kgatle. "The point is to not leave out an underprivileged child who doesn't have a gaming gadget or a smart device to download educational apps. We provide a very interactive learning environment through our standalone Educade machines. The service is cheap and utilizes the ancient 'play' culture."

The standalone arcades would be placed in public spaces near underserved schools. Private companies could advertise on the arcade cabinets in exchange for funding. The arcade cabinets would stay affordable through donated e-waste, which Kgatle would repurpose for her cause.

Despite the potential, securing an initial round of funding was challenging. "When I decided to start a business, I had difficulties. I think if I was a male, maybe a white male, I would have raised more money than I have for my business. There is still that stigma of disbelief that as a woman, you can actually run a tech company."

After hard work illustrating the potential of Educade, Kgatle was able to secure capital. "The Educades in Cape Town were sponsored by the municipality," she explained. "My primary business task is managing proposals to show that Educade is a valid complementary learning tool worth looking into. Or at least investing into as much as they are investing into books in the library."

CELEBRATING SOUTH AFRICAN CULTURE

Educade's games are contextualized within South African culture. *Memory Racer* challenges the player to remember placement of symbols within a series of blocks, and create matches to earn points. Points can be converted into fuel; the more fuel, the longer the race. "Respecting the realities that we are raised in is important," she said. "You are racing in the places that are familiar. You are not racing in a Ferrari, cruising past mansions. You are driving past places you would see daily, so you can better relate."

Her second game—*King Luki*—teaches mathematical equations. "In *King Luki* you are hiking in the mountains of Cape Town and collecting stones," she explained. "Each stone will contain a number or an operator, and after collecting enough stones, the player would have to solve the equation to progress." Getting the equation correct allows the player to continue hiking and reaching new places.

King Luki has resonated particularly well with young black girls. "They are hiking as a black girl who looks like them, which doesn't happen a lot in games," Kgatle said. "What I also find interesting is how they relate when they find out that I made the games. You can see them sparkling and taking more interest in the game. They begin to ask questions. It encourages their curiosity."

Inspiring young women of color is especially important to Kgatle. "I was hoping to meet more people like myself in the local community," she admitted. "But I'm always the only one who looks like myself. There are probably girls who are just as interested in games, but they don't have the network. They don't have access to the spaces that I have access to."

67GAMES FOR 67 SCHOOLS

In order to meet the demand of creating games to cover the entirety of South Africa's primary school curriculum, Kgatle came up with a plan. She created non-profit 67Games with the goal of designing 67 educational games for installation in 67 under-resourced schools across the country. In 2014, indie developers at local experimental games convention A MAZE pledged to design for 67 Games. She also opened up contributions designed with provided specifications from developers around the world.

Kgatle created and shared a list of game briefs that focused on the current school curriculum, as well as addressing larger societal issues. "There is difficulty understanding the concept of time. How many seconds make a minute; how many minutes make an hour; how many hours make a day/week," she said. "Also, life skills. We need to speak about dangerous environments and situations that children find themselves in. We need to create awareness about gangsters, rape, domestic violence, hyper-masculinity, and patriarchy. I know I'm pushing the curriculum. I've been making games exclusively to cover the curriculum, but I also asked, how do you complement it? There's no way in our curriculum you can talk about topics such as sexuality."

Kgatle's personal favorite game tackles that exact topic. "I designed a game called *There's a Monster for Everyone*, where you make monsters according to their characteristics," she described. "You start with physical descriptions—one eye versus two eyes—and then you match them into pairs not by what they look like, but what they are thinking in their speech bubbles. With that game I was trying to teach consent and sexuality. If this monster has one eye it does not necessarily mean that it's attracted to a monster that has one eye."

Kgatle also uses 67Games as a banner to teach under, hosting game jam sessions in areas without access to technology resources. The hope is that she may be training a future contributor to her cause. Although arcades are the foundation of Educade, Kgatle wants to make her games as widely available as possible. Therefore, she is working to have them installed in local libraries countrywide, and to provide them as free downloads on mobile devices.

"There is still that stigma of disbelief that as a woman, you can actually run a tech company."

Kgatle's programs have been noticed on an international scale. Facebook COO Sheryl Sandberg mentioned her in the context of women making change around the world. In 2012, Young People International Affairs named her as one of their "35 Under-35 African Leaders." In 2014 she was flown to the United States along with 24 other students from around the world to receive an award for youth changing lives through technology. She has been profiled by the *Mail & Guardian* as one of their 200 young South African leaders, and was featured recently in the August issue of *Elle South Africa*.

"I feel like I've positioned myself really well to help shape the serious gaming industry," she closed. "I want to see Educade as a leading game studio in the global game scene. The Japanese have their style; so does the United States. I would like Educade to establish the African style. I'm getting into the untapped mindset of the South African gaming industry, and I'm planning to expand it across the continent."

SOHA EL-SABAAWI

ADVOCATING INDUSTRY-WIDE DIVERSITY AND INCLUSION

 sokareemie

EXPERIENCE

FIRST INDUSTRY PROJECT: MOTHER MAY I?—DAMES MAKING GAMES GAME JAM (2013)

FAVORITE INDUSTRY PROJECT: MENTOR AT INDIGICADE (2015)

PROJECTS SHIPPED: 15+ GAMES

ACHIEVEMENTS UNLOCKED:

> 12 PUBLISHED ARTICLES
> 10+ PANEL APPEARANCES
> 8 ART EXHIBITIONS
> 5 UNIVERSITY LECTURES

STATS

INDUSTRY LEVEL: 6

CURRENT CLASS: MANAGER OF DIVERSITY AND INCLUSION PROGRAMS

CURRENT GUILD: RIOT GAMES—LOS ANGELES, USA

SPECIAL SKILLS: EXPERIMENTAL GAME DESIGN, DIVERSITY AND INCLUSION INITIATIVES, COMMUNITY MANAGEMENT, SOCIAL MEDIA, MENTORING, CAT PHOTOS

STANDARD EQUIPMENT

FAVORITE PLATFORM: PC

GO-TO GENRE: HORROR, SCI-FI, RPG

MUST-HAVE GAME: MASS EFFECT SERIES, SILENT HILL 2, FALLOUT: NEW VEGAS

BIO

Born a refugee in Saudi Arabia to an Iraqi mother and Palestinian father, Soha El-Sabaawi relocated to Canada with her family when she was young. She would spend her youth trying to understand her unique identity and, in some cases, mask it to better fit in. “Every six months a new Soha would emerge, with the least flattering being the Dead Kennedys-obsessed, punk-rocker Soha,” recalled El-Sabaawi. “Eventually, I decided to grow my plucked-too-thin eyebrows, hide my Sex Pistols CDs, and begin exploring the next phase—the gamer.”

El-Sabaawi consumed games casually at first. She has distant memories of playing the original *Prince of Persia*, *Moonwalker*, *Laura Bow 2: The Dagger of Amon Ra*, and *Doom II*. When a friend lent her a copy of *The Legend of Zelda: Ocarina of Time*, everything changed. She sat down and played the game in its entirely in a day and a half, and during that time found one of her most enduring identities.

Throughout her life, El-Sabaawi imagined herself as a human-rights lawyer, an educator of film and photography, and even deliberated archiving and museum work. “I never considered a career in the gaming industry until I was in university,” explained El-Sabaawi. “I was studying film and considered pursuing a career in cinematography to create cinematics for video games, but I was really conflicted about the additional schooling I thought I needed for that career path.” She eventually discovered the field of diversity and inclusion and, through it, found a unique and personal entry point into video games.

Easter Egg

Is obsessed with makeup and almost pursued a career as a makeup artist. She still does makeup for special events as a hobby, including weddings for family and friends.

DIVERSITY & INCLUSION

A local indie game community in Toronto facilitated El-Sabaawi’s first touch point with diversity and inclusion. “I fell in love with the scrappy, self-teaching programs by Dames Making Games, which is a non-profit organization to help women and non-binary folks create their first games using open-source tools in six weeklong incubations,” she explained. “They opened my eyes to what I was capable of doing, and that awakening made me want to help others pursue their dreams by crushing through obstacles in their way.” She would do this through running DMG-hosted seminars, expressing her unique viewpoint through games and online activism, eventually becoming a co-director for the organization.

El-Sabaawi also volunteered as a mentor for the Indigicade initiative, a collaboration between Dames Making Games and the Indigenous Routes Collective. "We mentored young indigenous women between the ages of 13 and 24," she explained. "It was my favorite project because watching indigenous youth create experiences on their own terms was so cathartic and fulfilling, especially as someone who comes from a displaced community."

In 2014 her efforts expanded beyond the Toronto games community. Tired of the lack of diverse representation on industry panels, El-Sabaawi helped formalize the "Plz Diversify Your Panel" campaign. "A few folks from the games industry came together to create 'Plz Diversify Your Panel,' a resource that listed marginalized people in the games community who would be perfect panelists at conferences and conventions," she explained. "I was on the team that originally started the list, and it really grew a mind of its own the more intersectional the resource became, to not only account for gender, but to boost people of color, people with disabilities, and people from across the globe to break our North American bias in the games industry."

GETTING PERSONAL

On a personal front, Dames Making Games had helped El-Sabaawi break from her long-held belief that one needed to be an experienced programmer to make games. Aided by the text-based game tool Twine, she began to create intensely personal games as both a form of self-expression and social activism.

Her first game, *Penalties*, explored her Palestinian identity through prose. The idea was born after she rediscovered her old passport. The words "Nationality: Stateless Refugee" was a stark reminder of the life she left behind. "*Penalties* is an escape-the-room horror game in which a nameless character wakes up in an unknown room with their mouth wired shut," she explained. "Its objective is not only to escape the room, but to believe that the room can be escaped. The process of making this game was rewarding and cathartic in ways that debating about Palestinian rights in political science classes or Internet comments sections are not. It voices the way it feels to be like me in this world: claustrophobic, terrifying, and horrifically quiet."

One of her more high-profile Twine games—*Reprogram*—had players point-and-click their way through El-Sabaawi's exploration of the ramifications on sexuality after abuse. The imagery is comprised of her own photography, edited to reflect the way she viewed the world at the time—chaotic and disconcerting.

RIOT GAMES

El-Sabaawi's education, activism, and passion resulted in her first formal industry job in 2013. "My first job in the gaming industry was as a community manager for mobile game studio Uken Games," she explained. "My role included a lot of customer support, which I had quite a lot of experience in because of the retail jobs I held throughout high school and university. Because I've been a gamer my whole life, it felt like second nature to apply the skills I learned in customer service to support players."

After leveling up her skills with Uken, El-Sabaawi moved from Toronto to Los Angeles in 2015 to work at one of the biggest companies in the world, on one of the biggest games in the world. "My current role is leading D&I initiatives at Riot Games," she said. "I've learned a lot about myself as a leader and how to collaborate with teams to create a positive impact. It was a large learning curve because it's my first time leading D&I at a bigger company, but I'm growing more confident and resilient, which is super exciting!"

El-Sabaawi hopes to ensure that D&I becomes a mainstay of the industry, and not a reaction to trends or consequence of bad behavior. "I want it to be accepted as a strategic advantage for every company across the globe," she said. "I want to be part of a larger movement that makes the future of games inviting for everyone who thinks they don't have what it takes to work in games."

> "I want to be part of a larger movement that makes the future of games inviting for everyone who thinks they don't have what it takes to work in games."

In her eyes, El-Sabaawi feels the current political climate has lit a fire within the games industry, moving toward positive change. "There's still a lot of resistance from different corners of toxic gaming communities that don't like this change or feel threatened by it," El-Sabaawi summarized. "But we're inching closer to industry-wide D&I progress, especially as minorities feel more empowered about coming forward with stories of marginalization. People in games are becoming braver, which only makes our industry stronger."

A DAY IN THE LIFE OF...

A VIDEO GAME JOURNALIST

As one would expect, video games journalism follows the tenets of traditional journalism, with an emphasis on covering interactive entertainment. Much like the larger occupational field, games journalism has recently undergone a rapid evolution to keep up with a changing landscape propelled by the rise of digital content, social media, live-streaming, influencers, and personality-driven blogs.

Some games journalists home in on an area of expertise called "beats," which allows them to provide a deeper layer of insights earned through years of specialization such as a specific platform, genre, or sub-industry such as indie gaming. Other games journalists prefer to be generalists. Dedicated news writers need more breadth than depth when it comes to industry knowledge in order to turn around informative stories soon after they break. Still others dedicate themselves to long-lead features and investigative articles, event coverage, or game reviews. Needless to say, there are many paths to pursue in games journalism.

Keza MacDonald has been well-known around the world for over a decade in games journalism, starting out in 2005. As a freelance writer, she's contributed to *Eurogamer*, *The Observer*, *Edge* magazine, and the official Xbox, Nintendo, and PlayStation magazines. In 2011 she joined industry giant IGN as their UK games editor, where she sourced, managed, and edited IGN's UK games content, helped define global editorial strategy, and won two industry awards for her own journalism, including Games Writer of the Year.

In 2014 she founded Kotaku's UK branch and served as editor for four years, establishing the site's editorial direction, running day-to-day operations, and writing plenty of content. Kotaku UK won an award for Best Editorial Team in both 2014 and 2016. MacDonald currently works at daily UK newspaper *The Guardian* as their games editor, and continues to regularly appear on countrywide media as a games expert, including appearances on the BBC and Channel 4 News.

KEZA MACDONALD

Kezamacdonald

theguardian.com/games

PROFESSION: VIDEO GAMES EDITOR, THE GUARDIAN—LONDON, UNITED KINGDOM

YEARS IN PROFESSION: 13

ASSOCIATED WITH: EUROGAMER, EDGE, IGN, KOTAKU, THE GUARDIAN

▶ EDUCATION

"I dropped out of school at 16 to become a video games journalist for a magazine at the other end of the country. As you can imagine, my parents weren't exactly delighted. I went back to university after a year and did a degree in Japanese and German, then a master's in comparative literature, whilst supporting myself with freelance journalism. My university education was enormously beneficial for me personally, but outside of transferable things like critical-thinking skills, I don't use it in my work. I largely learned journalism on the job.

"A journalism master's is a useful shortcut to showing a potential employer that you're serious about being a games journalist, rather than someone who just likes games—but they can be very expensive and are by no means essential."

▶ BREAKING IN

"I got very lucky in that I was offered work experience for a games magazine and then a job, which almost never happens now. I was one of two women at the entire company at the time, which wasn't easy—neither was being so young. It helped that I had already spent years writing for my own games website and reading voraciously about games; I wasn't a completely terrible writer when I started."

▶ EARLY INDUSTRY IMPRESSIONS

"I was surprised to learn that games journalists didn't play games all day! Reviewing and playing games is maybe 10-20% of a games journalist's working time. The rest is planning, research, interviewing, traveling, and, of course, writing. As an editor, working with other people's writing and running a publication, you get even less time to actually play."

▶ KEY QUALITIES

"To be a good reporter, you need curiosity and genuine interest in other people's stories. You need to be sure of your own ethics and care deeply about the truth. You need to be a good communicator, able to explain complex things in understandable words. To be a good critic, you need to read widely and be able to deconstruct what makes a game interesting and enjoyable (or not). To be a good games journalist—whether you are a reporter or a critic—you need to love games, or you'll get bored with the job pretty quickly."

▶ TOOLS OF THE TRADE

"Google's suite of text and office tools, and games consoles. That's about it."

▶ HOURS & ENVIRONMENT

"Over the years I have worked in offices, at home, at 3am, in front of cameras, from press conferences with a laptop balanced on my knees with rubbish Wi-Fi, and from maybe 10 different countries. One of the greatest things about being a journalist, for me, is the variety: depending on what you're working on, your location (and your hours) can vary."

▶ AN AVERAGE DAY

My average day involves working with writers to edit their copy and make their features the best they can be, planning coverage around upcoming games and current conversation points in the games industry, doing some of my own writing, and playing games when I can. Some days I interview game creators or players about something interesting they are doing, or travel to another country to cover a news event like E3 or play a new game at a studio."

▶ PROMOTIONAL PATH

"You start out as a writer. Sometimes a staff writer on a magazine or website, but these days, usually as a freelancer. You might then become a section editor, in charge of planning reviews or features for your publication. An editor-in-chief manages every writer and section editor at a publication. The further up the chain you get in media, the further away you get from spending all your time actually writing, but I love being an editor. Working with other people's words is as rewarding for me as my own."

▶ PROFESSIONAL PERKS

"I rarely pay for video games, which is pretty great. I get to speak to interesting creative people all the time. Often I play games before anyone else, though that can sometimes be as much of a frustration as a privilege when there's no day-one patch!"

▶ CAREER CHALLENGES

"Journalism in any field is not well-paid. Games journalism is worse than most as it relates to money. You and your work are also in the public eye all the time, which especially as it relates to women invites social media abuse. It takes time to stop caring about random strangers who take issue with your articles."

▶ FAVORITE PROJECT

"I wrote a book about *Dark Souls*, one of my favorite games, and the people who play it. I managed a huge investigation into *Star Citizen* at Kotaku UK—a game that raised millions and millions in crowdfunding but, at the time of this writing, has still yet to come out. I reviewed *Grand Theft Auto V* for the biggest games website in the world, IGN."

▶ BIGGEST MISTAKE

"I worked myself into the ground when I was a freelance writer, taking things on to ridiculous deadlines and ending up working until the early hours of the morning. I learned to be realistic about how much I'm capable of. It's better to ask for a later deadline than submit something that's not your best work because you've had to pull it together at the last minute."

▶ EXCITING ADVANCEMENTS

"The games media is a very different place now than it was when I started in 2005. Video, social media, and live-streaming all didn't exist when I started. Being part of the games media now can mean being a journalist, reporter, critic, editor, video producer, documentary maker, all sorts—and then there's the influencer side of things, with let's-players and YouTubers and streamers. If I've learned anything, it's that things change all the time."

PRO TIP!

"Have a plan B. Making a living from games journalism of any variety is ultimately rare. Having other interests and passions will both make you a more interesting writer and give you other career options."

INDIANA "FROSKURINN" BLACK

GRASSROOTS-TURNED-GLOBAL SHOUTCASTER

 Froskurinn  Froskur1nn

EXPERIENCE

FIRST INDUSTRY PROJECT: ELECTRONIC SPORTS LEAGUE GO4PRO TOURNAMENTS (2013, 2014)

FAVORITE INDUSTRY PROJECT: LEAGUE OF LEGENDS PRO LEAGUE (2017)

PROJECTS SHIPPED: CAST 22 TOURNAMENTS, HUNDREDS OF SERIES

ACHIEVEMENTS UNLOCKED:

> LEAGUE OF LEGENDS SPRING & SUMMER LPL FINALS CASTER (2017)
> LEAGUE OF LEGENDS WORLDS FINALS PRESHOW ANALYST (2017)
> LEAGUE OF LEGENDS 2018 MSI FINALS ANALYST (2018)
> LEAGUE OF LEGENDS RIFT RIVALS FINALS CASTER (2018)

STATS

INDUSTRY LEVEL: 5

CURRENT CLASS: LEAGUE OF LEGENDS SHOUTCASTER

CURRENT GUILD: RIOT GAMES—SHANGHAI, CHINA

STANDARD EQUIPMENT

FAVORITE PLATFORM: NINTENDO GAMECUBE

GO-TO GENRE: ROLE-PLAYING GAMES

MUST-HAVE GAME: FINAL FANTASY VII

BIO

Indiana "Froskurinn" Black was raised by a single mother juggling full-time employment and night classes while raising two children. "Our primary source of childcare was video games—the Game Boy being the real game changer," said Black. "For all the hours my mother couldn't give us direct attention due to her other responsibilities, heroes like Link, Sonic, Blue, Red, and Cloud covered the bases."

> "Our primary source of childcare was video games."

Despite a laden schedule, Black's mom would return home late and play the games that engrossed her children, eager to better understand the world of gaming, and ensure the age-appropriateness of each title. Her intentional outreach through games ultimately provided a crucial piece of guidance to Black. "The best piece of advice my mother ever gave me was that, in the coming age of employment, my generation would be tasked with creating jobs that didn't exist yet, and if I truly wanted to rise above my status, I would have to make my own job," she explained. And so Black did.

Easter Egg
Has two gaming-related tattoos.

FOR THE LOVE OF LEAGUE

In high school, Black continued her education outside the classroom. "I spent all of my free time in computer labs, making graphics and reading online tutorials about everything a computer could unlock for me creatively. The thing about ambition is that it doesn't really work without obsession, and I was obsessed," said Black with a note of self-deprecating humor. "But being called 'ambitious' sounds nicer."

Those hard-earned technical skills would become imperative in her early 20s, when Black homed in on her future career path—shoutcasting, the video game equivalent of sportscasting. "The primary reason I chased casting was because of my love for the game *League of Legends*," explained Black. "It allowed to me fill my competitive drive while maintaining friendships around the world. I was obsessed with the game and found that I not only had a knack for playing at a relatively high level, but communicating about it at a high level. It was then about training up my communication skills so that I could do something with *League of Legends* as a passion."

Shoutcasting as a profession was evolving in tandem with the booming esports scene. That being said, there was no road map or job notice that Black was attempting to answer. "In the early years (yesterday), shoutcasting didn't have any defined rules," she said. "In that sense, it was incredibly difficult for me to navigate the esports landscape, point in a general direction, and assume that it was the correct path to land in a position that only recently has a name to a larger audience."

> "The thing about ambition is that it doesn't really work without obsession—and I was obsessed."

SHOUTING INTO THE VOID

Without an established curriculum, Black began volunteering with esports organizations such as the Electronic Sports League. "My casting career started when I would do their Go4LoL amateur tournaments on the weekends before work," said Black. "I bounced around a couple of smaller third-party tournament organizers and communities. Trial-by-fire was the goal, and the sheer amount of reps that I cranked out in those early years cut the majority of my rough edges."

To refine her craft further, Black's peers became an invaluable resource. "I would wake up ridiculously early to cast an amateur tournament with my co-caster." After returning from work, they would chat again, loading up a video of established casters on a professional game. "We'd shoot the shit about the game but, more importantly, try to discuss what the professional casters were doing technically with each other. It would be years before I learned the established vocabulary and steps, but those late nights were the starting blocks to unpacking my future."

While she would work freelance for the better part of a year, Black's visibility rose considerably when she found a void to fill within *League of Legends*' global coverage. "I was most well-recognized for my grassroots coverage of the Chinese *League of Legends* Pro League (LPL), as it didn't have any English coverage," shared Black. "Working with a small team, we took a stream of eight viewers to 48,000 and flew to Twitch.tv's studio in San Francisco to cast and host the Summer Finals. Riot Games would shut us down shortly after, taking the rights to the broadcast and opening up their official coverage for the league in Sydney, Australia."

RETURNING TO THE LPL

Black worked for a variety of professional organizations after losing the rights to cast the LPL. "I worked the scene in North America, Europe, and Brazil—taking short-term contracts for teams to coach or do analyst work for their leagues or tournaments, such as the World Championship." Recognizing her invaluable contributions to the league, Riot reached out to Black in 2015 and asked her to join the official LPL broadcast in Australia. "The nice thing is that Riot Games recognized my passion for the LPL product and always kept me in close proximity for key decisions for the English broadcast content," said Black. "I really do feel that I've left a visible fingerprint and tone on the broadcast, not just in my own performance, but in the growth it's made today as it's traveled from my bedroom, to Sydney, and now to Shanghai."

> "I really do feel that I've left a visible fingerprint and tone on the [LPL] broadcast."

You wouldn't know that the LPL broadcast is the smallest of Riot's official broadcasts by looking at it, and that is a point of pride for Black. "While the Chinese league is the largest league in the world, as the secondary language broadcast, we are not high on priorities for resources," she explained. "We cast the most games with the smallest team of shoutcasters and have the least amount of tools or resources to help supplement content." That means the LPL shoutcasting team are all dual or triple threats, assisting with video editing, graphic design, writing, and directing. "It punches way above its weight and offers a very different work environment than the polished flagship broadcasts around the world."

TICKING A BOX

Black feels that sharing her knowledge and passion for the Chinese regional league with Western audiences is where she's had the most impact of her career. "But the majority of people say it's because I'm an openly gay woman who breaks up the monotony of whitewashed desks," admitted Black. She doesn't want this to be her legacy, though—being remembered for simply existing. Now that she's an established voice in the industry, she wants to use her station to help pull other minorities up.

That being said, it is difficult to ignore the importance of visibility within a trade hurting for diversity. "When I first entered the industry, it was suggested to me that I shouldn't disclose my sexuality and I should present to the audience as single to help appear more popular to the demographic," said Black. When it became clear that she didn't intend to mask her sexuality, they would try to fit Black into a specific box. "I've had producers from mainstream backgrounds ask if I was going to be 'sexy or sporty' for broadcast as my persona. I've been told that they 'don't mind the dyke thing' and that it could be a solid branding niche." But Black rebuffed the advice and chose to be open and genuine to herself. For a personality and popularity-driven profession, doing so can be a risk and, as such, is an act of defiance worth celebrating.

"I expected that my passion for gaming would lead me to become a designer, but instead it gave me the skill sets and drive to forge my own niche in the world," reflected Black. "Gaming taught me how to read, critically think, explore, fail, never give up—it essentially made me an expert at problem-solving and learning. These skills allowed me to goal-set and recognize what I actionably had to do to achieve my dreams and follow my passions."

LAILA SHABIR

HELPING GIRLS MAKE GAMES

GirlsMakeGames  Girls Make Games

 girlsmakegames.com

EXPERIENCE

FIRST INDUSTRY PROJECT: PENGUEMIC (2013)

FAVORITE INDUSTRY PROJECT: GIRLS MAKE GAMES (2014—CURRENT)

PROJECTS SHIPPED: 3 GAMES

ACHIEVEMENTS UNLOCKED:

> WHITE HOUSE-HOSTED GIRLS MAKE GAMES WORKSHOP (2016)

> ELECTRONIC SOFTWARE ASSOCIATION "VISIONARY AWARD" (2018)

> GIRLS MAKE GAMES EXPANDED TO 44 CITIES WORLDWIDE (2018)

STATS

INDUSTRY LEVEL: 5

CURRENT CLASS: FOUNDER & CEO

CURRENT GUILD: GIRLS MAKE GAMES & LEARNDISTRICT INC.—SAN JOSE, USA

SPECIAL SKILLS: ENTREPRENEURSHIP, LEADERSHIP, ECONOMICS, DATA ANALYSIS

STANDARD EQUIPMENT

FAVORITE PLATFORM: PC

GO-TO GENRE: MOBA

MUST-HAVE GAME: LEAGUE OF LEGENDS

BIO

When Girls Make Games founder Laila Shabir first met her husband, she was exasperated by the amount of time he sank into video games; she hadn't played games since her youth, nor followed the evolution of the industry. "One day I got really frustrated and told him to stop playing dumb games and learn something instead," she recalled. "That was a pivotal moment, because the conversations that followed were total eye-openers for me. He showed me a whole other dimension to games that I didn't know existed. How they could be so powerful and influential, and even educational."

That conversation was a catalyst to a great change. At the age of 25, Shabir and her husband quit their jobs and moved to California to start an educational media company.

ROLLING THE DICE

The move was a gamble, to say the least. Shabir had studied economics at MIT, but didn't have any formal training in running a game company. Her previous work experience included internships at Merrill Lynch, a research assistant position at the Federal Reserve Bank of Boston, and a portfolio risk analyst job for BlackRock financial services.

That being said, as a Pakistani immigrant raised in the United Arab Emirates, Shabir spent much of her youth teaching herself anything she could online. "I'm a big proponent for self-learning," said Shabir. In 2013, Shabir and her husband founded LearnDistrict. The company allowed her to work in the intersection of her longtime passion—education—and her newfound passion—video games.

LearnDistrict's first game aimed to support students prepping for SATs through a vocabulary game featuring penguins. *Penguemic* successfully raised $50,000 on Kickstarter in 2013.

Easter Egg

Played a total of zero video games between middle school—when obsessed with *Street Fighter* and *Tekken*—and age 26 when she picked up *League of Legends*.

GIRLS MAKING GAMES

"In the early days of Girls Make Games, I was very hard on myself," said Shabir. "Things were not moving fast enough; there wasn't enough time in the day. I was just frustrated. There was a lot I didn't know, but instead of pausing and learning, I just wanted to keep on moving and kept doing the same thing, expecting different results. Exhaustion kills creativity. This is one of the most important lessons I've learned."

Girls Make Games was founded on the goal of closing the gender gap in the video game industry. The first arm of Girls Make Games came in the form of three-week summer camps with a focus on academics and exposure. On the academic side, campers were taught the basics of game design, game art, and programming. Exposure included discussions and presentations with industry professionals, hands-on educational opportunities, and field trips to local game studios. At the end of the three weeks, each team of girls would have created a fully functional prototype for an original game idea.

> "Exhaustion kills creativity. This is one of the most important lessons I've learned."

Since the first camp kicked off in 2014, Girls Make Games has gone international—with over 40 summer programs offered across the United States, Canada, and Australia.

"I did face a lot of challenges that are standard to new entrepreneurs building and scaling a business," said Shabir. "However, once we established LearnDistrict and Girls Make Games, we found a lot of support in the indie game dev community, as well as at the corporate level."

Girls Make Games summer camps include tuition fees in order to grow the business, but offer scholarship opportunities for those without financial resources.

Summer camps are still at the core of Girls Make Games, but other programming, such as weekend workshops and game jams, has begun to augment the core curriculum. Girls Make Games has garnered worldwide press since its inception—and even caught the eye of the White House, who invited a group of future game designers to participate in an on-site workshop in 2016.

After the success of Girls Make Games, LearnDistrict opened a co-ed summer camp in 2017 for kids ages nine to 14, called the Game Dev Academy.

D-DAY

The girls who participate in yearly summer camps are single-mindedly working toward D-Day.

"Every year we host a national Demo Day, where the top five teams from our national summer camps are flown out to pitch their games to a panel of judges," explained Shabir. "This year's Demo Day was just so incredibly special. PlayStation, Nintendo, and Xbox had all come together to support the program and the girls, and the games being pitched were simply outstanding."

Demo Day began in 2014. After three weeks of hard work, participating teams pitched their game ideas to industry veterans Tim Schafer, Kellee Santiago, Shazia Makhdumi, and Tracy Fullerton. The winning concept—an RPG adventure game called *The Hole Story*—went on to raise over $31,000 on Kickstarter, and is now available to purchase on Steam. The 2015 winner—murder mystery *Interfectorem*—is also available for purchase online. The 2016 winner raised $32,000. Once the funds are raised, the LearnDistrict team helps bring the games to market.

WOMAN WITH A VISION

Shabir has made her mark on the industry in a very short time. In 2018 she was awarded the Electronic Software Association's Visionary Award, which she accepted to the sound of an audience of top industry talent cheering her on.

A new goal has been set for Girls Make Games. Shabir is on a mission to teach a million girls how to make video games through her workshops by 2020. "Working with budding game developers has been the most rewarding experience," said Shabir. "Knowing that Girls Make Games is helping young girls gain confidence in pursuing what they're interested in makes all the stressful, sleepless nights worthwhile."

NINA FREEMAN

EXPLORING INTIMACY, HONESTY, AND POETRY ON A SMALL SCALE

 hentaiphd  ninasays.so

EXPERIENCE

FIRST INDUSTRY PROJECT: LADYLIKE (2014)

FAVORITE INDUSTRY PROJECT: CIBELE (2015)

PROJECTS SHIPPED: 16 GAMES

ACHIEVEMENTS UNLOCKED:

- THE GAME AWARDS "GAMES FOR CHANGE" NOMINEE—CIBELE (2015)
- FORBES "30 UNDER 30: GAMES" (2015)
- INDEPENDENT GAMES FESTIVAL "NUOVO AWARD"—CIBELE (2016)
- INDEPENDENT GAMES FESTIVAL "EXCELLENCE IN NARRATIVE" NOMINEE—TACOMA (2018)

STATS

INDUSTRY LEVEL: 5

CURRENT CLASS: LEVEL DESIGNER

CURRENT GUILD: FULLBRIGHT—PORTLAND, USA

SPECIAL SKILLS: GAME DESIGN, LEVEL DESIGN, POETRY

STANDARD EQUIPMENT

FAVORITE PLATFORM: PC

GO-TO GENRE: NARRATIVE-DRIVEN GAMES

MUST-HAVE GAME: FINAL FANTASY X-2

BIO

"I started making games at about 23 years old," began indie game developer Nina Freeman. "I was out of college with my English degree and was trying to figure out what I wanted to do next. A combination of struggling with a new illness and working at a day job I wasn't passionate about led me to want to try something completely different. I had met some folks who were a part of the local games scene in New York City, and they introduced me to games like *Gone Home*, *Kentucky Route Zero* and *Cart Life*."

In Freeman's eyes, these games had echoes of poetry within them, which was her primary interest at the time. "I'd always loved games, technology, and storytelling, so game-making suddenly seemed like the perfect skill for me to pursue." Freeman studied English literature in college, and her writing had been published in several poetry journals during that time. Creating a game was an enticing new form of art.

LOVE, SEX, AND THE INTERNET

"I was fortunate to have some very supportive friends who helped me figure out how to best make games when I was getting started," said Freeman. "They took me to lots of game jams, and worked with me, and helped teach me through these small games we were making for fun. After I released five smaller games in that fashion, I became involved with New York University's Integrated Digital Media MS program." Freeman enrolled in the program, and began creating an ambitious game as the subject of her thesis. It would become her first commercial game, *Cibele*, released under her brand Star Maid Games.

In creating *Cibele*, Freeman got her first taste of long-term game development. "I didn't have much experience coordinating a whole team for a long-term project, so I had to figure out how to manage that throughout the development process," she said.

Easter Egg

When learning how to program, she taught herself how to use the command line and Git by writing a long poem in Terminal over the course of a few months.

"In addition to those more practical details, it was an experimental, personal game, which a lot of people would consider not to be commercially viable. Ultimately, myself and my team made it work despite all odds—we released the game, sold it successfully, and won a major award for it at the Independent Games Festival."

Cibele is autobiographical, based on real encounters from Freeman's past, exploring a relationship between a young man and woman who met through an online game. Told through vignette video footage of Freeman, voice-over, and the virtual world of a fictional MMO, players become intimately entangled with the pair as their relationship grows, eventually leading to a real-world meeting. Lauded as an authentic, mature, and bitingly honest portrayal of a modern-day romance, *Cibele* won the Nuovo Award at the 2016 Independent Games Festival.

"It was an experimental, personal game [*Cibele*], which a lot of people would consider not to be commercially viable."

While told from a very personal perspective, *Cibele* explored an increasingly common scenario. "I received an email from a young woman who had just played *Cibele*," recalled Freeman. "She reached out to me because she played the game, and felt like she was presently in a similar situation as the protagonist. She wanted me to know that the game really resonated with her, especially since her romantic relationship was so much like the one she saw in my game. I got a lot of emails like this from people who related to the story in *Cibele*, but her message particularly struck me as very honest because she sent it while traveling to visit a lover—just like the characters in my game."

Freeman has made a point to share her passion for vignette games with the industry at large, both by making them, and by championing them at conferences. "Vignette games are small games with an acute focus on a specific situation or character," she explained. "They don't need to be of any specific length or format, other than being deliberately focused on the specificity and details of one thing."

Sex and relationships are topics Freeman enjoys exploring in her vignette work. *Bum Rush* is an eight-player car-combat dating-sim racing game where college roommates sprint home with their hot date to secure the only private room in the house. Many of her games also feel autobiographical. *Lost Memories Dot Net* lets you play as 14-year-old Freeman as she builds her first website and chats about teenage drama with a friend. "I've often used personal stories to explore vignettes, like in *How Do You Do It*, a game about a young girl play-acting sex using her two Barbie dolls. I want people to feel like they can—and should—make games about something as small and honest as this." *How Do You Do It* was nominated for an IGF Nuovo Award in 2015. Browsing Freeman's portfolio of vignette games, it's easy to understand how they parallel poetry as a medium of self-expression.

In 2017, Freeman was asked to host the annual Independent Games Festival awards. "This is one of my favorite memories because it was such a unique, once-in-a-lifetime experience," she said. "As someone who had been attending those awards since I started making games, it was surreal to be able to stand onstage and help honor other game developers whose work I admired so much. It really made me feel connected to and proud of the games community."

FULLBRIGHT

All the while working on her personal projects, Freeman was establishing a future at Fullbright. "I got my first and current job as a level designer at Fullbright while I was still in school, after meeting my current bosses at the Game Developers Conference while showing a game there," she said. "I finished my degree and started it directly after graduation."

Freeman's first project for Fullbright was level design on *Tacoma*. This narrative-driven adventure game unfolds in an abandoned space station; the player is tasked with piecing together what happened to the previous crewmembers. "I contributed to *Tacoma* by doing things like paper-mapping levels, building gray-block architecture for those levels, gameplay-scripting, decorating environments," she explained. "I worked on many, many elements of *Tacoma* because our team was very small. The whole company consisted of about eight people, so we all wore many hats. I was one of three level designers."

Fullbright have established themselves as masters of nuanced narrative, able to elicit emotion and empathy from an array of players. "The team at Fullbright is currently more than half women," continued Freeman. "The co-founders, Karla Zimonja and Steve Gaynor, are fully dedicated to hiring and supporting women. I am really lucky to work with people who are passionate about this, because having a diverse team is healthy for the whole company and for the game itself. The stories we create benefit hugely from having a diverse team. It's also inspiring, as a woman in a male-dominated industry, to work with a team that really exemplifies the reality that you can create a gender-diverse team if you put the effort in."

Freeman intends to continue creating her small vignette games. "I love to come up with stories, and figure out how mechanics can best help the player embody the characters in those stories. Games have an incredible capacity for player-character embodiment—in other words, they're great for helping people step into another person's shoes. It's really rewarding as a game designer to help players see the world from a new perspective through the stories and mechanics in my work."

To Freeman, making small, personal games is a profitable pursuit. "I hope to continue to make games and reach an audience that is passionate about my work," she said in closing. "I want to continue my efforts at proving that small, honest games about real people are important, and that the creators deserve to be paid for their work. I hope to inspire a new generation of developers to share their own honest stories through games."

A DAY IN THE LIFE OF...

A VIDEO GAME MERCHANT

Armed with instincts, impressive data-driven tools, and detailed market research, video game buyers are forecasters with a finger on the pulse of the next big thing in gaming, giving voice to what a retailer should—and shouldn't—invest in. Merchants are also responsible for reviewing product performance in real time, planning promotions, and making informed purchases by regularly meeting with publishers to see in-development games.

Kayse Sondreal-Nene has spent most of her career as a video game merchant. In that time she's worked in hardware and software and been involved with console launches as far back as the Sega Dreamcast, Xbox, and PlayStation 2—as well as thousands of title launches in between.

KAYSE SONDREAL-NENE

PROFESSION: SR. MERCHANT, VIDEO GAMES AT BEST BUY—MINNEAPOLIS, USA

YEARS IN PROFESSION: 19

ASSOCIATED WITH: BEST BUY CO., INC.

▶ EDUCATION

"I have a Bachelor's degree in Business Administration, but as far as a career supporting retail goes, so much of it is learned on-the-job and is dependent upon the priorities and systems used by each company."

▶ BREAKING IN

"I have to say, I was extremely fortunate in this regard. I came to Best Buy as a Demand Planning Analyst and in that role you are assigned to a business team; I was lucky enough to be assigned to gaming and have been hooked ever since! The energy that comes from working on a constant flow of new releases and—for what is, in my opinion, the most enthusiastic consumer audience—has been fantastic."

▶ EARLY INDUSTRY IMPRESSIONS

"Being a casual gamer myself—the first system I had as a kid was the Atari 2600, but I spent a ridiculous number of hours across the street on my friend's NES, so I had some street cred—I was struck by how unpredictable the industry could be. Before we had sophisticated forecasting tools, you might see the quirkiest premise of a game strike like lightning, seemingly out of the blue. While the tools have improved dramatically, seeing a new and creative IP resonate with fans remains one of the most exciting elements of what we do."

▶ TOOLS OF THE TRADE

"In the office, we're constantly emailing and IM'ing to stay on top of things. We use Excel for analyzing sales and forecasting data, as well as planning our weekly promotions. We also have proprietary systems for inputting and tracking our financial forecasts. These allow necessary people from across the company to view and help prepare for what we expect will happen, whether it's a new product launch or a significant price drop. We have tools that allow us to see up-to-the-minute data from our website, where real-time feedback is more important now than ever."

▶ HOURS & ENVIRONMENT

"We work what I'd call 'modified traditional office hours,' meaning general office hours of 8-5 apply, but busier timeframes—major launches, Black Friday, holiday planning—result in longer hours as needed to ensure things go smoothly. Also, it's retail, so anything that doesn't go as planned can impact customers immediately; we take that responsibility very seriously and, as such, are highly accessible. My team sits together in a cube-type setting. It's professional, but we keep it fun with a variety of industry memorabilia, including a few larger-than-life-sized statues—Vault Boy being my favorite."

▶ AN AVERAGE DAY

"As far as an 'average' day goes, it usually starts with evaluating how the business is performing, whether at a more aggregate level or if a particular new product has launched, by reviewing that product's performance and sales trends against our expectations. If something new has launched, my team—the merchants—partners with our forecasting and demand planning groups to determine any potential changes to our replenishment plans, and we then determine whether any future promotional plans may need to be modified, so as not to advertise a product that might be sold out, for example.

"Once those more urgent matters have been addressed, our work typically follows a rhythm around planning ads and promotions. We do this both in meetings and outside of meetings with our internal team and with input and support from game manufacturers. A typical day often involves meeting with one or more of the manufacturers, as we meet with most of them weekly or every other week, to review current business performance and discuss opportunities around upcoming products, including possible gift-with-purchase offers. Because our team is responsible for a large number of products, we usually have one or two meetings each week with people from across a variety of functions that support the business, including demand planning, marketing, dot com, operations, and customer care. These are often very tactical in nature and allow our large group to discuss both short-and long-term action plans for the business."

▶ PROFESSIONAL PERKS

"Learning about or seeing upcoming games, sometimes while in their earliest stages of development, really is an honor. We see painstaking artistry at work on a regular basis and having a one-on-one discussion with a producer about an origin story or the passion behind a project brings it off the Excel spreadsheet—where much of our planning takes place—and into reality. These experiences make us all the more excited to help bring a new game to life for others and is something I don't take for granted as a huge privilege."

▶ CAREER CHALLENGES

"For the industry as a whole, maximizing the opportunities of digital gaming is a top challenge. Each platform owner has its own priorities and systems, and its own varying agenda, all of which make standardization very difficult. We have some highly engaged advocates across the industry trying to make it as efficient for gamers as possible, but even after several years, it's definitely still an uphill battle. That said, there are so many reasons to be excited about gaming's continued evolution!"

▶ FAVORITE PROJECT

"One particular project does stand out. I had a really interesting meeting one afternoon, but it was for a product that didn't really fall within my category. I was buying game peripherals at the time. In fact, it didn't naturally fall anywhere. A kind man named Charles set up shop with a ridiculously small TV I'd grabbed along the way to the meeting and he proceeded to show us a music game using a guitar as a controller. I remember my co-worker and I looking at each other like, 'Is this a major hit or an expensive novelty we should run from?' Then we played it and we were both sold. That was obviously *Guitar Hero* and I'm happy to say that after some convincing of our managers—who had not seen it for themselves—we placed the very first purchase order for the product. This began a strong partnership for us with Charles and Kai Huang, Doug Kennedy, and Red Octane, which continued throughout the franchise's life-cycle. We were able to be a real destination for that innovative experience and it remains one of my favorite projects."

▶ BIGGEST MISTAKE

"In my profession, making a 'bad buy' can be a highly-visible and enduring lesson. Before we had the modeling tools available now to forecast products, it was a bit more art than science and I can say I've had a few art projects go awry. The skills I was able to develop from these mistakes included taking responsibility for my decisions, diagnosing what went wrong—a meta score was terrible, or a marketing plan changed last-minute—and using that information to react as quickly as possible to mitigate the situation. Should you ever find yourself in a social setting with a group of buyers, playing 'What was your worst purchase?' is a real crowd-pleaser."

PRO TIP!

"Be open to new ideas and opportunities, because you never know when that next door might open and, as the industry evolves, so should we!"

REBECCA COHEN-PALACIOS

MAKING WAVES FOR WOMEN THROUGH INDUSTRY ACTIVISM

Rebheartsyou

Rebecca Cohen-Palacios

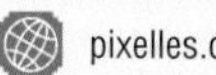

pixelles.ca

**The opinions expressed and the causes I advocate are my personal passions, and do not express the views or opinions of my employer.*

EXPERIENCE

FIRST INDUSTRY PROJECT: SHAPE UP (2014)

FAVORITE INDUSTRY PROJECT: SHAPE UP (2014)

PROJECTS SHIPPED: 5 GAMES

ACHIEVEMENTS UNLOCKED:

> GDC "TOP 50 SPEAKERS" (2016)

> IGDA "NEXT GEN LEADER" SCHOLARSHIP RECIPIENT (2017)

> IGDA "AMPLIFYING NEW VOICES" SCHOLARSHIP RECIPIENT (2016)

> FOSTERED CAREERS OF OVER 1000 PEOPLE AROUND THE WORLD THROUGH PIXELLES

STATS

INDUSTRY LEVEL: 5

DEV CLASS: USER INTERFACE ARTIST, BETHESDA GAMES STUDIOS

SUPPORT CLASS: CO-FOUNDER/DIRECTOR, PIXELLES—MONTRÉAL, CANADA

SPECIAL SKILLS: UI/UX DESIGN, PROGRAMMING, GRAPHIC DESIGN, ADVOCACY, COMMUNITY ORGANIZING

STANDARD EQUIPMENT

FAVORITE PLATFORM: PC

GO-TO GENRE: EXPLORATION AND NARRATIVE FOCUSED GAMES

MUST-HAVE GAME: "POSITIVE-ENERGY GAMES LIKE PIKMIN, OKAMI, SKYRIM, AND SPLATOON"

BIO

Rebecca Cohen-Palacios worked in web design before taking the plunge into video games—encouraged and mentored through her first game-making experience from women in the industry. A prime example of how women-in-games initiatives can have far-reaching influence, she in turn co-founded an organization to pay it forward.

"While I was living in Toronto, there was a program called the Difference Engine Initiative that helped six women make their first video game," recalled Cohen-Palacios."After going through that program, I realized that anyone could make a video game, including myself. It sparked something in me. Making video games—the culture and scene—was more of a fit than tech, start-ups, and web."

Cohen-Palacios' interest in graphic design began at an early age. "I spent a lot of time after school making layouts for *Sailor Moon* fan websites, *Neopets*, and LiveJournal. It's where I honed all my graphic design and scripting skills," she explained. "I'd see something cool that someone made and look up a tutorial online, or tinker around with the tool in Photoshop. I'd look at the source code of a website and break down how that script worked from CSS and JavaScript documentation." Formalizing her hobby as an adult, she earned a double major in computer science and computation arts.

Easter Egg

Scripted @UIChallengeBot, which tweets out daily, randomly-generated UI/UX design challenges for game developers to practice with.

PIXELLES

For several years, Cohen-Palacios developed her career as a graphic designer and web developer. After relocating to Montréal, she and Tanya Short co-founded the video-game outreach organization Pixelles. Pixelles is a non-profit organization that empowers and diversifies the landscape of game development through free workshops, mentorship, mid-career support, writers group, a "make-your-first-game" program, social gatherings, and building up a network of support within the Montréal games community. Some of these programs and activities have remote participation for anyone in the world, too.

Just as important as formalized programming, Pixelles provides a place of positive reinforcement for women. "A first positive experience in a space like Pixelles is a small action that creates a ripple effect into the future," explained Cohen-Palacics. "We make new friends who share our same experiences and help us to heal from the negative ones.

> "We [at Pixelles] make new friends who share our same eperiences and help us to heal from the negative ones."

In the safety of the space, we learn how to listen, grow confident, and support perspectives different from our own. The energies spent from being put down or constantly having to prove ourselves are gradually replenished."

One of the more unique events Pixelles offers is a yearly gathering called Teacade—a tea party with video games. "We wanted a 'radical' games event that would embrace softness, alternative games, and femininity where conversations with other games people didn't revolve around drinking alcohol," explained Cohen-Palacios. "Our first Teacade was a huge hit! It turns out that people are excited to spend an afternoon with games, new friends, and tea. We do the event every year now." Teacade has even expanded outside of Montréal. "We host a low-key tea social the night before the Game Developer Conference begins where recipients of various diversity- and inclusion-focused scholarships can network and make meaningful connections with other marginalized developers, which can be really overwhelming when the conference goes into full swing."

When Pixelles started five years ago, they were the only women-in-games organization in Montréal. "We received pushback and hate mail from people who were angry at what we were doing," she shared. "Nowadays, despite there still being some friction, but we are more supported than ever by the community, as marked by the growth in programs and events that Pixelles is organizing. Things have been changing for the better, albeit slowly. People are recognizing that change must happen and are listening more."

SHAPING UP

It wasn't until a full year after founding and directing Pixelles that Cohen-Palacios used the resources for herself. "After encouragement from other women in games and my mentor—thanks to the Pixelles mentorship program—I applied for a job at Ubisoft and two weeks later I was officially a game developer," she said.

Cohen-Palacios began her job at Ubisoft Montréal in 2013, brought on as a user interface developer, and quickly found that she wasn't alone in pivoting her career. "What surprised me the most was how so many other people had these wayward paths into video games! It's never too late to follow your dreams of being a game dev."

Creating UI for a new Xbox Kinect title kept Cohen-Palacios on her toes. "*Shape Up* was an exercise game for Kinect developed by a small team," she explained. "The challenges and workouts were themed like an arcade with lots of video game iconography, symbols, fun colors, and animations. Really different than your average fitness game."

Though she was originally hired to establish the game menus and HUD, her responsibilities expanded far beyond that. "The UI team for a while was just two people, myself and the presentation director," said Cohen-Palacios. "Towards the end of production, we expanded a bit to meet the deadlines. I did everything from coming up with some of the art, to doing animations in Flash, and eventually a lot of scripting to build the logic behind how the UI elements worked." She'd also routinely have to test out the effectiveness of the UI by actually doing the exercise, which meant getting really good at pushups, squats, and a whole lot of jumping around. "*Shape Up* will always have a place in my heart. I loved being on a small team where I could be doing art, animation, and programming all in the same day."doing art, animation, and programming in the same day."

After shipping *Shape Up*, Cohen-Palacios joined one of the biggest teams—working on one of the biggest franchises—in the world. She implemented, and animated menus in *Assassin's Creed: Syndicate* before moving on to *Assassin's Creed: Origins*. "*Origins* definitely had some of the more interesting challenges from a UI developer standpoint," she detailed. "The Ability menu is probably my favorite challenge because of the requirements surrounding it."

"There were a lot of changes coming in, and the deliverable timing was short," she continued. "I had to come up with a way to accommodate non-linear ability trees that were flexible enough to support changes by artists and game designers. With help from another programmer and the use of a pathing system made for navigation, we were able to spawn abilities along nodes and have them be modifiable on the data side. I love hard UI integration problems like that, where you need to be elegantly resourceful."

In early 2018, Cohen-Palacios moved to Bethesda Game Studios—remaining in Montréal—where she has returned to her creative roots, as a user interface artist, to work on the *The Elder Scrolls: Blades*, a game from one of her all-time favorite franchises.

MAKING WAVES

While working full-time and running Pixelles, Cohen-Palacios continued to offer her insight and mentorship wherever needed. In 2015 she co-organized Montréal's first GameLoop "unconference." GameLoop welcomes developers, journalists, academics, artists, and others interested in the industry to share ideas and engage in collaborative discussions.

Cohen-Palacios has also volunteered as a workshop leader and mentor at the Technology, Arts, and Games Lab at Concordia University, as well as teaching a variety of classes for Ladies Learning Code. Recently, her advocacy work has taken her to create a grassroots organization, Game & Color, to bring together and provide support to game developers of color in Montréal. Her portfolio of volunteer work earned industry recognitions including the IGDA Next Gen Leader and Amplifying New Voices Scholarships, allowing her influence to reach even further.

The advocacy work Cohen-Palacios fronted has made a quantifiable impact on the industry. "As the co-director of Pixelles, I've seen firsthand the Montréal games industry change over the last five years because of the hours of volunteering, organizing, and care that we put into empowering our community," she said in closing. "We've seen women whose first experience in game development was through Pixelles get their first industry job, ship games, come back to lead programs and workshops, and become these amazing, powerful role models for future generations."

BAHIYYA KHAN

SELF-DECLARED EMO, FRANZ KAFKA ENTHUSIAST, EXPERIMENTAL GAME DESIGNER

 Breakinbahiyya  bahiyya.itch.io

EXPERIENCE

FIRST INDUSTRY PROJECT: BOARD GAME ADAPTATION OF SCOTT PILGRIM VS. THE WORLD (2014)

FAVORITE INDUSTRY PROJECT: F THE SYSTEM (2016)

PROJECTS SHIPPED: 4 GAMES

ACHIEVEMENTS UNLOCKED:

> A MAZE FEST JOHANNESBURG "PINKEST GAME AWARD" (2017)

> A MAZE FEST BERLIN "HUMBLE NEW TALENT AWARD" (2018)

> FULL INDIE SUMMIT SPEAKER (2018)

> GIRLS MAKE GAMES GDC SCHOLARSHIP RECIPIENT (2018)

STATS

INDUSTRY LEVEL: 4

CURRENT CLASS: EXPERIMENTAL NARRATIVE MASTERS STUDENT, TUTOR

CURRENT GUILD: UNIVERSITY OF THE WITWATERSRAND—JOHANNESBURG, SOUTH AFRICA

SPECIAL SKILLS: GAME DESIGN, GAME WRITING, POETRY

STANDARD EQUIPMENT

FAVORITE PLATFORM: PC

GO-TO GENRE: EMOTIONAL NARRATIVE

MUST-HAVE GAME: BUTTERFLY SOUP

BIO

Content Warning! *This bio discusses subject matters that might be triggering, including sexual abuse.*

Bahiyya Khan—a young Muslim game designer from South Africa—struggles with feeling like she doesn't meet the narrative of what a game designer should be. Even more unexpected, there are times she considers making games a type of self-harm. Yet she keeps coming back to games as a cathartic form of self-expression, and as a way to stick up her middle finger at the stereotypes that try to gate-keep what games are, and who game designers should be.

Growing up in South Africa—a racially diverse country that is still very much divided due to the lingering effects of Apartheid—Khan never considered making games. She didn't even play games as a child. The part of Johannesburg where she grew up—and continues to live—is prone to car hijackings and robberies. From Khan's perspective, games seemed a distraction from the everyday challenges of life. Dedicating herself to creating a luxury form of entertainment seemed frivolous.

Easter Egg
Used to break into her high school after graduating and do pull ups.

INDIE INSPIRATION

When Khan discovered *Thomas Was Alone*—an indie game that managed to create an emotional tie between the player and a group of personified rectangles—she was struck by what was achieved through simple mechanics and minimal graphics. Khan realized that games were a medium she could use to tell stories. "I live in a very volatile area, and my people are subjected to many hardships," Khan began. "I want to tell our stories to the world because we deserve to be acknowledged and represented." With that realization, Khan enrolled in game design at the University of the Witwatersrand. She commuted two hours daily to attend class, staying late to use the Internet which wasn't available at home.

The first year at university was very difficult for her. Khan describes her natural disposition as "emo," not seeing it as a slight, but rather a symptom of the human condition; emotions are part of the essential wiring of humanity. Still, she found herself constantly filled with angst and focusing an unhealthy amount on the work of long-dead existentialist philosophers. The emotional struggles became a distraction from her schoolwork. She grappled with the thought of continuing to live in such an unfair system, which Khan didn't feel was going to change in her lifetime. A revelation came to Khan, however. She realized that games could be a cathartic release of the thoughts that consumed her, and perhaps, by expressing those feelings through games, she could help others too.

> "I want to tell our stories to the world because we deserve to be acknowledged and represented."

Khan's first game explored issues of gender constructs and sexuality. "To be a woman of color in 2017 means you are strong," she explained. "You have to be. One of the first games that I made was called *F the System*, a punk game about sexuality, patriarchy, and tweets longer than 140 characters."

This was the first game Khan felt true ownership over. Previous projects were made within specific constraints as schoolwork, not because she was compelled to create. "Making this game also taught me a lot about game design—I realized that there was so much I didn't know. I didn't grow up playing video games, so I didn't know how to communicate my ideas in a way that is usually done in games. Making it was such a learning curve for me." Khan is now a master's student focusing on experimental narrative, and tutors art and engineering at school.

> "To be a woman of color in 2017 means you are strong. You have to be."

WORKING AFTER HOURS

Khan's newest and highest-profile project is the most personal yet. "I'm currently working on a game called *after HOURS* as the game designer, narrative designer, director, and actress," explained Khan. "*after HOURS* is a vignette, FMV game that allows players a glimpse into the life of Lilith Gray—a young woman who was molested as a child and suffers from borderline personality disorder as a result." The game unfolds as the player spends a night alone with Lilith in her bedroom—and in her head—learning her story. "The player witnesses Lilith's story and pieces together why she behaves and responds as she does." Players also have access to the voices in Lilith's head, giving insights into how she sees herself in the world. Hand-drawn animations layered over filmed footage make the experience that much more tactile and real. *after HOURS* will release on Humble Bundle in the fall of 2018.

after HOURS is by far the most challenging game Khan has worked on to date. She admits that making games about your own life without critical distance can be haunting. "Interacting with these issues is so emotionally exhausting," she explained. "Another super difficult aspect of the game is watching people play it."

When showcasing *after HOURS* publicly, Khan says there is almost always a fellow survivor of sexual violence who chooses to play the game. "And then they speak to me about how reassuring it is to know they aren't crazy or alone in their feelings," she explained. "One of the young women who played my game asked if she could hug me when she finished it. It felt like my heart was simultaneously contracting and expanding—I was so flooded with emotions. I couldn't believe how a video game could connect people. That makes me feel like I'm contributing positively to the world."

PART OF THAT WORLD

Khan has presented her games and given talks at shows both local and international, taking home awards in the process. Khan's panels are as personal as her games are; "Crying in the Club: How to Make Games Despite the Crushing Weight of Being Alive" and "Emos in Africa: A Game Developer's Postmortem" both speak to why she feels motivated to make games. She often feels awkward speaking in front of an audience, but sees it as another level of relatability. "Often my students tell me that they watched my talks and didn't know that they could be awkward and human in this industry," explained Khan. "So the fact that I make people feel like they can be themselves—and that they don't have to try to be anything else—is really nice to me."

The year 2018 has been good for Khan's career. She spoke at A MAZE Berlin and was a recipient of the 2018 Girls Make Games GDC Scholarship. She is also scheduled to present at the Full Indie Summit in Vancouver in the fall. Despite the scholarships and speaking invitations, that feeling of being an outsider still follows her. "I don't know how 'in' the industry I am," Khan continued. "I often just feel like a kid whose luck is going to run out at any moment. I feel very weird being surrounded by so many white people as well, because I feel so far removed from them in terms of life experiences and opportunities, and it makes me feel very alone. I feel like being a financially unsecure woman of color in video games is an extreme sport."

At the same time, Khan has made many meaningful connections through games. "I've had some excellent opportunities that allowed me to travel and present my work and talk at expos. What surprised me was how kind many people were to me," she explained. "Helping me to travel and giving me useful feedback on my work and just being available to me as friends."

Khan has considered retiring many times because of the toll her work takes on her. Before she can, she is reminded of why she expresses herself through this medium. "Games like *Butterfly Soup*, *Thomas Was Alone*, and *The Temple of No*—games that remind me of my humanity and games that make me laugh because they highlight how absurd life is—they stoke the Dadaist fire within me to produce absolutely nonsense games. The belief that my work can have a positive impact on the world by cultivating empathy in people motivates me to continue," Khan concluded.

ALLY MCLEAN

STORYTELLER AND SENTIENT VACUUM CREATOR

AllyMcLeanGames  AllyMcLean11

 AllyMcLeanGames  ally-mcLean.com

EXPERIENCE

FIRST INDUSTRY PROJECT: THE WITCHER 3: WILD HUNT (2015)

FAVORITE INDUSTRY PROJECT: RUMU (2017)

PROJECTS SHIPPED: 4 GAMES

ACHIEVEMENTS UNLOCKED:

> WOMEN'S WEEKLY "WOMEN OF THE FUTURE AWARD—INNOVATION AND TECHNOLOGY" (2018)

> TRADE MEDIA WOMEN IN GAMES "CAMPAIGNER OF THE YEAR AWARD" PRESENTED BY XBOX (2018)

> TRADE MEDIA WOMEN IN GAMES "CREATIVE IMPACT AWARD" PRESENTED BY XBOX (2018)

> AUSTRALIAN WRITERS GUILD "INTERACTIVE MEDIA AWARD—RUMU (2018)

STATS

CURRENT CLASS: DIRECTOR

INDUSTRY LEVEL: 4

GUILD: THE WORKING LUNCH—SYDNEY, AUSTRALIA

SKILLS: ADVOCACY, COMMUNITY MANAGEMENT, CREATIVE, MARKETING, PRODUCTION, COSPLAY

STANDARD EQUIPMENT

FAVORITE PLATFORM: NINTENDO SWITCH

GO-TO GENRE: NARRATIVE TEAR-JERKERS

MUST-HAVE GAME: BIOSHOCK INFINITE

BIO

"I entered the games industry with no qualification and little experience," said Ally McLean. "There is space in games for people who are self-starters—people who have stories to tell."

McLean's own story is uncommon; one without years of careful calculation leading to a premeditated career. Her journey from the small ranks of Australia's first full-time cosplayers to a game industry professional came seemingly overnight. Crafting marathons were replaced with production crunches after her passion for gaming, professional drive, and emotional intelligence were funneled into a new path. At age 25, she's now considered a veteran in the Australian gaming scene—and with an indie hit under her team's belt—she's already looking to give back.

SELF-STARTING

"There was zero discussion of game development as a viable career option when I was growing up and choosing courses," recalled McLean, "so the whole process was such a mystery to me until I was physically in game studios watching it being done." Her access to the dev floor began with international cosplay work, firstly, as consultant on *The Witcher 3*, advising the community-centric CD Projekt Red on their global cosplay activations. *The Witcher* work was followed closely by collaborations with other AAA companies such as Blizzard, Ubisoft, and Activision. Skills earned through building and maintaining a successful personal brand as a public figure translated well to a production role on *Warhammer 40,000: Regicide*, which, according to McLean, "felt a lot more like my first game given I was full time, in the studio, in the trenches with the team trying to ship a product."

Despite a lack of formal education, McLean doesn't consider herself self-taught. "I had a lot of transferrable skills from fashion and marketing that got me in the door, and then I was really fortunate to be hired by a company that gave me opportunities to learn from some of the best in the world. I still spend a lot of my time at work and at home learning new skills through online courses like Udemy's Unity development classes."

As the Gamerunner of Robot House in Sydney, her first major project centered on a sentient robot vacuum and aimed to hit players right in the feels. "I pitched *Rumu* to the team, this story-rich game about a robot vacuum cleaner with feelings, expecting it to get shot down. Instead, I got to spend a year bringing it to life alongside some of the most talented and hardworking people I've ever met. The game has been incredibly well-received by players and critics alike. It's a dream come true to have been able to make Rumu."

Easter Egg

Has a habit of unknowingly befriending ghost hunters.

THE WORKING LUNCH

Although McLean carved her path into the industry through untraditional means, the lack of visible female leaders and innovators frequently made her feel like an outsider. She slowly found the role models that now remain mentors in her life. "My impression entering the industry was that women should stick to 'support' roles, and steer clear of hands-on development or high-power decision making. This impression largely shaped the way I saw myself and what the ceiling on my career would be. I think we still see that mindset reflected in the gender ratios across different games disciplines, though I do think the industry perceptions are evolving and entry-level women are able to see more pathways for success."

These experiences ignited a spark within McLean and she began working on a plan to make it easier for young women to find their footing in the industry. Her instrument for illuminating the diverse vocations within gaming is called The Working Lunch—a mentorship program officially funded by Australia & New Zealand's Interactive Games and Entertainment Association—of which she is the director. The Working Lunch pairs entry-level women with experienced industry alumni in an array of professions, including games PR, law, and journalism, in addition to more traditional roles such as production and design.

The Working Lunch includes six in-person workshops, two industry networking events, and tackles what Ally considers both "hard and soft skills"—the latter being often undervalued attributes that allow for effective collaboration. "When I was younger, I didn't realize how valuable my emotional intelligence was, or what an asset my soft skills would make me to a team. I wish I had backed myself more early on." The 2018 program includes "Self-Care under Pressure", "Networking Your Way", "Planning and Project Management", and "Freelancing 101", among others. Applications closed quickly with over 100 enthusiastic young women eager to participate.

"We're just wrapping up our first year, and we have a bright future ahead of us thanks to the support and recognition this year has brought us. Every time I feel lost or directionless in the industry the incredible mentees and mentors of The Working Lunch are the fire in my belly to keep going. It's my hope that we can make lasting change in the industry and eliminate the experience of being the only woman in the room."

"The industry as a whole is much broader and more segmented than I had expected. There are so many ways to work in games, so many disciplines, genres, platforms, audiences. From outside the industry I had a very narrow perception of what working in games entailed, but in reality the possibilities are nearly endless."

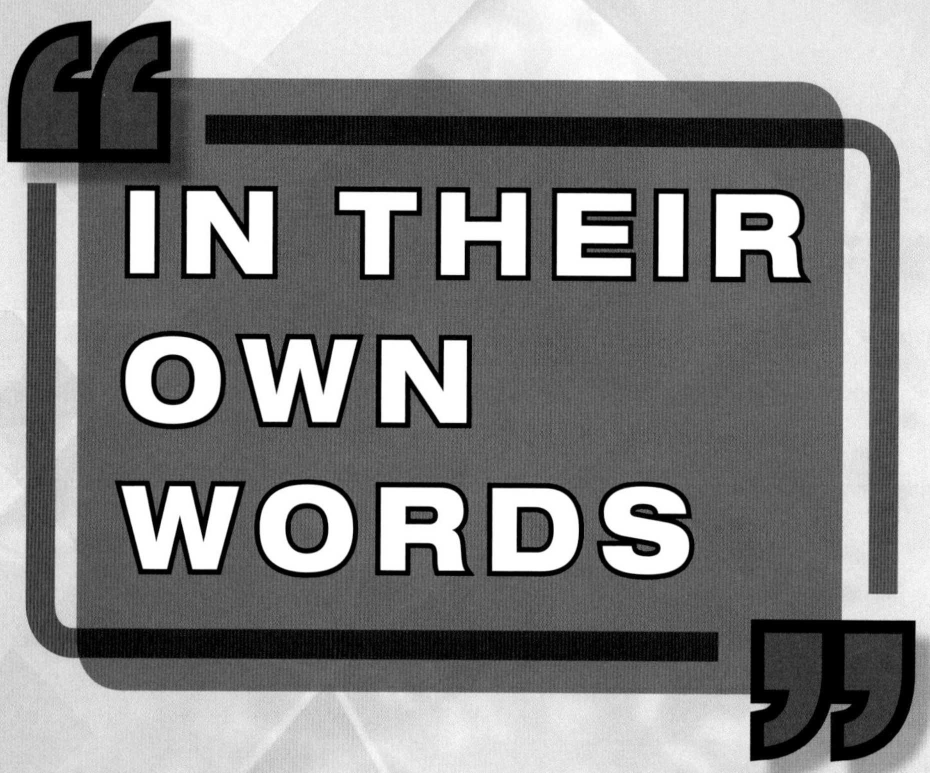

PRO-TIPS

If you could give an industry hopeful one piece of advice, what would it be?

"My biggest piece of advice is don't let doubt stand in your way. You have all the power over your life and no one can hold you down. If you want to work in gaming, take steps toward that. Start a blog, review games, talk to other women in those roles—heck, make a game! It can be the most terrifying thing to step outside of your comfort zone, but that's where the best opportunities are found. But as scary as it may seem, you can do it!"

Amanda Erickson | Social Media Manager | Rooster Teeth | Austin, USA

"Making games is like being a doctor; you need to study every day. The gaming world is always changing so anyone working in the industry, or wanting to, must be constantly updated on what's happening. About trends, about tech, about people. Never stop studying."

Giulia Zamboni | Producer | Gamera Interactive | Padua, Italy

---

"If you're still in school, and especially if you're studying computer science, take as many classes outside of your major as possible. You will spend the rest of your life doing deeply technical things, so this is your opportunity to follow a smaller passion you might have for film or philosophy or a language. More than my computer science degree, it was all those other things I studied at school that gave me the well-roundedness it takes to work on games. Definitely draw from things outside of games for your game ideas as much as you can. On a more practical note, make sure to get an internship at a game company while you are still in school to get a sense of what the atmosphere at a game studio is like and what you might need to brush up on while there's still plenty of time."

Anna Kipnis | Senior Gameplay Programmer | Double Fine Productions | San Francisco, USA

"Don't give up. There will always be hurdles and challenges, mistakes and misunderstandings, insanely busy times and pressure. Sometimes you may feel the world's weight on your shoulders. Step back and take one task at a time; don't be afraid to take advice and ask for suggestions. It's an amazing industry where people are so passionate."

Divya Sharma | Marketing Manager | Shooting Stars | Dubai, UAE

"Stay humble. I scored my first gig in the games industry out of sheer luck—being at the right place at the right time, but also by being very candid about my passion for games and very transparent about my lack of experience in the field. I always thought working in games was sort of like working in movies, that you had to know somebody to get a foot in the door. I think it's more of a combination of being honest and upfront, humble, being open-minded, and listening more than talking."

Geneviève St-Onge | Co-Founder | PopAgenda | San Francisco, USA

"Don't wait for someone, or something else, to give you permission. Start making games now, use the tools at hand. Buy and read books and follow online tutorials. Make mistakes! Have friends test your game and then listen to their feedback. Don't get defensive or over explain your choices. Take in all the feedback, sit with it for a while, and think about how you can change the system to solve any problems they discovered. But also, stay true to your own vision. Don't feel you have to make every change they suggested. The more you do this process, the better you'll have a feel for what works and doesn't."

Heather Kelley | Kokoromi Member & Assistant Teaching Professor | Carnegie Mellon University | Pittsburgh, USA

"You are in charge of your career. Don't wait around for your manager, or your peers, to determine what your next steps are, or what's best for you. Even the best manager won't be a better spokesperson for you than yourself. The best manager will listen to your goals and help you achieve them, but you have to speak up for yourself first."

Kari Toyama | Senior Producer | Private Division, Take-Two Interactive Software, Inc. | Seattle, USA

"I'd say there's no 'wrong way' to get into this industry. Make friends with people who are already working in games. Play all the games. Play games you love, not games you 'should.' Try new and different things. Find your like-minded group of nerds and spend time with them. Bask in the culture. Do whatever it takes to get your foot in the door… late nights, additional roles, empty the garbage if you need to. Once you're known for having a strong work ethic, a good sense of fun and a willingness to do the jobs no one else wants to do, the small indie studios will want to keep you. Once you ship your first game, any other studio will want you. If possible, volunteer at PAX, E3, GDC, or any other con. Find local game conventions, gaming groups, post-mortem nights, hackathons, or guest speaker events. Go to them. Stick out your hand and introduce yourself by telling others what you hope to do in gaming. Then, listen to them talk about their experiences. Take business cards and connect with people. Write little details about them right on the card, so when you follow up with them (did I mention to always follow up with anyone you meet at industry events?), you can ask about them in a personal and memorable way."

Katherine Postma | Community Manager | Stoic | London, Canada

---

"Just be yourself. Everyone brings their own unique experiences to games and it's easy to try to fit into a mold that's been ever-present. However, it's important to use your own voice and viewpoint because it's unique. No one else can come to the table with what you have to offer, and those experiences matter. Have confidence in yourself. The climate surrounding the games industry can be overwhelming and overtly negative. You shouldn't let that steer you away from what you stand for and how you intend to break in. Make your own mark in the industry."

Kimberley Wallace | Features Editor | *Game Informer* | Minneapolis, USA

"This industry is a passion play. That's why we are all here. If you don't love it, or if you fall out of love with it, don't be afraid to break up with it for a while. Take a breather and then come back to it."

Kimberly Unger | Mobile/VR Producer | Playchemy | Burlingame, USA

"My advice is for women involved in business development. You will often hear, even from people who really care for you, that you should step aside at certain moments of the business process because there are male dominant companies that would prefer talking to other men. My advice is, do things your way, never step out and you'll end up working with people who respect you."

Laia Bee | Co-Founder | Pincer Games | Punta del Este, Uruguay

---

"I would genuinely suggest to go out and learn new things, try something you've never tried. Don't be afraid of what the results might be or if it will be worth it. What you try might lead to new opportunities, new people, new perspectives. It might just be something you needed or something that might help you later. It's also good practice to not to seek reward in everything you do, but to simply enjoy it as is."

Lola Shiraishi | Producer | SEGA of America | Los Angeles, USA

"Have fun, do an honest job, be yourself, and make friends. Build your value on merit, not on political alliances."

Magdalena Tomkowicz | "Co-Founder, Narrative Designer, Boring Documents Writer" | Reikon Games | Warsaw, Poland

---

"Be open to accept constructive comments and criticisms both from players and their peers. As game creators, we easily get attached to our own ideas, but sometimes the only way to improve is to reevaluate them considering diverse points of view. You shouldn't be afraid to share your ideas at any stage of development, because you will surely get something valuable from other people's insights."

Maureen Berho | CEO & Producer | Niebla Games | Valparaíso, Chile

---

"The industry has proven to be both welcoming and beset with perils of prejudice. While it has improved, it has a way to go. Do not be timid, do not be complacent, and always remember that you are important."

Morrigan Johnen | Community & Social Media Manager | Crystal Dynamics | Redwood City, USA

"Keep on keeping on. Keep writing. Keep networking. Keep speaking to people. Keep doing what you love, no matter what that might be. Keep teaching yourself new things, because that is the only way you get better. Keep on keeping on."

Pippa Tshabalala | Video Game Reviewer/Presenter | *Glitched* | Johannesburg, South Africa

---

"Network. Get to know the people who do what you want to be doing. Understand the industry and the people in it. Show people that you are confident and capable and enjoyable to be around. Those relationships will be incredibly important at every stage of your career."

Rachel Day | Senior VFX Artist | Blizzard Entertainment | Irvine, USA

"The skills needed across the gaming industry can be built through the honest pursuit of almost any passion. Whether you draw anime or play water polo or program AI or raise pigeons, your experience can help inform the next great gaming event. When I talk to young people who want a future in video games, I tell them to lean into what they love now. Become the expert in the odd thing, investigate what makes *you* enjoy it, explore the mechanics of how it works, study the communities around it, mark your time and effort spent with publications/content/notes/versions. Then, draw the connections to gaming. The creator of *Pokémon* was a bug collector who wanted to share the joy of the hobby. I honed my emcee skills waitressing and evangelizing nerd culture through school. We're all a sidestep away from a gaming industry job."

Rachel "Seltzer" Quirico | esports Host | CSA | Irvine, USA

"If you want to make a game, make a game! We're living in an age of unprecedented access to resources, from paper prototypes to real-time game engines; access to education, from game design degrees to YouTube tutorials; and access to creators and devs, from conference highlights to Twitter and other social media. There's really no wrong way to get inspired, get your start, and get something out there. Want to make a game about opening a Marionberry Jam shop? Do it. A game about radishes that ride horses? Make it so. A game about a moon that wants to become a star? Why aren't you already making this game?! The independent games community is thriving and robust. There's no better time than now to be a creator or a lover of games."

Shana T Bryant | Senior Producer | Private Division, Take-Two Interactive Software, Inc. | Seattle, USA

"Dream big and take giant steps. Go to the people you admire and ask them for advice. Everything is within your reach if you give yourself the time and the flexibility."

Catherine Vandier | Marketing & Communications Manager | Electronic Arts | Guildford, UK

"When you're motivated and ready to work, the idea of taking your time to get ahead is not always the first approach. As humans we naturally gravitate toward instant gratification, forgoing the necessary building blocks that result in a fulfilling career and, as women, we are especially prone to that notion. We're constantly being told that we have limited time, that our biological clock is ticking, and that if we don't make our careers happen fast, we may never get there. It's BS that women are fed this message from the moment they enter the workforce and made to feel rushed, but it's an unfortunate reality. My advice is to put that perception in a box somewhere, because it will only serve as a distraction. Instead, focus on what's really important for any industry hopeful—and that is baby steps. Focus on accomplishing little, achievable goals every day. Keep your eye on the prize, but never be too anxious to get there. Every brick counts when building a house. If you skip bricks or take shortcuts, you may reach your goal but it might not be exactly what you hoped for. Parts of it will feel flimsy and you'll find yourself struggling to sustain it. Recognize the value in the small strides you make; they really matter. When you finally reach the height of your career, you'll be grateful you took your time with them."

Naomi Kyle | Actor, Host, & Producer | Los Angeles, USA

THE JOY AND LUCK OF BEING A FEMALE IN THE GAMING INDUSTRY

By Perrin Kaplan | *Co-Founder & Principal, Zebra Partners*

A change is coming. Oh, yes, it is. And whoever is reading this essay, I hope you are part of that change. But if you aren't yet, I sure hope you will be. If you love the industry of video games, you, too, can become part of the biggest shift in equality in gaming history.

My career journey in gaming came to me completely by accident. So, if you love this field, you already are way ahead of me.

What I hope to share here are some of the ways in which I found success and great satisfaction (and still do, every day) and why we are in a lucky time when it comes to women in this business.

YOU GET TO CHOOSE

For someone who studies to be a pilot or a grocery store manager, you don't really get to choose what part of it you will do, as those careers aren't as layered as gaming is. Don't mistake me. I am not degrading those roles—they are essential and definitely exciting if that's your field of choice. However, video gaming as a career is a kaleidoscope of possibilities.

I didn't even know who Mario was, honest to goodness. So, paint me lucky in being recruited by a wonderful company willing to bet on me. I love to sculpt brands and curate how products are seen in the eyes of the purchaser, so to oversee communications for a global brand—well, that was heaven. Little did I know I'd fall in love with the fields of video gaming and technology, nor would I have predicted I'd grow to mentor so many others.

You can go into any aspect of gaming and somewhat fluidly move to other areas when you are ready for something new. You can become an art and character designer. You can be a storyteller. You can write code and geek out inside the world of the computer. You can build communities.

You can make sure teams collaborate together and make progress against deadlines, plus create amazing game content and finally ship your product into gamers' hands. The possibilities really are limitless. And with new technologies coming to the fore, such as virtual and mixed reality, the toolbox just grew exponentially.

BE PROUD OF WHO YOU ARE

The best of the best companies in video gaming honor and encourage unique and different ideas. They want women to join their ranks to contribute to a better final outcome for gaming as a whole.

Find those companies and go there. Just like a plant in the sunshine, it's where you will grow and flourish. After all, some of the most inventive, wacky, deep-thinking, and successful game ideas have come from people being encouraged to focus far more on their art than their gender, race, or lifestyle.

Get comfortable with yourself and your ideas, and as you walk into the room, be confident. It isn't always about whether peers will accept you. It's more about the skin you are already in. Be you. Be confident, yet humble.

On the complete other side, if you find no sunshine at all, but instead, poor behavior or passive-aggressive tactics by peers, whether men or women, decide to exit to brighter pastures. Don't say to yourself, "I'll never find another job like this," because it's not accurate. Staying in a truly bad situation, unless your leaders will promptly resolve it with you, will only make you question yourself and your abilities. You can't succeed somewhere if you can't be proud of who you are.

In my career, whether at Nintendo or at my own company with my amazing partners (Zebra Partners), confidence has always lived in my pocket.

She is my best friend, especially when times feel rotten. I use my sixth sense to guide me on whether something is feeling really amazing or feeling bad. Then I decide what to do about it. Many others don't listen to their senses and stay put.

I credit confidence with my success, but more importantly and very honestly, the fact that I have worked with amazing people. I have had amazing male mentors because they were great professionals. I worked very hard to make sure the focal point was the work and never the gender. At least, that's how it's worked for me. I am definitely female and would choose it again in another life—times 10—but my work has always spoken for itself in terms of my curiosity, high expectation of performance, thinking at both a ground level in the immediate, and sharing a well-considered strategic perspective. With my early bosses, I felt like a person, not a gender. It may be luck, but my ethos as described in this essay has always been my biggest guide.

There have been wicked witches and monsterous men along the way, to be sure. I felt hurt, betrayed, misunderstood. But then I faced the sun again. A friend once told me, "Don't give anyone any more of you than they deserve." He was right.

KNOW YOUR STUFF

When Nintendo first hired me, there was no one there who knew how to do what I did. It's true that most people think they understand marketing and public relations, but most don't. You are born with a sixth sense for it, just like a longing for working in character design or coding.

I could have failed, but instead I used the opportunity to build something from the ground up, and once it started to bear fruit, my leaders saw its value.

Learn your art so that you can grow wonderful things, and teach others along the way by example. If you do it a few times well, that will be your continued path and hiccups will disappear more quickly. I would love to see more girls and young women enter gaming because it's multi-faceted. I encourage you to pursue areas outside marketing and communications because those are typically female fields. Help diversity become part of the every-day fabric by doing what the dudes have done for so long. Many amazing women have been doing this for years now. And guess what? They are badass and they are respected.

I learned a lesson early in my career. In a large meeting, I felt I needed to speak up to show that I was smart enough to be in the room. Or I might interrupt someone to make my point, thinking that it was crucial to share my idea. I really needed to stop and just listen to others and not sit on the edge of my chair waiting for a time to insert a comment

Should you speak up in meetings? Absolutely. If you have something to say. Besides bringing ideas, you could help expand on someone else's thinking, reaffirming it and adding more to the discussion, or challenge the overall approach, getting people to think more deeply. You can help explain a strategy you have in mind and why, and get buyoff. And, if it seems no one at the table is the leader moving the meeting into form, jump in and take the lead.

LOVE BEING IN VIDEO GAMES

You should want to come to work most of the time. We all have those other days where the clock can't move fast enough. But the joy and luck of being a female in this business is that by concept, it is one of the most exciting industries in the world. It's games! It's entertainment! It's technology! It's art! It's music! It's so many things, so pick the area that you think you will love and start there. The rest will guide you.

I have already mentioned my love for the apex between a product and when the consumer decides to dive in. I love the psychology, the messages and wording you can craft, the happiness they experience from playing the game.

I am often asked what I do for a living. I tell people that I sell joy for a living. I don't think any other words explain it as accurately and simply. I love what I do.

BEING FEMALE

I could go on with more personal and professional examples, or wax on about how my mother worked with Gloria Steinem in the early days and it made great scaffolding for my life. What I can say is that being female is great. And being a female in video gaming can be incredible.

A great management expert once taught me that it is not the "what" that you say or do, but "how" you say or do it. When she made that statement to me, it really stuck. I hope it sticks with you, too.

Women really are born with a unique ability to communicate. In general, we can read people and emotions well. We can use both heart and mind. So, if you want to be understood by the person(s) you are communicating with, think about the "how" and be purposeful with your intent.

Remember that there is a way to accomplish nearly anything. So many women have come before and paved the way to show that we belong in this industry, as leaders and creators. A change is coming—oh yes, it is. Be part of it so the next essay is written by you.

A DAY IN THE LIFE OF...

VIDEO GAME RETAIL

Working in video game retail is about establishing connections. The best video game retail workers can strike up a conversation, ask a few questions, and know exactly what game is right for the buyer by pulling from their wealth of product knowledge. Pairing purchasers with products is almost like a puzzle.

In 2009, Sharyn Vlastnik started her career as a Game Advisor at GameStop. Nearly a decade later, she manages her own store. The position allows her to connect with fellow passionate fans on a daily basis, but also comes with great responsibility. In addition to working the register, Vlastnik hires, trains, and manages staff, communicates stock levels to the district manager, tracks operational tasks, reconciles daily business transactions, implements loss prevention practices, and more. All this keeps the store running smoothly, and ensures games get into fans' hands.

SHARYN VLASTNIK

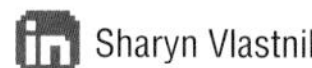

PROFESSION: STORE MANAGER AT GAMESTOP—SAN FRANCISCO, USA

YEARS IN PROFESSION: 9

ASSOCIATED WITH: GAMESTOP

▶ EDUCATION

"I have a bachelor's degree in Business Administration with a concentration in Management from Sonoma State University."

▶ BREAKING IN

"It wasn't difficult due to the fact that I knew someone who worked at the then 'Funcoland.' I had previous background working in the electronics section at Target, so it was an easy transition."

▶ EARLY INDUSTRY IMPRESSIONS

"I didn't expect all the 'selling' that was attached to video games and the detailed knowledge about every game that consumers demand. Luckily, I have played video games my entire life so it wasn't hard. Unfortunately people do like to test you—and I do mean quiz/test you—if they feel you don't look the part."

▶ KEY QUALITIES

"Energy. If you have ever worked in retail, you know how exhausting it can be. Having energy or being energetic can help make your day more enjoyable to yourself and those around you.

"Optimism. Retail can be an absolute killer on your mood if you let it get to you, so being optimistic can really help keep up your moral.

"Passion. Loving what you sell is what really helps any job. I often get the question 'Do you like working here?', and sometimes it's laced with confusion. I can confidently say I do everytime, which also makes the people I am talking to feel more comfortable around me. You are more likely to trust someone if they use the product and have a passion for it."

▶ TOOLS OF THE TRADE

"I am fortunate enough to work for a company that prides itself on giving information to their employees. GameStop supplies a training tool called 'Level Up' that updates every week with new quizzes to help employees learn about upcoming games, even the obscure and indie titles. It truly helps all of us have information at our fingertips if we want it. I personally am a huge fan of IGN and Game Informer, so I frequent their websites every morning for any video game news, which helps keep me on my toes."

▶ HOURS & ENVIRONMENT

"I work 44 hours a week in a mall in a city of 200,000 people. There are two malls in my city, but we are referred to as the 'big mall' or 'downtown mall.'"

▶ AN AVERAGE DAY

"An average day at work beings at 8:00 AM. If I am opening the store, I generally spend the first hour before opening doing manager type activities, such as leaving feedback for my team, tracking operational tasks, and checking performance. Most of my day is balanced between operational tasks, selling and managing performance, as well as keeping my team on task.

"Once the store opens, it's sell, sell, sell! My favorite part of working for GameStop is that they encourage you to sell people what they actually want, which makes engaging with people much more fun on the salesfloor. For example, if someone walks into my store, I'll generally try to find out what system they have, the last game they played, what game they can't put down—things like that. My favorite thing is to try and find a common 'love' between me and the person who walked in, because that's when people loosen up the most and a relationship starts between myself and the guest. For me, *Rainbow Six Siege* is my soft spot, so as soon as someone says *Rainbow Six* I'm hooked. There is a lot of cashiering and sometimes it's too busy to be on the salesfloor talking to people. However, when you get those people who are extremely passionate about what they love, those are the best conversations because that's when people open up the most."

▶ PROFESSIONAL PERKS

"It's definitely the people, whether it's who is on your team or the guest who walks into the store. Talking to people about video games all day really never gets old. Vendor gifts are also definitely a plus, as well as the employee discount. And who could forget about the GameStop Managers Conference in the fall!"

▶ CAREER CHALLENGES

"I often struggle with people not fully understanding how businesses work. There is a meme that floats around about GameStop that always makes me roll my eyes. It features a kid sitting in a bunch of video games and the quote underneath implies that GameStop gave him $2.00 for the lot. I have to explain that selling a game to your friend for $20 dollars is different then selling to a business for $7. Businesses have more expenses than the friend who would buy it for $20. The friend would certainly play the game, but with my business it may sit in a drawer for months until someone wants it and, in that time, we are still paying for staff, the building, and making some money in the middle."

▶ FAVORITE PROJECT

"The GameStop Manager's Conference is my favorite. Every year, all the vendors put on a conference for all the GameStop Store Leaders and it is filled with awesome activities and great shows. It's pretty much a 'mini E3' for GameStop Leaders."

▶ LIFE HACKS

"Delegation is key. As a new Store Leader, it is everyone's first instinct to do everything yourself because you know you can do it right. Teach your team right and you'll never have to worry about it being done wrong again."

▶ BIGGEST MISTAKE

"I was on a fast track for promotion and, due to a fear of failure, I let it get in the way and scared myself out of the promotional steps. I slowly backed out and returned to my normal position and thought I would be happy with it. Plot twist—I wasn't. Never let fear get in the way. My new motto in the morning is 'What's the worst that can happen?' Anxiety is a beast and I have chosen to not let it get the best of me, or get in my way."

▶ EXCITING ADVANCEMENTS

"Collectibles! My company bought a huge collectible company and boy, howdy, are we starting to get an awesome supply of nerdy things!"

PRO TIP!

"Strive to be the best at what you do. No matter what you are doing, it will make you better."

HAYAT SELIM

EGYPT'S FIRST FEMALE VIDEO GAME SOUNDTRACK COMPOSER

 Hayat Selim

 Hayatselimmusic

Hayat Selim

hayatselim.com

EXPERIENCE

FIRST INDUSTRY PROJECT: INITIA: ELEMENTAL ARENA (2015)

FAVORITE INDUSTRY PROJECT: INITIA: ELEMENTAL ARENA (2015)

PROJECTS SHIPPED: 7 GAMES

ACHIEVEMENTS UNLOCKED:

> NAMED "EGYPT'S FIRST FEMALE VIDEO GAME SOUNDTRACK OMPOSER" —CAIROSCENE (2016)

> GAME MUSIC COMPOSITION COMPETITION "YOUNG TALENT AWARD" (2016)

> ROYAL COLLEGE OF MUSIC LONDON "COMPOSITION FOR SCREEN COURSE" FULL SCHOLARSHIP HOLDER (2017)

STATS

INDUSTRY LEVEL: 4

CURRENT CLASS: COMPOSER AND SINGER-SONGWRITER

CURRENT GUILD: SELF-EMPLOYED—CAIRO, EGYPT & LONDON, UNITED KINGDOM

SPECIAL SKILLS: MUSIC COMPOSITION, SINGING, SONGWRITING, SOUND DESIGN, DANCE, ACTING

STANDARD EQUIPMENT

FAVORITE PLATFORM: GAME BOY

GO-TO GENRE: FANTASY/HISTORY

MUST-HAVE GAME: HARRY POTTER AND THE PHILOSOPHER'S STONE

Easter Egg

Treasured childhood memories include playing *Pokémon* and making custom clothing for Barbie.

BIO

Hayat Selim is Egypt's first female video game composer, a distinction that comes with both the privilege and responsibility of being a pioneer." Selim has been musically inclined as far back as she can remember, performing as both a pianist and vocalist at a young age. It wasn't until 2011, however, that she decided to pursue music as a career. "Songwriting is where my passion for writing music started," Selim explained. She was also passionate about games as a kid, rarely seen without a Game Boy in hand. "I would learn to play soundtracks from movies and games on the piano and would add my own lyrics to them. My piano teacher would often get angry when I escaped the classical repertoire to play soundtracks."

Despite these parallel passions, Selim didn't cater her university coursework towards composition. Instead, she earned a degree in digital media engineering and technology. Ultimately, Selim found the work unfulfilling and began taking private composition lessons to write music for film the next year.

"Being the first woman to do this in my country—and one of very few in the Middle East—has given me a great advantage when it comes to many opportunities," explained Selim. "My story was often very welcome and well listened to, which has helped a lot while trying to apply for scholarships and funding for different programs."

Selim received one such scholarship in 2015, providing an opportunity to study at Media Sound Hamburg. "This is the international summer academy for film music, game music, and sound design where I took a Masters class with the founders of Sound of Games in video game music," she said. "At the time, I also began exploring the video game industry in Egypt—my home country—which I had no idea existed. I stumbled upon a small yet very talented society and found myself despite having been fixated on pursuing film music only, suddenly discovering the options in the video game industry."

Many of Egypt's video game professionals graduated from the program at the Information Technology Institute in Cairo and, as such, were a tight-knit group. Selim began to introduce herself to others and was warmly welcomed into the field.

"The Egyptian game development scene is where I got my first job as a media composer. This society became my comfort zone and I had the honor of working with not just great talents, but very pleasant people."

"Almost every game developer in Egypt is under the age of 30," continued Selim, "and there is just so much room for flexibility, risk-taking, and throwing one's self out there. Many Egyptian studios have been able to compete with the international standards in a very short period of time."

One such studio—The Gentle Ghouls—brought on Selim for their game *Initia: Elemental Arena*. A first-person shooter that blended medieval and Celtic mythology; the genre and setting inspired her. "*Initia Elemental Arena* was—and still is at this moment—my favorite project. In 2016, I submitted the main theme of *Initia* to the 'Young Talent Award Game Music 2016' composition competition in Hamburg, Germany. Thankfully, it made first place. It was a completely unexpected and great experience. Her win was rewarded with the *Initia: Elemental Arena* soundtrack being played live in concert in Hamburg, an incredible honor for someone so young in their career.

Despite the abundance of talent, financial issues are a harsh reality of the game industry in Egypt. "Unfortunately, due to funding reasons, *Initia: Elemental Arena* did not get past alpha stage. Many projects start off very well until funding runs out and they are canceled, a lot of them with great potential. It takes quite a lot of energy to constantly seek new projects to be able to sustain one's self as a media composer, which is not always a very stable path especially with a fresh industry as this one," she explained. "However, I was lucky enough to have worked with very creative individuals with open minds who were very welcoming. It also taught me so much about this industry and was my first chance to build a strong portfolio that opened many doors."

Selim sees her visibility as an opportunity to inspire more women to join her field of work, and accessible tools are making these opportunities more abundant. "Writing music with pen and paper or classical notation in general is no longer the normal way for a media composer to write music to visual media. This is due to the popularity of digital audio workstations. Nowadays, media composers usually play virtual instruments using MIDI keyboard directly on a DAW (Digital Audio Workstation) and prepare sheet music usually only when the music will be recorded or played live," said Selim. "When there is no budget to record orchestra (which is very often the case), the soundtracks are released with well mixed virtual instruments. The size of an orchestration is no longer bound to recording budgets in media, since virtual sampled libraries can represent an entire orchestra nowadays and some libraries sound almost real. However, I believe the live aspect of music is one that cannot—and should never—be completely replaced. One or two live instruments in a soundtrack can push the quality very high and do not cost much to record."

"Writing music is beautiful but emotionally draining sometimes. When I have a sound design task, it is always a good break from the emotional investment."

Four years into her career, Selim works across multiple disciplines, which helps maintain equilibrium in her life. "I either work as a composer, singer-songwriter, or sound designer. I always need balance," she explained. "To me writing music will always be fulfilling, however, there is also a great beauty in sound design for me. There is an art behind foley and replicating sounds as close as possible to reality. It is creativity without the investment of emotions, which is more the case in music. Writing music is beautiful but emotionally draining sometimes. When I have a sound design task, it is always a good break from the emotional investment."

Projects continued to roll in for Selim, including *The Solar System* (2016), *Estimation Kings* (2016), and *Baloot Quest* (2017). "For *The Solar System*, I had to complete four soundtracks in two days; mainly in a more electronic direction, which I had barely tackled before. Somehow, I managed, the client was happy with the resulting soundtracks, and they were a great addition to my portfolio," she recalled. "I always believe one's best work is written under the pressure and adrenaline rush of a deadline—as much as formal training urges to take one's time. I believe time pressure forces one to act instinctively, which more often than not creates the best results. Having too much time for a creative process allows overthinking and overanalyzing, which may overshadow one's instinctive, creative ideas."

"I hope to keep encouraging and motivating women in the Middle East to enter this field usually dominated by men."

Selim hopes that her work is helping legitimize and raising awareness of the important role music plays in games as a creative medium. "I believe I may have helped the rising video game industry in Egypt see the importance of audio and music quality a little more than was the case before," she said. "Talks about sound, music, and video games were introduced for the first time in some major Egyptian events. This meant the audience was extended beyond video game developers and artists and started including sound designers, aspiring musicians, and voice artists. Also, media music is a field virtually untouched by women in the Middle East and I hope to keep encouraging and motivating women in the Middle East to enter this field usually dominated by men."

Selim continues to study and hone her craft while working on a new game—*Knights of Light* by Rumbling Games Studio. Always eager to learn, in 2017 Hayat was awarded a scholarship to study Composition for Screen at the Royal College of Music, London, and is currently working towards her Masters.

CAMILA GORMAZ

EXPLORING MILITARY MORALE THROUGH SYSTEMS DESIGN

 Burasto

 Long Gone Days Game

LGDays.tumblr.com

longgonedays.com

EXPERIENCE

FIRST INDUSTRY PROJECT: INVISIBLE APARTMENT (2014)
FAVORITE INDUSTRY PROJECT: LONG GONE DAYS (2018)
PROJECTS SHIPPED: 4 GAMES
ACHIEVEMENTS UNLOCKED:
> DAY OF THE DEVS "OFFICIAL SELECTION"—LONG GONE DAYS (2016)
> INDIEDB "INDIE OF THE YEAR TOP 100"—LONG GONE DAYS (2016)
> SQUARE ENIX COLLECTIVE OFFICIAL SELECTION—LONG GONE DAYS (2016)

STATS

INDUSTRY LEVEL: 4
CURRENT CLASS: GAME DEVELOPER
CURRENT GUILD: BURA—SANTIAGO, CHILE
SPECIAL SKILLS: ILLUSTRATION, WEBSITE DEVELOPMENT & DESIGN, SOCIAL MEDIA MARKETING, ANIMATION

STANDARD EQUIPMENT

FAVORITE PLATFORM: PC & PLAYSTATION 4
GO-TO GENRE: ANYTHING WITH A STRONG NARRATIVE
MUST-HAVE GAME: PAPERS, PLEASE

BIO

Although indie developer Camila Gormaz released her passion project *Long Gone Days* in March of 2018, she has been working on the title since the age of 12. Now that she's 27, the game illustrates a level of career clarity and dedication that few are lucky enough to find at such a young age.

"I was about eight or nine when I played *Kirby Super Star* for the first time and decided I wanted to make games," began Gormaz. "I didn't know anything about computers, so I would create my own levels on a piece of paper." Her skills progressed quickly. "A few years later I learned how to make hyperlink games, then dress-up dolls using Flash. When I was 12, I discovered RPG Maker. That is when I started writing what would become *Long Gone Days*."

Although working in gaming was the end goal, a lack of industry curriculum in Chile required Gormaz to pursue a different degree. "I went to college and earned a digital communications degree," explained Gormaz. "While I learned a lot about marketing, everything strictly related to game development has been self-taught or acquired through experience."

INDIE CRASH COURSE

Gormaz secured her first paid development gig in 2014. "I worked as the character designer and artist for the kinetic novel *Invisible Apartment 1* by Vysoko Anime Production." With a two-person team, the project acted as a crash course on indie game development. "I learned a lot about scheduling and business and it made me realize that becoming an indie dev was more achievable than I originally thought," said Gormaz.

During this period, Gormaz worked on *Long Gone Days* in her free time with friend Pablo Videla. The duo took a leap and pitched the game to indie-funding springboard Square Enix Collective in 2016. The game was officially selected, which resulted in a successful crowdfunding campaign

Gormaz and Videla founded Santiago-based independent game studio BURA soon after. Running a studio had its own challenges, though. "I had to gather a team, take charge of the business side of things, and all that stuff you normally wouldn't handle if you are just an employee." With staffing in place, a four-person team released the Early Access of *Long Gone Days* in early 2018.

Long Gone Days is described as a "2D modern-day character-driven military JRPG that combines elements from visual novels and dystopian fiction." It focuses on the emotional impact war takes on soldiers, drawing on Gormaz's extensive research on the real-life effects of war from those who have served. She lurked in military forums and studied conscript language, noting shared experiences such as fears and lingering trauma.

Wanting to ensure that the realities of war were less glamorized than Hollywood stories lead people to believe, she creatively expressed her findings through an array of in-game systems. A morale meter resulted in characters becoming less efficient as it depleted. To keep a soldier's morale up, the player needed to emotionally support them as a unique individual, taking cues through dialogue to discover their needs.

Easter Egg

Named her successfully crowdfunded game after Mad Season's song "Long Gone Day." She changed the title to *Long Gone Days* to make it easier to find on Google.

Gormaz also drew from the inherent feeling of isolation and constant proximity of the unknown in war. Players would need to recruit interpreters to join them on missions, or they wouldn't be able to speak with local non-playable characters. "It always amused me how, in media, foreigners are portrayed as English-speakers with ridiculous accents. By having these characters speak in their native tongue, it means the protagonist is the one who is not 'normal.' For the first time, he becomes the foreigner. He desperately needs and wants to communicate, but he's powerless without an interpreter. That feeling of isolation and inadequacy is what I wanted to convey." said Gormaz.

"*Long Gone Days* is the game I had always wanted to make, and it is the reason why I started my own studio," explained Gormaz. "I started writing it about 14 years ago when I was a teen, so the characters have been growing up with me, and it still makes me emotional to see how well-received it's been."

Looking back, Gormaz's drive and passion seemed to make working in the industry an inevitability, but she found herself apprehensive when taking her first steps into gaming. "I started working in games the same year Gamergate sparked, so I tried to keep a low profile. I hid my photos, used a nickname, and sometimes I'd hide the fact that I was a girl," said Gormaz.

Initial trepidation aside, she found her industry colleagues to be nothing but welcoming. "One of my favorite memories is when I gave my first talk at a local event, in front of several developers who had way more experience than me," said Gormaz. "I thought I would be laughed at, because working on an RPG as your first project is usually what everyone advises you against. But when I finished, everyone clapped and asked questions until time ran out. Honestly I've never been so overwhelmed in my life."

Now influential in the Chilean indie game scene, Gormaz hopes to raise awareness of the hurdles geography plays in international development. She understands how geography can be isolating. "Most major gaming events are hosted in the United States. Not to mention some developers can't even get issued a visa to attend those events. A lot of countries are not even allowed on popular storefronts or crowdfunding sites. Thankfully, the international press has been really supportive, and we have a lot of devoted fans who have made it easier for us to reach more people."

"I started working in games the same year Gamergate sparked, so I tried to keep a low profile. I hid my photos, used a nickname, and sometimes I'd hide the fact that I was a girl."

Gormaz no longer feels a need to hide her gender online, or in person. Rather, she's embraced it. "Some months ago, I gave a talk at an event aimed at young girls interested in technology. I wasn't sure if they would be interested, but as soon as the presenter said I was a game developer, the girls gasped in excitement," she recalled. "I told them how I began creating my first games when I was about their age, and by the end of it, a couple of them were asking me about game engines and how to get started. It was really, really cool to see them so motivated and interested!"

GLORIA O'NEILL

TELLING TRADITIONAL STORIES FROM INDIGENOUS CULTURES THROUGH VIDEO GAMES

 CITCAlaska

 Cook Inlet Tribal Council, Inc. | NYO Games Alaska

CITCAlaska

citci.org

EXPERIENCE

FIRST INDUSTRY PROJECT: NEVER ALONE / KISIMA INNITCHUNA (2014)

FAVORITE INDUSTRY PROJECT: NEVER ALONE / KISIMA INNITCHUNA (2014)

PROJECTS SHIPPED: 1 GAME

ACHIEVEMENTS UNLOCKED:

> ALASKAN COMMAND CIVILIAN ADVISORY BOARD (2005–PRESENT)

> BOARD DIRECTOR FOR THE ALASKA NATIVE JUSTICE CENTER (2016 – PRESENT)

> YWCA ALASKA/BP "WOMEN OF ACHIEVEMENT" AWARD (2004)

> ANCHORAGE ATHENA SOCIETY "LEADERSHIP AWARD" (2018)

 STATS

INDUSTRY LEVEL: 4

CURRENT CLASS: PRESIDENT & CEO, EXECUTIVE CHAIR & BOARD MEMBER

CURRENT GUILD: COOK INLET TRIBAL COUNCIL & E-LINE VENTURES, LLC—ANCHORAGE, USA

SPECIAL SKILLS: COLLABORATING, FOSTERING CONNECTIONS, YOUTH SUPPORT, COMMUNITY BUILDING, HIKING, FISHING

STANDARD EQUIPMENT

FAVORITE PLATFORM: PC

GO-TO GENRE: WORLD GAMES

MUST-HAVE GAME: NEVER ALONE / KISIMA INNITCHUNA (2014)

BIO

In 2014, Gloria O'Neill found herself working in video games, much to the surprise of her peers, and herself. "I am proud to say that while we only recently broke into the industry in 2014, we did it in such a meaningful way," shared O'Neill.

The nonprofit Cook Inlet Tribal Council, Inc. (CITC)—of which O'Neill is president and CEO—is in the people business. Their ultimate goal is to work with Alaska Native people and help them achieve their full potential through recovery and re-entry support services, child and family services, educational programs, and career connections.

> "The *Never Alone* game concept was bold, but also a risk."

"Making a video game was simply not on our radar," said O'Neill. CITC had, however, been looking into the area of social enterprise for some time. They aimed to ensure program participants had the tools to become self-sufficient. Partnering with the federal government in carrying out its federal trust responsibility to Alaska Native people, CITC had traditionally been dependent on federal funding and could not yet lead by example in terms of self-sufficiency. Being self-determined required a sustainable for-profit funding model.

O'Neill and her team had set aside a small pot of spending money over a period of several years, and they started exploring ways to invest it. Ideally they wanted to find a program that would share positive representation of Alaska Native people, and encourage youth to become more connected with their heritage in the process.

NEVER ALONE

Thus, the idea of investing in video games came about, and *Never Alone*—known as *Kisima Innitchuna* in the Iñupiaq language—was born. "The *Never Alone* game concept was bold, but also a risk," said O'Neill. "This was an arena we knew little about initially, so we had our work cut out for us. Once we honed the idea, we knew it had amazing potential. That's when, in 2012, we decided to establish a for-profit subsidiary of our nonprofit CITC." Upper One Games is CITC's for-profit subsidiary—a nod to Alaska being the northernmost state in the USA—and is the first indigenous-owned commercial game company in the country.

Knowing little about the gaming industry, Upper One Games started looking for partners, and was pointed repeatedly in the direction of E-Line Media. A developer and publisher, E-Line Media collaborates on projects with real-world impact. Their past games include real-world civic-engagement title *Our City*, and *MinecraftEdu*, an approved educational *Minecraft* mod used by teachers to promote learning.

O'Neill invited E-Line up Alaska in the frigid month of January for meetings, rationalizing that if the E-Line team was willing to brave the intense arctic conditions, they were truly invested in collaborating. They came and they were committed. After days of discussions, the proposal was taken to CITC's board, and they approved co-development of *Never Alone* with E-Line Media.

CULTURAL AMBASSADORS

Never Alone aimed to share stories as told through oral tradition of the Iñupiaq people from Arctic Alaska. Ensuring that the game would be both respectful and educational, over 24 cultural ambassadors were included in production, providing insight on everything from accurate tools and weapons, to spiritual guidance. "During an inclusive development process, we brought together elders, storytellers, youth, artists, and culture bearers who worked with video game industry professionals at every step of the production process, insisting we honor our culture, heritage, and people during this journey," shared O'Neill."

The tale followed a 12-year-old Iñupiaq girl named Nuna, paired with an ever-present snow-white fox. The player could seamlessly switch between controlling Nuna and her four-legged companion as needed to solve the puzzle-platformer challenges. Nuna's ultimate task was to discover the source of an endless blizzard that threatened her village. "She quickly experiences the richness and vastness of her brave and harsh world of the Arctic," said O'Neill. "During her travels, Nuna uses the environment, her culture, her community, and even spirit helpers to overcome obstacles and realize a new future for her people."

Nuna's place as protagonist in the world's first Alaska Native video game was a powerful and intentional statement. "We could have made the lead character anyone or anything we wanted, but Nuna was the obvious choice for me—strong, independent, family-oriented, and community-focused," explained O'Neill.

"Nuna [from *Never Alone*] was the obvious choice for me—strong, independent, family-oriented, and community-focused."

Adding more authenticity to the experience, *Never Alone* was narrated in the form of a legend, told in Iñupiaq through a tribal elder. Subtitles translated the story on-screen, which eventually became available in 16 different languages around the world, introducing the rich Alaska Native culture to new audiences. The player could also unlock over 30 minutes of video insights from the Iñupiaq community, exploring the practices, values, and culture that inspired the game. "In the process, we created a new genre of gaming—world games," said O'Neill, a genre she defines as using video games to share and extend culture throughout the world.

Never Alone was received with open arms. "I think what surprised me the most was the global response we had when we actually launched the game," O'Neill recalled. "The acclaim was instantaneous and almost overwhelming. It filled my heart that the world was so ready for a game, an idea, that shared the beauty of Alaska Native culture with the world, and we did it in a way that represented our culture and who we are as a people."

SELF-SUFFICIENCY

Never Alone would win dozens of awards, including a British Academy of Film and Television Arts (BAFTA) award for best storytelling, and best debut. Achieving their goal of profitability, *Never Alone* allowed the council to re-invest in the community it supports and begin the journey toward self-determination. The game had seen more than three million downloads since its launch. "It was quickly apparent that the project was a good investment from a commercial perspective, but the social impact it created was reinforced in many blogs and industry reviews. People were learning from the game and experiencing an indigenous culture. It had a positive effect within the Alaska Native community as well. Our young people were inspired by the game and how it reflected and their heritage."

Cook Inlet Tribal Council and E-Line Media now have a long-term partnership—CITC is currently a 30% stakeholder in E-Line—and will continue to expand their genre of world games. Their newest project is *Beyond Blue*, intended for release in 2019. The game will explore the unknowns of the deep ocean as told through the eyes of a scientist named Mirai. "The project embraces the same inclusive development process we used to create *Never Alone*," said O'Neill, "pairing world-class game makers with some of the field's leading ocean experts to craft an experience that reflects the awesome wonder and unbounded mystery that infuse our planet's beating blue heart."

The future seems bright for CITC and E-Line Media. "The technology and pace within the game industry gave us a level of understanding of potential future investments we can make to ensure we are creating the best opportunities and making the smartest investments so our young people can not only survive, but also thrive in this age of digitalization," concluded O'Neill. "It's through this lens that we will determine where we need to go as an organization to empower our young people."

Easter Egg

Grew up working on her father's commercial fishing boat in remote Alaska. As a young girl employed in a male-dominated industry, she believes the experience gave her a strong work ethic and sense of resilience that remain with her to this day.

NOURHAN ELSHERIEF

EGYPTIAN GAMES ENTREPRENEUR AND EVANGELIST

Tactrohs
Tactrohs
Tactrohs
Nourhan ElSherief

EXPERIENCE

FIRST INDUSTRY PROJECT: SEEDS (2014)
FAVORITE INDUSTRY PROJECT: KEYS TO SUCCESS (2015)
PROJECTS SHIPPED: 5 GAMES
ACHIEVEMENTS UNLOCKED:

> TEDXMANSOURA UNIVERSITY SPEAKER "POWER OF GAMES" (2015)
> IMAGINE CUP NATIONAL FINALS—FIRST PLACE, EGYPT REPRESENTATIVE IN BAHRAIN (2015)
> MICROSOFT "BEST GAME AWARD: GLOBAL GAME JAM EGYPT" (2015)
> TOKYO GAME SHOW INDIE GAMES GUEST (2016)

STATS

INDUSTRY LEVEL: 4
CURRENT CLASS: GAME DESIGNER AND DEVELOPER
CURRENT GUILD: INSTINCT GAMES—CAIRO, EGYPT
SPECIAL SKILLS: PROGRAMMING, GAME DESIGN, UNITY 3D, JAPANESE LANGUAGE, COSPLAY

STANDARD EQUIPMENT

FAVORITE PLATFORM: PLAYSTATION 4
GO-TO GENRE: RPG
MUST-HAVE GAME: THE WITCHER 3

BIO

When Nourhan ElSherief first enrolled at university, she had no visibility on the emerging gaming scene in Egypt. As such, computer science seemed like a practical field to feed her love of tech. Her discovery of a three-day workshop on developing games using Microsoft's XNA framework changed everything.

"I decided to Google some game-development basics because I had always loved games, but for some reason it never crossed my mind as a career," explained ElSherief. "For one, I was surprised to find that there were game studios in Egypt—indie ones, of course—and that they were striving to survive after the Egyptian Revolution in 2011."

The workshop opened new doors for ElSherief. After graduating with her computer science degree in 2013, she decided to take the plunge into gaming. "I applied for a nine-month game-development diploma offered by the Information Technology Institute in Smart Village, Cairo," said ElSherief. "I was accepted amongst eight other passionate developers, and started learning all about game development, its cycle, and even monetization."

TAKING A RISK

This decision was difficult—even risky. "For starters, the game-development industry was even smaller back then and applying for the nine-month diploma instead of obtaining experience in one of the fields that I have been studying was a bit of a risk," she explained. Friends and family approached, suggesting she reconsider her decision and pointing toward standard computer-science internships. "Looking back, I am glad that I did apply for the diploma, now that the gaming community here in Egypt is finally blooming bit by bit."

After finishing nine months of studies, ElSherief found a home at Cairo-based Appsinnovate. Primarily creating branded games for mobile, the position offered her regular work but wasn't as fulfilling as she hoped. ElSherief found herself frustrated by the fact that she wasn't working on the type of games that inspired her to pursue gaming in the first place.

Easter Egg

Studied Japanese for six years at the Japan Foundation in Cairo. Hopes to use her language skills in future games.

Taking control of her future, in 2014 she joined forces with several game-design students and founded 2024 Studios. "We believed we could work to publish our creative content, while also maintaining our day jobs as our main source of income." A year after founding 2024 Studios, ElSherief quit her job at Appsinnovate to focus solely on her indie work. She was the only one at the company to do so. "Since I was the only one full-time indie, I was appointed as studio coordinator and manager," she explained. "It was hard managing the studio's schedules and future plans, while also working on my own games."

KEYS TO SUCCESS

Despite the difficult balancing act, ElSherief kicked off her favorite solo project in 2015. "*Keys to Success* was born during the Global Game Jam in 2015, but has kept growing since then." In the puzzle platformer that explored positive psychology, the player had to find their lost friend—"success"—by collecting keys in the form of inspirational quotes. Each quote contained the key to solving a corresponding puzzle. "The game's main mechanic allowed the player to clone themselves to avoid trouble," expanded ElSherief. "This expressed the message that you can only reach success when you believe in yourself, and your capabilities, and rely on them."

Keys to Success opened new doors for ElSherief. She took first place in the Imagine Cup National Finals. "I also placed third in Microsoft's Pan Arab Semi-Finals in 2015, and later in 2016 was invited to showcase the game at Tokyo Game Show," she said. "Demoing *Keys To Success* at Tokyo Game Show was an eye-opener to me, to see what the indie scene abroad was like. It was great also because some people took the time to break their stereotypes about Muslims, and even helped me out with design ideas."

Despite the success, running a studio and developing a game solo proved to be unsustainable. The funds ElSherief won through the Imagine Cup began to dry up. "In the end, I had to work on anything but *Keys to Success* for income to be able to work on *Keys to Success*," said ElSherief. "That's the never-ending indie loop, I suppose." In 2017 she put the project on hold and stepped away from managing 2024 Studios, looking to discover her own keys to success.

"Working on my own projects for a studio I own was always my dream, but I might have passionately leaped into being full-time indie when I still have much to learn," said ElSherief. "And now, I am trying to study as much as I can before taking that leap again."

> "[Tokyo Game Show] was great also because some people took the time to break their stereotypes about Muslims, and even helped me out with design ideas."

Now working full-time at Instinct Games as a designer and developer, ElSherief succeeds despite unique cultural considerations. "Working late and staying overnight if needed is impossible," began ElSherief, describing an accepted Egyptian rule that women are not allowed to stay overnight in non-residential spaces. "Working in a studio that's mostly men poses a great problem when everyone else can put in extra hours, and you seem like you're not giving it your all because you're leaving early. I try to compensate for that by working harder and finishing my tasks faster, so that I don't appear like I'm dragging the team down."

EVANGELIZING LOCAL TALENT

In reality, no one could accuse ElSherief of lacking passion or commitment. In addition to her day job, she strives to raise awareness of the Egyptian game industry through extensive volunteer work. As a founder of the blog *Indie Games Corner*, ElSherief shares news and reviews about indie titles throughout Egypt and the Middle East. Additional extracurricular activities include lectures and workshops at institutes such as the Arab Academy for Science and Technology.

"It's harder to achieve something if you don't see stories of success out there," ElSherief explained. "In 2015 I was able to give a TED Talk. I had a huge number of people's attention for a whole 18 minutes to tell them about the game industry, and indie games in general. It was the first time I stood in front of so many people and talked about something I am so passionate about. I was approached by game enthusiasts after the talk and was able to guide some to where to start and how to actively enter the industry in Egypt."

While opportunities may be more abundant for ElSherief in other countries, she intends to stay local and continue to spark interest in the industry for the next generation of Egyptian developers. "I am not sure yet where my career will take me, but I hope to one day own a studio that could be one of Egypt's major gaming industry pillars. Through it, I wish to help undergraduates learn about game development and inspire them to pursue it."

LISY KANE

HIPSTER, HACKER, HUSTLER

 Lisyk

 Lisyk

Lisy Kane

lisykane.com

EXPERIENCE

FIRST INDUSTRY PROJECT: HAND OF FATE (2015)

FAVORITE INDUSTRY PROJECT: ARMELLO (2015)

PROJECTS SHIPPED: 1 GAME, 24 #MISSMAKESCODE EVENTS

ACHIEVEMENTS UNLOCKED:

> MCV PACIFIC "100 MOST INFLUENTIAL WOMEN IN GAMES" (2015, 2016)

> FORBES "30 UNDER 30 2017: GAMES"

> MCV PACIFIC "WOMEN IN GAMES OUTSTANDING ACHIEVEMENT OF THE YEAR" (2017)

> GDC XBOX WOMEN IN GAMES' RALLY KEYNOTE SPEAKER (2018)

STATS

INDUSTRY LEVEL: 4

CURRENT CLASS: PRODUCER & CO-FOUNDER

CURRENT GUILD: LEAGUE OF GEEKS & GIRL GEEK ACADEMY—MELBOURNE, AUSTRALIA

SPECIAL SKILLS: PRODUCTION, SOCIAL MEDIA, COMMUNITY MANAGEMENT, PUBLIC SPEAKING, BLOGGING, PUBLIC RELATIONS, VIOLIN

STANDARD EQUIPMENT

FAVORITE PLATFORM: PC

GO-TO GENRE: STRATEGY

MUST-HAVE GAME: DOTA 2

"It was one of those 'I think I've found my people' moments [attending GDC]."

BIO

After Lisy Kane dropped out of university a second time, it became clear that a career reassessment was needed. Something wasn't working—her chosen curricula didn't fit.

At the time, Kane made a living as an executive assistant at a major finance company. A career in game development had never crossed her mind—Kane's high school didn't offer IT training beyond Excel spreadsheets and basic computer studies. She would soon learn that she wasn't alone; there was a systemic issue within education that contributed to her lack of awareness of career options in science, technology, engineering, and mathematics (STEM). So when she discovered that making games was a viable career path, it was a paradigm shift. She had found her fit.

"I found out you could earn a degree in game design, and my world was flipped upside down," said Kane. "When you grow up in Australia, especially as a young woman, having a career goal of 'game producer' isn't something that was on my radar. It took me until my early 20s to even understand there *was* a games industry, let alone people in Australia making games." Kane enrolled at university for a third time, and this go-around, it stuck. She earned a double degree in PR and game design from the Queensland University of Technology.

Easter Egg

Prior to breaking into gaming, Kane performed in grimy pubs across Australia with her post-punk indie band.

JOINING THE LEAGUE OF GEEKS

After graduating in 2013, Kane moved to Melbourne—the heart of the Australian games industry. Within a year, she was hired into production work by indie studio League of Geeks. Kane's first year was a whirlwind that laid the foundation for her career. "I didn't know the amount I would learn and grow," she said. "The biggest thing I had to learn was understanding prioritization and self-discipline with my own workload. Learning to ask for help and pipe up when you're struggling is a tough thing to do, especially early on in your career." Happily, the local industry supported Kane as she learned the ropes. "I will always count myself as very fortunate that my pathway into the games industry was so welcoming," she continued. "The most surprising thing for me was the strong sense of community the Australian games industry has."

While her career in production was taking off, Kane wanted to ensure that young women had visibility on the industry at an earlier age. She now understood why STEM studies had a bad record with women, and it wasn't a lack of interest. "It really frustrates me when people say 'maybe women just don't want to work in games' or 'the stats show they shouldn't be in games,'" said Kane. "That's just not true—if it was, there'd be no women at all in the industry. Girls get pushed out of STEM studies from a young age due to early-established gendered beliefs that those subjects are 'not for them.'

Studies show these sentiments start at aged six. As a result, you get fewer girls electing STEM subjects in high school and then they become a minority gender in the university courses—which then trickles through into the workforce." Like any good producer, she realized there was a problem with the pipeline.

"It really frustrates me when people say 'maybe women just don't want to work in games.'"

A GIRL GEEK ACADEMY

To unblock the pipeline, Kane teamed up with four other female tech professionals and co-founded the Girl Geek Academy. "Girl Geek Academy is the start-up I wish had existed when I was finishing high school and looking to start my career," she said. "I've been in that position of being unsure of the tech sector, being scared and fearful of the unknown. Being able to empower more women to learn technology, start their own businesses, and help build the interest drives this passion and makes me incredibly proud of what we've achieved and continue to achieve."

Collaborating with companies, schools, governments, and even individual families, the Girl Geek Academy offers specialized programs aimed to increase the number of women in STEM fields. This is achieved through unique training programs, workshops, field trips, educational curricula, and scholarships offered out of Melbourne and Brisbane, as well as regional Victoria.

Girl Geek Academy's mission is to teach one million women technical skills by 2025. With such an ambitious goal, the academy had to hit the ground running. Kane did just that in 2015, when her first major program debuted to the public—#SheMakesGames. Australia's first all-women game-making day, the event included panels, discussions, networking, and other opportunities for industry hopefuls to learn. It was a hit and became an annual event for the Girl Geek Academy. Already making waves in the industry, Kane's work began to garner the notice of organizations. In 2015 she was awarded with a spot in *MCV Pacific*'s "100 Most Influential Women in Games."

BRINGING ARMELLO TO MARKET

Back at League of Geeks, Kane's development career was taking off with a promotion that dropped "associate" from her producer title. She worked full-time on the studio's debut title, *Armello*, as the scrum master and line producer for the code, art, and marketing teams. "Releasing *Armello* back in 2015 was incredibly challenging for me," said Kane. "It was my first big project; I'd only been working with the team for 11 months. It was a tough and stressful time, but it came with success on the other side."

Armello was nominated for awards at major industry shows such as the Indie Games Festival, IndieCade, the Australian Game Developers Awards, and SXSW. It took home Kotaku's Australian Game of the Year. The success of *Armello* put League of Geeks on the international map. In 2016, Kane flew out to San Francisco to represent League of Geeks at the Independent Games Festival award night. "We don't get to dress fancy very often, and we don't get to celebrate as much as we should," she said. "This was a sit-down, round-table event celebrating our nomination of Best Visual Art. Most developers don't even get to attend GDC until later in their careers, and here I was in my second year in the industry, sitting among game developers I'd respected and awed for years beforehand. It was one of those 'I think I've found my people' moments."

Kane continued to make waves with her personal endeavors. She made *MCV Pacific*'s "100 Most Influential Women in Games" again in 2016 and was nominated for their Woman of the Year and Creative Inspiration awards that same year. In 2017, she took home *MCV Pacific*'s "Women in Games Outstanding Achievement of the Year" award, and Film Victoria formally recognized her "outstanding contribution to the games industry." On a global stage in 2018, Kane made *Forbes*' annual "30 Under 30" list, and returned to San Francisco to give the keynote at Xbox's GDC Women in Games Rally.

Coming full circle, Kane was named an "Innovation and Entrepreneur Outstanding Alumni" of Queensland University of Technology and Innovation in 2018. After two false starts at university, she's now recognized as one of their best success stories.

"The projects I run and will continue to learn and iterate on at Girl Geek Academy are aiming to support and grow the pipeline of women we see making games, and working in the games industry," Kane concluded. "I want to continue to make and curate unique experiences for a global audience; this includes both making video games and the work I'm doing at Girl Geek Academy. I want to continue to be a leader and help bring more women and underrepresented people to this industry in a safe and supportive way."

PROFESSOR OAK'S AGE-OLD QUESTION

By Morrigan Johnen | *Community & Social Media Manager, Crystal Dynamics*

Character customization always starts the same old way.

Are you a boy or a girl?

It seems simple and straightforward. You're choosing how your avatar looks. You're picking whether shopkeepers greet you as "Sir" or "Lady." You're choosing which clothes your avatar will wear. In most cases, these differences are purely aesthetic at the surface level.

Yet the effects of your decision are extensive, impacting your character throughout the course of their adventure. This question is intrinsic to the identity of your character, defining them in perpetuity.

Character customization has grown to encompass such a wide variety of options available to players. As technology has developed through modern games such as *Black Desert Online* and *Dragon Age*, so have the avatars we've embodied. We can now make our characters with incredible particularity, defining us with such detail and definition. My representation in games can be crafted with artistic precision, making it visually unique among millions of combinations. Despite the many different ways I could portray myself, I never thought I had a choice with one selection.

Are you a boy or a girl?

Online games have developed worlds of opportunity for us to explore. When we play *EVE*, we explore the wide-open space of Nullsec and corporate warfare. When we log into *World of Warcraft*, we can traverse the wilds of Azeroth and embark on epic quests. These are worlds filled with incredible possibilities and wonder. But when I created my first online character, I was faced with that nagging question that just wouldn't go away.

Are you a boy or a girl?

Growing up with my friends, I was "one of the boys." We watched movies, played soccer, and always bought the latest video game. We were constantly at each other's houses playing games together. I spent many evenings up until 2:00 in the morning playing on the N64. Then the Internet arrived and everything changed. I remember the day my friend showed me the beta for *World of Warcraft* and how, if we got accounts, we could play together all the time—and we did.

When I made my first character in *World of Warcraft*, I created an Elf Hunter named Coriander. I quickly deleted her, because I didn't enjoy her play style. My next character stuck, though; it was a Warlock named Meli with her imp Jub Rin. She was a Human. My friends played radically different characters—Dwarves, Elves, Gnomes, and not one Human except mine. I was the outlier among my group of friends. For them, they wanted to explore what it was like being an Elf Warrior or a Gnome Mage. Meanwhile, I just wanted to explore what it was like to be Meli.

In the infancy of online games, people would typically assume a player's gender corresponded with their avatar. Almost every encounter with other players led them to assume that, much like my avatar, I was a woman. I never saw a reason to tell them otherwise, despite the unfortunate and rampant sexism that persists in online spaces—even to this day. Occasionally, my group of friends would interject trying to qualify my gender to a random stranger. I tried to not take it personally. Eventually, though, my group of friends grew tired of trying to "correct" others and settled on the inevitability of everyone referring to me as "she." They even began to refer to me, by virtue of my character, as "she."

This resulted in a pivotal and life-affirming opportunity that 16-year-old me cherished deeply. I had the freedom and chance to explore social spaces as my preferred gender, unabated by the preconceptions of those around me. I was able to safely explore my identity without fear. As a scared teenager confronting terrifying possibilities, this was absolutely crucial in giving me just enough confidence to take that leap. But as online games grew, people stopped always assuming that the female avatars they were talking to were consistently played by women. So once again...

Are you a boy or a girl?

This was the first time I ever told another human being that I was a girl.

I would continue to explore what this meant, built upon a world that afforded the safety net of self-discovery. In a game filled with players exploring epic raids filled with dragons, I was too busy exploring who I was. My guild mates fought through hordes of undead monsters, while I simply talked to others about who I was. This process would continue through and beyond my online game experience. Eventually I felt the safety and confidence to come out to the very same group of friends who had joined me at the beginning of my online play. Although we may not play *World of Warcraft* anymore, we still find time to play games together.

Massively multiplayer online games have a social aspect that is built upon the gameplay experience. Contained within the framework of the game, social constructs are developed. In more socially complex games, players develop a social culture that can utterly permeate gameplay. We've made lifelong friends built on many late nights of gameplay, found love across servers, and embarked on incredible journeys of self-discovery. The social value of games is so tied to human nature that scientists have studied MMORPGs such as *World of Warcraft* and the Corrupted Blood incident to find how groups of people would react to real-life epidemics. With video games permeating our society, it's hard to turn a blind eye to how our society has permeated video games.

As game developers, we're empowered with an incredible opportunity to craft entire worlds. Our decisions about which worlds we make and what we put in them can have an amazing effect on others. Gameplay is crucial; however, the structure by which our games empower others cannot be overlooked. Built within our games are the spaces and tools for others to go far beyond the limitations to which we as game developers can directly craft an experience. Through play, we can tell stories, confront scary truths, and learn more about who we are. We can make a space for others to cultivate and in so doing, grow themselves. These spaces are sacred and should be cherished.

Growing up I always knew that I was transgender. Despite knowing, it is still an overwhelming consideration to come to terms with. The daunting nature of exploring one's identity often requires a rough introspection made tougher by an unforgiving world around us. Yet with the advent of online spaces, video games, and representation therein, we can ask questions and experience possibility previously thought unobtainable. For some that experience may be flying through space or defeating countless waves of zombies. For myself and many others, it's the safe exploration of understanding who we are. Because of this, I'll never have to ask myself that old question ever again:

Are you a boy or a girl?

SITHE NCUBE

SUB-SAHARAN AFRICA GAME INDUSTRY EVANGELIST

_LadySith

_LadySith

Sithe Annette Ncube

Sithe Ncube

EXPERIENCE

FIRST INDUSTRY PROJECT: GAME DEVELOPMENT WEEKEND IN LUSAKA, ZAMBIA

FAVORITE INDUSTRY PROJECT: GAMES PLUS GIRLS WORKSHOP IN LUSAKA, ZAMBIA

PROJECTS SHIPPED: 13

ACHIEVEMENTS UNLOCKED:

> MOREMI INITIATIVE MILEAD FELLOW (2017)
> MISS AFRICA SEED FUND GRANT RUNNER-UP (2017)
> A MAZE./JOHANNESBURG SPEAKER (2016)
> GDC DIVERSITY SCHOLARSHIP RECIPIENT & SPEAKER (2016)

STATS

INDUSTRY LEVEL: 4

CURRENT CLASS: FOUNDER & DIRECTOR

CURRENT GUILD: UBONGO GAME LAB—LUSAKA, ZAMBIA

SPECIAL SKILLS: WRITING, GAME DESIGN, PROGRAMMING, HOBBY ELECTRONICS, COMMUNITY MANAGEMENT, TUTORING

STANDARD EQUIPMENT

FAVORITE PLATFORM: NINTENDO

GO-TO GENRE: COUCH-CO-OP

MUST-HAVE GAME: TEKKEN SERIES

BIO

When Sithe Ncube decided to dedicate her career to video games, she went all-in, simultaneously building an invaluable network of resources in Sub-Saharan Africa. As an advocate for the growing market, Ncube feels strongly that Africa is full of potential, yet remains a blind spot for video game publishers around the world. "If you make a game, you will make a lot of noise, because our market is a game vacuum," she explained. "Africa is a mobile-first continent, and I believe there is a huge opportunity for the game-development industry to develop locally here."

EXTRACURRICULAR ACTIVITIES

Helping others get a leg up seems to be a part of Ncube's DNA. While still in secondary school, she volunteered as a tutor for younger students, ensuring they were prepared for exams through tutoring, testing, and organizing hands-on science experiments that fit within the curriculum. Looking back, this was the foundation that Ncube's future as an educator was built on.

"I never expected myself to be a part of the industry in this way," she explained. "The first time I had a career interest in the video game industry was in high school when I was looking through university prospectuses on what I could do with my interest in computers and art. I came across multimedia engineering that involved working with programming, 2D and 3D animation in films and games, and I wanted to study that. But that idea was driven out of me as everyone around me encouraged me to take on mechanical or electrical engineering."

Easter Egg

Has been chased by a hippo twice in her life—first at age nine, and the second time at age 11. Unsurprisingly, she never wants to be near a hippo again.

Taking the advice to heart, Ncube left Zambia to study in South Africa in 2014, beginning her studies in a bachelor's degree in mechatronics, robotics, and automation engineering from Nelson Mandela Metropolitan University (now Nelson Mandela University). In 2016 she decided to change career paths and transferred to a different faculty at the same university to study a degree in computer science and mathematics.

To say that Ncube kept herself busy before university is an understatement. She accepted a three-month social media internship at a Zambian company called BongoHive—a technology and innovation hub that helps start-ups get off the ground. Before long she was promoted to social media executive, and assisted with drafting all external communications, managing editorial calendars, posting and monitoring content, providing insights into analytics, and growing the community.

"I decided it would be a great idea to host an event [Games Plus Girls] solely catered to women."

Ncube learned more than how to be a successful social media manager in this time. The entrepreneurial bug had bit her, and she began organizing opportunities to funnel together like-minded people. "My first local event in games was organizing a Game Development Weekend in Lusaka, Zambia to get youth interested in the idea of game development," said Ncube. The attendees participated in basic coding workshops, enjoyed a game design panel and sat to watch E3 2013 together, giving them perspective on the larger video wgame industry.

FOUNDING UBONGO GAME LAB & MAKERHUT

Local interest in the industry was growing, and so shortly after her internship began, Ncube founded two outreach organizations. Ubongo Game Lab is the first, where she is the acting director. "Ubongo Game Lab is a technology group interested in game development, gaming technology, and its use within Zambia," explained Ncube. "The overall interests of the group are to give visibility to the game-development scene in Zambia and encourage its growth."

More recently, the lab has created tailored programming to increase women's participation in game development, through an annual boot camp called Games Plus Girls. "My favorite project was our first Games Plus Girls in 2015," said Ncube. "We noticed that not a lot of women were participating in our game-development events in Lusaka. So I decided it would be a great idea to host an event solely catered to women. To this day it has been the most insightful event I've hosted. They provided insight into how women don't feel confident about themselves in gaming as players or creators and even specific incidences that deter them. It illustrated that there is a lot of room for improvement in our community."

MakerHut is the second outreach arm Ncube spearheaded, which she also runs as director. "MakerHut is a creative community and makerspace in Zambia, which is the first of its kind and explores projects and technology in the fields of electronics, arts, and industrial design as part of the Maker Movement," Ncube continued. "They empower curious minds by giving them access to technology, and in doing so provide hands-on learning and creative expression."

GOING INTERNATIONAL

Soon, Ncube's reach extended outside of Zambia. "The first international event I contributed to was Global Game Jam 2015 as a regional organizer for sub-Saharan Africa," she said. "As part of the world's largest game-development session, I am involved in reviewing and approving sites in sub-Saharan Africa in preparation for the annual Global Game Jam, as well as supporting them with the necessary information to ensure a successful experience leading up to the end of the jam weekend."

Ncube took up post as an assistant program manager to indie game show A MAZE in Johannesburg, helping curate talks, workshops, and other activities for the annual festival. She also contributes to their sister-show in Berlin. "A MAZE Johannesburg in 2016 is one of my best memories," she said. "It was my first time getting into the experimental games and South African game-development scenes. I read about some people online, but I didn't know how amazing they were in person."

All of the time and attention Ncube has given hasn't gone unnoticed. In 2016 Ncube was awarded a GDC Diversity Scholarship, granting her free access to an event that can be quite expensive. The local community rallied around her, successfully funding her Indiegogo campaign and covering her transportation and lodging expenses for the show. Ncube returned the favor by advocating for her hometown market while at GDC, speaking on the #1ReasonToBe panel. The discussion explored what it means to be a minority working in video games. Panelists shared their highs, lows, and hopes for a more inclusive industry.

"A lot of times, women and minorities will spend time asking themselves whether they belong in their respective community or industry," Ncube said, imparting hard-earned advice on others. "Sometimes people will be nice enough to welcome you and be accommodating. But sometimes you will face resistance or hostility even in the smallest of micro-aggressions. Make it your duty to take up space in that industry even if you have to make it your own. Don't waste time asking yourself if you belong here. You do! And we need your voice among us."

"Don't waste time asking yourself if you belong here [gaming industry]. You do!"

Once Ncube is finished with her undergraduate degree, she has even bigger plans to grow the game-development scene in Zambia. "I intend on turning Ubongo Game Lab into a full-time indie studio someday," she said. "My biggest hope is to help establish a unified sub-Saharan Africa game-development network, and something I really want to happen is seeing the success of a collective of African women in games."

"Something that has been on my mind lately is the future of games being a subscription service," she concluded. "It seems inevitable. I feel like that will alienate a lot of consumers in developing countries. It's a future I see that I'm not too excited about." This reality makes the work Ncube is doing more important than ever. While there may be a void in the African games market, Ncube is stepping into that void and encouraging others to join her. With hard work and continued advocacy, hopefully the next generation will fill it entirely.

TANYA DEPASS

EVOLVED A VIRAL HASHTAG INTO AN INDUSTRY-CHALLENGING NON-PROFIT

Cypheroftyr
 Cypheroftyr
Cypheroftyr.tumblr.com
cypheroftyr.com

EXPERIENCE

FIRST INDUSTRY PROJECT: DIVERSITY CONSULTING ON ROLL20APP (2016)

FAVORITE INDUSTRY PROJECT: UNANNOUNCED TITLE (2019)

PROJECTS SHIPPED: PARTICIPATED IN 100+ PANELS

ACHIEVEMENTS UNLOCKED:

> FACEBOOK WOMEN IN GAMING STORIES FEATURE (2018)

> VICTORIA & ALBERT VIDEOGAMES: DESIGN/PLAY/DISRUPT EXHIBIT FEATURE (2018)

> GAME DEVS & OTHERS: TALES FROM THE MARGINS EDITOR (2018)

> DIVERSITY ADVOCATES ROUNDTABLE & GDC MICROTALK: PLAYING WITH FIRE PRESENTER (2018)

STATS

INDUSTRY LEVEL: 3.5

CURRENT CLASS: FOUNDER & DIRECTOR

CURRENT GUILD: I NEED DIVERSE GAMES—CHICAGO, USA

SPECIAL SKILLS: CREATIVE WRITING, BLOGGING, SOCIAL MEDIA, PUBLIC SPEAKING, PODCASTING, CRITICAL THINKING, DIVERSITY & INCLUSION

STANDARD EQUIPMENT

FAVORITE PLATFORM: PLAYSTATION 4

GO-TO GENRE: WESTERN RPGS

MUST-HAVE GAME: DRAGON AGE II

BIO

Tanya DePass says her introduction to the industry was a "happy accident," although happy wasn't how she was feeling at the time. "There wasn't a particular age I wanted to get into the industry. I fell into this by mistake, to be blunt," confessed DePass. "I was mad about games—what they weren't doing for me and people like me—and #INeedDiverseGames came about. Seeing so many stories about the lack of female protagonists, and how hard it is to animate women, along with yet another year of games with mostly scruffy white dude leads led me here."

Easter Egg

Owns *Dragon Age: Inquisition* on PC, Xbox One, and PlayStation 4, and has maxed out all the save slots across each platform.

#INEEDDIVERSEGAMES

DePass has been a geek since youth, when she would lose herself in the first edition of *D&D* and spend her free time at arcades. Due to financial limitations, video games were a luxury not readily available to DePass growing up. As she got older and consoles became more affordable, DePass dived into video games with enthusiasm.

Coming from a tabletop fandom—a medium where character creation is often only limited by imagination—it isn't hard to understand why DePass began to feel deflated with the status of diversity in the video game industry. She began to speak up, voicing her concerns across a variety of mediums, including founding the *Fresh Out of Tokens* podcast. DePass also began to write freelance game critiques, focusing on the intersection of gaming and pop culture with diversity, feminism, and race. Her work has been featured on publications such as Uncanny Magazine, Polygon, Paste Games, Vice, Mic, and more.

In 2014, DePass took the conversation to Twitter, centralizing her concerns under the hashtag #INeedDiverseGames. "I did it because I was tired of not seeing myself in the games I have spent many years playing," said DePass.

"I was tired of being the trope, the joke, the one that gets fridged early in the game to fuel man-pain for the plot. I was tired of 'hero dude saves the world, gets the girl' plotlines. So I started that tag after being burned entirely out on the current offerings."

As the movement began to pick up steam, DePass had to contend with detractors who attempted to misrepresent the work she was doing. Often originating from individuals in a position of privilege, the comments tried to equate diversity initiatives to a zero-sum game. In this capacity, it became just as important to clarify what the hashtag *wasn't* about. "I Need Diverse Games is not some evil social-justice-warrior plot to undermine the gaming industry and take boys' toys away. It is not related to GamerGate, or created by someone involved in GamerGate. It is not some feminist gamer illuminati plot point," she explained, joking that she'd happily join a feminist gamer illuminati group if one did exist.

> "I did [#INeedDiverseGames] because I was tired of not seeing myself in the games I have spent years playing."

LEVELING UP TO NON-PROFIT

Before long it became obvious that I Need Diverse Games had potential beyond a hashtag—it was a rallying point for a movement that had been long coming. "I didn't know anyone doing diversity advocacy full-time, and honestly I still don't know a lot of people who make this their full-time gig," said DePass. She took a step into uncharted territory, and formalized I Need Diverse Games as a non-profit in 2016.

"I Need Diverse Games seeks to bring projects, works, and research by marginalized folks to light," reads the non-profit's mantra. "We also seek to discuss, analyze, and critique identity and culture in video games through a multifaceted lens rooted in intersectionality." DePass explained that they also aimed to provide a safe space online for gamers from any marginalized group to express themselves, and promote the work of underrepresented creators who would otherwise go unheard.

Under DePass's guidance the non-profit has grown considerably. She often speaks at events on the topic of diversity, or provides guidance to conventions looking to add diversity programming to their lineup. Additional initiatives include conference and convention sponsorships, which provide free entry to cost-prohibitive events. I Need Diverse Games has partnered with the Game Developers Conference to give away 25 industry badges a year through the program, a $1600 value per person. DePass and her team also continue to publish articles on diversity in games on their website, paying their contributors in addition to giving them the visibility boost.

On a personal level, DePass now dedicates a large amount of her time to providing diversity consultation services to big names in gaming. "Getting to speak at Ubisoft Montréal on diversity, and explaining why it is important and why it can't be a one-and-done thing, those are my favorite moments," said DePass of her invite to the mega-studio in Canada. Quite a bit of the consultation work DePass does is under NDA, which is heartening, as it signals her early involvement in unannounced games.

TALES FROM THE MARGINS

In 2018, DePass used her expertise to edit and publish an anthology called *Game Devs & Others: Tales from the Margins*. Told through a series of essays by sidelined industry professionals and gamers, *Tales from the Margins* marked a first for DePass. "It was the first time I'd edited an anthology. It was far more work than I expected, but in the end it worked out great," she said.

DePass continues to volunteer her time for causes that keep diversity at the forefront of development. She's the diversity liaison for GaymerX, a nonprofit convention focused on supporting LGBTQ+ people within the greater video game culture. She regularly speaks at conferences and conventions around the country, has been profiled by Facebook's Women in Gaming initiative, and had her work showcased in the Victoria & Albert *Videogames* exhibit *Design/Play/Disrupt*. DePass's *Fresh Out of Tokens* podcast ran 96 episodes, coming to a close in 2017. She now is a co-host on the *Spawn on Me* podcast, the "premier show about gaming featuring people of color."

DePass's ultimate goal is to make the work she does irrelevant. "I want to put myself out of business. I want there to be no need for the diversity conversation again and again, especially at the 101 level," she concluded. "I hope I can move on to do narrative design on games that make a difference." But for now, she knows her presence is making an impact. "When someone says thank you for being visible in the industry, knowing I can make a bit of a difference to someone who doesn't get to see themselves is worth it."

> "I want to put myself out of business. I want there to be no need for the diversity conversation again and again."

ARI GREEN

ACHIEVING SUCCESS THROUGH SPITE

 MuppetWolf  couplesix.com

EXPERIENCE

FIRST INDUSTRY PROJECT: LE LOUPGAROU (IN DEVELOPMENT)

ACHIEVEMENTS UNLOCKED:

> GDC SCHOLARSHIP "I NEED DIVERSE GAMES" WINNER (2017)

> MIAMI DADE COLLEGE "DEMAND SOLUTIONS" RUNNER-UP (2017)

STATS

INDUSTRY LEVEL: 3

CURRENT CLASS: STUDIO CO-FOUNDER, PROGRAMMER

CURRENT GUILD: COUPLE SIX—BARBADOS

SPECIAL SKILLS: PROGRAMMING, PRODUCTION, VISUAL ART, PHOTOGRAPHY

STANDARD EQUIPMENT

FAVORITE PLATFORM: NINTENDO HANDHELDS

GO-TO GENRE: RTS

MUST-HAVE GAME: POKÉMON RUBY

BIO

The video game industry has traditionally appeared opaque to outsiders and, as such, finding footing can seem impossible. Independent developers have recently helped disrupt this institution. In doing so, many budding professionals have been inspired to keep roots in local communities and celebrate making games with local talent, and local flavor.

One of those self-starters is Ari Green, a young developer from Barbados. "I think I was about 19 when I played *Bastion* for the first time, and it enchanted me. Then I found out it was made by a small team and I couldn't believe it," said Green. "It seems silly now, but it had never occurred to me that games could be made by anything other than huge studios with enormous budgets." She decided then and there to start making games herself.

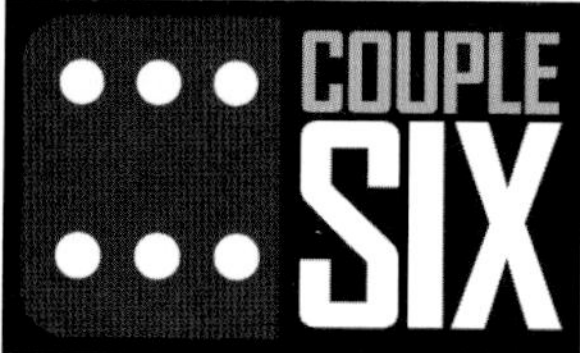

ENTERING A CHEAT CODE

Without an established video game industry in the Caribbean—there are no conferences, game jams, special interests groups, or grants specifically for video games—formal training wasn't in the cards for Green. It fell on her to blueprint her own education. "I'm a self-taught dev. I didn't have the money to pay for online courses, so I watched a lot of videos on YouTube and read as many tutorials and articles as I could get my hands on." Green cites the GDC Vault and the Extra Credits YouTube channel as major resources in her early education. "I taught myself programming the same way, by building small games with Python and C# using what I had learned." Free online resources and rapid prototyping paired with an abundance of ambition was a formula that proved fruitful.

In 2015 Green's aspirations grew beyond honing her own skills, and she founded a small development studio with longtime friend Mark Ramsay. "I put in the cheat code that allows you to enter the industry by starting a studio instead of going to work at an existing one. If I hadn't gone that route, I might have had difficulty padding out my portfolio as a programmer with enough interesting work to get a job in the industry."

Easter Egg

Has grapheme-color synesthesia, which gives her an advantage in *Sudoku.*

The Bajan variant of dominoes begins with play pieces shuffled and dealt. Whoever has the double six—colloquially called a "couple six"—starts the game. As the first game studio in Barbados, Green and Ramsay felt "Couple Six" was an apt moniker for them, since they too were "starting the game".

CARIBBEAN MAGIC

Couple Six makes "Games about You". While the studios five-person team aims to make games with widespread appeal, the "you" in question is an untapped demographic. Their ambition is to serve that audience by telling stories teeming with "Caribbean magic," and championing diversity by showcasing a "bariffle"—Bajan slang for a 'whole lot'—of people of color, the queer community, and other marginalized groups.

Their debut game *Le Loupgarou*—a narratively driven, stealth adventure game that weaves Caribbean folklore, history, and culture into the project's DNA —began development in 2015. Set in a fictionalized 1930s Barbados, Le Loupgarou is built around historical events with a twist. "While you play as the titular character, the real hero of this tale is Bertha, a civil rights activist masquerading as a maid whose story you discover even as you piece together the secrets of your own past," explained Green.

The player explores Barbados as Le Brun, an old man who harbors the immortal beast of local legend Le Loupgarou within him. While Le Brun must hunt souls to satiate the monster, the game is also about coming to understand one's own history and identity, and on the flipside, that of those he stalks.

Couple Six's hard work is slowly but surely paying off, as evidenced by their first public demo at AnimeKon 2015, the largest pop culture convention in the Caribbean. "The first time we showcased the game at Animekon in Barbados there was this one kid that kept coming back to our booth to play the prototype again and again," recalled Green. "He started timing himself and kept repeating the build to try to beat his time. Our first major fan was also our first speedrunner!" The lack of sleep leading to their first public demo lead to delirium on the convention floor, "but it was such a rewarding feeling to have made something that could be considered complete."

Le Loupgarou has been in development for three years now, and Couple Six's commitment to seeing it realized has been described as "borderline insanity." With a vertical slice nearly done, they've opened a Patreon, are seeking investors, and preparing for a crowdfunding campaign.

Green's successful contribution to Le Loupgarou hasn't gone unnoticed. "As a programmer, I feel a subconscious pressure to be perfect, to defy the stereotype that 'women just aren't natural coders.' I feel like a man could be average, and people would be okay with that, but if a woman is average, she is held up as an example of why women don't make good programmers," she explained. That being said, Green doesn't have much to worry about when it comes to her hard-earned programming skills. "I had a friend of mine look at the codebase for *Le Loupgarou* and tell me it was the cleanest code she had ever seen. She has a degree in Computer Science from McGill University and spent some time working at Ubisoft, so that meant a lot to me as a self-taught programmer."

HARNESSING SPITE

Green has come a long way since beginning her career in video games, but recognizes that the path ahead of her will be equally challenging. An unusual force motivates her to keep the course. "I make games out of sheer spite to succeed in a world that has not been welcome to me and my voice. We founded Couple Six to unabashedly show representations of people that look and live like us. To tell the stories of women and queer folk and anyone whose voice has been silenced or has never had one."

Green's passion, hard work, and visibility have already helped to inspire the next generation of Caribbean game developers who—much like her—didn't know it was a viable career option until recently. "In Barbados, I've had more than a few people ask me what I do and be stunned when I tell them I make video games. It's something most people haven't even realized was possible," said Green. We're demonstrating that you can become a developer without having to go overseas and doing an expensive degree."

CHERRY THOMPSON

CHAMPIONING INCLUSIVITY IN EVERY FORM

cherryrae

 cherryrae.com

cherryperson

 twitch.tv/cherryrae & mixer.com/cherryrae

EXPERIENCE

FIRST INDUSTRY PROJECT: IN-STUDIO CONSULTATION AT THE COALITION (2017)

FAVORITE INDUSTRY PROJECT: LECTURE—"A FRAUGHT LOVE LETTER TO THE GAMES INDUSTRY, FROM A DISABLED GAMER" (2018)

PROJECTS SHIPPED: 8 SPEAKING ENGAGEMENTS, 16 STUDIO CONSULTATIONS

ACHIEVEMENTS UNLOCKED:
> HAS CHEATED DEATH MORE THAN ONCE
> OWNS 10 LBS. OF TITANIUM
> OFFICIAL GDC SPEAKER (2018)
> COMPLETED BLOODBORNE

STATS

INDUSTRY LEVEL: 4

CURRENT CLASS: GAME-ACCESSIBILITY CONSULTANT, SPEAKER & STREAMER

CURRENT GUILD: FREELANCE—VANCOUVER, CANADA

SPECIAL SKILLS: VIDEO GAME ACCESSIBILITY, PUBLIC SPEAKING, CONSULTATION, VIDEO AND ART PRODUCTION, PATTERN RECOGNITION, ANIMAL WHISPERING

STANDARD EQUIPMENT

FAVORITE PLATFORM: IS GREEDY AND WANTS THEM ALL

GO-TO GENRE: ALL THE GENRES, REALLY

MUST-HAVE GAME: HORIZON ZERO DAWN

BIO

Note: Cherry Thompson is non-binary, meaning they do not identify exclusively with either binary gender as is commonly recognized today (male/female). However, Thompson is read—and therefore treated—as a woman in most social settings. As such, they have a shared understanding of what it is like to navigate a male-dominated industry as a marginalized person. Thompson's pronouns are them/they.

Cherry Thompson remembers reading an issue of *Edge Magazine* in the late '90s and being shocked to learn that some people were *actually paid* to create games. As an avid gamer, the realization laid the foundation for their future career.

In 2000, Thompson applied for a manager position at game shop Electronics Boutique, seeing it as a step in the right direction. "I was 18 and qualified, having worked in customer service since I was 15," they said. "The interview was an awful experience. A guy not much older than me was sat on the edge of a desk, peering over me. I was told I didn't like the right kinds of games, and the games I did like I only liked because I was a girl. I remember being really confused, because all my guy friends liked these games, too."

Feeling rejected, Thompson moved on, and eventually found work as a professional photographer, retoucher, and graphic artist. "After about eight years of that grind, I leveled up and expanded my career to fine art, and showed my paintings in galleries for a few years." Gaming remained their biggest hobby, though. "I always assumed it was 'too late' for me to even bother trying to switch careers and that I had the wrong skills, but I still daydreamed about it often."

Easter Egg

Is an actual cyborg, complete with several medical implants and upgrades, and gets around on wheels.

GAMES SAVE

In 2013, just as Thompson's art career was beginning to take off, they had a severe stroke. "It was an extremely rare spontaneous arterial rupture and led to a diagnosis of a progressive congenital disease that can result in profound disability," said Thompson. "I gave up my career in art because it was too physical, and I was in and out of the hospital unable to work regular hours."

With time, they came to terms with the diagnosis. "But the thing that kept me going was games," said Thompson. "It started out as hyperbole. I would joke that 'games saved my life,' but my jokes aren't that funny and are steeped in truth. That year was when I first discovered that games accessibility was a thing, and that it was also largely being neglected by development teams, usually due to a lack of knowledge or awareness."

> "I would joke that 'games saved my life,' but my jokes aren't that funny and are steeped in truth."

RAISING AWARENESS

As they started out trying to broach the subject of accessibility with developers and publishers, Thompson realized they weren't alone in the fight. A handful of dedicated industry advocates became mentors. "In the beginning, for me, it was extremely personal," Thompson said. "It felt like a matter of urgency because I was finding myself shut out from games, and while it wasn't the first time in my life, it really felt to me that if things didn't change, I would have to give up gaming, as well as everything else I'd already been forced to leave behind due to disability."

Thompson realized that their personal activism started with sharing. "I found that there was a lot of power in sharing my story with developers, and I learned ways to transfer the skills I'd gained exploring marginalized identity in film, art, and photography to making games more inclusive," said Thompson. "Today, I pride myself on being able to discuss the breadth of accessibility while also fostering and promoting the idea that the most valuable way to understand accessibility is to work directly with the players that need it."

THE INCLUSION COIN

"I work towards two sides of the inclusion coin: representation and accessibility," expanded Thompson. Both are incredibly important, make games better, and are often inescapably intertwined." On the accessibility front, Thompson's first major speaking event took place at the beginning of 2018. "I was afraid that because I was the last presentation of the entire conference, people would leave, bored of me halfway through." Instead, Thompson was met with a standing ovation.

Representation endeavors are inherently more challenging, says Thompson. "I'm currently writing a major talk on disability representation in games," they said. "It's challenging, sure, but it's also really scary." Thompson likens accessibility to a science with objective goals, challenges, and means to resolve barriers. Representation, however, is subjective and very personal. Representation can mean a different thing to different people. That and, as Thompson explains, not all disabled people want to be represented in games; some play games as a form of escapism and enjoy the fantasy.

When it comes to representation, Thompson stresses that you can't rely on only one perspective. "My aim is to be firm about the fact that my discussion and ideas for representation are inherently colored by my own lens, but to also try and include a few other voices and ideas, too. It comes down to the fact that it's impossible to cover the topic authentically with just one voice."

INDUSTRY ALLIES

Thompson's first big consulting gig involved a visit to *Gears of War* developer the Coalition, as part of Xbox's Games for Everyone initiative. Team members were looking to speak with subject-matter experts to gain insight into how they could make their games more accessible. "I talked with rotating teams in a workshop environment where they could ask whatever questions they wanted in a space that was nonjudgmental and welcoming," they said. "I shared several ideas for representation in their games, as well as what might be unnecessary barriers in terms of accessibility. It was a great experience of bouncing ideas off groups of really creative and motivated people."

Microsoft again proved themselves a major ally with the 2018 announcement of the Xbox Adaptive Controller. A customizable controller for gamers with limited mobility, it's designed to be highly adaptable to unique playstyles. Just as importantly, it's affordable; in the past, accessibility controllers have often been prohibitively expensive for those who need them.

"The Xbox Adaptive Controller has been monumental!" said Thompson. "For those of us who work in accessibility, we knew it was likely to be a big turning point, and that's part of why it was so exciting to see the industry respond in the way it did."

Thompson feels that the Adaptive Controller changed the discussion around accessibility. "We're no longer knocking on closed doors trying to get the industry to open up a little," they said. "Rather, we've got major figureheads championing accessibility and asking, 'How can we do better?' I still think there's a long way to go, but to see that snowball start rolling down the hill has been more exciting than I can describe."

VISIBILITY FOR THE MARGINALIZED

It isn't just Thompson's work in accessibility that has earned them accolades. They are also outspoken about being non-binary and having autism, providing positive visibility, solidarity, and support for groups who aren't often championed within the industry.

"I'm seeing more people being open and supportive of the fact that I came out as non-binary," said Thompson. "Still, just by being visible, positive presences in the games industry, marginalized people are putting themselves in harm's way. Even with progress, there's still so much room for improvement, whether that's inclusion, representation, or accessibility for all marginalized people from all backgrounds and all areas of the industry. Some areas have further to go than others, and there are still a number of tightly closed doors in the industry." This truth makes Thompson's unyielding visibility worth recognizing.

"The year 2018 has been a bumper year for accessibility—I'm busier than ever and having to turn down projects, which speaks volumes," said Thompson. "I can't express how meaningful it is to me when people tell me after panels or presentations that I've changed how they think of making games, or that I've reminded them why they do what they do."

Thompson intends to continue educating and motivating the industry toward a more inclusive future. "It's a really hard job to try and make change, and inclusion is about pushing for change," they shared. "If I can help people to keep doing that tiring job, I will."

MEAGAN BYRNE

EMPOWERING INDIGENOUS CREATIVITY

 Byrne_meagan

 meaganbyrne.carbonmade.com
byrneout.itch.io

EXPERIENCE

FIRST INDUSTRY PROJECT: WANISINOWIN | LOST (2015)

ACHIEVEMENTS UNLOCKED:

> FALL SHERIDAN FACULTY OF GAME DESIGN "SPRINT WEEK 3RD PLACE"—LAYERS OF MADNESS (2014)

> HOLLAND BLOORVIEW HOSPITAL "KIDS' CHOICE 2ND PLACE"—TINY PLANETS (2015)

> SHERIDAN COLLEGE "AWARD FOR EXCELLENCE IN GENERAL ARTS AND SCIENCE" (2016)

> LEVEL UP: FIRST FULL TIME JOB @IMAGINENATIVE

STATS

INDUSTRY LEVEL: 3

CURRENT CLASS: GAME DESIGNER

CURRENT GUILD: ACHIMOSTAWINAN GAMES—HAMILTON, CANADA

SPECIAL SKILLS: GAME DESIGN, NARRATIVE DESIGN, PUZZLE DESIGN, USER EXPERIENCE DESIGN, SWING DANCE, THEATER

STANDARD EQUIPMENT

FAVORITE PLATFORM: CONSOLES

GO-TO GENRE: JRPGS, ADVENTURE GAMES

MUST-HAVE GAME: OKAMI

BIO

Meagan Byrne has a perfectly rational reason for working in video games. "I liked games growing up, but I was always more interested in theater or animation," revealed Byrne. "After the last recession, it was obvious that I was never going to be able to make a career out of working in live production. I was low on options, and it was clear I was going to have to return to school."

This would be her third trip back to school; Byrne already earned a degree in visual art and art history, and a second in honors English and cultural studies. In order to make an informed choice on her future career, Byrne made the very practical decision to evaluate the economic forecast for 2013—an annual report by the Canadian government. She noticed that video games were one of the top areas of growth. "So I decided to try that out. I got into a game design program, joined as many industry groups as I could handle, did a lot of game jams, networked a lot, and it's been working out quite well for me so far."

Easter Egg

Had the top two highest scores on the SparkNotes Unintelligence Test in 2001, but didn't use her real name out of paranoia that her friends would find out.

Byrne knew that game design could be self-taught with all the resources available online, but recognized that a formal education was the best route for her. "I went to school for game design and I did that for two reasons: I needed structure and I needed knowledgeable feedback," she explained. An additional benefit was the built-in networking opportunities, with both classmates and instructors. "Being an anti-social lone wolf really doesn't cut it in game design, and I say this as someone with an anxiety disorder. It would have been easier for me to just do my work and head home every day, but if I wanted to succeed in game design, I had to push through my comfort zone."

FEELING LOST

University gave Byrne a chance to collaborate on a variety of student projects in various genres. Once graduated, she was eager to create something entirely from her own. Byrne chose a concept that explored the complex relationship she had with her Métis heritage growing up.

After a month of mentoring, Byrne was ready to tackle developing her first solo game—*Wanisinowin | Lost*. *Wanisinowin* is a word that encompasses everything that means "lost" in Cree. In the game the player takes control of Wani, a young girl from the spirit world. Wani's life is turned upside down when she learns she's not actually totally a spirit, but rather also a human. Through platforming and puzzles, the player can guide Wani to the human world, but the path is dangerous, which represents the difficulty of living between two worlds.

Byrne found herself in a similar situation growing up. "I wasn't told that I was Métis until I was at least a pre-teen. It wasn't really a shock; I guess it was something that permeated our home life even without being stated," she recalled. "But almost right away a friend of my aunt's dismissed my heritage because I didn't grow up on a reservation. I didn't feel comfortable going to 'native' events or Friendship Centers. 'Am I going to be rejected again?' was always in the back of my mind."

It took some healing to not feel like an outsider within the Métis community. "It was really only because of the growing Indigenous community at my school and our Indigenous Student Success Officer that I was able to find my path and begin to meet with other First Nations, Métis and Inuit students, and talk to elders," she continued. "I know I am not the only Indigenous person who feels this way. In fact, I'm starting to see it is very much a part of being Indigenous, this constant questioning of 'do I belong,' because there was and still is a deliberate mandate to absorb the first peoples into the dominant colonial structure. I often compare it to the Borg from *Star Trek*. Here you have this race that thinks it's the ideal and it goes around sucking up other cultures/races taking what serves them and discarding the rest, making everyone the same with a few cosmetic differences."

The message came across loud and clear through *Wanisinowin|Lost*, something that Byrne takes pride in. She recognized that the experience could be relatable to anyone with dual identities, which was validated when a Chinese Canadian student played the demo and expressed how connected she felt to the character.

ACHIMOSTAWINAN GAMES

"Achimostawinan" means "tell us a story" in Cree, and that is exactly what Byrne and Maliseet co-founder Tara Miller intend to do. Since 2016, the Achimostawinan Games team has staffed up from two to five, and is a majority-indigenous studio looking to tell indigenous stories.

Their first game, *Purity & Decay* began as a concept by Byrne and Miller, created in two days during Toronto's Feb Fatal game jam. A "cybernoir detective game in an indigenous future," the game unfolds as a choose-your-own-adventure with stylish black-and-white graphics. As the game designer, narrative designer, and project manager, Byrne wanted to incorporate Indigenous language, especially Cree, into *Purity & Decay*.

"Basically, all of the names of things are going to be in Cree and a few other Indigenous languages from the Ontario/Manitoba region," said Byrne.

This is the first game Byrne has intended to release as a full-fledged, for-profit title. Achimostawinan Games aims to release the game in 2020.

BUILDING A COMMUNITY

In addition to her indie development work, Byrne has currently found a home as a digital and interactive coordinator for the imagineNATIVE Film and media arts festival in Ontario.

She regularly finds time to share the skills she's earned and mentorship she's received, through running game design camps for indigenous youth, or volunteering for Canada Learning Code.

Dames Making Games is a "Space for genderqueer, non-binary, femmes, Two Spirit people, and trans and cis women to create games freely." The non-profit organization offers a large array of programming for individuals interested in creating games, including lectures, public workshops, quarterly roundtables on topics important to the community, game jams, and both 12- and six-week development workshops. Byrne sits on the board of directors for DMG.

She is also a co-director of Indigenous Routes, which helps to provide new-media training to indigenous youth in order to help them "level up" and use their artistic skills in digital media mediums, so that they can share their work on a global scale. Dames Making Games teamed up with Indigenous Routes in 2015 for the first-ever Indigicade, a workshop that teaches indigenous youth how to make games.

One of Byrne's motivations to share her skills with other indigenous creatives is because she feels there is an incredible amount of potential for Native stories to be told through games. "As a Métis woman, I would say what I see games doing that no other medium can do is preserve traditional knowledge and stories and let the knowledge be spoken well or understood more organically. When things are written down or recorded (through audio or film), you lose a lot of the life in that knowledge and, in so, lose some of the knowledge itself. Games and interactive media offer us a way of presenting traditional knowledge in a way that lets the receiver both hear and experience what they are being told. It also gives us a way to share life view and ways of being."

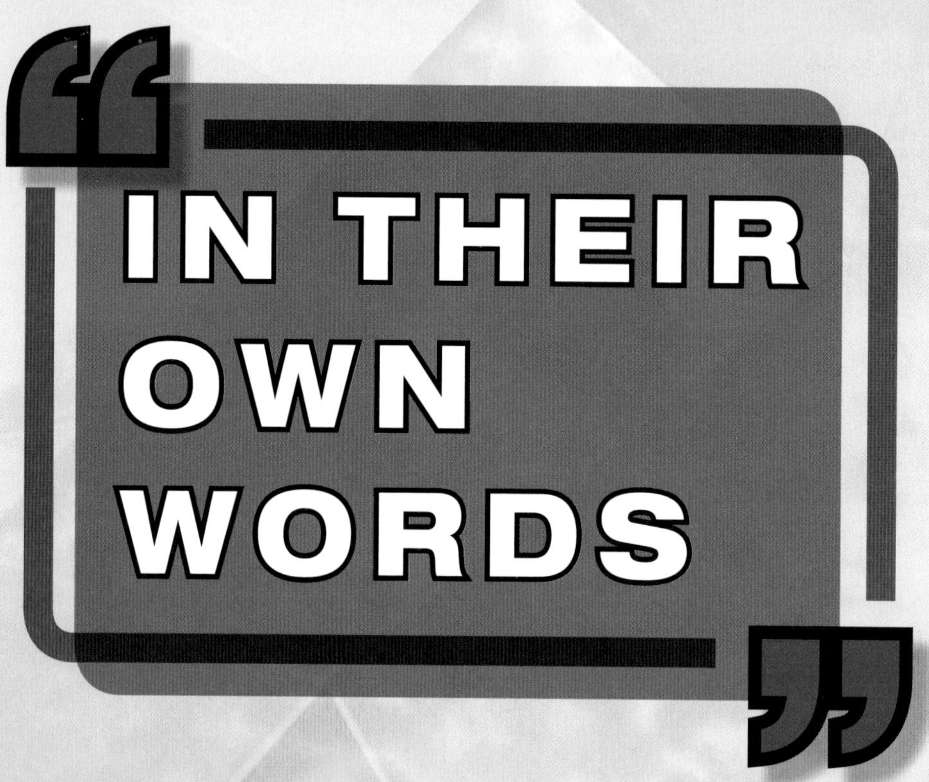

THE FUTURE

Where do you think the video game industry is headed? What are your hopes for the future of video games?

"I think indies are challenging even the most established developers, which makes everyone better. Given the flexibility in how we can all consume any type of content we enjoy, there's less room for complacency now than ever before. Also, I think the gaming community, as vocal as it is, is driving more development and financial decisions for major publishers. This past year certainly illustrated the power of 'voting with your dollars,' and it's shaping the future—without question."

Kayse Sondreal-Nene | Sr. Merchant, Video Games | Best Buy Co., Inc. | Minneapolis, USA

"As an art form, games are often classified between technology, art, and industry. As such, it sometimes makes it challenging to get arts funding for them the way you might for other forms of media. When games try for arts funding, they are often viewed as tech. When games try for tech funding, they're often viewed as creative media. When games try for creative media funding, they're pushed back to tech. You get the point. Games are capable of cultural critique and reflection, and in the coming years, it's my hope we'll see more artistic funding heading toward games to explore their potential."

Brenda Romero | Game Designer & CEO | Romero Games | Galway, Ireland

---

"I feel like the biggest advancements are coming from career training simulators. For example, the nXhuman project uses dynamic dialogue that adapts to user-driven conversation to better simulate complex patient-provider interactions, rather than simply using conversation trees. I'd love to see the ways we could implement this same technology to provide further immersion in video games."

Nikki Myers | Freelance Audio Designer | Nikki Myers Sound | Raleigh, USA

"I hope to continue seeing greater diversity in characters and the stories that are told about them. More risk-taking, stronger stories, less reliance on mindless gameplay. I'd like to see more and more games that have something of value to say about the human condition."

Christy Marx | Writer & Narrative Designer | Independent | Northern California, USA

"Motion capture plays a huge role in most AAA video games. The data quality is getting better and better as the processes are getting easier and more user friendly. I'm excited to see where the future of mocap takes us."

Tracy Jasperson | Senior Animator | Crystal Dynamics | Redwood City, USA

"For the sake of everyone trying to make a career in games and yet have some sort of functional life and stability away from the studio, I'd like to see a return to a time when studios treated managerial, technical, and content creator staff as valued team members, not just assets disposable at the end of a project. We should be building teams that aren't worried about being the first to get their résumés out to recruiters near the end of a project in order to be first in line for the next temporary gig."

Jennell Jaquays | Content Designer & Artist | Dragongirl Studios | Seattle, USA

"There's a lot of uncertainty in the industry, but I think it is growing pains. We're at an inflection point—our audience, our development practices, and our business models are all changing. As the cost of traditional, mainstream development increases, independent games are flourishing. We're seeing a democratization of game development like never before, thanks to digital distribution, affordable software tools and engines, and distributed development teams. This will enable a wider spectrum of experiences and a greater diversity of voices in our medium."

Amy Hennig | Sr. Creative Director & Writer | Independent | San Francisco, USA

"I believe that virtual reality is the future of video games. In the next 10 years, it will be dominating the industry as it is the media with the most power to engage players because it is the most immersive media we have so far. The only thing holding back VR to take over is its price range. Once it overcomes this issue, it will become mainstream."

Ana Ribeiro | Creator | Arvore Immersive Experiences | São Paulo, Brazil

---

"I feel like video games are only growing more popular as technology advances and might become populated by people crossing over from other fields. This will be interesting in terms of seeing the kinds of games that will be produced."

Bahiyya Khan | Experimental Narrative Masters Student & Tutor | University of the Witwatersrand | Johannesburg, South Africa

---

"The world is only becoming more connected. Our phones are our portals into mixed reality. Eventually, we'll have glasses or contact lenses or implants, or we'll have voice speakers and other networked objects in our homes and offices. In this world, what we know of as video games now will take many new forms, and will offer ways for us to entertain ourselves, new ways to educate ourselves, and even new ways to work and govern ourselves. As robots and AI automate many of our jobs, our relationship with education and work will change. I think the division between work and play is artificial and comes from a time when our education system had to prepare us for lives of grueling, boring factory work. But in the future, the jobs that will remain will be jobs of care, creation, curation, entertainment, and sport. We know from psychology that people enjoy discovering their unique traits and strengths and appreciate developing them. And play is how we naturally learn. I can imagine a future in which we educate ourselves and create things for each other inside video games or similar products."

Brie Code | CEO/Creative Director | TRU LUV | Montréal, Canada

---

"I really hope the game industry becomes more approachable for people in developing countries. Not only are most major gaming events hosted in the United States, a lot of countries are not even allowed on popular storefronts or crowdfunding sites, not to mention some of them can't even get issued a visa to attend those events."

Camila Gormaz | Game Developer | BURA | Santiago, Chile

"I would like to see less focus on violence and more focus on problem solving within the game content. Add more educational elements to more games."

Carol Kantor | Founder | Business Builders | Cupertino, USA

"It may sound funny, but the one thing I would change is calling the industry a 'gaming' one. I think nowadays the experience has become so real and tangible, it no longer feels like playing a 'game,' but rather a 'virtual interaction.'"

Hayat Selim | Composer & Singer-Songwriter | Self-Employed | Cairo, Egypt & London, UK

"I want every company to have a strong stance on ending toxic behavior in gaming communities, and to feel an unshakeable obligation to meet that end. So much of gamer identity is caught up in toxic behavior, and we simply don't need it and shouldn't enable or encourage it. It's time that we look out for each other as players, instead of tear each other down."

Soha El-Sabaawi | Manager of Diversity and Inclusion Programs | Riot Games | Los Angeles, USA

"I would love to see game companies adopt a two- to three-year turnaround policy for game creation. Another thing I'd like to see isn't specific to the gaming industry, but I'm big on labor laws that benefit the worker. Employees who are healthy and stress-free are much better producers of content. I would love to see a coalition of countries come together and set some serious labor laws. Things like a four-day work week, overtime starting at 30 hours, minimum 20-day annual vacation, full-health coverage, and a year-long maternal/parental leave plan. I'm actually really big on the maternal/parental leave, because those cover contracts are usually how game industry-hopefuls get their first big break."

Meagan Byrne | Game Designer | Achimostawinan Games | Hamilton, Canada

---

"It's easier to become a game developer than it ever has been thanks to tools and engines like Twine, Unity, and Unreal, and the proliferation of game development programs. But it's also harder to succeed as a professional game developer. I'd love to see us embrace game development as a hobby, not just a profession, and encourage more people to share their stories through game development. I'd also love to never have another conversation about diversity, not because people are tired of the topic, but because we have achieved an industry that is representative of our global population, and people simply understand that an inclusive community is the best community."

Jen MacLean | Executive Director | International Game Developers Association (IGDA) | Boston, USA

"I think the gaming industry seems like a gigantic monolith to those who aren't in the industry right now, and it seems like only the games that are the big players are the ones that people play. I'd like it to be easier for newcomers to join the market and feel as if their games will be noticed and seen. I think it's extremely discouraging to make a game and feel as if you haven't impacted anyone with it."

Jenny Xu | Studio Founder & Software Engineer | JCSoft Inc. | San Francisco, USA

"I believe the video game industry will continue to grow and redefine itself, opening new avenues for more people to experience gaming in new ways. I think we will continue to see developers take on building their own products versus relying on working at bigger companies. Bigger companies will continue to be much more risk averse, sticking to service-based models and using data to predict and drive various outcomes."

Karisma Williams | Product UI/UX Designer & Technical Program Manager | Microsoft | Seattle, USA

"Somehow make it more sustainable to make high-quality games without crunch. We, as an industry, have not figured out how to make games that offer a high value to players without requiring quite a lot of content to be made. That by itself is fine, but if you allow for an appropriate time to actually develop that content, games become so expensive that they aren't able to make a good return on investment. So, we crunch. And we pay people at lower salaries than they are able to make in any other tech-related field. This means that we are hemorrhaging many of our most skilled creators. Those are the people who are able to work much smarter, too, doing a lot more in a lot less time. Which then keeps us in the loop of having to hire less experienced game makers, who work less efficiently, necessitating crunch again, and so on and so on."

Kellee Santiago | Product Development Lead | Google Entertainment, VR/AR/XR | San Francisco, USA

"If I could change anything about the gaming industry, it would be the deep-rooted suspicion that if gamers aren't allowed to say whatever they want online (no matter how hateful or potentially harmful), that they will abandon their games or communities. There are certain cultural patterns in online gaming circles that are intentionally disruptive and harmful for the sake of testing boundaries and proving social shock value. The reality is that when these gamers are told that hateful behavior and words aren't acceptable in a gaming space, they usually accept it and find new ways to play."

Morgan "Rhoulette" Romine | Director of Initiatives | AnyKey | San Diego, USA

"We're seeing lots of advancements in cloud. In fact, we believe this will power all aspects of game, engine, and services. In its current state, cloud is already allowing for scalability in innovation, and for the player the experience today means extensive simulations, massive, persistent worlds, and multi-device access streaming. I believe that in the next 10 years, cloud will become the place where players consume and engage, and we'll see even more subscriptions, content, and services. Machine learning will also have a significant impact once we figure out how to design our games and game engines to leverage it."

Jade Raymond | SVP & Group General Manager | EA Motive Studios | Montréal and Vancouver Canada

---

"I wish we had more accessible, better-curated content platforms to discover, buy, and share games, with smart recommendation engines and social features. The choices we have now are rapidly becoming unsustainable for creators as well as players."

Leigh Alexander | Narrative Designer, Consultant, & Multi-Disciplinary Writer | Independent | London, UK

"Tech in general tends to lend itself to unhealthy work-life balance, and passion careers like gaming often pave the way for expectations that go above and beyond what someone should be expected to give, or feel, for a job. I hope that self-care and the discussions around mental health that are also prevalent in our industry right now will continue to help combat that."

Anna Prosser | Lead Producer | Twitch Studios | San Francisco, USA

"I would really change the way that games are funded. Right now, there's not a lot of funding available for experimental titles, predominantly because the biggest games are funded with the most money, but they also take the fewest risks. And I really wish that we had a more risk-centric model, and a robust incubation model inside of the publishers that really focused on making smaller investments in riskier projects, and then giving those teams more and more responsibility over time. But in general, it's very uncommon for funders to publish risky games. So the systems for that have now been sort of bubbling up alongside, and what that means is that a lot of really experimental designers work without pay, they work in their spare time, and they work at night. And I wish that there was a better funding model for those types of games, because I think that they're really what innovates and pushes the industry forward."

Robin Hunicke | CEO & Chief Creative Director | Funomena | San Francisco, USA

"I want my job to become obsolete and for me to have to find a new career again. What I mean by this is that I want games to be so inclusive that there's no need for someone like me. I want accessibility to be such an integral part of game design that people like me don't need to specifically educate developers on the need or process. Things are starting to change, but I want there to be more progress in the industry for hiring marginalized people, especially disabled people and people of colour. Games can't really be truly inclusive until those employed in the industry more accurately reflect those who play games."

Cherry Thompson | Game Accessibility Consultant | Freelance | Vancouver, Canada

---

"I hope that the way games are perceived in culture changes. I think that the fact that they are considered a 'lesser' medium than film or even television is holding them back in terms of content. If I could change that I would, because everything else I want for the industry would follow from that change."

Tracy Fullerton | Director & Professor | USC Game Innovation Lab | Los Angeles, USA

"I think we've reached the point in the industry where there are more game development graduates than job opportunities (at least in Singapore.) Many graduates end up starting their own studios due to the lack of opportunities to gain industry experience. It's no longer good enough to only teach students how to make a game, we're going to have to teach them how to start and run a business as well. I would really like to see a change that would prepare interested hopefuls for the reality and different challenges that await them."

Jess Ong | Senior Game Designer | PikPok | Wellington, New Zealand

---

"In traditional games PR we see the roles split between mainstream PR (popular newspapers, TV coverage, etc.) and specialist PR (popular gaming sites, gaming magazines, etc.). But thanks to the introduction and the varying needs of streamers, content creators and influencers, game publishers are having to create new roles to deal specifically with their requests. As long as these platforms continue to increase in reach and profile, so will the need to have people who cater to them directly and, for those who are used to the more traditional PR roles, taking this onboard can be a challenge."

Hollie Bennett | PlayStation UK Channel Manager | Sony Computer Entertainment Europe | London, UK

STRATEGY GUIDE

If you are working toward a career in video games, we hope the anecdotes and advice in this book left you feeling both inspired and informed. As an additional resource, we've curated a list of organizations that can help you along this career path.

DEV ORGANIZATIONS & EVENTS

FemDevs | Spain: FemDevs is a non-profit association that promotes the interests, participation and presence of women in video game development through events and workshops. [femdevs.org]

Pixelles | Canada: Pixelles is a non-profit organization dedicated to empowering more women to make games through free monthly workshops, mentorshiop, game jams, and more. [pixelles.ca]

Voxelles | USA: Voxelles is a Chicago-based group in favor of gender diversity in the video games industry that creates positive changes through a variety of events, workshops, and advocacy programs. [voxelles.com]

Women in Games Italia | Italy: Women in Games Italia is a non-profit organization that improves diversity in the Italian video games industry through sharing information and opportunities. [womeningamesitalia.org]

Dames Making Games | Canada: DMG is a Toronto-based, non-profit organization that offers accessible space, instruction, and mentorship for diverse game makers. [dmg.to]

Women in Games International | Global: Women in Games International promotes the inclusion of women in the global games industry with a focus on job placement and mentorship. [getwigi.com]

European Women in Games Conference | England: The European Women in Games Conference aims to educate and stimulate future generations, through keynote speeches, panel discussions, and workshops. [womeningamesconference.com]

The Working Lunch | Australia: The Working Lunch provides entry-level women programming and mentorship to aid them in their journey of working in video games. [workinglunch.online]

Women in Games (WIGJ) | United Kingdom: Women in Games is a not-profit network for women in video, mobile, online games, and eSports. [womeningames.org]

LadyCade | Sweden & United Kingdom: LadyCade is a gender-inclusive gaming event that provides welcoming spaces for women to network and create. [ladycade.org]

Japangame.org | Japan: JapanGame.org is a foundation that supports young game creators through networking and promotion. [japangame.org]

WiDGET | Australia: WiDGET is an organization that focuses on research, advocacy, and funding for women and non-binary game developers. [widgetau.com]

STEM ORGANIZATIONS

ChickTech | USA: ChickTech is a non-profit organization dedicated to increasing the number of women to achieve STEM-based careers through mentorship, events, and networking. [chicktech.org]

Women in Technology (WIT) | USA: Women in Technology is an organization that offers educational programs to promote creativity and innovation. [womenintechnology.org]

Technovation | Global: The Technovation offers young girls learning opportunities to develop skills to be in the technology field. [technovationchallenge.org]

Anita B.org | USA: Anita B.org is a social enterprise that connects, inspires, and guides women in technical fields. [anitab.org]

Womenize | Germany: Womenize is a program that promotes women in the workplace in the tech field. The conference provides inspirational people, job opportunities, and workshops. [gamesweekberlin.com/womenize]

Women Techmakers | Global: Google's Women Techmakers program focuses on providing visibility, resources, and community to women who work in tech. [womentechmakers.com]

Pink Programming | Sweden: Pink Programming is a non-profit organization focused on connecting women to the tech industry by promoting equality through workshops and courses. [pinkprogramming.se/en]

GLITCH | Global: GLITCH brings together a community that shares, learns, and promotes digital games as a culture and career. [glitch.mn]

Women Who Code | Global: Women Who Code is a non-profit organization that offers services and support for women pursuing careers in the technology field. [womenwhocode.com]

Canada Learning Code | Canada: Canada Learning Code is a charitable organization that promotes technological learning by offering courses and workshops to women and youth. [canadalearningcode.ca]

Code Liberation | NYC & London: Code Liberation works to catalyze the development of digital games and innovative technology by women and non-binary individuals through classes, workshops, game jams, hackathons, and more. [codeliberation.org]

she++ | USA: she++ is a non-profit organization that empowers women through programs that teach and spread technological culture among communities. [sheplusplus.com]

YOUTH PROGRAMS

Girl Geek Academy | Australia & USA: Girl Geek Academy is a movement teaching women to learn technology that includes coding, game development, design, and more. [girlgeekacademy.com]

Girls Who Code | USA: Girls Who Code is an organization that offers learning and job opportunities as a supportive community to girls and women seeking to work with technology. [girlswhocode.com]

Girls Make Games | Global: Girls Make Games offers international summer camps, workshops, and game jams designed to inspire the next generation of designers, creators, and engineers. [girlsmakegames.com]

Game Girl Workshop | Palestine, UAE, Sweden, & Denmark: Game Girl Workshop is a short and intensive workshop that teaches girls how to code and more. [gamegirlworkshop.org]

STEM for Her | USA: STEM for Her promotes education to create awareness, excitement, and opportunities among young women to launch successful careers. [stemforher.org]

Gameheads | USA: Gameheads is a youth program that uses videogame design and development to engage, prepare, and train low-income youth to the tech industries. [gameheadsoakland.org]

DigiGirlz | USA: DigiGirlz is a Microsoft YouthSpark program that provides middle and high school girls opportunities to learn about careers in technology, promoting workshops. [microsoft.com/en-us/diversity/programs/digigirlz]

Young Game Designers (YGD) | Global: The YGD is a BAFTA initiative that inspires young people to create, develop, and present their new game idea to the world. [ygd.bafta.org]

Black Girls Code | USA: Black Girls Code is a non-profit organization that provides technology and computer programming education for African-American girls. [blackgirlscode.com]

Native Girls code | USA: Native Girls Code is a Seattle-based program that provides computer coding skills for Native American girls through workshops, coaching, and teaching. [naahillahee.org/ngc.html]

Geek Girls Carrots | Global: Geek Girls Carrots is an organization focused on women in tech entrepreneurs, promoting meet-ups and workshops to inspire, learn, and share knowledge. [gocarrots.org]

CoderDojo | Global: CoderDojo is a community of free, non-profit programming clubs for young people that promotes learning in coding. [coderdojo.com]

Code.org | USA: Code.org is a non-profit organization that gives the opportunity for students to learn computer science at schools as they learn other subjects. [https://code.org/]

Girls in Tech (GIT) | Global: The GIT is a non-profit organization that empowers and educates girls who are interested in technology, also giving support to help women advance their careers in STEM fields. [girlsintech.org]

WORKSPACES & SHOWCASES

Hand Eye Society | Canada: The Hand Eye Society is a Toronto-based, non-profit organization aiming to provide support and promotion to local game projects. [handeyesociety.com]

ImagineNATIVE | Canada: ImagineNATIVE is an organization committed to creating a better understanding of indigenous people and cultures through digital media. [imaginenative.org]

Gamma Space | Canada: Gamma Space is a non-profit space for working, playing, and learning. It's a place to share skills and experiences for everyone interested in games. [members.gammaspace.ca]

Global Game Jam | Global: The GGJ focuses on creativity, collaboration, and experimentation through an event where small groups create new games. [globalgamejam.org]

ADVOCACY & AWARENESS

I Need Diverse Games | USA: I Need Diverse Games is a non-profit organization dedicated to bringing more projects, works, and research by marginalized people to light. [ineeddiversegames.org]

#GirlsBehindTheGames & #WomenBehindTheGames | 2018: These hashtags encouraged women to raise visibility of their work within the gaming industry.

#1ReasonToBe | 2012: #1ReasonToBe hashtagged discussions on social media illustrating the top reason the speaker choose to work in the video game industry.

Diversi | Sweden: Diversi is a collective working force that supports diversity within the gaming industry by promoting an inclusive culture.[diversi.nu]

GGP: Gay Game Industry Professionals | Global: GGP is a Facebook community for LGBTQ+ video game professionals. [facebook.com/groups/6628203394]

Gaming for Everyone @ Xbox | Global: A centralized blog for Microsoft's diversity and inclusivity initiatives related to video games. [news.microsoft.com/gamingforeveryone]

IGDA PROGRAMMING

IGDA Scholars | Global: The IGDA Scholars program provides selected students all-access passes to attend participating week-long industry conferences, as well as mentorship, networking, studio tours, and private Q&A opportunities. [igdafoundation.org]

IGDA Women in Games GDC Scholarship | Global: GDC Scholarship is a program for women who seek a degree in game development. It provides exclusive workshops and learning opportunities. [women.igda.org/]

IGDA Foundation Next Gen Leaders Program | Global: The Next Gen Leaders Program provides access to exclusive events and workshops related to career development and retention in the game industry. [igdafoundation.org]

IGDA Women in Games Ambassadors | Global: The Women in Games Ambassadors program supports an inclusive game development community providing a springboard for careers in game development. [igdafoundation.org]

IGDA Game Accessibility SIG | Global: A special interest group for advocating accessibility in video games. [igda-gasig.org]

IGDA LGBTQ+ SIG | Global: A special interest group for LGBTQ+ industry professionals and allies. [facebook.com/groups/IGDALGBTQSIG]

IGDA Women in Games SIG | Global: A special interest group that works towards gender balance in the workplace and marketplace. [women.igda.org]

ONLINE SAFTEY RESOURCES

Crash Override | Global: Crash Override is an advocacy group, resource, and crisis helpline for people experiencing online abuse. [crashoverridenetwork.com]

Speak Up & Stay Safe® | Global: An online security guide curated by Feminist Frequency, aimed to aid those targeted by digital violence. [onlinesafety.feministfrequency.com

ABOUT THE AUTHOR
MEAGAN MARIE

Written by Ally McLean, Director of The Working Lunch

 MeaganMarie

Meagan Marie

 MeaganMarie

 meaganmarie.com

EXPERIENCE

FIRST INDUSTRY PROJECT: EDITOR AT GIRLS ENTERTAINMENT NETWORK (2006)

FAVORITE INDUSTRY PROJECT: TOMB RAIDER (2013)

PROJECTS SHIPPED: 7 GAMES

ACHIEVEMENTS UNLOCKED:

> AUTHOR, GAME INFORMER WORLD EXCLUSIVE COVER STORY—PORTAL 2 (2010)

> AUTHOR, GAME INFORMER WORLD EXCLUSIVE COVER STORY—TOMB RAIDER (2011)

> AUTHOR, 20 YEARS OF TOMB RAIDER (2016)

> RAISED OVER $12,500 THROUGH HER COSPLAY CHARITY ORGANIZATION, CAUSEPLAY

STATS

INDUSTRY LEVEL: 12

CURRENT CLASS: SR. COMMUNITY & SOCIAL MEDIA MANAGER

CURRENT GUILD: CRYSTAL DYNAMICS—REDWOOD CITY, USA

SPECIAL SKILLS: SOCIAL MEDIA, COMMUNITY BUILDING, WRITING, PUBLIC SPEAKING, TRAVEL PHOTOGRAPHY, COSPLAY, PROP MAKING

STANDARD EQUIPMENT

FAVORITE PLATFORM: XBOX ONE

GO-TO GENRE: ACTION/ADVENTURE

MUST-HAVE GAME: ANYTHING TOMB RAIDER

BIO

Introducing my friend and role model, Meagan Marie feels, like an impossible task. Put simply, Meagan leaves everything better than she found it. A figure of profound positive impact on the communities she's involved in, Meagan holds herself, and those of us fortunate enough to be pulled into her orbit, to a higher standard. Above all else, in what can feel like hopeless times, Meagan continues to believe in and build a bright future for games, the people who make them, and the people who play them.

Meagan's ripple effect on the games industry began when she moved from honing her skills in college and later at the Girls Entertainment Network to become associate editor at *Game Informer* magazine in 2008. Always ahead of her time, Meagan was a vocal advocate for a present-day discussion point—the fundamental importance of accessibility in games. She also encouraged public discourse and developer accountability on topics related to gender—both in and out of game—through articles such as her 2010 investigative piece "The Gender Gap."

After the 2011 Tohoku earthquake and tsunami devastated Japan, Meagan auctioned off one of her most prized possessions—a Nintendo DS autographed by Shigeru Miyamoto, Koji Kondo, Eiji Aonuma, Charles Martinet, and Martin Leung. The high-profile auction raised over $4000 for the Japanese Red Cross, and catalyzed the formation of the industry-wide Play for Japan initiative. Dedicated industry professionals, Meagan included, organized auctions of donated industry memorabilia and raised over $100,000 for the cause.

Meagan's lifelong love of Lara Croft revealed itself to be prophetic when she took the role of community and communications manager at Crystal Dynamics in 2011, having opened the door for this career transition after debuting the brand-new, contemporary Lara Croft to the world via her *Game Informer* cover story. The impact Meagan continues to have as an organizer, moderator, creator, spokesperson and more on the franchise and its associated communities is almost unquantifiable in everything from events and social media to clothing lines to campaigning internally for the development of accessibility features. It would not be an exaggeration to say that beyond *Tomb Raider*, Meagan established a global gold standard of AAA community management that has seismically altered the landscape of the games industry and its relationship with its audience.

Aside from the public-facing community initiatives Meagan fosters, she is an advocate for strengthening communities through personal relationships and small-scale interactions. Many examples of this are unknown or uncredited publicly, whether it be quietly commissioning a custom Xbox controller for a webmaster with physical limitations, personally financing travel for community members without the resources to attend an important event, or sending studio-signed condolence cards signed to grieving fans.

With multiple successful releases under her belt and a list of accomplishments and accolades too long to name, Meagan left Crystal Dynamics for a brief six-month stint at the developer of one of the most popular video games in the world. Meagan's blog about her experiences at the company and the reasons for her departure was a crucial voice in the up swell that has led to the industry giant publicly acknowledging its poor treatment of women in the workplace and vowing to do better. This wasn't the first time Meagan raised her voice for the cause. Her 2013 blog, "What would you do if you weren't afraid?" went viral, raising awareness of systemic sexism and harassment in both professional and enthusiast sectors of the industry.

Returning to Crystal Dynamics and *Tomb Raider* in 2014, having literally written the book on Lara Croft (*20 Years of Tomb Raider*, 2016), Meagan is now senior community and social media manager, continuing to grow and shape the global voices and communities of Crystal Dynamics games, which have expanded to include the Marvel universe.

Easter Egg
Once played cello (terribly) for iconic *Final Fantasy* composer Noubo Uematsu during an after-hours Tokyo Game Show event. She casually mentioned playing cello in middle school, and shortly after—to her horror—one manifested out of thin air.

Running alongside all of these achievements, Meagan has also extended her natural ability for leadership, advocacy, and creation to the cosplay world. As a veteran international cosplayer, Meagan uses nearly 15 years of experience to raise industry standards for collaborations with cosplay professionals. In 2015 she created an international Lara Croft Cosplay Ambassador Program, which recognizes the effort of Lara cosplayers around the world by hiring them for official events. She illustrates that Lara Croft is a "state of mind" by hiring ambassadors for their passion (not similarity to the character), employing fans of all ethnicities, genders, and body types to represent Lara Croft at official events worldwide.

Meagan has converted her love of the craft and community into a powerful initiative for change. Started in 2014, the Causeplay Shop brings together cosplayers and creatives for annual sales that contribute to charitable causes. She also contributes by donating all personal cosplay-related earnings—including appearance fees and print sales—to local charities at the events she's invited to around the world. Over $12,500 has been raised under the Causeplay banner to date.

What all of this fails to communicate is Meagan's generous spirit and her seemingly endless well of energy when it comes to helping others get a fair shot. I first knew Meagan as Wonder Woman because of a costume she created that took the Internet by storm. After many years of her very specific brand of considerate, passionate, and intelligent friendship, I can confirm that the similarities to Wonder Woman do not stop at her sword and shield. I'm just one of many people working in games today whose career has been enriched and guided by Meagan Marie.

As the mammoth effort of this book demonstrates, Meagan does not do anything by halves. A cross-disciplinary powerhouse, a fierce champion for women in games, and a fearless voice for the underrepresented, Meagan Marie is a figure whose positive and far-reaching impact will be felt for many years to come.

AUTHOR NOTES

Author: Meagan Marie • **Project Manager :** Sebastian Haley • **Project Coordinators:** Jessica Moreno & Ben Borthwick

SPECIAL THANKS : AUTHOR'S SIDE

Getting in touch with over 100 women from the video game industry—some of which have been inactive for decades—is no easy task. I am incredibly thankful to all of the individuals who assisted with this monumental undertaking, including: Yutaka Okura, Dan "Shoe" Hsu, Ben Myres, Benj Edwards, Lauren Hall-Stigerts, Alex Wilmer, Geoff Keighley, Hollie Bennett, Cat Karskens, Tim Turi, Stephanie Palermo, Andrew Dovichi, Brian DiDomenico, Will Kerslake, Lydia White, Catherine Jones, Allie Page, Jeff Cork, Rachel Day, Allwyn D'souza, Gordon Walton, Nathan Mills, Alexa Ray Corriea, Steven Dengler, Arne Meyer, Isaac Cabrera, Jon Robins, Stan Barker, VG Chile, the Brave Wave Productions team, and the dozens of other individuals who offered assistance when I put a call out on social media. This book wouldn't be what it is without you.

Thank you to Lola Shiraishi, Takuya Kishimoto, JunJun Chen, and Alexander Aniel, who went above and beyond in conducting and translating interviews when language was a barrier.

Thank you to the diligent PR teams who helped facilitate interviews, especially when time was a precious commodity. Thank you to Ally McLean for generously agreeing to write my author bio, Luke Earle for the creative brainstorming that inspired our final book title, and Jessica Moreno and Ben Borthwick for stepping up to the plate in the final weeks to help take this book over the finish line.

Thank you to the team at Prima for trusting me with this opportunity, and to Tim for being in the trenches with me daily and advocating for the book at every opportunity, even if it resulted in a bigger workload on his plate.

Thank you to my coworkers at Crystal Dynamics for putting up with my deliriousness towards the end of this project, and to Rich Briggs for always encouraging me to take new career opportunities. Thank you to the talented and diverse women of Crystal, who provided insight and guidance in this book's formative period.

Thank you to all of the friends who encouraged me week after week of writing, including Hannah, Jenn, Ashley, Catherine, Tina, Meg, Katie, Morrigan, Ray, and Ben. Thank you to my extended Facebook friend circle, who was my sounding board for ideas this past year, and provided thoughtful answers and opinions to my constant onslaught of questions.

Thank you to Mom, Dad, Chris, and Hien for always supporting me in my professional and personal endeavors, and to Budman for the inspiration to always live my best life. Thank you to Donut and Sprinkles for being my emotional support cats and keeping me company through long sprints at my computer.

Thank you to Sebastian for not only stepping in as my project manager, but being a true partner who did everything possible to support me while writing this book. Thank you for keeping me alive with packed lunches, mandatory decompression periods, late-night candy runs, and helping me manage and adjust to my Fibro diagnosis when I had no resources left to take care of myself. Thank you for stepping in during the final weeks of this project to help with research, blocking, and anything else I requested. I literally couldn't have done this without you.

Thank you to the women who inspired me early in my career, including Lisa Mason, whose little yellow photo in *Game Informer*'s staff section was the first spark that made me feel I had a place in video games.

Although I said this in the "Note from the Author," it merits a second callout. Thank you to all of Women in Gaming: 100 Professionals of Play's contributors for trusting me to tell your stories, for dedicating your precious time to this project, and for challenging me with your feedback along the journey.

WOMEN IN GAMING

100 PROFESSIONALS OF PLAY

Written by Meagan Marie

DK/Prima Games, a division of Penguin Random House LLC
6081 East 82nd Street, Suite #400
Indianapolis, IN 46250

ISBN: 978-0-7440-1953-7

Printing Code: The rightmost double-digit number is the year of the book's printing; the rightmost single-digit number is the number of the book's printing. For example, 18-1 shows that the first printing of the book occurred in 2018.

21 20 19 18 4 3 2 1

001-311519-Dec./2018

Printed in Canada.

CREDITS

Publishing Manager
Tim Cox

Senior Product Manager
Jennifer Sims

Book Designer
Justin Lucas

Production Designer
Julie Clark

Creative Services
Tim Amrhein & Wil Cruz

Production
Elisabet Stenberg

Copy Editor
Serena Stokes

Proofreader
Tim Fitzpatrick

Cover Illustration
Inna Vjuzhanina

Pixel Portrait Illustrations
Darren "Daz" Tibbles

PRIMA GAMES STAFF

VP & Publisher
Mike Degler

Licensing
Paul Giacomotto

Marketing
Jeff Barton